Jimmy Swaggart Bible Commentary

Leviticus

JIMMY SWAGGART BIBLE COMMENTARY

For prices and information please call: 1-800-288-8350
Baton Rouge residents please call: (225) 768-7000
Website: www.jsm.org • E-mail: info@jsm.org

Jimmy Swaggart Bible Commentary

Leviticus

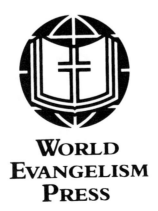

World Evangelism Press

ISBN 978-0-9769530-7-4

11-203 • COPYRIGHT © 2005 World Evangelism Press®
www.jsm.org • email: info@jsm.org
20 21 22 23 24 25 26 27 28 29 / Sheridan / 12 11 10 9 8 7 6 5 4 3

TABLE OF CONTENTS

INTRODUCTION

—■—

THE INTRODUCTION TO THE BOOK OF LEVITICUS

Leviticus has been called the *"Book of Worship."* Strangely enough, the Holy Spirit is not once named in this Book, and because His Office is to speak, not of Himself, but of Christ (Jn. 16:14).

The Hebrew title for this Book is *"And He Called."* It is a Book that treats of the offices, rites, services, and feasts of the Hebrew faith, as given in the charge of the Priests – the sons of Levi. The Talmudists called it *"The Law of the Priests,"* or *"The Law of the Offerings."* Either of these titles sufficiently describes it.

ITS AUTHOR

That Moses was the writer of this Book can hardly be doubted. In fact, I think it would not have been possible for anyone else to have written it.

As I think by now should be obvious, Moses was, without a doubt, one of the greatest men of God who has ever lived. History tells not of another like him, unless it be the Saviour, Whom he so much resembled. In fact, about one-fourth of the Old Testament was written by this remarkable man. It was through him that inspiration first broke forth in a steady and continued stream. He was, and remains, the great Lawgiver and historian of the world (Seiss).

As we see through the entirety of the Word of God, the Lord uses men, and by that term, we're speaking of both men and women. Even though the Old Testament, and especially the Book of Leviticus contains all the rituals, ceremonies, and offerings, it is still the man with whom the Lord deals and speaks.

This is totally different from the religions of the world. The individuals mean little, with the ritual or the ceremony being the primary spectacle. As someone has well said, all religions of the world function on the basis of an idea. Christianity, which is an offshoot of Judaism, functions on a Person, the Lord Jesus Christ, of Whom all the rituals and ceremonies of the Old Testament were types.

At this juncture of Old Testament history, Moses stands as the supreme leader. It is this man to whom God speaks, and who thereby leads the Children of Israel. But it is always the Lord Who is the final authority.

In the Book of Genesis, we have seen *"God's remedy for man's ruin"* in the promised seed – the Ark of Salvation, and in the rich unfoldings of Divine Grace to fallen and sinful man, especially to Abraham.

In the Book of Exodus we have seen *"God's answer to man's question."* There, man is not only outside of Eden, but he has fallen into the hands of a cruel and powerful enemy – he is the bond-slave of the world.

How can he be delivered from Egypt's furnace? God Alone could answer this question, and this He did in the Blood of the slain Lamb. In the Redemption-power of that Blood, every question is settled. It meets Heaven's highest claims, and man's deepest necessities (Mackintosh).

And now, in our meditations on the Book of Leviticus, we find *"God's provision for man's need,"* which pertains to the Sacrifice, the Priest, and the Place of Worship.

THE CROSS

As we go through this Book, I will take every opportunity afforded me to present to you, and to all concerned, the great Message of the Cross. As we have stated, the Standard or Foundation has already been laid, as it regards the Blood of the Lamb, which effected Israel's deliverance from Egyptian bondage even as we found in the Book of Exodus. Now, in Leviticus, we will find that *"Sacrifice is the basis of worship,"* and of course, sacrifice speaks of the Cross.

This means that acceptable worship to God must be based on a Sacrifice acceptable to Him. Man is guilty and unclean. As such, he needs a sacrifice to remove his guilt, cleanse him from his defilements, and fit him for the Holy Presence of God. The Scripture bluntly tells us, *"Without the shedding of blood is no remission"* (Heb. 9:22).

The Book of Leviticus portrays all of this, and as well, I think the guiding theme of this great work as given to us by the Holy Spirit through Moses, can be summed up in the *"Cross."* The Cross is in every Sacrifice, every ritual, every ceremony, and as stated, forms the basis of all worship. And let the Reader know and understand that as the Sacrifice formed the basis of worship in Leviticus times, it has not changed one iota as it regards the present. Sacrifice, i.e., *"the Cross,"* still forms the basis of all worship. If we do not come to God through the Blood of the Lamb, Who is Jesus Christ, the Holy Spirit will take special care to block all access (Eph. 2:13-18).

THE WORD OF THE LORD

Beautifully and strangely enough, the Book of Leviticus contains but little more than God's Own utterances. It is more entirely made up of the very Words of the Lord than any other Book of the Bible. Jehovah Himself speaks in every Chapter, and in almost every Verse, while Moses, it seems, sits by, and hears, and writes, as the Scribe of the speaking Lord.

But yet, this Book has probably been less read, and usually accounted less interesting and important, than almost any other Book of the Word of God. Many regard it as the mere record of an obsolete economy, inapplicable to our times, and containing little or nothing of practical value to us.

However, such thinking must be constituted as wrong, woefully wrong! So far from being a mere collection of ancient curiosity, it is a Book of impressive, sublime, evangelical instruction. Once again, if we can understand the great Levitical Principles, we will understand more about Christ. And anything that can teach us more about Christ is of such value as to defy all description.

Christ Himself says: *"Had you believed Moses, you would have believed Me, for he wrote of Me."* Part of that of which He spoke was Leviticus. And one might as well say that the whole Epistle to the Hebrews is one grand argument for Christianity, extracted from the rites and services of the Levitical economy.

I think we will find it astonishing, when we find how completely Christ is woven into the entire structure of the Book of Leviticus. Open the Book almost anywhere, and we are sure to find something of Jesus. Consequently, we might well say that this third Book of Moses could be called *"The Gospel according to Leviticus,"* just as the third Book of the New Testament is called *"The Gospel According To Luke."* The one tells of Jesus and Redemption through Him, as well as the other; and if we do not find it full and overflowing with clear and beautiful evangelical instruction, it is because we know not how to read it (Seiss).

THE PURPOSE OF THE BOOK OF LEVITICUS

What do we find to be its contents?

From beginning to end, everything bears the one pervading purpose, of showing the transgressor wherewithal he might come before the Lord, and obtain Justification and Peace. It is a great system of Salvation by Priestly mediation and bloody sacrifices. It is all meant to proclaim the price paid by Christ on the Cross of Calvary. It is meant to show the depths, the width, and the height of the Work of the Cross. In fact, unless we properly understand the great Book of Leviticus, I seriously doubt that we can understand the Cross. Quite possibly, because it is by and large unread and unstudied, do we have such a paucity of learning and understanding, as it regards the modern-day Christian, concerning the Cross.

Some may ask, why should we go back to these ancient types, when we have everything so plain in the writings of the New Testament? Why stop to contemplate a picture when we have the original?

The answer, once it is thought upon for a few moments, becomes quite simple. The Book of Leviticus helps us to more properly understand the writings of the New Testament, and does so by pointing out the tremendous significance of the great Sacrifice of Christ, which it does in all the Levitical Offerings.

For instance, there are five great Sacrifices listed in the first Chapters of this great Book. When these Sacrifices are properly understood, it helps us to know and realize exactly what Jesus accomplished at the Cross, and above all, how it affects us. This information can be found no place else.

Is that important for you to know? Undoubtedly, it is!

PERSONAL

As we go through this great Book, you will see yourself, and more particularly, and more important, you will see Christ. We will see Him as the answer to our question, the solution to our problem, the medicine for our sickness, the life for our death, the strength for our weakness, the light for our darkness, the Heaven for our Hell.

It is July 15, 2002, 3 p.m., as I begin the Commentary on this tremendous third Book of Moses. I would pray that you would take the time to study its contents. To do so will require meditation and study with an open heart and mind. But I believe it will be well worth your while.

Concerning this, Seiss said, *"God has spoken to us from the heavens – mercifully spoken – spoken to the intent that we might be saved; and while we do not refuse to listen to Him in His works, let us ever give a reverent attention to Him in His words."* Leviticus is a great part of these *"Words."*

"O perfect life of love! All, all is finished now;
"All that He left His Throne above to do for us below,
"No work is left undone of all the Father wills;
"His toil, His sorrows, one by one, the Scriptures have fulfilled;"

"No pain that we can share but He has felt its smart;
"All forms of human grief and care have pierced that tender heart;
"And on His thorn-crowned head, and on His sinless soul,
"Our sins in all their guilt were laid, that He might make us whole;"

"In perfect Love He dies; for me He dies, for me:
"O all atoning Sacrifice, I cling by Faith to Thee.
"In every time of need, before Thy gracious Throne,
"Thy work, O Lamb of God, I'll plead, Thy merit not my own."

THE
BOOK OF LEVITICUS

(1) "AND THE LORD CALLED UNTO MOSES, AND SPOKE UNTO HIM OUT OF THE TABERNACLE OF THE CONGREGATION, SAYING,

(2) "SPEAK UNTO THE CHILDREN OF ISRAEL, AND SAY UNTO THEM, IF ANY MAN OF YOU BRING AN OFFERING UNTO THE LORD, YOU SHALL BRING YOUR OFFERING OF THE CATTLE, EVEN OF THE HERD, AND OF THE FLOCK.

(3) "IF HIS OFFERING BE A BURNT SACRIFICE OF THE HERD, LET HIM OFFER A MALE WITHOUT BLEMISH: HE SHALL OFFER IT OF HIS OWN VOLUNTARY WILL AT THE DOOR OF THE TABERNACLE OF THE CONGREGATION BEFORE THE LORD.

(4) "AND HE SHALL PUT HIS HAND UPON THE HEAD OF THE BURNT OFFERING; AND IT SHALL BE ACCEPTED FOR HIM TO MAKE ATONEMENT FOR HIM.

(5) "AND HE SHALL KILL THE BULLOCK BEFORE THE LORD: AND THE PRIESTS, AARON'S SONS, SHALL BRING THE BLOOD, AND SPRINKLE THE BLOOD ROUND ABOUT UPON THE ALTAR THAT IS BY THE DOOR OF THE TABERNACLE OF THE CONGREGATION.

(6) "AND HE SHALL FLAY THE BURNT OFFERING, AND CUT IT INTO HIS PIECES.

(7) "AND THE SONS OF AARON THE PRIEST SHALL PUT FIRE UPON THE ALTAR, AND LAY THE WOOD IN ORDER UPON THE FIRE:

(8) "AND THE PRIESTS, AARON'S SONS, SHALL LAY THE PARTS, THE HEAD, AND THE FAT, IN ORDER UPON THE WOOD THAT IS ON THE FIRE WHICH IS UPON THE ALTAR:

(9) "BUT HIS INWARDS AND HIS LEGS SHALL HE WASH IN WATER: AND THE PRIEST SHALL BURN ALL ON THE ALTAR, TO BE A BURNT SACRIFICE, AN OFFERING MADE BY FIRE, OF A SWEET SAVOR UNTO THE LORD."

The structure is:

1. The Sacrifice or Offering addressed here is the *"Whole Burnt Offering."* It signified that God would give His all, which He did in the Person of His Son, and our Saviour, the Lord Jesus Christ. This alone would satisfy the demands of a thrice-Holy God.

2. God only accepted such Offerings as He Himself ordained.

3. The worshipper, imperfect and sinful in himself, was accepted in the perfection of the Offering.

4. The conscience, being a reflection of the Sacrifice, remained imperfect because the Leviticus Sacrifices were imperfect.

5. Christ's Sacrifice being perfect gives a perfected conscience; and, therefore, a peace that nothing can destroy.

6. The victim being a male without blemish signified the spotless Perfection of Christ's Manhood.

7. The entire Sacrifice was burnt on the Altar; that is, it was wholly for God. Such was the devotion of Christ's Heart.

8. The skin of the sacrifice was given to the Priests. Only the mere surface of Christ's offering up of Himself to God can be apprehended by the Believer, typified by the skin. The infinite depths of that great surrender are beyond human understanding.

9. The inwards were washed with water, so Christ's Emotions, as well as His Ways and

Words, when judged by the Word of God, were found to be sinless. With respect to Him, all within and without was without blemish.

COMMUNICATION

Verse 1 reads: *"And the LORD called unto Moses, and spoke unto him out of the Tabernacle of the congregation, saying."*

We find from the above Passage that the Lord has now taken up abode in the Tabernacle, actually in the Holy of Holies, where He dwelt between the Mercy Seat and the Cherubim. I think one can say without fear of contradiction that of the Godhead, it was the Holy Spirit Who occupied this place and position. Concerning the New Covenant, Paul said: *Do you not know that you are the Temple of God, and that the Spirit of God dwells in you?"* (I Cor. 3:16).

The Lord had spoken to Moses in various different means and ways, the last being in the giving of the Law on Mount Sinai. The fact that He now speaks to Moses from the Tabernacle, and more specifically the Holy of Holies, proclaims something of extreme importance.

The great Salvation Plan has been advanced forward to a great degree. While the Law definitely was not the answer for man's dilemma, it would serve as a substitute until the solution would come, namely the Lord Jesus Christ. Inasmuch as the Law contained the great sacrificial system, which was a Type and Shadow of what Christ would do, such made it possible for God to dwell much closer to His people. In fact, the Cross, which would fulfill all of these types, would place the Lord into the very hearts and lives of all Believers, and do so on a permanent basis (Jn. 14:17).

THE CALL OF GOD

It should be noted that the very first action of the Lord as it regards His taking up abode in the Holy of Holies was to explain the sacrificial system to Moses, and thereby, to Israel. We see then that the Cross of Christ is given preeminence. That's why Paul said, as it regards the Church: *"For Christ sent me not to baptize, but to preach the Gospel: not with wisdom of words, lest the Cross of Christ should be made of none effect"* (I Cor. 1:17).

NOTES

The emphasis must always be on the Cross, i.e., *"that which Christ did in order to redeem fallen humanity."*

We must not allow this lesson to be lost on us. There were many functions as it regards the Tabernacle, which must be explained and observed; however, it is the sacrificial system which God broached first. By doing this, He is telling us that the Sacrifice of Christ must always be preeminent. In fact, the Cross of Christ is not a mere doctrine, but rather the Foundation of all Doctrine. In other words, if we hold to any doctrine that is based on something other than the Cross, to the degree that it is separated from the Cross, to that degree will error be the result. In fact, the following will be the conclusion of such an effort:

"Now the Spirit (Holy Spirit) *speaks expressly* (pointedly), *that in the latter times* (the times in which we now live) *some shall depart from the Faith* (Jesus Christ and Him Crucified), *giving heed to seducing spirits, and doctrines of devils"* (I Tim. 4:1).

I am positive that Jesus considered that His Death on the Cross, with all of its implications, must be looked at as far more than a mere doctrine. No, and as stated, the Cross is and, in fact, must be, the Foundation of all Doctrine. The entirety of the Word of God bears this out, even as we now open our study of the great Book of Leviticus.

WORSHIP

As we go along, we will see the entirety of the process of the Tabernacle unfold before our eyes, with its central focus, as stated, being the sacrificial system. Actually, this great Book has been referred to as *"the Book of worship"*; in other words, all of these instructions were given in order that God's people could worship Him, their Creator. So we find that there can be no suitable worship, without the proper Sacrifice. And to be sure, that proper sacrifice is the Sacrifice of Christ.

FORGIVENESS

Without proper Sacrifice, and again we refer to Christ, there can be no forgiveness.

To my knowledge, in all the religions of the world, with Christianity excepted, there is no teaching on the subject of forgiveness, and that is because there is no Atonement. There are, in fact, whole races of men in whose vocabulary there is no word for forgiveness. The spirit of retaliation seems to be still as potent as ever, apart from the spirit of Christianity. Donald Trump, a real estate developer of some note, claims that the spirit of revenge must characterize our dealings with our fellowman. His great motto is, *"Get even!"* But Jesus said:

"You have heard that it has been said, An eye for an eye, and a tooth for a tooth: but I say unto you, that you resist not evil" (Mat. 5:38-39). He evidently meant that men should curb the impetuosity of personal vindictiveness, and leave their case in the hands of a more Perfect Justice, namely the Lord.

To cut straight through to the chase, the less the Believer knows about the Cross, the less he knows about forgiveness. If he properly understands the Cross, He will properly understand forgiveness, and function accordingly. Someone has well said, and rightly so: *"The world is very slow to forgive, and the Church forgives not at all!"*

That is tragic, but true! The Church little forgives, if at all, simply because it doesn't understand the Cross, which means that its trust and faith are little in the Cross, but rather other things.

MOSES

As well, we find that the great Plan of God was revealed here to a man – Moses. This is the way that it still is, and the way it has always been.

This means that God doesn't actually deal with committees, boards, or such like. He always selects a man or a woman!

As well, the way of the Lord is not anchored in the democratic process. In other words, it's not a democracy. It is rather a theocracy, which means that God rules all, and does so through His appointed representative. Such a person cannot be elected by popular ballot, and in fact is not elected by popular ballot. They are called of God, even as was Moses!

All of this pertains to the Government of God, which is not at all like the government of this world. Unfortunately, far too

often, the Church adopts the government of the world, which means that in doing so, the Government of God is abandoned. In fact, this is what ultimately destroyed the Early Church.

In Old Testament times, we find that God guided His Work primarily through Prophets. In New Testament times, which include the present, He uses Apostles. Paul said:

"Now therefore you are no more strangers and foreigners, but fellowcitizens with the Saints, and of the Household of God;

"And are built upon the foundation of the Apostles and Prophets, Jesus Christ Himself being the Chief Cornerstone" (Eph. 2:19-20).

THE OFFERING

Verse 2 reads: *"Speak unto the Children of Israel, and say unto them, If any man of you bring an Offering unto the LORD, you shall bring your Offering of the cattle, even of the herd, and of the flock."*

The Sacrifices or Offerings, which were instituted here, were not the beginning of the system, just the beginning as it pertained to the Tabernacle. There is every evidence that the Lord explained to the First Family how forgiveness could be obtained, and fellowship could be enjoined, and we speak of the relationship of fallen man with God. It could only be by Sacrifice of an innocent victim, namely a lamb, which would be a Type of Christ. We are given this example in Genesis, Chapter 4, as it regards Cain and Abel. The practice of offering up sacrifices was continued with Noah (Gen. 8:20), and greatly so with Abraham (Gen. 12:7-8; 13:4, 18). Isaac offered up sacrifices and so did Jacob (Gen. 26:25; 35:1, 7). So the sacrificial system wasn't new, but would now, under the Law of God, be regulated, thereby, expressing Christ even to a greater degree.

ANY MAN

There is no mention of any woman bringing an Offering to the Lord, as it regards the sacrifice of an animal. This was always done by a man.

Why?

Even though Eve sinned first, it was Adam who dragged down the human race. God had given the first pair the power of procreation, even as He has given such to all human beings. But the seed of that procreation is found in man, and not in woman. The only seed that a woman has had is the Lord Jesus Christ (Gen. 15:6).

Due to Adam being the fountainhead of the human race, whatever happened to him would pass on to the entirety of the human race, even forever. In other words, every baby that would be born would be born in original sin, which means that the child is born as a fallen creature.

This is the reason that Jesus had to come as the Last Adam, even as the Holy Spirit through Paul labeled Him (I Cor. 15:45). In other words, Jesus as the Last Adam had to undo what the first Adam did, which refers to the plunging of the human race into spiritual darkness, and to do what the first Adam did not do, which was to fully obey God. That He did, and in every capacity.

Although it is a moot point, if Eve alone had sinned, due to the fact that the seed of procreation did not reside within her, she could have asked forgiveness without her failure passing on to the human race. So the man would have to bring the Offering, inasmuch as he was the cause of all failure.

A CLEAN ANIMAL

Certain animals were labeled by God as clean, which included the bullock, the heifer, the lamb, the ram, the goat, the dove, and the pigeon. Of these animals, the lamb was most offered, and most epitomized Christ Who was to come. In fact, Jesus was referred to as *"the Lamb of God, which taketh away the sin of the world"* (Jn. 1:29).

A WHOLE BURNT OFFERING

Verse 3 reads: *"If his Offering be a Burnt Sacrifice of the herd, let him offer a male without blemish: he shall offer it of his own voluntary will at the door of the Tabernacle of the congregation before the LORD."*

There were five types of Sacrifices listed in the Levitical Law. Christ fulfilled all of them with His one Sacrifice of Himself. We will list them, but will give only a small amount of commentary at this time, addressing them more fully momentarily:

1. Whole Burnt Offering: All the animal

was burned on the Altar, with the exception of the skin, which was given to the Priests. It signified that God was giving His all, and in turn, would satisfy the demands of God Who was greatly offended. This Offering set the standard and suggested the themes which are manifested by all the other Levitical Offerings. It is thus a Biblical Type in the fullest sense of the word.

2. The Meat (Food) Offering: This was an Offering of Thanksgiving, and contained no flesh. It almost always accompanied the Whole Burnt Offering. Some of this Offering was burned on the Altar, with another part given to the Priests.

3. The Sin Offering: The Sin Offering is linked to the stages of our Christian growth. When we start out with the Lord, there are many things we still need to learn. In fact, we commit *"sins of ignorance,"* or to say it in a better way, we sin at times, simply because we do not know or understand God's Prescribed Order of Victory.

4. The Trespass Offering: As the Sin Offering pertains to our Christian growth, the Trespass Offering relates to our Christian *"Walk."* This Offering pertains more so to our sinning against our brother or sister in the Lord, than anything else.

5. The Peace Offering: In offering up the other Sacrifices, with the exception of the *"Meat Offering,"* most of the time, a Peace Offering would follow, meaning that the problem had been addressed, and the Peace of God is now resident within the Believer's heart. It was the only Offering of which the sinner could participate. Part was burned on the Altar, with part given to the Priests, and part was to be eaten by the offerer, who could call in his friends, if he so desired, for a feast.

A MALE

These animals were to be of the male species, because they were types of Christ. Although Christ was fully God, at the same time, He was fully Man. In fact, He was referred to as, *"The Man Christ Jesus"* (I Tim. 2:5). As well, it was a man, Adam, who dragged down the entire human race.

As we've already stated, Jesus came as the Last Adam (I Cor. 15:45). As *"The Man,"*

He would redeem the lost sons of Adam's fallen race, and He would do so by the giving of Himself in Sacrifice, on the Cross, of which these token sacrifices of the Levitical Law were symbols or types.

WITHOUT BLEMISH

The animal had to be without blemish, because again, it represented and symbolized Christ, and what He would do regarding the Salvation of souls.

Regarding the lambs which were offered at 9 a.m. (the morning Sacrifice) and 3 p.m. (the evening Sacrifice), it is said that the Priests would kill the animal, which would be done by the slitting of its throat, with the blood caught in a basin, and then the skin would be stripped from the carcass. At that point, they would take a razor-sharp knife, cut the carcass down the backbone, in effect, laying it open. They would minutely inspect the flesh, and if there was a blemish of any kind, even a discoloration, that animal would be discarded, and another chosen. It represented the One Who was to come; therefore, the representation must be correct.

The Perfection of Christ, of which these animals without blemish were but a type, and a poor type at that, for what could adequately portray the Son of God? His Perfection was total and complete in every respect. That's the reason He had to be born of the Virgin Mary. Had He been born as all other babies, of necessity, due to Adam's Fall, He would have been born in original sin. Had that been the case, He would not have qualified to be a Sacrifice that God would accept.

Ironically, many of the Jews of His day, which even continues unto this hour, claimed that He was born illegitimately, when in fact, His birth was the only totally legitimate birth that there ever was. Joseph was not His father; God was His Father. In fact, He was not the product of Joseph's seed or Mary's egg, but rather, of the Holy Spirit (Mat. 1:18; Lk. 1:35). This means that Jesus did not carry the traits of Joseph or Mary. What His appearance was, we aren't told; however, I think it is safe to say that He didn't look like His brothers or sisters, but was totally different in every respect.

Being born without original sin, He

NOTES

also lived without sin of any nature (Heb. 7:26). This means that He never sinned in word, thought, or deed! He was Perfect in every respect.

All of this was for many reasons, but the main purpose and reason of His Coming to this Earth was to go to the Cross. In fact, Peter said that His death on the Cross was *"foreordained before the foundation of the world"* (I Pet. 1:18-20).

Even before the world was brought back to a habitable state, and man was created, through foreknowledge, God knew that man would fall. To salvage His most noble creation, God would have to become man, and would do so in order to redeem man, which was done at the Cross. So the Cross was the destination of Christ. This means that it was not an accident, or an incident. It was a Sacrifice!

When He was placed on the Cross, He was Perfect in every respect; therefore, God accepted His poured out Life, in the shedding of His Blood, as payment for all the sin of mankind, past, present, and future, at least for all who will believe (Jn. 3:16; Eph. 2:13-18). He was truly *"without blemish."*

WHOSOEVER WILL

The phrase, *"He shall offer it of his own voluntary will,"* would probably be better translated, *"He shall offer it for His acceptance."* Pulpit says, *"The animal, representing the offerer, was presented by the latter in order that he might be himself accepted by the Lord."*

The animal was a substitute in the place of the offerer, symbolizing Christ Who was our Substitute as well.

As one advances in the Divine life, he becomes conscious that those sins which he has committed are but branches from a root, streams from a fountain; and, moreover, that sin in his nature is that fountain – that root. This leads to a far deeper exercise, which can only be met by a deeper insight into the work of the Cross. In a word, the Cross will need to be apprehended as that in which God Himself has *"condemned sin in the flesh"* (Rom. 8:3).

In reading that Passage in Romans, the Reader should observe that it does not say, *"sins in the life,"* but the root from where these have sprung, namely, *"sin in the flesh."* This is a truth of immense importance. Christ not merely *"died for our sins, according to the Scriptures,"* but He was *"made to be sin for us"* (II Cor. 5:21). This is the doctrine of the Sin-Offering (Mackintosh).

Him being *"made to be sin for us"* refers to the fact that He, by His death, addressed the root cause of sin, which, or rather who, is Satan. And how did He do that?

NAILING IT TO HIS CROSS

Paul gives us the answer to the above question, when he said: *"Blotting out the handwriting of ordinances that was against us, which was contrary to us, and took it out of the way, nailing it to His Cross;*

"And having spoiled principalities and powers, He made a show of them openly, triumphing over them in it" (Col. 2:14-15).

Breaking the Law of God, which refers to the Ten Commandments, is sin. The wages of that sin is death (Rom. 6:23).

In the Burnt Offering, with which the Book of Leviticus opens, we have a Type of Christ *"offering Himself without spot to God,"* hence the position which the Holy Spirit assigns to it. Concerning this, Mackintosh said, *"If the Lord Jesus Christ came forth to accomplish the glorious work of Atonement, His highest and most fondly cherished object in so doing was the Glory of God. 'Lo, I come to do Your Will, O God,' was the grand motto in every scene and circumstance of His Life, and in none more markedly than in the work of the Cross. Let the Will of God be what it might, He came to do it."* And what was that will?

Unequivocally, it was the offering up of Himself on the Cross, which paid the debt that man owed, which incidentally, man could not pay. Man had forfeited life by his failure in the Garden of Eden, and we speak of the Life of God, which of course brought death, which is separation from God, but which Jesus purchased back by the giving of His Perfect Life on the Cross. When He did this, He atoned for all sin, and that refers to past, present, and future (Jn. 3:16).

With this done, Satan and all of his cohorts of darkness were totally and completely defeated. Sin is the means by which Satan

holds man in bondage. He has a legal right to hold sinful man accordingly. But with all sin atoned, Satan's legal right is ended, at least if man will believe the Lord, thereby trusting Christ.

In this manner, Satan and all demon spirits and fallen angels were totally defeated, which was done at the Cross.

HOW WAS CHRIST MADE SIN FOR US?

Paul said: *"For He* (God the Father) *has made Him* (the Lord Jesus Christ) *to be sin for us* (a Sin-Offering), *Who knew no sin; that we might be made the Righteousness of God in Him"* (II Cor. 5:21).

God made Him to be sin for us, in that He made Him a *"Sin-Offering."* The Prophet Isaiah said: *"Yet it pleased the LORD to bruise Him; He has put Him to grief: when you shall make His soul an Offering for sin, He shall see His seed, He shall prolong His days, and the pleasure of the LORD shall proper in His hand"* (Isa. 53:10).

Jesus became sin only in the sense of becoming the Sin-Offering. If it is to be noticed, Paul didn't say, *"For He has made Him to be a sinner for us,"* but rather, *"To be sin for us."* To be a sinner one has to sin, and Jesus did not sin in any capacity. But He did become a Sin-Offering.

As we look at all the millions of lambs which were offered up under the Mosaic economy, those animals didn't sin, but they did bear the penalty of sin, which was death, and so did Christ, of Whom they were a Type.

Our Word of Faith friends claim that Jesus became a sinner on the Cross, took upon Himself the nature of Satan, died and went to Hell, and we speak of the burning side of Hell, where He was tormented there for some three days and nights, with Satan thinking that He was defeated, whenever God finally said, *"It is enough,"* implying that it was His suffering in Hell that redeemed mankind. Jesus, they say, was then *"born again,"* just like any sinner is born again, and then raised from the dead.

None of that is in the Bible, because none of that happened. In fact, that entire scheme is an aberration of the Atonement, which means that if a person believes that, thereby placing their faith in that, they are in effect trusting *"another Jesus,"* which means they forfeit their Salvation.

Our Salvation is 100 percent in Christ, and what He did for us at the Cross. He paid the price by shedding His Life's Blood, which paid the debt we could not pay (Eph. 2:13-18).

While Jesus did go to Hell, the Paradise part, and while He even made an announcement to fallen angels in the heart of the Earth who were locked up (I Pet. 3:19-20), there is no record whatsoever in the Bible that Jesus ever went to the burning side of Hell. The suffering of Christ was on the Cross, and not in Hell (I Pet. 3:18).

AT THE DOOR OF THE TABERNACLE

The offerer of the animal sacrifice had to go to a designated place. When the Israelites were traveling through the wilderness, this place was wherever the Tabernacle was. After the nation of Israel had been established, the offering place was in Jerusalem, because that was where God had chosen to place His Name.

Today, however, man does not have to go to a designated place to find God. He can find Him anywhere as he reaches out with his heart. But let us see how this happy development came about, for it was no mere accident.

God once dwelt between the Cherubim upon the Mercy Seat, and He was to be found only where the Tabernacle or the Temple was. But since Jesus Christ died on Calvary and broke down *"the middle wall of partition,"* which in a sense speaks of both the wall that separated the Gentiles from the Jews, as it regards the Temple Courts, and as well, the partition which divided the Holy Place from the Holy of Holies, for the Temple Veil has been rent asunder, it has become possible for man to approach God directly. Now the approach can be made anywhere, anyplace.

But we don't want to get ahead of ourselves. We need to think it through step by step. So let us now go back several thousand years to where we will be in a position to see – thanks to the different perspective – how the present contract between God and man, the New Covenant, is based on much better Promises.

NOTES

When the Bible says, *"At the door of the Tabernacle of the congregation of the LORD,"* it is pointing to a place where the Ark of the Covenant reposed. Let's look at this circumstance a bit more closely.

THE SACRIFICE

The offerer would come to the *"tent of meeting,"* or Tabernacle, leading his sacrifice. If it was a bullock, a ram, a lamb, or a goat, he would no doubt be leading it by the neck or head. If he was a very poor individual and could only afford a turtledove or a pigeon, he would no doubt have it cradled within his hands.

The approach to the place of meeting with God would have been awesome to him – and it would have been to you and me as well. If he advanced toward the Tabernacle in the daytime, then the offerer would have seen the Cloud hovering over the place as it always did. If, however, he were approaching the Tabernacle at night, then he would see the jagged forks of flames as they constantly played in the night air above the Holy of Holies, the Tabernacle of the Lord.

It would have been a fantastic, nearly stupefying sight. It would have struck terror in his heart. The sinner, the offerer of the sacrifice, would have known that right here was the living Power of Almighty God. And so if he did something wrong – once again did something wrong – the consequences could be disastrous. So he must follow to the letter Moses' instructions for all Israel. The sinner first had to come up to the fence that surrounded the Tabernacle. There would be a door, like a gate, which led through the fence at the front of the Tabernacle. Nearly 1,600 years later, Jesus would say:

"I am the Door: by Me if any man enter in, he shall be saved, and shall go in and out, and find pasture" (Jn. 10:9).

When Jesus uttered those words, every Jew there knew exactly what He was talking about. They knew that He was referring to the Tabernacle Gate of old. They knew He was referring to the fence that guarded the Tabernacle from intruders. They knew that He was referring to the Door that led the way to the Brazen Altar and the Sacrifices, and that He was saying: *"I am the Way, the Truth, and the Life: no man comes unto the Father, but by Me"* (Jn. 14:6).

THE BLOOD

Continuing our examination of the way in which the offerer experienced his personal sacrifice, the sinner would lead the animal through the gate with understandable fear and trembling. But then the scene that would meet his eyes would be totally unlike anything our minds could ever imagine.

It was ghastly. Other contrite and ashamed sinners would no doubt be lined up with their animals. Our sinner would look around and see these other people, and he would also see the sharp knives of the Levitical Priests flashing, and the hot blood of the doomed animals flowing into the basins.

And he would also see the Priests as they were taking blood to the Brazen Altar. His eyes would witness other Priests washing the blood off their hands and feet at the Brazen Laver. He would hear the bellowing of the animals as their throats were slit, and he would suddenly be half-sickened by the mingled scents of blood and entrails and oily black smoke and burning animal flesh.

As I think would be obvious, this was no Church picnic. This terrible place, however, was the very heart and center, the seat, of true Holiness.

And later, Calvary would afford no pleasant scene either. That hill would offer the most hideous, horrible spectacle that Heaven and Earth would ever see.

"Now from the sixth hour there was darkness over all the land unto the ninth hour" (Mat. 27:45).

In fact, the scene of Calvary would be so horrible that even God would not look upon it. God literally pulled the blinds, as it were, on the most appalling bloody sacrifice that would ever be offered in all of human history; for of all the millions of animal sacrifices that had been offered through the centuries, the Sacrifice on Calvary was to be the special one: *"The Lamb,"* Jesus Christ.

His beard would be pulled from His Face. The soldiers would beat His Face and Head with their bare fists and with reeds until He would cease to look human. He would appear *"as an animal,"* as Isaiah had prophesied.

Jesus' back would be cut to pieces by the lictor's lash. There is simply no way to describe the acute, awful suffering that He endured for you and me. When He dragged the Cross up to the top of Golgotha, Jesus dragged it over a trail of bloody footprints.

Calvary, in short, would be a scene so hideous, so horrible, so ghastly, that God would attempt to hide it even from Himself with a curtain of nature's darkness.

Similarly, what the Hebrew offerer of the ordinary animal sacrifice would see would be a dreadful scene too, because the scene would itself typify – would actually predict, signal, and virtually announce – the terrible and shocking price which the coming Redeemer would have to pay in order to bring about the Redemption, through Grace, of sinful mankind.

As our sinner comes, bringing the animal with him, with fear and trembling he now approaches the Priest.

BEFORE THE LORD

All sin is against God. It is an insult to God, a willful, flagrant, disavowal of His Word, which is the highest insult to the Creator. So inasmuch as all sin is committed against Him, it is before Him that we must come, in order to have sin forgiven and cleansed.

This is at least one of the reasons that the Catholic way is so very wrong! It claims that man can forgive or make Atonement for one's sins. Such does not lie within the domain of sinful, fallen man. Only the Lord can cleanse from sin (I Jn. 1:9).

Other than blaspheming the Holy Spirit, the greatest sin of all is rebelling against God's Prescribed Order of Salvation, and His Prescribed Order of Victory. That Prescribed Order is the Cross, which should be overly obvious in these Passages. So what do I mean by one rebelling against the Cross?

If the unredeemed man or woman thinks they can be saved by any other method than trusting Christ and what He has done for us at the Cross, they are rebelling against God's Prescribed Order of Salvation (Jn. 3:16). Of all the sins the unredeemed commit, and their lives are nothing but constant sin, this is the worst of all. Jesus said:

"And when He is come (the Holy Spirit),

He will reprove (convict) *the world of sin, and of righteousness, and of judgment:*

"Of sin, because they believe not on Me" (Jn. 16:8-9).

As it regards the Christian, of necessity they have trusted Christ as it regards their Salvation, but as it regards their Sanctification, most are trusting other things. The Christian who is doing this is living in a state of spiritual adultery (Rom. 7:1-4), which means they are rebelling against God's Prescribed Order of Sanctification.

Exactly as the believing sinner has to trust Christ and the Cross for Salvation, the believing Christian has to trust Him in the same manner, as it regards Sanctification. The Cross plays just as much a part in our Sanctification, as it did our Salvation (Rom. 6:3-14; 8:1-2, 11).

When Moses used the term *"before the Lord,"* he was in effect saying that all sin is committed against the Lord, and all sin must be atoned by the Lord. It cannot be removed any other way.

ATONEMENT

Verse 4 reads: *"And he shall put his hand upon the head of the Burnt Offering; and it shall be accepted for him to make Atonement for him."*

As the man would lead the animal to the Priest, he would then be told by the Priest to *"put his hand upon the head of the animal which would shortly be a Burnt Offering."*

Notice that Moses said, *"He shall put his hand upon the head of the Burnt Offering,"* which in effect, treated the animal as if it was already dead. It was referred to while still alive, as a *"Burnt Offering."*

When Jesus came to this world, He came for but one purpose, and that was to go to the Cross. Listen to what John said:

"In the beginning was the Word, and the Word was with God, and the Word was God" (Jn. 1:1).

This plainly tells us that Jesus Christ was the Living Word, and as well, that He was and is God.

John then said: *"And the Word was made flesh and dwelt among us"* (Jn. 1:14).

He was made flesh for one purpose and one reason only. Listen again to John:

NOTES

John the Beloved, quoting John the Baptist, said, *"Behold the Lamb of God, which taketh away the sin of the world"* (Jn. 1:29).

So in these three Verses, we see the purpose and reason for which Jesus came. He came as the *"Lamb of God,"* and as the Lamb of God, He would *"take away the sin of the world."* If it is to be noticed, it uses the word *"sin"* in the singular, meaning that he addressed the root cause of sin at the Cross.

The Priest would have told the offerer to lay his hand on the head of the animal, which was expressive of full identification. By that significant act, the offerer and the offering became one; and this oneness, in the case of the Burnt-Offering, secured for the offerer all the acceptableness of his offering.

The application of this to Christ and the Believer sets forth a truth of the most precious nature, and one largely developed in the New Testament, namely, the Believer's everlasting identification with, and acceptance in, Christ. *"As He is, so are we in this world."* *"We are in Him that is true, even in His Son Jesus Christ"* (I Jn. 4:17; 5:20).

Nothing, in any measure, short of this could avail. The man who is not in Christ is still in his sins. There is no middle ground: you must be either in Christ or out of Him. There is no such thing as being partly in Christ. Mackintosh says: *"If there is a single hair's breadth between you and Christ, you are in an actual state of wrath and condemnation; but, on the other hand, if you are in Him, then are you 'as He is' before God, and so accounted in the presence of infinite Holiness. Such is the plain teaching of the Word of God."*

NO DEGREES IN JUSTIFICATION

All of this means that all stand in one acceptance, in one Salvation, in one life, in one Righteousness. There are no degrees in Justification. In other words, there is no such thing as one being partially justified, 50 percent justified, etc. One is totally justified, or one is not justified at all!

The person who has just come to Christ, in other words, a babe in Christ, stands in the same Justification as the Saint of 50 years' experience.

While there may be various degrees in the

knowledge of the fullness and extent of Justification, and even various degrees in the ability to exhibit its power upon the heart and life, as it definitely is, we must never confuse that knowledge with the degree of Justification. Let us say it again: there are no degrees in Justification. Everyone truly justified is 100 percent truly justified.

WORKS

This is what makes the Gospel of *"works"* so deadly. One's Justification is judged by the amount of works, or the validity of works, which are ludicrous. While good works will always follow proper Justification, good works will never cause Justification.

The Church, at times, seems to believe in two Justifications – one for the sinner, and another for the Saint. In other words, they understand and accept the sinner coming to Christ, being saved, and thereby instantly justified. But when it comes to the Saint, far too often, the Church attempts to mix works with Faith.

Once justified, which takes place at the Born-Again experience, one is never unjustified, at least as long as one continues to believe in Christ. This means that the Christian who sins does not lose his Justification, as awful as sin is.

Because of this, some of the Christians during Paul's time, hearing the great Apostle speak of the Grace of God, had come to believe that sin was not a big factor after all. In other words, if Grace abounded more than sin, which it definitely does (Rom. 5:20), then sin is no big deal, so to speak.

Paul's answer to that was short and cryptic: *"Shall we continue in sin, that Grace may abound?*

"God forbid. How shall we, who are dead to sin, live any longer therein?" (Rom. 6:1-2).

If sin is committed, the Believer is to confess it before the Lord, Who has promised *"to forgive us our sins, and to cleanse us from all unrighteousness"* (I Jn. 1:9). But as bad as sin is, the Christian doesn't lose his Justification at this time.

And let the Christian ever understand, and the entirety of the Church, for that matter, that if sin is committed, there is only one way that it can be forgiven, washed, and

cleansed, and that is by continued Faith in Christ, and what He has done for us at the Cross. Works must never enter into this picture. For us to present any type of works before God, as an Atonement for sin, insults Christ to the highest degree, in effect saying, whether we realize it or not, that what He did at the Cross was not enough, and we need to add our two cents worth. I think once we see this in the cold light of what it really is, we can thereby see how blasphemous that such action actually is. It is always by Faith, and never by works (Gal. 5:6).

ANOTHER WORD ON JUSTIFICATION

We should as well understand that there is no such thing as progress in Justification. The Believer is no more justified today than he was yesterday; nor will he be more justified tomorrow than he is today. Any soul who is *"in Christ Jesus"* is as completely justified as if he were before the Throne. He is *"complete in Christ."* In fact, he is *"as Christ."*

While there may be, and certainly should be, progress in the knowledge of Justification, there can be no progress in Justification itself.

We should understand that the manner in which we look at Justification is the manner in which we look at Christ. He either paid it all, or He didn't! The Cross was either enough, or it wasn't! In fact, as one views the Cross, one will view Justification. This means if we have a false understanding of the Cross, we will have a false understanding of Justification, which can cause the Believer untold problems.

Everything is based upon the Divine protection of the Work of Christ on the Cross. Let the Reader understand this:

It was never a question of what the worshipper was; that was understood. It was always what the Sacrifice was. That's what makes Faith so important. Christ has done it, and we cannot do it. But our Faith in Him grants us all that He has done. In other words, when we claim Christ, and do so by Faith, God no longer looks at us, but looks at Him.

If He looks at us at all, it is at our Faith. That's why Paul said:

"Examine yourselves, whether you be in the Faith; prove your own selves, know ye not your

own selves, how that Jesus Christ is in you, except you be reprobates?" (II Cor. 13:5).

THE HEAD

If it is to be noticed, the sinner was to put his hand on the *"head"* of the animal. This tells us several things:

It tells us that sin so warps the individual, so twists the individual, so perverts the individual, that the person no longer thinks right, doesn't walk right, doesn't act right, and, in fact, is somewhat insane. There is an insanity to sin, typified by the head, which plays out to perverted actions on the part of the individual.

That's the reason for all the wars, man's inhumanity to man, criminal activity, crime, torture, and hurt in the world. Sin is the cause, and sin is a form of insanity! (Rom. 3).

Of course, there are degrees of sinful insanity. For instance, some sins are worse than others. The entire world has looked on in astonishment at the followers of Islam, who commit suicide in order to kill those whom they consider to be their enemies. The truth is, the people they are trying to kill aren't their enemies, but in reality, the Muslim religion itself is their enemy. But they can't see that, because they are blinded by spiritual insanity, and conduct themselves accordingly.

Anyone who doesn't know the Lord lives in spiritual darkness, hence the laying of hands on the head. That can be changed only in one way:

Jesus Christ must be accepted, Who is the Light of the world, but He must be accepted as one's Saviour, which can only be brought about by what He did at the Cross. So it's Faith in Him and what He did at the Cross that saves the sinner, whether at the beginning they understand such or not!

ATONEMENT

The phrase, *"And it shall be accepted for him to make Atonement for him,"* refers to the animal being accepted as a Substitute on behalf of the sinner, which will *"make Atonement for him."*

The Jew was not taught that the death of the animal was accepted instead of his punishment; but he was instructed to look upon it as a foreshadowing of a Perfect Offering to

come. This may not be apparent on a cursory glance in the writings of Moses (the Pentateuch); but the New Testament leaves no doubt on the question. *"It is not possible that the blood of bulls and of goats should take away sins"* (Heb. 10:4). The first Tabernacle was *"a figure for the time then present;" "the Law having a shadow of good things to come, not the very image"* (or full Revelation) *"of the things, can never with those sacrifices which they offered year by year continually make the comers thereunto perfect"* (Heb. 9:9; 10:1). This is not a contradiction of the Old Testament, but an explanation of the Mosaic dispensation.

All of this means that the Jews were never taught that the slaying or offering of the animal was an Atonement in itself. They knew that it was a foreshadowing, an educating of the world for the appreciation of the one Atonement which was to come in Christ.

In trying to explain the Atonement under the Old Testament economy, we cannot shut up the Doctrine of the Atonement under the naked formula that man must be punished on account of his sins unless someone else can be found to be punished for him; that the Justice of God must have suffering somewhere, if man is not to suffer.

However, to provide suffering was not the one only object of the Atonement; it was not merely to balance suffering against suffering that the one Great Sacrifice was offered.

To what, then, was satisfaction made? It is made on the basis of absolute justice, and we speak of the Truth of God; and it is made not only by the sufferings, but by the Perfect Life of Jesus as the Perfect Man, in obedience to the Law. Justice – not retaliation – demands that what a man sows, that shall he reap. Man sows sin, and reaps the necessary results – death, the forfeiture of God's Presence. Man cannot be pardoned and restored on his own merits. The merits of another, consequently, are offered to him. The picture of Atonement in the Old Testament is that of a covering of sins, and in the New Testament is reconciliation of man to God.

THE BLOOD

Verse 5 reads: *"And he shall kill the bullock before the LORD: and the Priests,*

Aaron's sons, shall bring the blood, and sprinkle the blood round about upon the Altar that is by the door of the Tabernacle of the congregation."

The man who offered up the sacrifice may not have understood all that took place. Likewise, we today do not really understand all that takes place when we come to the Lord Jesus Christ; but what we are actually doing, at that moment, when we accept Jesus personally, is entering into a whole different order of life and being. It is the Divine order . . . the order which operates in the Spiritual Life and, for that matter, in Heaven itself. We might think of this Heavenly System of governance as the *"economy of Grace."*

Because of our fallen nature, it is necessary that we choose to live in this Divine order. Sin is in all of us, and sin separates us from God. On our own, we poor sinners cannot possibly be at one with God. So Atonement – the word means *"at-one-ment"* – positively must occur if our souls are to be made right with God during our earthly strivings and if we are to be one with Him someday in Heaven.

Now in the Mind of God Himself, His Fellowship with wrongdoers is restored by the shedding of innocent blood. Innocent blood cures the estrangement. It makes God and the sinner *"at one"* again.

We have often heard it said, concerning the Old Testament sacrifices, that the sins of the individual were *"covered"* by the Atonement. That, in effect, is right; but it actually went further than that. Not only were the sins covered *"but the sinner was covered as well"* because, in reality, one cannot separate the sinner from the sin or the sin from the sinner.

Now in God's arrangement, not only is the sin treated, but the sinner is treated as well. This next area is subtle, however, and must be very carefully understood.

THE SHEDDING OF INNOCENT BLOOD

The only thing that stopped the Wrath of God from being poured out on the sinner, as we have said, was the shedding of innocent blood. It was this sacrifice of blood that provided a facing, a covering, or a shield between the Wrath of God and the sinner. In

effect, the sin was still there. It was not taken away – it was just covered over.

However, many centuries in the future, the Son of God would stand close to the River Jordan and John the Baptist would see Him coming and would say, *"Behold the Lamb of God, which taketh away the sin of the world"* (Jn. 1:29).

When John uttered the words, *"Lamb of God,"* every Jew standing nearby understood exactly what he was talking about. They knew that millions of little sacrificial lambs had been offered up through the centuries – lambs that were types, or symbolic predictions of the great Antitype, or unique One, Who was to come and be the Messiah, the Saviour of Israel, and as well, of the world. There by the Jordan, John was Himself recognizing the Lamb of God Who would be the Perfect Sacrifice. But it is the last part of John's statement that holds such a wealth of meaning for ourselves.

SIN IS TAKEN AWAY

John said, *"Which takes away the sin of the world."*

This was a startling Revelation by the Baptist to all nearby, and it is to us today also. Whereas the offering of the sacrifices of old only covered the sin and the sinner, now the Lamb of God would not just cover the sin; He would actually *"take it away!"*

This Lamb, God's Lamb, would actually separate the sin from the sinner. Jesus would not only atone – in other words, satisfy the Wrath of God – but He would make the person a brand-new creature (II Cor. 5:17). He would refer to the person as *"born again"* (Jn. 3:3).

John the Baptist, *"The Prophet of the Highest,"* did not just say that the Lamb of God was going to take away *"sins."* John didn't say *"sins"* in the plural form; he said *"sin"* in the singular meaning generic sin, all sin. In other words, Jesus, at the Cross, dealt with the very cause of sin, even as we've already explained.

KILL THE ANIMAL

The sinner himself had to personally kill the animal. He would no doubt be supplied a knife by the Priest, but due to the fact that he was the one who had sinned, he had to do the actual killing himself.

He would have to lay his hands on the head of the animal, thereby transferring his guilt and his sin to this innocent victim – just as his guilt and sin would, later on, be transferred in turn to the Lord Jesus Christ.

More than likely, the Priest would hold back the head of the victim, while the sinner slit the throat of the animal.

So to make the application, here is what we too must understand. It was our sins that nailed Jesus Christ to the tree. Each and every one of us had our share in that horrible, bloody death that He had to suffer. The Lord Jesus did not die for His sins; He died for our sins.

Now when the offerer, at the Tabernacle, would take the knife in his hand and put it to the throat of the animal, the thoughts that went to his mind must have been many. He knew this animal had done nothing amiss. He also realized that the animal was being made to pay the price that he should have paid himself.

He thus had to have a very sharp realization that his own sin was killing this little creature. In a sense, we did the same with the Lord Jesus Christ.

It is true, of course, that Christ the Lamb laid down His Life willingly and that no man took His Life from Him. But each one of us, every human being who has ever lived, had a part in it – in the thorns upon His Brow, in the beard plucked from His Face, in the whip laid across His Back, in the nails piercing His Hands, and in the spear that entered His Side.

One might say that we all had a hand in it. The Crucifixion and Death of the Lord Jesus was a horrible, bloody gang killing. We all did it!

THE SPRINKLING OF THE BLOOD ROUND ABOUT THE ALTAR

The assisting Priest would catch in a basin the blood that poured from the slain animal's throat. He would then take the blood to the Brazen Altar, and throw it around the bottom of the Altar. In some respects this was the most essential part of the ceremony, the blood representing the life (Lev. 17:11), which was symbolically received

at the hands of the offerer, and presented by the Priests to God. In the antitype, our Lord exercised the function of the sacrificing Priest when He presented His Own Life to the Father, as He hung upon the Altar of the Cross.

As it regards this particular Sacrifice, the *"Whole Burnt Offering,"* we must bear in mind that the grand point set forth therein is not the meeting of the sinner's need, but the presentation to God of that which was infinitely acceptable to Him, in order that the price be paid. This means that Christ as foreshadowed by the Burnt-Offering is not for the sinner's conscience, but for the heart of God. This is why, of all the Sacrifices, the Whole Burnt Offering was the foundation Offering, so to speak, of the five presentation Offerings. While each Sacrifice played its part, and served its purpose, even as we shall see, it was the Whole Burnt Offering that made everything possible, simply because it satisfied the Wrath of God.

Finally, *"Atonement,"* as seen in the Burnt Offering, is not merely commensurate with the claims of man's conscience, but with the intense desire of the heart of Christ to carry out the will and establish the counsels of God – a desire which stopped not short of surrendering up His spotless, precious Life, as *"a voluntary Offering"* of *"sweet savor"* to God.

THE MEANING OF THE SACRIFICE OF CHRIST

In the entire debacle of sin that originated with the Fall of Lucifer who dragged down one-third of the angelic hosts with him and then onto man, God's most prized creation, which the latter has soaked this Earth with blood and has brought unmitigated sorrow, God's honor, the very fiber of His Being, so to speak, that is if we can refer to God accordingly, has been trampled in the dirt. His Honor of Goodness, Grace, Mercy, Compassion, Longsuffering, and all of this in every capacity had to be satisfied, and there was no one or nothing which could fill this bill, except that God would pay the price Himself. This is at least one of the reasons, actually the primary reason, that the Atonement is of such significance. While it definitely met the need of sinful, fallen, depraved man, in fact, the entire spectacle of Adam's fallen race, above all, it satisfied the honor, the justice, and the character of God. We can judge the worth of this sacrifice by the magnitude of God, which of course is impossible for man to do!

That's the reason this great Book of Leviticus is at least one of the most important works in the entirety of the Word of God. It goes into detail in explaining what Christ has done for us, as it regards the Sacrifice of Himself on the Cross of Calvary, and does so by portraying and even detailing the sacrificial system of the Levitical Law.

THE PRIESTS

We must remember that it was *"The Priests,"* Aaron's sons, who brought the blood and sprinkled it round about upon the Altar that is by the door of the Tabernacle of the congregation, of which we will have more to say in a moment.

In this, we must also remember it is the *"blood of the Burnt-Offering,"* and not of the *"Sin-Offering,"* of which we speak. And what does that mean?

It doesn't mean that we as convicted sinners enter into the value of the blood of the sin-bearer, as important as that is within its own right. In effect, it is as *"Priests"* that we have to do with the Burnt-Offering. As John said, we are *"kings and priests unto God"* (Rev. 1:6). But we are that because of what Jesus did for us at the Cross, where He *"washed us from our sins in His Own Blood"* (Rev. 1:5).

The truth is, we as Believers are *"nothing at all"*; but in Christ, we are a purged worshipper. This means that we do not stand in the Sanctuary, so to speak, as a guilty sinner, but as a worshipping Priest, clothed in *"garments of glory and beauty."* In fact, to be occupied with guilt in the Presence of God is not humility as it regards myself, but unbelief as it regards the Sacrifice. And please understand, this is something we don't want to do!

As stated, the Burnt-Offering is not for the purpose of cleansing the conscience of the Believer, that having already been done; it is to satisfy the Justice and the Character of God.

If I contemplate Christ as the Sin-Offering, which we will do momentarily, I see Atonement made according to the claims of

NOTES

Divine Justice with respect to sin; but when I see Atonement in the Burnt-Offering, it is according to the measure of the willingness and ability of Christ, to accomplish the Will of God, which He did at the Cross. In fact, the Burnt-Offering aspect of Atonement is that about which the Priestly household, the Church of the Living God, may well be occupied in the courts of the Lord's House forever.

THE DOOR

The Brazen Altar, on which the sacrifice was laid, and on which the blood was poured, was very near the *"door,"* that led into the Holy Place of the Tabernacle. Jesus plainly said of Himself: *"I am the Door: by Me if any man enter in, he shall be saved, and shall go in and out, and find pasture"* (Jn. 10:9).

But what the Believer must know and understand is the great Biblical Truth, in fact, the foundational Truth of the Word of God, is that one cannot enter this Door, unless he goes by and through the Brazen Altar, which means that one cannot know Christ unless one comes by the Way of the Cross. There is simply no other way.

That's the reason that the Apostle Paul was so strong as it regarded the Cross. That's the reason that he vehemently came against any doctrine that impugned the Cross in any way, as did, in his time, the Law/Grace issue. That's the reason we presently take such a stand against the Word of Faith doctrine, which in reality is no faith at all, simply because it demeans the Cross, actually claiming that Salvation is brought about by one having faith in Jesus suffering three days and nights in Hell, with Him dying spiritually, they claim.

Were that true, then sinners could suffer three days and nights in Hell, and then be saved, simply because such suffering would atone for their sin. But of course, we know that is foolishness!

However, the sinner can definitely be saved, if He identifies with Christ on the Cross, even as Paul declared, and in fact, it's the only way he can be saved (Rom. 6:3-5; Jn. 3:16; Eph. 2:8-9; Col. 2:14-15).

THE FLAYING AND THE CUTTING

Verse 6 reads: *"And he shall flay the Burnt*

Offering, and cut it into his pieces."

To *"flay"* means to take the hide off, usually through whipping. With this done, the sacrificer or sinful offerer and the Priests or Levites assisting him needed to cut the animal into large pieces. The Priests then took over in following the Law that was set down regarding Sacrifices by laying these pieces on the Altar to be burned.

In the grizzly carving process, the head would be cut off and the fat would be severed from the muscle, tissue, and skin. The animal needed to be cut into pieces like this to signify two things:

1. It signified how horrible, how deep a thing sin is. Sin is not merely exterior; it is interior. It is not just outward; it is inward. Sin is a disease of our vitals. It affects every single part of the human being.

You have heard it said that *"A man is not a liar because he lies; he lies because he is a liar."* And similarly, *"A man is not a thief because he steals; he steals because he is a thief."*

In other words, at the time that he performs the sinful action, it is in his heart. Sin comes straight out of the vitals of a man or woman.

So as an effect of this, sin and sinfulness cannot be dealt with by simply changing a person's clothing, environment, geography, or social situation. Sin can only be dealt with through a change of heart, and only God Himself can get to our hearts. We are, by nature, so dense, so thick, and we have so many twists, deceptions, and *"kinks,"* as part of our sinful, inner beings, that it takes God Himself, our Maker, to pierce right through into the very fiber of our individuality.

2. The cutting up of the animal in order to lay it on the Brazen Altar to be burned further emphasized the horror and deep effect of sin. There is no part of the human being which it does not corrupt, be it mental, physical, financial, or spiritual.

THE FIRE

Verses 7 and 8 read: *"And the sons of Aaron the Priest shall put fire upon the Altar, and lay the wood in order upon the fire:*

"And the Priests, Aaron's sons, shall lay the parts, the head, and the fat, in order upon

the wood that is on the fire which is upon the Altar."

As it regards the *"fire,"* it would be well here to note that the Hebrew word that is rendered *"burn"* in the case of the *"Burnt-Offering"* is wholly different from that which is used in the *"Sin-Offering."* The Hebrew word that is rendered *"burn"* in connection with the *"Sin-Offering,"* signifies to burn in general; however, the Hebrew word used in *"Burnt-Offering,"* signifies *"incense."*

Now, we cannot imagine, for a moment, that this distinction is a mere interchange of words, the use of which is immaterial. Concerning this, Mackintosh said: *"I believe the wisdom of the Holy Spirit is as manifest in the use of the two words as it is in any other point of difference in the two Offerings."*

The idea is this: as we note in the concluding part of the Ninth Verse, the phrase is used, *"of a sweet savor unto the Lord,"* which signifies that the honor and justice of Jehovah have been satisfied, which of course refers to it being satisfied in the Cross.

As convicted sinners, we gaze on the Cross of our Lord Jesus Christ, and behold therein that which meets all our need. The Cross, in this aspect of it, gives perfect peace to the conscience. But then, as kings and priests, we can look at the Cross in another light – even as the grand consummation of Christ's Holy Purpose to carry out, even unto death, the Will of the Father.

We should have a very defective apprehension of the mystery of the Cross were we only to see in it that which meets man's need as a sinner. There were depths in that mystery which only the Mind of God could fathom. It is, therefore, important to see that when the Holy Spirit would furnish us with foreshadowings of the Cross, He gives us, in the very first place, one which sets it forth in its aspect Godward. This alone would be sufficient to teach us that there are heights and depths in the Doctrine of the Cross which man never could reach. There is in the Cross that which only God could know and appreciate. Hence it is that the Burnt-Offering gets the first place. It typifies Christ's death as viewed and valued by God Alone.

Strangely, but yet beautifully enough, from the Cross, we might well say that the

Father reaps His richest harvest of glory. In no other way could He have been so glorified as by the death of Christ. In Christ's voluntary surrender of Himself to death, the Divine Glory shines in its fullest brightness.

Creation never could have furnished such a basis. Moreover, the Cross furnishes a righteous channel through which Divine Love can flow. And in that flow of Love, every other Gift from the Father comes our way, but all made possible by the Cross.

And, finally, by the Cross Satan is eternally confounded, and *"principalities and powers made a show of openly."* These are glorious fruits produced by the Cross; and, when we think of them, we can see just reason why there should have been a type of the Cross exclusively for God Himself, and also a reason why that type should occupy the leading place – in other words, should stand at the very top of the list, even as does the Burnt-Offering. Lacking that, there would be a grievous blank in the page of inspiration (Mackintosh).

WASH IN WATER

Verse 9 reads: *"But his inwards and his legs shall he wash in water: and the Priest shall burn all on the Altar, to be a Burnt Sacrifice, an Offering made by fire, of a sweet savor unto the LORD."*

Going back to Verse 7, the fire that was placed on the Altar by the Priests was to never go out. Twenty-four hours a day it was to burn, signifying two things: God's anger against sin, and God's provision of Mercy.

The phrase *"burn all"* is not the common term for destroying by fire, but rather, it means, *"make to ascend."* The life of the animal has already been offered in the blood; now the whole of its substance is *"made to ascend"* to the Lord.

This means that the vapor that ascends is not something different from that which is burnt, but the very thing itself, its essence; which, having ascended, is, as previously stated, an *"incense,"* providing a *"sweet savor unto the Lord,"* which means that it is acceptable and well-pleasing to Him.

The *"Burnt-Offering,"* the *"Meat-Offering,"* and the *"Peace-Offering,"* are sacrifices of a *"sweet savor."* The expression is never used with regard to the *"Sin-Offering"* and

"Trespass-Offering."

Paul applies it to the Sacrifice of Christ in Ephesians 5:2, *"As Christ also loved us, and gave Himself for us an Offering and a Sacrifice to God for a sweet-smelling savor"*; thus, Paul indicated in an incidental manner, the connection between the Jewish sacrifices and the Sacrifice of Christ, as type and antitype (Pulpit). The *"Meat-Offering"* is a *"Thank Offering,"* which specifies that we thank God for giving His only Son. The *"Peace-Offering"* signifies that all sin has been assuaged, and done so because the proper sacrifice has been made, and now peace is restored. All of this, Christ giving Himself to satisfy the Honor and Justice of God, the thanksgiving on our part, and the peace we obtain, all made possible by Christ and what He did, provides a sweet savor unto the Lord.

The *"inwards"* typify the very being of Christ, while the *"legs"* typify His physical body. The *"washing"* signified the purity of Christ. Even though the animal was only a type, it had to be a type in every respect, and purity was an absolute requirement, hence the *"washing."* The parts would then be burned on the Altar, given up as a Sacrifice, and given up in totality.

THE WASHING AND THE CROSS

When Jesus went to the Cross, He did so Perfect in every respect. In a spiritual sense, He was Perfectly Clean, in fact, as no human being had ever been clean. This was demanded by God, because anything less than perfection could not be accepted.

This completely shoots down the theory that Jesus died spiritually (separated from God) on the Cross. The teachers of this blasphemy, and blasphemy it is, claimed that Jesus became one with Satan while on the Cross, and had to do such in order to redeem humanity, which Redemption was completed in the burning side of Hell. Of course, all of this is made up out of whole cloth, meaning that there is not a shred of Scriptural evidence to support these claims.

They teach that the fire on the Altar symbolizes the Hell to which Jesus had to go, and where, after some three days and nights of torture, He would then be born again.

The fire symbolized the Judgment of God,

and not Hell-fire. When the sacrifice was consumed completely, even the ashes were then moved away.

The ashes signified that all sin had been addressed, and there was nothing left, for everything had been atoned. When we think of something totally destroyed and consumed, we at times use the term, *"reduced to ashes."* It means that nothing is left.

So when Faith and trust are placed in Christ and what He did at the Cross, every sin is atoned, and nothing is left, in other words, *"My sins are gone."*

The Work of Christ on the Cross was a *"Finished Work"* (Heb. 1:3). This means that nothing remained to be done.

(10) "AND IF HIS OFFERING BE OF THE FLOCKS, NAMELY, OF THE SHEEP, OR OF THE GOATS, FOR A BURNT SACRIFICE; HE SHALL BRING IT A MALE WITHOUT BLEMISH.

(11) "AND HE SHALL KILL IT ON THE SIDE OF THE ALTAR NORTHWARD BEFORE THE LORD: AND THE PRIESTS, AARON'S SONS, SHALL SPRINKLE HIS BLOOD ROUND ABOUT UPON THE ALTAR.

(12) "AND HE SHALL CUT IT INTO HIS PIECES, WITH HIS HEAD AND HIS FAT: AND THE PRIEST SHALL LAY THEM IN ORDER ON THE WOOD THAT IS ON THE FIRE WHICH IS UPON THE ALTAR:

(13) "BUT HE SHALL WASH THE INWARDS AND THE LEGS WITH WATER: AND THE PRIEST SHALL BRING IT ALL, AND BURN IT UPON THE ALTAR: IT IS A BURNT SACRIFICE, AN OFFERING MADE BY FIRE, OF A SWEET SAVOR UNTO THE LORD."

The composition is:

1. The ritual of the Burnt Offering was the same, whether the victim was a bullock, sheep, or goat.

2. Even though the instructions are basically the same for the lamb as they had been for the bullock, they are meticulously given again. The significance lies in Who the Offering represented.

3. I think as we go along, we will find that the Book of Leviticus presents itself as priceless, as it regards the types that refer to Christ. To learn Christ is to learn life, and to learn Leviticus is to learn Christ.

THE LAMB

Verses 10 through 13 read: *"And if his Offering be of the flocks, namely, of the sheep, or of the goats, for a Burnt Sacrifice; he shall bring it a male without blemish.*

"And he shall kill it on the side of the Altar northward before the LORD: and the Priests, Aaron's sons, shall sprinkle his blood round about upon the Altar.

"And he shall cut it into his pieces, with his head and his fat: and the Priest shall lay them in order on the wood that is on the fire which is upon the Altar.

"But he shall wash the inwards and the legs with water: and the Priest shall bring it all, and burn it upon the Altar: it is a Burnt Sacrifice, an Offering made by fire, of a sweet savor unto the LORD."

Those who could not afford a bullock could bring a lamb or a goat; and those who were not able to do that would be accepted by God, even if they brought only a turtledove, or a pigeon. So the sacrificial system was made such that every single individual could participate, from the poorest to the richest, and because all needed to participate, and all would be accepted, that is if they followed the instructions given by the Lord.

It should be observable that the creatures chosen for sacrifice were most mild and gentle, but yet the bullock, as would be obvious, was very strong as well.

All of this typified Christ, Who was the strong of the strong, and we speak of spiritual sense, as well as mild and gentle.

In fact, whether more lambs or pigeons were offered, we aren't told; however, lambs are mentioned more than anything else as it regards the sacrifices. In fact, the *"lamb"* so typified Christ that the Prophet Isaiah said of Him: *"He is brought as a lamb to the slaughter"* (Isa. 53:7).

John the Baptist referred to Him as: *"The Lamb of God, which taketh away the sin of the world"* (Jn. 1:29).

(14) "AND IF THE BURNT SACRIFICE FOR HIS OFFERING TO THE LORD BE OF FOWLS, THEN HE SHALL BRING HIS OFFERING OF TURTLEDOVES, OR OF YOUNG PIGEONS.

(15) "AND THE PRIEST SHALL BRING

IT UNTO THE ALTAR, AND WRING OFF HIS HEAD, AND BURN IT ON THE ALTAR; AND THE BLOOD THEREOF SHALL BE WRUNG OUT AT THE SIDE OF THE ALTAR:

(16) "AND HE SHALL PLUCK AWAY HIS CROP WITH HIS FEATHERS, AND CAST IT BESIDE THE ALTAR ON THE EAST PART, BY THE PLACE OF THE ASHES:

(17) "AND HE SHALL CLEAVE IT WITH THE WINGS THEREOF, BUT SHALL NOT DIVIDE IT ASUNDER: AND THE PRIEST SHALL BURN IT UPON THE ALTAR, UPON THE WOOD THAT IS UPON THE FIRE: IT IS A BURNT SACRIFICE, AN OFFERING MADE BY FIRE, OF A SWEET SAVOR UNTO THE LORD."

The construction is:

1. The Jews say the sacrifice of birds was one of the most difficult services the Priests had to do. They would need to take as much care in offering this sacrifice as in any of the others.

2. This teaches us that the Lord loves the poor, who could afford only the pigeons, as much as He loves the rich, who could afford the bullocks.

3. The poor man's turtledoves, or young pigeons, are said to be an offering of a sweet savor, as much as that of an ox or bullock, or even a lamb.

THE TURTLEDOVES OR YOUNG PIGEONS

Verses 14 through 17 read: *"And if the Burnt Sacrifice for his Offering to the LORD be of fowls, then he shall bring his Offering of turtledoves, or of young pigeons.*

"And the Priest shall bring it unto the Altar, and wring off his head, and burn it on the Altar; and the blood thereof shall be wrung out at the side of the Altar:

"And he shall pluck away his crop with his feathers, and cast it beside the Altar on the east part, by the place of the ashes:

"And he shall cleave it with the wings thereof, but shall not divide it asunder: and the Priest shall burn it upon the Altar, upon the wood that is upon the fire: it is a Burnt Sacrifice, an Offering made by fire, of a sweet savor unto the LORD."

A turtledove or a pigeon could be had for a pittance; consequently, we find that the Lord

made it possible for the poorest of the poor to offer up sacrifices, which would be accepted by God, and done so just as much as if it had been a bullock or a lamb; therefore, no person in Israel, whatever their status in life, had any excuse for not obeying the Lord.

But yet, I think it would not be pleasing to the Lord if a person could afford to offer a bullock, or a lamb, but would instead offer a pigeon or a turtledove. The Lord, Who sees and knows all things, would probably not accept such a sacrifice, and because it would be dishonest. In fact, in later years, the Prophets, as the Holy Spirit spoke through them, would greatly charge the people for bringing sick animals, etc. (Mal. 1:13).

Is it not the same presently, when people give of their offerings to the Lord, and they give far less than they actually could give?

On my desk right now is a short note from a young couple in our Church, who has just written a sizeable check, in order that we may use it for SonLife Radio. In fact, this young couple has given a large portion of all that they have.

How does this measure up to those who are quite wealthy, and who give but a tiny, tiny portion of what they could actually give?

As we shall see, five different types of Sacrifices were demanded, with even different sacrifices among the types. This means that no one type could fully present Him. We needed to have Him reflected in life and in death – as a Man and as a Victim, Godward and usward; and we have Him thus in the Offerings of Leviticus.

"You are the everlasting Word
"The Father's only Son,
"God manifest, God seen and heard,
"The heavens' beloved One!"

"In You most perfectly expressed,
"The Father's Self does shine,
"Fullness of Godhead, too:
"The Blessed, Eternally Divine!"

"Image of Infinite Unseen,
"Whose Being none can know,
"Brightness of light no eye has seen,
"God's love revealed below!"

"The higher mysteries of Your fame
"The creature's grasp transcend;

*"The Father only Your blest Name
"Of Son can comprehend."*

*"Yet loving You, on Whom His love
"Ineffable does rest,
"The worshippers, O Lord, above,
"As one with You, are blest."*

*"Of the vast universe of bliss,
"The center You, and Son!
"The eternal theme of praise is this,
"To heavens' beloved One."*

CHAPTER 2

(1) "AND WHEN ANY WILL OFFER A MEAT OFFERING UNTO THE LORD, HIS OFFERING SHALL BE OF FINE FLOUR; AND HE SHALL POUR OIL UPON IT, AND PUT FRANKINCENSE THEREON:

(2) "AND HE SHALL BRING IT TO AARON'S SONS TO THE PRIESTS: HE SHALL TAKE THEREOUT HIS HANDFUL OF THE FLOUR THEREOF, AND OF THE OIL THEREOF, WITH ALL THE FRANK-INCENSE THEREOF; AND THE PRIEST SHALL BURN THE MEMORIAL OF IT UPON THE ALTAR, TO BE AN OFFERING MADE BY FIRE, OF A SWEET SAVOR UNTO THE LORD:

(3) "AND THE REMNANT OF THE MEAT OFFERING SHALL BE AARON'S AND HIS SONS': IT IS A THING MOST HOLY OF THE OFFERINGS OF THE LORD MADE BY FIRE."

The diagram is:

1. The Meat (meal) Offering prefigured Christ's spotless humanity.

2. The fineness of the flour predicted that in Him there should be no unevenness or roughness.

3. The flour was mingled with oil, and oil poured upon it. Such was the Man Christ Jesus. He was born of the Holy Spirit, and afterwards anointed by the Holy Spirit. (Mat. 1:20; Lk. 4:18-19).

THE MEAT OFFERING

Verse 1 reads: *"And when any will offer a Meat Offering unto the LORD, his Offering shall be of fine flour; and he shall pour oil upon it, and put frankincense thereon."*

Presently, *"meat"* refers to flesh; however, in Bible times, it just simply referred to food. In our interpretation presently, this Offering could be labeled a *"Food Offering,"* or a *"Meal Offering."*

The Hebrew word for *"Meat Offering"* is *"Minchah,"* and means *"a gift made by an inferior to a superior."* It actually was a *"gratitude or thanksgiving Offering."*

All the other Sacrifices are bloody sacrifices, but this Offering is a *"vegetable sacrifice,"* one might say!

While all of it refers to Christ, it does so in a different way. For instance, as the *"Burnt-Offering"* typified Christ in death, the *"Meat-Offering"* typified Him in *"life."*

In this particular Sacrifice, we find it a beautiful Type of Christ as He lived, walked, and served down here on this Earth. The Pure and Perfect Manhood of our blessed Lord is a theme which must command the attention of every true Christian.

This is very important, when one considers that many do not properly understand Christ, and more so do not understand the Incarnation, i.e., *"God becoming Man."* In fact, the expressions which one sometimes hears and reads are sufficient to prove that the fundamental doctrine of the Incarnation is not laid hold of as it ought to be, and as the Word of God presents it.

Considering that an entire Levitical Sacrifice was appointed by God, which refers to the Humanity of Christ, His Life, Living, and Walk, we should realize how important this is. Satan has diligently sought, from the beginning, to lead people astray in reference to this all-important aspect of our Saviour – His Humanity.

Concerning this, Mackintosh said: *"The Lord Jesus Christ was the only perfect Man Who ever trod this Earth. He was all perfect – perfect in thought, perfect in word, perfect in action. In Him every moral quality met in Divine and, therefore, perfect proportion. No one feature was out of kilter. In Him were exquisitely blended a majesty which overawed, and a gentleness which gave perfect ease in His presence."*

THE FINE FLOUR

The phrase, *"His Offering shall be of fine*

flour," presents the Type of this Perfect Manhood. It formed the basis of the Meat-Offering. There was not so much as a single coarse grain in this flour. This means there was nothing uneven, nothing unequal, nothing rough to the touch. What does all of this mean?

It means that Christ, no matter what the pressure, was never ruffled by any circumstance, or set of circumstances. He never had to retrace a step or recall a word. Come what might, He always met it in that perfect response and repose, which are so strikingly typified by the *"fine flour."*

Even though there have been Godly men and women in history, in fact, some which portrayed Christ beautifully, but yet, none could even remotely match the Perfection of the Son of God in any capacity, and especially in the portrayal of Life and Living, with all of its difficulties, problems, irritations, etc. I think we could say, without fear of exaggeration, that while some stand out over other men, none even remotely approaches Christ. In other words, that gap or chasm between Christ and man, is uncrossable.

As someone has well said, if a person could find on this Earth the individual of whom they think is the Godliest, the kindest, the most Christlike, the one in whom the Fruit of the Spirit functions to the greatest degree, upon close association with that individual, whomever they might be, one would quickly see the faults, flaws, and imperfections. And the longer one stayed around that person, again whomever that person might be, the more faults and flaws one would observe; however, the closer we get to Christ, the very opposite result is to be found. His Perfection becomes even greater perfection, if such is possible. His Attributes and Qualities are enlarged upon the closer that we inspect the Man from Galilee. Truly, one has to say, even as the Roman Governor of so long ago, *"I find no fault in this Man"* (Lk. 23:4). And no one else, at least if they are honest, has ever found any fault in this man.

THE LAST ADAM

There has always been much discussion about Christ, concerning the question as to whether He could have sinned or not. Many

take the position that inasmuch as He was God as well as Man, in effect, the God-Man, Jesus Christ, He could not sin, because God can't sin.

While it's certainly true that Jesus Christ was God, never ceased to be God, and in fact will always be God, still, when He became Man, He forever laid aside the expression of His Deity, while at the same time retaining possession of His Deity. In other words, even though He definitely is God, He functions as a man.

And I would remind the Reader that Jesus grew hungry, grew thirsty, grew tired, which are all characteristics of the flesh. And we know that God cannot get hungry, thirsty, or tired! So we must come back to the position that even though Jesus is God, and always will be God, due to the Incarnation, He now functions as a Man, and in fact, will forever function as a Man (Zech. 12:10; 13:6).

The purpose for Jesus becoming man (the Incarnation) was that He may serve as the *"Last Adam"* (I Cor. 15:45). In other words, He had to do what the first Adam did not do, which is to completely obey God, which He did, and as well, undo what the first Adam did, which was to plunge man into spiritual oblivion. He did the first by living a Perfect Life, which the *"Meat Offering"* typifies, and He did the second part, which was to effect the Redemption of humanity, which was undoing what Adam had done, by dying on the Cross, typified by the *"Burnt Offering."* Of course, the other Offerings played into this, even as we shall see.

To answer the question as to whether Jesus could have sinned or not, to be the *"Last Adam,"* He had to have the capacity to sin, or else He would not have fulfilled the Type.

Satan is deluded, deceived, and demented, but as we think of such, he's no fool. He would not have spent all the time he did tempting Christ, if there was no chance of success. But the truth was, in the Incarnation, God becoming Man, the Godhead reduced itself to its lowest possible denominator, one might say, which was the Man, Christ Jesus. In other words, everything was riding on Christ. Had He failed, which He had the capacity to do, it would have involved far more than the loss of humanity. It would have involved the loss of everything. In other words, Satan would have become the master of the universe; he would have taken the place of Jehovah as god.

Concerning Christ, Paul said: *"That in the dispensation of the fullness of times, He* (God the Father) *might gather together in one all things in Christ* (what Christ did at the Cross), *both which are in Heaven, and which are on Earth; even in Him"* (Eph. 1:10).

This means that what Jesus did affected not only this Earth, but Heaven as well!

Paul is actually referring in this Passage to a statement that he made in I Corinthians. He said: *"Then cometh the end, when He* (Christ) *shall have delivered up the Kingdom of God, even the Father; when He shall have put down all rule and all authority and power"* (I Cor. 15:24).

This will take place at the conclusion of the Millennial Reign, when Satan will be loosed out of his prison for a short period of time, and will make one more effort to take over the world, etc., but will be totally and completely defeated, and as well, cast into the Lake of Fire, along with all demon spirits and fallen angels (Rev. 20:7-15).

That will be the end of Satan's rebellion, and will be the end forever. In other words, Satan and all sin, which refers to all who served him, will be forever locked away, actually in the Lake of Fire, where they will be forever and forever. Then Jesus will deliver up the Kingdom to the Father, with the end result being that described in Revelation, Chapters 21 and 22.

Yes, in His earthly sojourn, Jesus could have sinned. But the facts are, He did not sin, whether in word, thought, or deed.

OIL

The phrase, *"And he shall pour oil upon it,"* refers to the oil being poured on the fine flour, which refers in Type to Jesus being filled with the Holy Spirit beyond measure (Jn. 3:34). In fact, the Holy Spirit led and guided Him, in all that He did (Lk. 4:18-19).

We find that the oil was applied in two ways: 1. The fine flour was *"mingled"* with oil; and then, 2. There was oil *"poured"* upon it.

This refers to the *"conception"* of Christ,

and then to His *"Anointing,"* all by the Holy Spirit (Mat. 1:18-23; 3:16; Lk. 4:18-19).

We must ever understand that Christ never took our fallen nature into union with Himself. He didn't do it at His Birth, not in His Life and Living, and not on the Cross, as some teach. At no point did He have a fallen nature. In fact, that was the reason for the Virgin Birth. Had He been born by normal procreation, He would have been born as all other babies, in original sin, which would have translated into a fallen nature. But to escape that fallen nature, He was born of the Virgin Mary. In fact, had He had a fallen nature, this would have meant that He was a sinner, and would have meant that He needed a Saviour Himself, which of course, is preposterous.

While Christ never unites with us in our fallen nature, we in fact, do unite with Him in His Divine Nature; in which case, His Divine Nature becomes ours (II Pet. 1:4). How is this done?

It was done totally and completely at the Cross, Paul said: *"But now in Christ Jesus you* (Gentiles) *who at one time were far off are made near by the Blood of Christ.*

"For He is our peace, Who has made both one (Jews and Gentiles), *and has broken down the middle wall of partition between us;*

"Having abolished in His flesh (His death on the Cross) *the enmity, even the Law of Commandments contained in ordinances* (the Ten Commandments); *for to make in Himself of twain* (both Jews and Gentiles) *one new man* (one Church), *so making peace;*

"And that He might reconcile both (Jews and Gentiles) *unto God in one body* (the Church) *by the Cross, having slain the enmity thereby* (removed the enmity by His death on the Cross)" (Eph. 2:13-16).

As should be overly obvious in these Passages, Jesus didn't do this by and through His Resurrection, but rather, through the Cross. While it is true that we are Resurrection people, which means that we enjoy Resurrection life, it is only because of what He did at the Cross. Paul plainly said:

"For if we have been planted together in the likeness of His death, we shall be also in the likeness of His Resurrection" (Rom. 6:5).

This plainly tells us that Resurrection

life is predicated solely on the *"likeness of His death,"* and our part in that death (Rom. 6:3-4).

While we dare not minimize the great significance of the Resurrection, which should be overly obvious, at the same time, we must not place undue emphasis on that all-important work. The individual should ever be directed to the Cross, whether the sinner being saved, or the Saint being righteous. All are tied to the Cross, and the Cross alone!

The Resurrection was a foregone conclusion, in that Jesus atoned for all sin. Had one sin been left unatoned (Rom. 6:23), Jesus could not have been raised from the dead. But inasmuch as all sin definitely was atoned, which means that Redemption was completed at the Cross, the Resurrection was never in doubt.

Some Christians think of Christ being raised from the dead, by struggling with Satan, along with demon spirits, and then finally breaking through them, and then walking out of the tomb. Nothing like that ever happened! To be factual, Satan or any demon spirit, do not want anything to do with Christ. In fact, they tremble in His Presence.

The Holy Spirit, typified by the oil on the fine flour, could occupy Christ as He did, simply because Christ was Perfect. The Holy Spirit can function in us accordingly, only because our Faith is in a Perfect Christ, Who has afforded a Perfect Redemption. Our Faith in Him gives us His Perfection, which makes it possible for the Holy Spirit to work with us as He does, which in fact could only be done after the Cross (Jn. 14:17).

FRANKINCENSE

The phrase, *"And put frankincense thereon,"* has a spiritual meaning as well, which should be obvious.

First of all, frankincense is *"white,"* which speaks of *"purity."* The Holy Spirit could function in Christ as He did simply because Christ was perfectly pure, symbolized by the frankincense.

As well, frankincense was bitter, which speaks of the bitterness that Christ had to undergo, not only in His Life and Living, but as well, in His Death on the Cross. Concerning His Life, the Scripture says: *"He is*

despised and rejected of men" (Isa. 53:3).

Concerning His Death on the Cross, the Scripture also says: *"And the LORD has laid on Him the iniquity of us all* (has laid on Him the penalty of our iniquity)*"* (Isa. 53:6).

THE ALTAR

Verses 2 and 3 read: *"And he shall bring it to Aaron's sons the Priests: he shall take thereout his handful of the flour thereof, and of the oil thereof, with all the frankincense thereof; and the Priest shall burn the memorial of it upon the Altar, to be an Offering made by fire of a sweet savor unto the LORD:*

"And the remnant of the Meat Offering shall be Aaron's and his sons': it is a thing most holy of the Offerings of the LORD made by fire."

So close was the union between the two sacrifices, and I speak of the Burnt-Offering and the Meat-Offering, that the Burnt-Offering was never offered without the accompaniment of the Meat-Offering (Num. 15:4).

When the Meat-Offering was brought to the Priests, and I speak of it being brought by Israelites who were offering up sacrifices, only about a handful was burned on the Altar, along with the Burnt-Offering, with the Priests taking the remainder for themselves, for this is what was ordered by the Lord.

According to the Pulpit Commentary, for every handful of flour burnt on the Altar, nearly a gallon went to the Priests. They had to eat it within the precincts of the Tabernacle, as was the case with all food that was *"most holy."* This included the *"Shewbread, and the flesh of the Sin-Offering and of the Trespass-Offering"* (Lev. 10:12). However, when the Priests personally offered Meat-Offerings, it was all wholly burnt, with none kept for themselves (Lev. 6:23).

THE MEMORIAL

The word *"memorial"* served a twofold purpose:

1. It pertained to the Believer not failing to remember what the Lord has done for him, and especially what Jesus has done for us.

2. As well, it pertains to the fact that God will not forget His Promises. The Psalmist said: *"The Lord remember all your offerings,*

and accept your burnt sacrifice" (Ps. 20:3).

The first part is carried over into that sacred Ordinance of the Church, referred to as the *"Lord's Supper."* Jesus said: *"Take, eat: this is My body, which is broken for you: this do in remembrance of Me."*

And then: *"This cup is the New Testament in My Blood: this do you, as oft as you drink it, in remembrance of Me"* (I Cor. 11:24-25).

The greatest Promise that God made, and in which the Meat-Offering was a Type, was that He would send a Redeemer into the world, to lift man out of this darkness. This One sent would be the Perfect One. How much the Israelites understood this, we cannot actually tell. It was supposed to have been explained to them. To be sure, Moses would have been faithful to this task, but how much the people would have heeded what he said about all of these things, is anyone's guess.

While Moses wrote all of this down, which constitutes the first five Books of the Bible, still, how many of the Israelites, who were former slaves, could actually read, again, is anyone's guess. So the instruction given to them would mostly have been given verbally.

A SWEET SAVOR UNTO THE LORD

This Offering was a sweet savor to the Lord, not so much because of the Offering itself, but rather What, or more particularly, Who it represented. It typified Christ in His Perfection. So we can understand how this would be a sweet savor. Correspondingly, this we must remember:

In all of our doing, we must present Christ! In all our believing, we must believe Christ! Nothing must come between us and Christ, and nothing must take the place of Christ. Christ and Him Crucified must always be the Foundation of our Faith. I think we can say without fear of contradiction that only Christ is a *"sweet savor unto the Lord."*

Consequently, how dare we offer anything else to the Lord, except Christ! And to be sure, the moment we do, I think we can safely say that we have just incurred upon ourselves the Wrath of God. Paul said: *"For the Wrath of God is revealed from Heaven against all ungodliness and unrighteousness of men, who*

hold the truth in unrighteousness" (Rom. 1:18).

MOST HOLY

The Offerings, it seems, were placed in two classes – that which was *"less holy,"* and that which was *"most holy."*

The Incense Offering, the Shewbread (Ex. 30:26; Lev. 24:9), the Sin and Trespass Offerings (Lev. 6:25-28; 7:1, 6; 14:13), and the Meat Offerings described here, belong to the *"most holy class."* Among other things, this meant that these Offerings could only be eaten in the Court of the Sanctuary by the Priests alone.

(4) "AND IF YOU BRING AN OBLATION OF A MEAT OFFERING BAKED IN THE OVEN, IT SHALL BE UNLEAVENED CAKES OF FINE FLOUR MINGLED WITH OIL, OR UNLEAVENED WAFERS ANOINTED WITH OIL.

(5) "AND IF YOUR OBLATION BE A MEAT OFFERING BAKED IN A PAN, IT SHALL BE OF FINE FLOUR UNLEAVENED, MINGLED WITH OIL.

(6) "YOU SHALL PART IT IN PIECES, AND POUR OIL THEREON: IT IS A MEAT OFFERING.

(7) "AND IF YOUR OBLATION BE A MEAT OFFERING BAKED IN THE FRYINGPAN, IT SHALL BE MADE OF FINE FLOUR WITH OIL.

(8) "AND YOU SHALL BRING THE MEAT OFFERING THAT IS MADE OF THESE THINGS UNTO THE LORD: AND WHEN IT IS PRESENTED UNTO THE PRIEST, HE SHALL BRING IT UNTO THE ALTAR.

(9) "AND THE PRIEST SHALL TAKE FROM THE MEAT OFFERING A MEMORIAL THEREOF, AND SHALL BURN IT UPON THE ALTAR: IT IS AN OFFERING MADE BY FIRE, OF A SWEET SAVOR UNTO THE LORD.

(10) "AND THAT WHICH IS LEFT OF THE MEAT OFFERING SHALL BE AARON'S AND HIS SONS': IT IS A THING MOST HOLY OF THE OFFERINGS OF THE LORD MADE BY FIRE."

The structure is:

1. The Meat-Offerings are mentioned after the Burnt-Offerings. This means that all which pertain to the Meat-Offerings are predicated on the Burnt-Offering, which typifies

the Cross, and what Jesus did there to appease the Wrath of God.

2. The price that God demanded was high, so high in fact that it beggars description. But we have no argument, seeing that He paid the price Himself.

3. Only the spotless Lamb of God could pay the price, and the Meat-Offering proclaims the Purity of Christ, in fact, a Perfect Purity.

UNLEAVENED

Verses 4 and 5 read: *"And if you bring an oblation of a Meat-Offering baked in the oven, it shall be unleavened cakes of fine flour mingled with oil, or unleavened wafers anointed with oil.*

"And if your oblation be a Meat-Offering baked in a pan, it shall be of fine flour unleavened, mingled with oil."

All of the instructions concerning the Meat-Offering were given for the Children of Israel. There were several ways that the Offering could be prepared, and instructions are given for each method.

The first type, as given in Verses 1 through 3, pertains to the uncooked Offering; Verses 4 through 10 pertain to that which is prepared before it is brought to the Priests.

If they were going to prepare this Offering fully, they must make certain that there be no leaven in any of the preparations.

In Hebrew life, leaven came to play an important part, not only in bread-making, but also in law, ritual, and spiritual teaching. It was made originally from fine white bran kneaded with the meal of certain plants such as fitch or vetch, or from barley mixed with water and then allowed to stand until it turned sour. As baking developed, leaven was produced from bread flour kneaded without salt and kept until it passed into a state of fermentation.

In bread-making the leaven was probably a piece of dough, retained from a former baking, which had fermented and turned acid. This was then either dissolved in water in the kneading-trough before the flour was added, or was *"hid"* in the flour (Mat. 13:33) and kneaded along with it. The bread thus made was known as *"leavened,"* as distinct from *"unleavened"* bread (Ex. 12:15).

The prohibition on leaven was possibly

made because fermentation implies disintegration and corruption, and to the Hebrew anything in a decayed state suggested uncleanness.

Doubtless for this reason it was excluded from the Offerings placed upon the Altar of Jehovah, which we are now studying.

Two exceptions to this rule should, however, be noted (Lev. 7:13). *"Leavened bread"* was an accompaniment of the Thank-Offering, and leavened loaves were used also in the Wave-Offering at the Feast of Pentecost, which we will study later.

THE ALTAR

Verses 6 through 10 read: *"You shall part it in pieces, and pour oil thereon: it is a Meat Offering.*

"And if your oblation be a Meat Offering baked in the frying pan, it shall be made of fine flour with oil.

"And you shall bring the Meat Offering that is made of these things unto the LORD: and when it is presented unto the Priest, he shall bring it unto the Altar.

"And the Priest shall take from the Meat Offering a memorial thereof, and shall burn it upon the Altar: it is an Offering made by fire, of a sweet savor unto the LORD.

"And that which is left of the Meat Offering shall be Aaron's and his sons': it is a thing most holy of the Offerings of the LORD made by fire."

The Reader lacking in spirituality may grow weary at the tedious instructions given, wondering why all of this was necessary.

All of this represents Christ and the Perfect Life that He lived, Who alone could serve as a Perfect Sacrifice; consequently, we should understand that anything that portrays Christ is of the utmost significance.

For instance, this Offering could not have, as previously stated, any *"leaven,"* mixed with its contents. As also stated, leaven represents decay and corruption, which of course was and is the opposite of Christ, Who had no sin. So, the more we understand about these instructions given, the more we understand Christ.

To be frank, it's not really that difficult to understand, if we'll only take the time to carefully digest the contents. In giving all of this, the Holy Spirit most definitely intended that we make full use of all that is portrayed here.

(11) "NO MEAT OFFERING, WHICH YOU SHALL BRING UNTO THE LORD, SHALL BE MADE WITH LEAVEN: FOR YOU SHALL BURN NO LEAVEN, NOR ANY HONEY, IN ANY OFFERING OF THE LORD MADE BY FIRE.

(12) "AS FOR THE OBLATION OF THE FIRSTFRUITS, YOU SHALL OFFER THEM UNTO THE LORD: BUT THEY SHALL NOT BE BURNT ON THE ALTAR FOR A SWEET SAVOR.

(13) "AND EVERY OBLATION OF YOUR MEAT OFFERING SHALL YOU SEASON WITH SALT; NEITHER SHALL YOU SUFFER THE SALT OF THE COVENANT OF YOUR GOD TO BE LACKING FROM YOUR MEAT OFFERING: WITH ALL YOUR OFFERINGS YOU SHALL OFFER SALT.

(14) "AND IF YOU OFFER A MEAT OFFERING OF YOUR FIRSTFRUITS UNTO THE LORD, YOU SHALL OFFER FOR THE MEAT OFFERING OF YOUR FIRSTFRUITS GREEN EARS OF GRAIN DRIED BY THE FIRE, EVEN GRAIN BEATEN OUT OF FULL EARS.

(15) "AND YOU SHALL PUT OIL UPON IT, AND LAY FRANKINCENSE THEREON: IT IS A MEAT OFFERING.

(16) "AND THE PRIEST SHALL BURN THE MEMORIAL OF IT, PART OF THE BEATEN GRAIN THEREOF, AND PART OF THE OIL THEREOF, WITH ALL THE FRANKINCENSE THEREOF: IT IS AN OFFERING MADE BY FIRE UNTO THE LORD."

The composition is:

1. In the part that was to be burned on the Altar, there could be no *"leaven"* or *"honey"* mixed with that part. Honey, as well as leaven, causes fermentation. There was neither error nor corruption in Jesus.

2. Any part of the Meat (Food) Offering presented, whether burned or otherwise, must have salt added. Salt is a Type of the Word of God. In Christ was very visible the salt of the incorruptible, preservative, and faithful Word of God.

3. Whether the Meat (Food) Offering was broken in pieces, baked in an oven, on a griddle, or in a frying-pan, it and all its pieces

NOTES

were alike precious, and because it represented Christ and His Life and Living.

NO HONEY

Verses 11 and 12 read: *"No Meat Offering, which you shall bring unto the LORD, shall be made with leaven: for you shall burn no leaven, nor any honey, in any Offering of the LORD made by fire.*

"As for the oblation of the firstfruits, you shall offer them unto the LORD: but they shall not be burned on the Altar for a sweet savor."

Why no honey in this particular Offering?

Honey, as leaven, can go into fermentation as well; however, there is an added thought respecting *"honey."*

Honey, as given here, represents all natural good, or at least that which man labels as good, which is in man outside of Christ. It would have something to do with the good side of the tree of the knowledge of good and evil, with all of that tree being forbidden (Gen. 2:17). In fact, this *"good"* is not only the greatest problem of the unredeemed, but it so happens to be the greatest problem of the redeemed as well!

The unredeemed man thinks that his *"good"* will save him, which it won't! And regrettably, the redeemed man often tries to live for God by the means of his so-called goodness. But let it be understood that this particular *"good,"* whether in the unredeemed or the redeemed, cannot be accepted at all by God. Listen to what Paul said:

"For I know that in me (that is, in my flesh,) dwelleth no good thing" (Rom. 7:18).

The only truly good that is within us, at least that which God will recognize, is that which comes exclusively by and through Christ, which refers to what He did at the Cross, and our Faith in that Finished Work. One of the Fruits of the Spirit is *"goodness,"* but we must remember that it is a Fruit of the Spirit, and not of us (Gal. 5:22-23).

All of this means that all goodness that proceeds from our flesh, is rejected by God, hence no *"honey."* Paul uses the word *"flesh"* in the sense of our own efforts, strength, ability, and power. Of course, all of this is exhibited from our own person, which means that it did not originate with the Lord. The idea is this:

Man, even redeemed man, from his own strength and ability, cannot originate anything that is good. This is because of the Fall. Now the problem with redeemed man is, he thinks that because he is now a new creation in Christ, in essence, a son or daughter of God, he can produce good things. And so he sets about by his own strength and ability to produce those particular things. He is then chagrined when he realizes that God cannot use these efforts, which sooner or later he will have to face. This is why the Cross is so very, very important.

The *"Meat-Offering"* as stated, typified the spotless, pure, perfect, uncorrupted Life of the Lord Jesus Christ. We make a great mistake when we look at that particular Life, and then try to imitate it by our own strength and ability. It cannot be done that way!

The only way that His Perfect Life can be ours, and the only way it is meant to be ours, is by and through what Christ did for us at the Cross. That's why Paul said, and concerning this very thing:

"I am crucified with Christ (this takes us back to Romans 6:3-5)*: nevertheless I live; yet not I, but Christ lives in me: and the life which I now live in the flesh I live by the Faith of the Son of God, Who loved me, and gave Himself for me"* (Gal. 2:20).

If it is to be noticed, all of Paul's life and living was predicated on the fact that he was *"crucified with Christ."* And to be sure, that's the only way that you and I are going to be able to give birth to goodness, and exhibit the same. It is all in Christ and what He did at the Cross, and our Faith in that Finished Work, which gives the Holy Spirit the latitude to bring about these things. Otherwise, it is goodness and works which God cannot accept.

BURNT ON THE ALTAR

While *"leaven and honey"* could be offered to the Lord as an Offering of Thanksgiving, Verse 12 tells us that they cannot be offered if the oblation (something offered in worship or devotion) is to be *"burnt on the Altar for a sweet savor."*

The Altar represents the Crucifixion of Christ, and the price that He would pay there; consequently, this is a price that we couldn't

pay, so our goodness, etc., is not to be added to the Finished Work of Christ.

SALT

Verse 13 reads: *"And every oblation of your Meat Offering shall you season with salt; neither shall you suffer the salt of the Covenant of your God to be lacking from your Meat Offering: with all your Offerings you shall offer salt."*

Salt is a preservative and, therefore, serves as a Type in the Old Testament of the Word of God.

As an example, after Elijah was taken up to Heaven, Elisha, now serving in his place, comes to the city of Jericho, where the men of the city tell him that the water is poisoned, and because of that, the ground is barren (II Ki. 2:19).

Elisha, no doubt, took this problem to the Lord, and then doing what the Lord told him to do, told the men to *"Bring him a new cruse* (a new clay pot), *and put salt therein."*

The Scripture then says, *"And he went forth unto the spring of the waters, and cast the salt in there, and said, Thus saith the LORD, I have healed these waters; there shall not be from thence any more death or barren land"* (II Ki. 2:20-21).

The new cruse was a Type of the Humanity of our Lord, and the *"salt"* in that new cruse, a Type of the Word of God, by which the Master functioned in totality.

In this Thirteenth Verse, the Lord told Moses, *"With all your Offerings you shall offer salt."* In fact, it is called *"the salt of the Covenant,"* referring to the enduring character of the Covenant. God Himself has so ordained it, in all things, which means that nothing can alter it, no influence can ever corrupt it, and because it is the unalterable, unchangeable, indescribable, eternal Word of Almighty God.

The *"salt"* proclaims, *"Thus saith the Lord,"* and as such, runs at cross-purposes with men's desires. Every true Preacher of the Gospel will have his Message *"seasoned with salt"* (Mat. 5:13; Col. 4:6).

For instance, when Jesus ministered in the Synagogue of Nazareth (Lk. 4:16-29), the people did *"bear Him witness, and wondered at the gracious words which proceeded out of His mouth.*" But when He proceeded to season those words with *"salt,"* which was so needful in order to preserve them from the corrupting influence of their national pride, they would have cast Him over the brow of the hill whereon their city was built, had not the Holy Spirit intervened.

If there is anything that the Church desperately needs today, it is the salt of the Word of God. But unfortunately, far too many in the modern Church seek to bend the Word to their perfidious ways, instead of conforming their ways to the Word of God. The trouble is, we've got too much *"honey"* in the modern Gospel, and not enough *"salt."*

MEMORIAL

Verses 14 through 16 read: *"And if you offer a Meat Offering of your firstfruits unto the LORD, you shall offer for the Meat Offering of our firstfruits green ears of grain dried by the fire, even grain beaten out of full ears.*

"And you shall put oil upon it, and lay frankincense thereon: it is a Meat Offering.

"And the Priest shall burn the memorial of it, part of the beaten grain thereof, and part of the oil thereof, with all the frankincense thereof: it is an Offering made by fire unto the LORD."

As we have seen in this Second Chapter of Leviticus, there were several ways that the Meat-Offering could be prepared. It speaks of being *"baked in an oven,"* or *"baked in a pan,"* or *"baked in a frying-pan."* Now the process of baking might suggest the idea of suffering; however, inasmuch as the Meat Offering is called *"a sweet savor,"* a term which is never applied to the Sin-Offering or Trespass-Offering, it should be evident that there is no thought of suffering for sin, no thought of suffering the Wrath of God on account of sin, no thought of suffering at the hand of Infinite Justice as the sinner's substitute, which means that the suggestion of suffering for sin is not intended here. Suffering, yes! But not for sin.

In His earthly Life and Walk, Christ suffered for Righteousness' sake, in which Believers now endure the same (I Pet. 4:13).

But when it came to suffering for sin, the Scripture plainly says, *"For Christ also has once suffered for sins"* (I Pet. 3:18). This

NOTES

means that whatever suffering that Christ endured, there was only *"one"* suffering which He endured for sins, and that was the Cross.

But as the Righteous Servant of God, He suffered in the midst of a scene in which all was contrary to Him, which the preparation of the Meat-Offering represented. But this was the very opposite of suffering for sin. It is of the utmost significance to distinguish between these two kinds of suffering. The confounding of them will lead to serious error. Suffering as a Righteous One standing among men on God's behalf is one thing, and suffering instead of man under the Hand of God is quite another. The Lord Jesus suffered for Righteousness during His Life: He suffered for sin in His Death.

During His Life, man and Satan did their utmost; and even at the Cross they put forth all their power; but when all that they could do was done, when they had traveled, in their deadly enmity, to the utmost limit of human and diabolical opposition, there lay, far beyond, a region of impenetrable gloom and horror into which the Sin-bearer had to travel, in the accomplishment of His Work. In other words, Jesus underwent a suffering on the Cross, when He suffered for sin, our sins, incidentally, and certainly not His Own, which no human being will ever be able to comprehend. But here is the point I wish to make:

SUFFERING FOR SIN

While the Believer may suffer because of sin, the sins of others or his own, there is no such thing as a Believer suffering for his sins, and we refer to such suffering as being an Atonement. To even think such, in effect, says that what Christ did at the Cross was not enough, and we, therefore, have to add to His Atonement by us suffering for sin as well. To think such, the Believer might as well go to a Cross, and attempt to hang himself on that wooden beam, which of course, is ridiculous! But yet, sadly and regrettably, much of the Church falls into the category of trying to make the *"Meat-Offering"* into something it was never intended to be. Let us say it again:

While the Believer will definitely suffer for Righteousness' sake, and while the Believer will at times definitely suffer because of the sins of others or even himself, he must ever understand that such suffering will never atone for sin.

PENANCE

The Catholic Church teaches penance, which in effect, is an attempt to atone for sin, which is a gross insult to Christ. (Penance is an act of self-abasement, or punishment of some kind, which is supposed to pay for sin.)

But yet, most in the Protestant world, while not quite as blatant, actually do the same thing.

One of my friends, a Lawyer, incidentally, was conversing with some Denominational leaders some time back. The leaders, in speaking of a particular individual, and concerning some things which had happened to him, made the statement, *"He has paid his dues, and, therefore, we can accept him."*

After that meeting ended, he called me and, relating this incident, said, *"Brother Swaggart, I soon realized that these men were advocating penance."*

He was right! That's exactly what they were advocating.

All of this stems from a lack of proper understanding as it regards the Cross, and what Jesus accomplished there. Or else, it evidences gross unbelief; of which I am concerned is actually the case.

THE MEANING OF THE MEAT OFFERING

Getting back to the Meat-Offering, and as it regards the suffering of Christ, there was absolutely nothing in His Humanity or in the nature of His associations which could possibly connect Him with sin, wrath, or death. He was *"made sin"* on the Cross; and there He endured the Wrath of God, and there He gave up His Life, as an all-sufficient Atonement for sin; but nothing of this finds a place in the Meat-Offering. True, we have the process of baking – the action of fire; but this is not the Wrath of God, at least in this instance. The Meat-Offering was not a Sin-Offering, but a *"sweet savor"* Offering. Thus, it's meaning is definitely fixed; and, moreover, the intelligent interpretation of it must ever guard, with holy jealousy, the

NOTES

precious truth of Christ's spotless Humanity, and the true nature of His associations, which the Meat-Offering represents.

When the Scripture speaks of our having fellowship with Christ's sufferings, it refers simply to His sufferings for Righteousness – His sufferings at the hand of man. That was the *"Meat-Offering."*

When it came to suffering for sin, He did so on the Cross, that we might not have to suffer for it; He endured the Wrath of God that we might not have to endure it. There He was the *"Sin-Offering,"* and the *"Trespass-Offering."*

Part of the Meat-Offering was to be burned on the fire, with evidence that frankincense was to be poured only on the part that was burned by fire, and not on the part given to the Priests. And incidentally, the word *"corn"* is an unfortunate translation. There was no such thing as corn in that part of the world, that being discovered as being grown by the Indians in North America, which discovery would not take place for some 2,000 years. It should have been translated *"grain."*

Inasmuch as part of the Meat-Offering was burned in the fire, and part eaten by the Priests, we should understand that this symbolized Christ in His Perfect Life, but yet a life that would be given on the Cross, hence the burning of the Meat-Offering on the Altar. This signifies as well that Christ came to this world but for one purpose, and that was to go to the Cross. His Life was Perfect, His Demeanor Perfect, His Way Perfect, His Manner Perfect, all for the purpose of being a Perfect Sacrifice.

So, as the Burnt-Offering symbolized Christ dying on the Cross, which was to appease the Wrath of God, in other words, that part of His Death was solely for God and not for man. The *"Meat* (Food) *Offering"* symbolized His Perfect Life. If it is to be noticed, the grain that was to be offered was to be out of *"full ears,"* which alone could symbolize the Perfection of Christ.

"Rejoice, the Lord is King; your Lord and King adore!
"Rejoice, give thanks, and sing, and triumph evermore.
"Lift up your heart, lift up your voice!

"Rejoice, again I say, rejoice!"

"Jesus the Saviour reigns, the God of truth and love;
"When He had purged our stains, He took His seat above.
"Lift up your heart, lift up your voice!
"Rejoice, again I say, rejoice!"

"His kingdom cannot fail; He rules over Earth and Heaven;
"The keys of death and Hell are to our Jesus given.
"Lift up your heart, life up your voice!
"Rejoice, again I say, rejoice!"

"Rejoice in glorious hope! Our Lord, the Judge, shall come,
"And take His servants up to their eternal home.
"Lift up your heart, lift up your voice!
"Rejoice, again I say, rejoice!"

CHAPTER 3

(1) "AND IF HIS OBLATION BE A SACRIFICE OF PEACE OFFERING, IF HE OFFER IT OF THE HERD: WHETHER IT BE A MALE OR FEMALE, HE SHALL OFFER IT WITHOUT BLEMISH BEFORE THE LORD.

(2) "AND HE SHALL LAY HIS HAND UPON THE HEAD OF HIS OFFERING, AND KILL IT AT THE DOOR OF THE TABERNACLE OF THE CONGREGATION: AND AARON'S SONS THE PRIESTS SHALL SPRINKLE THE BLOOD UPON THE ALTAR ROUND ABOUT.

(3) "AND HE SHALL OFFER OF THE SACRIFICE OF THE PEACE OFFERING AN OFFERING MADE BY FIRE UNTO THE LORD; THE FAT THAT COVERS THE INWARDS, AND ALL THE FAT THAT IS UPON THE INWARDS,

(4) "AND THE TWO KIDNEYS, AND THE FAT THAT IS ON THEM, WHICH IS BY THE FLANKS, AND THE CAUL ABOVE THE LIVER, WITH THE KIDNEYS, IT SHALL HE TAKE AWAY.

(5) "AND AARON'S SONS SHALL BURN IT ON THE ALTAR UPON THE BURNT

NOTES

SACRIFICE, WHICH IS UPON THE WOOD THAT IS ON THE FIRE: IT IS AN OFFERING MADE BY FIRE, OF A SWEET SAVOR UNTO THE LORD."

The construction is:

1. The infinite fullness of the atoning Sacrifice of Christ needed many offerings to show forth, even faintly, its plentitude.

2. The Burnt-Offering pictured Christ dying; the Meat (Meal) Offering, Christ living. The Peace-Offering presents Him as making peace by the Blood of His Cross, and so establishing for man communion with God.

3. The Burnt-Offering was a male only; the Peace-Offering, a male or female. In either case, without blemish.

THE PEACE-OFFERING

Verse 1 reads: *"And if his oblation be a sacrifice of Peace Offering, if he offer it of the herd; whether it be a male or female, he shall offer it without blemish before the LORD."*

Concerning the Peace-Offering, Mackintosh said: *"There is none of the Offerings in which the Communion of the worshipper so fully unfolded as in the 'Peace-Offering.' In the 'Burnt-Offering,' it is Christ offering Himself to God. In the 'Meat-Offering,' we have Christ's perfect humanity. Then, passing on to the 'Sin-Offering,' we learn that sin, in its root, is fully met. In the 'Trespass-Offering,' there is a full answer to the actual sins. But in none is the doctrine of the communion of the worshipper unfolded. This latter belongs to the 'Peace-Offering.'"*

THE SIN NATURE

In both the *"Peace-Offering,"* and the *"Trespass-Offering,"* we learn of the Presence of the Sin Nature in the heart and life of the Believer. But we find out, even more fully in the Peace-Offering, that even though the sin nature dwells in us, it is not to rule in us. In fact, Paul addressed this directly by saying:

"Let not sin (the sin nature) *therefore reign* (rule) *in your mortal body, that you should obey it in the lusts thereof"* (Rom. 6:12). Were there no sin nature, there would have been no need for the Peace-Offering, or the Trespass-Offering.

The more closely we view these Offerings,

the more fully do we see the necessity of the five Offerings, in order that Christ be properly portrayed, as it regards His Finished Work.

The Peace-Offering portrays communion with God, and the Believer's place and position in Christ, due to what Christ has done for us at the Cross. It was the only Offering in which the offerer could partake, which signified that Peace had now been restored.

A MALE OR FEMALE

In the Burnt-Offering, it had to be a *"male without blemish,"* whereas in the Peace-Offering, it might be either *"a male or a female."* Irrespective, whichever one was chosen, it had to be *"without blemish."* The Peace-Offering being concerned with communion, a female was permitted as expressive of the incapacity of the worshipper to fully comprehend the unsearchable riches of Christ's nature and work. There was no such limitation on the part of God; hence in the Burnt-Offering it was a male of the first year (Williams). Regarding the Peace-Offering, there was no restriction regarding the age of the animal, only that it be *"without blemish."* Of course, that was to portray Christ in all of His Perfection, as would be obvious.

The Peace-Offering was to be offered *"before the Lord"* (Vs. 1), *"unto the Lord"* (Vs. 3), and *"a sweet savor to the Lord"* (Vs. 5).

THE SACRIFICE

Verse 2 reads: *"And he shall lay his hand upon the head of his offering, and kill it at the Door of the Tabernacle of the congregation: and Aaron's sons the Priests shall sprinkle the blood upon the Altar round about."*

Much of the time the Sacrifices, whatever they were, were followed by a *"Meat Offering,"* which denoted thankfulness, and a *"Peace Offering,"* which referred to the fact that Peace had been restored.

The *"male or female"* of the animals being allowed stipulates that all, both man and woman, can have fellowship and peace with God.

THE DOCTRINE OF SUBSTITUTION AND IDENTIFICATION

When the individual brought his animals for sacrifice, as he generally brought two, one

would be for the Peace-Offering. After the Burnt, Sin, or Trespass Offering had been presented, followed by the Meat-Offering, it was now time for the Peace-Offering. He would then *"lay his hand upon the head of his Offering,"* which portrayed the beautiful doctrine of Substitution and Identification. The animal became the substitute in the sinner's place, and by the laying of his hand or hands on the head of his Offering, he identified with that substitute. That, in effect, is the heart of the Gospel. Christ became our Substitute, and we identify with Him, in all He did, but more particularly, what He did for us at the Cross. And how do we do that?

THE MANNER OF SUBSTITUTION AND IDENTIFICATION

It is always by Faith. Paul said: *"For in Jesus Christ neither circumcision availeth anything, nor uncircumcision; but Faith which works by love"* (Gal. 5:6).

This refers to the fact that identification cannot be made with Christ by works, but only by Faith.

So what did Paul mean when he said *"but Faith,"* or as it actually means, *"by Faith"*?

BY FAITH

To properly understand Faith, at least that which is given to us in the Word of God, we must understand the *"object of Faith."*

In truth, every human being in the world has faith. But only a tiny few have the right kind of Faith, which refers to the correct object of Faith, which is *"Jesus Christ and Him Crucified"* (I Cor. 1:17-18, 21, 23; 2:2).

So the nonreligious kind, and even the religious kind, which is not anchored in Christ and Him Crucified, is not recognized by God; therefore, when we speak of Faith, we must always understand that it's Faith in Christ and His Cross. The Cross must never be divorced from Christ, nor Christ from the Cross. No, by that we're not meaning that Christ is still on the Cross. In fact, He is presently in Heaven, seated by the right hand of the Father (Heb. 1:3). And as well, all true Believers are seated with Him, spiritually speaking (Eph. 2:6).

The Believer must understand that to properly have Faith in the Word is to have

Faith in the Cross, and if one doesn't have Faith in the Cross, one cannot properly have Faith in the Word. Listen to John the Apostle:

He said: *"In the beginning was the Word, and the Word was with God, and the Word was God"* (Jn. 1:1). This tells us that Jesus is the Living Word!

He then said: *"And the Word was made flesh and dwelt among us"* (Jn. 1:14). This speaks of the Incarnation of Christ, God becoming man.

John then recorded the words of John the Baptist, who said: *"Behold the Lamb of God, which taketh away the sin of the world"* (Jn. 1:29).

As stated, all of this tells us that Jesus is the Word, that He, as God, became flesh, and did so for the purpose of going to the Cross, which alone could *"take away the sin of the world."*

The manner in which Faith is exhibited in Christ, which brings about Peace with God, is that we are to understand that when Christ died, we were *"baptized into His death,"* were *"buried with Him by Baptism into death,"* and then, when Christ was raised from the dead by the Glory of the Father, we were raised with Him *"in newness of life"* (Rom. 6:3-4).

Of course, as should be obvious, we were not there when Christ died. But, Paul was speaking of us having Faith in what Christ did, which means to have Faith in the Cross, which is the identification with our Substitute. This is the key to all things. As should be obvious, this is something that one cannot earn by merit, so he has to come by this great and glorious life by Faith; and I trust that we have properly explained what Faith actually is.

Also, in Romans 6:3-4, when Paul spoke of *"Baptism,"* he wasn't speaking of Water Baptism, but rather the Crucifixion of Christ. He uses this word, because that's the strongest word that could be found to explain what actually happens in the Mind of God, when we evidence Faith in Christ, and what Christ did at the Cross. In God's mind, we are literally placed *"in Christ"*; and it means in what He did for us at the Cross as our Substitute.

THE DOOR OF THE TABERNACLE

As well, the person who brought the

Sacrifice had to personally kill it, and because he, the one who had brought it, was the one who had sinned.

In doing this, he must have felt the pangs of what he had done, which necessitated this action, realizing that an innocent victim was suffering in his stead. In fact, it was meant to portray this, in other words, was meant to have a great effect because it portrayed Christ Who was to come. It had to be done at the *"Door of the Tabernacle,"* even though the blood of this innocent animal couldn't get him through the door. That awaited Christ, Whom the *"Door"* typified (Jn. 10:9).

When the sinner killed the animal, the Priests caught the blood in a basin, and then sprinkled or splashed it at the foot of the Altar, once again, typifying the Blood that Jesus would shed. The Scripture says, concerning the Peace-Offering: *"But now in Christ Jesus you who in time past were far off are made nigh by the Blood of Christ.*

"For He is our peace, Who has made both one (both Jews and Gentiles), *and has broken down the middle wall of partition between us . . . And that He might reconcile both* (Jews and Gentiles) *unto God in one body by the Cross, having slain the enmity thereby"* (Eph. 2:13-16).

The final analysis of the Peace-Offering, which pertains to the man and his family, plus his friends, partaking of the Offering will not be addressed in this Chapter, but will be addressed in Chapter 7, which portrays the law of the various Offerings.

Of all the Offerings, with the exception of the Meal-Offering, the central core of the sacrifice was the shedding of blood, which was the life of the flesh. Eternal life had been forfeited in the Garden by the Fall of Adam, and now for that life to be regained, a perfect life would have to be given, which could only be supplied by Christ. Fallen man was and is totally inadequate. This completely shoots down the erroneous doctrine (totally erroneous) of the Word of Faith people, who teach that any Born-Again man could redeem fallen humanity. Such portrays a complete lack of knowledge, as it regards the Atonement, which is the worst error that can be believed.

THE ALTAR

Verses 3 through 5 read: *"And he shall offer of the Sacrifice of the Peace Offering an Offering made by fire unto the LORD; the fat that covers the inwards, and all the fat that is upon the inwards,*

"And the two kidneys, and the fat that is on them, which is by the flanks, and the caul above the liver, with the kidneys, it shall he take away.

"And Aaron's sons shall burn it on the Altar upon the Burnt Sacrifice, which is upon the wood that is on the fire: it is an Offering made by fire, of a sweet savor unto the LORD."

The first three Offerings, the Burnt-Offering, the Meal-Offering, and the Peace-Offering are referred to as a *"sweet savor."* The Sin-Offering and the Trespass-Offering are not referred to as such.

When we view Christ in the Peace-Offering, we must remember that He does not stand before us as the bearer of our sins, as in the Sin and Trespass Offerings, but (having already borne) as the ground of our peaceful and happy fellowship with God. If sin-bearing were in question, it could not be said, *"It is an Offering made by fire, of a sweet savor unto the LORD."*

Concerning this, Mackintosh said, *"Still, though sin-bearing is not the thought, there is full provision for one who knows himself to be a sinner, else he could not have any portion therein. To have fellowship with God, we must function 'in the light' (I Jn. 1:7). And to function or be 'in the light,' we must understand that only on the ground of that precious statement, 'The Blood of Jesus Christ God's Son cleanses us from all sin,' can this be. The more we abide in the light, the deeper will be our sense of everything which is contrary to that light; and the deeper, also, our sense of the value of that Blood which entitles us to be there."*

We must never forget that it is blood which is sprinkled on the Altar round about, which means that fellowship with God must be encircled by Atonement, and only exists within it. Thus, God and the worshipper are brought into fellowship. Peace is established. Worship that's not based fully

NOTES

on the death of Christ is not worship that God would recognize.

Its eternal and unshakable foundation is not the worthfulness of the worshiper, but the preciousness of the sprinkled blood.

All the fat was wholly burnt upon the Altar as a sweet savor. The fat and the blood symbolized the priceless life and the precious inward affections of the Lamb of God (Williams).

(6) "AND IF HIS OFFERING FOR A SACRIFICE OF PEACE OFFERING UNTO THE LORD BE OF THE FLOCK; MALE OR FEMALE, HE SHALL OFFER IT WITHOUT BLEMISH.

(7) "IF HE OFFER A LAMB FOR HIS OFFERING, THEN SHALL HE OFFER IT BEFORE THE LORD.

(8) "AND HE SHALL LAY HIS HAND UPON THE HEAD OF HIS OFFERING, AND KILL IT BEFORE THE TABERNACLE OF THE CONGREGATION: AND AARON'S SONS SHALL SPRINKLE THE BLOOD THEREOF ROUND ABOUT UPON THE ALTAR.

(9) "AND HE SHALL OFFER OF THE SACRIFICE OF THE PEACE OFFERING AN OFFERING MADE BY FIRE UNTO THE LORD; THE FAT THEREOF, AND THE WHOLE RUMP, IT SHALL HE TAKE OFF HARD BY THE BACKBONE; AND THE FAT THAT COVERS THE INWARDS, AND ALL THE FAT THAT IS UPON THE INWARDS,

(10) "AND THE TWO KIDNEYS AND THE FAT THAT IS UPON THEM, WHICH IS BY THE FLANKS, AND THE CAUL ABOVE THE LIVER, WITH THE KIDNEYS, IT SHALL HE TAKE AWAY.

(11) "AND THE PRIEST SHALL BURN IT UPON THE ALTAR: IT IS THE FRUIT OF THE OFFERING MADE BY FIRE UNTO THE LORD."

The overview is:

1. All the information regarding the Peace-Offering is not given in this Third Chapter. It will be detailed in Chapter 7.

2. Whether the poor man's lamb or goat were offered, or the rich man's heifer, all were precious in God's sight, and received the same ceremony.

3. The Peace-Offering and the partaking thereof proclaims the fact that the Whole

Burnt Offering, or Sin-Offering, or Trespass-Offering have been accepted.

A SACRIFICE OF PEACE-OFFERING

Verses 6 through 8 read: *"And if his Offering for a Sacrifice of Peace Offering unto the LORD be of the flock; male or female, he shall offer it without blemish.*

"If he offer a lamb for his Offering, then shall he offer it before the LORD.

"And he shall lay his hand upon the head of his Offering, and kill it before the Tabernacle of the congregation: and Aaron's sons shall sprinkle the blood thereof round about upon the Altar."

The lesson taught by the Peace-Offering was the tremendous blessing of being in union with God as His Covenant people, and the joys since this union, carried out by celebrating a festival meal, eaten reverently and thankfully, with a part being given to God's Priests, and a part symbolically consumed by God Himself (Pulpit). In simple terminology, it means that sin had been committed, but a sacrifice had been offered, whether Burnt, Sin, or Trespass Offering, which had atoned. A Peace-Offering was now sacrificed, of which the worshipper would receive a part, in which he, his family, and friends could celebrate. It was to be, as stated, a joyous occasion. The sin had been forgiven and atoned, brought about by the Sacrifice, and now Peace had been restored. As stated, we will study this more minutely when we come to Chapter 7.

Due to Christ not yet having come, these various sacrifices were instituted in order to symbolically proclaim to the people what Christ would do when He actually came. How much of this they understood is anyone's guess; however, the Type beautifully portrayed Christ in all that He would do.

Jesus told the Pharisees: *"Search the Scriptures; for in them you think you have eternal life: and they are they which testify of Me."*

He then said, *"And you will not come to Me, that you might have life"* (Jn. 5:39-40).

The Master plainly tells us here that the Old Testament Scriptures, for that's what He was speaking of, testified of Him. To be sure, the Sacrifices testified most of all!

NOTES

So this means that the Children of Israel should have known.

THE FIRE

Verses 9 through 11 read: *"And he shall offer of the Sacrifice of the Peace-Offering an Offering made by fire unto the LORD; the fat thereof, and the whole rump, it shall he take off hard by the backbone; and the fat that covers the inwards, and all the fat that is upon the inwards,*

"And the two kidneys, and the fat that is upon them, which is by the flanks, and the caul above the liver, with the kidneys, it shall he take away.

"And the Priest shall burn it upon the Altar: it is the fruit of the Offering made by fire unto the LORD."

The fire speaks of the Judgment of God. It speaks of Judgment poured out on His Only Son, with the sacrifice of the animal serving as the Substitute. As the animal is totally consumed, in other words, reduced to ashes, the idea presented is that of our sins being reduced to nothingness. When anyone speaks of something being reduced to ashes, they are simply meaning that there is nothing left, nothing salvageable; it is totally consumed. And so are our sins. Christ took the judgment for our sins, and how did He do that?

THE PRICE THAT WAS PAID

He paid the price, thereby taking the judgment that by all rights was due us, and did so by the giving of His Life. This was accomplished by the shedding of His precious Blood, for the life of the flesh is in the blood. Hence Peter saying: *"Forasmuch as you know that you were not redeemed with corruptible things as silver and gold . . . But with the precious Blood of Christ, as of a lamb without blemish and without spot"* (I Pet. 1:18-19).

The fire does <u>not</u> represent Hell, as some teach.

THE JESUS DIED SPIRITUALLY DOCTRINE

This teaching is propagated by the Word of Faith people, claiming that Jesus not only died physically on the Cross, but as well, died spiritually. By that, they mean that He actually became a sinner on the Cross, becoming one with Satan, died as a sinner, and went to Hell, and we speak of the burning side of Hell. They claim that He suffered there in the flames for three days and nights, with Satan thinking that he had won the day. When at the end of that three days and nights, God the Father said, *"It is enough,"* and Jesus was then born again, even as any sinner is born again. He was then, according to their teaching, raised from the dead.

There's not a shred of any of this in the Bible. In other words, it is pure fiction.

In the teaching of this subject, they belittle the Cross, claiming that it was the *"worst defeat in human history."* I quote Kenneth Hagin verbatim. He said, *"The Cross is actually a place of defeat, whereas the Resurrection is a place of victory."* He went on to say, *"When you preach the Cross, you're preaching death."* This is derived from his April 2002 edition of his monthly magazine.

Some may claim that all of this is merely a matter of semantics, which is a play on words. In other words, they are claiming that we are both teaching the same thing about the Cross, he's just teaching it in another way. No, that is basely incorrect!

When one refers to the Cross as the *"greatest defeat in human history,"* that is clearly and plainly the very opposite of what the Bible teaches.

The Cross was the destination of Christ, which means that it was the supreme reason for which He came. In fact, the Cross was planned, as Peter said, from before the foundation of the world (I Pet. 1:18-20). The truth is, any individual who believes the doctrine of the Word of Faith teachers is believing gross error; and furthermore, it is the worst type of error inasmuch as it is error concerning the Atonement. To have a hangnail is one thing, but to have heart problems is something else altogether. The hangnail won't kill you, but the heart will! And to be wrong about the Atonement is to be wrong about the very heart of the Gospel.

As well, the *"fire"* on the Altar does not represent Hellfire into which Jesus had to go, as they erroneously teach. Were that

NOTES

the case, then any sinner, upon going to Hell, could burn there for three days and nights, and his sin would then be atoned, and he would then be saved. No, the fire doesn't save anyone; it is what Jesus did at the Cross, in the giving of His Life, by the pouring out of His precious Blood, which effects Salvation, and that alone (Eph. 2:13-18; Col.. 2:14-15)!

THE FAT

All the fat, along with particular body parts, were to be burned on the Altar. This specified that God gave His best, as it regards the giving of His Only Son, and it also states that all of our prosperity comes totally and completely from and through Jesus Christ, and what He has done for us at the Cross.

(12) "AND IF HIS OFFERING BE A GOAT, THEN HE SHALL OFFER IT BEFORE THE LORD.

(13) "AND HE SHALL LAY HIS HAND UPON THE HEAD OF IT, AND KILL IT BEFORE THE TABERNACLE OF THE CONGREGATION: AND THE SONS OF AARON SHALL SPRINKLE THE BLOOD THEREOF UPON THE ALTAR ROUND ABOUT.

(14) "AND HE SHALL OFFER THEREOF HIS OFFERING, EVEN AN OFFERING MADE BY FIRE UNTO THE LORD; THE FAT THAT COVERS THE INWARDS, AND ALL THE FAT THAT IS UPON THE INWARDS.

(15) "AND THE TWO KIDNEYS, AND THE FAT THAT IS UPON THEM, WHICH IS BY THE FLANKS, AND THE CAUL ABOVE THE LIVER, WITH THE KIDNEYS, IT SHALL HE TAKE AWAY.

(16) "AND THE PRIEST SHALL BURN THEM UPON THE ALTAR: IT IS THE FOOD OF THE OFFERING MADE BY FIRE FOR A SWEET SAVOR: ALL THE FAT IS THE LORD'S.

(17) "IT SHALL BE A PERPETUAL STATUTE FOR YOUR GENERATIONS THROUGHOUT ALL YOUR DWELLINGS, THAT YOU EAT NEITHER FAT NOR BLOOD."

The exegesis is:

1. The Peace-Offering represented the blessedness and joyousness of communion between God and man.

2. As someone has said, *"The character

of these Feasts cannot be mistaken. It was that of joyfulness tempered by solemnity, of solemnity tempered by joyfulness."

3. Like the Passover, the Peace-Offering at once commemorated an historical event, and prefigured a blessing to come. The Passover, for instance, always looked backwards to the deliverance from Egypt, but yet forward to *"Christ our Passover sacrificed for us."* In like manner, the Peace-Offering commemorated the making of the Covenant, and prefigured the blessed state of communion to be brought about by the Sacrifice of the Cross.

THE GOAT

Verses 12 through 14 read: *"And if his Offering be a goat, then he shall offer it before the LORD.*

"And he shall lay his hand upon the head of it, and kill it before the Tabernacle of the congregation: and the sons of Aaron shall sprinkle the blood thereof upon the Altar round about.

"And he shall offer thereof his Offering, even an Offering made by fire unto the LORD; the fat that covers the inwards, and all the fat that is upon the inwards."

As is obvious, in this one Chapter, the Lord portrays three different animals as potential Offerings – the heifer, the lamb, and the goat. The instructions for the offering of each were basically the same.

This is to impress upon us the fact that even though the heifer was of greater value, as would be obvious; still, it was the intent of the Sacrifice, and what it represented, at least in the Eyes of God, that really mattered.

More than likely, the goat was the least valuable of the three animals. But yet, this particular sacrifice had to be given the same attention as the sacrifice of the heifer. The idea is this:

All of these sacrifices, which necessitated the shedding of innocent blood, represented Christ. It was not so much what the animal was, providing it was one specified by the Lord, as to what was done with the animal as it regards the sacrifice. Its blood was shed, which referred to the giving of its life, and all because sin had been committed.

I've had some to ask me the question, *"Are*

we saved because of Who Jesus is, or What Jesus has done?"

WHO JESUS WAS, AND WHAT JESUS DID!

In the first place, what was done, and I speak of the Cross, could not have been done by anyone other than Christ. So it should go without saying that Who He was, which refers to the God-Man, Jesus Christ, was an absolute necessity, for Redemption to be brought about. The ridiculous idea put forth by the Word of Faith teachers that any Born-Again man could have redeemed humanity is worse than ridiculous; it borders on blasphemy. For a perfect sacrifice to be offered, only Jesus, the Son of God, could do such a thing.

However, I must remind the Reader that Jesus has always been God. As God, He had no beginning, was not formed, was not made, was not created, and in fact, has always been. But I also remind the Reader that as God, He did not redeem anyone. Now think about that for a moment! If the mere fact of Who He was would redeem people, then the Cross was unnecessary.

No, while it was definitely necessary that Christ be Who He was, it was What He did, and I refer to the Cross, which brought about Redemption.

The Virgin Birth, as wonderful and necessary as it was, didn't save anyone. The miracles and healings of Christ, as wonderful and necessary as they were, didn't save anyone. For men to be saved, Christ had to go to the Cross, and give Himself, which He did. Paul said: *"Who gave Himself for our sins, that He might deliver us from this present evil world, according to the Will of God and our Father"* (Gal. 1:4).

THE OBJECT OF OUR FAITH

Almost all Christians talk about Faith. When they do so, they are speaking of Faith in the Word, Faith in Christ, Faith in the Lord, etc., which are all correct terms, at least as far as they go. In fact, *"the object of our Faith,"* or *"the correct object of Faith,"* are terms that most Christians have little heard, if at all. But yet, there is nothing more important than the correct object of one's Faith. What do we mean by that?

For Faith to be that which God will recognize, it has to have the Finished Work of Christ as its object. In fact, to just merely say and stop there, *"I have Faith in the Lord,"* or *"I have Faith in the Word,"* while correct as far as it goes, really does not say, as stated, much of anything.

In fact, most Christians have been taught that if they need something, and whatever it might be, they should find two or three Scriptures which seem to apply themselves to that particular need, memorize them, and then quote them over and over. Somehow, at least according to this teaching, this is supposed to move God to action, etc.

In truth, it doesn't move God to anything. While memorizing the Scriptures is wonderful, and should be done by all Believers, and while quoting the Scriptures is even more wonderful, and should be done by all Believers, our thinking that doing such in this fashion will bring about some positive result, is actually *"white magic."* This is the very opposite of *"black magic,"* which attempts to manipulate the spirit world of darkness, in order to appease demon spirits, or get them to do something positive for you. This has to do with witchcraft, etc.

"White magic" is that which seeks to manipulate the spirit world of Righteousness, to get the Lord to do something for you, etc. Both, as should be obvious, are wrong!

The Lord responds to one thing only, and that is Faith (Gal. 5:6), but it must be Faith in the correct object, and that correct object is *"Jesus Christ and Him Crucified"* (I Cor. 1:23).

Any other type of so-called faith that a person would seek to exhibit falls into the category of manipulation. And it should be understood that God cannot be manipulated by anyone. He sees through whatever is on the surface, even to the very heart, and knows the motive behind all things. While our intention may not be to manipulate Him, still, if we are functioning in a wrong manner, it constitutes manipulation, whether we intend it or not, which God can never honor.

The Believer must ever understand that all Faith, at least the type that God recognizes, must have as its object the Sacrifice of Christ. Whenever the Lord dealt with Abraham, and the Scripture says that *"Abraham believed God, and God accounted it to him for Righteousness,"* we must ask the question as to what Abraham believed.

Jesus answered that Himself by saying to the Children of Israel: *"Your father Abraham rejoiced to see My day, and he saw it, and was glad"* (Jn. 8:56).

Abraham wasn't merely believing that there was a God; he was believing rather what God had said about Redemption. In other words, through Abraham and Sarah, a child would be born, and somewhere in the future through this lineage, the Redeemer would be born into the world, Who would give His Life, in order to bring about Redemption for Adam's fallen race. In effect, Abraham had placed his Faith in Christ and Him Crucified. Even though he might not have understood those terms, that's actually what he was doing.

In fact, if you as a Believer properly understand the statement, *"Abraham believed God, and God accounted it to him for Righteousness,"* you can understand, in effect, the entirety of the Bible. And if you don't properly understand that term, you really cannot rightly understand the Word.

RIGHTEOUSNESS

This tells us that all Righteousness comes entirely through one's Faith, and never by works. Paul said: *"I do not frustrate the Grace of God: for if Righteousness come by the Law, then Christ is dead in vain"* (Gal. 2:21).

This means that if anyone can earn Righteousness in any manner, then Christ simply did not have to come down here and die on a Cross. Worse than that, His Death was all in vain. But what is actually happening?

What is actually happening pertains to the fact that most of the modern Church is seeking to earn Righteousness in some way. They think by belonging to a certain Church, or a certain Denomination, that this will bring Righteousness. Many think that being baptized in water brings about Righteousness, or taking the Lord's Supper, or joining the Church, etc. In fact, the list is long!

Even though these things may or may not be good in their own right, none of them bring about Righteousness, for Righteousness cannot be bought, purchased, or earned. The Peace-Offering was a perfect representation of that.

Sin had been committed! A Sin-Offering or Trespass-Offering had been presented, and I might quickly add, along with a *"Meat (grain) Offering."* This atoned for sin, because it represented Christ Who was to come. With sin atoned, Righteousness now is the sole object in the life of the Believer. In recognition of that, a Peace-Offering is presented, with part being burned on the Altar, which means it was given to God, and part being eaten by the Priests, who were a Type of Christ, and part being eaten by the sinner, his family, and his friends. It was a joyous occasion, because peace had been restored, and had been restored because of what Christ would do at the Cross.

As we have stated at the beginning of this Commentary on Leviticus, the Jew was not taught that the death of the animal was accepted instead of his punishment; but he was instructed to look upon it as a foreshadowing of a Perfect Offering to come. This may not be apparent regarding a cursory glance at the Pentateuch; but the New Testament commentary leaves no doubt on the question. Paul said, *"It is not possible that the blood of bulls and goats should take away sins"*; and, the first Tabernacle was *"a figure for the time then present"*; and then, *"the Law having a shadow of good things to come, and not the very image"* (or full Revelation). And finally, *"Of the things, can never with those sacrifices which they offered year by year continually make the comers thereunto perfect."* As the writer said, *"This is not a contradiction of the Old Testament, but at explanation of the Mosaic dispensation."*

In fact, Jesus said to Israel, *"Had you believed Moses, you would have believed Me: for he wrote of Me."* That the Sacrifices were nothing in themselves is a lesson constantly brought before the Jews. Through the Prophets, the Lord said to them, *"To what purpose is the multitude of your sacrifices unto Me? saith the LORD: I am full of the Burnt Offerings of rams, and the fat of fed beasts; and I delight not in the blood of bullocks, or of lambs, or of he-goats."* This

meant, as should be overly obvious, that there was nothing in the sacrifices themselves that was effective in themselves for Atonement. Israel, thinking that it was, was merely a perversion of the Truth.

Unfortunately, we seem to be doing the same thing presently, by making the Church, or some man-made rule or regulation, the object of our Faith, instead of Christ and Him Crucified. Righteousness can never be attained in this manner.

IS THE OBJECT OF FAITH THAT IMPORTANT?

I'll tell you how important it is!

Israel lost her way, so badly in fact that she didn't even know her Messiah when He came, and all because the object of her Faith was moved from what the sacrifices represented, namely Christ, to something else. It really didn't matter what the something else was, whether the sacrifices themselves, or the ritual of the Law itself, or whatever. Unless it was Faith in Christ and Him Crucified, then it wasn't Faith that God would recognize.

Ditto as it regards the modern Church. Satan tries to pull the Faith of Believers away from the Cross to other things. And he really doesn't care too very much what those other things are. They may be good in their own right, but still, if they become the object of one's faith, then that means the object of one's faith is not the Cross, which in effect, puts that Believer in a position of making war on God (Rom. 8:7).

THE CARNAL MIND AND THE SPIRITUAL MIND

Paul said, *"For to be carnally minded is death; but to be spiritually minded is life and peace"* (Rom. 8:6).

What did Paul mean by that?

Were I to ask most Christians as to what *"carnally minded"* meant, their answers would be mostly in this vein:

They would claim that it refers to watching too much television, going fishing too often, or being too interested in the Stock Market, or a hundred and one other similar things.

The truth is, those things, which may or may not be harmful, have absolutely nothing to do with what Paul is addressing here, as it regards being *"carnally minded."*

To be *"carnally minded"* refers to the Believer who is trusting in anything other than *"Christ and Him Crucified."* And without going into a lot of detail, let the Reader understand that when we say *"anything,"* we are meaning *"anything."* For your victory, your power, your strength, your Holiness, your Righteousness, your Christlikeness, and in fact, every single thing that we receive from the Lord, we must ever understand that it all comes, and without exception, through Christ and what He did at the Cross. When you understand that, believe that, and act upon that, that's being *"spiritually minded"* (Rom. 8:1-2). To believe something else, which means to make something else other than the Cross the object of one's faith, is being *"carnally minded."*

Paul then said: *"Because the carnal mind is enmity against God: for it is not subject to the Law of God, neither indeed can be"* (Rom. 8:7).

The word *"enmity"* as it is used here, refers to *"hatred or war."* In other words, the carnal mind has declared war against God. That's a strong statement, but we must remember that the Holy Spirit is the One Who has said this, using Paul as his instrument.

It is a shame when we realize that the majority of Christians, even those who truly love God, and are sincerely trying to serve Him, are in fact, at war with God. They are seeking to bring about nearness to Him through means other than simple Faith in Christ and the Cross, which puts them at cross purposes with God. In other words, whether they realize it or not, they have declared war on God, and that's a perilous situation for a Believer to be in.

Let the Believer understand that it's not so much what we do, as what we believe. And to be sure, what we believe is going to play out to what we do. But the correct doing cannot be brought about until we have correct believing (Jn. 3:16; Eph. 2:8-9; Rom. 6:3-14).

THE FAT AND THE BLOOD

Verses 15 through 17 read: *"And the two kidneys, and the fat that is upon them, which is by the flanks, and the caul above the liver, with the kidneys, it shall he take away.*

"And the Priest shall burn them upon the

Altar: it is the food of the Offering made by fire for a sweet savor: all the fat is the LORD's.

"It shall be a perpetual Statute for your generations throughout all your dwellings, that you eat neither fat nor blood."

The fat, as stated, represented God giving His best, which was and is the Lord Jesus Christ. It also represents the prosperity of Israel, and as well of the Saint presently. In other words, all true prosperity comes from the Lord, and is made possible by what Christ did at the Cross, hence the fat being burned upon the Altar. Actually, this is what Jesus was speaking about when He said: *"Seek ye first the Kingdom of God, and His Righteousness; and all these things shall be added unto you"* (Mat. 6:33).

The true prosperity Gospel, and it definitely is prosperity, is *"Jesus Christ and Him Crucified."* The fat represented that. As well, it tells us how this prosperity is obtained, symbolized by the fat being burned on the Altar, which was a Type of Christ and His Crucifixion.

The *"Blood"* represented the price that Christ would pay, in order for this prosperity to be brought about, whether spiritual or otherwise, hitherto the prohibition of eating fat or blood.

This prohibition was carried over into the New Covenant, when James, the Lord's brother, stated: *"For it seemed good to the Holy Spirit, and to us, to lay upon you no greater burden than these necessary things;*

"That you abstain from meats offered to idols, and from blood, and from things strangled, and from fornication: from which if you keep yourselves, you shall do well" (Acts 15:28-29).

The prohibition given here against the eating of *"blood,"* pertained as well to *"fat."*

"I know not when the Lord will come,
"Or at what hour He may appear,
"Whether at midnight or at morn,
"Or at what season of the year."

"I know not what of time remains,
"To run its course in this low sphere,
"Or what awaits of calm or storm,
"Of joy or grief, of hope or fear."

"I know not what is yet to run

"Of spring or summer, green or sere,
"Of death or life, of pain or peace,
"Of shade or shine, of song or tear."

"The centuries have come and gone,
"Dark centuries of absence drear;
"I dare not chide the long delay,
"Nor ask when I His voice shall hear."

"I do not think it can be long,
"Till in His glory He appears;
"And yet I dare not name the day,
"Nor fix the solemn advent year."

CHAPTER 4

(1) "AND THE LORD SPOKE UNTO MOSES, SAYING,

(2) "SPEAK UNTO THE CHILDREN OF ISRAEL, SAYING, IF A SOUL SHALL SIN THROUGH IGNORANCE AGAINST ANY OF THE COMMANDMENTS OF THE LORD CONCERNING THINGS WHICH OUGHT NOT TO BE DONE, AND SHALL DO AGAINST ANY OF THEM:

(3) "IF THE PRIEST THAT IS ANOINTED DO SIN ACCORDING TO THE SIN OF THE PEOPLE; THEN LET HIM BRING FOR HIS SIN, WHICH HE HAS SINNED, A YOUNG BULLOCK WITHOUT BLEMISH UNTO THE LORD FOR A SIN OFFERING.

(4) "AND HE SHALL BRING THE BULLOCK UNTO THE DOOR OF THE TABERNACLE OF THE CONGREGATION BEFORE THE LORD; AND SHALL LAY HIS HAND UPON THE BULLOCK'S HEAD, AND KILL THE BULLOCK BEFORE THE LORD.

(5) "AND THE PRIEST THAT IS ANOINTED SHALL TAKE OF THE BULLOCK'S BLOOD, AND BRING IT TO THE TABERNACLE OF THE CONGREGATION:

(6) "AND THE PRIEST SHALL DIP HIS FINGER IN THE BLOOD, AND SPRINKLE OF THE BLOOD SEVEN TIMES BEFORE THE LORD, BEFORE THE VEIL OF THE SANCTUARY.

(7) "AND THE PRIEST SHALL PUT SOME OF THE BLOOD UPON THE HORNS OF THE ALTAR OF SWEET INCENSE BEFORE THE LORD, WHICH IS IN THE TABERNACLE OF THE CONGREGATION; AND SHALL POUR ALL THE BLOOD OF THE BULLOCK AT THE BOTTOM OF THE ALTAR OF THE BURNT OFFERING, WHICH IS AT THE DOOR OF THE TABERNACLE OF THE CONGREGATION.

(8) "AND HE SHALL TAKE OFF FROM IT ALL THE FAT OF THE BULLOCK FOR THE SIN-OFFERING; THE FAT THAT COVERS THE INWARDS, AND ALL THE FAT THAT IS UPON THE INWARDS,

(9) "AND THE TWO KIDNEYS, AND THE FAT THAT IS UPON THEM, WHICH IS BY THE FLANKS, AND THE CAUL ABOVE THE LIVER, WITH THE KIDNEYS, IT SHALL HE TAKE AWAY,

(10) "AS IT WAS TAKEN OFF FROM THE BULLOCK OF THE SACRIFICE OF PEACE-OFFERINGS: AND THE PRIEST SHALL BURN THEM UPON THE ALTAR OF THE BURNT-OFFERING.

(11) "AND THE SKIN OF THE BULLOCK, AND ALL HIS FLESH, WITH HIS HEAD, AND WITH HIS LEGS, AND HIS INWARDS, AND HIS DUNG,

(12) "EVEN THE WHOLE BULLOCK SHALL HE CARRY FORTH WITHOUT THE CAMP UNTO A CLEAN PLACE, WHERE THE ASHES ARE POURED OUT, AND BURN HIM ON THE WOOD WITH FIRE: WHERE THE ASHES ARE POURED OUT SHALL HE BE BURNT."

The diagram is:

1. Chapter 4 represents the *"Sin-Offering."* Christ became a Sin-Offering on the Cross (Isa. 53:10).

2. The words in the Second Verse, *"through ignorance,"* signify that a person, irrespective of his knowledge of the Word of God, cannot really know what sin actually is.

3. The Church, in its foolishness, paints some sins as heinous, with others even more heinous being ignored altogether.

4. Man has a tendency to speak lightly of his own sin irregardless of its dreadfulness.

5. The efficacy (effectiveness) of Christ's Atonement for sin is not to be measured by man's consciousness of sin, but by God's measurement of it.

6. Sin is sin, regardless of who commits it, or when it is committed.

7. So, according to Scripture, God deals

with all who sin on the same basis.

8. In the *"Burnt-Offering,"* the sinlessness of the victim was transferred to the worshipper. In the *"Sin-Offering,"* the sinfulness of the sinner was transferred to the victim.

9. The sprinkling of the blood some seven times before the Lord portrays a perfect Restoration, for the number *"seven"* proclaims the Perfection, Totality, and Completeness of God.

10. The Fifth Verse says, *"And the Priest who is anointed shall take."* Christ was anointed above all His fellows. He Alone can take the blood to the Altar of Worship and sprinkle it before God, thereby restoring fellowship. This is His High Priestly role.

11. The *"Blood upon the horns of the Altar,"* speak of the total dominion which Calvary brought about, and which was brought about for Believers. In other words, the Cross proclaims the fact that the Believer can have victory over all sin.

IGNORANCE

Verses 1 and 2 read: *"And the LORD spoke unto Moses, saying,*

"Speak unto the Children of Israel, saying, If a soul shall sin through ignorance against any of the Commandments of the LORD concerning things which ought not to be done, and shall do against any of them."

The Burnt-Offering, the Meal-Offering, and the Peace-Offering were Sweet-Savor Offerings. The *"Burnt-Offering"* portrayed Christ satisfying the demands of a thrice-Holy God.

The *"Meal-Offering,"* was an Offering of Thanksgiving, that would be presented along with the Burnt-Offering, signifying thankfulness that the Offering had been accepted.

The *"Peace-Offering,"* signified Restoration, and was almost always offered in conjunction with the Burnt-Offering, as well as the Sin or Trespass-Offerings. All of these, as stated, were Sweet-Savor Offerings, but Sacrifices for sin, which included *"Sin-Offerings"* and *"Trespass-Offerings,"* were not Sweet-Savor Offerings.

As we study the Sin-Offerings, hopefully we will learn, at least as far as much as a human being can know, of the awfulness of sin, and the price that was paid by the Saviour, to

NOTES

rid us of this evil monster.

The Sin-Offering typifies the Sacrifice of our Lord Jesus Christ upon the Cross, as the great Sin-Offering for mankind, whereby the Wrath of God was propitiated, and an expiation (to pay the penalty for, to atone) for the sins of man was wrought, bringing about reconciliation between God and man. (*"Propitiation"* means, *"to appease or to conciliate."*)

The *"sins of ignorance,"* addressed here portray to us amazing truths – truths we desperately need to know. When we think upon the Atonement, what Jesus did for us, we soon find out that what was accomplished at the Cross addressed far more than the mere satisfaction of the conscience. In fact, even though the conscience may have reached a state of refined spirituality, which means that one is deep in the Lord, and has an excellent understanding of His Word; still, this cannot be a guide as it regards the terrible problem of *"sin."*

We know beyond the shadow of a doubt that the Cross of Christ addressed every aspect of sin, in all of its horror and all of its effect. In fact, the Holy Spirit through Paul said: *"Knowing this, that our old man is crucified with Him, that the body of sin might be destroyed, that henceforth we should not serve sin"* (Rom. 6:6).

This tells us that not only was the power of sin broken at the Cross, but as well, the guilt of sin was taken away.

As well, what Jesus did at the Cross not only addressed sin as it appears on this Earth, and especially in the hearts and lives of men, but also, it went to the very root of sin, which is Satan himself, and all that he did in his revolution against God. Again, Paul said: *"That in the dispensation of the fullness of times He* (God the Father) *might gather together in one all things in Christ, both which are in Heaven, and which are on Earth; even in Him"* (Eph. 1:10).

This tells us that the Cross not only addressed the Earth, but Heaven as well!

So the more we learn of the Cross, which these Sacrifices teach us, the more we will learn of the horror of sin. And the more we learn of that horror, the more we will learn that it was only the Cross which could address this monster. Man is foolish to think that his efforts to assuage sin can have any effect. Irrespective as to what he does, how much the intellect may address the problem, or how much money is thrown at the problem, the fact remains that all man can do is address the external, which really presents only the effects of sin. The core of sin begins with Satan, and has incorporated itself in the hearts of the unredeemed. It can only be addressed by the individual being *"born again."* Jesus told Nicodemus: *"Verily, verily, I say unto you, except a man be born again, he cannot see the Kingdom of God"* (Jn. 3:3).

MAN'S STANDARD VERSUS GOD'S STANDARD

Concerning this, Mackintosh said, *"The Holiness of God's dwelling-place, and the ground of His association with His people, could never be regulated by the standard of man's conscience, no matter how high the standard might be. There are many things which man's conscience would pass over – many things which might escape man's cognizance – many things which his heart might deem alright, which God could not tolerate; and which, as a consequence, would interfere with man's approach to, his worship of, and his relationship with God.*

"Wherefore if the Atonement of Christ merely made provision for such sins as come within the compass of man's apprehension, we should find ourselves very far short of the true ground of peace. We need to understand that sin has been atoned for, according to God's measurement thereof – that the claims of His Throne have been perfectly answered – that sin, as seen in the light of His inflexible Holiness, has been Divinely judged. This is what gives settled peace to the soul. A full Atonement has been made for the Believer's sins of ignorance, as well as for his known sins."

GOD'S PRESCRIBED ORDER FOR VICTORIOUS LIVING

The Cross deals not only with the Salvation of the sinner, but as well, the Sanctification of the Saint. God's prescribed order in this capacity, even as we have addressed several times, is Faith on both counts – Faith

NOTES

in Christ and His Cross as it regards Salvation from sin, and Faith in Christ and His Cross as it regards victory over sin, in our continued walk.

The following two diagrams will hopefully explain more fully what we are saying:

1. Focus: The focus of the Believer must ever be on Christ and Him Crucified (Rom. 6:3-14).

2. Object of Faith: The focus being the Cross, the object of Faith must always be the Finished Work of Christ (I Cor. 1:17-18, 23).

3. Power Source: If our focus is right, which means our object of Faith is correct, our Power Source will then be the Holy Spirit, without Whom we can do nothing (Rom. 8:1-2, 11).

4. Results: What we've given you is God's prescribed order, and that order followed will always bring victorious results, and will do so perpetually. No, that doesn't mean sinless perfection, for the Bible doesn't teach such. But it does mean that sin will not have dominion over such a Believer (Rom. 6:14).

Now let's look at this order that has been perverted, even as it has presently by the majority of the Church, and because the Church has had so little teaching on the Cross. The following is a diagram of defeat:

1. Focus: The Cross is ignored, with *"works"* becoming the focus.

2. Object of Faith: Works now being prominent, our performance becomes the object of our faith.

3. Power Source: The focus being on works, with the object of faith now being our performance, the power source becomes *"self."* The Holy Spirit will not function in such an atmosphere.

4. Results: Trying to live this life in the fashion we've just described, atmosphere, guarantees failure on every hand.

But yet, the far greater majority of the modern Church is trying to live for God by functioning according to the second diagram. Most are doing this through ignorance.

THE MODERN SINS OF IGNORANCE

To try to function outside of God's prescribed order, which is, as repeatedly stated, *"Jesus Christ and Him Crucified,"* meaning that our Faith must ever be in the Finished

Work of Christ, which then gives the Holy Spirit latitude to work within our lives, is pure and simple, rebellion against God, which in effect is a sin of the highest order. It is an insult to Christ, actually in effect saying, whether we realize it or not, that what He did at the Cross was not enough, and we need to add to His Sacrifice. It puts us in the position of trying to do what no human being has ever done, and in fact, which no human being can ever do. If man could somehow save himself, which refers to making himself holy, or righteous, then Jesus would not have had to come down to this Earth, and die on a Cross. Paul bluntly says: *"If Righteousness come by the Law, then Christ is dead in vain"* (Gal. 2:21).

Most people do not think of such action as sin. But it is not only sin; it is sin of the highest order, as stated, rebellion against God, and in fact, against the entirety of the Plan of God. It is committing the same sin that Cain committed, when he attempted to offer to God a sacrifice of the labor of his own hands, instead of offering up that which God had demanded, an innocent victim, i.e., *"a lamb."* Unfortunately, the problem didn't die with Cain; it remains with the human race unto this hour. In fact, the problem today is worse than ever. As we've said repeatedly, the Church in the last several decades has had so little teaching on the Cross that for all practical purposes, it is presently Cross-illiterate. Being in that condition, it has only one recourse, and that is to try to *"sail this ship alone."* That is sin against God, because it's rebellion against His prescribed order, and even though it's done in ignorance, it is still sin, and it will still reap the terrible consequences that sin reaps.

THE CROSS

Every iota of Salvation, of victory, of blessings from the Lord, of worship as it regards the Lord, all and without exception pertain to the Cross. To the degree that we understand the Cross, to that degree will we have victory in all of these things mentioned, and many things not mentioned. To the degree that we do not understand the Cross, to that degree we will suffer!

That's one reason that Satan fights the

Cross so hard, and why all false doctrine has its roots, in some way, in opposition to the Cross. During Paul's time, the great opposition to the Cross was the Message of the Judaizers, which was the Law/Grace issue. In other words, teachers out of Jerusalem and Judea, while professing Christ, were also pushing and promoting the Law. In other words, they were trying to get Gentile Believers to accept the Law of Moses, or at least parts of the Law. Paul, in answering this false message, said: *"Christ is become of no effect unto you, whosoever of you are justified by the Law* (seek to be justified by the Law); *you are fallen from Grace"* (Gal. 5:4).

While there have been many false doctrines down through the many centuries from the time of the Early Church to the present, perhaps the worst of all, and because we're nearing the very end, is the so-called Word of Faith doctrine. The Reader may not quite understand as to why we address this issue so very, very much. We do so because this doctrine bitterly opposes the Cross. In fact, one could only say as it regards its teachers and adherents, *"For many walk, of whom I have told you often, and now tell you even weeping, that they are the enemies of the Cross of Christ."*

The Apostle went on to say: *"Whose end is destruction, whose god is their belly, and whose glory is in their shame, who mind earthly things"* (Phil. 3:18-19).

THE SIN-OFFERING

Verse 3 reads: *"If the Priest who is anointed do sin according to the sin of the people; then let him bring for his sin, which he has sinned, a young bullock without blemish unto the LORD for a Sin-Offering."*

The sin that is committed here, which is a sin of ignorance, and committed by a Priest, in some way has a negative effect on the people. That is what is meant by the words, *"According to the sin of the people."* In some way, his sin caused them to sin, or to do things wrong, etc.

The Priest is to select for a Sin-Offering a young bullock, which is to be offered up to God. It is to be *"without blemish."* Before we deal with this particular sin, let's first of all address ourselves to the Sin-Offering per se.

Nothing can more forcibly express man's incompetency to deal with sin than the fact of there being such a thing as a *"sin of ignorance."* Man's ignorance of sin proves his total inability to put it away.

To more fully understand the Sin-Offering, perhaps it would be best to compare it with the Burnt-Offering. In doing this, we will find the two very different aspects of Christ. But although these aspects may be different, it is still one and the same Christ; and hence the sacrifice in each case was to be *"without blemish."*

In the Burnt-Offering, Christ is seen meeting the Divine demands; in the Sin-Offering, He is seen meeting the depths of human need. In the former, we learn of the preciousness of the Sacrifice; in the latter, the hatefulness of sin.

In the first place, when considering the Burnt-Offering, we observe that it was a voluntary Offering. *"He shall offer it of his own voluntary will."* Now, the word *"voluntary"* does not occur in the Sin-Offering (Mackintosh).

In the Sin-Offering, we have quite a different line of truth unfolding. The Sin-Offering introduces Christ as the Bearer of that terrible thing called *"sin,"* and as well, the endurer of all its appalling consequences. The Sin-Offering alone furnishes the fitting Type of the Lord Jesus as the One Who poured forth those accents of intense agony; for in it alone do we find the circumstances which evoked such accents from the depths of His Spotless Soul. The *"young bullock"* signifies Christ as a young man and without sin, dying in man's place. In other words, He *"without blemish unto the Lord"* became *"a Sin-Offering."* In the *"Burnt-Offering,"* the sinlessness of the victim was transferred to the worshipper. In the *"Sin-Offering,"* the sinfulness of the sinner is transferred to the victim. So, there is a vast difference in the Burnt-Offering as a Type of Christ, which it was, than the Sin-Offering, which was also a Type of Christ.

As we go further into the Text, we shall see exactly how the Sin-Offering so typified Christ.

THE SIN OF THE PREACHER

While there is no more Office of the Priest, that having been fulfilled in Christ,

NOTES

the Church now has *"Apostles, Prophets, Evangelists, Pastors, and Teachers"* (Eph. 4:11). When Preachers or Teachers explain to people how to live for God, how to walk in victory, and do so wrongly, which means that they direct them to that other than the Cross, such direction will cause the people to sin. The Preacher is sinning when he gives them such false direction, and such false direction will always result in them sinning as well.

There is only one way to have dominion over sin, and that is by understanding the Cross and our part in that Finished Work (Rom. 6:3-5, 14).

While all of this, the sin committed by the Preacher, and the resultant sin of the people, is done in ignorance, it is still sin. It will still reap bitter results, and it must be washed by the blood and put away.

As well, the Preacher giving such wrong direction is living a life of spiritual failure himself. It cannot be otherwise! If he knew and understood the Cross, he would be preaching the Cross (I Cor. 1:17-18, 21, 23; 2:2). But not knowing and understanding the Cross, he preaches something else as the answer, which of course, is no answer at all. But let all understand, such a Preacher, even though God may be using him, and he at the same time may be very sincere before the Lord, still, without understanding the Cross, he cannot live a life of spiritual victory. In some way the *"works of the flesh"* are functioning through him. If he'll be honest with himself, which is not easy to do, he will admit that something is wrong (Gal. 5:19-21). There can never be settled peace upon this ground. There will always be the painful apprehension that there is something wrong underneath. If the heart be not led into settled repose by the Scripture testimony that the inflexible claims of Divine Justice have been answered, there must, of necessity, be a sensation of uneasiness, and every such sensation presents a barrier to our worship, our communion, and our testimony.

The truth is, if one is uneasy in reference to the settlement of the question of sin, one cannot properly worship, one cannot properly enjoy communion with God, or His people, nor can one be an intelligent or effective witness for Christ. The heart must be at rest before God as to the perfect remission of sin, or else, we cannot *"worship Him in spirit and in truth."* If there be guilt on the conscience, and most definitely, if the Preacher is preaching something that's not Scriptural, even though done in ignorance, there must be terror at the same time in the heart, even though one may try to cover such terror, or even refuse to admit such.

It is only from a heart filled with that sweet and sacred repose, which the Blood of Christ imparts, that true and acceptable worship can ascend to the Father (Mackintosh).

THE HAND LAID ON THE HEAD

Verse 4 reads: *"And he shall bring the bullock unto the Door of the Tabernacle of the congregation before the LORD; and shall lay his hand upon the bullock's head, and kill the bullock before the LORD."*

The *"Priest who is anointed,"* as given in Verse 3, refers to the High Priest. If he sinned through ignorance or otherwise, it was required of him that a *"bullock"* be sacrificed. While all sin is terrible, and while it is a terrible thing for anyone to sin, the sin of a leader, as typified here by the High Priest, causes far more damage to the Work of God, as certainly would be obvious. To be sure, the remedy for his sin is the same as the remedy for all others; even as there can be no other remedy; however, a bullock was demanded to be offered, the most valuable of all the clean animals that could be offered for sacrifice, in order that it may be known and understood, the import of such a sin.

For instance, when David sinned by committing adultery with Bathsheba, and then murdering her husband Uriah, the impact on the Work of God, not to speak of David, was awful to behold. While many others in Israel no doubt committed the same sin, at one time or the other, although just as heinous, irrespective as to who would have committed it, still, the impact was far greater when committed by David. But yet, the blood of the lamb was David's recourse, just as it is with all others (Ps. 51).

THE DOOR

The *"Door"* stood for the Tabernacle

proper, but included the Brazen Altar, and even the Brazen Laver. It actually pertained to the entire apparatus of the Plan of God.

The *"Door"* as given here, was a Type of Christ (Jn. 10:9). This means that it is through Christ and Christ Alone that sin can be addressed, washed, cleansed, and put away. Of course it is done, even as we shall see, by and through what Christ did at the Cross.

While our Lord is God, and in fact, has always been God, and always will be God, it was not as God per se, that He gives us all these things. It is as the Man, Jesus Christ, that all of this is done (Jn., Chpt. 10). But more particularly, it is the reason that He became a Man, which was to go to the Cross, and which He did, that makes all these things possible. And when I say *"all these things,"* I am referring to every single thing the Lord does for us, irrespective as to what it might be, but most particular, I'm referring to sin. Sin cannot be addressed, cannot be cleansed and removed, cannot be handled correctly, except by and through Jesus Christ, and what He has done for us at the Cross. Concerning this, Paul said: *"But this Man* (the Lord Jesus Christ), *after He had offered one Sacrifice for sins* (the only Sacrifice that God would accept, which was the Sacrifice of Himself) *forever sat down on the Right Hand of God* (which refers to the task being completed and thereby accepted)*"* (Heb. 10:12).

Through and by this great Sacrifice, Paul went on to say: *"From henceforth expecting till His enemies be made His footstool"* (Heb. 10:13).

This means that Calvary has defeated every single enemy, irrespective as to what it might be. This means that you, through Christ, which refers to Faith in His Cross, can vanquish every enemy. Paul also said: *"And has put all things under His feet, and gave Him to be the head over all things to the Church, which is His body, the fullness of Him Who fills all in all"* (Eph. 1:22-23).

In other words, the Church, and I speak of the True Church, is the Body of Christ, and understanding that the *"feet"* are on the body, this means that Christ overcame, which He did at the Cross, in order that we might be the overcomer that we must be, which can only be by and through Faith in Christ and what He has done for us in His great Sacrifice.

Unfortunately, most of the modern Church, the Pentecostal varieties included, are telling people to take their sin to Psychologists, i.e., *"the psychological way."* Let me give you an example:

In the Assemblies of God and the Church of God, the two largest so-called Pentecostal Denominations, and which probably includes most, if not all, the others as well, if a Preacher has a problem with sin of any nature, before he can be accepted in good standing with these Denominations, he must be signed off by a Psychologist, which demands several months of so-called psychological therapy.

There could be no higher insult to Christ than this abominable practice. In the first place, humanistic psychology is a lie from beginning to end. It holds no answer, has no help, can provide no satisfaction whatsoever, as it regards victory over sin. It is humanistic wisdom, which James said is *"earthly, sensual, and devilish"* (James 3:15).

Such a direction can be construed as none other than ungodly! And for such to be demanded, in effect, is a vote of no confidence as it regards Christ and His Cross.

The problem is, most of the Church doesn't understand at all what the Cross means as it regards the Sanctification of the Saint. This refers to how one is to live for God. As I have stated in one way or the other over and over in this Volume, the Church, for all practical purposes, seeks to live for God in all the wrong ways. In other words, it simply doesn't know how to live for the Lord. The reason for that is that it doesn't understand the Cross as it regards Sanctification. And once again, please bear with my repetition.

The entirety of Paul's teaching centers up on this very subject, and is done so in all of his 14 Epistles. The following is very abbreviated, but is basically what the great Apostle taught, even as it was given to him by Christ (Gal. 1:12).

THE CROSS

Paul said: *"Don't you know, that so many of us as were baptized into Jesus Christ were baptized into His death?*

"Therefore we are buried with Him by

NOTES

Baptism into death: and like as Christ was raised up from the dead by the Glory of the Father, even so we also should walk in newness of life.

"For if we have been planted together in the likeness of His death, we shall be also in the likeness of His Resurrection" (Rom. 6:3-5).

This, along with so many other Passages, tells us that everything comes to us by the Cross. Salvation is made possible by and through the Cross alone, even as is everything else.

So the Believer should settle the fact in his or her mind that every single thing we receive from the Lord, and irrespective as to what it is, is all made possible, and in totality, by Christ, and what He did for us in the Sacrifice of Himself. This means that the Believer should be zeroed in on the Cross at all times, actually making that, which of course is the Work of Christ, his emphasis. That's why Paul also said:

"For Christ sent me not to baptize, but to preach the Gospel: not with wisdom of words, lest the Cross of Christ should be made of none effect" (I Cor. 1:17).

The Apostle is not demeaning Water Baptism, but rather making the point that the emphasis must always be on the Cross, and nothing else, even as important as the other things might be in their own right. And incidentally, in Romans, Chapter 6, Verses 3 through 5, Paul is not speaking of Water Baptism, but rather using the word *"Baptism"* to describe what Christ did on the Cross, and how that we, by Faith, are literally *"in Him"* as it refers to that great Work.

FAITH

The Apostle also said: *"Likewise reckon ye also yourselves to be dead indeed unto sin, but alive unto God through Jesus Christ our Lord"* (Rom. 6:11). This refers to Faith. In other words, Jesus Christ and Him Crucified must ever be the object of our Faith.

Even as we have said over, and over again, the object of Faith is all-important. If Satan trips up the Believer, this is where he does it most of all.

The Evil One tries to get our Faith moved from the Cross of Christ to other things. He doesn't much care what the other things are, just as long as it isn't the Cross.

Once we begin to question Christians, we can quickly find out what the object of their Faith actually is. And you would be surprised, simply because it covers the waterfront, so to speak.

Without going into all type of detail, let the Reader understand that the object of Faith must always be the Cross of Christ. And as stated, this is where Satan fights the hardest. That's why Paul again said:

"Fight the good fight of Faith, lay hold on eternal life, whereunto you are also called" (I Tim. 6:12).

Actually, in the original Text, the definite article is placed in front of the word *"Faith,"* making it read *"the Faith,"* which refers to the *"body of Faith,"* not so much the *"act of Faith."* In fact, the term *"the Faith,"* refers to *"Jesus Christ and Him Crucified,"* just as the term *"in Christ"* refers to the same.

The idea is, if your faith isn't anchored in the Cross of Christ, then what you have might be faith, but it's not *"the Faith."* So, the Cross of Christ must always, and without exception, be the object of our Faith.

THE HOLY SPIRIT

Listen again to Paul: *"But if the Spirit (Holy Spirit) of Him (God the Father) Who raised up Jesus from the dead dwell in you, He Who raised up Christ from the dead shall also quicken your mortal bodies by His Spirit Who dwells in you"* (Rom. 8:11).

This is not speaking of the coming Resurrection, although it certainly does include that. It is rather speaking of the working of the Holy Spirit within our hearts and lives, to help us live the life we ought to live.

This means that the same power that raised Jesus from the dead is available to us, and is available at all times. Now if we properly understand that, we certainly should realize that victory should be ours in every respect.

The Holy Spirit doesn't demand a lot of us, but He does demand that our Faith be anchored in Christ and what Christ did for us in the Sacrifice of Himself.

Jesus said of the Holy Spirit: *"He shall glorify Me: for He shall receive of Mine, and*

shall show it unto you" (Jn. 16:14).

When Christ speaks of the Holy Spirit glorifying Him, this refers to what Jesus did at the Cross.

With Faith properly placed, and with it properly remaining there, Paul also said: *"For sin shall not have dominion over you: for you are not under the Law but under Grace"* (Rom. 6:14).

When we get to the blood applied to the horns of the Altar, as given to us in Verse 7, we will deal with this more directly.

But what I have given you above, and have done so in a very abbreviated way, is in fact, *"God's Prescribed Order of Victory."* And I might quickly add, it's His only Prescribed Order of Victory. Other than the Cross of Christ, He has no other, and because no other is needed!

SHALL LAY HIS HAND UPON THE BULLOCK'S HEAD

This act was common both to the Burnt-Offering and the Sin-Offering; but in the case of the former, even as we've already stated, it identified the offerer with an unblemished Offering; in the case of the latter, it involved the transfer of the sin of the offerer to the head of the Offering (Mackintosh).

What, then, is the Doctrine set forth in the laying on of hands? In the words of Mackintosh, it is this:

"Christ was 'made sin for us, that we might be made the Righteousness of God in Him' (II Cor. 5:21). He took our position with all its consequences, in order that we might get His position with all its consequences. He was treated as sin upon the Cross, that we might be treated as Righteousness in the presence of Infinite Holiness. He was cast out of God's Presence for a short period of time, because He had sin on Him by imputation, that we might be received into God's House, and into His bosom because we have a perfect Righteousness by imputation. He had to endure the hiding of God's countenance, that we might bask in the light of that countenance. He had to pass through three hours' of darkness, that we might walk in everlasting light. He was forsaken by God for a short period of time, that we might enjoy His Presence forever."

WHAT IS IMPUTATION?

1. The word *"impute"* or *"imputation,"* means, *"to lay the responsibility or blame for something on someone, when they do not rightly deserve it."* For instance, God imputed the penalty of all of our sins on Christ, even though He had never sinned, and did not deserve such, as would be obvious. As well, He imputed the Righteousness of Christ upon us, even though we were sinners, and did not at all deserve such Righteousness.

In the Biblical account, it refers to *"setting to one's account or reckoning something to a person."*

For instance again, it is said in Genesis 15:6 that God reckoned Righteousness to believing Abraham, which means that He gave Abraham something which Abraham did not have within himself, and in fact, did not deserve such. Paul quotes this Passage in arguing man's Justification by God through Grace alone. If Abraham had been able to justify himself by works he might boast, but man is unable to save himself.

The meaning is not that God accepted Abraham's Faith instead of perfect Righteousness as the meritorious ground for his Justification. It is rather that God accepted Abraham because he trusted in God rather than in anything that he could do. To make it simple, God imputed Righteousness to Abraham, even though Abraham didn't deserve such, and in fact, could not do anything to attain such, at least as far as works were concerned. This means that the Righteousness that Abraham had, God had to impute it unto Him, just exactly as He does with us presently.

In fact, this reckoning, or imputation, of Righteousness to the Believer lies at the heart of the Biblical Doctrine of Salvation.

Paul uses the phrase *"Righteousness of God"* nine times (Rom. 1:17; 3:5, 21; 10:3; II Cor. 5:21), and in most of these instances, it is mentioned in order to teach that God grants the sinner a new legal standing, i.e., *"he is counted righteous even while a sinner."*

Men are not righteous within themselves; consequently, we need God's Righteousness, which has been made manifest in Christ, and in Christ Alone. Paul also said: *"Not having*

a Righteousness of my own, based on law, but that which is through Faith in Christ, the Righteousness from God that depends on Faith" (Phil. 3:9).

This Righteousness is imputed, or reckoned, so that while, strictly speaking, it is not our own, yet God reckons it to us so that we are justified, even though we certainly do not deserve such.

The imputation of the Righteousness of Christ to the sinner lies at the heart of the Doctrine of Salvation.

THE LORD JESUS CHRIST

2. The second sense in which the word imputation is used in Christian Doctrine is the reckoning of man's sin to Jesus Christ. This is exemplified in the *"Sin-Offering."* The sinner would lay his hand on the head of the bullock, just before he killed the animal, in effect, imputing his sin to the innocent animal, which was a Type of Christ, and would be fulfilled in Christ, when He died on the Cross. Whenever the believing sinner evidences Faith in Christ and what Christ did at the Cross, he is in effect, transferring his sins from himself to Christ, the same as the Israelite did in Old Testament times. Of course the difference is very great.

The blood of bulls and goats could not take away sins, only cover them in a sense, while our Faith in Christ takes our sins completely away, and in every respect.

But when this happens, even as we've already stated, not only are our sins imputed to Christ, which refers to their penalty, but as well, His Perfect Righteousness is in turn imputed to us.

The imputation of our sin to Christ is not that Christ actually becomes a sinner, for all of the Gospel contradicts that position. It is rather that by virtue of His identification with the human race that sin is reckoned to Him. Although it is not explicitly said in Scripture that sin is reckoned or imputed to Christ, the meaning is clear.

It is said that He *"bore our sins in His Body on the tree"* (I Pet. 2:24), that *"the LORD has laid on Him the iniquity of us all"* (Isa. 53:6), that He was made to *"bear"* the iniquities of His people (Isa. 53:11; Heb. 9:28).

Each of these Passages of Scripture has in mind the Old Testament institution of sacrifice in which guilt was symbolically and ceremoniously transferred to an animal with the laying on of hands of the head of the victim. Applied to Christ, to Whom the sacrifices of the Old Testament pointed, the teaching is that *"He bore the punishment of our sin vicariously* (to suffer in place of another), *its guilt having been imputed to Him."*

PAUL

The same teaching is set forth graphically by Paul in Galatians 3:13, where Christ is said to have *"become a curse for us."* The meaning is that He bore the penalty for human sin, that, as Luther declared, God dealt with Him as though He were the greatest of sinners. Sin was imputed, or reckoned to Him, so that man might be forgiven. Imputation is thus bound together with the teaching of the Vicarious Salvation.

All of this completely refutes the modern teaching that *"Jesus died spiritually."*

THE ERRONEOUS JESUS DIED SPIRITUALLY DOCTRINE

This teaching claims that Jesus not only died physically on the Cross, but as well, died spiritually. This means that He died as a lost sinner, actually becoming one with Satan, taking upon Himself the Satanic nature. Of course, dying as a sinner, He then went to the burning side of Hell where, they teach, He was tortured for some three days and nights in the burning flames, etc. After three days and nights of punishment in Hell, they then teach that God said, *"It is enough,"* and Jesus was then born again, even as any sinner must be born again. He was then raised from the dead. That's the reason that they also teach that any born-again man could redeem humanity, etc.

This teaching is pure fiction, and as one might say, made up out of whole cloth. And let the Reader understand the following:

This teaching completely abrogates the Cross and the shed Blood of Jesus Christ, making it of no effect. In fact, Kenneth Copeland somewhat speaks out of both sides of his mouth, while in one breath claiming the veracity of the shed Blood of Christ, and

in the next breath, denying its effectiveness.

He states that the day Jesus died on the Cross, thereby shedding His Life's Blood, that hundreds of others died on crosses in the Roman Empire as well, thereby reckoning the shed Blood of Christ, as no different than any other man. He then goes on to state that it was necessary for Christ to then go to the burning side of Hell and be tortured there for three days and nights, for the Redemption process to be completed. So as is obvious, he is claiming one thing, while contradicting it in the next breath.

What he seems to fail to realize is, while it is true that many others died that day on crosses, those others were not Jesus Christ. He Alone was the Perfect Sacrifice, and because He was Perfect in every respect, a Sacrifice which God could accept, and in fact, did accept. Listen again to Paul:

"But now in Christ Jesus you who in times past were far off are made nigh by the Blood of Christ (notice that he said it was by the Blood of Christ, and not by Christ burning in Hellfire) . . . *Having abolished in His flesh* (the word *'flesh'* means that He died physically, and not spiritually, as these false teachers claim) *the enmity* (hatred), *even the Law of Commandments contained in Ordinances* (Jesus satisfied the claims of the broken Law by and through His death)*; for to make in Himself of twain one new man* (the Body of Christ), *so making peace;*

"And that He might reconcile both (Jews and Gentiles) *unto God in one body* (the Church) *by the Cross, having slain the enmity thereby"* (Eph. 2:13-16). Again notice that Paul said this was done *"by the Cross,"* which means it was not done in Hell.

In short, the Jesus died spiritually doctrine is blasphemy! It is an attack on the Atonement, and as well, an attack that is so serious that it strikes at the very heart of the Salvation Plan, which is the Cross. In other words, if one believes that doctrine, one cannot be saved. To believe that doctrine means that one is *"preaching another Jesus, whom Paul did not preach, which means it has been received by another spirit, which is not the Holy Spirit, which translates into another gospel, which cannot be accepted"* (II Cor. 11:4).

KILL THE BULLOCK
BEFORE THE LORD

The sin was committed before the Lord, as all sin is committed before the Lord, which refers to sin being an affront to God. Consequently, the animal must be killed before the Lord, which refers to the fact that the sinner acknowledges his guilt, and that the One this Sacrifice represents, namely Christ, is his only hope. And that hope lies completely within its death. Concerning this, Williams said:

"Directly the sinner laid his hand upon the substitute it was put to death; but in the Burnt-Offering it was not so (1:4). The Burnt-Offering was indeed also put to death; but before being killed the words 'It shall be accepted for him to make an Atonement, (i.e., a covering) for him,' are introduced. These two Passages explain substitution. In the Burnt-Offering the sinlessness of the victim is transferred to the worshipper; in the Sin-Offering, which we are now studying, the sinfulness of the sinner is transferred to the victim. Personal identification with Christ brings peace; for it means the taking away of sin and the reception of Righteousness."

THE BLOOD SPRINKLED
SEVEN TIMES

Verses 5 and 6 read: *"And the Priest that is anointed shall take of the bullock's blood, and bring it to the Tabernacle of the Congregation:*

"And the Priest shall dip his finger in the blood, and sprinkle of the blood seven times before the LORD, before the Veil of the Sanctuary."

The *"Priest who is anointed,"* refers to the High priest, who was a Type of Christ. Christ was anointed above all His fellows. He Alone can take the Blood to the Altar of worship and sprinkle it before the Lord, thereby restoring fellowship.

The blood sprinkled seven times before the Lord speaks of a complete Restoration; of a complete Redemption; of a complete Relationship. For a Christian not to know that his sin is gone, and gone forever is to cast a slight upon the Blood of his Divine Sin-Offering; it is to deny that there has been

the Perfect presentation – the sevenfold sprinkling of the blood before the Lord.

BEFORE THE VEIL OF
THE SANCTUARY

This latter phrase of the Sixth Verse pertains to the Altar of Worship, which sat immediately before the Veil, which separated the Holy Place from the Holy of Holies.

If we are to notice, the blood was sprinkled seven times on the Altar of Incense (the Altar of Worship), before it was then poured out at the base of the Brazen Altar, exclaimed in the Seventh Verse. Why was it done this way?

It was done in this manner that we might know and understand that when we as a Believer sin, as bad as that sin is, we do not have to get saved all over again for Relationship to be restored. But yet, even as the Seventh Verse proclaims, all that pertains to the Altar of Incense, which speaks of our Relationship with Christ, and His Intercessory Work on our behalf, are based strictly on what had transpired originally at the Brazen Altar, speaking of the Whole Burnt Offering, which typified the death of Christ. The Cross of Christ, typified by the Brazen Altar, is the foundation of all that we are in Christ, and all that we ever shall be. In other words, everything is based on that Finished Work.

Mackintosh says, and concerning the Sin-Offering: *"The full assurance of sin put away ministers, not to a spirit of self-confidence, but to a spirit of praise, thankfulness, and worship. It produces, not a spirit of self-complacency, but of Christ-complacency, which, blessed be God, is the spirit which shall characterize the redeemed throughout eternity. It does not lead one to think little of sin, but to think much of the Grace which has perfectly pardoned it, and of the blood which has perfectly cancelled it. It is impossible that anyone can gaze on the Cross – can see the place where Christ died – can meditate upon the sufferings which He endured – can ponder on those three terrible hours of darkness, and at the same time think lightly of sin."*

He then went on to say: *"When all these things are entered into, and the Power of the Holy Spirit, there are two results which must follow, namely, an abhorrence of sin in all its forms, and a genuine love for Christ, His people, and His cause."*

THE HORNS AND THE BRAZEN ALTAR

Verse 7 reads: *"And the Priest shall put some of the blood upon the horns of the Altar of sweet incense before the LORD, which is in the Tabernacle of the congregation; and shall pour all the blood of the bullock at the bottom of the Altar of the Burnt-Offering, which is at the Door of the Tabernacle of the Congregation."*

We learn two things from this particular Verse:

1. The blood applied to the four horns of the Altar of Incense speaks to the fact that even though forgiveness for Believers is available at all times, which the Sin-Offering proclaims, the horns, which speak of dominion, testify to us that we in fact should have dominion over all sin. But it also testifies to the fact that such dominion cannot come about except by the Cross of Christ and our Faith in that Finished Work, typified by the *"blood"* applied to the *"horns."*

Salvation is not a sinning and repenting, sinning and repenting, spectacle. It is rather one of dominion over sin. Paul plainly told us:

"For sin (the sin nature) *shall not have dominion over you: for you are not under the Law, but under Grace"* (Rom. 6:14).

In effect, the Apostle is definitely telling us that if we attempt to have dominion over sin by *"law,"* i.e., *"rules and regulations, works, etc.,"* victory will never be obtained in this manner. It can only be obtained *"under Grace."* Now what does that mean?

GRACE

Grace refers to the Goodness of God extended to undeserving Believers. It actually refers to all the work the Holy Spirit performs within our hearts and lives, which He Alone can do. We obtain this, not by works of the Law, but by simply believing in Christ, and what Christ has done for us at the Cross. If we try to function through Law, we will find ourselves committing *"spiritual adultery,"* with which the Holy Spirit will have no part (Rom. 7:1-4). The idea is this:

The believing sinner is saved by trusting in Christ and what Christ has done at the Cross (Jn. 3:16). He, in fact, may understand very little about Christ, or what Christ has done, but if he believes at all, thereby calling on the Lord, he will be saved (Rom. 10:13).

After the believing sinner comes to Christ, in order to maintain his Salvation, and even to grow in Grace and the knowledge of the Lord, he must as well maintain his Faith in the Cross of Christ, even that which saved him. But the problem is, after being saved, many Christians transfer their Faith from the Cross to other things. As stated, this makes one a spiritual adulterer.

WHAT IS SPIRITUAL ADULTERY?

In brief, it is the Christian being unfaithful to Christ. How can a Christian do that?

It refers to trusting in things other than Christ, whatever those things might be. Let us explain:

In Romans 7:1-4, Paul uses, as an example, a woman who is married to a particular man, and then at the same time, marries someone else. The Apostle said, *"She shall be called an adulteress,"* he then said, *"but if her husband be dead, she is free from that law; so that she is no adulteress, though she be married to another man"* (Rom. 7:3).

He then stated, in effect, that we are married to Christ, and we are, therefore, to trust Him for all things. We are *"dead to the Law,"* meaning that what we were, we are no more. We died with Christ (Rom. 6:3-14). We are raised a *"new man,"* and are married to Christ. Consequently, we are to trust Him for everything.

If we place our faith in our works, we have gone back to Law, which means that we are now living the life of a spiritual adulterer, meaning that we are being unfaithful to Christ. Of course, the Holy Spirit will not help us in such a situation, as should be obvious, and because we are functioning under Law, and not under Grace.

The sad fact is, most modern Christians are *"spiritual adulterers,"* and because they are not trusting Christ and what He has done for us at the Cross, but rather other things.

WHAT DOES IT MEAN TO
FULLY TRUST CHRIST?

I suppose that almost every Christian would claim that he is trusting Christ, and doing so fully. But the sad fact is, at least for most, this is actually not the case.

For one to fully trust Christ, one must trust in what Christ has done for us at the Cross. The Cross was the very reason that Jesus came. Peter said that Christ, in the Mind of God, was given up to the Cross even before the foundation of the world (I Pet. 1:18-20).

The destination of Christ, despite all the other things that He did, was ever the Cross. His Virgin Birth, although necessary, couldn't save anyone. His healings and miracles, although necessary, couldn't save anyone. It took the Cross, for which He came, in order for man to be redeemed.

So, for a Believer to fully trust Christ, that Believer must place his Faith totally and completely in what Christ has done, which refers to the Cross. He must understand that not only did his Salvation come by that means, but as well, his Sanctification also! Even as these sacrifices of the Old Testament economy point out over and over, and in every way possible, everything hinges on the Cross. That's why Paul said:

"But God forbid that I should glory, save in the Cross of our Lord Jesus Christ, by Whom the world is crucified unto me, and I unto the world" (Gal. 6:14). This is all proven by our next point.

THE BLOOD POURED OUT AT THE
BASE OF THE BRAZEN ALTAR

2. The effectiveness of the blood applied to the horns of the Altar of Incense, which speaks of dominion over sin in every capacity, is all based upon the fact that a Whole Burnt Offering had been originally offered on the Brazen Altar, which means that everything is predicated on that (vs. 18).

In the Redemption of the transgressor, the Priest did everything; the man, nothing. He stood, he looked, he listened, he believed! Like action today in relation to Christ on the Cross insures conscious Salvation.

Let the Believer ever understand that the

"Cross" is the key to everything. It is what Jesus did there.

Satan will do everything within his power to push the faith of the Believer away from the Cross to other things. He doesn't much care what these other things are, because he knows that within themselves, as right as they may be in their own place, faith placed therein will not bring about victory. Only the Cross can do that.

This means that the modern Christian placing his faith in his confession, in his Denominational ties, or anything for that matter, which is not the Cross, will bring no victory. In fact, all of these other things are merely the result of a *"carnal mind."* And Paul plainly said concerning that: *"For to be carnally minded is death; but to be spiritually minded is life and peace"* (Rom. 8:6).

WHAT DID PAUL MEAN BY BEING
CARNALLY MINDED OR
SPIRITUALLY MINDED?

To be *"carnally minded"* is to place one's faith in anything except the Cross. To be *"spiritually minded"* is to place one's faith exclusively in the Cross.

Most Christians, when they thing of being *"carnally minded,"* they think it refers to watching too much television, being too interested in sports, or anything of that nature, for that matter.

While those things may or may not be wrong, they have nothing to do with what Paul is speaking about here.

Likewise, most Christians, when they think of being *"spiritually minded,"* they think of one reading so many Chapters a day in the Bible, praying so much each day, or witnessing to a certain number of souls each day, etc.

While those things are spiritual, that's not what Paul is speaking of. In fact, the entire gist of Paul's discussion in Romans, Chapters 6, 7, and 8, refer to the Cross.

As well, all of this is beautifully typified, even as we are attempting to explain, in these Levitical Sacrifices.

THE FINAL DESTRUCTION OF
ALL THAT IS SINFUL

Verses 8 through 12 read: *"And he shall*

take off from it all the fat of the bullock for the Sin-Offering; the fat that covers the inwards, and all the fat that is upon the inwards,

"And the two kidneys, and the fat that is upon them, which is by the flanks, and the caul above the liver, with the kidneys, it shall he take away,

"As it was taken off from the bullock of the sacrifice of Peace-Offerings: and the Priest shall burn them upon the Altar of the Burnt-Offering.

"And the skin of the bullock, and all his flesh, with his head, and with his legs, and his inwards, and his dung,

"Even the whole bullock shall he carry forth without the camp unto a clean place, where the ashes are poured out, and burn him on the wood with fire: where the ashes are poured out shall he be burnt."

As we shall see, the carcass of the slain animal was not to be burned upon the Brazen Altar, but rather taken to a place "without the camp," and burned there. Why?

This means that when the Christian sins, as bad as it is, the Christian doesn't have to get saved all over again. In the "Sin-Offering" we see the means and the manner by which relationship is restored.

If it was commanded that the animal, constituting the Sin-Offering, was to be burned on the Altar, as was the animal of the Whole Burnt-Offering, this would mean that the person would have to get saved all over again, every time he sinned. But of course, the Bible doesn't teach that, and graphically so, illustrates the very opposite in the Sin-Offering, and the way it was handled.

But yet, and even as we have previously studied, the blood of that slain animal had to be sprinkled seven times on the Altar of Incense, as well as smeared on its four horns, and then poured out at the base of the Brazen Altar. This signifies that the Crucifixion of Christ, which constituted the shedding of His Precious Blood, which paid for all of the sin of humanity, at least for all who will believe, even though accomplished many centuries ago, has continuing results. And in fact, these results will never be discontinued. The Blood of Christ continues to avail today, exactly as it did 2,000 years ago, or whenever! However, even as all of

this typifies, the Believer must maintain his Faith in that shed Blood, which means that he must ever maintain his Faith in the Cross.

THE FAT

And yet the "fat," plus some of the physical organs of the animal, such as the kidneys and the caul (intestines), were to be burned on the Brazen Altar. Why this and not the whole bullock?

The "fat" constitutes the prosperity of Christ, while the organs constitute daily living.

This means that if we do not approach sin in the right manner, meaning that the Sacrifice of Christ alone can handle sin, as Believers, we will lose our spiritual prosperity, which will greatly affect, in a negative way, our daily living. This is one of the reasons that Jesus said:

"If any man will come after Me, let him deny himself (deny his own strength and ability) and take up his cross daily, and follow Me (this means to trust daily in the benefits that come to us from the Cross, and the Cross alone).

"For whosoever will save his life shall lose it (try to live outside of the Cross of Christ): but whosoever will lose his life for My sake, the same shall save it (will place his life exclusively in Christ)" (Lk. 9:23-24).

WHERE THE ASHES ARE POURED OUT

After the items mentioned above were removed from the carcass of the animal, and burned upon the Altar, the remainder of the carcass, which constituted almost all of it, was to be taken "without the camp unto a clean place, where the ashes are poured out." There it was to be burned and consumed.

As we've already stated, the carcass of the animal being burned outside of the camp signified that the Believer, when he sins, doesn't have to be saved all over again; however, he definitely does have to confess his sin before the Lord, typified by the Sin-Offering (I Jn. 1:9), and then renew his Faith in Christ, and what Christ has done for him at the Cross, typified by the animal being slain, and its blood poured out at the base of the Brazen Altar. Fellowship is restored by the blood being sprinkled seven times on the Altar of Incense and smeared on the four horns. But all, as stated, is predicated on what was done originally at the Brazen Altar.

The animal being burned without the camp signifies that while the Believer, and because of his sin, should in fact be banned *"without the camp,"* instead, the sins are taken without the camp and banished. The animal being burned signifies that God cannot abide sin in any form, and it must be totally and completely eradicated. In fact, this typifies the final removal of sin from God's Kingdom, and the final destruction of all that is sinful.

Paul states in Hebrews that one of the points in which our Lord was the antitype of the Sin-Offering was that He *"suffered without the gate,"* that He might sanctify the people with His Own Blood (Heb. 13:12).

(13) "AND IF THE WHOLE CONGREGATION OF ISRAEL SIN THROUGH IGNORANCE, AND THE THING BE HID FROM THE EYES OF THE ASSEMBLY, AND THEY HAVE DONE SOMEWHAT AGAINST ANY OF THE COMMANDMENTS OF THE LORD CONCERNING THINGS WHICH SHOULD NOT BE DONE, AND ARE GUILTY;

(14) "WHEN THE SIN, WHICH THEY HAVE SINNED AGAINST IT, IS KNOWN, THEN THE CONGREGATION SHALL OFFER A YOUNG BULLOCK FOR THE SIN, AND BRING HIM BEFORE THE TABERNACLE OF THE CONGREGATION.

(15) "AND THE ELDERS OF THE CONGREGATION SHALL LAY THEIR HANDS UPON THE HEAD OF THE BULLOCK BEFORE THE LORD: AND THE BULLOCK SHALL BE KILLED BEFORE THE LORD.

(16) "AND THE PRIEST THAT IS ANOINTED SHALL BRING OF THE BULLOCK'S BLOOD TO THE TABERNACLE OF THE CONGREGATION:

(17) "AND THE PRIEST SHALL DIP HIS FINGER IN SOME OF THE BLOOD, AND SPRINKLE IT SEVEN TIMES BEFORE THE LORD, EVEN BEFORE THE VEIL.

(18) "AND HE SHALL PUT SOME OF THE BLOOD UPON THE HORNS OF THE ALTAR WHICH IS BEFORE THE LORD, THAT IS IN THE TABERNACLE OF THE CONGREGATION, AND SHALL POUR OUT ALL THE BLOOD AT THE BOTTOM OF THE ALTAR OF THE BURNT-OFFERING,

WHICH IS AT THE DOOR OF THE TABERNACLE OF THE CONGREGATION.

(19) "AND HE SHALL TAKE ALL HIS FAT FROM HIM, AND BURN IT UPON THE ALTAR.

(20) "AND HE SHALL DO WITH THE BULLOCK AS HE DID WITH THE BULLOCK FOR A SIN-OFFERING, SO SHALL HE DO WITH THIS: AND THE PRIEST SHALL MAKE AN ATONEMENT FOR THEM, AND IT SHALL BE FORGIVEN THEM.

(21) "AND HE SHALL CARRY FORTH THE BULLOCK WITHOUT THE CAMP, AND BURN HIM AS HE BURNED THE FIRST BULLOCK: IT IS A SIN OFFERING FOR THE CONGREGATION."

The structure is:

1. Verses 13 through 21 make it clearly known that when sin has been committed through ignorance, but is now found out, it must be immediately addressed.

2. God, being just, passes over sin until it is made known by the conscience, the Word, and the Holy Spirit. Then He holds sinners responsible and will judge and punish them if the sin is allowed to continue (Jn. 16:7-11; Rom. 2:12-16).

3. We will see in the following commentary how that sins of ignorance are committed presently.

SIN COMMITTED THROUGH IGNORANCE

Verses 13 through 16 read: *"And if the whole congregation of Israel sin through ignorance, and the thing be hid from the eyes of the assembly, and they have done somewhat against any of the Commandments of the LORD concerning things which should not be done, and are guilty;*

"When the sin, which they have sinned against it, is known, then the congregation shall offer a young bullock for the sin, and bring him before the Tabernacle of the congregation.

"And the Elders of the congregation shall lay their hands upon the head of the bullock before the LORD: and the bullock shall be killed before the LORD.

"And the Priest that is anointed shall bring of the bullock's blood to the Tabernacle of the congregation."

To which we have already touched upon, but because it is so very, very important, I think it would be profitable to address the subject again of *"sinning through ignorance."*

The modern Believer may well understand how Israel of old could do such a thing, and even do it as a corporate body, considering all the many rules and regulations contained in the Law of Moses. It would be very easy to miss one or more, or more particularly, to misunderstand what was said.

But let the Reader understand that even though the infraction was committed in ignorance, God still labeled it as *"sin."*

So how is it that modern-day Christians can sin through ignorance?

MODERN CHRISTIANS AND
THE SIN OF IGNORANCE

If the Christian doesn't understand the Cross, as it regards Sanctification, through ignorance that Christian will attempt to live for God through and by his own strength and ability, which are always woefully inadequate. To rebel against God's prescribed order, which is *"Jesus Christ and Him Crucified,"* even though done in ignorance, even as it is by most, is sin. Paul plainly said: *"Because the carnal mind is enmity* (war) *against God: for it is not subject to the Law of God, neither indeed can be.*

"So then they who are in the flesh cannot please God" (Rom. 8:7-8).

As we've already explained, the *"carnal mind"* is the effort by the individual to live for God outside of total dependence on Christ and the Cross.

A PERSONAL EXPERIENCE

This of which I speak, I have lived. I know what it is to understand the Cross as it regards Salvation, but understand it not at all as it regards Sanctification. Regrettably, almost all of the modern Church presently falls into the latter category. It has no understanding of the Cross, as it refers to our everyday living before God, i.e., *"our walk."* That being the case, the Believer will attempt to live for the Lord in all the wrong ways.

Even in this state, as are most Christians, the Lord was using me mightily. We were

NOTES

seeing literally hundreds of thousands of souls brought to a saving knowledge of Jesus Christ, which fruit remains unto this hour. Let me explain that:

FUNCTION AND FAITH

The Call of God on a person's life regards their function, in other words, what He has called them to do. Even if that person doesn't understand Sanctification as it was taught by Paul, the Lord will still use them as it regards their function. Many Christians misunderstand this. They think if the Lord is using someone, and it is obvious that He is doing so, this means that such a Preacher is close to perfect. Regrettably, that's not the case at all.

It doesn't matter how much the Lord is using a person, and He will definitely do so, that is, if the person is truly Called of God, and truly believes Him, if that Preacher (or whomever), doesn't understand the Cross as it regards Sanctification, then in some way, that Preacher is going to be living a life of spiritual failure – and despite the fact that God is using him (or her)! However, the following must quickly be said:

Without understanding the Cross as it regards Sanctification, no matter how sincere, no matter how earnest, no matter how honest, such a Christian simply will not be able to live a life of spiritual victory, at least on a perpetual basis. God has made one provision for sin, which includes victory over sin, and that is the Cross of Christ. It pertains, as should be obvious, to the sinner being saved, and the Saint being Sanctified.

The Child of God can never outgrow the Cross, hence Paul referring to it as *"The Everlasting Covenant"* (Heb. 13:20). But as stated, the moment the Believer seeks to live this life outside of the Cross of Christ, that Believer is rebelling against God's Prescribed Order of Victory, and even though it be done in ignorance, it is sin, and will reap bitter results. In fact, there are untold millions at this very moment, who are struggling, and have been struggling for years, trying to overcome a problem or problems within their hearts and lives, but have been unable to do so. In fact, despite all of their struggles, the problem has grown steadily worse. As we've said, we'll say again: the problem, for the most part, is ignorance.

UNBELIEF

However, I have found in dealing with many people, and especially Preachers, that the problem for many is not ignorance, but rather unbelief. In other words, they simply do not believe that what Jesus did at the Cross is the answer for mankind. Why?

It is like Abraham. He did not at all enjoy giving up Ishmael, even though God said he must do so. Ishmael was the fair work of his flesh, and he loved the young man. While Abraham definitely obeyed, there are many who do not obey.

They love the labor of their hands, the works of their flesh, and in fact, they have invested much into these particular *"works,"* and they do not take kindly to being told that they must give them up, and give them up completely.

In fact, many Preachers would have to change their entire Ministry, if they look to the Cross, instead of their own efforts. Let me give you an example:

DELIVERANCE MINISTRY

Most of the Ministries which go under the guise of a *"Deliverance Ministry,"* for the most part, work under the auspices of the *"laying on of hands."* While the *"laying on of hands"* is certainly Scriptural, at least for healing, and for blessing, it will do no good as it regards deliverance from bondages of sin and darkness, etc. And yet, that statement needs some qualification:

If in fact, the Preacher understands the means and the way in which true deliverance does come, and also, if the person coming for deliverance understands as well, then the laying on of hands will definitely be of benefit to the individual. But otherwise, it won't! Let me explain:

Jesus said: *"You shall know the Truth, and the Truth shall make you free"* (Jn. 8:32). In other words, manifestations, as Scriptural as they might be in their own right, will not set anyone free. Momentarily, I will explain what the *"Truth"* actually is.

If it is to be noticed, Jesus also said: *"The Spirit of the Lord is upon Me, because He*

has anointed Me to . . . preach deliverance to the captives" (Lk. 4:18).

If it is to be noticed, He didn't say that the Holy Spirit had anointed Him to deliver the captives, but rather to *"preach deliverance to the captives."* It is a subtle difference, but very important!

He is actually saying that one cannot truly be delivered until the Truth is given to that particular person. Now what is the Truth?

THE TRUTH

The Truth is, *"Jesus Christ and Him Crucified"* (I Cor. 2:2). It is explained in detail in Romans, Chapter 6. In fact, some have spoken of this Chapter as the *"mechanics of the Holy Spirit,"* with the Eighth Chapter of Romans spoken of as *"the dynamics of the Holy Spirit."* In other words, the Sixth Chapter of Romans tells us what we are in Christ and how we obtained it, which is through Faith in what Christ did at the Cross. Once the Cross of Christ is the object of our Faith, which it must ever be, then we will witness *"what"* the Holy Spirit will do within our lives, as outlined in the Eighth Chapter of Romans. It is *"how He does it,"* in Chapter 6, and *"what He does, once we know how He does it,"* in Chapter 8.

The person can truly experience deliverance only if they understand Christ and what Christ has done for them at the Cross. That's the reason that Paul also said:

"I am crucified with Christ (Paul takes us back to Romans 6)*: nevertheless I live; yet not I, but Christ lives in me: and the life which I now live in the flesh I live by the Faith of the Son of God, Who loved me, and gave Himself for me"* (Gal. 2:20).

THE SAME REMEDY

Verses 17 through 21 read: *"And the Priest shall dip his finger in some of the blood, and sprinkle it seven times before the LORD, even before the Veil.*

"And he shall put some of the blood upon the horns of the Altar which is before the LORD, that is in the Tabernacle of the congregation, and shall pour out all the blood at the bottom of the Altar of the Burnt-Offering, which is at the door of the Tabernacle of the congregation.

NOTES

"And he shall take all his fat from him, and burn it upon the Altar.

"And he shall do with the bullock as he did with the bullock for a Sin-Offering, so shall he do with this: and the Priest shall make an Atonement for them, and it shall be forgiven them.

"And he shall carry forth the bullock without the camp, and burn him as he burned the first bullock: it is a Sin-Offering for the congregation."

The only difference in this ritual, as it regards the Priests who had sinned, and the entirety of Israel, as described in Verses 13 through 21, is that instead of the Priest laying his hand on the head of the bullock before it is killed, thereby transferring his sins, the Elders are to perform that task as it regards the whole nation of Israel.

As it regards the Elders of Israel, there were 70 of these men, so we know that a representative group must perform this task. It is said that it was ordained that during the second Temple, three of their members should lay their hands upon the sacrifice. Besides this Sin-Offering, there was only one other congregational Offering upon which there was this laying of hands, which was the scapegoat (Lev. 16:21).

The rest of the regulations are exactly the same as those prescribed in the Sin-Offering for the High Priest himself, as described in Verses 5 through 12.

(22) "WHEN A RULER HAS SINNED, AND DONE SOMEWHAT THROUGH IGNORANCE AGAINST ANY OF THE COMMANDMENTS OF THE LORD HIS GOD CONCERNING THINGS WHICH SHOULD NOT BE DONE, AND IS GUILTY;

(23) "OR IF HIS SIN, WHEREIN HE HAS SINNED, COME TO HIS KNOWLEDGE; HE SHALL BRING HIS OFFERING, A KID OF THE GOATS, A MALE WITHOUT BLEMISH:

(24) "AND HE SHALL LAY HIS HAND UPON THE HEAD OF THE GOAT, AND KILL IT IN THE PLACE WHERE THEY KILL THE BURNT-OFFERING BEFORE THE LORD: IT IS A SIN OFFERING.

(25) "AND THE PRIEST SHALL TAKE OF THE BLOOD OF THE SIN-OFFERING WITH HIS FINGER, AND PUT IT UPON THE HORNS OF THE ALTAR OF BURNT-OFFERING, AND SHALL POUR OUT HIS BLOOD AT THE BOTTOM OF THE ALTAR OF BURNT-OFFERING.

(26) "AND HE SHALL BURN ALL HIS FAT UPON THE ALTAR, AS THE FAT OF THE SACRIFICE OF PEACE-OFFERINGS: AND THE PRIEST SHALL MAKE AN ATONEMENT FOR HIM AS CONCERNING HIS SIN, AND IT SHALL BE FORGIVEN HIM."

The construction is:

1. The *"Ruler"* of Verse 22 refers to a king. But as well, it could probably refer to members of the Sanhedrin, the highest Jewish court, or even to lesser courts, and most likely, as well, to any one of the 70 Elders. Incidentally, there was a political Sanhedrin and a religious Sanhedrin, with the latter mostly made up of Priests; therefore, the former would have probably been included, with the latter excluded.

2. If it is to be noticed, the remedy is basically the same for sin, irrespective as to who commits it, with the exception of some minor particulars.

3. Irrespective as to who sins, ultimately the person must be led to the Cross, because the Cross is the only answer. There is no other!

THE REMEDY IS THE SAME

Verses 22 through 26 read: *"When a Ruler has sinned, and done somewhat through ignorance against any of the Commandments of the LORD his God concerning things which should not be done, and is guilty;*

"Or if his sin, wherein he has sinned, come to his knowledge; he shall bring his Offering, a kid of the goats, a male without blemish:

"And he shall lay his hand upon the head of the goat, and kill it in the place where they kill the Burnt-Offering before the LORD: it is a Sin-Offering.

"And the Priest shall take of the blood of the Sin-Offering with his finger, and put it upon the horns of the Altar of Burnt-Offering, and shall pour out his blood at the bottom of the Altar of Burnt-Offering.

"And he shall burn all his fat upon the Altar, as the fat of the sacrifice of Peace-Offerings: and the Priest shall make an Atonement for him as concerning his sin,

and it shall be forgiven him."

As we shall see, there were some differences in the ritual, but the ultimate point is, it was the shed blood which brought about forgiveness of sin, all pointing to the coming Christ.

The difference in the ritual, as it regarded a Ruler or the Priest or congregation, was that the blood of the Sin-Offering was put on the four horns of the *"Altar of Burnt-Offering,"* instead of the Altar of Incense, as it regarded the other two.

Why this difference?

It is the same with the sin of the common people, as we will study in Verses 27 through 35. The blood there, as well, is applied to the horns of the Brazen Altar, instead of the Altar of Incense.

The first two include the Priest and the entirety of the congregation of Israel. The latter two include Rulers and the common people.

The Priest was a Type of Christ, with the entirety of the nation consisting of God's Plan. The latter two pertained to individuals, among the people, which would pertain even to a king, etc.

Inasmuch as the Priest represented Christ and the entire nation represented His Plan, the blood had to be sprinkled seven times on the Altar of Incense, and then applied to the four horns, with the remainder taken to the Brazen Altar, and poured out at its base. Intercession was at stake with the first two, and because of who they were, and Intercession pertains to the Altar of Incense. So for the first two, Intercession and Atonement were required. For the latter two, only Atonement was required, which in their cases would automatically include Intercession, but which evidently was not automatic with the first two.

(27) "AND IF ANY ONE OF THE COMMON PEOPLE SIN THROUGH IGNORANCE, WHILE HE DOES SOMEWHAT AGAINST ANY OF THE COMMANDMENTS OF THE LORD CONCERNING THINGS WHICH OUGHT NOT TO BE DONE, AND BE GUILTY;

(28) "OR IF HIS SIN, WHICH HS HAS SINNED, COME TO HIS KNOWLEDGE: THEN HE SHALL BRING HIS OFFERING,

NOTES

A KID OF THE GOATS, A FEMALE WITHOUT BLEMISH, FOR HIS SIN WHICH HE HAS SINNED.

(29) "AND HE SHALL LAY HIS HAND UPON THE HEAD OF THE SIN-OFFERING, AND SLAY THE SIN OFFERING IN THE PLACE OF THE BURNT-OFFERING.

(30) "AND THE PRIEST SHALL TAKE OF THE BLOOD THEREOF WITH HIS FINGER, AND PUT IT UPON THE HORNS OF THE ALTAR OF BURNT-OFFERING, AND SHALL POUR OUT ALL THE BLOOD THEREOF AT THE BOTTOM OF THE ALTAR.

(31) "AND HE SHALL TAKE AWAY ALL THE FAT THEREOF, AS THE FAT IS TAKEN AWAY FROM OFF THE SACRIFICE OF PEACE-OFFERINGS; AND THE PRIEST SHALL BURN IT UPON THE ALTAR FOR A SWEET SAVOR UNTO THE LORD; AND THE PRIEST SHALL MAKE AN ATONEMENT FOR HIM, AND IT SHALL BE FORGIVEN HIM.

(32) "AND IF HE BRING A LAMB FOR A SIN-OFFERING, HE SHALL BRING IT A FEMALE WITHOUT BLEMISH.

(33) "AND HE SHALL LAY HIS HAND UPON THE HEAD OF THE SIN-OFFERING, AND SLAY IT FOR A SIN-OFFERING IN THE PLACE WHERE THEY KILL THE BURNT-OFFERING.

(34) "AND THE PRIEST SHALL TAKE OF THE BLOOD OF THE SIN-OFFERING WITH HIS FINGER, AND PUT IT UPON THE HORNS OF THE ALTAR OF BURNT-OFFERING, AND SHALL POUR OUT ALL THE BLOOD THEREOF AT THE BOTTOM OF THE ALTAR:

(35) "AND HE SHALL TAKE AWAY ALL THE FAT THEREOF, AS THE FAT OF THE LAMB IS TAKEN AWAY FROM THE SACRIFICE OF THE PEACE-OFFERINGS; AND THE PRIEST SHALL BURN THEM UPON THE ALTAR, ACCORDING TO THE OFFERINGS MADE BY FIRE UNTO THE LORD: AND THE PRIEST SHALL MAKE AN ATONEMENT FOR HIS SIN THAT HE HAS COMMITTED, AND IT SHALL BE FORGIVEN HIM."

The composition is:

1. As is obvious here, in the Eyes of God, sin is sin, irrespective as to who commits it.

It must be addressed, and in essence, addressed the same way, even if it's a *"common person,"* or a *"Ruler,"* or a *"Priest,"* or even the entirety of the nation of Israel.

2. The fat of the Sin-Offering for a *"common person"* was burned upon the Altar for a *"sweet savor."* This is not said of the Offering for the Priest, for the congregation, or for the Ruler. If Christ's death for a multitude is sweet to God, His Death for an individual sinner of the common people is especially sweet. Such is Grace!

3. As it regards a *"common person"* a female animal was to be brought. Evidently, the others required were to be males. Why a female?

All the Priests were men, and a Type of Christ. A Ruler was as well a man, or almost always! Also, the nation of Israel as a whole was looked at in the same capacity. But when it came to the common people, it must include, of necessity, both males and females. So a female animal was demanded in this instance, which would cover both men and women, for both at times sinned. However, only the men were allowed to bring the animals for sacrifice.

COMMON PEOPLE

Verses 27 through 30 read: *"And if any one of the common people sin through ignorance, while he does somewhat against any of the Commandments of the LORD concerning things which ought not to be done, and be guilty;*

"Or if his sin, which he has sinned, come to his knowledge: then he shall bring his Offering, a kid of the goats, a female without blemish, for his sin which he has sinned.

"And he shall lay his hand upon the head of the Sin-Offering, and slay the Sin-Offering in the place of the Burnt-Offering.

"And the Priest shall take of the blood thereof with his finger, and put it upon the horns of the Altar of Burnt-Offering, and shall pour out all the blood thereof at the bottom of the Altar."

As we have stated, and as in this explanation of the Sin-Offering, which is overly obvious, God cannot abide sin in any capacity. Whether it is the High Priest, who was a Type of Christ, the nation as a whole, or a

NOTES

king, or now the common people, sin is sin, and must be dealt with. Furthermore, it can only be dealt with in one manner, and that is by the Sacrificial, Atoning Death of Christ on the Cross, of which these Sacrifices were a Type.

As we've also stated, Israel wasn't washed, cleansed, and forgiven because of these animal sacrifices, simply because the blood of animals was woefully insufficient, but rather, by what the sacrifices represented, namely the Lord Jesus Christ, and what He would do at the Cross on behalf of Adam's fallen race. While their understanding of this would have been dim, still, the original command had pointed to the *"Seed of the woman,"* which was to come, and Who would bruise Satan's head (what Jesus would do at the Cross), even though Satan would bruise His heel (what Jesus would suffer at the Cross) (Gen. 3:15). In fact, this had been graphically spelled out in Genesis, Chapter 4, as it regards the episode of Cain and Abel.

Unfortunately, in later years, Israel turned the sacrifices into a ritual, completely ignoring What and Who they represented, which in essence, made the sacrifices ineffectual.

Christ is the subject of the entirety of the Bible, and that from Genesis 1:1 through Revelation 22:21. The idea ever was that He would come as the Second Man, i.e., *"the Last Adam"* (I Cor. 15:45-50), and do what the first Adam failed to do, which was to render perfect obedience to God, but as well, to address the broken law, of which every man was guilty, and which Christ did at the Cross. In fact, God, through foreknowledge, planned all of this, even before the foundation of the world (I Pet. 1:18-20).

In fact, Paul tells us that under the Old Covenant, which we are now studying, that the animal sacrifices, even though they were a Type of Christ and what He would do at the Cross, could not salve the conscience. He said:

"Which was a figure for the time then present (which pertained to the old Levitical system, including the sacrifices), *in which were offered both gifts and sacrifices, that could not make him who did the service perfect, as pertaining to the conscience"* (Heb. 9:9).

So how could one know under the old Levitical Law that one was saved?

THE BLOOD AND THE WORD

The knowledge that he was saved was founded upon two facts outside of himself:

1. The value of the Blood shed for him.
2. The trustworthiness of the Word spoken to him.

In fact, on this Divine foundation, the Blood and the Word, not only rested the Jew under the old economy, but as well, is where the Christian's peace rests also. The knowledge that Christ's Blood is of infinite value to cleanse all sins, which declares that whoever trusts that Saviour shall never be confounded, is trustworthy, and as stated, is the Divine Foundation. This double knowledge establishes assurance of Salvation.

So, one can see that the object of Faith was identical in Old Testament times, as it is presently – the Cross. But yet, the result of that Faith, and I now speak of Old Testament Times, was not nearly as glorious as it is presently, and because of the weakness of animal blood by comparison to the Blood of Christ. Listen again to Paul:

"*How much more shall the Blood of Christ, Who through the Eternal Spirit offered Himself without spot to God, purge your conscience from dead works to serve the Living God?*"

Paul went on to say:

"*And for this cause He* (Christ) *is the Mediator of the New Testament* (the New Covenant), *that by means of death* (the Cross), *for the Redemption of the transgressions that were under the First Testament* (the Cross addressed itself also to all the sins of Old Testament Times), *they which are called might receive the promise of eternal inheritance.*"

And then: "*And almost all things are by the Law* (Old Testament Law) *purged with blood; and without shedding of blood is no remission* (meaning there is no remission of sin)" (Heb. 9:14-15, 22).

So, when any one of the people of Israel sinned, and this sin was called to their attention, in other words, they knew they had sinned, they were to take a "*kid of the goats*" (a baby goat), "*a female without blemish*"

NOTES

or a lamb (Vs. 32), and offer it up in sacrifice. He was, as well, to "*lay his hand upon the head of the Sin-Offering,*" thereby, transferring his sin to this innocent victim, which was a Type of Christ, and then he was to personally kill the animal, with the Priest then carrying out the balance of the ritual.

The blood would be applied with the finger of the Priest upon the four horns of the Altar of Burnt-Offering, which was the Brazen Altar. Those four horns signified not only dominion, but that Salvation was the same for all, even as the horns pointed in all directions, north, south, east, and west. The problem for all of mankind is the same, sin, and the solution for mankind is the same, Christ and Him Crucified, of which the Altar was a Type.

THE SWEET SAVOR

Verses 31 through 35 read: "*And he shall take away all the fat thereof, as the fat is taken away from off the sacrifice of Peace-Offerings; and the Priest shall burn it upon the Altar for a sweet savor unto the LORD; and the Priest shall make an Atonement for him, and it shall be forgiven him.*

"*And if he bring a lamb for a Sin-Offering, he shall bring it a female without blemish.*

"*And he shall lay his hand upon the head of the Sin-Offering, and slay it for a Sin-offering in the place where they kill the Burnt-Offering.*

"*And the Priest shall take of the blood of the Sin-Offering with his finger, and put it upon the horns of the Altar of Burnt-Offering, and shall pour out all the blood thereof at the bottom of the Altar:*

"*And he shall take away all the fat thereof, as the fat of the lamb is taken away from the sacrifice of the Peace-Offerings; and the Priest shall burn them upon the Altar, according to the Offerings made by fire unto the LORD: and the Priest shall make an Atonement for his sin that he has committed, and it shall be forgiven him.*"

There is one difference in this which the Priest did for the common person, than he would do for the others.

The Scripture says that when he burned the fat upon the Altar, it went up before the Lord as a "*sweet savor,*" which was not said concerning the others.

Why did it use the term *"sweet savor"* here, without relating such when the fat was burned regarding sins of ignorance concerning the Priests, the nation of Israel, and rulers?

Of course, and as would be obvious, the far, far greater number of sacrifices were offered for the common people, than for the others. As a result, the Grace of God was portrayed to a greater extent, a far greater extent!

This signified the fact that when Jesus died on the Cross, His Death was so effective that it paid for all sin, past, present, and future, at least for all who would believe (Jn. 3:16). In fact, there are three Greek words for Redemption used in the New Testament. They are:

1. Garazo: To purchase out of the slave market.

2. Exgarazo: To purchase in such totality and with such finality that the subject will never again be offered as a slave.

3. Lutroo: The price that was paid, which was the Blood of Christ, was so sufficient that no creature in eternity past, eternity present, or eternity future will ever be able to say that it was insufficient. So, it is a *"sweet savor unto the Lord."*

*"One day when Heaven was filled with
   His praises,
"One day when sin was as black as
   could be,
"Jesus came forth to be born of a Vir-
   gin,
"Dwelt among men, my example is
   He!"*

*"One day they led Him up Calvary's
   Mountain,
"One day they nailed Him to die on
   the tree;
"Suffering anguish, despised and re-
   jected:
"Bearing our sins, my Redeemer is He!"*

*"One day they left Him alone in the
   Garden,
"One day He rested, from suffering free;
"Angels came down o'er His tomb to
   keep vigil;
"Hope of the hopeless, my Saviour is
   He!"*

"One day the grave could conceal Him

*no longer,
"One day the stone rolled away from
   the door;
"Then He arose, over death He had con-
   quered;
"Now is ascended, my Lord evermore!"*

*"One day the Trumpet will sound for
   His Coming,
"One day the skies with His Glory will
   shine;
"Wonderful day, my Beloved One's
   bringing;
"Glorious Saviour, this Jesus is mine!"*

CHAPTER 5

(1) "AND IF A SOUL SIN, AND HEAR THE VOICE OF SWEARING, AND IS A WITNESS, WHETHER HE HAS SEEN OR KNOWN OF IT; IF HE DO NOT UTTER IT, THEN HE SHALL BEAR HIS INIQUITY.

(2) "OR IF A SOUL TOUCH ANY UNCLEAN THING, WHETHER IT BE A CARCASS OF AN UNCLEAN BEAST, OR A CARCASS OF UNCLEAN CATTLE, OR THE CARCASS OF UNCLEAN CREEPING THINGS, AND IF IT BE HIDDEN FROM HIM; HE ALSO SHALL BE UNCLEAN, AND GUILTY.

(3) "OR IF HE TOUCH THE UNCLEANNESS OF MAN, WHATSOEVER UNCLEANNESS IT BE THAT A MAN SHALL BE DEFILED WITHAL, AND IT BE HID FROM HIM; WHEN HE KNOWS OF IT, THEN HE SHALL BE GUILTY.

(4) "OR IF A SOUL SWEAR, PRONOUNCING WITH HIS LIPS TO DO EVIL, OR TO DO GOOD, WHATSOEVER IT BE THAT A MAN SHALL PRONOUNCE WITH AN OATH, AND IT BE HID FROM HIM; WHEN HE KNOWS OF IT, THEN HE SHALL BE GUILTY IN ONE OF THESE.

(5) "AND IT SHALL BE, WHEN HE SHALL BE GUILTY IN ONE OF THESE THINGS, THAT HE SHALL CONFESS THAT HE HAS SINNED IN THAT THING:

(6) "AND HE SHALL BRING HIS TRESPASS OFFERING UNTO THE LORD FOR HIS SIN WHICH HE HAS SINNED, A FEMALE FROM THE FLOCK,

A LAMB OR A KID OF THE GOATS, FOR A SIN OFFERING; AND THE PRIEST SHALL MAKE AN ATONEMENT FOR HIM CONCERNING HIS SIN.

(7) "AND IF HE BE NOT ABLE TO BRING A LAMB, THEN HE SHALL BRING FOR HIS TRESPASS, WHICH HE HAS COMMITTED TWO TURTLEDOVES, OR TWO YOUNG PIGEONS, UNTO THE LORD; ONE FOR A SIN OFFERING, AND THE OTHER FOR A BURNT OFFERING."

The overview is:

1. The Trespass-Offering was provided to atone for trespass against God, and trespass against man, for any sin against man is also, at the same time, a sin against God.

2. The words in the Seventh Verse, *"And if he be not able to bring a lamb,"* then go on to say that he can bring *"two turtledoves, or two young pigeons."* God always makes it possible for anyone to meet His Terms of Reconciliation. This is why He permitted different kinds of Offerings for the rich, poor, and the very poor – from rams to turtledoves, and pigeons to a handful of flour.

3. We find in all of this that there are, despite some claims to the contrary, lingering defilements and trespasses adhering to man, even though he be justified, consecrated, and in fellowship with God.

THE TRESPASS OFFERING

Verse 1 reads: *"And if a soul sin, and hear the voice of swearing, and is a witness, whether he has seen or known of it; if he do not utter it, then he shall bear his iniquity."*

There are many who claim that the first 13 Verses of this Chapter should have been included in the previous Chapter, because it is claimed that they pertain to the Sin-Offering and not the Trespass-Offering. That may very well be correct; however, I think not!

First of all, the Trespass-Offering has to do with sins against God and man, even as the First Verse of this Chapter proclaims. As well, the Sixth Verse mentions the *"Trespass-Offering."*

SIN

Seiss said: *"With all his efforts, prayers, and joys, the best Christian is still very faulty."*

He went on to say: *"Christ has taught us to pray daily, 'Forgive us our trespasses;' but why continue praying for forgiveness, if we have not continual trespasses to be forgiven? I know and preach that 'the Blood of Jesus Christ cleanses from all sin.' That is a precious Truth to me. But did He not continue a Priest forever, daily presenting His atoning Blood anew in our behalf, we should most certainly come into condemnation. It is only because 'He continues ever,' that He is 'able to save them to the uttermost who come unto God by Him, seeing He ever lives to make intercession for them.' If He did not ever live to make intercession for us, we could not stand for a single day."*

Men tend to attempt to put sins into categories. While most definitely some sins are worse and greater than others, let it ever be understood that the Catholic teaching of *"venial"* sins and *"mortal"* sins has no Scriptural validity. While men may talk of *"little sins,"* God never does. However small they may be, they are big enough to sink the soul to everlasting death, if uncancelled by the Saviour's Blood. Let me quote Seiss again:

"And there is not a Christian on Earth, however eminent, who does not, every day he lives, accumulate guilt enough to ruin him forever, were it not that he has 'an Advocate with the Father, Jesus Christ the Righteous.'"

BLOOD

As we have already seen, and will continue to see, there are literal rivers of blood demanded from the slaughter of innocent animals, which would serve as a stopgap measure, regarding the sins of the people. Until Christ came and shed His Life's Blood, the problem of sin was not totally addressed. The blood of bulls and goats simply could not take away sins.

A PERSONAL EXPERIENCE

While we now have a state-of-the-art Recording Studio at the Ministry, for years I recorded in Nashville. On one particular session when the backup singers came in, one of the young girls, who happened to be Jewish, complained that many of the songs were about the Blood. She remarked as to how this was somewhat gruesome, etc.

Our producer recalled to her the Old Testament Sacrificial System, which was originated by the Lord, and how that it was actually given to the Jewish people. Evidently she had not studied the Word of God at all, but she did have enough knowledge to understand what was being told her, and then answered accordingly.

It is easy to understand how some people will be offended by the continual displays of blood, blood, blood, as these accounts are given in the Old Testament. They conclude all of this as unworthy of God, and repulsive to man. But they do this, simply because they do not understand the terrible power of sin, and the price that had to be paid, which God incidentally paid Himself, which was the shedding of innocent blood, and I now speak of the Blood of God's Son, the Lord Jesus Christ (Eph. 2:13-18).

Though there is a constant recurrence of blood in the Old Testament, as well as in the New, it is all full of great significance. It tells of guilt, and of death, and ruin merited by that guilt. It tells of our condemnation, and of the way in which that condemnation is removed in Christ Jesus. It shows us the awful penalty which we have incurred, and how our Saviour undertook to bear it in His Own Body on the tree.

When we begin to understand this, then we begin to see that the reason for the blood is because of our sins, from which we could never be saved, were it not for the ever efficacious (effective) Blood of the Lamb of God Who was slain for us.

INIQUITY

The last phrase of the First Verse says, *"Then he shall bear his iniquity,"* proclaims the fact that each individual will have to answer for his own personal sin. I cannot answer for the sins of another, and neither can you. But the Holy Spirit, through Moses, is definitely telling us here that we must answer for our own sins. No one is exempt! And how do we answer?

That's what all of this instruction is all about. Under the Mosaic Law, the individual who had sinned had to bring a particular animal to the Tabernacle or Temple, when the latter would ultimately be constructed.

NOTES

While he was to be given instruction as to what type of animal was to be brought, which would be according to who He was, and the type of sin committed, that was actually all that he was required to know. The Priests, after questioning him as to the type of sin committed, would then carry out the necessary ritual concerning the blood and the disposal of the carcass, according to the instructions given to them by Moses. As is obvious, it was a very cumbersome process, very costly, very time consuming, and because sin is such a terrible business.

Under the New Covenant, incidentally, and as should be obvious, based upon much better Promises, the procedure is entirely different.

When a Christian sins presently, he is to simply confess that sin before the Lord, in which he is then promised forgiveness (I Jn. 1:9). In order for this to be done, he doesn't have to go to a Church, a Priest, a Preacher, or anyone else for that matter, only to the Lord.

When Jesus Christ died on the Cross of Calvary, he fulfilled in total all of the Sacrificial System, making it no longer necessary. He died on the Cross, shedding His Life's Blood, and the one Sacrifice of Himself was and is totally sufficient, and in fact, will ever be sufficient. Paul said:

"But this Man (the Lord Jesus Christ), *after He had offered one sacrifice for sins forever* (which was the Sacrifice of Himself), *sat down on the Right Hand of God"* (Heb. 10:12).

THE UNCLEAN THING

Verses 2 through 5 read: *"Or if a soul touch any unclean thing, whether it be a carcass of an unclean beast, or a carcass of unclean cattle, or the carcass of unclean creeping things, and if it be hidden from him; he also shall be unclean, and guilty.*

"Or if he touched the uncleanness of man, whatsoever uncleanness it be that a man shall be defiled withal, and it be hid from him; when he knows of it, then he shall be guilty.

"Or if a soul swear, pronouncing with his lips to do evil, or to do good, whatsoever it be that a man shall pronounce with an oath, and it be hid from him; when he knows of it, then he shall be guilty in one of these.

"And it shall be, when he shall be guilty in one of these things, that he shall confess that he has sinned in that thing."

Even though addressing dead animals, and specifying that they were of the unclean type, which refers to animals other than the heifer, the ox, the bullock, the goat, the lamb, and the ram, the emphasis seems to be on the fact of death itself.

Death, and in all its forms, is a result of sin. It, as nothing else, portrays the horror of sin. In fact, concerning this, Paul said:

"Forasmuch then as the children are partakers of flesh and blood, He (Christ) *also Himself likewise took part of the same; that through death* (the Crucifixion on the Cross) *He might destroy him who had the power of death, that is, the Devil;*

"And delivered them who through fear of death were all their lifetime subject to bondage" (Heb. 2:14-15).

The idea is, before the Cross, Satan had the power of death, and that was because of man's sin. When Jesus died on the Cross, thereby atoning for all sin, past, present, and future, this in effect destroyed Satan and his power. Sin being the legal right which gave Satan the power to hold man in bondage, has now been conquered, and was conquered by what Christ did at the Cross (Col. 2:14-15).

The uncleanness of man, as described in Verse 3, had to do, among other things, with one who had leprosy, or had touched a leper, or had been defiled because he had touched a dead body, and had not yet been purified, etc. All of this, in a sense, was a type of sin, and the touching of such a person would defile the individual, which would be sin on his part as well! Consequently, he would need cleansing, forgiveness, and restoration.

As I'm certain that we can see here, sin, even in its simplest form, cannot be passed over by God. So let us not think that certain little sins, which we might refer to as such, can be left in our lives. To be sure, the Holy Spirit, if allowed to have His Way, will definitely convict us of all sin, irrespective as to what it might be (Jn. 16:8). In fact, there are many things which God constitutes as sin, but which we do not; however, irrespective as to what we might think, it's what God

thinks that counts, as should be obvious.

The very attitude of some Christians is sin.

FAITH AND SIN

Paul said: *"Whatsoever is not of Faith is sin"* (Rom. 14:23).

Even though the definite article *"the"* is not used in front of the word *"Faith,"* at least in this instance, still, the gist of the sentence is toward *"the Faith,"* which is a synonym for the Christian experience.

What does it mean that a lack of Faith constitutes sin?

Understanding that what Paul said was inspired by the Holy Spirit, which means that it's the Word of God, means that we should pay careful attention.

The lack of Faith addressed here has to do with one having Faith in Christ and what Christ has done at the Cross. Everything should be hinged on the foundation of *"Jesus Christ and Him Crucified"* (I Cor. 2:2). Everything must stem from that particular aspect.

If in fact we as Believers are attempting to guide our lives, to guide our walk, to live as we ought to live, by trusting in things other than the Cross, such a position constitutes sin. It is a rebellion against God's prescribed order, which in effect, is the foundation sin of all sin. So if one's Faith is not in Christ and His Finished Work, automatically, that person is living in a state of sin. That may come as a shock to Christians, but it is the Truth!

When we presently think of sin, almost always, we think of acts of sin. That is labeled as *"works of the flesh"* (Gal. 5:19-21). The reason for the *"works of the flesh"* is that the Believer, and Paul is addressing Believers here, is operating from the premise of *"flesh"* (Rom. 8:8). That's the realm of the carnal mind (Rom. 8:6).

WHAT IS THE FLESH?

Even though we have addressed this subject already in this Volume, considering that it is at least one of, if not the single most important aspect of the Christian experience, I think it would be difficult to over-discuss the subject.

When Paul uses the term *"flesh,"* he is

speaking of one's own individual power, strength, and ability; in other words, what we can do from the human standpoint. In fact, those things aren't sin within themselves, but if we depend on them, instead of Christ and what He has done for us at the Cross, we sin! Due to the Fall, man lives in a polluted atmosphere, and is, as well, polluted himself. Even though Believers fall into the category of *"new creations in Christ Jesus,"* still, we have not yet been glorified, and due to that fact, whatever is done in our lives to help us live for God must be instigated by the Holy Spirit (Rom. 8:11). He will function within our hearts and lives, helping us on a continuing basis, only on the premise of what Christ has done at the Cross, and our Faith in that Finished Work (Rom. 8:2). If we try to live for God in any other manner, and I speak of Faith in the Cross, we automatically sin, and because we have stepped outside of God's prescribed order. The Holy Spirit will not, and in fact, cannot function in that atmosphere. In fact, such a person, and which regrettably, includes almost all of modern Christianity, is constituted as living in *"spiritual adultery"* (Rom. 7:1-4). This refers to an individual who is saved by the Blood of Jesus, thereby married to Christ, but is being unfaithful to Christ, and is being unfaithful by trusting in things other than Christ and the Cross. I would trust by now that the Reader has been made aware of the fact that everything hinges on the Cross, of which all of these Sacrifices were types.

ATONEMENT

Verses 6 and 7 read: *"And he shall bring his Trespass-Offering unto the LORD for his sin which he has sinned, a female from the flock, a lamb, or a kid of the goats, for a Sin-Offering; and the Priest shall make an Atonement for him concerning his sin.*

"And if he be not able to bring a lamb, then he shall bring for his trespass, which he has committed two turtledoves, or two young pigeons, unto the LORD: one for a Sin-Offering, and the other for a Burnt-Offering."

If sin was committed, sacrifice had to be offered. And as is obvious here, if the person's financial status didn't allow him to bring a lamb or a goat, he could bring

two turtledoves or two young pigeons. And if he was so poor that he couldn't afford that, as Verse 11 tells us, he could bring a portion of fine flour. As is obvious, every strata of society was accommodated, but the fact is, and must not be overlooked, sacrifice must be offered for sin, irrespective as to whom the person might be.

As should be noted here, the type of sacrifices, especially in the first seven Verses of this Chapter, are somewhat intermingled. In fact, the *"Trespass-Offering"* was but a *"Sin-Offering"* of distinct types to make Atonement for the trespasses named in the sins. Consequently, the first pigeon or turtledove was a *"Sin-Offering,"* which required the shedding of blood, and the second was a *"Burnt-Offering"* symbolizing satisfaction to God by perfect obedience to Him in making Atonement. Both symbolized the Perfect Obedience of Christ as man's Substitute.

(8) "AND HE SHALL BRING THEM UNTO THE PRIEST, WHO SHALL OFFER THAT WHICH IS FOR THE SIN-OFFERING FIRST, AND WRING OFF HIS HEAD FROM HIS NECK, BUT SHALL NOT DIVIDE IT ASUNDER:

(9) "AND HE SHALL SPRINKLE OF THE BLOOD OF THE SIN-OFFERING UPON THE SIDE OF THE ALTAR; AND THE REST OF THE BLOOD SHALL BE WRUNG OUT AT THE BOTTOM OF THE ALTAR: IT IS A SIN-OFFERING.

(10) "AND HE SHALL OFFER THE SECOND FOR A BURNT-OFFERING, ACCORDING TO THE MANNER: AND THE PRIEST SHALL MAKE AN ATONEMENT FOR HIM FOR HIS SIN WHICH HE HAS SINNED, AND IT SHALL BE FORGIVEN HIM.

(11) "BUT IF HE BE NOT ABLE TO BRING TWO TURTLEDOVES, OR TWO YOUNG PIGEONS, THEN HE WHO SINNED SHALL BRING FOR HIS OFFERING THE TENTH PART OF AN EPHAH OF FINE FLOUR FOR A SIN-OFFERING; HE SHALL PUT NO OIL UPON IT, NEITHER SHALL HE PUT ANY FRANKINCENSE THEREON: FOR IT IS A SIN-OFFERING.

(12) "THEN SHALL HE BRING IT TO THE PRIEST, AND THE PRIEST SHALL TAKE HIS HANDFUL OF IT, EVEN A MEMORIAL THEREOF, AND BURN IT ON THE

ALTAR, ACCORDING TO THE OFFERINGS MADE BY FIRE UNTO THE LORD: IT IS A SIN-OFFERING.

(13) "AND THE PRIEST SHALL MAKE AN ATONEMENT FOR HIM AS TOUCH-ING HIS SIN THAT HE HAS COMMITTED IN ONE OF THESE, AND IT SHALL BE FORGIVEN HIM: AND THE REMNANT SHALL BE THE PRIEST'S, AS A MEAT-OFFERING."

The exegesis is:

1. The Priest made an Atonement, and the sinner was forgiven. To *"forgive"* is to unbind. Forgiveness means the unbinding from off the soul of the death sentence bound upon it by the committed sin.

2. Life surrendered could alone unbind the sentence. In the slain lamb, or the crushed wheat, this judgment appears. The Priest, the lamb, the crushed wheat – all symbolized Christ and His Atoning Work.

3. In Verse 1, the voice of swearing was the action of the Hebrew judge in adjuring by God a witness to *"utter"* the truth. To refuse to answer was to sin against Jehovah. We find an example of this in Jesus before Caiaphas, who at once replied. This is the Divine method of swearing a witness.

FORGIVENESS

Verses 8 through 10 read: *"And he shall bring them unto the Priest, who shall offer that which is for the Sin-Offering first, and wring off his head from his neck, but shall not divide it asunder:*

"And he shall sprinkle of the blood of the Sin-Offering upon the side of the Altar; and the rest of the blood shall be wrung out at the bottom of the Altar: it is a Sin-Offering.

"And he shall offer the second for a Burnt-Offering, according to the manner: and the Priest shall make an Atonement for him for his sin which he has sinned, and it shall be forgiven him."

As we have stated, the very word *"forgive"* means *"to unbind."* The person who is forgiven by God is loosed from the sentence of death, which was incurred because of the sin. Christ has taken the penalty which we should have taken, but if we had taken that penalty, we would have been lost forever. Of course, such forgiveness is predicated solely upon the

confession of the sin by the Believer, which must be done to God (I Jn. 1:9). And as bad as sin is, there is no limitation on the number of times that God will forgive. As long as the person confesses the sin, and at the same time, which means that he is sorry for the sin, and is trying to rid himself of such, forgiveness will always be granted.

A Believer can forgive another Believer, and in fact must do so, if wrong has been committed against him. Unless the one who has committed the wrong admits the wrong, which is proper confession, the effect of forgiveness in such a case cannot actually be consummated. For forgiveness to be total and complete, it necessitates the action of two parties.

If we sin against the Lord, we must confess our sin to Him; He will then forgive, and in fact, has promised to do so (I Jn. 1:9). But if the Believer who has sinned will not confess the sin to the Lord, in other words, will not admit that he has sinned, forgive-ness cannot be enjoined.

While we Believers are commanded to for-give those who trespass against us, irrespec-tive as to whether they confess it or not, that is done for our good. As a Believer, we can-not allow resentment or grudge to build up in our heart. So we are commanded to for-give in order that such not be done; how-ever, as stated, fellowship between the two parties cannot be enjoined unless both par-ties conduct themselves Scripturally. That means that the person who has committed the wrong must confess it to the individual whom he has wronged, and the one who has been wronged must make certain that he for-gives the wrong done to him. Fellowship can then be restored.

If a lamb or a goat was brought, it would be handled in the customary way. But if two birds were brought (turtledoves or pigeons), one was to be offered as a *"Sin-Offering,"* with the other offered as a *"Burnt-Offering."* Why were the birds treated different than the lamb or the goat? In other words, concern-ing these two fowls, why was a Burnt-Offer-ing needed, when it wasn't needed regarding the goat or the lamb?

The Sin-Offering must make way for the Burnt-Offering. After the Sin-Offering, which made Atonement, came the Burnt-Offering, an acknowledgement of the great Mercy of God, in appointing and accepting the Atonement. The Burnt-Offering was required, because not enough blood was shed, regarding the Offering of the first bird as a Sin-Offering.

The *"Burnt-Offering,"* irrespective of the animal, presents a Type of Christ *"offering Himself without spot to God."* In other words, His Sacrifice of Himself on the Cross was carried out in order that the Righteousness of a thrice-Holy God might be satisfied. In the Burnt-Offering the sinlessness of the victim (Christ) is transferred to the worshipper; in the Sin-Offering the sinfulness of the sinner is transferred to the victim.

As the Christian advances in this Divine life, he becomes conscious that those sins he has committed are but branches from a root, streams from a fountain; and, moreover, that sin in his nature is that fountain – that root. This leads to far deeper exercise, which can only be met by a deeper insight into the Work of the Cross. In a word, the Cross will need to be apprehended as that in which God Himself has *"condemned sin in the flesh"* (Rom. 8:3).

If one is to notice, it does not say, *"sin in the life,"* but the root from which these have sprung, namely, *"sin in the flesh."* This is a Truth of immense importance. Christ not merely *"died for our sins, according to the Scriptures,"* but He was *"made sin for us"* (II Cor. 5:21). This latter is the doctrine of the *"Sin-Offering."*

In the *"Burnt-Offering,"* we are conducted to a point beyond which it is impossible to go, and that is, the Work of the Cross, as accomplished under the immediate Eye of God, and as the expression of the unswerving devotion of the heart to Christ. In all cases, we begin with the Cross and end with the Cross. If we begin with the Burnt-Offering, we see Christ, on the Cross, doing the Will of God – making Atonement according to the measure of His Perfect Surrender of Himself to God. If we begin with the Trespass-Offering, we see Christ on the Cross, bearing our sins, and putting them away according to the Perfection of His Atoning Sacrifice; while in each and all we behold the

NOTES

Excellency, the Beauty, and the Perfection of His Divine and adorable Person.

THAT ALL MAY COME

Verses 11 through 13 read: *"But if he be not able to bring two turtledoves, or two young pigeons, then he who sins shall bring for his Offering the tenth part of an ephah of fine flour for a Sin-Offering; he shall put no oil upon it, neither shall he put any frankincense thereon: for it is a Sin-Offering.*

"Then shall he bring it to the Priests, and the Priest shall take his handful of it, even a memorial thereof, and burn it on the Altar, according to the Offerings made by fire unto the LORD: it is a Sin-Offering.

"And the Priest shall make an Atonement for him as touching his sin that he has committed in one of these, and it shall be forgiven him: and the remnant shall be the Priest's, as a Meat-Offering."

In this beautiful application, we find that provision is made for all of humanity. Whether the sinner was rich or poor, provision was made that a suitable Offering could be rendered.

For the poorest of the poor, one who could not afford a lamb or a goat, or even two turtledoves, or two young pigeons, they could bring the amount of flour required, which was small. So we see here that sin had to be dealt with, irrespective as to whom the person might be. The Lord could not overlook the rich person, and neither could He overlook the poor person. So provision was made, which in effect, portrayed the Cross. The one Sacrifice of Christ answered every need in every heart and life, irrespective of the need, and irrespective of the person, at least for those who will believe (Jn. 3:16).

But let it be understood, the non-bloody substitute, namely the flour, being permitted was only an exception for the benefit of the very poor, and only in the cases specified, which does not invalidate the general rule that without the shedding of blood there is no remission of sin.

No oil was to be added to the flour, with oil being a Type of the Holy Spirit. The reason is, there was no shedding of blood in this particular Offering. His work is accomplished only through the Cross, but which could not be carried out except in some minor type, before the Cross. So this Offering of flour could be carried out, without great harm being done.

As well, as is stated in Verse 11, frankincense was not to be added either, and because it represented the Perfect Life of Christ which would be given on the Cross in Sacrifice.

Why was it prohibited with the *"Sin-Offering,"* and added to the Thanksgiving-Offering? (Lev. 2:1).

The Thanksgiving-Offering, or Meat-Offering, to which it was Biblically referred, was not a sacrifice Offering which required the shedding of blood. It was a Thanksgiving-Offering that was supposed to be rendered because the Sin-Offering, or Trespass-Offering, had been accepted by God, and the one who had failed had now been restored to fellowship. The Meat-Offering was not an Offering for sin; it was a Thank-Offering in that sin had now been atoned.

(14) "AND THE LORD SPOKE UNTO MOSES, SAYING,

(15) "IF A SOUL COMMIT A TRESPASS, AND SIN THROUGH IGNORANCE, IN THE HOLY THINGS OF THE LORD: THEN HE SHALL BRING FOR HIS TRESPASS UNTO THE LORD A RAM WITHOUT BLEMISH OUT OF THE FLOCKS, WITH YOUR ESTIMATION BY SHEKELS OF SILVER, AFTER THE SHEKEL OF THE SANCTUARY, FOR A TRESPASS-OFFERING.

(16) "AND HE SHALL MAKE AMENDS FOR THE HARM THAT HE HAS DONE IN THE HOLY THING, AND SHALL ADD THE FIFTH PART THERETO, AND GIVE IT UNTO THE PRIEST: AND THE PRIEST SHALL MAKE AN ATONEMENT FOR HIM WITH THE RAM OF THE TRESPASS-OFFERING, AND IT SHALL BE FORGIVEN HIM.

(17) "AND IF A SOUL SIN, AND COMMIT ANY OF THESE THINGS WHICH ARE FORBIDDEN TO BE DONE BY THE COMMANDMENTS OF THE LORD; THOUGH HE DID IT THROUGH IGNORANCE, YET IS HE GUILTY, AND SHALL BEAR HIS INIQUITY.

(18) "AND HE SHALL BRING A RAM WITHOUT BLEMISH OUT OF THE FLOCK, WITH YOUR ESTIMATION, FOR A TRESPASS-OFFERING, UNTO THE PRIEST:

NOTES

AND THE PRIEST SHALL MAKE AN ATONEMENT FOR HIM CONCERNING HIS IGNORANCE WHEREIN HE ERRED AND KNEW IT NOT, AND IT SHALL BE FORGIVEN HIM.

(19) "IT IS A TRESPASS-OFFERING: HE HAS CERTAINLY TRESPASSED AGAINST THE LORD."

The diagram is:

1. We find in the Trespass-Offering, by the fifth part being added, that through the Cross, God has not merely received back what was lost, but has actually become a gainer. He has gained more by Redemption than ever He lost by the Fall.

2. He reaps a richer harvest of glory, honor, and praise from the Cross of Redemption, than ever He could have reaped from those of creation.

3. The wrong has not only been perfectly atoned for, but an eternal advantage has been gained by the Work of the Cross.

4. Actually, the Cross involved a mysterious wisdom *"which none of the princes of this world knew; for had they known it, they would not have crucified the Lord of Glory"* (I Cor. 2:8).

5. As well, as it regards the Believer, Faith evidenced in the Cross will give him back all that was lost, and more besides. As the Lord, he is a gainer also.

6. In no way is this meant to glorify sin. In other words, the idea of sinning that Grace may abound is foolish indeed! Most sin, in fact, is committed by Christians, not because they want to do such, but simply because they do not know God's Prescribed Order of Victory. In other words, through their ignorance, Satan has stolen much from them. The Cross gets it all back, and more!

THE FIFTH PART

Verses 14 through 16 read: *"And the LORD spoke unto Moses, saying,*

"If a soul commit a trespass, and sin through ignorance, in the holy things of the LORD; then he shall bring for his trespass unto the LORD a ram without blemish out of the flocks, with your estimation by shekels of silver, after the shekel of the Sanctuary, for a Trespass-Offering.

"And he shall make amends for the harm

that he has done in the holy thing, and shall add the fifth part thereto, and give it unto the Priest: and the Priest shall make an Atonement for him with the ram of the Trespass-Offering, and it shall be forgiven him."

We have here, in the law of the Trespass-Offering, one of the most wonderful promises found anywhere in the Word of God. It has to do with the fifth being added, which explanation, I think, will prove to be beautifully enlightening.

We find in the Law of the Trespass-Offering, which is given in the next Chapter, that this sin pertains to harm done to one's neighbor or fellow Believer. In other words, we sin against another Believer. Concerning this, Mackintosh says: *"There is a fine principle involved in the expression, 'against the Lord.' Although the matter in question was a wrong done to one's neighbor, yet the Lord looked upon it as a trespass against Himself. Everything must be viewed in reference to the Lord. It matters not who may be affected; Jehovah must get the first place. Thus, when David's conscience was pierced by the arrow of conviction, in reference to his treatment of Uriah, he exclaims, 'I have sinned against the LORD' (II Sam. 12:13). This principle does not in the least interfere with the injured man's claim."*

The Law of the Trespass-Offering was that the person who had wronged his brother in the Lord must make amends for that wrong, and then add a fifth or 20 percent. To make it easy to understand, we suggest the following:

If, through negligence, an Israelite was responsible for the loss of a lamb of another Israelite, he was required by law to pay for the lamb, plus add 20 percent to whatever the lamb was worth.

This seemed to apply only to property. It would be impossible to measure harm done to someone through lies or malicious gossip, etc.

TO RESTORE MORE THAN HAS BEEN LOST

We must look at the Law of this particular Offering from both the standpoint of God the Father, and as well, the standpoint of the Believer.

We should very well understand that God has been robbed of much, as it regards the revolution of Satan and fallen angels against Him, and as well the terrible Fall of man. He has been insulted and impugned in every capacity. His prized creation, man, has been all but destroyed. So it would be difficult for us to properly comprehend how in the world that He could be rightly compensated for His terrible loss! And yet, we will show you how that through the Cross, the Lord has not only been compensated for His loss, but due to the fifth required to be added, He will actually come out as a net-gainer. But it was only done through the Cross. Let me give you an example:

Man was originally created to live forever; however, due to the Fall, death entered the picture, and the results are obvious. But due to the Cross, at the Resurrection, redeemed man will be given a Glorified Body, which will be far superior to that which was originally intended.

As well, due to the Cross, the New Jerusalem will be brought down to this Earth, with there actually being a new heaven and a new Earth, as stated, all made possible by the Cross. We find this in the last two Chapters of Revelation. The reason we know that the Cross is responsible for this is because, in those last two Chapters, with Satan, demon spirits, and fallen man locked away forever and forever, and with there being no hint of sin left on this Earth, or in the universe, still, Christ is mentioned seven times as the *"Lamb."* This tells us that all of these great things have come to pass, all because of what Jesus did at the Cross.

So, in the Work of the Cross, God has not merely received back what was lost, but as well, He is an actual gainer. He has gained more by Redemption than ever He lost by the Fall. He reaps a richer harvest of glory, honor, and praise in the Work of Redemption than ever He could have reaped from those of creation. Let's say it another way:

"The sons of God" could raise a loftier song of praise around the empty tomb of Jesus than ever they raised in view of the Creator's accomplished work. The wrong has not only been perfectly atoned for, but an eternal advantage has been gained by the

Work of the Cross. This is a stupendous Truth. God is a gainer by the Work of Calvary.

Concerning this, Mackintosh said, *"Who could have conceived this? When we behold man, and the creation of which he was lord, laid in ruins at the feet of the enemy, how could we conceive that, from amid those ruins, God should gather richer and nobler spoils than any which our unfallen world could have yielded? Blessed be the Name of Jesus in all of this! It is to Him we owe it all. It is by His precious Cross that ever a truth so amazing, so Divine, could be enunciated. Assuredly, the Cross involves a mysterious wisdom 'which none of the princes of this world knew; for had they known it, they would not have crucified the Lord of Glory'"* (I Cor. 2:8).

No wonder that the Holy Spirit gave forth the solemn decree, *"If any man love not the Lord Jesus Christ, let him be cursed"* (I Cor. 16:22).

Every knee shall bow at the feet of Jesus, whether in Heaven, Earth, or under the Earth, and every tongue shall confess that He is Lord, to the Glory of God the Father (Phil. 2:10-11), and all because of what He did at the Cross.

THE CROSS OF CHRIST

The first thing we must ever realize is that through the Cross all victory has been won, all victory is being won, and all victory shall be won. I speak of the human race from the very beginning, even into eternity future. As a Believer you must understand that, comprehend that, and believe that!

Second, you must act upon that tremendous premise; in other words, you must conduct yourself in the realm and respect of what Jesus did at the Cross. It must ever be the object of your Faith. That is the only way, and I mean the only way, that you can live a victorious, overcoming, Christian life. It is the only way that you can enjoy the *"more abundant life,"* of which Jesus spoke in St. John 10:10. This is the only way that the powers of darkness can be defeated in your life, and you walk and live as a Child of God should walk and live.

It's all in the Cross. That's the reason that Paul said: *"But God forbid that I should*

NOTES

glory, save in the Cross of our Lord Jesus Christ, by Whom the world is crucified unto me, and I unto the world" (Gal. 6:14). If it is to be noticed, he didn't say that I should glory, save in the Resurrection . . . or the Throne . . . or anything else for that matter. No, by all means, we aren't denigrating the Resurrection, or the Throne of God, or anything that pertains to the Lord. We are saying that it was at the Cross and the Cross alone where all victory was won, and you as a Believer must understand that.

THE BELIEVER

Considering all of this, and going back to the fifth that is added, we must as well come to the conclusion that man, as well as God, is a positive gainer by the Cross. By that I'm not merely referring to the fact that Salvation comes by the Cross. Of course, that is very, very important, in fact all-important! But I am speaking rather of the following:

I am saying that due to the Cross, man will gain more than he lost by the Fall. No, by no means am I saying that it was good that Adam fell. In fact, it was the most horrible thing that one could ever begin to imagine. But where sin abounded, Grace did much more abound (Rom. 5:20).

In other words, in essence, the Lord has said to Satan, and all the cohorts of darkness, *"Inasmuch as you have done this to My prized creation, man, through the Cross, I will give him back what he has lost, and even more besides"* (Gen. 3:15). Now let me look at the second part of this scenario:

There are some of you holding this book in your hands who love the Lord supremely. But until you heard the Message of the Cross, Satan got the upper hand in your life time and time again. In other words, he robbed, plundered, mutilated, exactly as Jesus said he would do, i.e., *"he steals, kills, and destroys"* (Jn. 10:10).

But now that you've heard the Message of the Cross, and you have believed the Message of the Cross, and you have started to act upon this foundation of the Faith, for in effect, the Cross is *"the Faith,"* the Lord, through the Cross, is going to give you back all that Satan has plundered from you, plus he's going to give you even more than you lost. It's the Law of the Trespass-Offering. Satan took from you that which was rightly yours, and now it will be restored, plus. . . .

GRACE

Paul said: *"For sin shall not have dominion over you: for you are not under the Law, but under Grace"* (Rom. 6:14).

What did Paul mean by that statement?

He meant that the Law of God, oftentimes referred to as the Law of Moses, which constituted the entirety of the Old Testament economy, has totally and completely been fulfilled in the Lord Jesus Christ. He fulfilled the keeping of it in His perfect Life, and satisfied its righteous, just demands, by His sacrificial, atoning death on the Cross of Calvary (Col. 2:14-15). Consequently, the Law of God, which in effect, is the Righteousness of God, has been fulfilled in Christ, and our acceptance of Him places us in the category of being Law-keepers instead of Law-breakers.

But having said that, the Holy Spirit, through the Apostle is telling us that our lives now are not to be lived by law, and that refers to rules and regulations, ceremonies and rituals, etc., but rather by Grace. And what does that mean?

The Grace of God is simply the Goodness of God extended to undeserving Saints. It pertains to the work that the Holy Spirit does within our hearts and lives, making us what we ought to be (Gal. 2:20).

We obtain that Grace, and its uninterrupted flow, by simply expressing Faith in Christ and what Christ has done for us at the Cross (Gal. 5:1-6). All that is required of us is that we ever understand, as already stated, that the Cross of Christ is the intersection point of all things. That must ever be the object of our Faith.

That being the case, the Holy Spirit, Who is God, and Who can do all things, will perfect His Fruit within our hearts and lives, ever making us more and more Christlike, ever giving us more and more of abundant life (Jn. 10:10).

The *"Life"* flows from Christ, and of course, it can also be said that it flows from the Father and the Divine Spirit. But we look at it as from Christ, and because Christ has made

that Life available to us, by and through what He did at the Cross (Eph. 2:13-18).

But it is the Holy Spirit Who is the Superintendent of that Life (Rom. 8:2, 11). He is the One Who distributes this life to our hearts and lives, making it more and more pertinent and prevalent within our living. And as we have repeatedly stated, He does all of this on the premise of the Cross (Jn. 14:17), and our Faith in that Finished Work.

SATAN

Consequently, we might look at the Law of the Trespass-Offering in the following manner:

Satan must give back to you all that he has stolen from you, which refers to *"the principal"* and as well, add *"the fifth."*

However, I'm saying that in that manner, only as a way of explanation. The truth is, Satan doesn't give anyone anything, simply because he doesn't have anything to give, at least that's worth anything. The true meaning pertains to him being forced aside, while God lavishes upon you all that Satan has taken from you, plus . . . the Evil One, despite your failures of the past, cannot do anything about the scenario. All he can do is to stand helplessly by. It's the Law of the Trespass-Offering!

GUILT

Verses 17 through 19 read: *"And if a soul sin, and commit any of these things which are forbidden to be done by the Commandments of the LORD; though he knew it not, yet he is guilty, and shall bear his iniquity.*

"And he shall bring a ram without blemish out of the flock, with your estimation, for a Trespass-Offering, unto the Priest: and the Priest shall make an Atonement for him concerning his ignorance wherein he erred and knew it not, and it shall be forgiven him.

"It is a Trespass-Offering: he has certainly trespassed against the LORD."

The expressions *"through ignorance"* and *"wist it not,"* or *"knew it not,"* dispose of the popular fallacy that sincerity secures Salvation.

As well, and as we have repeatedly stated, even though these transgressions were done in ignorance, the Lord still looked at it as sin, and to be sure, it would have negative results. The moment that true knowledge came to such an individual, he was to offer up the Trespass-Offering. In other words, he couldn't, and neither can we, plead ignorance, as it regards the Word of God.

Years ago, I was reading behind a particular English Preacher, who has long since gone on to be with the Lord. He made a statement, which at the time, I knew to be true, but I really did not quite understand exactly as to how it was true.

He stated, or words to this effect, *"The Church must repent, not only of the bad things it has done and is doing, but as well of the good things."*

When I read that, I knew instinctively that it was correct; but yet, I did not fully understand as to how it was correct. It is obvious that anyone must repent over things which we know to be bad, but good things?

What he meant was this, and which I have come to understand since the Cross has been opened up to me: it is sin for the Believer, or the Church as a whole, to place trust in the good things we do, thinking that it may earn us something with the Lord.

Now almost everyone would read that and say, *"Well, I've always known that!"* And most of the time, those who say that are even at that very moment trusting in things other than the Cross. Let me say it in a different way:

It is impossible for a Believer who doesn't understand the Cross, and I'm referring to the Cross as it regards Sanctification, to properly live for the Lord. Every single time, that person will have his or her faith in something other than the Cross, which in fact, is a given. In other words, as Believers, we're going to make the object of our Faith something, and even though we may load it up with Scriptures, and even though it may sound right, if it's not the Cross, it's not right, and in fact, we are sinning. All of these things are *"good things,"* in our sight, and in fact, may definitely be good things; however, our Faith must ever rest in Christ and Him Crucified (I Cor. 2:2). Anything else is sin. Paul said:

"Examine yourselves, whether you be in the Faith; prove your own selves. Know ye not your own selves, how that Jesus

Christ is in you, except you be reprobates?" (II Cor. 13:5).

*"God of eternity, Saviour and King,
"Help us to honor You, help while we sing;
"Now may the clouds of night break into splendor bright
"Jesus, our life and light, our Lord and King!"*

*"God of eternity, Ancient of Days,
"Glorious in majesty, Author of Praise;
"Hear You our earnest call, while at Your feet we fall,
"Jesus our all in all, our Lord and King!"*

*"God of eternity, Ruler Divine,
"Strength of the mighty hills, all power is Thine;
"Boundless Thy reign shall be, wondrous Thy victory,
"Earth shall be filled with Thee, our Lord and King!"*

*"God of eternity, Love is Your Name,
"God of the Earth and sea, Thee we proclaim;
"Love, through Thine only Son, Thy work of Grace has done;
"O blessed Three in One, our Lord and King!"*

CHAPTER 6

(1) "AND THE LORD SPOKE UNTO MOSES, SAYING,

(2) "IF A SOUL SIN, AND COMMIT A TRESPASS AGAINST THE LORD, AND LIE UNTO HIS NEIGHBOR IN THAT WHICH WAS DELIVERED HIM TO KEEP, OR IN FELLOWSHIP, OR IN A THING TAKEN AWAY BY VIOLENCE, OR HAS DECEIVED HIS NEIGHBOR;

(3) "OR HAVE FOUND THAT WHICH WAS LOST, AND LIES CONCERNING IT, AND SWEARS FALSELY; IN ANY OF ALL THESE THAT A MAN DOES, SINNING THEREIN:

(4) "THEN IT SHALL BE, BECAUSE HE HAS SINNED, AND IS GUILTY, THAT HE SHALL RESTORE THAT WHICH HE

TOOK VIOLENTLY AWAY, OR THE THING WHICH HE HAS DECEITFULLY GOTTEN, OR THAT WHICH WAS DELIVERED HIM TO KEEP, OR THE LOST THING WHICH HE FOUND,

(5) "OR ALL THAT ABOUT WHICH HE HAS SWORN FALSELY; HE SHALL EVEN RESTORE IT IN THE PRINCIPAL, AND SHALL ADD THE FIFTH PART MORE THERETO, AND GIVE IT UNTO HIM TO WHOM IT APPERTAINS, IN THE DAY OF HIS TRESPASS-OFFERING.

(6) "AND HE SHALL BRING HIS TRES-PASS-OFFERING UNTO THE LORD, A RAM WITHOUT BLEMISH OUT OF THE FLOCK, WITH YOUR ESTIMATION, FOR A TRES-PASS-OFFERING, UNTO THE PRIEST:

(7) "AND THE PRIEST SHALL MAKE AN ATONEMENT FOR HIM BEFORE THE LORD: AND IT SHALL BE FORGIVEN HIM FOR ANYTHING OF ALL THAT HE HAS DONE IN TRESPASSING THEREIN."

The structure is:

1. It is my thinking that the Fifth Chapter should have continued down through Verse 7 of the Sixth Chapter. Irrespective, we have taken it as the Chapters are presented to us in the King James Version, and because it makes it easier, I think, to understand, as it regards the Reader or student.

2. A sin against one's neighbor, even as the Second Verse proclaims, is the same as a sin against God. In fact, in some way, all sin is against God!

3. Once again in Verse 5, the Holy Spirit brings it out through Moses that if property is wrecked or stolen in any way, the guilty party, that is if he wants to be right with God, must restore in like value, and as well add 20 percent. The truth contained in this statement is phenomenal, to say the least! To be brief, it tells us that if we will believe God, all that Satan has stolen from us will be restored, plus more will be added on top of that. Such is Grace!

SIN AGAINST A FELLOW BELIEVER

Verses 1 through 4 read: *"And the LORD spoke unto Moses, saying,*

"If a soul sin, and commit a trespass against the LORD, and lie unto his neighbor in that which was delivered him to keep, or

NOTES

in fellowship, or in a thing taken away by violence, or has deceived his neighbor;

"Or have found that which was lost, and lies concerning it, and swears falsely; in any of all these that a man does, sinning therein:

"Then it shall be, because he has sinned, and is guilty, that he shall restore that which he took violently away, or the thing which he has deceitfully gotten, or that which was delivered him to keep, or the lost thing which he found."

While all sin, as stated, is ultimately against God, the greater thrust of the Tres-pass-Offering, I think, pertains to one Believer sinning against another Believer in some way. Of course, under the old economy, it would have been one Israelite sinning against another Israelite. As should be obvious, this is a grievous sin as it regards the Lord, and it is not overlooked, even though it is between Believers. In fact, I think it is obvious in these Passages that God looks upon such a sin as worse than other sins. To sin against unbelievers is terrible to say the least, but to sin against a fellow Believer is beyond abominable. But tragically so, it happens, sad to say, everyday!

As Believers, we must be very, very careful as to our conduct toward anyone, irrespective as to whom that person might be; however, if we're dealing with other Christians, irrespective as to what they might do, we must ever understand that if they are, in fact, a true Believer, Jesus died for them, and in fact, they belong to Christ. Knowing and understanding that, our treatment of them and our attitude and conduct toward them must be according to Whom they belong, namely the Lord!

In such a case, even though the Believer in question may not own up to his perfidiousness, still, the Lord always, and without exception, knows the truth of any and every matter. And to the one who is in the wrong, irrespective of their claims, the Scripture concerning this plainly says, *"Avenge not yourselves, but rather give place unto wrath: for it is written, Vengeance is Mine; I will repay, says the Lord"* (Rom. 12:19).

To be sure, nothing escapes the eye of God, and concerning everything, all must be accounted for, and all must give account!

No one, but no one, gets by with wrong-doing. Jesus said, and plainly so: *"Judge not, that you be not judged.*

"For with what judgment you judge, you shall be judged: and with what measure you mete, it shall be measured to you again" (Mat. 7:1-2).

So, whatever we maliciously say about others, ultimately and eventually, it will be said about us. Whatever we do to others, and I speak of that which is wrong, ultimately and eventually, it will be done to us.

Such judgment can be escaped, if the one who has done the wrong will properly confess the wrong, and seek forgiveness, both from the offended party, and especially from God. But regrettably, most are loathe to admit their wrongdoing, even when it is so very obvious!

THE FIFTH PART MORE

Verses 5 through 7 read: *"Or all that about which he has sworn falsely; he shall even restore it in the principal, and shall add the fifth part more thereto, and give it unto him to whom it appertains, in the day of his Trespass-Offering.*

"And he shall bring his Trespass-Offering unto the LORD, a ram without blemish out of the flock, with your estimation, for a Trespass-Offering, unto the Priest:

"And the Priest shall make an Atonement for him before the LORD: and it shall be forgiven him for anything of all that he has done in trespassing therein."

The Holy Spirit saw fit to address the fifth part the second time, with the first time being in Verse 16 of the previous Chapter. As always, this is done with purpose. The Holy Spirit wants us to know how important it is as to what is being said. As well, He wants us to garner the truth that is being given, which as it is with all Scripture, is of vital significance.

To be brief, and as we've already stated in Chapter 5, the great truth presented here, which of course is in conjunction with the Sacrificial Offering itself, which of course speaks of what Christ did on the Cross, we have the restitution demanded for wrongdoing, at least when the property of fellow Believers has been harmed

in some way, and as well, we have the fifth part which is to be added.

As it concerns you the Reader, this means that every single thing that Satan has stolen from you, if you will believe the Lord, place your Faith and trust totally in Him, referring to Christ in His Finished Work of the Cross, everything you've lost to the Evil One will be restored, plus 20 percent more will be added. To be sure, those numbers are not mine, but they belong to the Holy Spirit. And to be sure, the Lord will definitely do that which He has promised. So you as a Believer ought to understand this, believe this, and expect this!

As is seen in Exodus 22:1-9, when a person was guilty of any of the offenses specified there, the offender was condemned to make a fourfold restitution. The Passage before us proclaims this amount as being reduced to the restitution of the principal with the addition of the fifth part. The reason for this difference is that the Law in Exodus deals with a culprit who is convicted of his crime in a court of justice by means of witnesses, while the Law before us deals with an offender who, through compunction of mind, voluntarily confesses his offense, and to whom, without this voluntary confession, the offense could not be recognized and known. It is in this difference which constitutes it a case for a Trespass-Offering.

(8) "AND THE LORD SPOKE UNTO MOSES, SAYING,

(9) "COMMAND AARON AND HIS SONS, SAYING, THIS IS THE LAW OF THE BURNT-OFFERING: IT IS THE BURNT-OFFERING, BECAUSE OF THE BURNING UPON THE ALTAR ALL NIGHT UNTO THE MORNING, AND THE FIRE OF THE ALTAR SHALL BE BURNING IN IT.

(10) "AND THE PRIEST SHALL PUT ON HIS LINEN GARMENT, AND HIS LINEN BREECHES SHALL HE PUT UPON HIS FLESH, AND TAKE UP THE ASHES WHICH THE FIRE HAS CONSUMED WITH THE BURNT-OFFERING ON THE ALTAR, AND HE SHALL PUT THEM BESIDE THE ALTAR.

(11) "AND HE SHALL PUT OFF HIS GARMENTS, AND PUT ON OTHER GARMENTS, AND CARRY FORTH THE ASHES WITHOUT

THE CAMP UNTO A CLEAN PLACE.

(12) "AND THE FIRE UPON THE ALTAR SHALL BE BURNING IN IT; IT SHALL NOT BE PUT OUT: AND THE PRIEST SHALL BURN WOOD ON IT EVERY MORNING, AND LAY THE BURNT-OFFERING IN ORDER UPON IT; AND HE SHALL BURN THEREON THE FAT OF THE PEACE-OFFERINGS.

(13) "THE FIRE SHALL EVER BE BURNING UPON THE ALTAR; IT SHALL NEVER GO OUT."

The composition is:

1. Beginning with Verse 8 through the Seventh Chapter, we have the Law of the Burnt-Offering, the Meal-Offering, the Sin-Offering, the Trespass-Offering, and the Peace-Offering. We also have the Law of the High Priest's Consecration-Offering.

2. The order in which the Offerings are placed does not correspond here with that found in the opening Chapters of the Book. There, the Sin-Offering comes last; here, the Peace-Offering. This shows design. Only an absolutely Perfect Victim, the Lord Jesus Christ, could put away sin by the Sacrifice of Himself; hence the Sin-Offering is placed last; but only a fully accomplished Atonement can give peace to the conscience and, therefore, in the Laws affecting the Sacrifices, the Peace-Offering is put last.

3. The Burnt-Offering was to burn all night. In the morning, dressed in his clean linen garments, the Priest was to gather its ashes and place them beside the Altar, and then, in his garments of beauty, bring them with befitting glory unto a clean place. This represents the coming Kingdom Age, which of course, speaks of a cleansed Earth.

4. Through this night of mystery the fragrance of Christ's offering up of Himself to God ascends continually. *"In the morning"* He will appear to His people Israel in His double glory as the white-robed Priest, and the glory-crowned Mediator.

5. The fire that consumed the Burnt-Offering originally came from Heaven (Lev. 9:24), and was maintained perpetually burning by the unwearied Ministry of the Priests.

6. It was lacking in the second Temple. It testified on the one hand to the unceasing delight of God in the Sacrifice of Christ, and

NOTES

on the other hand, to His unceasing hatred of sin. False teachers today put this fire out by denying the Doctrines of the Atonement and of the Wrath to come (Williams).

THE LAW OF THE BURNT-OFFERING

Verses 8 and 9 read: *"And the LORD spoke unto Moses, saying,*

"Command Aaron and his sons, saying, This is the Law of the Burnt-Offering: it is the Burnt-Offering, because of the burning upon the Altar all night unto the morning, and the fire of the Altar shall be burning in it."

The Ninth Verse could read: *"It, the Burnt-Offering* (the evening Sacrifice), *shall burn upon the hearth upon the Altar all night unto the morning."*

Verse 8 records the fourth instance in which the formula, *"The LORD spoke unto Moses,"* is used in Leviticus (Lev. 4:1; 5:14; 6:1, 8), and as in the former Passages, introduces a further communication from the Lord to Moses.

Previously, the Law pointed out to the people under what circumstances, and how they are to bring their sacred oblations, now directions are given to the Priests how to conduct the sacrificial service of the people.

THE LINEN GARMENT

Verse 10 reads: *"And the Priest shall put on his linen garment, and his linen breeches shall he put upon his flesh, and take up the ashes which the fire has consumed with the Burnt-Offering on the Altar, and he shall put them beside the Altar."*

Of course, the Priest doing the officiating is a type of Christ, even as the Whole Burnt-Offering is a type of Christ.

As we have stated, the Whole Burnt-Offering typified Christ satisfying the demands of the thrice-Holy God. Only a Perfect Sacrifice could do such, hence the officiating Priests dressed in the *"linen garment,"* which typified that Righteousness.

Christ was perfectly Righteous, which means that His birth was perfect, his life was perfect, which means that it was without sin of any shape, form, or fashion, which means that He satisfied the demands of the Law, which typified the Righteousness of God, and which God demanded of all men. As our

Substitute, Christ kept the Law perfectly in every respect, and did so as a Man, the Man Christ Jesus, the Second Man, as Paul referred to Him, and the Last Adam (I Cor. 15:45-50).

Irrespective as to how many people died on crosses that day throughout the Roman Empire, even had they attempted to die as a sacrifice, the giving of themselves could not have been accepted by God, simply because all men, due to original sin, were and are spiritually polluted. Christ Alone could fit this description of perfect Righteousness, and Christ Alone did fit this description.

This blows to pieces the grossly erroneous doctrine of the Word of Faith people, which claim that the blood of any born again man could redeem humanity. The difference in the born again man and Christ is stupendous to say the least.

First of all, we have to be *"made the Righteousness of God,"* while Christ *"is the Righteousness of God"* (II Cor. 5:21). The difference there is vast! Imputed Righteousness, which is actually what we have, is not the same as the perfection of Righteousness which Christ is.

The Whole Burnt-Offering transfers the Righteousness of the victim to the sinner, while the Sin-Offering transfers the guilt of the sinner to the innocent victim, namely Christ.

ASHES

After the fire had burned all night, and had totally consumed the Sacrifice, the Priest was to take the ashes off the Altar, and deposit them on the ash-heap to the east of the Altar.

Considering that the Sacrifice had been totally consumed, this refers to the fact that the Sacrifice of Christ was total and complete. In other words, the *"ashes"* represented the fact that the totality of the sin problem, the root of sin, had been dealt with. This refers not only to man's condition, but what caused man's condition, which was the revolution of Satan in eternity past.

Preachers argue over whether certain things, such as healing, are in the Atonement. To be sure, Divine Healing is in the Atonement, as is every single thing that was

lost in this terrible rebellion and revolution against God. Jesus left nothing unaddressed.

While it is true that we do not have, at the present time, all for which He has paid the price, that awaiting the coming Resurrection, we do have enough now to live a victorious, overcoming, Christian life, in regard to the settled fact, according to the Scripture, that *"sin shall not have dominion over us"* (Rom. 6:14).

If sin in some way is dominating the Child of God, this means that the Believer is not properly availing himself of the great victory purchased by Christ at the Cross. And considering the price that He paid, it is a travesty of the highest sort for us not to avail ourselves of all that for which He has paid, at least that which we can have at present.

The phrase, *"Unto the morning,"* found in the Ninth Verse, proclaims the fact that the day or morning is coming when the long night of sin will be totally and completely finished, which speaks of the coming Kingdom Age, when Jesus will come back to rule on this Earth; however, it's greater meaning pertains to the coming time of the new heavens and the new Earth, when *"former things will have passed away"* (Rev. 21:4), even as is described in the last two Chapters of the Book of Revelation. The Scripture then says: *"For there shall be no night there"* (Rev. 21:25).

OTHER GARMENTS

Verse 11 reads: *"And he shall put off his garments, and put on other garments, and carry forth the ashes without the camp unto a clean place."*

To remove the ashes to a clean place, the Priest was to change his sacred robes in which he had ministered at the Altar. He was to put on other garments, though less holy, but not common, since the removing of the ashes was still a sacred function.

Great care was taken that the place to which the ashes were removed was well sheltered, so that the wind should not blow them about. The Priest was not allowed to scatter them, but had to deposit them gently. No stranger was permitted to gather them, or to make profit by the ashes (Ellicott).

The Priest being required to change his garments, that is when he removed the ashes each morning, presented itself as a portrayal of the fact that Christ, of Whom the Priest was a type, had finished His Work, which pertained to the satisfying of the Righteousness of God, which was the holiest of all, hence it required the *"linen garments,"* and now Christ would embark upon another aspect of His Ministry, which is to serve as our High Priest, constantly making intercession for us (Heb. 7:25; 9:24).

This is the reason that the *"Burnt-Offering"* was a Sweet-Savor Offering, exactly as were the *"Meal-Offering"* and the *"Peace-Offering."* The sacrifices for sin were not Sweet-Savor Offerings, which constituted the *"Sin-Offerings,"* and the *"Trespass-Offerings."*

The Law of the Burnt-Offering, which we are now studying, tells us that this was the holiest Work of Christ. In other words, the Cross came up before God as the holiest Work of the Saviour, eclipsing any and everything else which He had done. That's the reason that Paul said: *"But God forbid that I should glory* (boast), *save in the Cross of our Lord Jesus Christ, by Whom the world is crucified unto me, and I unto the world"* (Gal. 6:14).

THE CROSS IS THE FOUNDATION OF ALL DOCTRINE

Verse 12 reads: *"And the fire upon the Altar shall be burning in it; it shall not be put out: and the Priest shall burn wood on it every morning, and lay the Burnt-Offering in order upon it; and he shall burn thereon the fat of the Peace-Offerings."*

Concerning this, Ellicott says: *"This is introduced here in this fashion, in order to caution the Priest whose function it is to remove the ashes, that when engaged in this act, he is to take great care that in taking off the ashes from the Altar, he does not knock away the pieces of fat of the Burnt-Offering, which constitute the fuel, which could cause the fire to go out.*

"Each morning, the Priest was to replenish the wood on the Altar which had been consumed during the night."

It is said that there were three separate piles of wood on the Altar, and kept that way at all times. The largest one was for the daily sacrifice to be burned, which was a Whole Burnt-Offering, and which was offered

up twice a day, 9 a.m. and 3 p.m.

The second pile of wood was that which provided the coals of fire, which could be put into the censers, and in fact were done so twice a day, at the time of the morning and the evening sacrifices, and placed on the Altar of Incense, with Incense poured over these coals of fire, which filled the Holy Place with a sacred fragrance and a sacred smoke. This was a type of the Intercessory Work of Christ, which is carried on in Heaven, unto this very hour.

The third pile of wood was said to be the perpetual fire from which the other two portions were fed. It was not quenched, we are told, until the destruction of the Temple by Nebuchadnezzar.

The fact that the fire was to never go out proclaims the fact that the Cross alone is the answer to the sins of mankind, and furthermore, that it will ever be the answer. The fact that it was to never go out also proclaims the absolute necessity that we understand that the Cross is the Foundation of our Faith. It is not a mere doctrine, but rather the Foundation of all Doctrine.

While it can be spoken of as a doctrine, it must be understood that it is the Foundational Truth, from which all supplemental doctrine springs. I'm sure that Jesus addressed what He had done on the Cross as more than a mere doctrine among doctrines.

If one properly understands the Cross, then one has a working knowledge of the Bible. To not understand the Cross means that in some way, the individual has a perverted view of the Word of God. In fact, the story of the Cross is, in effect, the story of the Bible. This is so closely intertwined that we might even turn it around and it would work accordingly, meaning that the story of the Bible is the story of the Cross. Once one begins to understand the Cross, then what I have just stated becomes overly obvious. The study of the Tabernacle and of the Sacrificial System, which we are studying now, all and in totality are a study of the Cross.

THE FAT OF THE PEACE-OFFERINGS

With the *"Burnt-Offering,"* the *"Sin-Offering,"* and the *"Trespass-Offering,"* a *"Peace-Offering"* was to be presented and offered with each one of these Offerings, and every time they were offered.

The *"Peace-Offering,"* which we will study momentarily, presents the fact that the other Offering, whatever it might have been, was accepted by God, and peace was thereby restored to the one who had sinned. It was the Offering of a Finished Work, and Faith in that Finished Work.

THE FIRE SHALL NEVER GO OUT

Verse 13 reads: *"The fire shall ever be burning upon the Altar: it shall never go out."*

It is believed that when Moses dedicated the Tabernacle, meaning that it had been constructed and now erected, exactly as the Lord had demanded, the Lord sent fire down from Heaven and ignited the wood on the Altar (Ex. 40:29-38; Lev. 9:24).

The fire on this Altar, which was ignited originally by God, was to be kept perpetually by the Priests, which means that it was to never go out, because the need of the people was ever present, as it regarded cleansing from sin.

Presently, and I speak of the time of the New Covenant, even though it is a Finished Work, we are to ever look at the Cross as the answer for the ills of man, and in fact the only answer, which means that we are to preach the Cross continually, i.e., *"that it never go out."*

The truth is, there is less preaching of the Cross presently than there has been at any time, I believe, since the Reformation. This means that the Church presently is in worse condition than it has been at any time since the Reformation. The Holy Spirit is given less and less place, and because the preaching of the Cross has been given less and less place. The two, the Cross and the Holy Spirit, go hand-in-hand.

Unfortunately, the Denominational world attempted to preach the Cross without the Holy Spirit, and presently, they are basically left preaching much of nothing. The Pentecostals tried to preach the Holy Spirit without the Cross, which incidentally, the Holy Spirit will not tolerate, and they are basically left now as little more than a hollow shell. In fact, they are chasing spirits, thinking it's the Holy Spirit!

The Scripture is emphatic, *"This fire is to never go out!"* But I'm afraid it is going out, making the Altar, i.e., *"the Cross,"* totally ineffective. The Cross is Christianity, and to remove the Cross is to take the heart out of Christianity, leaving it as no more, as stated, than a hollow shell.

(14) "AND THIS IS THE LAW OF THE MEAT-OFFERING: THE SONS OF AARON SHALL OFFER IT BEFORE THE LORD, BEFORE THE ALTAR.

(15) "AND HE SHALL TAKE OF IT HIS HANDFUL, OF THE FLOUR OF THE MEAT-OFFERING, AND OF THE OIL THEREOF, AND ALL THE FRANKINCENSE WHICH IS UPON THE MEAT-OFFERING, AND SHALL BURN IT UPON THE ALTAR FOR A SWEET SAVOR, EVEN THE MEMORIAL OF IT, UNTO THE LORD.

(16) "AND THE REMAINDER THEREOF SHALL AARON AND HIS SONS EAT: WITH UNLEAVENED BREAD SHALL IT BE EATEN IN THE HOLY PLACE; IN THE COURT OF THE TABERNACLE OF THE CONGREGATION THEY SHALL EAT IT.

(17) "IT SHALL NOT BE BAKED WITH LEAVEN. I HAVE GIVEN IT UNTO THEM FOR THEIR PORTION OF MY OFFERINGS MADE BY FIRE; IT IS MOST HOLY, AS IS THE SIN-OFFERING, AND AS THE TRESPASS-OFFERING.

(18) "ALL THE MALES AMONG THE CHILDREN OF AARON SHALL EAT OF IT. IT SHALL BE A STATUTE FOREVER IN YOUR GENERATIONS CONCERNING THE OFFERINGS OF THE LORD MADE BY FIRE: EVERY ONE WHO TOUCHES THEM SHALL BE HOLY."

The construction is:

1. We are to now study the Law of the Meat-Offering, which in effect, was a grain or cereal Offering, which could be constituted as a *"Thank-Offering."*

The word *"Meat"* then was used for all types of food, whereas meat at present refers to the flesh of animals. In fact, in this Offering, there was no blood shed, and because it was a grain Offering. It was offered along with the Peace-Offering, which latter was a blood Sacrifice, every time the other Offerings were presented to God.

2. The Meal-Offering, as the other Offerings,

was first for God and His Glory, and then for man and his need.

3. As the Sin-Offering, and the Trespass-Offering, so was it *"most holy."* Thus, the Holy Spirit testifies to the sinlessness of Christ as a Man, and at the moment in which He was *"made sin"* upon the Cross.

THE LAW OF THE MEAT-OFFERING

Verse 14 reads: *"And this is the Law of the Meat-Offering: the sons of Aaron shall offer it before the LORD, before the Altar."*

In the first part of Chapter 2, the people were told as to what this Offering consisted of, and what portion belonged to the Priests. Now we find that additional directions are given to the Priests about the eating of the portions which belonged to them and about the treatment of the residue.

As we've already stated, this was not a bloody Offering, which means it was not an animal sacrifice. In fact, it was the only sacrifice of the five that was not bloody. It was a *"Thank-Offering,"* or as one might say, a *"Thanksgiving-Offering,"* intended to be presented to the Lord, in thanksgiving, that the Burnt, Sin, or Trespass Offerings had been accepted.

While the *"Sons of Aaron"* here did represent the actual sons of the High Priest, the phrase is intended to comprise his lineal descendants who succeeded to the Priestly Office.

A SWEET SAVOR

Verse 15 reads: *"And he shall take of it his handful, of the flour of the Meat-Offering, and of the oil thereof, and all the frankincense which is upon the Meat-Offering, and shall burn it upon the Altar for a Sweet Savor, even the memorial of it, unto the LORD."*

As is by now obvious, the *"Meat-Offering"* was unlike the Whole Burnt-Offering in that it was not a bloody sacrifice. As the Burnt-Offering taught the totality of the Atonement, as effected by Christ, so the Meat-Offering taught the recognition of God's supremacy and submission to that supremacy. The Burnt-Offering and Meat-Offering taught these attitudes in two ways: first, by requiring that a living creature, one substituting for the offerer himself, namely

Christ, be surrendered up, and second, by calling for the offerer to also hand over to God, as a gift, a portion of some of the good things that he had originally received from God, in the form of thanksgiving.

The lesson taught to the Jew was that of the necessity of loyal service to God. By the Meat-Offering he was taught thanksgiving. Actually, the Meat-Offering was such that it could well have been referred to as a *"Thanksgiving-Offering."* The individual was also taught the need of purity and incorruption of spirit, this quality being symbolized by the prohibitions against leaven and honey, and the command to use salt (Lev. 2:11-13).

It is said that the relationship between the two sacrifices, that of the Whole Burnt-Offering and of the Meat-Offering, was so close that the Burnt-Offering was seldom offered without the accompaniment of the Meat-Offering (Num. 15:2-4). This would hold true to a lesser extent, for its accompaniment of the Sin-Offering and the Trespass-Offering.

THE GREATNESS OF CHRIST

The Glory of the Lord Jesus Christ is so great that no one Offering could symbolize His grandeur and greatness, regarding Who He was, and What He did, and we refer to the Cross. It, therefore, took some five separate Offerings, those prescribed in this Book of Leviticus, to encompass the Christ symbolism – and even then the symbols pale into insignificance alongside the reality.

Likewise, man's oblation to God could not be symbolized by one Offering. It would take several Offerings to encompass man's worship of God. As we have just mentioned, the very heart of this particular Offering is thanksgiving. And of course, it is obvious that thanksgiving must be done out of a free will (Lev. 2:1).

In fact, Israel's major problem was the sin of thanklessness or ingratitude. This is illustrated in their constant murmurings against Moses and against the Lord.

"And the people murmured against Moses, saying, What shall we drink?" (Ex. 15:24).

Understanding that, is it not possible that one of the most prevalent sins in the Body of Christ today is that of thanklessness? Is it not true that we today are mostly unappreciative and ungrateful to God, despite all the good things that He does for us? Paul said:

"Because that, when they knew God, they glorified Him not as God, neither were thankful" (Rom. 1:21).

THE FLOUR

The phrase, *"And he shall take of it his handful, of the flour of the Meat-Offering,"* pertains to Christ.

The flour of the Meat-Offering was to be a fine flour. The grain had to be thoroughly ground to a powder consistency. There were to be no lumps in it anywhere, no foreign material of any kind.

This powdery, pure white flour speaks of the perfection and purity of spirit which marked our Lord. He was perfect in everything that He did. He never had to apologize for a single statement in all of His life. He never lost His temper, nor did He ever speak crossly to anyone. He never had to say, *"I am sorry."* He was never gripped by jealousy, pettiness, vengefulness, stubbornness, or hatred in the way that we are. The fine flour truly symbolized His perfect character, His perfect humanity.

In essence, the fine flour represented the perfect humanity of our Lord, in fact, the only perfect humanity that has ever existed.

THE HANDFUL

This particular Sacrifice called for only a small portion to be offered up at the Brazen Altar. The balance of the Offering was to go to the Priests for their own use. The Meat-Offerings, therefore, must have gone far toward supplying the Priests with food, since for every handful of flour burned on the Altar, nearly one gallon went to the Priests. They were required to eat foods made with this flour within the precincts of the Tabernacle, as was the case with the animal sacrifices that were considered most holy. So what does this tells us?

The greater portion going to the Priests proclaims to us the fact that all that Jesus did on the Cross, typified by the *"handful of flour there placed,"* was done for our benefit. Considering that almost all of the Offering went to the Priests, we learn from this that all that He did on the Cross was

entirely for our benefit. In other words, He didn't die for Himself, for Angels, for God the Father, but altogether for us. While it is true that the Whole Burnt-Offering was in effect for God, that is, that His Righteousness be satisfied, still, this was necessary if man was to be redeemed. So in essence, it was done for us!

THE OIL

The phrase, *"And the oil thereof,"* signifies the Holy Spirit.

The part that was to be burned on the Brazen Altar was to have a liberal portion of oil poured on it. The word *"pour"* in Leviticus 2:6 demands this. It was to be a liberal application. This tells us three things:

1. Jesus was anointed with the Holy Spirit above anyone who has ever existed (Ps. 45:7).

2. The Holy Spirit not only superintended the life of the Saviour in every respect, but as well, superintended His death on the Cross, in effect, even telling Him when to die (Heb. 9:14).

3. The Believer is to be literally baptized with the Holy Spirit, with the word *"baptize"* or *"baptism,"* referring, as is obvious, to a total inundation (Acts 1:4-5).

FRANKINCENSE

Frankincense is a bitter white substance, a resin, that came from piercing a tree which grew in the cracks of marble rock. There was very little fluid in this type of tree that produced this type of incense, so any fluid that was extracted from it, of necessity, would be precious.

The Frankincense was not mixed with the oil and the flour, or with the salt, as a constituent element of the Offering. It was, rather, scattered over all the components, and was burnt together with them in the *"memorial."* This use of frankincense symbolized Intercession – that of Christ on our behalf.

Frankincense was also used in the Incense which was placed on the Altar of Worship – the Incense which routinely produced the cloud of beautiful fragrance in the Holy Place. This was done twice a day, at the time of the morning and evening Sacrifices.

Just as the frankincense produced a Sweet Savor unto the Lord as it was offered on the

Altar of Worship in the Holy Place, likewise it would produce a Sweet Savor unto the Lord when it was offered on the Brazen Altar as part of the offerer's Sacrifice of Thanksgiving (Lev. 2:2).

After the Priest placed a handful of the mixture on the Brazen Altar and the flames burned through the flour, causing the oil to ignite, the sweet aroma of the frankincense would fill the air for a few moments. This would be a testimony to the glory and wonder of Christ and what He would do at the Cross, all on our behalf, which made His Intercession possible.

THE MEMORIAL

The phrase, *"And shall burn it upon the Altar for a Sweet Savor, even the memorial of it, unto the LORD,"* refers to something that must be remembered. This means that a memorial is something that keeps remembrance alive – but remembrance of what?

Jesus Himself told us:

"And when He had given thanks, He broke it, and said, Take, eat: this is My Body, which is broken for you: this do in remembrance of Me" (I Cor. 11:24).

In a sense, *"The Lord's Supper"* is a form of the Meat-Offering in a spiritual sense. It is done as a memorial *"till He come,"* and we must never forget what He has done for us.

I'm afraid that much of the modern Church is forgetting the great Sacrificial Offering of Christ on the Cross. They are forgetting that this is the very foundation of the Faith, in effect, *"the Faith."* They are forgetting that there is no Salvation outside of Faith in Christ and the Cross. They are forgetting that it's impossible for the Saint to live a holy life, without continued Faith in the Sacrifice of Christ. And how do I know that?

I know it because the Cross, more and more, is relegated to a place of insignificance. This is proven by the foray of the modern Church into humanistic psychology. There was a time that theology was the queen of the sciences in the universities of our land. Today, humanistic psychology has taken its place.

There was a day that the Cross was held up as the answer to man's dilemma, but today, even as with the universities, the

NOTES

Church instead holds up humanistic psychology as the answer. What a travesty! What an abomination!

Likewise, the Word of Faith people, who have made such inroads into the modern Church, and all because false doctrine is always easily accepted, actually repudiates the Cross. They refer to it as *"the greatest defeat in human history."* Their teachers openly proclaim that the Cross should not be preached.

Kenneth Hagin, in the April 2002 issue of his monthly publication, plainly stated that if we preach the Cross, we are preaching death! He then encouraged Preachers to preach the Resurrection or the Throne. That seems strange, considering that Paul said:

"I determined not to know anything among you, save Jesus Christ, and Him Crucified" (I Cor. 2:2).

And then: *"I am crucified with Christ"* (Gal. 2:20).

And then: *"For Christ sent me not to baptize, but to preach the Gospel: not with wisdom of words, lest the Cross of Christ should be made of none effect"* (I Cor. 1:17).

He then said: *"For the preaching of the Cross is to them who perish foolishness; but unto us which are saved it is the Power of God"* (I Cor. 1:18).

And finally: *"But we preach Christ Crucified"* (I Cor. 1:23).

He didn't say, *"We preach Christ on the Throne,"* or *"We preach Christ resurrected."* He rather said, *"But we preach Christ Crucified."*

Yes, the Meat-Offering was to ever be a memorial of what Christ would do at the Cross. We must never forget that! It must be sung in our songs, proclaimed in our Messages, explained in our teaching, and in effect, the very center of all that we are in Christ and all that we believe. It is *"the Cross!" "The Cross!" "The Cross!"*

MOST HOLY

Verses 16 through 18 read: *"And the remainder thereof shall Aaron and his sons eat: with unleavened bread shall it be eaten in the Holy Place; in the Court of the Tabernacle of the congregation they shall eat it.*

"It shall not be baked with leaven. I have given it unto them for their portion of My

Offerings made by fire: it is most holy, as is the Sin-Offering, and as the Trespass-Offering.

"All the males among the children of Aaron shall eat of it. It shall be a statute forever in your generations concerning the Offerings of the LORD made by fire: every one who touches them shall be holy."

The Meat-Offering contained no blood, as is obvious, but it was conjoined with an Offering that was literally soaked in blood, and we speak of the Burnt-Offering. So, too, our private offerings of thanksgiving contain no great sacrifice of our own; yet, even so, God looks upon our Praise or Thanksgiving-Offering as a sacrifice. The reason He does so is because of His Son, Jesus Christ. God willingly receives and accepts our display of thankfulness – even knowing that we have been given great blessings despite our basic unworthiness – because the ground around that Cross was literally soaked with the Blood of His Only Son.

So when we thank God, we must always realize that He accepts our thanksgiving only because of His Son, the Lord Jesus Christ. Our thanksgiving in itself cannot please Him; our praises within themselves cannot please Him. If He is pleased, it is only because we do these things in remembrance of His Only Son, Who died and rose again from the dead. Even as the Meat-Offering was attached totally and completely to the Whole Burnt-Offering, our worship, thanksgiving, and praises must ever be attached to the Cross, or else it will not be accepted (Eph. 2:13-18).

The part eaten by Aaron and his sons, and all the Priests who followed thereafter, was in a sense a symbolic picture of what Jesus was speaking about when He said to Israel: *"Except you eat the flesh of the Son of Man, and drink His Blood, you have no life in you.*

"Whoso eats My flesh, and drinks My Blood, has eternal life; and I will raise him up at the last day.

"For My flesh is meat indeed, and My Blood is drink indeed.

"He who eats My flesh, and drinks My Blood, dwells in Me, and I in him" (Jn. 6:53-56).

Christ was not talking about literally eating His flesh and drinking His Blood, for He then said: *"It is the Spirit that quickens; the flesh profits nothing: the words that I*

NOTES

speak unto you, they are spirit, and they are life" (Jn. 6:63).

Our Lord was speaking of His death on the Cross. And by Him using the terminology which He did, He in essence was saying that His great Work on the Cross must be accepted as more than a mere philosophical quest. Faith must be tendered completely in Christ and what He did for us in the Sacrifice of Himself. When this is done, and I speak of such Faith being registered, God literally places us *"in Christ."* In other words, in the Mind of God, we were literally *"in Christ,"* when He died on the Cross, in effect, *"baptized into His death,"* and then *"buried with Him by baptism into death,"* and then raised with Him in *"newness of life"* (Rom. 6:3-5).

Untold millions accept Christ in a philosophical sense. By that I speak of Him being a great Healer, a great Miracle-Worker, or even a great Prophet, etc. But that's not enough! That will save no one!

For Christ to be accepted, He must be accepted totally and completely, which was symbolized by the Passover Lamb being eaten totally and completely, with none of it left remaining (Ex. 12:10).

To reject the Cross is to reject Christ. In effect, if the Cross is rejected or ignored in any way, the Believer will find himself worshipping *"another Jesus,"* and doing so by *"another spirit,"* which produces *"another gospel"* (II Cor. 11:4).

NO LEAVEN

When the Priests would prepare this particular Offering of their own consumption, they must not add any leaven to it. Leaven is a type of yeast, which causes the corruption or fermentation of that in which it is placed; therefore, it was not to be used in this Offering.

If leaven would have been blended into the flour, along with the oil and the frankincense, the mixture would no doubt have swelled and frothed, thus creating the repulsive *"festering"* appearance which we find used throughout the Mosaic legislation as an image of moral evil.

In fact, when the Passover was to be observed, a detailed ritual was to be carried out, which referred to the cleaning of the house of any leaven. The family was to search and scrub the house so that no crumb of bread would be left in the house. Leaven, as stated, represents corruption; therefore, it should be readily understandable that no leaven would be included in this Thanksgiving-Offering.

If there is unconfessed sin in our lives, which refers to leaven, God will not hear our prayers; and, therefore, our Meat-Offering is made in vain. This flour was a type of Christ, and inasmuch as there was no sin in Him whatsoever, no leaven was to be put into this concoction, which in effect, typified sin. His body was pure, perfect, and holy, which means that it was a Perfect Sacrifice.

We saw, in the Whole Burnt-Offering, what sin does to the individual. Its effect was symbolized perfectly in the required cutting up of the carcasses. The grizzly act of quartering and sectioning the slain animal symbolized the penetrating property of sin, which goes down into the very vitals of human beings. This helps to explain why Jesus had to pay the supreme sacrifice to rid man not only of the guilt of sin, but also of the very root of sin.

Why was this Offering *"most holy"*? It is *"most holy"* because it is an Offering to the Lord *"made by fire."* What does this mean?

Any Offering that was placed on the fiery Brazen Altar and consumed by the Altar's fire was considered *"most holy."* Totally and completely, this refers to the Cross of Christ. That connection, and that alone, is what made the Offering most holy.

The garments of the offerer did not make it holy. The detailed preparations did not make it holy. The *"style"* by which the Offering was handed over to the Priests did not make it holy.

The fire represented Calvary, and the Offering's ingredients represented Christ; therefore, the Holiness was in the Christ of Calvary, and in nothing else!

How confused we get when we think our efforts somehow produce Holiness! We wear out hair a certain length, and we think that the *"look"* we've achieved is holy. Our sleeves are a certain length, and we think that somehow this style is holy. We attend Church so many times during the year, and in our

minds we think of this as being holy. We praise the Lord in a certain way, and this is supposed to denote some type of Holiness.

We build our own little religion, in other words; and because we strictly adhere to it, we think of ourselves as holy. And, conversely, we come to think of those who do not adhere to our own man-made standards as being *"not holy,"* or unholy, or somehow unclean. We call ourselves people of *"Holiness,"* because we adhere to some set of rules.

When will we wake up and realize that our works and our own talents or abilities cannot produce any Holiness? When will we see that all of our Holiness, and in totality, comes from the Sacrifice of our Lord Jesus Christ at Calvary's Cross, and our Faith in that Sacrifice, which in effect, constitutes a Holiness made by fire?

The point is, true Holiness cannot be attained by works and even by religious observances; it can only be *"made by fire."* Holiness cannot be created by man's efforts; it can only be *"made by fire."* Satan will not bow before our man-made Holiness, but he bows and trembles at that which is *"made by fire"* i.e., *"the Cross of Christ."* We are holy simply and truly by having Faith in Christ and what Christ has done for us at the Cross, and that alone!

THE MALES

Only the males among the children of Aaron could eat this, symbolizing that it was through man, namely Adam, that sin was imposed upon the human race, and in effect, affected its destruction.

The Law of the Meat-Offering closed with the words, *"Every one who touches them shall be holy,"* which referred to the Offerings made by fire. It is the same presently!

Christ Alone and what He did at the Cross makes one holy. Only the Priests could touch it in those days. But thank God, at this present time, and in fact, since the Cross, it is possible for anyone to *"touch"* that most holy Sacrifice. When they do, a Perfect Righteousness is imputed to them, and they are holy.

(19) "AND THE LORD SPOKE UNTO MOSES, SAYING,

(20) "THIS IS THE OFFERING OF AARON AND OF HIS SONS, WHICH THEY

SHALL OFFER UNTO THE LORD IN THE DAY WHEN HE IS ANOINTED; THE TENTH PART OF AN EPHAH OF FINE FLOUR FOR A MEAT-OFFERING PERPETUAL, HALF OF IT IN THE MORNING, AND HALF THEREOF AT NIGHT.

(21) "IN A PAN IT SHALL BE MADE WITH OIL; AND WHEN IT IS BAKED, YOU SHALL BRING IT IN: AND THE BAKED PIECES OF THE MEAT-OFFERING SHALL YOU OFFER FOR A SWEET SAVOR UNTO THE LORD.

(22) "AND THE PRIEST OF HIS SONS THAT IS ANOINTED IN HIS STEAD SHALL OFFER IT: IT IS A STATUTE FOREVER UNTO THE LORD; IT SHALL BE WHOLLY BURNT.

(23) "FOR EVERY MEAT-OFFERING FOR THE PRIEST SHALL BE WHOLLY BURNT: IT SHALL NOT BE EATEN."

The composition is:

1. Verses 19 through 23 form a parenthesis. It treats of the special relationship of the High Priest to the Meal-Offering.

2. His Meal-Offering was to be offered morning and evening.

3. It was to be *"baked,"* and *"well kneaded,"* and wholly burnt, not eaten (Heb., Chpt. 7).

4. Aaron, though High Priest, and all who would follow in his place, was a sinner, and twice everyday had to shelter himself in type, behind a sinless Saviour.

THE MORNING AND EVENING SACRIFICES

Verses 19 and 20 read: *"And the LORD spoke unto Moses, saying,*

"This is the Offering of Aaron and of his sons, which they shall offer unto the LORD in the day when he is anointed; the tenth part of an ephah of fine flour for a Meat-Offering perpetual, half of it in the morning, and half thereof at night."

It seems that much was worked around the two Sacrifices that were offered daily, namely the morning Sacrifice, which was a Whole Burnt-Offering, and carried out at 9 a.m., and the evening Sacrifice, which was another Whole Burnt-Offering, and carried out at 3 p.m. Along with the High Priest preparing this on a daily basis, which he was required to do, the wicks on the Golden

Lampstand would be cleaned twice a day, at this particular time, as well. Also, Incense was offered on the Golden Altar at this time.

Jesus was put on the Cross at the time of the morning Sacrifice, and He died at the time of the evening Sacrifice, meaning that He stayed on the Cross for six hours. Consequently, he fulfilled the type in totality.

While the High Priest was to offer the *"Meat-Offering"* everyday, the ordinary Priests were to offer it only once, and that was on the day that he was consecrated to his Office.

It seems that it was offered after the Sacrifice of the Whole Burnt-Offering, and before the Drink-Offering.

It is to this practice that the Apostle refers when he says, *"For such a High Priest became us . . . Who needeth not daily, like those High Priests, to offer up sacrifice first for His own sins"* (Heb. 7:26-27).

A SWEET SAVOR

Verses 21 through 23 read: *"In a pan it shall be made with oil; and when it is baked, you shall bring it in: and the baked pieces of the Meat-Offering shall you offer for a Sweet Savor unto the LORD.*

"And the Priest of his sons that is anointed in his stead shall offer it: it is a statute forever unto the LORD; it shall be wholly burnt.

"For every Meat-Offering for the Priest shall be wholly burnt: it shall not be eaten."

This small amount of fine flour, which typified the perfect humanity of Christ was to be sprinkled with oil, and then baked. Along with the Meat-Offering, it was to be placed on the Brazen Altar, and then offered for a *"Sweet Savor unto the Lord."*

This was to be carried out by Aaron, who was High Priest, and all who would follow in his stead, even down through the centuries. It was not to be eaten; it was to be *"wholly burnt."*

As should be obvious, the High Priest typified Christ. But more particularly, this ritual typified what Christ would do as it regards the Redemption of humanity. This Offering being burned on the Brazen Altar signified the death that Christ would suffer, in essence, the price that He would pay. But there was one vast difference:

Whereas the earthly High Priests, despite

their office, were sinful men and, therefore, had to repeat this everyday, Christ, being perfect in every respect, would have to offer up this sacrifice, the Sacrifice of Himself, only once. That would forever suffice (Heb. 10:12).

(24) "AND THE LORD SPOKE UNTO MOSES, SAYING,

(25) "SPEAK UNTO AARON AND TO HIS SONS, SAYING, THIS IS THE LAW OF THE SIN-OFFERING: IN THE PLACE WHERE THE BURNT-OFFERING IS KILLED SHALL THE SIN-OFFERING BE KILLED BEFORE THE LORD: IT IS MOST HOLY.

(26) "THE PRIEST WHO OFFERS IT FOR SIN SHALL EAT IT: IN THE HOLY PLACE SHALL IT BE EATEN, IN THE COURT OF THE TABERNACLE OF THE CONGREGATION.

(27) "WHATSOEVER SHALL TOUCH THE FLESH THEREOF SHALL BE HOLY: AND WHEN THERE IS SPRINKLED OF THE BLOOD THEREOF UPON ANY GARMENT, YOU SHALL WASH THAT WHEREON IT WAS SPRINKLED IN THE HOLY PLACE.

(28) "BUT THE EARTHEN VESSEL WHEREIN IT IS SODDEN SHALL BE BROKEN: AND IF IT BE SODDEN IN A BRAZEN POT, IT SHALL BE BOTH SCOURED, AND RINSED IN WATER.

(29) "ALL THE MALES AMONG THE PRIESTS SHALL EAT THEREOF: IT IS MOST HOLY.

(30) "AND NO SIN-OFFERING WHEREOF ANY OF THE BLOOD IS BROUGHT INTO THE TABERNACLE OF THE CONGREGATION TO RECONCILE WITHAL IN THE HOLY PLACE, SHALL BE EATEN: IT SHALL BE BURNT IN THE FIRE."

The overview is:

1. The following is the Law of the Sin-Offering.

2. The Sin-Offering was killed in the place where the Burnt-Offering was slain, and its body (the Sin-Offering) burned outside the camp.

3. So desperate a malady is sin that anything that came in contact with the Sin-Offering had to be washed, broken, or scoured.

4. The Sin-Offering, whose blood was brought into the Sanctuary, symbolizes Christ bearing before God the sin of the whole world.

NOTES

5. The Sin-Offering, whose blood was not so brought in, but whose flesh was eaten by the Priest, presents Christ as making His Own the sins of the individual sinner who believes upon Him.

6. The Burnt-Offering and the Sin-Offering being slain upon the one spot sets out the unity of the death of Christ in its two aspects. At Golgotha, He was at once in the same moment, accursed of God as the Sin-Offering, and beloved of the Father as the Burnt-Offering.

THE LAW OF THE SIN-OFFERING

Verses 24 and 25 read: *"And the LORD spoke unto Moses, saying,*

"Speak unto Aaron and to his sons, saying, This is the Law of the Sin-Offering: In the place where the Burnt-Offering is killed shall the Sin-Offering be killed before the LORD: it is most holy."

The personal Holiness of Christ is more strikingly presented in the Sin-Offering, than in any of the other Sacrifices. The Holy Spirit, through Moses, said, *"It is most holy."* He even went so far as to say, *"Whatsoever shall touch the flesh thereof shall be holy . . . All the males among the Priests shall eat thereof: it is most holy"* (Lev. 6:27, 29).

This was said of the *"Meat-Offering," "Sin-Offering,"* and the *"Trespass-Offering."*

Concerning this, Mackintosh said: *"This is most marked and striking. The Holy Spirit did not need to guard with such jealousy the personal Holiness of Christ in the Burnt-Offering; but lest the soul should, by any means, lose sight of that Holiness while contemplating the place which the Blessed One became the Sin-Offering, we are again and again reminded of it by the words, 'It is most holy.'"*

Mackintosh went on to say: *"The same point is observable 'in the Law of the Trespass-Offering' (Lev. 7:1-6). Never was the Lord Jesus more fully seen to be 'the Holy One of God' than when He was 'made sin' upon the cursed tree. The vileness and blackness of that with which He stood identified on the Cross, only served to show out more clearly that He was 'most holy.' Though a sin-bearer, He was sinless; though enduring the Wrath of God, He was the Father's delight; though deprived of the light of God's countance, He dwelt in the Father's bosom."*

As should be obvious, this completely shoots down the erroneous theory of the Jesus died spiritually doctrine. This is taught by those of the Word of Faith group, which in effect states that Jesus became one with Satan on the Cross, died as a sinner, and went to the burning side of Hell, where He was tortured for three days and nights, until God said *"It is enough."* At that time, they continue to say, Jesus was born again, as any sinner must be born again in order to be saved. He was then resurrected from the dead, etc.

Consequently, their Faith is not in what He did at the Cross, but rather of what He did, they claim, in the burning side of Hell.

In the first place, there is not one shred of this in the Bible. It is pure fiction from beginning to end. Also, the *"Law of the Sin-Offering,"* and that it was *"most holy"* in the eyes of the Lord, completely debunks the idea of Jesus dying spiritually on the Cross.

Once again, we go back to the fact that many of these erroneous doctrines are perpetrated on false ideas, simply because the person doing the perpetrating doesn't know and understand the Old Testament. This is at least one of the many reasons that the Book of Leviticus is of such significance. In the five Sacrifices presented, it beautifully portrays the one Sacrifice of Christ, thereby giving us its vast significance, at least as far as we can understand such. The truth is, we will never, as human beings, be able to fully comprehend and understand all that Christ did for us at the Cross. He not only addressed the human need, but as well, He addressed what Satan did in his revolution against God, which originated sin (Eph. 1:10).

The Scripture is emphatic that, *"In the place where the Burnt-Offering is killed shall the Sin-Offering be killed before the LORD: it is most holy."*

As we have stated, the Burnt-Offering stipulated Jesus Christ offering to God His total perfection, and doing so in Sacrifice, that the Righteousness of God might be satisfied. There had to be a perfect victim who would give up his life, and that Perfect Victim was Christ, and because that Perfect Victim could only be Christ. No one else could fit the bill, so to speak!

In the Sin-Offering, Christ would be the sin-bearer of the whole world, but in this, He would be looked at by God as even more holy than in the representation of the Burnt-Offering.

HOLY

Verses 26 and 27 read: *"The Priest who offers it for sin shall eat it: in the Holy Place shall it be eaten, in the Court of the Tabernacle of the congregation.*

"Whatsoever shall touch the flesh thereof shall be holy: and when there is sprinkled of the blood thereof upon any garment, you shall wash that whereon it was sprinkled in the Holy Place."

God gave the Sin-Offering as food for the Priests to bear the iniquity of the congregation, and to make Atonement for them (Lev. 10:17). Once again, we go back to St. John, Chapter 6, in the eating of the flesh and the drinking of the blood regarding Christ.

The flesh provided by the Sin-Offering constituted a part of the livelihood of the Priests, as it constitutes our spiritual livelihood presently (Ezek. 44:28-29). The officiating Priest to whom fell this obligation could invite not only his family, but other Priests and their sons to partake of it. Covetous Priests abused this gift (Hos. 4:8).

It was to be eaten in the Holy Place of the Sanctuary. In fact, eight of the Offerings (there were others beside the blood sacrifices) had to be eaten in the precincts of the Sanctuary:

1. The flesh of the Sin-Offering (Lev. 4:26).
2. The flesh of the Trespass-Offering (Lev. 7:6).
3. The Peace-Offering of the congregation (Lev. 23:19-20).
4. The remainder of the Omer (Lev. 23:10-11).
5. The Meat-Offering of the Israelites (Lev. 2:3-10).
6. The two loaves (Lev. 23:20).
7. The Shewbread (Lev. 24:9).
8. The leper's log of oil (Lev. 14:10-13).

THE BLOOD

So peculiarly sacred was the Sin-Offering, that when any of its blood chanced to spurt upon the garment of the officiating Priest, or the one who brought the Sacrifice, the spot which received the stain had to be washed in the room of the Court provided for this purpose, wherein was a well which supplied the water for the Sanctuary, thus preventing the blood from being profaned outside the Holy Place (Ellicott).

This proclaims to us the preciousness of the Blood.

It was to be handled in two ways. If it pertained to the Priest who had sinned, or the nation as a whole, some of the blood of the Sacrifice was to be sprinkled seven times on the Golden Altar, with blood then applied to the four horns of that Altar. The balance of the Blood was to be poured out at the base of the Brazen Altar.

If it was a ruler who sinned, or the common people, the blood was not to be sprinkled on the Golden Altar, or applied to its horns, but was rather to be applied to the horns of the Brazen Altar, and then poured out at its base.

All of this means that extra care had to be taken that none of the blood was spilled any other place. If even one drop was spilled upon the garment of the Priest who was doing the officiating, as stated, his garment had to be washed immediately, and done so in a particular place, i.e., *"the Holy Place."*

As stated, this proclaims the preciousness of the blood, and as well, that it was the shed Blood of Christ that brought about our Salvation, and because it represented the poured out life of Christ on the Cross (Eph. 2:13-18).

THE AWFULNESS OF SIN

Verses 28 through 30 read: *"But the earthen vessel wherein it is sodden shall be broken: and if it be sodden in a brazen pot, it shall be both scoured, and rinsed in water.*

"All the males among the Priests shall eat thereof: it is most holy.

"And no Sin-Offering, whereof any of the blood is brought into the Tabernacle of the congregation to reconcile withal in the Holy Place, shall be eaten: it shall be burnt in the fire."

We learn from this of the awfulness of sin. So desperate a malady is sin that anything that came in contact with the Sin-Offering had to be washed, broken, or scoured.

All these regulations were calculated to express the polluting nature of sin, and the translation of guilt from the sinner to the Sacrifice. We learn from this, as well, that there are no such things as venial sins (small sins); the least sin deserves death.

THE BELIEVER AND SIN

This means that if we properly understand sin as we ought to, at the same time, in order to have peace, we, as well, must understand the Cross. In fact, many Believers, because of the guilt of condemnation, have been led to a mental and emotional anguish, that has robbed them of all peace. In fact, some have even committed suicide under such stress.

If a Believer *"walks after the flesh"* (Rom. 8:1), such a Believer will have a miserable lifestyle, and because of condemnation. He may confess the opposite, may deny such, but trying to ignore a 3,000 pound elephant in one's living room takes a stretch of the imagination. In other words, it cannot be done!

The more consecrated a Believer is, the more this problem presents itself. Such a Believer wants to live right, wants to walk right, wants to be right, but finds themselves, despite all of their efforts otherwise, doing wrong, with the wrong continually getting worse. In fact, the Seventh Chapter of Romans bears this out. It concludes with Paul saying: *"O wretched man that I am! Who shall deliver me from the body of this death?"* (Rom. 7:24). Regrettably, that's the exact state which most of Christendom presently finds itself. They do not know how to address sin, at least according to the Word of God, which means they don't know how to have victory over sin.

THE BELIEVER AND THE CROSS

The only answer for sin, which is the problem, is the Cross. While many in the Church may allude to other things, may claim other things, the truth is, sin is the problem. This is abruptly clear in the teaching given us in the Law of the various Offerings. Some may claim the problem to be physical, while others claim it to be emotional. Others may claim that it is domestical, or material; however, irrespective as to what the problem might be, the root cause in some way is sin. It may be the sin of someone else, or it may be the sin of the individual in question, but the cause, indirect or direct, is sin, and is always sin! That's the reason it is hopeless and helpless to try to address the problem any other way. That's the reason that humanistic psychology is such a crock; and as well, the same can be said for those who promote this wisdom of the world.

Humanistic psychology, nor any other effort by man, can address itself to the sin question. It is the Cross and the Cross alone that answers this horrible malady of the human race. And let us say it again:

There is no answer for sin but the Cross. If we try something else, we try in vain! If we look to anything else, we look in vain! If we claim anything else, we claim such in vain!

WHAT IS THE CHURCH DOING ABOUT THE CROSS?

Now let me ask this question:

How is the modern Church addressing its problems? The answer to that is obvious. It is looking to anything and everything except the Cross. Let me give you an example:

Concerning the Assemblies of God, the largest Pentecostal Denomination, if a Preacher has a problem, unless he is signed off by a Psychologist, he can never be accepted in good standing. This means that there is no Faith in the Cross, but rather the frail efforts of pitiful man. And to be sure, most every other Pentecostal Denomination falls into the same category, at least those of which I am aware.

But the Holy Spirit is bringing the Message of the Cross into full view of the Church, to where it has absolutely no choice but to either publicly reject it, or accept it. As we've said repeatedly, the Cross of Christ is the dividing line between the True Church and the apostate Church. In fact, it has always been that way; however, the Holy Spirit is making the Cross of Christ, and all for which it stands, so prominent that it can no longer be ignored (I Cor. 1:17-18, 21, 23; 2:2; Eph. 2:13-18; Col. 2:14-15; Gal. 6:14).

CHRIST AND HIS SACRIFICE

The *"Sin-Offering,"* whose blood was brought into the Sanctuary, symbolizes

NOTES

Christ bearing before God the sin of the whole word. The *"Sin-Offering,"* whose blood was not so brought in, but whose flesh was eaten by the Priests presents Christ as making His Own the sins of the individual sinner, who believes upon Him.

The meaning of Verse 30 is this:

Regarding the sins of Priests and of the nation of Israel as a whole, the blood was to be brought into the Tabernacle, sprinkled seven times on the Golden Altar, and as well, with blood applied to the four horns. The flesh of this animal, which served as the Sin-Offering, was not to be eaten by the Priests, but was to be taken out to a clean place, in fact where the ashes were taken, and there, *"burnt in the fire."*

If it was a Sin-Offering, which referred to Rulers and the common people, the blood then was not taken into the Holy Place, but was rather applied to the four horns of the Brazen Altar, and then poured out at the base. Of the flesh of this particular animal, the Priests could partake.

It all had to do with where the blood was applied.

This tells us, as should be obvious, that the sins of Priests, and of the nation as a whole, which latter was probably carried out because of the sins of the Priests, and we speak of sins of ignorance, constituted itself as that which was more serious. So the flesh of such an Offering could not be eaten, but had to be burned.

As previously stated, it is the same presently, with the thousands of Preachers who sin ignorantly, thereby causing the Church to sin, when they tell people how to live for God, but in all the wrong ways. In other words, they are telling them to live for the Lord outside of the boundaries of the Cross, which is sin! With many of these Preachers, it is done through ignorance, but it is still sin, and it will still cause great problems in the Body of Christ. The only answer to the dilemma is for the Preacher to understand the Cross, and then to preach the Cross to his people. This is why Paul said: *"We preach Christ Crucified"* (I Cor. 1:23).

"Five bleeding wounds He bears,
"Received on Calvary;

"They pour effectual prayers,
"They strongly speak for me;
"Forgive him, O forgive, they cry,
"Nor let that ransomed sinner die."

"The Father hears Him pray,
"His dear Anointed One;
"He cannot turn away,
"Cannot refuse His Son;
"His Spirit answers to the Blood,
"And tells us we are born of God."

CHAPTER 7

(1) "LIKEWISE THIS IS THE LAW OF THE TRESPASS-OFFERING: IT IS MOST HOLY.

(2) "IN THE PLACE WHERE THEY KILL THE BURNT-OFFERING SHALL THEY KILL THE TRESPASS-OFFERING: AND THE BLOOD THEREOF SHALL HE SPRINKLE ROUND ABOUT UPON THE ALTAR.

(3) "AND HE SHALL OFFER OF IT ALL THE FAT THEREOF; THE RUMP, AND THE FAT THAT COVERS THE INWARDS,

(4) "AND THE TWO KIDNEYS, AND THE FAT THAT IS ON THEM, WHICH IS BY THE FLANKS, AND THE CAUL THAT IS ABOVE THE LIVER, WITH THE KIDNEYS, IT SHALL HE TAKE AWAY:

(5) "AND THE PRIEST SHALL BURN THEM UPON THE ALTAR FOR AN OFFERING MADE BY FIRE UNTO THE LORD: IT IS A TRESPASS-OFFERING.

(6) "EVERY MALE AMONG THE PRIESTS SHALL EAT THEREOF: IT SHALL BE EATEN IN THE HOLY PLACE: IT IS MOST HOLY.

(7) "AS THE SIN-OFFERING IS, SO IS THE TRESPASS-OFFERING: THERE IS ONE LAW FOR THEM: THE PRIEST WHO MAKES ATONEMENT THEREWITH SHALL HAVE IT.

(8) "AND THE PRIEST WHO OFFERS ANY MAN'S BURNT-OFFERING, EVEN THE PRIEST SHALL HAVE TO HIMSELF THE SKIN OF THE BURNT-OFFERING WHICH HE HAS OFFERED.

(9) "AND ALL THE MEAT-OFFERING THAT IS BAKED IN THE OVEN, AND ALL THAT IS DRESSED IN THE FRYINGPAN, AND IN THE PAN, SHALL BE THE PRIEST'S WHO OFFERS IT.

(10) "AND EVERY MEAT-OFFERING, MINGLED WITH OIL, AND DRY, SHALL ALL THE SONS OF AARON HAVE, ONE AS MUCH AS ANOTHER."

The exegesis is:

1. The Trespass-Offering was most holy as well.

2. The requirements for the Trespass-Offering were very similar to the Sin-Offering. Both were intended as remedies for the sins of spiritual weakness, attending upon life still subject to the trials and temptations of this world.

3. One point of difference between them was in the mode of disposing of the blood. Both were bloody Offerings, but the blood in the case of the Sin-Offering was to be put on the four horns of the Altar, and in the Trespass-Offering, it was to be sprinkled *"round about upon the Altar."*

THE LAW OF THE TRESPASS-OFFERING

Verses 1 through 5 read: *"Likewise this is the Law of the Trespass-Offering: it is most holy.*

"In the place where they kill the Burnt-Offering shall they kill the Trespass-Offering: and the blood thereof shall he sprinkle round about upon the Altar.

"And he shall offer of it all the fat thereof; the rump, and the fat that covers the inwards,

"And the two kidneys, and the fat that is on them, which is by the flanks, and the caul that is above the liver, with the kidneys, it shall he take away:

"And the Priest shall burn them upon the Altar for an Offering made by fire unto the LORD: it is a Trespass-Offering."

As stated, the Meat-Offering, the Sin-Offering, and the Trespass-Offering were labeled *"most holy."* The Whole Burnt-Offering and the Peace-Offering were *"holy,"* but they were not labeled as *"most holy."*

Why?

Without what Christ did at the Cross, sinful man couldn't be saved. That's the reason the Sin-Offering and the Trespass-Offering are labeled *"most holy."* The Meat-Offering falls into the same category, simply because in essence, it refers to thankfulness on our part for what He has done to deliver us from sin.

All of the instructions given here, by and large, pertain to the Priests. This means that the far greater responsibility lay with the Priests. As well, the glory of our Salvation does not lie with us, the sinner; it lies with the Lord Jesus Christ. About all the person could do under the old economy was to bring his Offering and to believe the instructions he was given concerning the Atonement. Likewise, at this particular time, under the New Covenant, all the failing Believer can do is to present himself before the Lord and believe. All the work is done by our Great High Priest.

According to Verses 2 through 5, the Priests were given careful instructions regarding the *"kidney,"* the *"caul,"* and the *"fat."* This represented the prosperity, the life, and the living of the individual, and that the Lord is the Author of such.

If it is to be noticed, the blood of the Trespass-Offering is not to be placed on the horns of the Altar, as was the rule in the ordinary Sin-Offering, but cast against the inner side of the Altar, as with the Burnt-Offering and Peace-Offering.

In all of these Sacrifices, with the exception of the Meat-Offering, there was an ample display of blood.

THE BLOOD

The Psalmist sings: *"How amiable are Your Tabernacles, O LORD of Hosts!"* (Ps. 84:1).

Concerning this, Seiss says: *"Approaching those admirable Courts, our attention would have been attracted on all sides with marks of blood. Before the Altar, 'blood'; on the horns of the Altar, 'blood'; in the midst of the Altar, 'blood'; on its top, at its base, on its sides, 'blood'; and tracked along into the deepest interior of the Tabernacle, 'blood'!"*

Most of humanity would think of such as disgusting, but he who has learned to look at things from a spiritual sense, thereby to see the blood in the realm of forgiveness and the Grace of God to lost sinners, will know how precious the blood is, and very well, how to appreciate it.

Paul said that the preaching of Christ

NOTES

Crucified was to the Jews a stumbling block, and to the Greeks foolishness; but to those of us who know what sin actually is, and what is implied in Redemption from it, will ever hail the announcement of the Cross as the most glad tidings that ever fell upon the ear of Earth.

MOST HOLY

Verses 6 through 10 read: *"Every male among the Priests shall eat thereof: it shall be eaten in the Holy Place: it is most holy.*

"As the Sin-Offering is, so is the Trespass-Offering: there is one law for them: the Priest who makes Atonement therewith shall have it.

"And the Priest who offers any man's Burnt-Offering, even the Priest shall have to himself the skin of the Burnt-Offering which he has offered.

"And all the Meat-Offering that is baked in the oven, and all that is dressed in the fryingpan, and in the pan, shall be the Priest's who offers it.

"And every Meat-Offering, mingled with oil, and dry, shall all the sons of Aaron have, one as much as another."

We may grow weary at all of these tedious instructions, which is the reason the Book of Leviticus is seldom read; however, if we fully understand the sin question, and what it took to redeem humanity from its awful clutches, which of course was the Cross, to which all of these instructions point, then we would linger long over every word, asking the Holy Spirit to more and more reveal the meanings to our hearts.

Understanding the Meat-Offering, the Sin-Offering, and the Trespass-Offering, as most holy, proclaims to us, in no uncertain terms, the absolute Holiness, the *"most Holiness,"* of the Cross of Calvary.

The *"Sin-Offering"* and the *"Trespass-Offering"* were so very similar that there was actually one Law for the both of them. The same rule, as stated in Leviticus 6:27-28, applies to both Offerings; hence what is omitted in the regulation of the one must be supplied from the directions given in the other (Ellicott).

THE BURNT-OFFERING

Attached to the instructions given regarding

the Trespass-Offering, there are various instructions again given, as it regards the Burnt-Offering, and the Meat-Offering.

For instance, the Burnt-Offering was consumed totally on the Altar, with the exception of the skin. This was to be stripped from the carcass, and given to the officiating Priests.

As well, as it regarded the Meat-Offering, with the exception of the memorial part, which was burnt upon the Altar, it was to go to the particular Priest who offered it.

All the Priests were to share equally, according to the instructions given by the Lord.

(11) "AND THIS IS THE LAW OF THE SACRIFICE OF PEACE-OFFERINGS, WHICH HE SHALL OFFER UNTO THE LORD.

(12) "IF HE OFFER IT FOR A THANKS-GIVING, THEN HE SHALL OFFER WITH THE SACRIFICE OF THANKSGIVING UN-LEAVENED CAKES MINGLED WITH OIL, AND UNLEAVENED WAFERS ANOINTED WITH OIL, AND CAKES MINGLED WITH OIL, OF FINE FLOUR, FRIED.

(13) "BESIDES THE CAKES, HE SHALL OFFER FOR HIS OFFERING LEAVENED BREAD WITH THE SACRI-FICE OF THANKSGIVING OF HIS PEACE-OFFERINGS.

(14) "AND OF IT HE SHALL OFFER ONE OUT OF THE WHOLE OBLATION FOR AN HEAVE-OFFERING UNTO THE LORD, AND IT SHALL BE THE PRIEST'S WHO SPRINKLES THE BLOOD OF THE PEACE-OFFERINGS.

(15) "AND THE FLESH OF THE SAC-RIFICE OF HIS PEACE-OFFERINGS FOR THANKSGIVING SHALL BE EATEN THE SAME DAY THAT IT IS OFFERED; HE SHALL NOT LEAVE ANY OF IT UNTIL THE MORNING.

(16) "BUT IF THE SACRIFICE OF HIS OFFERING BE A VOW, OR A VOLUNTARY OFFERING, IT SHALL BE EATEN THE SAME DAY THAT HE OFFERS HIS SACRI-FICE: AND ON THE MORROW ALSO THE REMAINDER OF IT SHALL BE EATEN:

(17) "BUT THE REMAINDER OF THE FLESH OF THE SACRIFICE ON THE THIRD DAY SHALL BE BURNT WITH FIRE.

(18) "AND IF ANY OF THE FLESH OF

NOTES

THE SACRIFICE OF HIS PEACE-OFFER-INGS BE EATEN AT ALL ON THE THIRD DAY, IT SHALL NOT BE ACCEPTED, NEI-THER SHALL IT BE IMPUTED UNTO HIM WHO OFFERS IT: IT SHALL BE AN ABOMINATION, AND THE SOUL THAT EATS OF IT SHALL BEAR HIS INIQUITY.

(19) "AND THE FLESH THAT TOUCHES ANY UNCLEAN THING SHALL NOT BE EATEN; IT SHALL BE BURNT WITH FIRE: AND AS FOR THE FLESH, ALL THAT BE CLEAN SHALL EAT THEREOF.

(20) "BUT THE SOUL THAT EATS OF THE FLESH OF THE SACRIFICE OF PEACE-OFFERINGS, AND THAT PERTAIN UNTO THE LORD, HAVING HIS UNCLEAN-NESS UPON HIM, EVEN THAT SOUL SHALL BE CUT OFF FROM HIS PEOPLE.

(21) "MOREOVER THE SOUL THAT SHALL TOUCH ANY UNCLEAN THING, AS THE UNCLEANNESS OF MAN, OR ANY UNCLEAN BEAST, OR ANY ABOMINABLE UNCLEAN THING, AND EAT OF THE FLESH OF THE SACRIFICE OF PEACE-OFFERINGS, WHICH PERTAIN UNTO THE LORD, EVEN THAT SOUL SHALL BE CUT OFF FROM HIS PEOPLE."

The diagram is:

1. Verses 11 through 21 portray the *"Law of the Sacrifice of Peace-Offerings."*

2. Verse 12 tells us that the *"Peace-Offer-ings"* were at times offered as a *"thanksgiving."*

3. In Verse 13, the offerer is instructed to use *"leavened bread with the Sacrifice."* This was permitted in the *"Thank-Offering,"* even though it was a form of corruption, and thereby a type of sin, because this was the spontaneous expression of devotion from lives that were not entirely rid of sin and evil in every case.

4. The eating of the *"leavened bread"* was a constant reminder that the offerer was a poor, weak sinner, and that all of the Grace was in the Lord Jesus Christ.

5. There were some Offerings of Thanks-giving that were given with *"unleavened cakes,"* which signify the perfect, unblem-ished, sinless body of the Lord Jesus Christ.

6. Verse 15 indicates that the offerer of the Peace-Offering could have a feast with his friends, which would symbolize the Bless-ings of the Lord.

7. Verse 19 speaks of *"touching any unclean thing."* This principal, which made one unclean, also applied to touching any holy thing which made one clean or holy. It typifies two things: first of all, the touching of Satan (his works) makes one unholy, and touching Christ makes one holy.

THE LAW OF THE SACRIFICE OF PEACE-OFFERINGS

Verses 11 through 15 read: *"And this is the Law of the Sacrifice of Peace-Offerings, which he shall offer unto the LORD.*

"If he offer it for a Thanksgiving, then he shall offer with the Sacrifice of Thanksgiving unleavened cakes mingled with oil, and unleavened wafers anointed with oil, and cakes mingled with oil, of fine flour, fried.

"Besides the cakes, he shall offer for his Offering leavened bread with the Sacrifice of Thanksgiving of his Peace-Offerings.

"And of it he shall offer one out of the whole oblation for an Heave-Offering unto the LORD, and it shall be the Priest's who sprinkles the blood of the Peace-Offerings.

"And the flesh of the Sacrifice of his Peace-Offerings for Thanksgiving shall be eaten the same day that it is offered; he shall not leave any of it until the morning."

The Law of the Peace-Offering commanded unleavened cakes (Vs. 12) and leavened bread (Vs. 13). The first symbolized the sinless humanity of Christ; the other, the sinful humanity of the worshipper. The One had sin on Him, actually our sin, but not in Him; the latter, the sinful worshipper, had sin in him, and on him.

The Peace-Offerings could be offered as a *"Thanksgiving-Offering,"* even as the Meat-Offering. This would be an acknowledgment of special mercies received from God, for whatever! It is to this Sacrifice that Paul alludes when he says, *"By Him therefore let us offer the Sacrifice of Praise to God continually"* (Heb. 13:15).

In Verses 12 through 14, no mention is made of the number of cakes or the quantity of oil. Consequently, this must have been left up to the decision of the Administrators of the laws, etc.

These *"cakes"* were to be eaten with the flesh of the Peace-Offering, and had to be baked before the victim was slaughtered.

These particular *"cakes"* were to be unleavened, and because they represented the sinless humanity of Christ.

But along with these cakes, he was to also offer, *"leavened bread,"* which he would also eat. It was *"leavened"* simply because it represented the life of the offerer, which was not completely free from sin, as no human being is completely free from sin.

The Peace-Offering was offered at times after the other Offerings. It was the only Offering of which the offerer could partake. A small portion was to be burnt on the Brazen Altar, a portion given to the Priests, of which we will address momentarily, with the offerer taking the remainder. With this, he could have a feast with his friends and family, signifying that Peace with God had been restored. Sin, in whatever form, destroys that peace; consequently, the proper sacrifices have to be offered in order to atone for the sin. Then the Peace-Offering could be offered.

There were four different kinds of cakes – *"unleavened cakes mingled with oil,"* *"unleavened wafers anointed with oil,"* *"cakes mingled with oil, of fine flour, fried,"* and lastly, there was the *"leavened bread."*

Of these four different types of cakes or bread, the officiating Priest was to wave one of each of the four kinds before the Lord as a *"Heave-Offering"* (Ex. 29:24, 28). After he waved them before the Lord in Thanksgiving to the Lord, he could have these four loaves as his portion, with the rest or the remaining cakes belonging to the owner of the Sacrifice, which he could partake of with the roasted flesh of the Sacrifice.

To the Priest was given the *"breast"* and the *"shoulder,"* of the animal. The one bringing the Sacrifice would be given that which remained, with the exception of the fat, etc., which was burned on the Altar (Lev. 7:4-5). But there was one stipulation:

All of the flesh of the Peace-Offering had to be eaten the same day it was offered. None was to be left until the morning.

This typified that we must partake of all of Christ, and not merely a part of Christ. Many desire Him as Saviour, but reject Him as the Baptizer with the Holy Spirit. In fact, this list is long, with many picking and choosing.

Sorry! According to the Scriptures, such cannot be done. It is all of Christ, or none of Christ!

BLESSINGS AND THE CROSS

Verses 16 through 18 read: *"But if the Sacrifice of his Offering be a vow, or a voluntary Offering, it shall be eaten the same day that he offers his Sacrifice: and on the morrow also the remainder of it shall be eaten:*

"But the remainder of the flesh of the Sacrifice on the third day shall be burnt with fire.

"And if any of the flesh of the Sacrifice of his Peace-Offerings be eaten at all on the third day, it shall not be accepted, neither shall it be imputed unto him who offers it: it shall be an abomination, and the soul that eats of it shall bear his iniquity."

The Peace-Offering for Thanksgiving was eaten the same day that it was offered; the Peace-Offering for a vow, the same day or the next day – because a vow, or a voluntary Offering, necessarily affected the heart more than an ordinary Thanksgiving. Concerning this, Williams said:

"This Law taught the offerer to closely associate the death and sufferings of the slain lamb with the blessings for which he gave thanks.

"It teaches men today the same lesson. To disassociate worship and thanksgiving from the anguish and blood-shedding of the Lord Jesus, in other words, to separate all of this from the Cross, is to offer to God an abomination, and to bring death into the soul and into the Church."

UNCLEANNESS

Verses 19 through 21 read: *"And the flesh that touches any unclean thing shall not be eaten; it shall be burnt with fire: and as for the flesh, all that be clean shall eat thereof.*

"But the soul that eats of the flesh of the Sacrifice of Peace-Offerings, that pertain unto the LORD, having his uncleanness upon him, even that soul shall be cut off from his people.

"Moreover the soul that shall touch any unclean thing, as the uncleanness of man, or any unclean beast, or any abominable unclean thing, and eat of the flesh of the

NOTES

Sacrifice of Peace-Offerings, which pertain unto the LORD, even that soul shall be cut off from his people."

Ceremonial cleanliness was obligatory before eating the Peace-Offering. Disobedience in this matter entailed death. To profess Faith in the Person and Atonement of Christ, and claim fellowship with Him, and be secretly unclean, ensures the Wrath of God. This proclaims the following truth vividly:

Jesus Christ saves us from sin, not in sin. The idea that the Believer is no different from the unbeliever, with the exception of Faith in Christ, could not be more wrong. The idea that we can claim Faith in Christ, while at the same time continuing in the sin business, as well, could not be more wrong. These Old Testament types completely repudiate such erroneous thinking.

THE WAY OUT OF SIN

The Lord has a way that the Believer can overcome the *"law of sin and death."* It is by the *"Law of the Spirit of Life in Christ Jesus"* (Rom. 8:2). By the word *"Law"* being used, this means that the Holy Spirit works within the confines of that formulated by the Godhead. And what are those confines?

The phrase *"in Christ Jesus,"* explains what it is, and it refers to what Christ did at the Cross, and exclusively as to what Christ did at the Cross.

The Believer is to express Faith in Christ and His Finished Work, and to do so at all times. The Holy Spirit, Who works within the boundaries of the Finished Work of Christ, upon such Faith, will then work mightily on behalf of the Child of God, giving such a Believer total and complete victory over *"the law of sin and death."* But let it be understood that the *"Law of the Spirit of Life in Christ Jesus,"* is the only Law in the world that is more powerful than the law of sin and death. If the law of sin and death is approached in any other manner, there will be nothing but failure and wreckage. The Cross is the answer for sin, and the Cross alone is the answer for sin!

(22) "AND THE LORD SPOKE UNTO MOSES SAYING,

(23) "SPEAK UNTO THE CHILDREN OF ISRAEL, SAYING, YOU SHALL EAT NO

MANNER OF FAT, OF OX, OR OF SHEEP, OR OF GOAT.

(24) "AND THE FAT OF THE BEAST THAT DIES OF ITSELF, AND THE FAT OF THAT WHICH IS TORN WITH BEASTS, MAY BE USED IN ANY OTHER USE: BUT YOU SHALL IN NO WISE EAT OF IT.

(25) "FOR WHOSOEVER EATS THE FAT OF THE BEAST, OF WHICH MEN OFFER AN OFFERING MADE BY FIRE UNTO THE LORD, EVEN THE SOUL THAT EATS IT SHALL BE CUT OFF FROM HIS PEOPLE.

(26) "MOREOVER YOU SHALL EAT NO MANNER OF BLOOD, WHETHER IT BE OF FOWL OR OF BEAST, IN ANY OF YOUR DWELLINGS.

(27) "WHATSOEVER SOUL IT BE THAT EATS ANY MANNER OF BLOOD, EVEN THAT SOUL SHALL BE CUT OFF FROM HIS PEOPLE."

The structure is:

1. The fat of the Peace-Offering was to be wholly given to God, because it symbolized the excellent affections of His dearly-beloved Son, and as well, the spiritual prosperity that comes to Believers through His Son.

2. The fat of any animal that died, or was accidentally killed, might be used for other purposes, but not eaten. Similarly was the blood precious.

3. The blood was precious for two reasons: first of all, the life of the flesh is in the blood; second, the Precious Blood of Christ, which was shed on the Cross, provides the saving factor for Redemption (Jn. 3:16).

THE FAT

Verses 22 through 25 read: *"And the LORD spoke unto Moses, saying,*

"Speak unto the Children of Israel, saying, You shall eat no manner of fat, of ox, or of sheep, or of goat.

"And the fat of the beast that dies of itself, and the fat of that which is torn with beasts, may be used in any other use: but you shall in no wise eat of it.

"For whosoever eats the fat of the beast, of which men offer an Offering made by fire unto the LORD, even the soul that eats it shall be cut off from his people."

Fat is first mentioned in the Bible in Genesis 4:4, where it is said that Abel offered the

fat of the firstlings of his flock to the Lord. Evidently, in giving instructions to the first family, the Lord had instructed them that the fat of sacrificed animals belonged exclusively to Him.

The fat of sacrificial animals, such as heifers, sheep, or goats, could not be eaten, irrespective as to whether the animal was to be offered in Sacrifice or not. But the fat of other tame or wild animals that are clean, such as deer, etc., was lawful to be eaten.

Why this prohibition of fat, and as well, that it had to be burned on the Altar as belonging to Jehovah, and must be burned the same day the sacrificial animal was slain?

The best animals were to be offered in Sacrifice, as would be obvious, and the fat of the animal signified its health and prosperity. Consequently, it served as a type of God giving His very best as it regards the Lord Jesus Christ, from Whom we receive all things from the Lord.

As well, the fat being burned on the Altar symbolizes the means by which all of these good things come to us, and that is through the Cross.

THE BLOOD

Verses 26 and 27 read: *"Moreover you shall eat no manner of blood, whether it be of fowl or of beast, in any of your dwellings.*

"Whatsoever soul it be that eats any manner of blood, even that soul shall be cut off from his people."

The prohibition against the eating of blood was brought over into the New Covenant (Acts 15:19-20).

Concerning this, Williams said, *"The reverence due to the Person and to the Work of the Messiah was enjoined by the two laws respecting the 'fat' and the 'blood.' They express excellency and efficiency. 'This is My Beloved Son' declared the one; and 'Peace through the Blood of His Cross,' proclaimed the other"* (Col. 1:20).

(28) "AND THE LORD SPOKE UNTO MOSES, SAYING,

(29) "SPEAK UNTO THE CHILDREN OF ISRAEL, SAYING, HE WHO OFFERS THE SACRIFICE OF HIS PEACE-OFFERINGS UNTO THE LORD SHALL BRING HIS OBLATION UNTO THE LORD OF THE

SACRIFICE OF HIS PEACE-OFFERINGS.

(30) "HIS OWN HANDS SHALL BRING THE OFFERINGS OF THE LORD MADE BY FIRE, THE FAT WITH THE BREAST, IT SHALL HE BRING, THAT THE BREAST MAY BE WAVED FOR A WAVE-OFFERING BEFORE THE LORD.

(31) "AND THE PRIEST SHALL BURN THE FAT UPON THE ALTAR: BUT THE BREAST SHALL BE AARON'S AND HIS SONS'.

(32) "AND THE RIGHT SHOULDER SHALL YOU GIVE UNTO THE PRIEST FOR AN HEAVE-OFFERING OF THE SACRIFICES OF YOUR PEACE-OFFERINGS.

(33) "IIE AMONG THE SONS OF AARON, WHO OFFERS THE BLOOD OF THE PEACE-OFFERINGS, AND THE FAT, SHALL HAVE THE RIGHT SHOULDER FOR HIS PART.

(34) "FOR THE WAVE BREAST AND THE HEAVE SHOULDER HAVE I TAKEN OF THE CHILDREN OF ISRAEL FROM OFF THE SACRIFICES OF THEIR PEACE-OFFERINGS, AND HAVE GIVEN THEM UNTO AARON THE PRIEST AND UNTO HIS SONS BY A STATUTE FOREVER FROM AMONG THE CHILDREN OF ISRAEL.

(35) "THIS IS THE PORTION OF THE ANOINTING OF AARON, AND OF THE ANOINTING OF HIS SONS, OUT OF THE OFFERINGS OF THE LORD MADE BY FIRE, IN THE DAY WHEN HE PRESENTED THEM TO MINISTER UNTO THE LORD IN THE PRIEST'S OFFICE;

(36) "WHICH THE LORD COMMANDED TO BE GIVEN THEM OF THE CHILDREN OF ISRAEL, IN THE DAY THAT HE ANOINTED THEM, BY A STATUTE FOREVER THROUGHOUT THEIR GENERATIONS.

(37) "THIS IS THE LAW OF THE BURNT-OFFERING, OF THE MEAT-OFFERING, AND OF THE SIN-OFFERING, AND OF THE TRESPASS-OFFERING, AND OF THE CONSECRATIONS, AND OF THE SACRIFICE OF THE PEACE-OFFERINGS;

(38) "WHICH THE LORD COMMANDED MOSES IN MOUNT SINAI, IN THE DAY THAT HE COMMANDED THE CHILDREN OF ISRAEL TO OFFER THEIR OBLATIONS UNTO THE LORD, IN THE

NOTES

WILDERNESS OF SINAI."

The construction is:

1. The following is the Law of the Sacrifice of Peace-Offerings.

2. The wave breast and the heave shoulder were to be eaten by the Priests.

3. Before it was eaten, the *"breast"* was to be lifted up on high by the Priest, and then waved before the Lord. The *"shoulder"* before it was eaten, was to be heaved, which means to be lifted up before God as expressive of its preciousness and acceptability to Him.

4. The *"breast"* that was *"waved"* was to be waved to the four corners of the Earth as setting forth the sufficiency of this Offering to give life to the world, namely Christ.

5. Further, Christ's shoulder upholds, and His breast consoles, all those who trust in Him.

THE LAW OF THE SACRIFICE OF THE PEACE-OFFERINGS

Verses 28 and 29 read: *"And the LORD spoke unto Moses, saying,*

"Speak unto the Children of Israel, saying, He who offers the Sacrifice of his Peace-Offerings unto the LORD shall bring his oblation unto the LORD of the Sacrifice of His Peace-Offerings."

The Peace-Offerings, as stated, were actually what their name specified. The Peace-Offering being offered to God signified that peace had been interrupted by sin, and now had been restored. The Offering of their Sacrifice generally followed the Sacrifices of the Burnt-Offering, and even the Sin-Offering, and Trespass-Offering.

In the Burnt-Offering, sin was not directly involved. This Sacrifice represented Christ giving His Life, satisfying the demands of a thrice-Holy God. Only a perfect Sacrifice could serve, and only Christ, God's only Son, could fit that particular bill. But of course, irrespective as to the reason Christ was on the Cross, the necessity of such was all because of sin. In fact, until the Law of Moses was given, all the Offerings from the time of Abel were, in fact, Whole Burnt-Offerings.

In that peace was restored, the one who offered the Sacrifice would be given a portion, that he might have a feast with his family and friends, signifying the restoration. It was to be a festive occasion of joy! The Priests were to receive a portion as well, which we will address momentarily. In the realm of the fat, which was to be burned on the Altar, as it always was to be burned, God, as well, would receive His portion. This signified that He had accepted the Sacrifice.

In fact, in a sense, He always accepted the Sacrifices, irrespective as to the condition of the offerer. In fact, it was the Sacrifice which was minutely inspected, and never the offerer of the Sacrifice. If the Sacrifice was accepted, the offerer was accepted as well. It is the same presently!

We are accepted by God not at all because of who we are, but rather because of Who and What Christ is. He has been inspected minutely by God the Father, and accepted on all points, thereby, Faith in Him guarantees our acceptance (Jn. 3:16; Eph. 2:8-9, 13-18; Col. 2:14-15).

THE WAVE OFFERING AND THE HEAVE OFFERING

Verses 30 through 34 read: *"His own hands shall bring the Offerings of the LORD made by fire, the fat with the breast, it shall he bring, that the breast may be waved for a Wave-Offering before the LORD.*

"And the Priest shall burn the fat upon the Altar: but the breast shall be Aaron's and his sons'.

"And the right shoulder shall you give unto the Priest for an Heave-Offering of the Sacrifices of your Peace-Offerings.

"He among the sons of Aaron, who offers the blood of the Peace-Offerings, and the fat, shall have the right shoulder for his part.

"For the wave breast and the heave shoulder have I taken of the Children of Israel from off the Sacrifices of their Peace-Offerings, and have given them unto Aaron the Priest and unto his sons by a Statute forever from among the Children of Israel."

1. The one who offered a *"Peace-Offering"* was to give a portion of it to the Priest. The Priest was a type of Christ, and as such, the part being given to Him shows that He Alone could effect *"peace."* As stated, the *"fat"* burned on the Altar from the Sacrifice, signified the manner in which Christ has made it possible for Believers to have

peace. It is by Faith and trust solely in the Cross of Christ.

2. The *"right shoulder"* was to be given to the Priest offering the *"blood"* of Atonement and who burned the *"fat."* The *"shoulder"* and the *"breast"* signify the *"strength"* and the *"love"* of the Lord Jesus Christ given unto His people.

3. The *"Wave-Offering"* derived its name from the fact that whatever was offered was waved first of all toward the Brazen Altar, symbolizing the price that Christ would pay, and thanking Him for paying it, and then the Priest would turn, continuing to lift the Offering high, and wave the breast toward the four corners of the universe, in effect saying that what Christ would do at the Cross would suffice for all.

4. The *"Heave-Offering"* was a little bit different than the *"Wave-Offering"* in that the *"Heave-Offering"* was lifted up and down several times, up as a symbol of offering it to God Who is above, and down again as a symbol of God coming to this Earth and becoming man in the form of the Lord Jesus Christ.

A STATUTE FOREVER

Verses 35 through 38 read: *"This is the portion of the anointing of Aaron, and of the anointing of his sons, out of the Offerings of the LORD made by fire, in the day when he presented them to minister unto the LORD in the Priest's Office;*

"Which the LORD commanded to be given them of the Children of Israel, in the day that He anointed them, by a Statute forever throughout their generations.

"This is the Law of the Burnt-Offering, of the Meat-Offering, and of the Sin-Offering, and of the Trespass-Offering, and of the consecrations, and of the Sacrifice of the Peace-Offerings;

"Which the LORD commanded Moses in Mount Sinai, in the day that He commanded the Children of Israel to offer their oblations unto the LORD, in the wilderness of Sinai."

The *"portion"* mentioned here speaks of the *"Wave-Offering,"* and the *"Heave-Offering,"* which belonged to the Priests, which they could eat on the day of the offering of the Sacrifice.

The *"Statute"* that these two parts of the

Peace-Offering are to be given to Aaron and his descendants who may officiate at the Sacrifice, is binding upon the Israelites as long as the Priesthood lasts (Ellicott).

All of this was given to Moses on Mount Sinai. It was the greatest legislation by far that the world had ever known. It was in totality instituted by God. Man had no part whatsoever in this which was given, all originating by the Lord.

However, all of this given was totally and completely formulated for man. The Lord, as should be obvious, didn't need such. This tells us several things:

First of all, it tells us of the awfulness of sin. I'm afraid that we do not quite realize the deadliness of this horror. We may chaff at the minute instructions given, meaning little to us presently; however, if we understand all of these Laws and Statutes, as referring to the Lord Jesus Christ, and what He would do at the Cross, then they take on a brand-new meaning.

In fact, it is impossible for one to properly understand the New Testament unless one properly understands the Old Testament. And then when we are made to realize that Jesus has paid it all, in other words satisfying every single rule and regulation, and did so by the Sacrificial Offering of Himself on the Cross, then we are made to realize the greatness of Christ.

"Marvelous message we bring,
"Glorious carol we sing,
"Wonderful Word of the King:
"Jesus is coming again!"

"Forest and flower exclaim,
"Mountain and meadow the same,
"All Earth and Heaven proclaim:
"Jesus is coming again!"

"Standing before Him at last,
"Trial, and trouble all past,
"Crowns at His feet we will cast:
"Jesus is coming again!"

CHAPTER 8

(1) "AND THE LORD SPOKE UNTO

MOSES, SAYING,

(2) "TAKE AARON AND HIS SONS WITH HIM, AND THE GARMENTS, AND THE ANOINTING OIL, AND A BULLOCK FOR THE SIN-OFFERING, AND TWO RAMS, AND A BASKET OF UNLEAVENED BREAD;

(3) "AND YOU GATHER ALL THE CONGREGATION TOGETHER UNTO THE DOOR OF THE TABERNACLE OF THE CONGREGATION.

(4) "AND MOSES DID AS THE LORD COMMANDED HIM; AND THE ASSEMBLY WAS GATHERED TOGETHER UNTO THE DOOR OF THE TABERNACLE OF THE CONGREGATION.

(5) "AND MOSES SAID UNTO THE CONGREGATION, THIS IS THE THING WHICH THE LORD COMMANDED TO BE DONE.

(6) "AND MOSES BROUGHT AARON AND HIS SONS, AND WASHED THEM WITH WATER.

(7) "AND HE PUT UPON HIM THE COAT, AND GIRDED HIM WITH THE GIRDLE, AND CLOTHED HIM WITH THE ROBE, AND PUT THE EPHOD UPON HIM, AND HE GIRDED HIM WITH THE CURIOUS GIRDLE OF THE EPHOD, AND BOUND IT UNTO HIM THEREWITH.

(8) "AND HE PUT THE BREASTPLATE UPON HIM: ALSO HE PUT IN THE BREASTPLATE THE URIM AND THE THUMMIM.

(9) "AND HE PUT THE MITRE UPON HIS HEAD; ALSO UPON THE MITRE, EVEN UPON HIS FOREFRONT, DID HE PUT THE GOLDEN PLATE, THE HOLY CROWN; AS THE LORD COMMANDED MOSES."

The composition is:

1. This Chapter pertains to the consecration of the Priests.

2. Even though Aaron had been chosen by the Lord as the Great High Priest, he and his sons, who were Priests as well, had to undergo the same Sacrificial Offerings as the worst sinner in Israel.

3. All of this was a reminder that even though Aaron was called, anointed, and directed by God, still, he was flawed flesh and needed a Redeemer.

4. The *"Anointing Oil"* was a Type of the Holy Spirit.

5. The *"bullock for the Sin-Offering"* and

"two rams" as well as the *"unleavened bread"* stood for sacrifice and cleansing, with the *"unleavened bread"* standing for the perfection demanded by God that could never be obtained except by Sacrifice.

6. All of the congregation of Israel were commanded to observe these rituals, that they may know and understand that Aaron, even though the Great High Priest, was still a poor mortal, exactly as they were.

7. The Fourth Verse speaks of commands. Note that these were not suggestions; they were commands. Moses must carry them out to the letter.

8. The *"washing with water"* spoke of cleansing, and was a type of that accomplished by the Blood and the Word.

9. *"The Coat"* speaks of Christ's Deity.

10. The *"Girdle"* spoke of the service of Christ to humanity.

11. The *"Robe"* spoke of His Righteousness.

12. The *"Ephod"* was that which had the names of the Children of Israel on each shoulder – six to a side. The Lord would carry His people on His shoulders.

13. The *"Breastplate"* of the Eighth Verse contained the 12 precious stones listing the names of the 12 Tribes of Israel. It was over the heart of the Great High Priest, referring to the fact that the Lord carries His people on His heart, as well as His shoulders.

14. In a pouch under the Breastplate were the *"Urim and the Thummim."* The two words meant *"lights and perfection."* They concerned the leading of the Holy Spirit.

15. The *"Mitre"* of the Ninth Verse speaks of authority. Jesus is the *"Head"* of the Church.

THE CONSECRATION OF THE PRIESTS

Verses 1 and 2 read: *"And the LORD spoke unto Moses, saying,*

"Take Aaron and his sons with him, and the garments, and the Anointing Oil, and a bullock for the Sin-Offering, and two rams, and a basket of unleavened bread."

As we study this Book of Leviticus, we will find that its major subject is *"a Sacrifice, a Priest, and a Place of Worship."* Chapters 8, 9, and 10 pertain to Priesthood. But Sacrifice is the foundation of it all. This speaks of the Cross of Christ. The sinner needs a Sacrifice; the worshipper needs a

Priest. Christ is both. The Place of Worship consummates in the Heavens, even as it originates in the Heavens.

Williams says: *"These three Chapters make prominent the following:*

1. *"The Authority of the Bible,*
2. *"The Preciousness of the Blood,*
3. *"The Power of the Holy Spirit."*

Even though all of this is very intricate, very detailed, and very complicated, but yet, all of it, and in every detail, points to Christ and what He would do to redeem humanity, which refers to the Cross. There is no way that any serious Bible student could study Leviticus and not see this of which we speak. The Book drips with blood, all speaking of the Blood that Christ would shed at the Cross. In some way, every single thing points to His Perfection, His Sacrifice of Himself, and His High Priestly Ministry, which continues unto this hour.

As a Sacrifice, and only as a Sacrifice, He introduces His people into a settled relationship with God; and as a Priest, our Great High Priest, He maintains us therein, according to the Perfection of what He is.

As sinners, by nature and by practice, we are *"brought near to God by the Blood of the Cross"*; we are brought into an established relationship with Him; we stand before Him as the fruit of His Own Work. He has put away our sins in such a manner as suits Himself, so that we might be before Him to the praise of His Name, as the exhibition of what He can accomplish through the power of death and Resurrection (Mackintosh).

OUR GREAT HIGH PRIEST

As this Chapter portrays the anointing of Aaron as the Great High Priest, the type of Christ, we are made to know and realize our need for the services, and in fact, the continued services, of our Great High Priest, the Lord Jesus Christ.

Even though we have been totally and completely delivered from all sin, and done so by our Faith in Christ and what He has done for us at the Cross, thereby perfectly accepted in the Beloved – though so complete in Christ – though so highly exalted (Eph. 2:6), yet are we still, in ourselves, poor feeble creatures, ever prone to wander, ready to stumble, exposed to manifold temptations, trials, and snares.

As such, and any honest Believer will have to admit such, we need, in fact we must have, the ceaseless Ministry of our *"Great High Priest,"* Whose very Presence in the Sanctuary above maintains us in the full integrity of that place and relationship in which, through Grace, we stand. Paul beautifully, but even bluntly writes: *"He ever lives to make Intercession for us"* (Heb. 7:25).

The truth is, we could not stand for a moment down here if He were not living for us up there. *"Because I live, you shall live also"* (Jn. 14:19).

WHAT IS INTERCESSION?

As it pertains to Christ, it is simply His Presence at the Throne of God, all on our behalf (Heb. 1:3), meaning that God has accepted Him, has accepted His Sacrifice of Himself, has accepted its Finished Work, and His very Presence before God guarantees Intercession on our behalf. If He had to do anything else, that would mean that the Work at Calvary was incomplete, which we know is not the case (Heb. 1:3).

Some Christians have the erroneous idea that Jesus has to pray for us, or plead our case before the Father, etc. While the spirit of that is definitely present, and because He most surely is our *"Advocate"* (I Jn. 2:1-2), still, He is that by His Presence, and His Presence Alone. If it is to be noticed, the Scripture says: *"For Christ is not entered into the holy places made with hands, which are the figures of the true* (referring to the Old Testament Tabernacle and Temple)*; but into Heaven itself, now to appear in the Presence of God for us"* (Heb. 9:24).

If it is to be noticed, the word *"appear"* is used here, meaning that His Presence before God guarantees Intercession.

In our understanding of the Scriptures, we must always comprehend the fact that Calvary paid it all. There is nothing left owing, nothing left to be done; it has all been done. In fact, religion says, *"do,"* while the true Gospel says, *"done!"*

As well, it's Heaven, and not Earth, which is the sphere of Christ's Priestly Ministry, although the effects of that Ministry are

definitely felt and experienced by all Believers. Christ is our Great High Priest.

In fact, there is no such thing now, and I speak of time since the Cross, that God recognizes any Priest upon this Earth. In fact, to be a Priest, one would have to show his descent from Aaron, and unless he can trace his pedigree to that ancient source, he has no right to exercise the Priestly Office. And in fact, even the sons of Aaron have no right, since Jesus has fulfilled all of the Old Testament types and shadows, which were designed to point to Him anyway, and which He settled by His Work at the Cross. Christ is our Mediator, and our Mediator alone, and there is no need for another. So for a man to say that he is a *"Priest,"* he is in effect saying, whether he realizes it or not, that Christ didn't finish His Work, and that He still needs the help of poor mortals. Because a Priest, and the only ones who were ever recognized as Priests were those under the Mosaic Covenant, actually serves as a mediator. This refers to a go-between, between to God and man. But since Jesus went to the Cross, He forever did away with the need for Earthly Priests. The Scripture plainly says: *"For there is one God, and one Mediator between God and men, the Man, Christ Jesus"* (I Tim. 2:5). Notice that the Scripture says *"one,"* not 1,000, not 500, not 10, not even two, just *"One,"* and that *"One"* is the Lord Jesus Christ. So the Priesthood of the Catholic Church, or any other religion for that matter, is an abomination in the eyes of God. It is the highest insult that can be tendered toward Christ and His Finished Work.

Incidentally, this Eighth Chapter of Leviticus goes back to Chapter 29 of Exodus, providing far more detail.

THE ANOINTING OIL

The oil was a Type of the Holy Spirit, which should be obvious. However, Aaron, even though a type of Christ, while having the Holy Spirit to help him regarding his Office, still, only had His help in a very limited way.

Before the Cross, while the Holy Spirit was definitely present in the world, and has been from the very beginning, his activities were very limited due to the fact that the blood of bulls and goats could not take away sins (Heb. 10:4). This means that the terrible sin debt, and we speak of original sin, etc., still hung over the heads of every Believer, so to speak, even the greatest ones of the Old Testament. In fact, this is the very reason that Jesus said of John the Baptist, who was the last great Prophet before Christ: *"Verily I say unto you, among them who are born of women there has not risen a greater than John the Baptist: notwithstanding he who is least in the Kingdom of Heaven is greater than he"* (Mat. 11:11).

What did Jesus mean by that statement?

He wasn't meaning that we are better morally or character wise than John the Baptist, but rather, since the Cross, we have far better privileges than those under the Old Covenant. Since the Cross, which incidentally paid the total sin debt, past, present, and future, at least for those who will believe, the Holy Spirit can now come into the heart and life of the Believer, which He does at conversion, to abide forever (Jn. 14:16). The Cross, and the Cross alone, has made everything possible.

THE BULLOCK, THE TWO RAMS, AND THE BASKET OF UNLEAVENED BREAD

As we enter into the consecration of the Priesthood, we find that even though Aaron was to be the Great High Priest, the closest type to Christ of any human being under the old economy, he and his sons, who were also Priests, had to undergo the same Sacrificial Offerings as the worst sinner in Israel.

As we look at these Sacrifices, we must be made to realize that even though a Righteous Sovereign may feel for and pity those whom He has created, still, He dare not have fellowship with them, except on the basis of judgment satisfied, hence the necessity of the Sacrifices, which would point to the One Who was to come, Who would be the Sacrifice, namely, the Lord Jesus Christ.

There is a great chasm between man and his God. The fallen one goes on sinning, and the wronged Sovereign must go on maintaining His Righteous administration. Man cannot of himself come to God, and is terrified when he thinks of His Presence; and God cannot sacrifice His sovereignty or tarnish His Throne, by advancing with favors to those

NOTES

who continue to trample everything sacred under their feet. In fact, the whole bent and drift of man's natural affections are against God. It is not in man to turn or change himself; and God cannot reverse His Own immutability, or retire from His eternal constitution of Righteousness and Holiness. The simple fact is, *"They who are in the flesh cannot please God"* (Rom. 8:8). And then Jesus said: *"No man comes unto the Father, but by Me"* (Jn. 14:6).

Nothing can recover a man from sin, not the powers and workings of nature, not good works, not money, not education, nothing but Christ, and in fact, Faith in Christ and what Christ has done for us at the Cross. Christ without the Cross could not have saved anyone!

KNOWLEDGE OF GOD

Even when men had a right knowledge of God, all of these things we have mentioned were not competent within themselves, as to keep that knowledge alive in them. The Scripture plainly says: *"Because that, when they knew God, they glorified Him not as God, neither were thankful; but became vain in their imaginations, and their foolish heart was darkened.*

"Professing themselves to be wise, they became fools,

"And changed the glory of the uncorruptible God into an image made like to corruptible man, and to birds, and four-footed beasts, and creeping things.

"Wherefore God also gave them up to uncleanness through the lusts of their own hearts, to dishonor their own bodies between themselves:

"Who changed the Truth of God into a lie, and worshiped and served the creature more than the Creator, Who is blessed forever. Amen" (Rom. 1:21-25).

This is Scripture, and it is also history. Seiss said, *"Nor is it difficult to trace the philosophy of it. It requires only a little attention and analysis of our most common and most inward impressions and experiences under the workings of nature."*

So, we see from Aaron and his sons, who incidentally, were chosen by God, anointed by God, and directed by God, that all men must have a Sacrifice.

First of all, they were to offer up a *"bullock for the Sin-Offering,"* and because they were sinful men, as are all men. They were then to offer *"two rams,"* one for a Whole Burnt-Offering, and the other for a Consecration-Offering. The latter was to be done with unleavened bread. In effect, four great Offerings were sacrificed; but in this order: the Sin-Offering first, followed by the Burnt-Offering, the Meal-Offering, and the Peace-Offering.

THE HOLY SPIRIT

That which the Holy Spirit is impressing upon us in these instructions is man's internal need for a Saviour, and that the Saviour is obtainable only on the premise of justice satisfied. That justice, and we speak of the Justice of God, was satisfied, and in fact could only be satisfied, by the Sacrificial, Atoning Death of Christ on the Cross.

When we look closely at false doctrine, in some way, it will always be found that the error begins with a wrong interpretation of the Atonement. In other words, if one perverts the Cross, one will pervert the entirety of the Word of God. If one properly understands the Cross, which serves as a proper foundation, then one will understand the Bible, which serves as the story of the Cross, and that alone! While the story as the Bible presents it may have broad aspects, and in fact does, still, all of those aspects, and whatever they might be, always center up on the Cross. I speak of all the great Doctrines of the Bible!

ALL OF ISRAEL

Verse 3 reads: *"And you gather all the congregation together unto the Door of the Tabernacle of the congregation."*

There were upwards of three million people in the wilderness at this time. This was only about one year since they had been delivered from Egyptian bondage.

Considering the great number of people, even though all were commanded together, many, even the far greater majority, could not have witnessed the proceedings as far as firsthand information was concerned. But still, they were commanded to be there.

No doubt, when Moses began to carry out

NOTES

the consecration rituals, those who in fact did see what was happening, would have told all who stood nearby, until the entirety of the congregation would have had some knowledge as to what was taking place.

At least one of the reasons for the Lord telling Moses that they must gather close is that they may understand that even the highest among them, namely Aaron in this case, was still dependent on the Sacrifice, and that as much as the worst sinner among them. I am positive this lesson was not lost on those who were gathered.

THE CROSS AT PRESENT

From this example, we must understand that just as much as the Sacrifice was applicable to all in Moses' time, it is still applicable to all presently, and in fact always has been. The Cross of Christ was the answer at the very beginning for man's dilemma (Gen. 3:15; Chpt. 4), and it is the answer now. The only way to God is through Jesus Christ (Jn. 14:6), and the only way to Christ is through the Cross (Jn. 1:1-2, 14, 29).

The problem with Church presently is, it has substituted for *"Jesus Christ and Him Crucified,"* a Crossless Christ! Paul said to do such only brings about *"another Jesus"* (II Cor. 11:4).

Whenever the Church promotes humanistic psychology as the answer to man's dilemma, and in any shape, form, or fashion, they are presenting to the world a Crossless Christ. Whenever the Word of Faith people make faith the object of faith, instead of Christ and Him Crucified, they too, present a Crossless Christ.

THE COMMANDS OF THE LORD

Verses 4 and 5 read: *"And Moses did as the LORD commanded him; and the assembly was gathered together unto the Door of the Tabernacle of the congregation.*

"And Moses said unto the congregation, This is the thing which the LORD commanded to be done."

These are a repeat of the instructions given in Exodus 29:1-37. According to tradition, this ceremony took place on February 23.

I want the Reader to pay careful and strict attention to the phrase, *"This is the thing* which the LORD commanded to be done." These are priceless words.

He did not say, this is the thing which is expedient, agreeable, or suitable; neither did He say, this is the thing which has been arranged by the fathers, the decree of the elders, or the opinion of the doctors. In fact, Moses knew nothing of such so-called authority. He knew only the Voice of the Lord, and that Voice alone he followed.

Furthermore, he would bring every member of the congregation of Israel under the sound of that voice, so to speak. In fact, there was no room left for tradition, for the opinions of men, or for the ideas of man in any capacity.

Concerning this, Mackintosh said: *"Had the Word been disregarded, the glory would not have appeared. The two things were intimately connected. The slightest deviation from 'Thus saith Jehovah' would have prevented the beams of the Divine Glory from appearing to the congregation of Israel. Had there been the introduction of a single rite or ceremony not enjoined by the Word, or had there been the omission of ought which that Word commanded, the Lord would not have manifested His glory. He could not sanction, by the glory of His Presence, the neglect or rejection of His Word. He can bear with ignorance and infirmity (spiritual weakness), but He cannot sanction neglect or disobedience."*

THE GREAT SIN OF THE MODERN CHURCH

And this, ignoring the Word, changing the Word, adding to the Word, or taking from the Word, is the great sin of the modern Church. How long will it take us to learn that God means what He says, and says what He means?

For instance, the modern Church promotes humanistic psychology as the answer to the aberrations and perversions of man. It does this despite the fact that the Holy Spirit through Peter said: *"According as His Divine Power has given unto us all things that pertain unto Life and Godliness, through the knowledge of Him Who has called us to glory and virtue:*

"Whereby are given unto us exceeding

NOTES

great and precious promises, that by these you might be partakers of the Divine Nature, having escaped the corruption that is in the world through lust" (II Pet. 1:3-4).

Due to the Word presently being handled so loosely, many take exception to our insistence that the attack on the Atonement is so basely wrong, as carried out by the Word of Faith people, when they claim that the Cross is of little consequence. The truth is, their erroneous doctrine, as it concerns the Atonement, and almost everything else, will cause Christians to be wrecked, and souls to be eternally lost. So there could be nothing worse than that!

A PERSONAL EXPERIENCE

As few people in the world, I think, I have been made to realize how necessary it is that we adhere strictly to the Word. Even when we stray from the Word through ignorance, or through ignorance do not know how to apply the Word, such ignorance cannot be overlooked by God, and to be sure, will reap its bitter fruit.

As it regards the great Message of the Cross, which is actually the foundation of all doctrine as it regards the Word of God, I understood that Message as it regards Salvation, and strongly preached it all over the world, with the result being that hundreds of thousands were brought to a saving knowledge of Jesus Christ; and I exaggerate not! However, as the Message of the Cross regards Sanctification, this I understood not at all. As a result, and despite my sincerity, despite my zealousness, and despite the fact that I tried so very, very hard, not understanding God's prescribed order of victory as it regards the Cross respecting Sanctification, I re-lived the Seventh Chapter of Romans all over again, even as virtually all modern Christians are doing presently. To be sure, if we do not understand the Message of the Cross as it refers to Sanctification, we definitely will re-live that Seventh Chapter, even as Paul lived it. To be sure, it will not be a pretty picture.

We sometimes think that sincerity, or zealousness, will suffice. It won't! There must be a strict adherence to the Word, and for that adherence to be strict, it must be properly taught and preached behind the Pulpit.

That's why Paul emphatically stated: *"We preach Christ Crucified"* (I Cor. 1:23).

That's why he also said: *"For Christ sent me not to baptize, but to preach the Gospel: not with wisdom of words, lest the Cross of Christ should be made of none effect"* (I Cor. 1:17).

As we've already said repeatedly in this Volume, the Church has been pushed away from its true foundation of the Cross to such an extent that it hardly knows where it's been, where it is, or where it's going. In fact, and I say this with great sadness of heart, the Church is in worse condition presently, I believe, than it has been since the Reformation.

That's at least one of the reasons, I also believe, that the Lord has raised up SonLife Radio.

SONLIFE RADIO

In the latter part of 1998, had you mentioned to me SonLife Radio, I would have paid scant attention. In fact, Radio was the furthest thing from my mind. But in the early part of 1999, the Lord suddenly opened up to me what He wanted me to do, as it regards that in which we are presently engaged. At that time, the Ministry owned two Radio Stations. I speak of WJFM–FM, 88.5 in Baton Rouge, and WJYM-AM, 730, in Bowling Green, Ohio. And actually, we had tried repeatedly to sell the Station in Bowling Green, but without success. Now I know why!

We were operating those Stations like most other Christian Stations are operated, which means that they effected little positive result for the Kingdom of God.

All of a sudden, and I speak of that which took place in only a matter of days, if that, the Lord gave me the vision of SonLife Radio. He told me how to program the Stations, which was totally different than they were presently being programmed, and totally different than anything I had ever heard previously. All programming was to come totally and completely from Family Worship Center.

He then instructed me to apply to the F.C.C. in Washington, for FM Translator frequencies, which we immediately began to do. Actually, we installed about 50 of these Translators all over the nation.

NOTES

Translator Stations are Radio Stations in every respect, except they are very small, i.e., *"low power."*

After we got the programming situated, the Lord then instructed me to make the bulk of our teaching the Cross of Christ. That we began to do, actually utilizing six hours a day for this purpose, and I speak of a 24-hour day, and doing so seven days a week, with the exception of service nights, etc. All of this time is spent on teaching the Message of the Cross of Christ. We utilize 90 minutes every morning, beginning at 7 a.m. (seven days a week), C.S.T. That program is re-aired every night at 7 p.m., with the exception of Service nights. We also re-air the same programs about one year later, at 1 a.m., and 1 p.m., seven days a week.

Through the Message of the Cross, lives are being gloriously changed, and to an extent that I have not previously seen in my Ministry. As well, other Preachers are beginning to preach the Cross, as they come into the understanding of the Cross as it refers not only to Salvation, but as well to our Sanctification.

In November 2001, the Lord began to broaden this vision, instructing me to purchase full-power Stations, some of them reaching upwards of several millions of people, instead of continuing to install the Translators. The Translators helped us to get started, but then I realized that to reach the entirety of the nation, and even the world by the Internet, we must employ full-power Stations, which we immediately began to do. At the present time (August 2002), we have nine full-power Stations, and are presently negotiating for seven more. These seven are scattered all over the nation. In fact, we believe the Lord has told us to cover the entirety of the nation, and because it's imperative that all hear the Message of the Cross.

This Message changed my life, even as it has changed the lives of untold millions. In fact, anything and everything that the Lord has done for the human race has been done exclusively by and through the Cross of Christ. That's why Paul said: *"But God forbid that I should glory, save in the Cross of our Lord Jesus Christ, by Whom the world is crucified unto me, and I unto the world"* (Gal. 6:14).

DESPERATION PRECEDES REVELATION

I don't know if that is true with everyone, but I do know it was true with Paul, and I definitely know that it was true with me.

In late Fall of 1991, I laid my Bible on the table in front of me, and said to a group of friends who were there, *"I don't know the answer, but I know the answer is found in the Word of God. And by the Grace of God, I intend to find that answer."*

To be sure, those words were not stated matter-of-factly. They were stated from the hurt of a broken heart, and through bitter tears. I meant what I said!

For some five years, day and night, I sought the Lord, and with tears, asking Him to show me the answer to my dilemma, and in fact, the dilemma of the entirety of the Church world. In the summer of 1996, He began to answer that prayer. First of all, He took me to Romans, Chapter 6. He began to unfold to me that which He had given to Paul so long, long ago. That's the reason I constantly say that what we are teaching isn't new, but actually that which was taught by Paul.

I will never forget that morning when the Lord began to move upon me as it regards the answer to my petition. I was studying the Sixth Chapter of Romans. And from that great Chapter, the Holy Spirit began to move upon my heart, opening it up to me, and instantly I knew that this was the answer. I will never forget that day, and I will never forget what the Lord has done, and in fact, continues to do, even unto this hour, which I trust will ever continue, and because it is impossible to exhaust the potential of the Cross.

As the Lord began to give me this Revelation, I don't think it would be possible to reveal the joy that flooded my soul, and continues unto this moment.

I know what it is to say as Paul, *"O wretched man that I am! Who shall deliver me from the body of this death?"* (Rom. 7:24).

I also now know what it is to say: *"There is therefore now no condemnation to them which are in Christ Jesus, who walk not after the flesh, but after the Spirit.*

"For the Law of the Spirit of Life in Christ Jesus has made me free from the law of sin and death" (Rom. 8:1-2).

If we adhere to the Word, we will reap the benefits of the Word! If we stray from the Word, we will reap that direction as well, but it definitely won't be benefits.

THE CROSS AND THE MODERN CHURCH

It is my belief that the Church is in such terrible condition, actually epitomizing the Laodicean Church of Revelation 3:14-22, because it has strayed from the foundation of the Cross of Christ. To put it bluntly, the Church no longer preaches the Cross. It preaches psychology, it preaches various fads, it preaches intellectualism, and it preaches a plethora of works, but it is no longer preaching the Cross.

As a result, the Churches are full of people who aren't saved. And the few who are saved, for the most part, are, as one of my Associates said, *"miserably saved!"* In other words, modern Believers, and I speak of true Believers, simply do not know how to live for God. And they don't know how to live for God, simply because they do not know and understand the Message of the Cross as it refers to Sanctification. And the Laity in the pew is in this condition, because the Preachers behind the Pulpits do not know the Message of the Cross.

THEOLOGICAL OR MORAL

The Message of the Cross is not a difficult Message. In fact, it is very simple. Paul told the Corinthians: *"But I fear, lest by any means, as the serpent beguiled Eve through his subtilty, so your minds should be corrupted from the simplicity that is in Christ."* He then went on to say: *"For if he who comes preaches another Jesus, whom we have not preached, or if you receive another spirit, which we have not received, or another gospel, which you have not accepted, you might well bear with him"* (II Cor. 11:3-4).

The Message of the Cross, regarding both Salvation and Sanctification, is not difficult to understand. In effect, the Holy Spirit through Paul referred to this Message as the *"simplicity of Christ."* So this means, if

Preachers or anyone reject the Cross, it is definitely not from theological reasons. In other words, it is not because it is too difficult to understand. This means that the reason for rejecting the Cross is definitely not theological, but rather is moral.

What do we mean by *"moral"*?

It means that men reject the Cross, simply because of pride and self-will. Like Cain of old, they do not refuse to offer up Sacrifice; in fact, they offer up beautiful sacrifices. But it's a sacrifice of their own hands, and not that of Christ, i.e., *"Christ and Him Crucified."* And as I've already said several times in this Volume, the Holy Spirit is drawing the line, in which on one side is the True Church, and on the other side is the apostate church. That line is the Cross of Christ. As Martin Luther said so long ago, *"As men view the Cross, so they view the Reformation."* I'll say the same thing presently:

"As men view the Cross, so they view Christ!"

In fact, the Cross has always been the dividing line. But the Holy Spirit is making it more prominent now than ever before, and for all the obvious, Scriptural reasons.

Concerning the Cross, may we in effect say as Moses of old, *"This is the thing which the Lord commanded to be done."*

THE WASHING

Verse 6 reads: *"And Moses brought Aaron and his sons, and washed them with water."*

The very first initiation as directed by the Lord, as it concerned the rite of consecration, was the bathing of Aaron and his sons, which symbolized their purification from sin. This denoted the washing or bathing of the entirety of the body. This was not done in the presence of the people, as would be obvious, but in a baptistery, so to speak, behind a curtain.

All of this represented Christ, both in the person of Aaron and his sons, and as well, in the ritual of washing. This was meant to portray the sublime purity of Jesus Who *"was holy, harmless, undefiled, separate from sinners."*

Concerning this, Seiss says, *"It was partly in token of this pureness and separation that John, as another Moses, so to speak, baptized*

NOTES

Christ in the River Jordan. In fact, Christ needed no cleansing. He always was pure. But, to indicate this purity, and to enter upon His Priesthood in the regular way, He consented to be washed, as was Aaron. In fact, His Baptism was part of his Priestly installation. It is one of the items of proof that He meant to be, and is, a Priest."

THE LEVITICAL LAW

As we look at the Levitical Law, whether it pertains to the Tabernacle, its sacred furniture, the Sacrificial System, or the Priesthood, we must always understand that the object of all of this was Christ. More particularly, it was Christ and what He would do for humanity, by dying on the Cross. It pointed to Him in this respect, in every capacity.

If our eyes and our attention fasten merely onto the individuals here involved, we will miss the entirety of the picture. To get the full import of what all of this meant, we must ever look away to Christ, realizing that all of this, and in every detail, represented Him in His Atoning, Mediatorial, and Intercessory Work. Failure to see that will bring back a failure of understanding. Christ atoned through the Cross; Christ mediates through the Cross; Christ intercedes because of the Cross!

THE SACRED VESTMENTS OF AARON

Verses 7 through 9 read: *"And he put upon him the Coat, and girded him with the Girdle, and clothed him with the Robe, and put the Ephod upon him, and he girded him with the Curious Girdle of the Ephod, and bound it unto him therewith.*

"And he put the Breastplate upon him: also he put in the Breastplate the Urim and the Thummim.

"And he put the Mitre upon his head; also upon the Mitre, even upon his forefront, did he put the Golden Plate, the Holy Crown; as the LORD commanded Moses."

Regarding this part of the installation and the consecration, the whole of the congregation of Israel had to be gathered together to witness this solemn occasion. And to be sure, this scene must have presented an imposing spectacle.

In the background stood Mount Sinai in

solemn silence, terrible yet in the imaginations of the people, for the fires that had so lately enveloped it, and the Holy Law that had thundered down from its summit.

In the valley beneath the Mount stood the thousands of Israel. In fact, there were probably nearly three million people present that day. The princes of Jacob would have stood about the door of the Sanctuary in devout expectancy. They would have conveyed all that was happening to the many thousands of Israel who awaited all of this with bated breath. Of course, it would not have been possible for all of these people to have personally observed these proceedings, and because many would have to stand far back from the actual site of the consecration, due to the large number. But it is certain that they were informed as to what was taking place, even as it took place.

In the center of all this hung the cloudy pillar, stretching high into the heavens, its shadow resting upon the Holy Tabernacle. As stated, all of this had to have been an imposing sight.

As imposing as it was, I'm sure that the far greater majority of the congregation of Israel little understood the full import of what was taking place. In fact, I don't think it was possible at that time for them to properly understand. It was then veiled in type and symbol. Paul referred to it as a *"shadow of things to come"* (Col. 2:17).

So, one might well ask, how were they saved in those days, by comparison to the present?

In fact, they were saved then exactly as we are now. The Sacrifices were a symbol of the One Who was to come. They were to have Faith in the One Who was to come, of Whom the Sacrifices represented. Faith in that coming One guaranteed Salvation, even as Faith in the One Who has come, now guarantees Salvation (Rom. 10:9-10; Eph. 2:8-9).

As someone has well said, *"The Old Testament Saints were saved by looking forward the Cross, while we are saved by looking backward to the Cross."*

All of Israel was to witness this occasion, because it affected all of Israel. The Gospel of Jesus Christ is not for a select few; it is for all!

SYMBOLIC OF CHRIST

1. The Coat: This item was worn next to the skin. It typified the Deity of Christ.

At the Fall in the Garden of Eden, the Scripture says: *"Unto Adam also unto his wife did the LORD God make coats of skins, and clothed them"* (Gen. 3:21).

In effect, these *"Coats"* made by the Lord God for Adam and Eve, proclaim the fact that God would become Man, and would die on a Cross in order to provide a covering for lost humanity. That covering, and that covering alone, will do!

While the humanity of Christ was portrayed outwardly, the Deity was always within. While He willingly laid aside the expression of His Deity, He never for a moment lost possession of His Deity.

2. The Girdle: This spoke of His humanity, and more particularly, His humanity as it regarded service. John said: *"And took a towel, and girded Himself"* (Jn. 13:4).

The Girdle was a narrow, long band or belt of linen, tied around the waist to confine the Ephod close to the body.

3. The Robe: This was sometimes referred to as the *"Robe of the Ephod,"* and was a seamless garment, curiously embroidered with blue, purple, scarlet, and gold. Its lower border was ornamented with a roll of red pomegranates, denoting *"fruit,"* and with little golden bells encircling the entire Robe in alternate succession. It was a garment which extended from the shoulders to a little below the knees. It portrayed the Righteousness of Christ.

4. The Ephod: This was the distinctive vestment of the High Priest. It was a sleeveless garment, and was worn over the shoulders. It was made of blue, purple, scarlet, and fine twined linen, interwoven with golden threads. It signified the working, moving, and operation of the Holy Spirit, within, and upon Christ (Jn. 3:34).

5. The Curious Girdle: This could be referred to as a *"band,"* which was attached to the Ephod, which wrapped around the waist of the High Priest, and tied at the front. As the Ephod typified the Holy Spirit upon Christ, the *"Curious Girdle"* typified the Work of the Spirit within the Life of

Christ (Lk. 4:18-19).

6. The Breastplate: This is called more fully, *"The Breastplate of Judgment."*

This was a fabric about nine inches square, set with 12 different jewels, large and well arranged. Its two upper corners had gold rings, by which it was connected with jeweled shoulder pieces, with wreathed chains of gold. At its lower corners it was fastened to the Girdle with blue ribbons.

The 12 jewels stood for the 12 Tribes of Israel, and each jewel had upon it the name of its Tribe. They were the most precious things belonging to the Priest's attire.

In its total complication, it signifies not only Israel of old, but as well, spiritual Israel, which speaks of the Church. It is that for which Christ died, therefore, it was worn over the heart of the High Priest.

7. The Urim and the Thummim: These were inserted in a pouch, which was made into the back of the Breastplate. The two words *"Urim"* and *"Thummim,"* mean *"Lights"* and *"Perfection."* The Scripture doesn't say exactly what they were. Many believe they could have been two precious stones, with the word *"yes,"* inscribed on one, and the word *"no"* inscribed on the other. They were used by the High Priest for spiritual direction. An example is David enquiring of the High Priest, as found in I Samuel 30:7-8.

8. The Mitre: This was a hat or a turban of sorts, made of fine linen. It represents authority, and portrays Christ as the *"Head"* of the Church (Col. 1:18).

9. The Golden Plate: This was a golden plate which fitted over the Mitre, and on the front of this shining gold appeared the solemn inscription – *"Holiness to the Lord."* This, of course, represented the absolute Holiness of Christ.

Thus did God direct for the clothing of the High Priest *"for glory and for beauty"*; and thus it typified Christ!

(10) "AND MOSES TOOK THE ANOINTING OIL, AND ANOINTED THE TABERNACLE AND ALL THAT WAS THEREIN, AND SANCTIFIED THEM.

(11) "AND HE SPRINKLED THEREOF UPON THE ALTAR SEVEN TIMES, AND ANOINTED THE ALTAR AND ALL HIS VESTMENTS, BOTH THE LAVER AND HIS

NOTES

FOOT, TO SANCTIFY THEM.

(12) "AND HE POURED OF THE ANOINTING OIL UPON AARON'S HEAD, AND ANOINTED HIM, TO SANCTIFY HIM.

(13) "AND MOSES BROUGHT AARON'S SONS, AND PUT COATS UPON THEM, AND GIRDED THEM WITH GIRDLES, AND PUT BONNETS UPON THEM; AS THE LORD COMMANDED MOSES.

(14) "AND HE BROUGHT THE BULLOCK OF THE SIN-OFFERING: AND AARON AND HIS SONS LAID THEIR HANDS UPON THE HEAD OF THE BULLOCK FOR THE SIN-OFFERING.

(15) "AND HE SLEW IT; AND MOSES TOOK THE BLOOD, AND PUT IT UPON THE HORNS OF THE ALTAR ROUND ABOUT WITH HIS FINGER, AND PURIFIED THE ALTAR, AND POURED THE BLOOD AT THE BOTTOM OF THE ALTAR, AND SANCTIFIED IT, TO MAKE RECONCILIATION UPON IT.

(16) "AND HE TOOK ALL THE FAT THAT WAS UPON THE INWARDS, AND THE CAUL ABOVE THE LIVER, AND THE TWO KIDNEYS, AND THE FAT, AND MOSES BURNED IT UPON THE ALTAR.

(17) "BUT THE BULLOCK, AND HIS HIDE, HIS FLESH, AND HIS DUNG, HE BURNT WITH FIRE WITHOUT THE CAMP; AS THE LORD COMMANDED MOSES.

(18) "AND HE BROUGHT THE RAM FOR THE BURNT-OFFERING: AND AARON AND HIS SONS LAID THEIR HANDS UPON THE HEAD OF THE RAM.

(19) "AND HE KILLED IT; AND MOSES SPRINKLED THE BLOOD UPON THE ALTAR ROUND ABOUT.

(20) "AND HE CUT THE RAM INTO PIECES; AND MOSES BURNT THE HEAD, AND THE PIECES, AND THE FAT.

(21) "AND HE WASHED THE INWARDS AND THE LEGS IN WATER; AND MOSES BURNT THE WHOLE RAM UPON THE ALTAR: IT WAS A BURNT SACRIFICE FOR A SWEET SAVOR, AND AN OFFERING MADE BY FIRE UNTO THE LORD; AS THE LORD COMMANDED MOSES."

The exegesis is:

1. The *"Anointing Oil,"* which was applied to the Tabernacle, and all the furniture therein, along with the Brazen Altar,

which Altar was anointed seven times, with the Brazen Laver then anointed as well, and with the Anointing Oil poured upon Aaron's head, all of this proclaims the fact of the absolute necessity of the Holy Spirit, of which the *"oil"* was a type, upon everything we do.

2. Verse 14 proclaims the fact that even though Aaron stood in the place of the Great High Priest, which means he was called and anointed by God, still, he was a sinner and, thereby, *"laid their hands upon the head of the bullock for the Sin-Offering."*

3. This signifies that their sins were transferred to the animal that became their substitute.

4. The animal then being slain testified to the death of Christ.

5. The blood poured out at the bottom of the Altar typified the Blood of Jesus that would be shed at Calvary.

6. The word *"reconciliation,"* as used in Verse 15, proclaims the first time it is used in the Bible, and applies to the doing away of an enmity, the bridging over of a quarrel.

7. It is interesting to notice that no Bible Passage speaks of Christ as reconciling God to man. Always, the stress is on man's being reconciled to God. It is man's sin which has caused the enmity.

8. This enmity in no way impacts or changes God's Love. The Bible is very clear that God's love to man never varies, no matter what man may do. Indeed, the whole atoning Work of Christ stems from God's great love.

9. However, God's Love in no way overlooks our sin. Love alone could not do away with sin. The price had to be paid for sin for the enmity to be taken away. It was paid by the death of Christ at Calvary.

10. The words in Verse 17, *"without the camp,"* signified that the Lord paid for Redemption of man *"without the camp"* (Heb. 13:12).

THE HOLY SPIRIT

Verses 10 through 12 read: *"And Moses took the Anointing Oil, and anointed the Tabernacle and all that was therein, and sanctified them.*

"And he sprinkled thereof upon the Altar seven times, and anointed the Altar and all

NOTES

his vestments, both the Laver and his foot, to sanctify them.

"And he poured of the Anointing Oil upon Aaron's head, and anointed him, the sanctify him."

There are two things of which the modern Church is greatly lacking. The first is its understanding, or rather, the lack thereof, of the Cross. Second, the Church little understands the Holy Spirit. As I have previously stated, the Denominational Church world, at the turn of the Twentieth Century, attempted to preach the Cross, without the Power of the Holy Spirit. They ultimately concluded by basically preaching much of nothing.

The Pentecostal world has tried to preach the Holy Spirit without the Cross, and they are now almost bereft of the Holy Spirit, while still claiming to be Pentecostal, but I might quickly add, in name only!

The two, the Cross, which the Text addresses a little later in this Chapter, as it refers to the Blood, and the Holy Spirit are so directly connected or intertwined, as to be inseparable. In other words, if one properly understands the Cross, one will properly understand the Holy Spirit, and vice versa.

For instance, and to which we have already alluded, Revelation 5:6 graphically displays that of which I speak.

In John's great Vision of the Throne of God, he saw the *"Book"* held in the right hand of God the Father, Who sat on the Throne. A strong Angel cried with a loud voice, asking, *"Who is worthy to open the Book, and to loose the seals thereof?"*

The Scripture then tells us that *"no man"* was worthy.

John then wept, because it seems that he understood the significance of this Book being opened.

The Scripture then tells us that one of the Elders spoke to John, telling him to weep not, and then said, *"Behold, the Lion of the Tribe of Judah, the Root of David, has prevailed to open the Book, and to loose the seven seals thereof."*

And then John looked, but he did not really see a *"Lion,"* but rather a *"Lamb."* What does that tell us?

That tells us that we cannot have the power of the *"Lion,"* in other words, the power of the *"Lion of the Tribe of Judah,"* until we first recognize Jesus as the *"Lamb."* In other words, we can't have the *"power"* without first recognizing the *"price"* that has been paid, which refers to the Cross. Unfortunately, millions are trying to do just that! They are ignoring the Cross, while at the same time claiming the power, which in effect, places them in the position of serving *"another Jesus"* (II Cor. 11:4).

To emphasize the fact, the Scripture says that what John saw was, *"a Lamb as it had been slain,"* which signifies the Cross. This means that we cannot get to the Throne, unless we come through the Cross. So those who would try to preach the Resurrection, or the Throne, without the Cross, will in fact, never reach the Throne. The answer and the key are, *"Jesus Christ and Him Crucified"* (I Cor. 1:23).

The Scripture then tells us that the *"Lamb"* had *"seven horns and seven eyes, which are the seven Spirits of God sent forth into all the Earth"* (Rev. 5:1-6).

The *"seven horns"* speak of total dominion, which in effect, is supposed to be our dominion, which Jesus purchased for us at the Cross. The *"seven eyes"* speak of total illumination, meaning that without understanding the Cross, one cannot properly understand the Word.

We know that there aren't seven Holy Spirits. The idea is, the number *"seven"* speaks of total dominion, total illumination, and as well, the total work of the Spirit. In fact, we are told what this total work is in Isaiah 11:1-2.

The point is, the slain Lamb, and the Holy Spirit are both so closely intertwined that they seem to be one and the same. That's how close the Holy Spirit works within the parameters of the Finished Work of Christ (Rom. 8:2).

THE MOVING AND OPERATION OF THE HOLY SPIRIT

Anything and everything done by the Lord on Earth is done totally and completely through the Person, Office, Ministry, and Power of the Holy Spirit. The only thing done on this Earth that the Holy Spirit did not Personally do was the Redemption Work

accomplished by Christ on the Cross. Even then, the Holy Spirit superintended the Conception, Birth, Life, Ministry, Death, Resurrection, Ascension, and Exaltation of Christ (Mat. 1:18; Lk. 4:18-19). In fact, the Holy Spirit was at the Cross when Jesus died, and actually told Him when to die (Heb. 9:14).

Before the Preacher preaches, he should earnestly seek the Lord as to what the Message ought to be, which the Holy Spirit will give to him. He should then ask the Lord to anoint him as he delivers the Message, which again, the Holy Spirit will definitely do. In fact, if this doesn't happen, nothing is going to be accomplished for Christ.

The truth is, the Believer, Preacher or otherwise, should seek the Lord earnestly for the leading and guidance of the Holy Spirit on a continuing basis (Jn. 16:13-14). In fact, we should have the leading of the Spirit in every single thing we do, and in fact, can have, if we will only seek the Face of the Lord.

Regrettably, most Christians have the mistaken idea that we are to do all that we can within our own strength and power, and then when we cannot do anymore, the Holy Spirit will step in and help us. Nothing could be further from the Truth. In fact, that to which the Holy Spirit does not give birth, to be sure, He will have no association with such.

THE BAPTISM WITH THE HOLY SPIRIT

I do not personally believe, due to the light that has presently been shed in this world as it regards the Holy Spirit, which actually began at the turn of the Twentieth Century, and could be referred to as the *"latter rain"* (Joel 2:23), that one can have the leading of the Spirit, without being first Baptized with the Holy Spirit. I believe the Bible teaches the following as it regards the Holy Spirit:

1. While the Spirit of God definitely comes into the heart and life of the Believer, and does so at conversion, that is different than what Jesus was speaking of in Acts 1:4-5. There is a vast difference in being *"born of the Spirit,"* than being *"Baptized with the Spirit."*

2. We believe that the Bible teaches that the Baptism with the Holy Spirit is an experience different and apart from Salvation. It does not make one more saved, for it's

impossible to be more saved, which comes by trusting what Christ did at the Cross, all on our behalf. The Baptism with the Holy Spirit is given to equip us for service, among other things (Mat. 3:11-12).

3. We believe that the Bible teaches that the Baptism with the Spirit is always, and without exception, accompanied by speaking with other tongues (Acts 2:4; 10:44-48; 19:1-7).

4. We believe the Bible teaches that the Holy Spirit works entirely within the confines of the Sacrifice of Christ. In other words, He will do nothing outside of the price that Jesus paid (Jn. 16:13-14). This is so much a fact that it is referred to as a *"Law"* (Rom. 8:2). This means if the Believer is to have the Holy Spirit work within his life, he is to exhibit Faith in the Cross of Christ at all times, understanding that everything comes to him through the Cross (I Cor. 1:17-18, 21, 23; 2:2, 5; Rom. 6:3-14).

With Faith evidenced in the Cross constantly, the Holy Spirit will work within our lives, using the same power with which He raised Christ from the dead (Rom. 8:11).

THE PRIESTHOOD

Verse 13 reads: *"And Moses brought Aaron's sons, and put coats upon them, and girded them with girdles, and put bonnets upon them; as the LORD commanded Moses."*

Aaron and his sons together represent Christ and His Priestly house; Aaron alone represents Christ in His Sacrificial and Intercessory function; Moses and Aaron together represent Christ as King and Priest (Mackintosh).

Now let us remember that all these Chapters contain is but *"a shadow of good things to come."* In fact, the entire Mosaic economy must be put in that category (Heb. 10:1).

THE SIN-OFFERING

Verses 14 and 15 read: *"And he brought the bullock for the Sin-Offering: and Aaron and his sons laid their hands upon the head of the bullock for the Sin-Offering.*

"And he slew it; and Moses took the blood, and put it upon the horns of the Altar round about with his finger, and purified the Altar, and poured the blood at the bottom of the Altar, and sanctified it, to

make reconciliation upon it."

Though duly consecrated, Aaron and his sons had first to be purged of their sins before they could commence their Priestly functions in the Sanctuary.

In fact, Aaron and his sons stood as penitent sinners by the side of the Sin-Offering, which was now offered for the first time. The *"Sin-Offering"* was called *"most holy,"* and because it cleansed the sinner from sin. In the *"Whole Burnt-Offering,"* Christ took His perfection, and gave it to the sinner. In the *"Sin-Offering,"* Christ took the sinner's sin, and made it His own, thereby justifying the sinner, and because Christ had paid the price for that sin, and in fact, all sin (I Jn. 2:2).

Let the Reader understand that all of the emphasis is totally and completely on the Crucifixion of Christ, and very little on the Resurrection, Ascension, and Exaltation of Christ, as important as those things actually are. However, I will remind the Reader that these latter things were a foregone conclusion, once the price was paid at the Cross.

So whenever certain Preachers in the Word of Faith philosophy claim that the preaching of the Cross is the preaching of death, meaning that it should not be preached, such a statement presents itself as being about as unbiblical as anything could ever be. Paul said:

"For the preaching of the Cross is to them who perish foolishness, but to we who are saved, it is the Power of God" (I Cor. 1:18).

The laying on of hands upon the head of the bullock for the Sin-Offering represented their sins being transferred to this innocent victim, typifying Christ taking our sins upon Himself.

Aaron then had to kill the animal, even as all had to kill the animal brought for their Sacrifice. In other words, the guilty party had to personally kill the innocent animal. This no doubt made him very much aware of his guilt, and that an innocent victim was suffering in his place.

When the throat of the animal was cut, Moses caught the blood in a basin, as all Priests following him would do. He then put the blood upon the four horns of the Altar, and then poured the balance of the blood out at the bottom of the Altar, which sanctified it. This tells us three things:

1. The blood signified Christ shedding His Life's Blood on the Cross of Calvary. Faith in that shed Blood was and is an absolute must, in order for a person to be saved. The shedding of the blood signified that life had been given, for the life of the flesh is in the blood.

2. The blood applied to the four horns of the Altar signified that God's Plan of Redemption was for the entirety of the universe, even as the four horns pointed in all four directions of the compass.

3. The Brazen Altar, which was but a type of the Cross, had to be sanctified, and was sanctified, by the blood being poured out at its base. This signified its purpose, and its purpose alone! The *"Altar"* is the place of death, and more specifically, it was the place of the Death of Christ.

Whenever you trusted Christ as a believing sinner, you were *"baptized into His Death,"* *"buried with Him by baptism into death,"* *"and then raised with Him in newness of life"* (Rom. 6:3-5).

And please understand, the word *"baptized,"* has absolutely nothing to do with Water Baptism. It speaks of what Jesus did at the Cross, all on our behalf. When we evidenced Faith in Him when we were originally saved, in the Mind of God, we were literally baptized into His death.

This is all done by us exhibiting Faith in Him. No physical act is involved, just Faith, but Faith in Christ, and what Christ has done at the Cross (Jn. 3:16).

THE FAT

Verses 16 and 17 read: *"And he took all the fat that was upon the inwards, and the caul above the liver, and the two kidneys, and their fat, and Moses burned it upon the Altar.*

"But the bullock, and his hide, his flesh, and his dung, he burnt with fire without the camp; as the LORD commanded Moses."

The *"fat"* signified that the very best animal had been offered. A sick, wasted animal would have very little fat, if any. The *"fat"* signified that God had given His best, and in a sense, represented the prosperity that comes from Christ, spiritual, physical, and material.

Even though the *"fat"* was burned on the Altar, the bullock itself could not be burned

NOTES

on the Altar, because it was a *"Sin-Offering."* In fact, of the four bloody Offerings, it was only the Whole Burnt-Offering which could be burned totally upon the Altar, and because it represented the Perfection of Christ, and not sin. Anything which represented sin, and we speak of the Peace-Offering, the Sin-Offering, and the Trespass-Offering, had to be disposed of in other manners.

THE RAM

Verses 18 through 21 read: *"And he brought the ram for the Burnt-Offering: and Aaron and his sons laid their hands upon the head of the ram.*

"And he killed it; and Moses sprinkled the blood upon the Altar round about.

"And he cut the ram into pieces; and Moses burnt the head, and the pieces, and the fat.

"And he washed the inwards and the legs in water; and Moses burnt the whole ram upon the Altar: it was a Burnt Sacrifice for a Sweet Savor, and an Offering made by fire unto the LORD; as the LORD commanded Moses."

Whereas the bullock was offered up as a Sin-Offering, the ram, as one of two rams, was offered up as a Whole Burnt-Offering. This means that all of it was burned on the Altar, and because it represented the Perfection of Christ.

In the Sin-Offering, the guilt of the sinner, Aaron and his sons in this case, were transferred to Christ. Now that reconciliation has taken place, the Perfection of Christ is now passed to Aaron and his sons, represented by the ram, and it being offered totally on the Altar.

The Perfection of Christ, i.e., *"the Righteousness of Christ,"* cannot be imputed to the believing sinner, until sin has first been dealt with.

The Whole Burnt-Offering, the Meat (Cereal) Offering, and the Peace-Offering, were all spoken of as a *"Sweet Savor"* before the Lord. They all spoke of Christ as it regards the Perfect Sacrifice of His Perfect Self, thanksgiving for that Sacrifice represented by the Cereal-Offering, and now Peace restored, represented by the Peace-Offering.

(22) "AND HE BROUGHT THE OTHER

RAM, THE RAM OF CONSECRATION: AND AARON AND HIS SONS LAID THEIR HANDS UPON THE HEAD OF THE RAM.

(23) "AND HE SLEW IT; AND MOSES TOOK UP THE BLOOD OF IT, PUT IT UPON THE TIP OF AARON'S RIGHT EAR, AND UPON THE THUMB OF HIS RIGHT HAND, AND UPON THE GREAT TOE OF HIS RIGHT FOOT.

(24) "AND HE BROUGHT AARON'S SONS, AND MOSES PUT OF THE BLOOD ON THE TIP OF THEIR RIGHT EAR, AND UPON THE THUMBS OF THEIR RIGHT HANDS, AND UPON THE GREAT TOES OF THEIR RIGHT FEET: AND MOSES SPRINKLED THE BLOOD UPON THE ALTAR ROUND ABOUT.

(25) "AND HE TOOK THE FAT, AND THE RUMP, AND ALL THE FAT THAT WAS UPON THE INWARDS, AND THE CAUL ABOVE THE LIVER, AND THE TWO KIDNEYS, AND THEIR FAT, AND THE RIGHT SHOULDER:

(26) "AND OUT OF THE BASKET OF UNLEAVENED BREAD, THAT WAS BEFORE THE LORD, HE TOOK ONE UNLEAVENED CAKE, AND A CAKE OF OILED BREAD, AND ONE WAFER, AND PUT THEM ON THE FAT, AND UPON THE RIGHT SHOULDER:

(27) "AND HE PUT ALL UPON AARON'S HANDS, AND UPON HIS SONS' HANDS, AND WAVED THEM FOR A WAVE-OFFERING BEFORE THE LORD.

(28) "AND MOSES TOOK THEM FROM OFF THEIR HANDS, AND BURNT THEM ON THE ALTAR UPON THE BURNT-OFFERING: THEY WERE CONSECRATIONS FOR A SWEET SAVOR: IT IS AN OFFERING MADE BY FIRE UNTO THE LORD."

The composition is:

1. Verses 22 through 26 portray *"the consecration ram."*

2. Whether we contemplate the Doctrine of Sacrifice, or the Doctrine of Priesthood, we find the shedding of blood gets the same important place.

3. A blood-stained ear was needed to hearken to the Divine communications, a blood-stained hand was needed to execute the services of the Sanctuary, and a blood-stained foot was needed to tread the courts of the

NOTES

Lord's House (Mackintosh).

4. The shedding of blood was the grand foundation of all sacrifice for sin, and it stood connected with all the vessels of the Ministry and with all the functions of the Priesthood.

5. The very presence of Christ in Heaven, and we speak of His appearance at the Throne of the Majesty, presents the value of all that He has accomplished on the Cross. His presence on the Throne attests the worth and acceptableness of His Atoning Blood (Heb. 1:3).

6. He did it all for us.

7. Back to Verse 12, we find Aaron being anointed alone. This was before the sacrifice of the animals, with the blood applied. In this we have a type of Christ, Who, until He offered Himself upon the Cross, stood entirely alone. There could be no union between Him and His people save on the ground of death and resurrection.

8. The unleavened cake spoke of the perfection of the humanity of Christ.

9. The *"Wave-Offering"* signified that Christ and His Perfection were recognized by those who believe on Him, and thankfulness to God was offered up for the Gift of His Son.

10. The unleavened cake, plus the oiled bread, and one wafer, along with the fat and the right shoulder of the animal, were all offered up as a Burnt-Offering, signifying Christ, Who Alone could satisfy the righteous demands of a thrice-Holy God.

11. It was a *"Sweet Savor,"* and because it represented the full Redemption Plan, which specified the death of the Son of the Living God.

THE RAM OF CONSECRATION

Verse 22 reads: *"And he brought the other ram, the ram of consecration: and Aaron and his sons laid their hands upon the head of the ram."*

The *"ram of consecration"* was the concluding Sacrifice, which in form, resembles the Thank-Offering and the Peace-Offering, and was designed to typify the consecration of Aaron and his sons, and in effect, all Priests who would follow in their train over the many centuries. The next Verse proclaims what this *"consecration"* entails.

THE BLOOD

Verses 23 and 24 read: *"And he slew it; and Moses took of the blood of it, put it upon the tip of Aaron's right ear, and upon the thumb of his right hand, and upon the great toe of his right foot.*

"And he brought Aaron's sons, and Moses put of the blood upon the tip of their right ear, and upon the thumbs of their right hands, and upon the great toes of their right feet, and Moses sprinkled the blood upon the Altar round about."

This tells us what the consecration was.

Concerning this, Williams said, *"Cleansed, clothed, and crowned though they were, yet the moment their hands touched the sacrifice, the sinless victims were slain. Such is the nature and the doom of sin.*

"The ear, the hand, and the foot were first cleansed with blood, and then anointed with oil. The cleaning of the precious blood, and the energizing of the Holy Spirit alone fit even the noblest character for entry into God's Service."

The *"blood"* of the slain ram was taken by Moses, in which he first of all put blood on the tip of Aaron's right ear, and then Aaron's sons. This meant that his ear was now consecrated to God Alone. He was to hear only from the Lord.

The *"Blood"* was then applied to the thumb of Aaron's right hand, and that of his four sons as well. This means that their *"doing,"* i.e., *"hands,"* would be consecrated totally to the Lord. They were to *"do"* only what He desired.

The blood was then applied to the big toe of Aaron, plus those of his sons as well, which typified their *"going."* They would *"go"* only where He directed them to go. This was their consecration.

So we have the *"hearing,"* the *"doing,"* and the *"walking."*

THE FAT, THE UNLEAVENED BREAD, THE OILED BREAD, THE WAFER, AND THE RIGHT SHOULDER

Verses 25 through 28 read: *"And he took the fat, and the rump, and all the fat that was upon the inwards, and the caul above the liver, and the two kidneys, and their fat,*

and the right shoulder:

"And out of the basket of unleavened bread, that was before the LORD, he took one unleavened cake, and a cake of oiled bread, and one wafer, and put them on the fat, and upon the right shoulder:

"And he put all upon Aaron's hands, and upon his sons' hands, and waved them for a Wave-Offering before the LORD.

"And Moses took them from off their hands, and burnt them on the Altar upon the Burnt-Offering: they were consecrations for a Sweet Savor: it is an Offering made by fire unto the LORD."

The *"unleavened bread"* represents the perfect humanity of Christ. The *"oiled bread"* represents Him being filled with the Holy Spirit above measure (Jn. 3:34). The *"wafer"* symbolized His perfect body, which would be offered in Sacrifice, as Verse 28 proclaims. The *"fat"* symbolized His prosperity, in that God had given Heaven's best. The *"right shoulder"* of the ram signified the strength of this which would be offered to the Lord.

THE WAVE-OFFERING

Aaron and his sons were to take these ingredients in their hands, in essence, all putting their hands on the concoction, and then they were to wave it before the Lord, signifying thanksgiving unto Him, and that He was the Author of Salvation.

THE BURNT-OFFERING

Then, these things, all representing Christ, were placed upon the Altar, and offered up as a Burnt-Offering, signifying that Christ would give His all on the Cross. This was a *"Sweet Savor"* to the Lord.

VICTORIOUS LIVING

These things done to and with the Priests, such as the blood being applied to the ear, etc., as well as being anointed with oil, and even the Sacrifices, were all symbolic. However, as should be obvious, it had to do with daily living.

Unfortunately, the modern Church, little understanding the Cross, and little understanding the Holy Spirit, little knows how to live for God. And this despite the fact that all true Believers have the Holy Spirit. When it comes to the Cross, about all that modern Believers know is, *"Jesus died for me."* While that is certainly true, and is in fact the greatest statement ever made, still, that's about the gist of the understanding of most Christians as it regards the Cross. In other words, they have no knowledge whatsoever of the part the Cross plays in the Sanctification process, which has to do with our victory, and our daily living.

As I've said many times, I think one of the main reasons for this is because the modern Church little understands the Bible, and especially it little understands the Old Testament.

The consecration of the Priests, as outlined in this Eighth Chapter of Leviticus, pertains to daily living. But as stated, these Priests could only have the symbol of what was yet to come, namely Christ. And only having the symbol, they could not actually walk in victory as modern Christians can do, that is, if modern Christians understand God's prescribed order.

Looking at these things closely, we must understand that *"blood"* was applied to the ear, thumb, and big toe. The blood was from the ram that had been killed, and was to be offered up, at least in part, as a Burnt-Offering. The point I'm making is this:

The *"blood applied"* signified that it's impossible to live the life we ought to live, unless we understand the Cross, and I'm speaking of the Cross as it refers to our Sanctification. The bullock as a Sin-Offering had already been offered. Its blood was shed, and its fat was offered on the Brazen Altar, with the carcass of the animal taken out and *"burned with fire without the camp."*

This particular Offering pertained to Salvation, one might say. The two rams were offered for consecration, and had to do with daily living. However, the one Offering of Christ sufficed for all. But as the sinner must believe in Christ and what Christ has done at the Cross, in order to be saved, although he understands very little about it, likewise, the Believer, after becoming a Christian, must continue to believe in the Cross, and which his knowledge of this Finished Work will now be greatly increased.

NOTES

The point I'm attempting to make is, the Believer cannot successfully live for the Lord, cannot walk in perpetual victory, unless he understands that all of this comes through the Cross, with the Cross having given the Holy Spirit the legal means to work within our lives.

The Bible is not much on formulas; however, the little formula below will perhaps make it easier to understand. We might even refer to it as *"God's Prescribed Order of Victory."*

THE CROSS

The Believer is to understand, as it regards his daily living, his daily walk before the Lord, his Christlikeness, his Righteousness and Holiness, the Fruit of the Spirit being developed within his life, his prosperity, along with Grace, Peace, Love, and in fact all things that come from the Lord, are made possible, and in totality, by what Christ did at the Cross.

Nothing must be added to that, and nothing must be removed from that. If we try to go beyond the Cross, we lose our way.

FAITH

Understanding that everything comes to us through the Cross, the great Sacrifice of Christ must ever be the object of our Faith. This must not change, irrespective as to what might happen.

Faith is the key, but it's the correct object of Faith, which makes Faith in God what it ought to be. Millions of Christians claim to have Faith in God, but they really don't know what that actually means. Others will say the same thing regarding the Word, but they don't actually know what that means either. Others claim Faith in Christ, even as we all should; however, most don't really know what these terms mean, at least as they should. They have a semblance of knowledge, but not to any degree.

When we speak of Faith, we must always understand that it ever must have as its object *"Christ and Him Crucified."* That's why Paul said, *"We preach Christ Crucified"* (I Cor. 1:23). That's why he also said: *"I determined to know nothing among you, save Christ and Him Crucified"* (I Cor. 2:2). That's why he gave us the entire Sixth Chapter of

Romans, which deals with this subject. It is all by Faith, but that term must be understood in the realm of the correct object of Faith, which always is the Cross.

THE HOLY SPIRIT

Due to what Christ did at the Cross, all Believers since the Cross have the Holy Spirit living within them (Jn. 14:16-17). In fact, every single thing done in our lives, and I speak of things done for the Lord, must be done exclusively by the Holy Spirit. Anything else constitutes the *"flesh,"* which God can never honor (Rom. 8:8).

The *"flesh"* refers to our own strength, efforts, and personal ability. While that within itself is not wrong, it becomes wrong if we depend on that instead of the Lord. The truth is, no matter how strong you might be, you simply cannot live for God within your own strength and ability. It cannot be done! But with the Holy Spirit, all things can be done. This is what Paul was talking about when he said:

"But if the Spirit (Holy Spirit) *of Him* (God the Father) *Who raised up Jesus from the dead dwell in you, He Who raised up Christ from the dead shall also quicken your mortal bodies by His Spirit Who dwells in you"* (Rom. 8:11).

Most Christians read this and think that Paul is speaking of the Resurrection of the dead, which is yet to come. No, he's not! At the coming Resurrection, our bodies will be instantly glorified. We shall be changed in a moment, in the twinkling of an eye (I Cor. 15:51-54). That will be the glorified body.

Paul is not speaking in the Eighth Chapter of Romans about the glorified body, but rather *"our mortal bodies."* He tells us, if we make the Cross of Christ the object of our Faith (Rom. 8:2), the Holy Spirit, Who works exclusively within the parameters of the Finished Work of Christ, will *"also quicken our mortal bodies."* In other words, we can then yield the members of our bodies to Righteousness instead of unrighteousness (Rom. 6:13). But we simply cannot do that, no matter how sincere we are, and no matter how hard we try, if we do not maintain our Faith in the Finished Work of Christ, which then gives the Holy Spirit the legal

NOTES

right to work accordingly within our daily living. This is so much circumscribed that it is referred to as a *"Law"* (Rom. 8:2).

This is the manner in which the Holy Spirit works, and in fact, the only manner in which He works.

Christians, for the most part, don't know how the Holy Spirit works; consequently, He is by and large ignored, or else we approach Him all wrong. It's because we do not understand the Cross and the price that Jesus paid there. Properly understanding the Cross gives the Holy Spirit latitude to work within our lives, which guarantees, *"rest in Christ"* (Mat. 11:28-30), and victorious living (Rom. 6:3-14).

This is what this Eighth Chapter of Leviticus teaches us, as should be obvious.

(29) "AND MOSES TOOK THE BREAST, AND WAVED IT FOR A WAVE-OFFERING BEFORE THE LORD: FOR OF THE RAM OF THE CONSECRATION IT WAS MOSES' PART; AS THE LORD COMMANDED MOSES.

(30) "AND MOSES TOOK OF THE ANOINTING OIL, AND OF THE BLOOD WHICH WAS UPON THE ALTAR, AND SPRINKLED IT UPON AARON, AND UPON HIS GARMENTS, AND UPON HIS SONS, AND UPON HIS SONS' GARMENTS WITH HIM; AND SANCTIFIED AARON, AND HIS GARMENTS, AND HIS SONS, AND HIS SONS' GARMENTS WITH HIM.

(31) "AND MOSES SAID UNTO AARON AND TO HIS SONS, BOIL THE FLESH AT THE DOOR OF THE TABERNACLE OF THE CONGREGATION: AND THERE EAT IT WITH THE BREAD THAT IS IN THE BASKET OF CONSECRATIONS, AS I COMMANDED, SAYING, AARON AND HIS SONS SHALL EAT IT.

(32) "AND THAT WHICH REMAINS OF THE FLESH AND OF THE BREAD SHALL YOU BURN WITH FIRE.

(33) "AND YOU SHALL NOT GO OUT OF THE DOOR OF THE TABERNACLE OF THE CONGREGATION IN SEVEN DAYS, UNTIL THE DAYS OF YOUR CONSECRATION BE AT AN END: FOR SEVEN DAYS SHALL HE CONSECRATE YOU.

(34) "AS HE HAS DONE THIS DAY, SO THE LORD HAS COMMANDED TO DO, TO

MAKE AN ATONEMENT FOR YOU.

(35) "THEREFORE SHALL YOU ABIDE AT THE DOOR OF THE TABERNACLE OF THE CONGREGATION DAY AND NIGHT SEVEN DAYS, AND KEEP THE CHARGE OF THE LORD, THAT YOU DIE NOT: FOR SO I AM COMMANDED.

(36) "SO AARON AND HIS SONS DID ALL THINGS WHICH THE LORD COMMANDED BY THE HAND OF MOSES."

The diagram is:

1. Aaron and his sons had already been anointed with oil and had the blood applied. It is now done again, which were fitting conclusions to their consecration. It was meant to show that the Sanctification process is an ongoing process, thereby, the necessity of continued trust in the Blood and the need of continued anointing with the Holy Spirit.

2. Beautiful and costly as was the raiment of Aaron, yet the oil and the blood were applied. This simply means that the beauty and glory of Salvation, typified by the garments of Aaron, are all made possible by what Jesus did at the Cross.

3. That which remained of the ram of consecration was now to be eaten, along with the unleavened bread, etc. This typified the statement of Christ: *"Except you eat the flesh of the Son of Man, and drink His Blood, you have no life in you"* (Jn. 6:53).

Once again, we go back to the Cross! *"Eating His flesh, and drinking His Blood,"* was not meant in a literal sense, but referred to Faith in Christ and what Christ would do at the Cross. It literally referred to entering into His Death, Burial, and Resurrection (Rom. 6:3-5).

4. The Priests were to remain in the Court of the Tabernacle for seven days and nights. On each of these days, the same sacrifices were to be repeated, the Sin-Offering, the Burnt-Offering, and the Consecration-Offering, along with all the other parts of the ritual. The number *"seven"* typified perfection, completion, and totality. In other words, it was a total consecration.

THE WAVE-OFFERING

Verse 29 reads: *"And Moses took the breast, and waved it for a Wave-Offering*

NOTES

before the LORD: for of the ram of consecration it was Moses' part; as the LORD commanded Moses."

Inasmuch as Moses was officiating that day in accordance with the directions given in Exodus 29:26, this was to be his sacrificial meal, since he was Divinely appointed to perform the Priestly service. Ordinarily this would have been for the Priests in general, but Moses was instructed by the Lord to consume it himself.

This signified that even Moses had to partake of Christ, as do all.

THE OIL AND THE BLOOD

Verse 30 reads: *"And Moses took of the Anointing Oil, and of the Blood which was upon the Altar, and sprinkled it upon Aaron, and upon his garments, and upon his sons, and upon his sons' garments with him; and sanctified Aaron, and his garments, and his sons, and his sons' garments with him."*

We learn from this Passage that there is never a time that the *"blood,"* i.e., *"the Cross,"* and the *"oil,"* i.e., *"the Holy Spirit,"* aren't needed.

Aaron was outfitted in these beautiful garments which only the High Priest could wear. As well, his sons were outfitted in their garments, but still, the *"oil"* and the *"blood"* were sprinkled all over Aaron and his sons, referring to their garments, which spoke of the sanctifying process. This tells us three things:

1. It tells us that the glory and beauty of Salvation, typified by these beautiful garments, cannot be ascertained by the Believer, without the proper application of the *"oil"* and the *"blood."* In other words, after Salvation, all the glorious and wonderful things accomplished by Christ at the Cross can be ours, only by our Faith in that Finished Work. Faith properly placed, which refers to the Cross of Christ, guarantees the help of the Holy Spirit, typified by the *"oil."*

2. We learn from this that the Sanctification process is a progressive work. In other words, it is ongoing.

3. We learn that this Sanctification process can be carried out, and in fact, is carried out, solely by and through the Holy Spirit, Who works exclusively within the

parameters of the Finished Work of Christ.

If it is to be noticed, the *"Anointing Oil"* is mentioned first. This signifies the fact that that Holy Spirit works continuously, but does so on the basis of the *"shed Blood of the Lamb."*

THE FEAST

Verses 31 and 32 read: *"And Moses said unto Aaron and to his sons, Boil the flesh at the Door of the Tabernacle of the congregation: and there eat it with the bread that is in the basket of consecrations, as I commanded, saying, Aaron and his sons shall eat it.*

"And that which remains of the flesh and of the bread shall you burn with fire."

These Verses furnish a fine type of Christ and His people feeding together upon the results of the accomplished Atonement.

Feasting on Christ, which once again has to do with John 6:53-58 pertains to continued Faith in His Finished Work. We are not to mistake the Lord's Supper with this Feast. It is merely a symbol of this Feast, and points one to the Sacrifice of Christ, always to the Sacrifice of Christ.

It is impossible to know Christ, to understand Christ, to enjoy the benefits of Christ, without a proper understanding of the Cross. When one understands that, thereby maintaining his Faith in that Finished Work, that is feasting upon Christ, and that is the enjoyment of *"more abundant life"* (Jn. 10:10).

BURNED WITH FIRE

Verse 32 proclaims the fact that all which was not eaten had to then be burned with fire, that nothing remain. This signifies the fact that all of Christ must be consumed. In other words, it's all of Christ, or it's none of Christ! He cannot be accepted in part, so to speak.

SEVEN DAYS

Verses 33 through 36 read: *"And you shall not go out of the Door of the Tabernacle of the congregation in seven days, until the days of your consecration be at an end: for seven days shall he consecrate you.*

"As he has done this day, so the LORD

NOTES

has commanded to do, to make an Atonement for you.

"Therefore shall you abide at the Door of the Tabernacle of the congregation day and night seven days, and keep the charge of the LORD, that you die not: for so I am commanded.

"So Aaron and his sons did all things which the LORD commanded by the hand of Moses."

Aaron and his sons were to remain in the confines (the Court) of the Tabernacle for seven days and seven nights. On each of these days, the entire Sacrificial ritual was to be engaged.

The number *"seven"* typifies totality and completion. In other words, that which the Lord does is perfect, and is often typified by the number *"seven."*

Then everything was done in symbolism, because it was the only way it could be done. But now, due to what Christ has done at the Cross, all of this is carried out by the Holy Spirit in reality. It is done upon the basis of our Faith in Christ, and what Christ has done for us in the giving of Himself on the Cross of Calvary. It is always, *"The Cross!" "The Cross!" "The Cross!"*

"The Saviour Who loves me and suf
    fered the loss of heavenly glory to
    die on the Cross,
"The Babe of the manger, though born
    without stain,
"This Jesus is coming, is coming
    again!"

"The Angels, rejoicing and singing His
    praise to Bethlehem shepherd's of
    earlier days,
"Will come in the glory, attending His
    train,
"When Jesus, my Saviour, is coming
    again!"

"The Saints will be with Him, O heav-
    enly bliss! How tearful the parting
    from faces we miss!
"But clouds are descending, and we
    who remain
"Are caught up to meet them with
    Jesus again!"

"O hearts that are weary, and sinful,
    and sad, we carry the tidings that
    make us so glad;

"We publish the Saviour over mountain and plain;

"The Lord Who redeemed us is coming again!"

CHAPTER 9

(1) "AND IT CAME TO PASS ON THE EIGHTH DAY, THAT MOSES CALLED AARON AND HIS SONS, AND THE ELDERS OF ISRAEL;

(2) "AND HE SAID UNTO AARON, YOU TAKE A YOUNG CALF FOR A SIN-OFFERING, AND A RAM FOR A BURNT-OFFERING, WITHOUT BLEMISH, AND OFFER THEM BEFORE THE LORD.

(3) "AND UNTO THE CHILDREN OF ISRAEL YOU SHALL SPEAK, SAYING, YOU TAKE A KID OF THE GOATS FOR A SIN-OFFERING; AND A CALF AND A LAMB, BOTH OF THE FIRST YEAR, WITHOUT BLEMISH, FOR A BURNT-OFFERING;

(4) "ALSO A BULLOCK AND A RAM FOR PEACE-OFFERINGS TO SACRIFICE BEFORE THE LORD; AND A MEAT-OFFERING MINGLED WITH OIL: FOR TODAY THE LORD WILL APPEAR UNTO YOU.

(5) "AND THEY BROUGHT THAT WHICH MOSES COMMANDED BEFORE THE TABERNACLE OF THE CONGREGATION; AND ALL THE CONGREGATION DREW NEAR AND STOOD BEFORE THE LORD.

(6) "AND MOSES SAID, THIS IS THE THING WHICH THE LORD COMMANDED THAT YOU SHOULD DO: AND THE GLORY OF THE LORD SHALL APPEAR UNTO YOU."

The structure is:

1. This Chapter describes Aaron in his role of mediation as the High Priest. It symbolizes Christ in this intercessory role, which He now occupies (Heb. 7:25).

2. Aaron, on the eighth day, was a fore-picture of Christ sanctified, anointed with the Holy Spirit, and sent into the world in order to put away its sin by the Sacrifice of Himself.

3. *"The Glory of the Father"* raised Him from the dead, thus accepting His Person

and His Work.

4. *"The eighth day"* represents the Resurrection of Christ, Who was raised from the dead on the first day of the week, i.e., *"the eighth day, which was eight days from the first Sabbath."*

5. Aaron, although the Great High Priest, still, was a sinner who needed the saving Grace of Christ, which the Sacrifices were a type. Consequently, as he began his duties, he had to offer up a Sin-Offering, and a Burnt-Offering for himself.

6. He was to then offer a Sin-Offering, a Burnt-Offering, a Peace-Offering, and a Meat-Offering for the congregation of Israel.

7. With the proper Offerings, the promise was, *"Today the Lord will appear unto you."* The only way He will appear, and to any degree, is by and through the Cross of Christ, and our Faith in that Finished Work.

8. All the congregation was commanded to draw near to the Tabernacle, which they did. It was meant to impress upon them that all of these ceremonies and rituals concerning the sacrifices and the blood, etc., were all done on their behalf.

THE EIGHTH DAY

Verse 1 reads: *"And it came to pass on the eighth day, that Moses called Aaron and his sons, and the Elders of Israel."*

The eighth day followed the seven days of consecration. According to ancient tradition, this was the first day of March.

This corresponds with Jesus being raised from the dead, which He was, in essence, on the eighth day. He was raised on the first day of the week, which was eight days after a full Sabbath week. After the Ascension and sending back the Holy Spirit, at least the Spirit coming in a new dimension, Christ would begin His High Priestly Work, of which this Ninth Chapter is a type.

Some have placed this into the Second Coming of Christ, when He will come back to redeem Israel, in which His Glory at that time, will then cover the Earth. While it certainly could lean toward that, it is my thought that the Second Coming, which will be followed by the Millennium, little needs shadows and types for its portrayal. So I think the heavier meaning deals with the

Resurrection of Christ, after He has redeemed lost humanity, in which He will now begin His High Priestly Work, which in fact, continues unto the hour.

THE SIN-OFFERING AND
THE BURNT-OFFERING

Verse 2 reads: *"And he said unto Aaron, You take a young calf for a Sin-Offering, and a ram for a Burnt-Offering, without blemish, and offer them before the LORD."*

As stated, even though Aaron was the Great High Priest, thereby a type of Christ, still, he was a poor mortal in need of a Saviour, which meant that he was a sinner. Sin – sin – sin – in everything there is remembrance made of sin, as man's great, ever-present, crushing burden, and of the bloody Sacrifice of Christ Jesus as its only remedy. Concerning this, Seiss said:

"Everywhere, even in our holiest moods and most sacred doings, there still flashes out the stern and humiliating accusation – 'O man, you are a sinner! All your goodness is but abomination apart from Christ! Your only hope is in Him Whose body was broken and Whose Blood was shed for the remission of sins!'"

All of this means that our hand must be ever kept on the brow of the Atoning Lamb. We must never cease to rest upon Jesus and His offering of Himself for us. We must ever look to the Cross. The songwriter said:

"Sit, forever viewing
"Mercy streaming in His Blood."

This, His Sacrificial, Atoning Death, the shedding of His Blood, this and this alone underlies everything else. There is no heavenly consecration, at least that which God will recognize, which does not take in this. It is the beginning, the middle, and the end of all human Sanctification. And without resting upon Christ as the Sin-Offering, we can never come to the high honors of the Priesthood of Saints. We are no longer our own; we are bought with a price – *"With the precious Blood of Christ as of a lamb without blemish and without spot."*

Oh dear Reader, can you not sense the Presence of God, even as we utter these words? Can you not sense the total reliance we must place upon Him, Who has paid for all of our sins?

Even though Aaron and his sons were called of God and robed in beautiful garments, and, thereby, stood as leaders of the people, they were poor, frail, flawed, sinful mortals, and, thereby, must have the same Sacrifice as the worst sinners in Israel.

SIN

If one has a proper view of the Cross, then one will have a proper view of sin.

While it is true that we are new creations in Christ Jesus, with old things having passed away, and all things having become new (II Cor. 5:17), while we are definitely *"kings and priests"* (Rev. 1:6), and in fact are perfect in Christ, we must at the same time, properly understand what all of that means.

Yes, we are all of this in Christ, which refers to what He did for us at the Cross. In other words, when God looks at us, He can do so only as He looks at Christ. Every victory won by Christ, every price paid by Christ, every Sacrifice made by Christ, all and in totality were developed and carried out strictly for us – for sinners. He did none of that for Himself, not at all for His Father in Heaven, neither for Angels, but altogether for us.

The idea is, what He is, I am, but all because of the Cross, and my Faith in His Cross (Rom. 6:3-14; 8:1-2, 11; I Cor. 1:17-18, 21, 23; 2:2; Gal. 5:1-6; 6:14; Eph. 2:13-18; Col. 2:14-15).

That's what I am in Christ, and because of Christ, and solely because of Christ, which again refers to His Cross.

But despite all of this, I must recognize the fact that the sin nature is ever present within me (Rom. 6:1-2, 6-7, 12-18, 20, 22-23). For those who would claim that the Believer no longer has a sin nature, I would counter by saying, if that is so, the Holy Spirit wasted a lot of time through Paul, explaining something that didn't exist.

Find the holiest man or woman on Earth, whomever that might be, and through that individual, in one day, and sometimes even one hour, enough evil thoughts and evil passions arise in that heart to doom that soul forever and forever. Such is the horror and the power of sin. Were it not so powerful, such a great price would not needed to have been paid.

To the Believer who will not admit his personal frailty, faults, and failures, to such a Believer deception has become the rule. John said: *"If we say that we have no sin, we deceive ourselves, and the Truth is not in us"* (I Jn. 1:8).

That being the case, and it most definitely is, even among the best of us, what is then our hope?

THE BLESSED HOPE

Our hope from beginning to end, from the first to the last, altogether is in Christ. But it is in Christ according to the Sacrifice of Himself on the Cross. He must never be separated from the Cross, as it regards its benefits. Through the Cross, He opened up the way to the Holy of Holies. Without the Cross, man would never have been able to bridge that great gulf. But the Cross bridged it, which means that Jesus became our Sin-Offering. This means that He became the sin-bearer, the penalty-taker, if you will, the Sin-Offering, and in this, He was *"most holy"* (Lev. 2:3, 10; 6:17-18, 25, 29; 7:1).

THE BURNT-OFFERING

The Sin-Offering was offered first, with the Burnt-Offering following.

The *"Sin-Offering"* proclaims Christ as the victim, and a perfect victim at that, taking the sins of the sinner upon Himself, in effect becoming the sin-bearer, suffering its penalty, which was death.

The *"Burnt-Offering"* typified the perfect Christ giving His Perfection, i.e., *"Righteousness,"* to the sinner, who within himself had no Righteousness. In fact, it took five Offerings to properly portray the one Offering of Christ.

Now that all sin had been atoned, and done so by the Sin-Offering, the Perfect Righteousness, typified by the Burnt-Offering, could be lavished upon Aaron, and in fact, all who trust Christ.

THE SACRIFICES FOR THE PEOPLE

Verses 3 through 6 read: *"And unto the Children of Israel you shall speak, saying, You take a kid of the goats for a Sin-Offering; and a calf and a lamb, both of the first year, without blemish, for a Burnt-Offering;*

NOTES

"Also a bullock and a ram for Peace-Offerings to sacrifice before the LORD; and a Meat-Offering mingled with oil: for today the LORD will appear unto you.

"And they brought that which Moses commanded before the Tabernacle of the congregation; and all the congregation drew near and stood before the LORD.

"And Moses said, This is the thing which the LORD commanded that you should do: and the Glory of the LORD shall appear unto you."

On *"the eighth day"* Aaron, robed in linen and anointed, came forth out of the Tabernacle to offer up the four great Sacrifices for the people, i.e., the *"Sin-Offering,"* the *"Burnt-Offering,"* the *"Meal-Offering,"* and the *"Peace-Offering."* A public proclamation was made that God would accept him and his Sacrifice by a special manifestation of His Glory. This came to pass (Williams).

All of Israel was commanded to bring forth the specified Sacrifices, which no doubt the Elders of Verse 1 did, on behalf of all the people.

There were six Sacrifices in all regarding Israel; (there were two *"Burnt-Offerings"* and two *"Peace-Offerings"*, plus one *"Sin-Offering"*) five of them bloody Sacrifices (vss. 3-4).

It was promised that the Lord that day would appear unto them, that is, would manifest Himself in some way, which He did! However, it must be remembered, and without fail, that the Lord could not manifest Himself, until the proper Sacrifices could be offered.

Likewise presently, if the Lord is in some way to appear among us, again, to manifest Himself in some way, He will not do so unless Christ and what He has done at the Cross be given the proper place as it regards our Faith. Regrettably, the flesh parades itself, and Christians by the untold thousands, who know little of the Word of God, think it's the Lord, when it's not!

Worse than that, Satan, with his ministers, parade themselves under the guise of angels of light, and much of the Church doesn't know the difference (II Cor. 11:13-15).

Why?

How?

Christ and His Glory cannot at all manifest Himself unless we go through the Cross. There is no other way. Preachers who would try to tell you of other ways are only speaking of manufactured ways, which are the ways of man, and not of God. The only way to the Holy of Holies is through the Blood of Christ. Concerning this, Paul said: *"Having therefore, Brethren, boldness to enter into the Holiest by the Blood of Jesus,*

"By a new and living way, which He has consecrated for us, through the veil, that is to say, His flesh" (Heb. 10:19-20).

I think what Paul says speaks for itself. We can go into the Holiest only by the Precious Blood of Jesus, and in the shedding of His Blood, He gave His Life, i.e., *"His flesh,"* i.e., *"the Cross."*

ALL THE CONGREGATION

The entirety of Israel drawing near and standing before the Lord means that they were standing before the Tabernacle. There were at least three million of these people, so many of them could little see the Tabernacle, if at all, but no doubt, it was related to them by others who were closer, exactly as to what was taking place. It would have been an awesome sight!

The cloudy pillar would have rested above the Tabernacle, with its awesome presence. They knew this was God, and that He dwelt between the Mercy Seat and the Cherubim, in the Holy of Holies.

They were told that with the proper Sacrifices offered, which they were, that the *"Glory of the Lord would appear unto them,"* and that He did, which we will study at the close of this Chapter.

(7) "AND MOSES SAID UNTO AARON, GO UNTO THE ALTAR, AND OFFER YOUR SIN-OFFERING, AND YOUR BURNT-OFFERING, AND MAKE AN ATONEMENT FOR YOURSELF, AND FOR THE PEOPLE: AND OFFER THE OFFERING OF THE PEOPLE, AND MAKE AN ATONEMENT FOR THEM; AS THE LORD COMMANDED.

(8) "AARON THEREFORE WENT UNTO THE ALTAR, AND KILLED THE CALF OF THE SIN-OFFERING, WHICH WAS FOR HIMSELF.

(9) "AND THE SONS OF AARON BROUGHT THE BLOOD UNTO HIM, AND HE DIPPED HIS FINGER IN THE BLOOD, AND PUT IT UPON THE HORNS OF THE

NOTES

ALTAR, AND POURED OUT THE BLOOD AT THE BOTTOM OF THE ALTAR:

(10) "BUT THE FAT, AND THE KIDNEYS, AND THE CAUL ABOVE THE LIVER OF THE SIN-OFFERING, HE BURNED UPON THE ALTAR; AS THE LORD COMMANDED MOSES.

(11) "AND THE FLESH AND THE HIDE HE BURNT WITH FIRE WITHOUT THE CAMP.

(12) "AND HE SLEW THE BURNT-OFFERING; AND AARON'S SONS PRESENTED UNTO HIM THE BLOOD, WHICH HE SPRINKLED ROUND ABOUT UPON THE ALTAR.

(13) "AND THEY PRESENTED THE BURNT-OFFERING UNTO HIM, WITH THE PIECES THEREOF, AND THE HEAD: AND HE BURNT THEM UPON THE ALTAR.

(14) "AND HE DID WASH THE INWARDS AND THE LEGS, AND BURNT THEM UPON THE BURNT-OFFERING ON THE ALTAR."

The construction is:

1. Atonement means reconciliation. Its ultimate conclusion is the reconciliation of God and man through the Sacrificial Death of Jesus Christ.

2. After the calf was killed, Aaron *"dipped his finger in the blood, and put it upon the horns of the Altar, and poured out the blood at the bottom of the Altar."* Without the shedding of blood, and only a particular blood at that, there is no remission of sins (Heb. 10:4).

3. The fat, along with certain physical organs, were burned on the Altar, with the carcass and the hide being burned with fire without the camp.

That which was burned with fire *"without the camp,"* symbolizes complete expiation (to do away with the guilt incurred). The whole curse fell upon the substitute. An Atonement was not completed until the whole Sacrifice was consumed.

4. The *"Burnt-Offering"* portrayed in Verse 12 was for Aaron as well. It symbolized Jesus Christ as the one all-sufficient Offering to God, which alone could satisfy His righteous demands.

ATONEMENT

Verse 7 reads: *"And Moses said unto*

Aaron, Go unto the Altar, and offer your Sin-Offering, and your Burnt-Offering, and make an Atonement for yourself, and for the people: and offer the Offering of the people, and make an Atonement for them; as the LORD commanded."

Atonement is mentioned over and over in the Old Testament, while it is mentioned only once in the New; and then, it should have been translated *"Reconciliation"* (Rom. 5:11). As stated, it refers to, and means, that man has been reconciled to God, through the atoning, Sacrificial Death of the Lord Jesus Christ. That being the case, and as important as it is, why is the word Atonement mentioned only once in the New Testament?

In the Old Testament, Atonement was something that had to be done over and over again, and because the blood of animals was not sufficient to take away sins (Heb. 10:4). So, inasmuch as the ritual of Sacrifice had to be repeated over and over, in fact, unceasing and unending, it was necessary that the word *"Atonement"* be used as well over and over.

As well, the Atonement effected in the Old Testament was in reality only a stopgap measure. It was what one might say, Atonement on credit. In fact, it was a very incomplete Atonement.

The four Gospels record the true Atonement, in the Sacrificial, Atoning Death of Jesus Christ on the Cross of Calvary, to which all the animal sacrifices had pointed. When it was done, once for all, it was a completed work and, therefore, didn't have to be mentioned again and again. It was mentioned again and again in the Old Testament, as stated, because in reality, the work was actually never done, demanding repeated sacrifices.

However, the Apostle Paul explained over and over again, in all of his 14 Epistles, the results of the completed Atonement in Christ. *"Jesus died for me"* in essence, explains the Atonement. He died as my Substitute, taking my place, thereby reconciling me to God. But there remains the results of the Atonement, which Paul graphically explained, and which we have attempted to explain over and over again, even in this Volume.

If it is to be noticed, the results of Atonement were never explained in the Old Testament, and because Old Testament Atonement

was never actually complete. The results were alluded to, but only in passing. The Lord spoke through the Prophet Ezekiel, saying: *"And I will give them one heart, and I will put a new spirit within you; and I will take the stony heart out of their flesh, and will give them an heart of flesh:*

"That they may walk in My Statutes, and keep My Ordinances, and do them: and they shall be My people, and I will be their God" (Ezek. 11:19-20).

But if it is to be noticed, these Passages speak of a future tense, when Christ would come, effecting a completed Atonement.

THE BLOOD

Verses 8 and 9 read: *"Aaron therefore went unto the Altar, and killed the calf of the Sin-Offering, which was for himself.*

"And the sons of Aaron brought the blood unto him, and he dipped his finger in the blood, and put it upon the horns of the Altar, and poured out the blood at the bottom of the Altar."

Why was blood so important?

First of all, it was important, vastly so, because it spoke of Christ Who would give His Own Life, and do so by shedding His Blood. As the Scripture says, *"The life of the flesh is in the blood"* (Lev. 17:11).

God is not flesh and blood, but rather *"Spirit."* For Him to pay the price for dying humanity, He would have to become man, which means that the Creator, in a sense, would have to become a creation, which is beyond our comprehension. In doing so, which was a necessity, that is, if man was to be redeemed, He would have to become flesh, blood, and bone.

God cannot die, and death was required, if man was to be redeemed. So God would have to become man.

Why would He have to become man?

When God created Adam, He gave Adam latitude and discretion, which it seems, were not given even to the Angels. It seems from Genesis 1:26-27 that tremendous dominion was given to man. In fact, Psalms 8:4-6 imply that this dominion included all of God's creation.

Psalms 8:5 says: *"For You have made him a little lower than the Angels, and have crowned him with glory and honor."*

The word *"Angels"* in this Verse is an improper translation. The actual Hebrew reads, *"For you have made him a little lower than the Godhead,"* which means that man was originally created superior to the Angels, which means that man was and is God's highest creation.

The tragedy is, man is a fallen creature. This means that he fell from total God-consciousness, down to the far lower level of self-consciousness. So we do not now see man, which includes redeemed man, as God originally made him. In fact, Jesus Christ was the Perfect Man, the Man that God originally intended; however, Jesus was God manifested in the flesh, which refers to the Incarnation.

THE FIRST ADAM AND THE LAST ADAM

Everything that God gave to the original Adam, in a sense, was lost in the Fall. Death became the mainstay, instead of life. Darkness became the emphasis instead of light. Inasmuch as God had created man in this fashion, in effect, making him the Image of God, man could not be redeemed by mere fiat or decree. In other words, the Righteousness of God demanded satisfaction. While God has the power to do anything, His power is always subjected to His Nature and His Righteousness. So for man to be properly redeemed, another Adam would have to be sent into the world, Who would do what the first Adam didn't do, which pertains to perfect obedience, and to undo, in fact, what the first Adam had done, which was to allow sin into this world, i.e., *"Satan;"* Jesus came to destroy the works of the Devil (I John 3:8). That Second Man, Whom Paul referred to as the *"Last Adam,"* was and is the Lord Jesus Christ (I Cor. 15:45-50).

He is referred to as the *"Last Adam"* simply because the term means that there will never be the need for another. So, what would the Last Adam do, in order to redeem humanity?

THE CROSS

From before the foundation of the world, God through foreknowledge knew that He would create man, and that man would fall.

NOTES

Foreknowledge as well knew the manner in which man would be redeemed. Love created man, and love would have to redeem man.

Concerning this, Peter said: *"Forasmuch as you know that you were not redeemed with corruptible things, as silver and gold, from your vain lifestyle received by tradition from your fathers;*

"But with the Precious Blood of Christ, as of a lamb without blemish and without spot:

"Who verily was foreordained before the foundation of the world, but was manifest in these last times for you" (I Pet. 1:18-20).

So, from this Passage, and others similar, we know that the Cross was not an incident or an accident. In fact, we know that Jesus came to this world not only to live, but as well, to die. Furthermore, He specifically came to die on a Cross.

WHY A CROSS?

In Israel of old, the Law stated (the Law of God) that if a man *"committed a sin worthy of death,"* and this speaks of a heinous sin, he was to be put to death. As a sign of his terrible sin, which means that he was cursed by God, his body was to be hung on a tree. He was to be placed accordingly, to serve as a spectacle of his terrible crime.

But his body was not to remain on the tree into the night, but before dark was to be taken down and buried (Deut. 21: 22-23).

In other words, we are speaking of the worst type of sin, which means that the Cross was demanded, because Jesus died not only for sin in general, but the worst type of sin that man could imagine, even the very root of sin. So, His death had to include the worst among the worst, and to be sure, it did. This means that He atoned for all sin, irrespective of its nature, or degree. This is why the Cross was demanded.

In fact, the Holy Spirit through Peter said: *"Who His Own Self bear our sins in His Own Body on the tree, that we, being dead to sins, should live unto Righteousness: by Whose stripes you were healed"* (I Pet. 2:24).

Paul said: *"Christ has redeemed us from the curse of the Law, being made a curse for us: for it is written, Cursed is every one who hangs on a tree"* (Gal. 3:13).

So the Cross was a necessity, because Jesus

had to atone for all sin, even the most hideous of sins.

THE PRICE

The price for that Redemption was high. In fact, it was so high that no man could pay the price. And if the Lord had left it there, demanding that man pay the price, man possibly might have an argument; however, due to the fact that God paid the price Himself, then man is left with no argument.

To redeem fallen man, a perfect life would have to be given. As should be understood, due to original sin, no man could supply that perfect life. Therefore, as stated, God would have to become Man, which He did, *"the Second Man"* (I Cor. 15:45-50).

Christ would live a perfect life, sinning not even one time, failing not even one time, which meant that He did what the first Adam did not do. He rendered a perfect obedience.

But there remained the terrible sin debt that had to be addressed. His perfect life could not address that sin debt, only His perfect death. Therefore, as the Perfect Sacrifice, He offered up Himself on the tree, i.e., *"Cross,"* shedding His Life's Blood, which was untainted by sin, and, thereby, which God readily accepted. This means that Christ by pouring out His Life's Blood, gave His life, which atoned for all sin, hence the constant application of the blood respecting the Old Testament Sacrifices (Eph. 2:13-18).

We were not purchased with such corruptible things as silver or gold, even as Peter said, which is the most valuable commodity in the world, but which was insufficient. We were rather purchased by His Precious Blood; perfect Blood, incidentally, which no other individual had (I Pet. 1:18-20). For life to be regained, a perfect life would have to be given, which was the price that the Nature and Righteousness of God demanded. Jesus paid that price, and that's the reason that Paul said: *"But God forbid that I should glory, save in the Cross of our Lord Jesus Christ, by Whom the world is crucified unto me, and I unto the world"* (Gal. 6:14).

WHY WAS BLOOD PUT ON THE HORNS OF THE ALTAR?

The Brazen Altar was the first vessel of all

NOTES

the sacred vessels. It sat outside of the Tabernacle in the Court. One other sacred vessel stood between it and the Tabernacle, which was the Brazen Laver.

On each of the four corners of the Brazen Altar was a horn. Each one pointed outward, north, south, east, and west.

This referred to the fact that God's Redemption Plan was one Plan, and was for the entirety of mankind all over the world. This means that every other supposed plan of Redemption, whatever it might be, was not acceptable by God, and in fact, was cursed by God (Gal. 1:8-9). Furthermore, this Plan, which was symbolized by all of these sacred vessels, all and without exception, pointed to Jesus Christ as the Saviour of the world. That's the reason that Jesus said: *"I am the Way, the Truth, and the Life: no man comes unto the Father, but by Me"* (Jn. 14:6).

He also said: *"I am the Door: by Me if any man enter in, he shall be saved, and shall go in and out, and find pasture"* (Jn. 10:9).

The Lord commanding Aaron, and all Priests who would follow after him, to apply blood from the Sin-Offering, at least in this type of Sacrifice, to the four horns of the Altar, was done so in order to proclaim the *"way"* and the *"manner"* in which this Plan of Redemption would be put into force. The blood coming from the slain victim, and part of that victim being burned on the Altar, specified that Christ would effect Redemption by and through the Cross, and by and through the Cross alone!

This means that man can be saved only by trusting in Christ, and what Christ has done for us at the Cross.

The balance of the Blood was then poured out at the bottom of the Altar, which signified that Jesus would die on an Altar, i.e., *"a Cross."* The *"Altar"* was always a place of death!

WITHOUT THE CAMP

Verses 10 and 11 read: *"But the fat, and the kidneys, and the caul above the liver of the Sin-Offering, he burned upon the Altar; as the LORD commanded Moses.*

"And the flesh and the hide he burnt with fire without the camp."

As is obvious here, only a part of the

carcass of the Sin-Offering was burned on the Altar, that being the *"fat"* and certain other organs, while the balance was taken *"without the camp,"* and there *"burnt with fire."* This says two things:

1. The carcass being taken *"without the camp,"* and there burned completely proclaims the fact that all sin would be completely expiated in the Death of Christ, which means, *"to do away with the guilt incurred."* The whole curse fell upon the Substitute. The Atonement was not completed until the whole sacrifice was consumed. In fact, the Sin-Offering was to be burned in a clean place, actually *"where the ashes are poured out"* (Lev. 4:12).

2. The majority of the Sin-Offering being burned outside of the camp coincides with the statement as given by Paul: *"Wherefore Jesus also, that He might sanctify the people with His Own Blood, suffered without the gate"* (Heb. 13:12).

THE BURNT-OFFERING

Verses 12, 13, and 14 read: *"And he slew the Burnt-Offering; and Aaron's sons presented unto him the blood, which he sprinkled round about upon the Altar.*

"And they presented the Burnt-Offering unto him, with the pieces thereof, and the head: and he burnt them upon the Altar.

"And he did wash the inwards and the legs, and burnt them upon the Burnt-Offering on the Altar."

As we have stated, the *"Sin-Offering"* was *"most holy,"* and symbolized Christ taking the guilt of the sinner, and making it His Own. The *"Burnt-Offering"* symbolized the Perfection of Christ, and Him giving that Perfection to the sinner.

The process of cutting up the carcass is not mentioned here, because it is implied in the fact that the ritual on this occasion was exactly the same as in the Offerings made by Moses.

Aaron's sons handed the dismembered victim to him piece by piece, which was done in this manner for a reason.

The idea is twofold:

First of all, it points to the great price paid by Christ, especially His separation from the Father, from 12 noon, to 3 p.m., when He was on the Cross. During this time, the Earth,

or at least that part of the world, turned black, because a thrice-Holy God couldn't look upon His Son, as He did bear the sin penalty of mankind. During that time, He was separated from the Father, at least as it regards the union He had always known.

As well, the dismemberment of the victim is also meant to portray the terrible ravages of sin upon the human heart and life. That's why Jesus said of Satan that he, *"steals, kills, and destroys"* (Jn. 10:10).

WASH THE INWARDS

All of the Burnt-Offering was consumed on the Brazen Altar, all that is, with the exception of the hide.

But yet, certain parts of the physical organs were washed, and then placed on the Altar along with the carcass.

This was meant to show the veracity of the Atonement. In other words, what Christ would do at the Cross would be far more than a mere external application. It would go to the very vitals, the very soul, and spirit of the individual, hence the *"inwards being washed."*

This is the reason that man's solutions never work. He can only deal with externals. He tries to deal with the internals through humanistic psychology, but such is a fruitless effort. In fact, it is worse than useless! When the person comes to Christ, he or she is *"born again,"* which means that the person has become a new creation, and done so both inwardly and outwardly (II Cor. 5:17).

(15) "AND HE BROUGHT THE PEOPLE'S OFFERING, AND TOOK THE GOAT, WHICH WAS THE SIN-OFFERING FOR THE PEOPLE, AND SLEW IT, AND OFFERED IT FOR SIN, AS THE FIRST.

(16) "AND HE BROUGHT THE BURNT-OFFERING, AND OFFERED IT ACCORDING TO THE MANNER.

(17) "AND HE BROUGHT THE MEAT-OFFERING, AND TOOK AN HANDFUL THEREOF, AND BURNT IT UPON THE ALTAR, BESIDE THE BURNT SACRIFICE OF THE MORNING.

(18) "HE SLEW ALSO THE BULLOCK AND THE RAM FOR A SACRIFICE OF PEACE-OFFERINGS, WHICH WAS FOR THE PEOPLE: AND AARON'S SONS PRESENTED UNTO HIM THE BLOOD, WHICH

HE SPRINKLED UPON THE ALTAR ROUND ABOUT.

(19) "AND THE FAT OF THE BULLOCK AND OF THE RAM, THE RUMP, AND THAT WHICH COVERED THE INWARDS, AND THE KIDNEYS, AND THE CAUL ABOVE THE LIVER:

(20) "AND THEY PUT THE FAT UPON THE BREAST, AND HE BURNT THE FAT UPON THE ALTAR:

(21) "AND THE BREAST AND THE RIGHT SHOULDER AARON WAVED FOR A WAVE-OFFERING BEFORE THE LORD; AS MOSES COMMANDED.

(22) "AND AARON LIFTED UP HIS HAND TOWARD THE PEOPLE, AND BLESSED THEM, AND CAME DOWN FROM OFFERING OF THE SIN-OFFERING, AND THE BURNT-OFFERING, AND PEACE-OFFERINGS.

(23) "AND MOSES AND AARON WENT INTO THE TABERNACLE OF THE CON-GREGATION, AND CAME OUT, AND BLESSED THE PEOPLE: AND THE GLORY OF THE LORD APPEARED UNTO ALL THE PEOPLE.

(24) "AND THERE CAME A FIRE OUT FROM BEFORE THE LORD, AND CON-SUMED UPON THE ALTAR THE BURNT-OFFERING AND THE FAT, WHICH WHEN ALL THE PEOPLE SAW, THEY SHOUTED, AND FELL ON THEIR FACES."

The composition is:

1. Four different Offerings at this time were offered for the people. In fact, this was the very first time that this was done. It was the *"Sin-Offering"* for Israel's Atonement. It was the *"Burnt-Offering"* which gave to Is-rael the Perfection of Christ. It was the *"Meat-Offering"* which was to render thanks, for God accepting the Offerings that had been pre-sented. It was the *"Peace-Offering"* which signified that due to God accepting the Offer-ings, the people now had *"peace"* with God.

2. Verses 22 and 23 proclaim the blessing of the people. The lifting up of hands be-came a custom of Priests in blessing the people when completing their duties for them in the rituals.

3. Exactly what Moses said would happen, did happen. *"The Glory of the Lord appeared unto all the people."* How did this happen?

NOTES

Verse 24 tells us *"And there came a fire out from before the Lord, and consumed upon the Altar the Burnt-Offering and the fat."*

THE PEOPLE'S OFFERING

Verses 15 through 18 read: *"And he brought the people's Offering, and took the goat, which was the Sin-Offering for the people, and slew it, and offered it for sin, as the first.*

"And he brought the Burnt-Offering, and offered it according to the manner.

"And he brought the Meat-Offering, and took an handful thereof, and burnt it upon the Altar, beside the Burnt Sacrifice of the morning.

"He slew also the bullock and the ram for a Sacrifice of Peace-Offerings, which was for the people: and Aaron's sons presented unto him the blood, which he sprinkled upon the Altar round about."

As we have previously stated, it took five great Offerings to properly portray the one Sacrifice of Christ. As Aaron and his sons for the very first time offered up sacrifices for the people, four of these Offerings were presented, leaving out the Trespass-Offering. This was left out because the Offerings were general, instead of personal. While they defi-nitely had a personal result, they were in fact, offered for the entirety of the nation.

The *"Trespass-Offering"* mostly concerned itself with differences or wrongs done to a neighbor. After the sacrifices were properly explained to the people *"Trespass-Offerings"* were no doubt presented, beginning at that time. But for now, the four Sacrifices men-tioned here dealt with the entire nation, and in general.

Most surely, we find in the description of all these Offerings, plus the entirety of the Bible for that matter, that Redemption by blood is the great theme of the Scriptures, from beginning to end. This may be repul-sive to some, and no doubt is; however, it is only because they do not understand the ter-rible ravages of sin, even though sin is even at that moment destroying them.

We must ever remember that we're not dealing here merely with this life, but for eternity. The sin is great; the price was high for cleansing as it regards this terrible malady;

but God paid the price, when He became man, and gave Himself on the Cross of Calvary. Even as Paul said: *"Who gave Himself for our sins, that He might deliver us from this present evil world, according to the Will of God and our Father"* (Gal. 1:4).

Had that not occurred, of which all of these sacrifices were types and shadows, we would have died in our sins, forever lost; and to be sure, the thought of eternal darkness is beyond comprehension!

THE WAVE-OFFERING

Verses 19 through 21 read: *"And the fat of the bullock and of the ram, the rump, and that which covered the inwards, and the kidneys, and the caul above the liver:*

"And they put the fat upon the breast, and he burnt the fat upon the Altar:

"And the breast and the right shoulder Aaron waved for a Wave-Offering before the LORD; as Moses commanded."

For the Sin-Offering a *"goat"* was offered. For the Burnt-Offering a calf and a lamb were offered (vs. 3). For the Peace-Offerings the bullock and the ram were sacrificed.

What did the different animals mean?

In this instance, the goat represented sin more than any of these other animals, which Christ took upon Himself.

The lamb and the calf are the most docile of the animals, representing the humility of Christ, in the offering up of Himself as an Offering to God.

The bullock typified sin forgiven, and done so because of Christ, while the ram specified the High Priestly Work of Christ, both proclaiming that Peace had been restored. Regarding the Peace-Offerings, the fat of the bullock and the ram, as well as other parts, were burnt upon the Altar, signifying that all Blessings come from God, of which these things were a type.

Aaron then took the *"breasts"* and the *"right shoulder"* of both the bullock and the ram, lifted them up, and waved them for a *"Wave-Offering before the Lord."*

The *"Wave-Offering"* signified that all Blessings came from above, which means that Redemption would come from above, and would do so in the form of the Lord Jesus Christ, of which these sacrifices were types.

NOTES

THE BLESSING

Verse 22 reads: *"And Aaron lifted up his hand toward the people, and blessed them, and came down from offering of the Sin-Offering, and the Burnt-Offering, and Peace-Offerings."*

As stated, the lifting up of the hands of the Priests became a custom in blessing the people when completing their duties for them in the rituals. What the Priests said to them on this occasion is not stated, but it could have been what was established for Priests in Numbers 6:24-26.

"The Lord bless you, and keep you:

"The Lord make His Face shine upon you, and be gracious unto you:

"The Lord lift up His countenance upon you, and give you peace."

THE APPEARANCE OF THE GLORY OF THE LORD

Verses 23 and 24 read: *"And Moses and Aaron went into the Tabernacle of the congregation, and came out, and blessed the people: and the Glory of the LORD appeared unto all the people.*

"And there came a fire out from before the LORD, and consumed upon the Altar the Burnt-Offering and the fat, which when all the people saw, they shouted, and fell on their faces."

Concerning this, Ellicott says: *"The Sacrifices being ended, there still remained the burning of the Incense on the Golden Altar which stood in the Holy Place of the Tabernacle. Hence Aaron, conducted by Moses, left the Court where the Altar of Burnt-Offering stood, and where the Sacrifices had been offered, and went into the Holy Place where the Altar of Incense stood to perform this last act of the ritual (Ex. 30:7).*

"Having already delivered to Aaron the charge of all the things connected with the Sacrifices in the Court, Moses now also committed to him the care of the things within the Sanctuary, showing him at the same time, how to offer the Incense, how to arrange the Shewbread on the Table, how to light and trim the Lamps of the Lampstand, all of which were in the Sanctuary."

This being done, both of them came out,

after which they had no doubt prayed and asked the Lord for His guidance, and then they blessed the people.

And then it happened!

The fire did not come directly from Heaven, but rather came from God Who dwelt between the Mercy Seat and the Cherubim. A literal tongue of flame came from the Holy of Holies through the Veil without burning it, and struck the Brazen Altar, and consumed the *"Burnt-Offering and the fat."* In fact, it was visible to all of Israel.

When the people saw this, they shouted, and fell on their faces, which of course, is understandable!

Some claim that this particular fire was the first fire on the Altar; however, according to Leviticus 8:16 and 9:10, this is not correct. Fire had already been kindled on the Altar, in order for Aaron to offer up sacrifices for himself and his sons.

This being the case, fire from God manifested His Divine Presence and that He had accepted the Sacrifice, which He consumed with the tongue of flame.

This means that what the Lord had commanded had been faithfully obeyed by Moses, as he instructed Aaron and Aaron's sons. All was complete. There was nothing lacking and, therefore, the Divine Glory appeared, and the whole assembly fell prostrate in adoring worship.

But let us not forget that the Glory of God, represented by the tongue of flame, and which came from the Holy of Holies, was the result of the proper Sacrifice. In other words, it was the Cross, which the Altar and the Sacrifices represented, which God acknowledged and honored. More particularly, it was His Son, Who would die on that Cross, which guaranteed Atonement, and brought about the manifestation.

How important it is that we understand these things! This is the reason that we preach the Cross! This is why Paul said that nothing must be emphasized to the extent that the *"Cross of Christ is made of none effect"* (I Cor. 1:17).

We see here Israel brought into the full enjoyment of the results of accomplished Atonement, at least as much as could be done at that particular time. They shouted

because God had accepted the Atonement. Unfortunately, we are all too often shouting over other things, which have little significance. Let me say it again:

It is ever *"the Cross!" "The Cross!" "The Cross!"*

"Lo, He comes, with clouds descending,
"Once for our Salvation slain;
"Thousand Angel hosts attending,
"Swell the triumph of His train."

"Every eye shall then behold Him,
"Robed in mighty majesty;
"Those who set at naught and sold Him,
"Pierced, and nailed Him to the Tree."

"Now Redemption long expected,
"See in solemn pomp appear:
"All His Saints, by men rejected,
"Now shall meet Him in the air:"

"Yea, Amen; let all adore Thee,
"High on Thine eternal Throne;
"Saviour, take the power and glory;
"Claim the kingdoms for Your Own."

CHAPTER 10

(1) "AND NADAB AND ABIHU, THE SONS OF AARON, TOOK EITHER OF THEM HIS CENSER, AND PUT FIRE THEREIN, AND PUT INCENSE THEREON, AND OFFERED STRANGE FIRE BEFORE THE LORD, WHICH HE COMMANDED THEM NOT.

(2) "AND THERE WENT OUT FIRE FROM THE LORD, AND DEVOURED THEM, AND THEY DIED BEFORE THE LORD.

(3) "THEN MOSES SAID UNTO AARON, THIS IS IT THAT THE LORD SPAKE, SAYING, I WILL BE SANCTIFIED IN THEM WHO COME NIGH ME, AND BEFORE ALL THE PEOPLE I WILL BE GLORIFIED. AND AARON HELD HIS PEACE.

(4) "AND MOSES CALLED MISHAEL AND ELZAPHAN, THE SONS OF UZZIEL THE UNCLE OF AARON, AND SAID UNTO THEM, COME NEAR, AND CARRY YOUR BRETHREN FROM BEFORE THE SANCTUARY OUT OF THE CAMP.

(5) "SO THEY WENT NEAR, AND CARRIED

THEM IN THEIR COATS OUT OF THE CAMP; AS MOSES HAD SAID.

(6) "AND MOSES SAID UNTO AARON, AND UNTO ELEAZAR AND UNTO ITHAMAR, HIS SONS, UNCOVER NOT YOUR HEADS, NEITHER REND YOUR CLOTHES; LEST YOU DIE, AND LEST WRATH COME UPON ALL THE PEOPLE: BUT LET YOUR BRETHREN, THE WHOLE HOUSE OF ISRAEL, BEWAIL THE BURNING WHICH THE LORD HAS KINDLED.

(7) "AND YOU SHALL NOT GO OUT FROM THE DOOR OF THE TABERNACLE OF THE CONGREGATION, LEST YOU DIE: FOR THE ANOINTING OIL OF THE LORD IS UPON YOU. AND THEY DID ACCORDING TO THE WORD OF MOSES."

The overview is:

1. Chapter 10 portrays the Judgment of God upon the sinner instead of the Sacrifice.

2. It was because of *"strange fire,"* the same *"strange fire"* that is so abundant in false doctrines, false sacrifices, and false prophets, even in this day and age.

3. The fire they used, while it definitely was fire, did not come from the Brazen Altar, and as such, was not a type of Christ and Him Crucified and, therefore, could not be recognized by God, but in effect, had to be judged by God. It was the sin of Cain.

4. They were devoured by fire from the Holy of Holies, the same fire which consumed the Sacrifice in the previous Chapter. This tells us that if our Faith is anchored in Christ and Him Crucified, there are untold blessings connected with the Gospel; otherwise, it is death, i.e., *"spiritual death."*

STRANGE FIRE

Verses 1 and 2 read: *"And Nadab and Abihu, the sons of Aaron, took either of them his censer, and put fire therein, and put Incense thereon, and offered strange fire before the LORD, which He commanded them not.*

"And there went out fire from the LORD, and devoured them, and they died before the LORD."

The previous Chapter closes with fire coming out from the Lord, Who dwelt between the Mercy Seat and the Cherubim in the Holy of Holies, and consuming the Sacrifice on the Brazen Altar, which was a display of the

NOTES

Glory of God, and which greatly benefited the people (Lev. 9:4, 6, 23-24). But now, the same fire comes from the Lord from the same place, but rather kills two of the Priests, Nadab and Abihu, sons of Aaron. The first fire was Glory; the second was Judgment, although the same fire. A powerful lesson, one of the greatest in the Bible, is to be learned here.

First of all, what was this *"strange fire"*?

Twice a day, at the time of the morning and the evening Sacrifices (9 a.m. and 3 p.m.), the Priests were to burn holy Incense before the Lord, and it was to be done in the following manner:

They were to take coals of fire from the Brazen Altar, and only from the Brazen Altar, and put those coals of fire on the Golden Altar, which sat immediately in front of the Veil, which hid the Holy of Holies, where God dwelt between the Mercy Seat and the Cherubim.

Incense was to be poured over these coals of fire, which would fill the Holy Place.

As stated, this fire had to come from the Brazen Altar, which was a type of Christ and His great Sacrifice of Himself on the Cross of Calvary. This is what the Brazen Altar typified.

So, the fire that Nadab and Abihu used didn't come from this source, but more than likely from one of the fires which had been made for boiling the sacrificial flesh. That being the case, it definitely would have been fire used for spiritual purposes, but it was not fire from the Brazen Altar.

The idea is, it doesn't really matter where the fire comes from, from whatever ignition, if it's not from the Brazen Altar, it could not be accepted. It is the same presently.

THE BRAZEN ALTAR, A TYPE OF CALVARY

As stated, the coals of fire which were to be placed on the Golden Altar, had to come from the Brazen Altar (Lev. 16:12). God would accept no other, and as I think is overly obvious, looked at the presentation of other fire as a most grave offense, which brought death to two Priests.

I think one can say without fear of contradiction that the Brazen Altar was the crowning vessel of all of the sacred vessels. One may think that the Ark of the Covenant, covered by the Mercy Seat, over which looked the Cherubim, was the crowning piece. While that definitely was the place where God dwelt, which typified His Throne, the idea is, that august place could not be reached, unless it was reached by way of the Brazen Altar. The Brazen Altar, typifying Calvary, was the key to all things. The Sacrifices were offered on this Altar, and this Altar alone. In fact, God absolutely forbid Sacrifices to be offered on the Golden Altar. The blood alone could be applied to the horns of the Golden Altar, or sprinkled, but Sacrifices there must not be offered, nor strange incense, nor Meat-Offerings, and neither must any Drink-Offering be poured thereon (Ex. 30:9). In other words, to do such was, in effect, to bypass Calvary, which God could not tolerate. Man can come before God only on one premise, and that is by and through the shed Blood of the Lord Jesus Christ. That and that alone, which the Brazen Altar and its Sacrifices typified, gains entrance to God in any form. When Jesus said, *"No man cometh to the Father but by Me,"* He was speaking of what He would do at the Cross of Calvary, which would make all of this possible (Jn. 14:6).

Whenever Nadab and Abihu, who were Priests of God, which means they were ordained of God, called of God, and anointed by God, ignored the Cross, which is actually what they did, the results of judgment were immediate. It is no less presently!

THE SIN OF THE MODERN CHURCH

Regarding most of the modern Church, the Cross has been ignored, set aside, and even repudiated in some cases. In fact, the modern Church is a Crossless Church, which worships a Crossless Christ. As such, it worships *"another Jesus"* (II Cor. 11:4).

Most of the worship is *"will worship,"* of which we will have more to say in a moment, which means that it is worship which does not originate at the Cross.

All false doctrine, in some way, has its origination in a false interpretation of the Cross. Paul said: *"For many walk, of whom I have told you often, and now tell you even

NOTES

weeping, that they are the enemies of the Cross of Christ:*

"Whose end is destruction, whose god is their belly, and whose glory is in their shame, who mind earthly things" (Phil. 3:18-19).

The Message of the Cross in reality is the foundation of all doctrine. Within itself, even though it may be referred to as a doctrine, it is not merely a doctrine, but rather the foundation on which all doctrine is built, at least if it's true Biblical Doctrine. I am absolutely positive that Jesus looked at the Sacrificial Offering of Himself on the Cross of Calvary as more than a mere doctrine. No! As stated, it is the foundation of all doctrine.

And if it's not the foundation of doctrine, then in some way, that which is presented is strange fire.

Let the Reader understand that it definitely was *"fire"* in which Nadab and Abihu offered. It looked just like the fire from the Brazen Altar. But even though it looked like that fire, and in fact by mere observation, could not be distinguished from that fire, God knew it was strange fire, and acted accordingly.

All types of strange fire are being offered up today in Christendom. It looks right, and it looks real, but it does not originate with the Cross. As a result, it cannot be right, and most definitely, it will ultimately be judged by God.

Rather than trying to name the types of *"strange fire,"* suffice to say, anything that ignores the Cross, or registers unbelief toward the Cross, or repudiates the Cross, is *"strange fire,"* irrespective of how good it may look on the surface.

We believe that the Word of God teaches that when Jesus died on the Cross, He addressed Himself to every single problem facing the human race, in other words, everything that was lost at the Fall. While it is true that in the Atonement, there are some things, such as the glorified body, which we will not have until the coming Resurrection, still, everything was addressed. Not only did Paul say so, but Peter did as well (II Pet. 1:3-4). When it comes to sin, and it doesn't matter what the bondage might be, whatever the sin might be, whether it's judged to be little, or large, Jesus answered it at the

Cross. There, He defeated Satan, along with every single demon spirit and fallen angel. He did it by atoning for all sin, past, present, and future (Col. 2:14-15). So, if the Preacher is not preaching the Cross, then he's not preaching the Gospel. He might be preaching about the Gospel, and as such, say some good things, but until he preaches the Cross, he's not preaching the Gospel (I Cor. 1:17-18, 21, 23). Paul said:

"For after that in the wisdom of God the world by wisdom knew not God, it pleased God by the foolishness of preaching (preaching the Cross) *to save them who believe"* (I Cor. 1:21).

The Holy Spirit through Paul is not claiming here that preaching is foolishness, or that preaching the Cross is foolishness, but that this is the way the world looks at the situation. He also said:

"For the preaching of the Cross is to them who perish foolishness; but unto us which are saved it is the Power of God" (I Cor. 1:18).

Therefore, this means that the foray of the Church into humanistic psychology is a slap in the face of Christ, in effect, a repudiation of the Cross, which states, whether admitted or not, that the Cross is insufficient, and that worldly wisdom is needed as well. What a travesty! What stupidity! What an abomination! That's at least one of the reasons that Jesus said:

"You are they which justify yourselves before men; but God knows your hearts: for that which is highly esteemed among men is abomination in the sight of God" (Lk. 16:15).

THE CROSS OF CHRIST, THE DIVIDING LINE

As should be plainly and clearly obvious, the Cross is not something that can be ignored. Anyone, even as we have previously stated, who honestly reads the Bible, cannot help but see the Cross as the central theme of the entirety of the Word of God. Once again, as we've already said a number of times, the Holy Spirit is making the Cross at this present time so visible that it can no longer be ignored. One will either have to accept it or reject it. In other words, there will be no neutral Christians, as it regards the Cross of Christ.

NOTES

Those who reject the Cross, or ignore the Cross, or even try to link it with something else, are going to be placed on the side of the apostate church. There is no place else to be as it regards this particular position. Those who embrace the Cross will be in the True Church.

In fact, this is the way that it has always been. The Cross has ever been the dividing line, and so this is not something new; however, I personally feel that the emphasis which the Holy Spirit is now placing on the Cross, one might say, is new. These are the last of the last days, and the world is saddled with a Church that says, *"I am rich, and increased with goods, and have need of nothing."* But Christ says: *"And knowest not that you are wretched, and miserable, and poor, and blind, and naked"* (Rev. 3:17).

I personally feel as well that the Lord has raised up this particular Ministry (Jimmy Swaggart Ministries) to take this Message of the Cross to the world. He is giving us the means to do so, through Television and Radio. In fact, at this particular time (August 2002), we are now airing Television in some 40 countries of the world. Also, and of great significance, at least as far as the spread of the Gospel is concerned, the Ministry is purchasing Radio Stations all over the nation, and in fact, will continue to do so, until we cover the entirety of the United States, and the world by Internet.

As well, the Lord is raising up other Preachers all over this world, who are preaching the Message of the Cross, and that number will increase almost on a daily basis.

Of all the things the Lord has helped us to do and helped us to see in past years, I do believe that this which He is presently doing will help us to have a greater impact on the Church than ever before, as well as seeing untold numbers of people brought to a saving knowledge of Jesus Christ. In fact, I think this is the very reason, or at least one of the primary reasons, why the Lord has given to me the Revelation of the Cross. It is not for me only, as would be obvious, but it is for the entirety of the Body of Christ.

WILL WORSHIP

Acceptable worship can only be in the

energy of the Holy Spirit, in the truth of the shed Blood, and in obedience to the inspired Word. The fire of the Holy Spirit associates itself alone with the Blood of the Crucified Saviour; now the Believer must understand this, and must understand it perfectly, because we are speaking here of the fate of the eternal soul. One must know that all other fire is *"strange fire."*

Of necessity, the Lord must pour out His Righteous Judgment upon all false worship, though He will never *"quench the smoking flax nor break the bruised reed."* The thought of this is most solemnizing, when one calls to mind the thousands of censers, so to speak, smoking with strange fire throughout the wide domain of modern Christendom (Mackintosh).

Everyone who knows, through Grace, the pardon of his sins through the Atoning Blood of Jesus, can worship the Father in Spirit and in Truth. And to be sure, these things can only be known in a Divine way. They do not belong to the flesh, or to nature. In fact, they do not even belong to this Earth. They are spiritual and they are heavenly.

In fact, and sadly so, very much, if not most, of that which passes among men for the worship of God is but *"strange fire."* It is fire that has been brought from man's own ingenuity, strength, and ability. In other words, no matter how good it looks, no matter that it is real fire, it did not come from the Brazen Altar, which means that it did not come from the Cross, which means that it cannot be accepted by God.

However, let it be readily known that rejection by God, at the same time, demands judgment.

JUDGMENT

The Lord is patient with all of us, and we thank God for that a thousand times over. Where would any of us be if His patience was not as it is?

But whenever the time comes that the *"Light"* is shone in all of its full glory, if that Light is rejected, Judgment, just as it was with Nadab and Abihu, is swift and sure. So what am I saying?

I'm saying that the Holy Spirit is now making the Message of the Cross clear and

plain to the entirety of the Church. They're going to have to make a choice. With many it will mean giving up their respective Church, even their respective Denomination. With many it will mean giving up their circle of friends. But if we stop and think a moment, that's exactly what Jesus demanded. He plainly said:

"If any man will come after Me, let him deny himself, and take up his cross daily, and follow Me.

"For whosoever will save his life shall lose it: but whosoever will lose his life for My sake, the same shall save it" (Lk. 9:23-24).

The fire of judgment will consume the Sacrifice, i.e., *"Christ,"* or else it will consume the individual. In other words, we go Christ's way, which is the Cross, or else we face the Judgment of God.

I WILL BE SANCTIFIED IN THEM WHO COME NEAR ME

Verses 3 through 5 read: *"Then Moses said unto Aaron, This is it that the LORD spoke, saying, I will be sanctified in them who come near Me, and before all the people I will be glorified. And Aaron held his peace.*

"And Moses called Mishael and Elzaphan, the sons of Uzziel the uncle of Aaron, and said unto them, Come near, and carry your brethren from before the Sanctuary out of the camp.

"So they went near, and carried them in their coats out of the camp; as Moses had said."

Quite possibly, Moses inquired of the Lord, as to why Nadab and Abihu were stricken dead. The answer was straightforward: *"I will be sanctified in them who come near Me, and before all the people I will be glorified."*

The Lord is saying by this statement that if men place on His Altar the workings of their own corrupt will, what must be the result? Judgment! Sooner or later, judgment must come! It may linger, but it will come. It cannot be otherwise.

What did the Lord mean by the statement, *"I will be sanctified in them who come near Me, and before all the people I will be glorified"*?

In essence, He is meaning that things will be done His way, or judgment will come. *"To be sanctified"* means *"to be set apart."* In this instance, it means *"to be set apart to God's Way."*

And what is that way?

I think it is overly obvious as to what that way is, as presented here in this Tenth Chapter of Leviticus.

His Way is, *"Jesus Christ and Him Crucified"* (I Cor. 1:23). If another way is instituted by man, it is a way that is abominable to God, irrespective as to how religious it may seem to be on the surface.

To be sure, Cain did not refuse to offer a sacrifice. In fact, he offered a beautiful sacrifice, but it just happened to be a sacrifice that God could not accept. It was the labor of Cain's own hands, which means that it's polluted to begin with.

There is only one Sacrifice that God will recognize, and that is the Sacrifice of Christ. When we recognize that Sacrifice, place all of our faith and hope in that Sacrifice, we are then sanctifying God. When we fail to do so, God will not fail to be sanctified. He will pour out judgment upon that which rebels against Him, which as well sanctifies Him.

LEST YOU DIE

Verses 6 and 7 read: *"And Moses said unto Aaron, and unto Eleazar, and unto Ithamar, his sons, Uncover not your heads, neither rend your clothes; lest you die, and lest wrath come upon all the people: but let your brethren, the whole house of Israel, bewail the burning which the LORD has kindled.*

"And you shall not go out from the Door of the Tabernacle of the congregation, lest you die: for the Anointing Oil of the LORD is upon you. And they did according to the word of Moses."

We find here that Aaron, his other two sons, Eleazar and Ithamar, as well as the entirety of the nation of Israel, were now in great danger of the Wrath of God being poured out upon them as well.

Why was this so?

While it would have been proper for the people of Israel to have mourned the deaths of these Priests, the High Priest and his remaining sons must prove their submission to the Divine chastisement by crushing their individual feelings of sorrow. In fact, a murmur on their part would have brought God's

NOTES

Wrath on themselves, and even on Israel as a whole, whom they represented.

These Priests could not stop their duties for one moment, even for the sake of burying their dead. Others would have to perform this task.

For the Priests to have mourned would, in essence, have been saying that the Cross was of little significance. And regrettably, that's what many modern Preachers are now saying.

They pray, or at least what little they do pray, with no thought of the Cross. They worship, but rather that which God does not recognize as worship, simply because they attempt to approach God without the benefit of the shed Blood of the Lamb. They send needy souls to humanistic psychologists, which means that they are expressing a vote of no confidence as it regards the Cross.

The truth is, with many of these Preachers, they, nor the people whom they lead, are not even saved. But for those who definitely are saved, and some definitely are, chastisement is about to follow. If that is rejected, judgment will follow, and it will not be a pretty picture.

The Lord plainly told the Priests through Moses, you will do as I say, or you will die!

Is it any different now?

THE DAY OF GRACE

Many think that because this is the Dispensation of Grace, and it definitely is, that God withholds all judgment. Nothing could be further from the truth. The facts are, God makes greater demands now, and I speak of this Dispensation of Grace, even than He did under Law. Listen again to Paul:

"And the times of this ignorance (before the Cross), *God winked at; but now* (this Day of Grace) *commandeth all men everywhere to repent"* (Acts 17:30).

Under Grace, which has been brought about by the Cross, much more light is given to a darkened world; consequently, much more is expected, once again, as should be obvious!

While the Judgment of God presently may not be as obvious and as pointed, as it was with these two Priests; still, I greatly suspect that if the truth be known, many things which presently happen to individuals, although thought of as being for certain causes and reasons, and we speak of Believers, or at least those who profess, what is actually taking place is the Judgment of God. We must never take lightly the Divine Nature of God. For those who stray, chastisement will come. If that fails, Judgment will follow.

While God is love, His Nature will never allow His Righteousness to be impugned. In fact, He cannot allow such to happen. If He did, the entire structure of Righteousness would collapse. He who loves must at the same time judge. If He doesn't then it's not really love that's being shown. This means that the Judgment of God is also the Love of God.

Man can only be saved in one way, and that is by Faith in the slain Lamb (Jn. 3:16; Rom. 5:8; Rev. 5:6).

(8) "AND THE LORD SPOKE UNTO AARON, SAYING,

(9) "DO NOT DRINK WINE NOR STRONG DRINK, YOU, NOR YOUR SONS WITH YOU, WHEN YOU GO INTO THE TABERNACLE OF THE CONGREGATION, LEST YOU DIE: IT SHALL BE A STATUTE FOREVER THROUGHOUT YOUR GENERATIONS:

(10) "AND THAT YOU MAY PUT DIFFERENCE BETWEEN HOLY AND UNHOLY, AND BETWEEN UNCLEAN AND CLEAN;

(11) "AND THAT YOU MAY TEACH THE CHILDREN OF ISRAEL ALL THE STATUTES WHICH THE LORD HAS SPOKEN UNTO THEM BY THE HAND OF MOSES.

(12) "AND MOSES SPOKE UNTO AARON, AND UNTO ELEAZAR AND UNTO ITHAMAR, HIS SONS WHO WERE LEFT, TAKE THE MEAT-OFFERING THAT REMAINS OF THE OFFERINGS OF THE LORD MADE BY FIRE, AND EAT IT WITHOUT LEAVEN BESIDE THE ALTAR: FOR IT IS MOST HOLY:

(13) "AND YOU SHALL EAT IT IN THE HOLY PLACE, BECAUSE IT IS YOUR DUE, AND YOUR SONS' DUE, OF THE SACRIFICES OF THE LORD MADE BY FIRE: FOR SO I AM COMMANDED.

(14) "AND THE WAVE BREAST AND HEAVE SHOULDER SHALL YOU EAT IN A CLEAN PLACE; YOU, AND YOUR SONS, AND YOUR DAUGHTERS WITH YOU: FOR THEY BE YOUR DUE, AND YOUR SONS'

NOTES

DUE, WHICH ARE GIVEN OUT OF THE SACRIFICES OF PEACE-OFFERINGS OF THE CHILDREN OF ISRAEL.

(15) "THE HEAVE-SHOULDER AND THE WAVE-BREAST SHALL THEY BRING WITH THE OFFERINGS MADE BY FIRE OF THE FAT, TO WAVE IT FOR A WAVE-OFFERING BEFORE THE LORD; IT SHALL BE YOURS, AND YOUR SONS' WITH YOU, BY A STATUTE FOREVER; AS THE LORD HAS COMMANDED."

The exegesis is:

1. The Law given here by the Lord has led to the thought that Nadab and Abihu had acted under the excitement of intoxicating drink. In other words, they were drunk.

2. We have in the Ninth Verse a prohibition against any type of strong drink.

3. The Children of Israel were to be taught the entirety of the Law as it had been given to Moses, as the Eleventh Verse records.

4. Aaron and his two remaining sons, Eleazar and Ithamar, were to partake of the *"Meat-Offering,"* which made the Perfection of Christ their own, and as well, expressed thanksgiving, because the *"Meat-Offering"* represented the Perfection of Christ, and thankfulness to God that Christ would ultimately be given to the human race.

5. The Meat-Offering was *"most holy,"* simply because some of it was burned on the Brazen Altar, which was a type of the Crucifixion of Christ.

It was to be eaten by the Priests in the *"Holy Place,"* which was the first or the larger room of the Tabernacle, which totally represented Christ.

They were to take the *"Wave-Breast"* and the *"Heave-Shoulder"* of the *"Peace-Offering,"* which was the portion of the Priests, and could be eaten by them and their families, and in fact could be eaten anywhere in the camp that was ceremonially clean.

6. But before it was eaten, they were to present it to the Lord as a *"Wave-Offering,"* signifying that God was the Giver of all good things, but that the best of those things was His giving of Christ to the world.

STRONG DRINK

Verses 8 through 10 read: *"And the LORD spoke unto Aaron, saying,*

"Do not drink wine nor strong drink, you, nor your sons with you, when you go into the Tabernacle of the congregation, lest you die: it shall be a Statute forever throughout your generations:

"And that you may put difference between holy and unholy, and between unclean and clean."

The Law as given by the Lord at this juncture indicates that Nadab and Abihu had acted under the excitement of intoxicating drink. In other words, they were drunk.

Some have claimed from these Passages that it's satisfactory to drink in moderation, providing it's done at the right time and the right place, etc.

That's not what the Scripture is saying here.

In fact, this is a prohibition against strong drink in any capacity. The Lord is telling these Priests, and all Priests who would follow thereafter, that if they partook of strong drink regarding their duties in the Tabernacle or Temple, with the latter yet to come, that they would run the risk of being stricken dead.

While they might not be stricken dead if they partook of strong drink outside of the Tabernacle, etc., most definitely, they would be courting disaster, if they did so within the confines of the Tabernacle of its Courts.

But in no way do these Passages make allowance for social drinking, etc.

SOCIAL DRINKING!

I believe the Bible teaches total and complete abstinence from all alcoholic beverage of any kind, and at all times. Considering the heartache and sorrow that alcohol has caused, I cannot even remotely see how any Christian, striving to be a good example, would think it satisfactory to partake of alcohol in any capacity. It is a known fact, concerning most crimes committed, that the individual committing the crimes is under the influence of alcohol. While there are thousands of evil things that could be said about strong drink, there isn't one good thing that can be said, of which I am aware.

Let's briefly look at some of the instances in the Bible, which some have claimed gives license to moderate drinking, etc.

NOTES

DID THE SAVIOUR USE INTOXICATING WINE IN THE LORD'S SUPPER?

No!

First of all, in the description of the Lord's Supper, the Bible never uses the word *"wine."* We are told, *"He took the cup, and gave thanks, and gave it to them, saying, Drink ye all of it"* (Mat. 26:27). Mark says: *"He took the cup, when He had given thanks, He gave it to them"* (Mk. 14:23). Luke says: *"He took the cup, and gave thanks, and said, Take this, and divide it among yourselves"* (Lk. 22:17). Jesus called this drink the *"fruit of the vine"* (Mat. 26:29; Mk. 14:25; Lk. 22:18).

It seems the Holy Spirit carried this directive right on through even into the Early Church. The Apostle Paul said: *"After the same manner also He took the cup, when He had finished supper, saying, This cup is the New Testament in My Blood"* (I Cor. 11:25). Then, following, He mentioned *"this cup,"* and then, later on, *"that cup."* It becomes clear, when these Passages are read consecutively, that God intended for us to use grape juice. I also think the Holy Spirit took particular pains not to use any words that could be construed as referring to any kind of intoxicating beverage. There is not a single reference in the Word of God that a person should use intoxicating wine for the Lord's Supper.

THE SYMBOL OF DECAY

The very meaning of fermented wine makes it unsatisfactory to represent the Blood of the Lord Jesus Christ, which the juice taken in the Lord's Supper is definitely to represent.

Fermented wine is grape juice in which decay (or rot) has taken place. In other words, the process of fermentation is the breakdown of large molecules caused by the influence of bacteria or fungi. Wine, then, results from the degenerative action of germs on pure substances.

Fermented wine used in Communion would actually symbolize tainted, sinful blood, and not the pure and perfect Blood of Jesus Christ, that had to be made evident to be a perfect cleansing for our sins. Pure, fresh grape juice tends toward life, but fermented wine tends toward death. Alcohol used for drinking purposes is both a narcotic and a poison. It could hardly be used as a symbol for the Blood of the Lord Jesus Christ. Please consider the following:

The Jews were required to use unleavened bread with the Passover Feast, and they were commanded that during that time *"there shall no leavened bread be seen with you, neither shall there be leaven seen with you in all your quarters"* (Ex. 13:7). In other words, there was not even to be any leaven in the house.

As early as this, bread which had been tainted with bacteria or yeast, which comprises leaven, was considered unsuitable at the spiritual events celebrated by the Jews. Jesus also used unleavened bread in initiating the Lord's Supper. (However, the New Testament makes no special issue of unleavened bread, and because this particular type of bread was a type of the Perfection of the Lord Jesus Christ, which He fulfilled in totality in His Personal Life, making the symbol unnecessary anymore.)

Consequently, the point that I make is this: if the Lord specifically chose bread that had no bacteria, no fungus spores in it, to picture His broken body, do you honestly think He would choose alcoholic wine, fermented wine, which is directly the product of fungi or bacteria, to represent His Blood? I hardly think so! The pure Blood of Jesus Christ, as stated, is best represented by pure grape juice.

THE MORAL STATUTES

In the Passage of our study, the Lord, in addressing the High Priest, along with all other Priests under the old economy, commanded of them: *"Do not drink wine nor strong drink . . . when you go into the Tabernacle of the congregation, lest you die: it shall be a Statute forever throughout your generations."*

You must remember, these Priests entering into the Tabernacle were types of the Lord Jesus Christ, Who is our Great High Priest. Now I ask you a question: would Jesus, the night He was betrayed, drink intoxicating wine before going to the Crucifixion and entering into His High Priestly Work? I think not! It

would have been a rejection and a contradiction of His Own Word which we are now studying in this Tenth Chapter of Leviticus.

We must always remember that the word *"wine"* as used in the Bible simply means, *"the fruit of the vine."* It can mean either unfermented grape juice or intoxicating wine. So, when the word is read, whether it is New Testament or Old Testament, this distinction must always be kept in mind.

No, the beverage that Jesus used at the Lord's Supper was not intoxicating wine, and neither is it proper or permissible for us to use intoxicating wine in the Lord's Supper presently, or any other time for that matter.

WAS THE WATER THAT JESUS TURNED INTO WINE IN SAINT JOHN, CHAPTER 2, THE KIND OF WINE THAT WILL MAKE ONE DRUNK?

Again, no!

If the wine referred to here is understood to be intoxicating wine, our Lord is automatically placed in the position of providing men who had already *"well drunk"* (Jn. 2:10) with more wine. If it was wine, as we think of wine today, which it is an intoxicating beverage, the Lord then would have been breaking His Own Law against temperance. The total amount of water turned to wine was about 150 gallons. If this had been an intoxicating beverage, it would have served as an invitation to drink, and would have placed our Lord in the unsavory position of providing a flood of intoxicants for the people who had already consumed a considerable amount.

GOOD WINE

The word *"good"* was used to describe what the Lord had miraculously brought about. It is the Greek word *"kalos"* and is defined in *"Vine's Expository Dictionary of New Testament Words"* as denoting what is intrinsically good. Now the pure, sweet juice of the grape could rightly be denoted as *"intrinsically good"*; but the rotted, fermented, decayed, spoiled, intoxicating kind of wine could hardly be called good. It is easy to think of the term *"good"* in describing whatever the Lord makes. For example, in describing the creation, Moses said, *"And God saw everything that He had made, and, behold, it was very good"* (Gen. 1:31).

It is unthinkable that our Lord would have made corrupted, fermented wine at Cana and called it *"good."* You see, fermentation is a kind of decomposition, just as are putrefaction, and decay. It would be almost blasphemous to call that *"good"* in connection with our Lord.

Pliny (an ancient Greek Scholar) said that *"good wine"* was a term used to denote the juice destitute of spirit. Albert Barnes says, *"The wine referred to here was doubtless such as was commonly drunk in Palestine."* That was the pure juice of the grape; it was not brandied nor drugged wine. Nor was it wine compounded of various substances, such as people drink in this land. The common wine of that day, which was drunk in Palestine, was the simple juice of the grape.

As well, it is tantamount to blasphemy, in my opinion, to suppose that the first miracle that Christ preformed after being filled with the Holy Spirit (compare Mk. 1:9-12; Lk. 4:1) was an act of creating intoxicating wine for a crowd of celebrants, the kind of wine that would make them drunk. It is unthinkable!

Still another fact from the record in John, Chapter 2, is this: those men who had already drunk a considerable amount praised the bridegroom for having kept the *"good wine"* until the last. Now, it is a simple fact that alcohol, drunk to any excess, will deaden the taste buds of the drinker. If the wine in Cana of Galilee, that the guests had already been partaking of, was intoxicating wine (and they had already partaken of quite a bit at this point), then when the wine that Jesus had miraculously made was given to them, they could not have detected its taste. Their taste buds would have been deadened. To be honest with you, they would have been drunk by this time, or almost so. Only if they had been drinking the form of the vine's fruit that we know as grape juice, and then had been provided some fresh grape juice, would the governor of the feast have been able to make the observation he did.

WINE IN BIBLICAL TIMES

Even though there are several words in the Bible which denote wine, there are two

words which are used more than any other. In the New Testament it is the Greek word *"oinos,"* which can mean either fermented or unfermented wine.

Dr. Ferrar Fenton, a Biblical translator (The Holy Bible In Modern English), lists six different meanings of the word *"oinos"*: (1) grapes, as fresh fruit; (2) raisins; (3) thick grape syrup; (4) a thick jam; (5) fresh grape juice; and (6) fermented grape juice. The last type would make you drunk.

Dr. Lyman Abbott said that fermented wine in Bible times was the least common of all wines. Even in the fermented kind, the percentage of alcohol was small.

In the Old Testament, the most often used Hebrew word for wine is *"yayin."* That word is found 141 times in the Old Testament, and is used interchangeably, depending on the context.

Also, it is unthinkable that the Lord would have broken His Own Word. *"Wine is a mocker, strong drink is raging: and whosoever is deceived thereby is not wise . . . Who has woe? Who has sorrow? Who has contentions? Who has babbling? Who has wounds without cause? Who has redness of eyes? They who tarry long at the wine; they who go to seek mixed wine. Do not look upon the wine when it is red, when it gives his color in the cup, when it moves itself aright. At the last it bites like a serpent, and stings like an adder"* (Prov. 20:1; 23:29-32).

The reasons given above are sufficient proof that Jesus did not change water to the kind of wine that would make one drunk. Instead, it was a pure, sweet grape juice.

PROHIBITION

Before Prohibition *"wine"* was considered to be exactly as it was in Bible times. However, when Prohibition was enacted in 1929, the term had to be defined more closely. Consequently, *"wine"* was designated to mean something that would make one drunk. The other kind of non-intoxicating beverage was called by whatever name desired, grape juice or whatever. Consequently, many people today confuse the simple word *"wine"* as it was used in the Bible with our understanding of that word presently, but that is not universally true.

No, Jesus' first miracle was not the making of wine that would make a person drunk. It was pure, sweet, fresh grape juice; and I believe that Scripturally, scientifically, and legally we have proof of that.

THE HOLY AND THE UNHOLY

As it was then, there is presently that which is holy and that which is unholy, that which is clean, and that which is unclean. Alcohol falls into the category of the unholy and the unclean, as ought to be overly obvious.

As well, there are many things presently in the world which are unholy and unclean, with which a Believer should not associate himself.

These things would consist of that which would be of harm to the physical body, which is the Temple of the Holy Spirit. This is at least one of the reasons that Paul said: *"And be not drunk with wine, wherein is excess; but be filled with the Spirit;*

"Speaking to yourselves in Psalms, and Hymns, and Spiritual Songs, singing and making melody in your heart to the Lord" (Eph. 5:18-19).

The idea is that Believers be drunk with the Spirit, instead of spirits.

As well, much of what comes through Television, almost all that comes through the movies, and much of what comes over the Internet, falls into the category of the *"unclean,"* and, therefore, *"unholy."*

Concerning one of the major companies in the world, I was told the other day that an anonymous poll was taken among their white collar people. These are people, as would be obvious, with a much higher educational average, some who were millionaires, and many who concluded themselves to be Christians. The shocking thing is, sixty percent admitted to being hooked on Internet pornography.

When I was given this information, incidentally by one of their top men, to be frank, I did a double-take. I said to him, *"Say that again."* He answered, *"You heard me right the first time."*

These people could fill out the questionnaire without signing their names, so the honesty factor was far higher than would be normal. But to think of sixty percent of these people, who are some of the elite of

the nation, being hooked on Internet pornography, is beyond comprehension. But that is what is happening out there.

I'm going to make some statements that should be made, and at the same time, show you a way that the *"holy"* and the *"clean"* can prevail, even in these immoral times.

GOD'S PRESCRIBED ORDER OF VICTORY

Many Christians have the erroneous idea that once they have come to Christ, they now have the willpower to say *"yes"* or *"no,"* to sin at their leisure. They embark upon such a course, which always leads to spiritual failure.

While the *"yes"* and *"no"* factor is correct, it is correct only in a specific way.

In other words, we as Believers have the capacity to say *"yes"* or *"no"* to Christ, but that's about where it begins and ends. This means that if you as a Believer set out to live this Christian life by addressing sin with a *"yes"* or *"no,"* you have just bought yourself some problems. But yet that's where most Christians presently are. Many Preachers claim that all the Christian has to do is just to simply say *"no"* to sin. That's not the way, and simply because it is a dependence on *"self."* Such a dependence deprives the Believer of the help of the Holy Spirit, Whose help we must have, if we are to live this Christian life (Rom. 8:1).

THE LAW OF SIN AND DEATH

As we've already said in this Volume, the second most powerful law in this world is *"the law of sin and death"* (Rom. 8:2). The unredeemed cannot overcome this law at all, as should be obvious. The Believer can overcome this law only by bringing into play *"The Law of the Spirit of Life in Christ Jesus"* (Rom. 8:2). This particular Law incidentally, is the most powerful law in the world, and as stated, the only Law that can overcome *"the law of sin and death."*

To be frank, most Christians, even though they have read Romans 8:2 a few times, have never heard a single Message preached, or a single word taught, on these two particular *"Laws."* That's tragic, when they face the law of sin and death every single day of their lives. And please understand, no Christian without being properly taught, is going to understand *"The Law of the Spirit of Life in Christ Jesus."* Without it being properly taught, it cannot be properly understood. So this means that the far, far greater number of Christians are stumbling through this Christian experience, trying to live the life, but in essence, failing on a continuous basis; and failing because they do not understand this *"Law of the Spirit of Life."*

IN CHRIST JESUS

If it is to be noticed, this *"Law of the Spirit of Life"* is *"in Christ Jesus."* Every time Paul uses this term, or one of its many derivatives, which he does about 170 times in his 14 Epistles, he is speaking without exception of what Jesus did at the Cross. So, this particular Law, which is the most powerful in the world, and which is the only Law that can overcome sin, is all wrapped up in what Christ did at the Cross. In other words, the Holy Spirit, Who is the *"Spirit of Life,"* works entirely within the parameters of the Sacrifice of Christ. He superintends the life that comes from Christ, which is made possible to Believers as a result of the Cross. Everything hinges on the *"Cross."*

As a Believer, you are to understand that every single thing comes to you through and by *"the Cross of Christ."*

Second, the Cross of Christ is to ever be *"the object of your Faith."*

Third, when this is done, *"the Holy Spirit"* will then work mightily within your heart and life, overcoming the *"law of sin and death."* Otherwise, you will not be able, even though you are a Christian, even though you are Spirit-filled, to live a *"holy"* and *"clean"* life. The Lord has only one prescribed order of victory, not five, not three, not even two, only one! That one way is *"Jesus Christ and Him Crucified"* (I Cor. 1:23; 2:2, 5).

SELF-RIGHTEOUSNESS

The unfortunate thing as it regards the Christian experience, and in fact which has been with us from the time of the Garden of Eden, is the problem of self-righteousness.

The Believer can have the Righteousness of Christ, only by believing in what Christ

has done at the Cross. That being done, and continuing to be done, the Righteousness of Christ is freely imputed to the Believer. This takes place when the person gets saved, and it continues throughout our Salvation experience.

But if the Believer begins to look elsewhere, in other words, making other things the object of his Faith, rather than the Cross, he will only succeed in developing self-righteousness. And that was not only the bane of Israel, it is, as well, the bane of the modern Church, and in fact, has always been the problem. Concerning Israel, Paul said:

"For they (Israel) *being ignorant of God's Righteousness, and going about to establish their own righteousness, have not submitted themselves to the Righteousness of God"* (Rom. 10:3).

That's the major problem of Believers presently, exactly as it was in Israel of old; we've tried to establish our own Righteousness. That is self-righteousness.

Now let me make this statement, to help us understand it even more:

Any Believer who doesn't understand the Cross as it pertains to our Sanctification, which means that the object of his faith is not the Cross, but rather other things, will, of necessity, function from a position of self-righteousness. There are only two types of righteousness in this world, Righteousness which comes from Christ and what He did at the Cross, and self-righteousness.

As well, almost all Believers who are functioning in self-righteousness claim to be trusting Christ. And the truth is, many think they are. But again I state, if that Believer doesn't understand the Cross, which as well demands an understanding of Faith, along with the Holy Spirit, despite the claims, such a Believer is going to function in self-righteousness.

Considering that very few modern Christians understand the Cross, which means that very few modern Preachers understand the Cross, that means the Church is presently functioning almost entirely from a position of self-righteousness. This is a road to spiritual disaster. This is what destroyed Israel of old, and it is what is destroying most Christians.

INSTRUCTION IN THE
WAYS OF THE LORD

Verse 11 reads: *"And that you may teach the Children of Israel all the Statutes which the LORD has spoken unto them by the hand of Moses."*

We learn here that the Priests, which number would grow extensively very shortly, were to teach the people the Law of Moses. It is the same now as Apostles, Prophets, Evangelists, Pastors, and Teachers, proclaiming and explaining the Word of God to the Church.

The task then would have been somewhat harder, because many of the people couldn't read, and beside that, there were no printing presses in those days. Whatever copies of the Law there were had to be copied laboriously by hand, which many were.

So it was left up to the Priests to teach all the people the Word of God, which then consisted of the Law, referred to at times as *"the Law of Moses."* If the Priests did not sufficiently teach the people, they simply could not learn, which spells disaster.

In later years, the Priests neglected this all-important duty. Concerning this, the Lord through the Prophet Ezekiel said: *"Her Priests have violated My Law, and have profaned My holy things: they have put no difference between the holy and the profane, neither have they showed difference between the unclean and the clean."* In other words, they did not teach the people the difference (Ezek. 22:26).

I'm afraid that this sin of ancient Israel is our sin presently as well. Christians, presently, simply do not know the Word of God. That's at least one of the reasons that they fall so easily for false doctrine.

I read sometime back of an Assemblies of God Church, which was devoting its Wednesday nights to a discussion on what the Radio talk show host, Rush Limbaugh, had said that past week. Wednesday nights in most Churches are normally given over to Bible study.

I do not know who this Pastor was, but I do know that he isn't much of a Pastor. In fact, the people who are so foolish to attend that particular Church will wreck themselves

spiritually. That's how bad the situation is, and, regrettably, that's how bad it is in the far greater majority of Churches. Some few proclaim the Gospel, and do so with the Power of the Holy Spirit. The majority does not!

It is incumbent upon every Believer to know the Word of God. In fact, every Believer ought to make the study of the Bible a part of his daily consecration. That's at least one of the reasons that we strongly encourage every Believer, at least over whom we might have some small amount of influence, to obtain these Commentaries. I know that their study will open up the Word of God, and nothing could be greater than learning the Word.

THE MEAT-OFFERING

Verses 12 and 13 read: *"And Moses spoke unto Aaron, and unto Eleazar and unto Ithamar, his sons who were left, Take the Meat-Offering that remains of the Offerings of the LORD made by fire, and eat it without leaven beside the Altar: for it is most holy:*

"And you shall eat it in the Holy Place, because it is your due, and your sons' due, of the Sacrifices of the LORD made by fire: for so I am commanded."

This information was given to Aaron, and his two sons, immediately after the terrible calamity which had just befallen them. It seems that Moses is most anxious to guard him and his two younger sons against transgressing any other part of the ritual connected with the same Sacrifices, lest they also should incur a similar penalty. We will find in later Verses that Aaron, in fact, did do something wrong, but it was not done intentionally, and was done under the terrible stress of the moment; consequently, the Lord took no action.

But in all of this, we should understand that God says what He means, and means what He says. If we take His Word lightly, the results will not be pleasant.

A part of the Meat-Offering had evidently been burned on the Brazen Altar, and now Moses instructs Aaron, along with his two remaining sons, to eat it, as they had been instructed to do. They were to eat it without leaven, and do so beside the Altar.

The *"Meat-Offering"* was the only Offering

of the five Sacrifices, which was an unbloody Sacrifice. In other words, even though it was referred to as a *"Meat-Offering,"* in fact, it had no meat, but rather grain, which was ground into a fine flour. In those days, *"meat"* referred to all manner of food, whereas presently, it refers to the flesh of certain animals.

This Offering signified Christ in His Perfection, and as well, it signified thanksgiving to God, for giving humanity such a gift (Jn. 3:16).

No *"leaven"* could be used in this concoction, simply because leaven was a type of fermentation or rot. This fine flour, ground to a powdery substance, was meant to typify Christ without blemish. Leaven would have indicated corruption, which in no way typified Christ.

It was to be eaten *"beside the Altar,"* which referred to the *"Brazen Altar."* In fact, and as stated, a small portion was to be burnt on the Altar, all of it typifying Christ.

The idea was, that which was burned on the Altar represented what Christ would do as it regards His Crucifixion, in order to redeem humanity. There he would atone for all sin. The eating of the portion assigned to the Priests proclaims the fact that this perfection can belong to the Saint of God, but only through what Christ did at the Cross. We obtain this simply be exhibiting Faith in Christ and His Finished Work, in which the Holy Spirit then makes His perfection real to us. This is what Paul was speaking of when he said:

"I am crucified with Christ: nevertheless I live; yet not I, but Christ lives in me: and the life which I now live in the flesh I live by the Faith of the Son of God, Who loved me, and gave Himself for me.

"I do not frustrate the Grace of God: for if Righteousness come by the Law, then Christ is dead in vain" (Gal. 2:20-21).

MOST HOLY

Three of the Sacrifices were labeled as *"most holy."* They were the *"Meat-Offering,"* the *"Sin-Offering,"* and the *"Trespass-Offering."*

Why were these three labeled as *"most holy,"* when the other two, *"Whole Burnt-Offering,"* and the *"Peace-Offering,"* referred to only as *"holy"*?

The three labeled *"most holy"* had to do with the very purpose and reason that Christ died on the Cross, which was to break the terrible bondage of sin that held mankind in its awful grip. This was the purpose, the reason, for Calvary. Of course, many other things were addressed at Calvary, in fact, everything lost at the Fall, but it was freedom from dominion of sin which occasioned the great Sacrifice.

This means that Jesus <u>didn't</u> go to the Cross merely that we might trade our Neon in on a Cadillac, or increase our paycheck from $500 a week to $1,000 a week, etc. But regrettably, almost the entirety of the Charismatic Church world has gone in that direction, which is none other than the *"way of the flesh."* Man's problem is not economic, nor agricultural, nor social, nor educational, nor scientific. Man's problem is spiritual. In other words, he is a sinner, a lost sinner, which means he is in the domain of darkness, and darkness only, and it is the Sacrifice of Christ alone which saves man. Everything else, and irrespective as to what it might be, is no more than waving a palm branch at a hurricane. That's why these three Sacrifices are referred to as *"most holy."* They dealt with the sin question, and they dealt with it through the Cross of Calvary.

THE CROSS OF CALVARY

There are some who may think that I say too much about the Cross. There are some who think that I emphasize this great Finished Work of Christ too much. But if they think so, it is because they do not understand the Word of God, and in fact, neither do they understand their perilous condition as they should, which is a condition of sin. No, it's not possible to emphasize the Cross too much!

One day, by the Grace of God, when we cross the threshold into the portals of Glory, and we walk into that City built foursquare, and we hear Him say, *"Well done, good and faithful servant,"* we will be there for one reason, and for one reason only, because of what Jesus did on that Cross.

If it is to be noticed, none of these sacred vessels were types of the Resurrection. And by that, we are definitely not meaning that the Resurrection was unimportant. In fact, the Resurrection was all-important. But it was not the Resurrection which set the captive free; it was the Cross of Calvary.

RESURRECTION LIVING

When the believing sinner comes to Christ, he instantly receives *"Resurrection Life"* (Jn. 14:6). But sadly and regrettably, most Christians, even though they have *"Resurrection Life,"* do not know how to enjoy *"Resurrection Living."*

Why?

Millions of Christians talk about their *"Resurrection Living,"* or words to that effect, but they little know that of which they speak. They refer to themselves as Resurrection people, or *"Resurrection Saints,"* etc., and in effect, many, if not most, of these people are denigrating the Cross.

What they don't understand is, for us to have and to enjoy *"Resurrection Living,"* we must first understand the Cross, knowing that it is the Cross which made the Resurrection possible, and in fact, the Ascension, and even the Exaltation of Christ. Paul said:

"For if we have been planted together in the likeness of His death, we shall be also in the likeness of His Resurrection" (Rom. 6:5).

While he does allude here to the coming Resurrection, when the dead in Christ shall be changed, etc., his major emphasis is placed on *"Resurrection Living."* The Apostle in effect says that we cannot have *"Resurrection Living,"* unless we first understand *"the likeness of His death"* and our part in that death.

He has just told the Romans, and all other Believers as well, that the moment we were saved, we were *"baptized into His death."* We were then *"buried with Him by baptism into death,"* and then raised with Him *"in newness of life"* (Rom. 6:3-4).

This *"newness of life,"* refers to *"Resurrection Living."* But to try to have this *"Living,"* this *"manner of life,"* which is the most glorious life there is, we must always understand that it comes by the Way of the Cross, and our Faith in that Finished Work. Otherwise, the Believer will not know or enjoy *"Resurrection Living,"* irrespective of how much he may claim such.

NOTES

The phrase in Verse 13, *"And you shall eat it in the Holy Place,"* should have been translated, *"And you shall eat it in a holy place."* In fact, it was to be eaten *"beside the Altar,"* which refers to the Brazen Altar.

THE WAVE BREAST AND THE HEAVE SHOULDER

Verses 14 and 15 read: *"And the Wave-Breast and Heave-Shoulder shall you eat in a clean place; you, and your sons, and your daughters with you: for they be your due, and your sons' due, which are given out of the Sacrifices of Peace-Offerings of the Children of Israel.*

"The Heave-Shoulder and the Wave-Breast shall they bring with the Offerings made by fire of the fat, to wave it for a Wave-Offering before the LORD; and it shall be yours, and your sons' with you, by a Statute forever; as the LORD has commanded."

The *"breast"* and the *"shoulder"* of the *"Peace-Offerings"* belonged to the Priests, for the maintenance of themselves and their families. However, before partaking of this, it had to be acknowledged in a certain way.

They were to take the *"breast"* and to *"wave"* it before the Lord, signifying that the Cross has made it possible for *"Peace"* to be restored to fallen mankind.

The *"Heave-Shoulder"* was to be heaved up and down, whereas the *"Wave-Offering"* was to be stretched out over the heads of the Priests. The idea of the *"Heave-Offering"* was an acknowledgement that God would ultimately come down to this Earth in the form of man, in order to redeem mankind, which He did. The *"heave-up"* signified that this God-Man would come from Heaven; the *"heave-down"* signified that He would come down to this Earth.

These *"Offerings"* were ever reminders that all of this in the Levitical Law were meant to be temporal, and would be fulfilled in totality, when the Son of Man would come. It forever pointed to the fact that the Cross of Christ would be the redeeming factor.

(16) "AND MOSES DILIGENTLY SOUGHT THE GOAT OF THE SIN-OFFERING, AND, BEHOLD, IT WAS BURNT: AND HE WAS ANGRY WITH ELEAZAR AND ITHAMAR, THE SONS OF AARON WHICH

WERE LEFT ALIVE, SAYING,

(17) "WHEREFORE HAVE YOU NOT EATEN THE SIN-OFFERING IN THE HOLY PLACE, SEEING IT IS MOST HOLY, AND GOD HAS GIVEN IT TO YOU IN ORDER TO BEAR THE INIQUITY OF THE CONGREGATION, AND TO MAKE ATONEMENT FOR THEM BEFORE THE LORD?

(18) "BEHOLD, THE BLOOD OF IT WAS NOT BROUGHT IN WITHIN THE HOLY PLACE: YOU SHOULD INDEED HAVE EATEN IT IN THE HOLY PLACE, AS I COMMANDED.

(19) "AND AARON SAID UNTO MOSES, BEHOLD, THIS DAY HAVE THEY OFFERED THEIR SIN-OFFERING AND THEIR BURNT-OFFERING BEFORE THE LORD; AND SUCH THINGS HAVE BEFALLEN ME: AND IF I HAD EATEN THE SIN-OFFERING TODAY, SHOULD IT HAVE BEEN ACCEPTED IN THE SIGHT OF THE LORD?

(20) "AND WHEN MOSES HEARD THAT, HE WAS CONTENT."

The diagram is:

1. Aaron and his two remaining sons should have eaten the goat of the Sin-Offering; so making the sins of the people his own. But his personal grief unfitted him for bearing their sorrows.

2. How different the True Aaron in John 16:22. He laid His Own immeasurable griefs aside, and His loving heart engaged itself with those of His Disciples. It was not disobedience on Aaron's part, but human infirmity and sorrow.

3. Priests in the Sanctuary were not to bewail, but to worship – they were not to weep, as in the presence of death, but to bow their anointed heads in the Presence of the Divine visitation.

THE SIN-OFFERING

Verses 16 through 18 read: *"And Moses diligently sought the goat of the Sin-Offering, and, behold, it was burnt: and he was angry with Eleazar and Ithamar, the sons of Aaron which were left alive, saying,*

"Wherefore have you not eaten this Sin-Offering in the Holy Place, seeing it is most holy, and God has given it to you in order to bear the iniquity of the congregation, and to make Atonement for them before the LORD?

NOTES

"Behold, the blood of it was not brought in within the Holy Place: you should indeed have eaten it in the Holy Place, as I commanded."

The rule was that, when the blood was presented in the Tabernacle on the Golden Altar, the flesh was to be burned; when it was not burned, the flesh was eaten by the Priests. In the present case, the blood had not been brought within the Holy Place, and yet the flesh had been burned instead of being eaten (Lev. 6:25-26, 30).

Concerning the Sin-Offering as it is portrayed here, it was to be eaten by Aaron and his two remaining sons. Had they brought the blood of the animal into the Holy Place, and put it on the four horns of the Golden Altar, and sprinkled it seven times on the Golden Altar, they were then to take the carcass to a clean place outside the camp, *"where the ashes are poured out, and burn the carcass on the wood with fire"* (Lev. 4:12).

Inasmuch as the blood was not carried into the Holy Place as it regarded this particular Sacrifice, it should have been eaten by the Priests.

By the eating of the sin-laden victim, the sins of the offerer were, in type, laid upon the Priests to be taken away by him, thus prefiguring Christ, Who would be both Priest and Sacrifice.

When Moses began to inquire into this particular *"rite,"* he found that no blood had been brought into the Holy Place, and that the carcass of the Sin-Offering had been mistakenly burned, when it should have been eaten.

The Scripture says that the Lawgiver was angry!

All of this happened very shortly after Nadab and Abihu had been stricken by the Judgment of God. Moses was concerned that if any part of the ritual was mishandled, misinterpreted, or ignored, that the Judgment of God would now fall on the remaining Priests.

From all of this, I would hope that we could see the vast significance of what was taking place. Every single thing that was done was ordained by God. Every ritual, every ceremony, down to the minute details – all and without exception were designed by Jehovah.

As well, its significance was beyond our comprehension. It had to do with the eternal souls of men, and in this case, the souls of those of Israel. So I'm sure that it now becomes obvious that much was at stake.

When Moses used the term, *"And God has given it to you to bear the iniquity of the congregation, to make Atonement for them before the Lord,"* there is fear in this statement. The Lawgiver was concerned, not only for his brother Aaron, and his two nephews, Eleazar and Ithamar, but as well, for the entirety of the nation of Israel. Judgment could readily have fallen upon them also.

The Priests stood between them and God, thereby acting as mediators. If they did not attend their duties, and do it right, as we've already seen, judgment must be, of necessity, poured out. They were not playing games here.

While, no doubt, hundreds of thousands who were standing outside the Tabernacle began to bewail the situation, at least some of these people must have known that they were in danger as well. So the bewailing was more so for the entirety of the situation, than merely for Nadab and Abihu.

THE EXPLANATION

Verses 19 and 20 read: *"And Aaron said unto Moses, Behold, this day have they offered their Sin-Offering and their Burnt-Offering before the LORD; and such things have befallen me: and if I had eaten the Sin-Offering today, should it have been accepted in the sight of the LORD?*

"And when Moses heard that, he was content."

The explanation as given by Aaron satisfied Moses.

Aaron mentions the fact that all the other sacrificial duties in which he and his sons were engaged on the same day, prior to the great calamity, were performed in strict accordance with the prescribed ritual. His sons assisting him had offered their (the people's) Sin and Burnt-Offerings (Lev. 9:15-16), thus far in due compliance with the requirements of the Law, and hence could never have meant to transgress intentionally.

Concerning this, Ellicott says, *"But while he, Eleazar, and Ithamar were thus duly performing the sacrificial rites, Nadab and Abihu, his other two sons, transgressed, and were*

suddenly struck down dead, thus overwhelming the survivors with sorrow, and rendering them unfit to partake of the Sacrifices."

Aaron proclaims, as Ellicott continues, *"Unfitted as they thus were by mourning and the sense of their own sinfulness, that if they had partaken of this solemn meal it would not have been acceptable to the Lord."*

They were right!

Moses acknowledged Aaron's plea to be just, and that he had himself spoken hastily. Hence Jewish tradition ascribes the mistake to Moses, and not to Aaron.

Jewish tradition further says, when Moses heard it, he approved of the explanation. Whereupon he sent a herald through the whole camp of Israel, saying, *"It is I from whom the Law had been hid, and my brother Aaron brought it to my remembrance."*

THE THRICE-HOLY GOD

While God is no different presently than He was in Old Testament Times, the Cross has made all the difference.

Due to the Cross, and the price paid there, because of Christ, men can now enter into the most sacred precinct of the Holy of Holies, actually into the very Presence of God, guaranteed by the Holy Spirit. Concerning this, Paul said:

"Having abolished in his flesh the enmity, even the Law of Commandments contained in Ordinances; for to make in Himself of twain one new man, so making peace;

"And that He might reconcile both (Jews and Gentiles) *unto God in one body* (the Church) *by the Cross, having slain the enmity thereby:*

"And came and preached peace to you which were afar off (Gentiles), *and to them who were near* (the Jews).

"For through Him (what He did at the Cross) *we both* (Jews and Gentiles, equally) *have access by one Spirit unto the Father"* (Eph. 2:15-18).

In other words, the Holy Spirit guarantees access for the Believer, who has placed his faith entirely in Christ, and what Christ did at the Cross. We speak of *"access"* into the very Presence of God. The Holy Spirit guards this access, as Verse 18 proclaims.

If one attempts to come into the Presence

of God, in a way other than by the Cross, the Holy Spirit will block access. It is only *"through Him,"* i.e., *"through Jesus Christ, and His Sacrificial, Atoning Work."*

Jesus Himself said: *"Verily, verily, I say unto you, he who enters not by the Door into the sheepfold, but climbs up some other way, the same is a thief and a robber"* (Jn. 10:1).

And let me remind the Reader that this *"Door"* is a *"bloody Door"* (Ex. 12:7, 13).

"There's a light upon the mountains,
and the day is at the spring,
"When our eyes shall see the beauty
and the glory of the King:
"Weary was our heart with waiting,
and the night-watch seemed so long,
"But His triumph-day is breaking, and
we hail it with a song."

"In the fading of the starlight, we may
see the coming morn;
"And the lights of men are paling in
the splendors of the dawn;
"For the eastern skies are glowing, as
with light of hidden fire.
"And the hearts of men are stirring,
with the throbs of deep desire."

"There's a hush of expectation, and a
quiet in the air,
"And the breath of God is moving, in
the fervent breath of prayer;
"For the suffering, dying Jesus, is the
Christ upon the Throne,
"And the travail of our spirit, is the
travail of His Own."

"He is breaking down the barriers, He
is casting up the way;
"He is calling for His Angels, to build
up the gates of day:
"But His Angels here are human, not
the shining hosts above;
"For the drum-beats of His army, are
the heart-beats of our love."

"Hark! We hear a distant music, and
it comes with fuller swell;
"'Tis the triumph-song of Jesus, of our
King, Immanuel!
"Go ye forth with joy to meet Him!
And, my soul, be swift to bring
"All your sweetest and your dearest,
for the triumph of our King!"

CHAPTER 11

(1) "AND THE LORD SPOKE UNTO MOSES AND TO AARON, SAYING UNTO THEM,

(2) "SPEAK UNTO THE CHILDREN OF ISRAEL, SAYING, THESE ARE THE BEASTS WHICH YOU SHALL EAT AMONG ALL THE BEASTS THAT ARE ON THE EARTH.

(3) "WHATSOEVER PARTS THE HOOF, AND IS CLOVEN FOOTED, AND CHEWS THE CUD, AMONG THE BEASTS, THAT SHALL YOU EAT.

(4) "NEVERTHELESS THESE SHALL YOU NOT EAT OF THEM THAT CHEW THE CUD, OR OF THEM THAT DIVIDE THE HOOF: AS THE CAMEL, BECAUSE HE CHEWS THE CUD, BUT DIVIDES NOT THE HOOF; HE IS UNCLEAN UNTO YOU.

(5) "AND THE CONEY, BECAUSE HE CHEWS THE CUD, BUT DIVIDES NOT THE HOOF; HE IS UNCLEAN UNTO YOU.

(6) "AND THE HARE, BECAUSE HE CHEWS THE CUD, BUT DIVIDES NOT THE HOOF; HE IS UNCLEAN UNTO YOU.

(7) "AND THE SWINE, THOUGH HE DIVIDE THE HOOF, AND BE CLOVEN-FOOTED, YET HE CHEWS NOT THE CUD; HE IS UNCLEAN TO YOU.

(8) "OF THEIR FLESH SHALL YOU NOT EAT, AND THEIR CARCASS SHALL YOU NOT TOUCH; THEY ARE UNCLEAN TO YOU."

The structure is:

1. Priesthood having been established, to it was now committed the judgment of that which was defiled (Williams).

2. The Priest stood nearest to God. Thus, the lesson was taught, and it still operates, that to exercise a right judgment in moral and doctrinal matters, continuous and close fellowship with God is absolutely necessary.

3. The Laws of this Chapter and following for several Chapters were not only a test of obedience, and a loving provision for the health and happiness of the people, but they also give a humbling picture of the weakness and corruption of fallen human nature.

4. It should be noted that the Word of

the Lord was the one and only Judge in all these matters.

THE CLEAN AND THE UNCLEAN

Verses 1 and 2 read: *"And the LORD spoke unto Moses and to Aaron, saying unto them,*

"Speak unto the Children of Israel, saying, These are the beasts which you shall eat among all the beasts that are on the Earth."

We find first of all that the introduction has changed somewhat. Heretofore it was, *"And the Lord spoke unto Moses."* Now it says, *"And the Lord spoke unto Moses and to Aaron."* And this despite the fact that Aaron had miserably failed the Lord in the matter of the golden calf, some months earlier. However, the Sacrifices which he offered for himself, which he was ever compelled to do, pointed to the One Who was to come, and Faith in Him, and I speak of the Lord Jesus Christ, effected cleansing for Aaron, even as it did for all others. In other words, every single individual in the nation of Israel was in dire need of the Sacrifices, whether the two which were offered each day (doubled on the Sabbath), are in personal Sacrifices brought to the Tabernacle.

This included Moses, as well! The great Lawgiver, being a Levite, from which Tribe the Priesthood came, either came under the heading of the Priests, or the general population of the people. But let it be understood that Moses needed the Sacrifices, as all others.

The Scripture plainly says, and which hits us hard, *"There is none righteous, no, not one"* (Rom. 3:10).

This means that none could stand before God, including Moses, and every other Bible great at that, unless they stand there by Faith in Christ and His glorious Sacrifice. Oh, how I sense the Presence of God in these words, even though clumsily given.

How I thank God for the precious, shed Blood of the Lord Jesus Christ! Because of the Sacrifice of Himself, I am saved, and so are you, and so is every other person who has expressed Faith in that glorious Name.

THE CEREMONIAL LAW

Verses 3 through 8 read: *"Whatsoever parts the hoof, and is cloven-footed, and chews the*

cud, among the beasts, that shall you eat.

"Nevertheless these shall you not eat of them that chew the cud, or of them that divide the hoof: as the camel, because he chews the cud, but divides not the hoof; he is unclean unto you.

"And the coney, because he chews the cud, but divides not the hoof; he is unclean unto you.

"And the hare, because he chews the cud, but divides not the hoof; he is unclean unto you.

"And the swine, though he divide the hoof, and be cloven-footed, yet he chews not the cud; he is unclean to you.

"Of their flesh shall you not eat, and their carcass shall you not touch; they are unclean to you."

First of all, why would the Lord give specific instructions of this nature, as it regarded the eating of certain animals and fowls, etc.?

We know that in Acts, Chapter 10, as it regards the vision given to Simon Peter, all of these rulings were rescinded. In fact, as it regards Christianity, which is the outgrowth of true Judaism, there are no prohibitions whatsoever of this nature, and actually few commands at all.

First of all, the Law, as we are studying here in Leviticus, was never meant to be permanent, but was temporary only. It was given to show God's Standard of Righteousness, which portrayed the way that man ought to live. It was also given to show man that despite his best efforts, he was incapable of keeping the Law of God, considering the results of the Fall. Consequently, it was to show man that he needed one who could keep the Law, to whom the Sacrificial System pointed, namely the Lord Jesus Christ. In fact, every single thing about the Law, excepting nothing, pointed totally and completely to Christ. In other words, in some way, it was a symbol of Him and His Perfect Work, and we speak of the Cross.

When Christ came, He kept the Law perfectly in His Life and Living, thereby portraying its Righteousness, and as well, He answered its demands as it regarded it being broken. He willingly died to satisfy the demands of the broken Law, thereby, clearing the guilty, which pertained to all, at least for those who will believe (Jn. 3:16; Eph. 2:13-18; Col. 2:14-15).

THE REASON THESE INSTRUCTIONS WERE GIVEN

Israel was raised up from the loins of Abraham and the womb of Sarah, for a specific purpose and reason. Those reasons are as follows:

1. The Lord would give His Word to the Prophets of Israel, who were to give it to the world, which they did.

2. They were to serve as the womb of the Messiah, so to speak, fulfilling the promise given by the Lord concerning the *"Seed of the woman"* in Genesis 3:15.

3. They were to take the *"good news"* of the *"Seed of the woman,"* namely, the Lord Jesus Christ, to the entirety of the world.

They fulfilled the first two, but with great difficulty. They fulfilled the third point in a limited way, with the Apostle Paul, who of course was Jewish, being the Masterbuilder of the Church, which Gospel has gone to the ends of the Earth (I Cor. 3:10).

Inasmuch as Israel was to be the womb of the Messiah, all of these instructions were given to her, and many more. When the Messiah came, which He did, these things were no longer necessary.

In fact, as should be obvious, none of these rulings are *"moral,"* but rather *"ceremonial."* Moral rulings are inculcated in the Ten Commandments, which in effect, cannot change, and because they are *"moral."* But ceremonial things can and do change, according to the need of the time.

One might say, and rightly so, that obedience or disobedience to these commands was definitely moral. That is correct; however, the actual commands themselves, concerning the eating of certain animals and fowls, etc., contained nothing that was moral.

ARE THERE LESSONS, HOWEVER, WE CAN LEARN AS MODERN CHRISTIANS FROM THESE INSTRUCTIONS?

Most definitely!

In this Eleventh Chapter, as is obvious, the God of Israel entered with amazing detail into the daily food of His people, in order to teach them to make a difference between

NOTES

the unclean and the clean, as stated, because of Christ. In fact, love was the basis of this legislation.

With respect to animals, those only that chewed the cud and divided the hoof were to be eaten.

"Chewing the cud" expresses the natural process of *"inwardly digesting"* that which one eats.

Concerning this, Mackintosh said, *"The one who feeds upon the green pastures of the Word of God, and inwardly digests what he takes in – the one who is enabled to combine calm meditation with prayerful study, will, without doubt, manifest that character of outward walk, to which we will address ourselves momentarily, which is to the praise of Him Who has graciously given us His Word to form our habits and govern our ways."*

To be specific, the *"chewing of the cud"* relates spiritually to digesting the Word of God, which means to fully understand what it says, which means that we avidly seek to learn what the Lord is telling us. Reading the Word, and digesting the Word, are two different things altogether. In fact, one may read Chapter after Chapter, even Book after Book, and not digest so much as a single line.

That's the reason I plead with people to get these Commentaries, and after they get them, to study them. I believe the Lord has told me to write them, has helped me to write them, and if in fact that is the case, the contents contained will help you to digest the Word, and nothing could be more important than that.

THE CROSS AND DIGESTING THE WORD

Unless one has a proper understanding the Cross, and I speak of how the Cross effects both Salvation and Sanctification, I seriously doubt that such a Believer can properly digest the Word. While they might digest some things about the Word, proper digestion simply cannot take place unless there is a proper understanding of what the Word is all about, namely the Cross.

While Paul amply explained the Atonement as it refers to Salvation in Romans, Chapters 4 and 5, and elsewhere as well, the far greater majority of his teaching, in effect, what the Lord gave to him, is directed toward what the Atonement meant, as it regards our Sanctification. One is saved in a moment's time, but Sanctification continues throughout the living of our life. As I've also stated elsewhere, every single Believer has *"Resurrection Life,"* which they obtained at the moment of conversion; however, most Believers do not enjoy *"Resurrection Living."* The reason for this terrible problem, and terrible it is, is simply because they do not understand the Cross as it regards Sanctification, i.e., *"our everyday life and living."*

To understand it, one has to properly digest the Word, and more particularly, that Word which the Holy Spirit gave to us through Paul. And to be even more specific, I speak of Romans, Chapters 6, 7, and 8.

Why Paul?

While of course, every single word in the Bible is the Word of God, and of supreme significance, and that which we should learn minutely, the reason I mentioned Paul is because it was to the great Apostle that the Lord gave the meaning of the New Covenant (Gal. 1:10-12).

Once the Lord began to open up to me the Revelation of the Cross, I now see the Cross in every line of the Word of God, exactly as it ought to be seen. I have read the Bible completely through approximately 50 times. But for the greater majority of these times, I was not really digesting the Word.

HOW DOES ONE DIGEST THE WORD?

There are two things which must happen, in order for the Believer to properly *"digest the Word,"* i.e., *"chew the cud."*

First of all, the Holy Spirit Alone can help us to do this. Paul wrote: *"But the natural man receives not the things of the Spirit of God: for they are foolishness unto him: neither can he know them, because they are spiritually discerned"* (I Cor. 2:14).

So the avid Bible student, of which every Believer ought to be, should constantly ask the Lord to help him understand the Word. There is absolutely nothing more important than this. If we misunderstand the Word, to what degree it is misunderstood, or misinterpreted, to that degree we will suffer loss. And to be sure, that loss will fall out to hurt

NOTES

on our part, and possibly great hurt. The Word of God is the *"Lamp unto our feet, and the Light unto our path"* (Ps. 119:105). According to our understanding of the Word, accordingly we will have light. Little understanding, little light! Much understanding, much light!

Second, and once again as Paul said: *"And He* (Christ) *gave some, Apostles; and some, Prophets; and some, Evangelists; and some, Pastors and Teachers;*

"For the perfecting of the Saints, for the Work of the Ministry, for the edifying of the Body of Christ:

"Till we all come in the unity of the Faith, and of the knowledge of the Son of God, unto a perfect man, unto the measure of the stature of the fullness of Christ:

"That we henceforth be no more children, tossed to and fro, and carried about with every wind of doctrine by the sleight of men, and cunning craftiness, whereby they lie in wait to deceive" (Eph. 4:11-14).

Probably I can say without fear of exaggeration that presently, there are less God-called men and women, as it respects these particular Offices, in the modern Church, than any time since the Reformation. Presently, the modern Church is not so much different from the Israel of the time of Christ. The Scripture says: *"But when He saw the multitudes, He was moved with compassion on them, because they fainted, and were scattered abroad, as sheep having no shepherd"* (Mat. 9:36).

Oh yes, there were plenty of shepherds, but not the right kind! There are plenty today, but not the right kind!

It will be difficult, if not impossible, for you the Believer to properly understand the Word, unless that Word is properly taught by Godly Preachers.

HOW DO WE KNOW WHAT IS THE PROPER INTERPRETATION OF THE WORD?

Our Lord Himself told us how. He said:

"Beware of false prophets, which come to you in sheep's clothing, but inwardly they are ravening wolves.

"You shall know them by their fruits" (Mat. 7:15-16).

All kind of people and all kind of Preachers say all kind of things; however, to properly judge what Ministry is right or wrong, we should look at the fruit of that Ministry.

Are there souls being saved? Believers being Baptized with the Holy Spirit? The sick truly being healed? Lives truly being changed? Bondages truly being broken? Is the Fruit of the Spirit being developed in hearts and lives? Is Christlikeness, which is Righteousness and Holiness, being developed?

Let's look at one particular popular doctrine. I speak of the modern Word of Faith doctrine. What are the fruits of that doctrine?

It's certainly not those things mentioned above, not at all! And if those things mentioned above are not the fruit of particular Doctrines, then pure and simple, it's not of God.

To cut straight through to the bottom line, unless the Preacher is preaching the Cross, there can be no *"good fruit,"* only *"bad fruit"* (Rom. 6:3-14; 8:1-2, 11; I Cor. 1:17-18, 21, 23; 2:2, 5; Gal., Chpt. 5; 6:14; Eph. 2:13-18; Col. 2:14-15).

This means that we should be fruit inspectors. That doesn't mean that we are to be fault finders, but it does mean that every Believer must evaluate according to the Scriptures, that which is being taught, preached, and practiced. Again, judge the fruit.

SUBMISSION

It is erroneously taught presently, and this teaching is widespread, that people should meekly submit to Preachers, and never question them, as it regards what they are teaching. It is taught that to question Preachers is to question the authority of God, etc. Nothing could be further from the Truth!

In the first place, the Word of God is the final authority in all things, and not Preachers; and any God-called Preacher, who is truly functioning under the leading and guidance of the Holy Spirit, and according to the Word, will say exactly what I've just said.

I actively encourage Believers to minutely inspect every word that I say, and every word that I write, and do so by comparing it to the Word of God. Any true Preacher will do the same. Jesus said: *"Making the Word of God of none effect through your tradition"*

NOTES

(Mk. 7:13). This plainly tells us that the Word of God is to be the final authority in all things.

The idea that Believers are to meekly submit to Preachers, and never question what they say, has taken untold millions to Hell, and is presently taking untold millions to Hell.

When it comes to God, there is always a vertical submission enjoined upon all Believers. In other words, we are always to submit to Him, which is to submit to His Word.

When it comes to Believers, submission is always horizontal. The Scripture plainly says: *"Submitting yourselves one to another in the fear of God"* (Eph. 5:21).

The idea of a vertical submission as it regards Believers is not taught in the Word of God. I am referring to the popular teaching that the Laity is to always submit to the Pastor, irrespective as to what he says or does, and that the Pastor is to submit to some elected official in a religious Denomination, etc. Nothing of that nature is taught in the Word of God, and nothing of that nature is Scriptural. As I've already stated, if that criteria is followed, it will bring about spiritual wreckage for all concerned.

If Believers humbly submit one to another, even as the Scripture teaches, such will abrogate the *"lone ranger"* attitude, and as well, will keep Scriptural government in the Church, instead of substituting man's government, which phony submission does.

SPIRITUAL AUTHORITY

While we're on the subject, we might as well deal with it to its proper conclusion.

Also, it is erroneously taught in the modern Church, at least in many circles, that Preachers have spiritual authority over the laity, and that certain Preachers elected to some particular religious office have spiritual authority over other Preachers, etc. Again, nothing could be further from the truth.

There is no such thing in the Word of God as one Believer having authority over another. While there definitely is spiritual authority, it is always in the sense of the spirit world. Let me explain.

Every Believer has spiritual authority over demon spirits, and even over Satan himself. We have this authority under Christ, consequently, being allowed to use the Name of Jesus. The Master said: *"And these signs shall follow them who believe; in My Name shall they cast out devils; they shall speak with new tongues;*

"They shall take up serpents (put away demon spirits)*; and if they drink any deadly thing, it shall not hurt them; they shall lay hands on the sick, and they shall recover"* (Mk. 16:17-18).

As well, Jesus said: *"Behold, I give unto you power to tread on serpents and scorpions* (metaphors for demon spirits)*, and over all the power of the enemy: and nothing shall by any means hurt you"* (Lk. 10:19).

There is nothing in the Word of God that teaches that Believers, or Preachers, or even Apostles or Prophets, have spiritual authority over other Believers, etc.

Some particular Denominations attempt to proclaim such an idea, claiming they have spiritual authority, because they have been elected to some religious office, some of them on the tenth or twelfth ballot. Again, nothing could be further from the truth!

While I love and respect all Believers, and all Preachers, and will do my very best to be kind and gracious to them, and will do whatever they request, providing it's Scriptural, and it's something I should do, I definitely will not follow them blindly, and neither should you. Jesus addressed this by saying: *"Let them alone: they be blind leaders of the blind* (He was speaking of the Pharisees). *And if the blind lead the blind, both shall fall into the ditch"* (Mat. 15:14). Regrettably, the Pharisee spirit presently is alive and well in our midst.

Once again, there are millions of people in Hell presently because they were told they must obey some Preacher or Priest, because he had spiritual authority, and whatever he said do, they must obey. This is not a new trick with Satan, but rather something which he has nurtured from the very beginning.

On the other hand, if the true Preacher of the Gospel is preaching to you the Truth, and you ignore that Truth, the end result will definitely not be well. But it's because you have rebelled against the Word of God. That always brings disaster!

By this, I am not at all meaning to denigrate

in any way the high and holy Offices of the *"Apostle, Prophet, Evangelist, Pastor, and Teacher."* These are gifts to the Church, given by Christ. You are to love Preachers, respect them, and revere their high and holy Callings. And you are to follow them, but only as they follow Christ. Blessed greatly are the man and woman who have a Church to attend, whose Pastor is Godly, and who preaches the Truth. Sadly and regrettably, such a Church and such a Preacher are not always easy to find. There are some, but not many. You would do yourself wise to search diligently, asking the Lord to help you find such a Church.

THE PARTED HOOF

The parted or divided hoof marked the animal's *"Walk."* However, let it be understood that the divided hoof was insufficient within itself, if not accompanied by the *"chewing of the cud."* *"The swine though he divide the hoof and be cloven-footed, yet he chews not the cud; he is unclean to you"* (vs. 7).

The *"inward life"* (chewing of the cud) and the *"outward walk"* (daily Sanctification) must go together. In fact, there are tens of thousands who claim to know the Word, and who can quote many Scriptures, and are in fact, very educated; however, their *"outward walk"* doesn't measure up to their claims. Both must go together, and to be sure, if the *"cud is rightly chewed,"* i.e., *"the Word rightly digested,"* then the *"walk"* will be correct as well. The hog had the parted hoof, but he did not chew the cud. Such a *"walk"* as it regards the Christian will be a *"self-righteous walk."* It will not be a *"walking after the Spirit,"* but rather a *"walking after the flesh"* (Rom. 8:1).

WALKING AFTER THE SPIRIT AND WALKING AFTER THE FLESH

I've already addressed this, but due to its vast importance, let us briefly look at it again. In fact, it would be difficult, if not impossible, to overstate this case.

What is walking after the Spirit, even as Paul addressed himself in Romans 8:1?

Romans 8:2 tells us what it is. It is placing our Faith and trust exclusively *"in Christ Jesus,"* which refers to what He did for us at the Cross. Considering that the Holy Spirit works exclusively within the parameters of the Finished Work of Christ, our Faith must ever be in that Finished Work. That is *"walking after the Spirit."*

"Walking after the flesh," which is the very opposite of *"walking after the Spirit,"* refers to us trusting in our own strength and ability, or even in religious things, but not in the Cross of Christ.

The *"walk"* of the Child of God, which refers to our daily living, can only be carried out properly if we *"walk after the Spirit."* That is a simple matter of Faith, but more particularly, Faith in the correct object, which ever is the Cross of Christ (Rom. 8:2, 11). Otherwise, our *"walk"* will not be as it ought to be, and because we are *"Walking after the flesh,"* which regrettably and sadly, seems to be the case of the majority of the modern Church.

(9) "THESE SHALL YOU EAT OF ALL THAT ARE IN THE WATERS: WHATSOEVER HAS FINS AND SCALES IN THE WATERS, IN THE SEAS, AND IN THE RIVERS, THEM SHALL YOU EAT.

(10) "AND ALL THAT HAVE NOT FINS AND SCALES IN THE SEAS, AND IN THE RIVERS, OF ALL THAT MOVE IN THE WATERS, AND OF ANY LIVING THING WHICH IS IN THE WATERS, THEY SHALL BE AN ABOMINATION UNTO YOU:

(11) "THEY SHALL BE EVEN AN ABOMINATION UNTO YOU; YOU SHALL NOT EAT OF THEIR FLESH, BUT YOU SHALL HAVE THEIR CARCASSES IN ABOMINATION.

(12) "WHATSOEVER HATH NOT FINS NOR SCALES IN THE WATERS, THAT SHALL BE AN ABOMINATION UNTO YOU.

(13) "AND THESE ARE THEY WHICH YOU SHALL HAVE IN ABOMINATION AMONG THE FOWLS; THEY SHALL NOT BE EATEN, THEY ARE AN ABOMINATION: THE EAGLE, AND THE OSSIFRAGE, AND THE OSPRAY,

(14) "AND THE VULTURE, AND THE KITE AFTER HIS KIND;

(15) "EVERY RAVEN AFTER HIS KIND;

(16) "AND THE OWL, AND THE NIGHT HAWK, AND THE CUCKOW, AND THE HAWK AFTER HIS KIND,

NOTES

(17) "AND THE LITTLE OWL, AND THE CORMORANT, AND THE GREAT OWL,

(18) "AND THE SWAN, AND THE PELICAN, AND THE GIER EAGLE,

(19) "AND THE STORK, THE HERON AFTER HER KIND, AND THE LAPWING, AND THE BAT.

(20) "ALL FOWLS THAT CREEP, GOING UPON ALL FOUR, SHALL BE AN ABOMINATION UNTO YOU.

(21) "YET THESE MAY YOU EAT OF EVERY FLYING CREEPING THING THAT GOES UPON ALL FOUR, WHICH HAVE LEGS ABOVE THEIR FEET, TO LEAP WITHAL UPON THE EARTH;

(22) "EVEN THESE OF THEM YOU MAY EAT; THE LOCUST AFTER HIS KIND, AND THE BALD LOCUST AFTER HIS KIND, AND THE BEETLE AFTER HIS KIND, AND THE GRASSHOPPER AFTER HIS KIND.

(23) "BUT ALL OTHER FLYING CREEPING THINGS, WHICH HAVE FOUR FEET, SHALL BE AN ABOMINATION UNTO YOU."

The construction is:

1. Fish that had both fins and scales were clean.

2. Birds that flew, and that had legs above their feet to leap withal were clean.

3. As to creeping things, those that had many feet, and that dragged their body along the earth were unclean.

THE FISH

Verses 9 through 12 read: *"These shall you eat of all that are in the waters: whatsoever has fins and scales in the waters, in the seas, and in the rivers, them shall you eat.*

"And all that have not fins and scales in the seas, and in the rivers, of all that move in the waters, and of any living thing which is in the waters, they shall be an abomination unto you:

"They shall be even an abomination unto you; you shall not eat of their flesh, but you shall have their carcasses in abomination.

"Whatsoever has not fins nor scales in the waters, that shall be an abomination unto you."

The manner in which the instructions are given here might serve as an example for modern Christians, and would fall into the following category:

Williams says, *"Fish that had both fins and scales were clean. Fins to enable them to move through the water, and scales to resist its action. A Christian is to be in the world, but he must not let the world be in him. He is to resist its influence and swim against its current. Spiritual life and energy can alone give this resistance and progression."*

I think we can learn through these instructions given by the Lord, even though the practical side no longer applies.

The Christian must have spiritual energy to be able to move through the elements of temptation, the elements of opposition, which surround us, and the power to preserve us from its action. This is found only in the Holy Spirit. And without the Baptism with the Holy Spirit, which Jesus commanded all Believers to receive (Acts 1:4-5), the Holy Spirit is greatly hindered in that which He Alone can do for us.

The Child of God is, in effect, a stranger to the present system of this world. We are in the world, but not of the world; at least we are not supposed to be of the world. John said: *"Love not the world, neither the things that are in the world. If any man love the world, the love of the Father is not in him.*

"For all that is in the world, the lust of the flesh, and the lust of the eyes, and the pride of life, is not of the Father, but is of the world" (I Jn. 2:15-16).

If we are friendly with the system of this world, then that tells us that we cannot be friendly with the Lord. One or the other must go.

SATAN'S SUBTERFUGE

We're living in an age, and I speak of the present time, when far too many Preachers are trying to accommodate the world and the Christian at the same time. They are afraid if they preach against the system of this world, warning of its influence, that their people will leave. However, the Preacher must understand that it's not our business as to how many people come or go, but rather that we stay true to the Word of God, irrespective of how it is accepted or rejected.

The Lord has given this Ministry, and I speak of Jimmy Swaggart Ministries, the responsibility of preaching the Cross, and to

do so with such authority that those who refer to themselves as *"Christians,"* will either have to accept it or reject it. To be sure, this is not my responsibility only, but the responsibility of all Preachers (I Cor. 1:17-18, 21, 23; 2:2).

The Revelation of the Cross began in 1996, and continues unto this hour, and by that, I speak of a continued enlargement of information. I would trust that it ever shall continue.

THE DRAWING POWER OF THE CROSS

I have learned some things since this Revelation began. I have learned that the Cross addresses each individual Christian as to exactly where he or she is, spiritually speaking. The Cross points out false doctrine, as nothing else! The Cross charts the course, and does so in unmistakable terms. Consequently, it demands all of the Believer, which means that if that Believer is to truly follow Christ, he will have to deny himself, and take up the Cross daily (Lk. 9:23-24).

In the doing of this, he may have to leave his Church, or even his Denomination, and quite possibly, his family might turn against him. He may lose all of his friends, because the Cross demands total allegiance to Christ.

Looking at modern Christendom, about fifty percent has been infected by the so-called Word of Faith Doctrine, which means that they openly repudiate the Cross. Consequently, very few of these people will respond favorably to the Message of the Cross.

Of the other fifty percent, about forty-nine percent have no interest. In other words, they want to refer to themselves as *"Christians,"* but they still want to hang onto the world. The Cross draws a line between the world and Christ, so this eliminates many Christians. They want no part of the Cross!

That leaves about one percent, who truly love the Lord, and who truly want to follow Christ, and do so all the way. While these figures are mine, I fear they are close to being correct.

Satan's subterfuge is that the Christian can have the world, and all that is in the world, and at the same time have the Lord. The Christian swallows this bait, thinking they can join the world, while at the same time maintaining their Christian experience. By no means is this a new temptation. It is an old dodge, that the Evil One has been using for a long, long time, in fact, since the very beginning.

Very soon, the nice sins, as if there were such, disappear, with the hard vice taking over, and now the trap has been sprung, and the Christian is caught, and he or she will find to their utter dismay that the bright lights of the world are not exactly what they thought they would be.

Jesus said: *"The thief* (meaning the Devil) *cometh not, but for to steal, and to kill, and to destroy"* (Jn. 10:10). He knew what He was talking about.

SO WHAT IS THE DRAWING POWER OF THE CROSS?

Jesus said: *"And I, if I be lifted up from the earth, will draw all men unto Me"* (Jn. 12:32).

When He spoke in this manner, He was speaking of the Cross. Verse 33 says: *"This He said, signifying what death He should die."*

He wasn't meaning that all the world would flock to Him, and especially considering that He would die on a Cross, nor was He inferring that the Church would flock to Him. In fact, most won't.

He meant that through the Cross, and the Cross alone, He would break the bondages which did bind humanity; He would bring spiritual life to those who had nothing but spiritual death; He would bring the light to those who sat in great darkness. There is no other way that humanity can know freedom, except by the Cross.

This addresses the unsaved who are altogether in sin. It also addresses the Believer, as well! The Believer must continue to look to the Cross, because it was there that all victory was won.

THE WORD OF FAITH ERROR

I personally feel that the word *"error"* is far too mild, as it regards this spurious doctrine. While some doctrines, although in error, do claim a way of Salvation; this particular doctrine claims nothing of the sort. It deals not at all with the unsaved, and because it is impossible for the unsaved to hear

NOTES

this particular doctrine, and by that doctrine, accept Christ. While there might be some few, precious few, who are saved in these particular meetings, to be sure, they are saved by trusting in Christ and what He did at the Cross, which they heard somewhere else. There is no moving of the Holy Spirit in this doctrine, whether in convicting power to the unsaved, or whether in anointing power as it regards Believers. While these Preachers speak of the anointing constantly, once again, that of which they speak is not the Anointing of the Holy Spirit, but rather the anointing of *"spirits."*

We must come to the realization that all false doctrine, and whatever it might be, or however good it might look on the surface, was instituted by demon spirits. Paul said:

"Now the Spirit (Holy Spirit) *speaks expressly, that in the latter times* (the times in which we now live) *some shall depart from the Faith, giving heed to seducing spirits, and doctrines of devils"* (I Tim. 4:1).

Pure and simple, the Word of Faith doctrine is a *"doctrine of devils."*

I have a Bible in my possession that is printed by these particular people. It is referred to as *"The Word."* As far as the Bible itself is concerned, it is a King James Version, just like any other King James Version.

At the back of this particular Bible, however, the publisher has printed Messages from some of their primary Preachers, addressing many Bible Doctrines. If I remember correctly, there are possibly 10 or 12 of these Messages. They deal with Salvation, Faith, the Holy Spirit, financial prosperity, healing, how to live a victorious life, etc.

I read them all, and not one single time in any of these Messages is the Cross of Christ mentioned – not one single time.

This past week (August 2002), someone sent us by e-mail 75 or 80 pages, if I remember correctly, concerning a particular book written by one of their scholars, defending the *"Jesus died spiritually doctrine."* This doctrine is the mainstay of the Word of Faith people.

I read, I suppose, 30 or 40 pages, and basically, this is what the dear Brother was teaching, and it is what the Word of Faith people teach:

They basically state, *"The Blood of Jesus Christ does not atone."* If you ask them point blank, they would probably answer you, *"Oh yes, the Blood of Jesus atones,"* and then they will attempt to add something else to the shed Blood of Christ. That which they will add is their claim that when Jesus hung on the Cross, He actually became a sinner, and then He died as a sinner, and went to the burning side of Hell, where He was tormented by demon spirits, and even Satan himself, for some three days and nights. At that time, God said, *"it is enough,"* and Jesus was then *"born again,"* just like any sinner is born again, and then resurrected from the dead.

Never mind that there is not a shred of this found anywhere in the Word of God; this is what they teach. And basically, Jesus supposedly going to Hell is the object of their faith. They actually have no faith in the Blood of Christ.

They claim that the Blood of Christ was merely a physical thing, and by itself could effect no Salvation. But the Bible doesn't say that. It does say:

"Being justified freely by His Grace through the Redemption that is in Christ Jesus:

"Whom God has set forth to be a propitiation through Faith in His Blood, to declare His Righteousness for the remission of sins that are past, through the forbearance of God" (Rom. 3:24-25).

And then: *"Much more then, being now justified by His Blood, we shall be saved from wrath through Him"* (Rom. 5:9).

And then: *"In Whom we have Redemption through His Blood, the forgiveness of sins, according to the riches of His Grace"* (Eph. 1:7).

And then: *"But now in Christ Jesus you who sometimes were far off are made nigh by the Blood of Christ"* (Eph. 2:13).

And then: *"In Whom we have Redemption through His Blood, even the forgiveness of sins"* (Col. 1:14).

And then: *"And, having made peace through the Blood of His Cross, by Him to reconcile all things unto Himself; by Him, I say, whether they be things in Earth, or things in Heaven"* (Col. 1:20).

Peter said: *"Forasmuch as you know that you were not redeemed with corruptible*

things, as silver and gold . . . But with the Precious Blood of Christ, as of a lamb without blemish and without spot" (I Pet. 1:18-19).

John said: *"But if we walk in the light, as He is in the light, we have fellowship one with another, and the Blood of Jesus Christ His Son cleanses us from all sin"* (I Jn. 1:7).

And then: *"And from Jesus Christ, Who is the Faithful Witness, and the First Begotten of the dead, and the Prince of the kings of the Earth. Unto Him Who loved us, and washed us from our sins in His Own Blood"* (Rev. 1:5).

And finally: *"And they sung a new song, saying, You are worthy to take the Book, and to open the seals thereof: for You were slain, and have redeemed us to God by Your Blood out of every kindred, and tongue, and people, and nation"* (Rev. 5:9).

In fact, the entirety of the Book of Hebrews paints the picture, in no uncertain terms of *"Blood Atonement."* And of course, the Book of Leviticus, which we are now studying, epitomizes this of which we speak, also in no uncertain terms.

To add something to the shed Blood of Christ, claiming that the added measure, whatever it might be, is needed, in order for men to be saved, is to abrogate the Blood of Christ. In fact, it is an insult to Christ of the highest order.

If Jesus going to Hell for three days and nights, and burning in the flames for that period of time, which incidentally He didn't do, could redeem humanity, then that would mean that every sinner who died and went to Hell could suffer there for three days and nights, and then be saved. How preposterous can we be! If Jesus died spiritually, which He didn't, then He would have to remain in Hell forever and ever. After death there is no second chance. First, second, and even multitudes of opportunities, are on this side of the grave. The idea of being saved after death is not taught in Scripture.

HOW SERIOUS IS THE ERROR OF THE WORD OF FAITH DOCTRINE?

It is so serious that I personally believe it is even worse than the Law/Grace issue faced by Paul. I'll tell you why.

We're nearing the very end of the Church Age. The Rapture could take place at any time, incidentally, in which, most of the Word of Faith people do not believe. Satan is getting ready for his final thrust, as he attempts to take over the world, which information is given to us throughout the Bible, but especially in Revelation, Chapters 6 through 19. He has, I believe, saved his biggest guns for the last.

Due to the particular time in which we live, I personally feel that the Word of Faith doctrine, which is in actuality no faith at all, at least that which God will recognize, is Satan's final hand, before the Rapture. I believe, as well, that the Lord has raised up our particular Ministry, among others, to present the Message of the Cross, which in fact, has been lost to the Church for the past several decades, and mostly due to the Word of Faith doctrine. The Holy Spirit is striving to bring the Church back to the Cross.

To be sure, this erroneous doctrine of which we speak is not the only culprit. Satan is working in every capacity in order to push the Church away from the foundation Doctrines of the Word of God. While many Denominations still have the correct Foundation of the Faith in their constitution and by-laws, far too often, they are what they claim in name only.

The only answer for all of this is the Message of the Cross. Nothing else will suffice, as nothing else is meant to suffice.

FADS

In the decade of the 1990's, one fad after the other has sprang up, burned brightly for a short period of time, and then died, in that there aren't even any spiritual embers left.

In each one of these fads, whatever they may have been, they were touted as the answer to the dilemma of the Church. But yet, the Church keeps drifting further and further away from Christ, with more and more Christians failing, and sadly and regrettably, more Preachers failing at this particular time, than ever before. In other words, the *"works of the flesh"* are rampant (Gal. 5:19-21).

I realize that what I am saying is not popular. In fact, such preaching never is!

Consequently, I do not look for great multitudes to flock to the banner of the Cross. In fact, they never have.

But for those who love the Lord, and who truly want to grow in Grace and the knowledge of the Lord, to ever draw closer to Him, for the Fruit of the Spirit to be manifested in their lives, they will find that the Cross will open that door wide, because it opens the door to Christ. In fact, no other door does (Jn. 10:1).

Back to our original subject, there is no way that the Believer can throw aside the pressures of the world and the powers of darkness, without the Holy Spirit (Rom. 8:11). It simply cannot be done!

And the only way that the Holy Spirit will work within our lives, giving us victory over the world, the flesh, and the Devil, is that our Faith be anchored clearly and plainly in the Finished Work of Christ, through which the Holy Spirit works exclusively (Rom. 8:1-2).

THE FOWLS

Verses 13 through 23 read: *"And these are they which you shall have in abomination among the fowls; they shall not be eaten, they are an abomination: the eagle, and the ossifrage, and the ospray,*

"And the vulture, and the kite after his kind;

"Every raven after his kind;

"And the owl, and the night hawk, and the cuckow, and the hawk after his kind,

"And the little owl, and the cormorant, and the great owl,

"And the swan, and the pelican, and the gier eagle,

"And the stork, the heron after her kind, and the lapwing, and the bat.

"All fowls that creep, going upon all four, shall be an abomination unto you.

"Yet these may you eat of every flying creeping thing that goes upon all four, which have legs above their feet, to leap withal upon the Earth;

"Even these are them you may eat; the locust after his kind, and the bald locust after his kind, and the beetle after his kind, and the grasshopper after his kind.

"But all other flying creeping things, which have four feet, shall be an abomination unto you."

Birds that flew, and that had legs above their feet to leap withal, were clean; but those that could not so leap, or that fed upon flesh, were unclean.

As to creeping things, those that had many feet, and that dragged the body along the earth, were unclean.

From this we find, and now I speak of the fowls, the native air of the Christian is the upper air. On the wings of Faith he is to mount up thither; his food is not to be carnal; and when, of necessity, he must touch Earth, he to touch it as lightly as possible, and not to rest thereon, so to speak.

As well, Paul said that minding earthly things is an evidence of hostility to the Cross of Christ (Phil. 3:18-19).

(24) "AND FOR THESE YOU SHALL BE UNCLEAN: WHOSOEVER TOUCHES THE CARCASS OF THEM SHALL BE UNCLEAN UNTIL THE EVENING.

(25) "AND WHOSOEVER BEARS OUGHT OF THE CARCASS OF THEM SHALL WASH HIS CLOTHES, AND BE UNCLEAN UNTIL THE EVENING.

(26) "THE CARCASSES OF EVERY BEAST WHICH DIVIDES THE HOOF, AND IS NOT CLOVEN-FOOTED, NOR CHEWS THE CUD, ARE UNCLEAN UNTO YOU: EVERY ONE WHO TOUCHES THEM SHALL BE UNCLEAN.

(27) "AND WHATSOEVER GOES UPON HIS PAWS, AMONG ALL MANNER OF BEASTS THAT GO ON ALL FOUR, THOSE ARE UNCLEAN UNTO YOU: WHOSO TOUCHES THEIR CARCASS SHALL BE UNCLEAN UNTIL THE EVENING.

(28) "AND HE WHO BEARS THE CARCASS OF THEM SHALL WASH HIS CLOTHES, AND BE UNCLEAN UNTIL THE EVENING: THEY ARE UNCLEAN UNTO YOU.

(29) "THESE ALSO SHALL BE UNCLEAN UNTO YOU AMONG THE CREEPING THINGS THAT CREEP UPON THE EARTH; THE WEASEL, AND THE MOUSE, AND THE TORTOISE AFTER HIS KIND,

(30) "AND THE FERRET, AND THE CHAMELEON, AND THE LIZARD, AND THE SNAIL, AND THE MOLE.

(31) "THESE ARE UNCLEAN TO YOU AMONG ALL THAT CREEP: WHOSOEVER

NOTES

DOES TOUCH THEM, WHEN THEY BE DEAD, SHALL BE UNCLEAN UNTIL THE EVENING.

(32) "AND UPON WHATSOEVER ANY OF THEM, WHEN THEY ARE DEAD, DOES FALL, IT SHALL BE UNCLEAN; WHETHER IT BE ANY VESSEL OF WOOD, OR RAIMENT, OR SKIN, OR SACK, WHATSOEVER VESSEL IT BE, WHEREIN ANY WORK IS DONE, IT MUST BE PUT INTO WATER, AND IT SHALL BE UNCLEAN UNTIL THE EVENING; SO IT SHALL BE CLEANSED.

(33) "AND EVERY EARTHEN VESSEL, WHEREINTO ANY OF THEM FALLS, WHATSOEVER IS IN IT SHALL BE UNCLEAN; AND YOU SHALL BREAK IT.

(34) "OF ALL MEAT WHICH MAY BE EATEN, THAT ON WHICH SUCH WATER COMES SHALL BE UNCLEAN: AND ALL DRINK THAT MAY BE DRUNK IN EVERY SUCH VESSEL SHALL BE UNCLEAN.

(35) "AND EVERYTHING WHEREUPON ANY PART OF THEIR CARCASS FALLS SHALL BE UNCLEAN; WHETHER IT BE OVEN, OR RANGES FOR POTS, THEY SHALL BE BROKEN DOWN: FOR THEY ARE UNCLEAN AND SHALL BE UNCLEAN UNTO YOU.

(36) "NEVERTHELESS A FOUNTAIN OR PIT, WHEREIN THERE IS PLENTY OF WATER, SHALL BE CLEAN: BUT THAT WHICH TOUCHES THEIR CARCASS SHALL BE UNCLEAN.

(37) "AND IF ANY PART OF THEIR CARCASS FALL UPON ANY SOWING SEED WHICH IS TO BE SOWN, IT SHALL BE CLEAN.

(38) "BUT IF ANY WATER BE PUT UPON THE SEED, AND ANY PART OF THEIR CARCASS FALL THEREON, IT SHALL BE UNCLEAN UNTO YOU.

(39) "AND IF ANY BEAST, OF WHICH YOU MAY EAT, DIE; HE WHO TOUCHES THE CARCASS THEREOF SHALL BE UNCLEAN UNTIL THE EVENING.

(40) "AND HE WHO EATS OF THE CARCASS OF IT SHALL WASH HIS CLOTHES, AND BE UNCLEAN UNTIL THE EVENING: HE ALSO WHO BEARS THE CARCASS OF IT SHALL WASH HIS CLOTHES, AND BE UNCLEAN UNTIL THE EVENING."

The composition is:

1. An unclean animal, fish, bird, or reptile, when dead, defiled whatsoever it touched.

2. The one thing it would not defile was an abundant spring of water, and seed-corn. Christ the Lord, as man, was undefiled by contact with sinners and with sin. He was, and is, the Living Water that springs up into everlasting life, and He is the corn of wheat that brings forth much fruit (Jn., Chpt. 12).

3. These Passages speak of the death of these unclean animals, fowls, or reptiles, etc. Even their dead carcass would defile. This is because death is a direct result of sin.

DEATH

Verses 24 through 31 read: *"And for these you shall be unclean: whosoever touches the carcass of them shall be unclean until the evening.*

"And whosoever bears ought of the carcass of them shall wash his clothes, and be unclean until the evening.

"The carcasses of every beast which divides the hoof, and is not cloven-footed, nor chews the cud, are unclean unto you: every one who touches them shall be unclean.

"And whatsoever goes upon his paws, among all manner of beasts that go on all four, those are unclean unto you: whoso touches their carcass shall be unclean until the evening.

"And he who bears the carcass of them shall wash his clothes, and be unclean until the evening: they are unclean unto you.

"These also shall be unclean unto you among the creeping things that creep upon the earth; the weasel, and the mouse, and the tortoise after his kind,

"And the ferret, and the chameleon, and the snail, and the mole.

"These are unclean to you among all that creep: whosoever does touch them, when they be dead, shall be unclean until the evening."

Not only were these certain animals, fowls, or reptiles pronounced as unclean, which means they were not fit to be eaten, their dead carcass was declared unclean as well. In other words, if an individual touched the carcass of one of these particular creatures, he would be unclean, and

would be so unto nightfall.

The primary reason for this prohibition was the fact of death. Death is a product of sin, and has affected the entirety of creation, some worse than others.

And if these particular animals, fish, or fowls declared to be unclean would be inspected carefully, most of them would be found in some way to subsist on dead carcasses, etc. While it wouldn't apply to all, it definitely, I think, would apply to most. All of this speaks of the result or wages of sin. In fact, death is such an example of sin, which speaks of its terrible results, that it made one unclean to even touch the dead body of a human being, even one who had been Godly in life and living before death (Num. 19:2-17).

Even the animals which were deemed by the Lord to be clean, which had not been properly slaughtered, and had died from disease or accident, if one touched that particular carcass, they would be considered unclean until nightfall. This was not applicable to birds and fish (vs. 39).

THE TOUCH OF DEATH

Verses 32 through 40 read: *"And upon whatsoever any of them, when they are dead, does fall, it shall be unclean; whether it be any vessel of wood, or raiment, or skin, or sack, whatsoever vessel it be, wherein any work is done, it must be put into water, and it shall be unclean until the evening; so it shall be cleansed.*

"And every earthen vessel, whereinto any of them falls, whatsoever is in it shall be unclean; and you shall break it.

"Of all meat which may be eaten, that on which such water comes shall be unclean: and all drink that may be drunk in every such vessel shall be unclean.

"And everything whereupon any part of their carcass falls shall be unclean; whether it be oven, or ranges for pots, they shall be broken down: for they are unclean and shall be unclean unto you.

"Nevertheless a fountain or pit, wherein there is plenty of water, shall be clean: but that which touches their carcass shall be unclean.

"And if any part of their carcass fall upon

any sowing seed which is to be sown, it shall be clean.

"But if any water be put upon the seed, and any part of their carcass fall thereon, it shall be unclean unto you.

"And if any beast, of which you may eat, die; he who touches the carcass thereof shall be unclean until the evening.

"And he who eats of the carcass of it shall wash his clothes, and be unclean until the evening: he also who bears the carcass of it shall wash his clothes, and be unclean until the evening."

All of this may seem to be tedious to the unspiritual eye and mind; however, we must understand that God desired to keep His people free from the defilement consequent upon touching, tasting, or handling that which was unclean. They were not their own, and hence they were not to do as they pleased. They belonged to Jehovah; His Name was called upon them; they were identified with Him. As a result, His Word was to be their grand regulating standard in every case.

Other nations might eat what they pleased, but Israel enjoyed the high privilege of eating that only which was pleasing to Jehovah. As a result, in rendering obedience, they not only satisfied the spiritual requirements, but were no doubt healthier than the surrounding nations.

Not only was what they were to eat jealously guarded, even bare contact was forbidden, even as we see in the Verses of our study. They could not even touch that which was unclean without contracting defilement, and that referred as well to vessels which a carcass had touched, etc.

HOLINESS?

Of course, we would ask ourselves the question as to whether the keeping of all these rules and regulations actually made one holy.

The answer to that is somewhat ambiguous; *"yes"* and *"no!"*

The keeping of these rules and regulations did not make one holy, even as the Sacrifices did not save one. But what it all represented definitely did have a bearing and effect upon these individuals. So one might clumsily say that they were *"holy on credit, even as they were saved on credit."*

In some way, all of these things, and whatever they might have been, pointed to Christ. The complete truth is, the only true Righteousness and Holiness that one can have is that which comes from Christ, which is received by Faith only, and not at all by the keeping of rules and regulations, etc. That's why Paul referred to these things as *"a shadow of good things to come"* (Heb. 10:1).

HOLINESS WHICH COMES FROM CHRIST

If one had asked an Israelite of old, *"Why do you shrink so from that reptile which crawls along the path?"* He would have replied, *"Jehovah is holy, and I belong to Him."*

So also now, if a Christian be asked why he walks apart from the 10,000 things in which the men of this world participate, his answer is simply to be, *"My Father is holy."*

Concerning this, Mackintosh said, *"This is the true foundation of personal holiness. The more we contemplate the Divine Character, and enter into the power of our relationship to God, in Christ, by the energy of the Holy Spirit, the holier we must, of necessity, be."*

He went on to say, *"There can be no progress in the condition of Holiness into which the Believer is introduced, but there is and ought to be progress in the apprehension, experience, and practical exhibition of that Holiness. These things should never be confounded. All Believers are in the same condition of Holiness or Sanctification, but their practical measure may vary to any conceivable degree."*

And finally, as he continues, *"This is easily understood. The condition arises out of our being brought near to God by the Blood of the Cross; the practical measure will depend upon our keeping near by the power of the Spirit."*

POSITIONAL HOLINESS AND CONDITIONAL HOLINESS

To help us properly understand what we have just stated, perhaps it could be better explained in the following fashion:

Every Believer has a position of Holiness which does not vary, simply because it is in Christ. In other words, it's not judged by what the Believer does or doesn't do, but by what Christ has already done, and our Faith in that Finished Work. That *"position"* does not vary, simply because Christ does not vary.

But we all know that the *"position,"* which we have in Christ, does not necessarily guarantee that our *"condition"* is the same as our *"position."* It ought to be, and to be sure, the Holy Spirit is working constantly in order to effect our place and position, in that our *"condition"* will be brought up to our *"position."* But the *"condition"* will vary with different Believers, and in fact, will constantly vary with the individual Believer. That's why Peter said that we are to *"grow in Grace and the knowledge of the Lord"* (II Pet. 3:18).

However, our *"growing in Grace,"* thereby living the victorious, Christian life, which refers to our *"condition"* being brought up to our *"position,"* all in Christ, cannot be done without the Christian having a proper understanding of the Cross. By that statement, I'm not meaning that it will be more difficult without the Cross, but positively impossible. Listen to Paul:

"I do not frustrate the Grace of God: for if Righteousness come by the Law, then Christ is dead in vain" (Gal. 2:21). He then said:

"Behold, I Paul say unto you, that if you be circumcised, Christ shall profit you nothing."

He said again, *"Christ is become of no effect unto you, whosoever of you are justified by the Law; you are fallen from Grace"* (Gal. 5:2, 4).

Paul is not preaching against circumcision. He is merely stating that if we take our Faith away from Christ and Him Crucified, and make circumcision, or anything else, for that matter, the object of our Faith, *"Christ shall profit us nothing."* Or if we seek to be justified by the Law, which refers to our own efforts and ability, in other words, anything other than the Cross of Christ, *"Christ is become of no effect unto us."*

What does he mean by being *"fallen from Grace"*?

FALLEN FROM GRACE

Most Christians think he is speaking of a Christian sinning. No, that's not falling from

NOTES

Grace. In fact, that's the time that the Christian needs Grace more than ever.

"Falling from Grace," refers to the Believer, as the entire Fifth Chapter of Galatians brings out, placing his faith in something other than Christ and Him Crucified. When we do that, we frustrate the Grace of God.

The Grace of God is the Goodness of God extended to undeserving Saints. Grace comes to us strictly, totally, and completely, by and through what Christ did for us at the Cross. In fact, it is the Holy Spirit Who carried out the Work of Grace within our hearts and lives. He works exclusively within the Finished Work of Christ, which of course, is the Cross.

In other words, it is the Cross which gives the Holy Spirit the legal means to do all that He does within our hearts and lives. Paul again said: *"For the Law of the Spirit of Life in Christ Jesus has made me free from the law of sin and death"* (Rom. 8:2).

As we've already said in this Volume, this which the Holy Spirit does, and more particularly, the manner in which He does it, is so ironclad that it is referred to as *"the Law."* It's not the Law of Moses, as should be understood, but in reality, the Law that was devised by the Godhead in eternity past, which designates the manner in which the Holy Spirit works within our lives. It is called, *"The Law of the Spirit of Life."* It functions *"in Christ Jesus,"* which always and without exception refers to what Christ did at the Cross.

So, the only way in which the Believer can attain to a condition of Holiness, which is brought up to our position, is by exhibiting Faith in the Cross of Christ, which refers to what He did there.

(41) "AND EVERY CREEPING THING THAT CREEPS UPON THE EARTH SHALL BE AN ABOMINATION; IT SHALL NOT BE EATEN.

(42) "WHATSOEVER GOES UPON THE BELLY, AND WHATSOEVER GOES UPON ALL FOUR, OR WHATSOEVER HAS MORE FEET AMONG ALL CREEPING THINGS THAT CREEP UPON THE EARTH, THEM YOU SHALL NOT EAT; FOR THEY ARE AN ABOMINATION.

(43) "YOU SHALL NOT MAKE YOURSELVES ABOMINABLE WITH ANY

CREEPING THING THAT CREEPS, NEITHER SHALL YOU MAKE YOURSELVES UNCLEAN WITH THEM, THAT YOU SHOULD BE DEFILED THEREBY.

(44) "FOR I AM THE LORD YOUR GOD: YOU SHALL THEREFORE SANCTIFY YOURSELVES, AND YOU SHALL BE HOLY; FOR I AM HOLY: NEITHER SHALL YOU DEFILE YOURSELVES WITH ANY MANNER OF CREEPING THING THAT CREEPS UPON THE EARTH.

(45) "FOR I AM THE LORD WHO BROUGHT YOU UP OUT OF THE LAND OF EGYPT, TO BE YOUR GOD: YOU SHALL THEREFORE BE HOLY, FOR I AM HOLY.

(46) "THIS IS THE LAW OF THE BEASTS, AND OF THE FOWL, AND OF EVERY LIVING CREATURE THAT MOVES IN THE WATERS, AND EVERY CREATURE THAT CREEPS UPON THE EARTH:

(47) "TO MAKE A DIFFERENCE BETWEEN THE UNCLEAN AND THE CLEAN, AND BETWEEN THE BEAST THAT MAY BE EATEN AND THE BEAST THAT MAY NOT BE EATEN."

The diagram is:

1. Because Israel was elected to be a peculiar treasure to God, therefore, she was to cleanse herself from all filthiness of the flesh and spirit, and to be holy, for God was holy.

2. The word *"Holiness"* as *"Sanctification,"* refers to *"being set apart exclusively unto God."*

3. Spiritually speaking, the same command, although on a more general sense, is given to modern Christians. The Holy Spirit through Paul said: *"Wherefore come out from among them, and be ye separate, saith the Lord, and touch not the unclean thing; and I will receive you"* (II Cor. 6:14-18; 7:1).

SANCTIFY YOURSELVES

Verses 41 through 47 read: *"And every creeping thing that creeps upon the Earth shall be an abomination; it shall not be eaten.*

"Whatsoever goes upon the belly, and whatsoever goes upon all four, or whatsoever has more feet among all creeping things that creep upon the Earth, them you shall not eat; for they are an abomination.

"You shall not make yourselves abominable with any creeping thing that creeps,

neither shall you make yourselves unclean with them, that you should be defiled thereby.

"For I am the LORD your God: you shall therefore sanctify yourselves, and you shall be holy; for I am holy: neither shall you defile yourselves with any manner of creeping thing that creeps upon the Earth.

"For I am the Lord Who brought you up out of the land of Egypt, to be your God: you shall therefore be holy, for I am holy.

"This is the Law of the beasts, and of the fowl, and of every living creature that moves in the waters, and of every creature that creeps upon the Earth:

"To make a difference between the unclean and the clean, and between the beast that may be eaten and the beast that may not be eaten."

Quite a number of times, Israelites were told to *"sanctify themselves,"* even as stated in Verse 44. Nothing of this nature is mentioned in the New Testament. The closest would be that given by Peter when he said: *"But sanctify the Lord God in your hearts"* (I Pet. 3:15). However, sanctifying the Lord God in our hearts, and sanctifying ourselves, are basically two different things.

While every Believer should sanctify the Lord in our hearts, which means that we give Him our all, setting ourselves apart from the world, that He may have not only first place in our lives, but in fact, every place.

So, what did Moses mean, when he told Israel that they must *"sanctify themselves"*?

As we have mentioned regarding Holiness, Sanctification would fall into the same category, for in essence, both come from the same root word. As it regards Sanctification and Holiness, Believers before the Cross didn't have the Holy Spirit abiding permanently within their hearts and lives, as Believers do since the Cross. Consequently, the Sanctification process was more in the realm of rules and regulations, as we are studying here, with the admonition being that the Believer should sanctify themselves, by adhering to these rules as closely as possible.

This means that Sanctification and Holiness would be more symbolic than anything else. Only the Holy Spirit can truly bring one to a place of Holiness and Sanctification, which we've already explained. But due

NOTES

to the fact that the blood of bulls and goats could not take away sins, this greatly hindered the Holy Spirit from having access then, as He does now.

If it is to be remembered, John the Baptist said of Christ, even at the beginning of the Ministry of our Lord, *"Behold the Lamb of God, which taketh away the sin of the world"* (Jn. 1:29). Every Jew standing nearby would have understood perfectly what John was saying. Under the Old Covenant, sins were not taken away, only covered; consequently, the sin debt remained. But when Jesus came, and paid the price on the Cross, all sin was taken away, which means that Atonement was made for all sin, past, present, and future.

That's the reason that Paul said: *"But now has He* (Christ) *obtained a more excellent Ministry, by how much also He is the Mediator of a Better Covenant, which was established upon Better Promises"* (Heb. 8:6).

IT IS THE CROSS WHICH HAS MADE IT ALL POSSIBLE

Does the Reader tire of me holding forth the Cross? If the Reader does, then the Reader does not properly understand the Cross.

Would those who had been slaves have grown tired of hearing about the Emancipation Proclamation? I think not!

At the close of the Civil War, a group known as Quantrill's Raiders was apprehended by the Union forces. A goodly number of these men were tried and judged, and sentenced to die by hanging. One of those men, in fact, was an 18 year old boy.

On the day of the hanging, just before the young man was to be taken to the scaffold, an elderly gentleman stepped out of the crowd, who was not a relative of this boy, and in fact, had never seen him before.

He said that day to the Judge, who was present, *"Justice demands a life; can I take this boy's place?"*

He then added, *"This young man is just a boy. I've lived my life, and I don't have long left. If it would be satisfactory to the Court, would the Court allow me to take his place?"*

The Judge looked at him a few moments, and then asked a few more questions. He finally said, *"Yes, if that's what you want to do. You can give your life in place of his."*

That day, the elderly gentleman was hung in the place of this young man.

The boy bought a tombstone and placed it at the head of the man's grave. He inscribed the words on it:

"Here lies Willie Lee.

"He took my place in the line for me."

It is said that he visited this man's grave at least once every year, laying fresh flowers next to the tombstone, and did so until he died.

I don't think he ever tired of telling this wonderful story over and over, of how this man gave him back his life.

When Jesus died on the Cross, He in effect, took my place in the line for me, and He took your place in the line for you. Other than that Sacrificial, Atoning death, you and I would have been eternally lost, and so would all of mankind.

As someone has rightly written and sung, *"The Old Rugged Cross made the difference!"* Yes, it did!

"When the Trump of the great Archangel, its mighty tones shall sound,
"And the end of the world proclaiming, shall pierce the depths profound,
"When the Son of Man shall come in His Glory, with all the Saints on high,
"What a shouting in the skies from the multitudes that rise,
"Changed in the twinkling of an eye."

"When He comes in the clouds descending, and they who loved Him here,
"From their graves shall awake and praise Him, with joy and not with fear,
"When the body and the soul are united, and clothed no more to die,
"What a shouting there will be, when each other's face we see,
"Changed in the twinkling of an eye."

"O the seed that was sown in weakness, shall then be raised in power,
"And the songs of the Blood-bought millions, shall hail that blissful hour;
"When we gather safely home in the morning, and night's dark shadows fly,
"What a shouting on the shore, when

we meet to part no more,
"Changed in the twinkling of an eye."

CHAPTER 12

(1) "AND THE LORD SPOKE UNTO MOSES, SAYING,

(2) "SPEAK UNTO THE CHILDREN OF ISRAEL, SAYING, IF A WOMAN HAVE CONCEIVED SEED, AND BORN A MANCHILD: THEN SHE SHALL BE UNCLEAN SEVEN DAYS; ACCORDING TO THE DAYS OF THE SEPARATION OF HER INFIRMITY SHALL SHE BE UNCLEAN.

(3) "AND IN THE EIGHTH DAY THE FLESH OF HIS FORESKIN SHALL BE CIRCUMCISED.

(4) "AND SHE SHALL THEN CONTINUE IN THE BLOOD OF HER PURIFYING THREE AND THIRTY DAYS; SHE SHALL TOUCH NO HALLOWED THING, NOR COME INTO THE SANCTUARY, UNTIL THE DAYS OF PURIFYING BE FULFILLED.

(5) "BUT IF SHE BEAR A MAID CHILD, THEN SHE SHALL BE UNCLEAN TWO WEEKS, AS IN HER SEPARATION: AND SHE SHALL CONTINUE IN THE BLOOD OF HER PURIFYING THREESCORE AND SIX DAYS."

The structure is:

1. This Chapter humbles and comforts. It humbles, because it declares that man by nature is defiled, and needs cleansing. It comforts, because it provides a Redemption without money and without price – for two young pigeons could be had for nothing (Williams).

2. The birth of a child recalled the sin and disobedience of Eden, and that woman was the instrument of that rebellion.

3. Hence, after the birth of a little boy, the mother was shut out of the Tabernacle for 40 days, and, in the case of a girl, for 80 days; nor was she permitted to touch any hallowed thing (Williams).

A PORTRAYAL OF SIN AND ITS RUIN

Verses 1 through 5 read: *"And the LORD spoke unto Moses, saying,*

"Speak unto the Children of Israel, saying, If a woman have conceived seed, and

NOTES

born a manchild: then she shall be unclean seven days; according to the days of the separation of her infirmity shall she be unclean.

"And in the eighth day the flesh of his foreskin shall be circumcised.

"And she shall continue in the blood of her purifying three and thirty days; she shall touch no hallowed thing, nor come into the Sanctuary, until the days of her purifying be fulfilled.

"But if she bear a maid child, then she shall be unclean two weeks, as in her separation: and she shall continue in the blood of her purifying threescore and six days."

This Chapter portrays sin and its terrible ruin. While man may try to deny the fact of sin, he cannot deny the results of sin.

But at the same time, this Chapter portrays the remedy for sin, which is *"Christ and Him Crucified"* (I Cor. 1:23), and portrays it as the only remedy. While the world and even the Church may attempt to present other proposed remedies, this Chapter tells us, and in fact the entirety of the Bible, that there is no other remedy but Christ and Him Crucified. The Cross is the answer to man's dilemma, and as well, the Cross is the only answer to man's dilemma.

Mackintosh said, *"The effect of all Scripture, when properly interpreted to one's own soul, which is done directly by the power of the Holy Spirit, is to lead us out of self to Christ. Wherever we see our fallen nature, at whatever stage of its history we contemplate it – whether in its conception, at its birth, or at any point along its whole career, from the womb to the coffin, it wears the double stamp of infirmity and defilement."*

As it regards sin, there is not a corner of the Earth, nor a member of the race, which the great contamination has not touched. The soil of sin is upon every conscience, and its uncleanness is more or less in every heart. This means that it is man who corrupts society, and not society that corrupts man.

Seiss said, *"The one may react very powerfully upon the other, but the errors and corruptions in both must have a common seat and source. What is that seat? Where are we to find this prolific fountain? Penetrating to the moral signification of the Twelfth Chapter of Leviticus, we have the true answer."*

Sin is not something that is without man, in other words, that is exterior. It is a manifestation which comes from within. It is a corruption, if you will, of man's entire being, his thought processes, the very seat of his soul. Every part of man, and whatever it may be, is tainted by the terrible, putrid corruption of sin. The truth is, we are unclean, and not because of contact with a bad world, but that we are innately impure. Man as a result of the Fall is what he is, not only by education and association, but also by the seat and the soul of his very being. Uncleanness is upon the very seat of life, and attaches to every one of us from our very coming into the world. *"We were conceived in sin. We were shaped in iniquity"* (Ps. 51:5).

We will deal more graphically with the solution to this terrible dilemma regarding commentary on the latter part of this Chapter.

THE WOMAN

While the Lord spoke to both Moses and Aaron as it referred to the Law concerning clean and unclean animals, etc., characterized in the previous Chapter, He speaks here to Moses alone. Why?

The case of defilement as it regards the instructions given in the previous Chapter is a result of the teaching given in Chapter 12. Chapter 11 dealt with results, while Chapter 12 deals with the cause; hence, the Lord would direct this to the Lawgiver alone.

Why is the woman singled out here?

Two reasons:

1. It was Eve who first fell (Gen. 2:16-17; 3:1-6; II Cor. 11:3). In fact, she would bear that stigma until the coming of Christ, and His Sacrificial, Atoning Death on the Cross. There, Jesus leveled the playing ground, so to speak, taking away the reproach from women, at least as it regards those who trust Christ.

2. By the method of procreation, which God ordained at the beginning, it is woman who brings humankind into this world. As the result of the Fall of her husband, that which she brings into the world is the result of original sin, and is perpetuated by the birth process.

In fact, the seed of procreation is in the man. That means it is perpetuated through

NOTES

the man. This means had Adam not fallen, the human race would not have been destroyed. Eve could have asked for forgiveness for her sin, which would have been granted, and the wreckage and ruin would have stopped with her. But inasmuch as Adam sinned, and inasmuch as he was the federal head, so to speak, of the human race, the ruin passes down through him, but is brought forth by the woman. Actually, woman in all of her existence has only had one *"Seed,"* and that was the Lord Jesus Christ (Gen. 3:15).

When a boy baby was born, she was unclean for 40 days. When a little girl was born, she would be unclean for 80 days.

Though the discharge of blood and effluence lasts from two to three weeks, the period is nearly doubled, to include exceptional cases.

The 80 days of defilement as it regards the birth of a little girl, which as is obvious, is doubled, was meant to portray the fact that it was Eve who had first sinned.

THE BLOOD

The idea of all of this is that the blood is impure after birth, and remains impure for a period of time. But the root meaning is the life of the flesh is in the blood, and the blood of man is polluted because of original sin.

All of this is meant to declare to us, even in language not to be misunderstood, that man is *"an unclean thing."* And that he needs the blood of Atonement to cleanse him, which humanity could not provide, and because of sinful pollution.

If we properly look at this Chapter as we ought to, and thereby properly understand its contents, the pride, pomp, dignity, and self-righteousness, which all of us are so prone to have, would speedily vanish, and instead thereof, we would find the solid basis of all true dignity, as well as the ground of Divine Righteousness, which is in the Cross of our Lord Jesus Christ, and His Cross alone!

The idea is, and as we shall see, the blood of the human being is defiled, and its defilement comes from original sin. As such, we must have Atonement, and that speaks of pure blood, which is unsullied, and untainted, which can only speak of the Blood of the Lord Jesus Christ, which He shed for us.

CIRCUMCISION

The shadow of the Cross passes before us in a double way in this Chapter. First, it is in the circumcision of the *"manchild,"* and second, it is in the Burnt-Offering and the Sin-Offering, whereby the mother was restored from every defiling influence, and which we will study next.

The circumcision of the little boy baby was carried out on the eighth day, which specifications had been given to Abraham, some 400 years earlier (Gen. 17:21).

It is said that on the eighth day of the life of the little boy, his blood properly coagulates. If done before this, the child could bleed to death.

Circumcision consisted of the foreskin being cut as it regards the little boy's member. Spiritually, this symbolized several things:

1. The cutting symbolized separation from this world unto God. In a sense, it was a sign of Sanctification.

2. The shedding of blood which accompanies circumcision proclaims the fact that man is redeemed, not by such corruptible things as silver or gold, but by the Precious Blood of the Lord Jesus Christ (I Pet. 1:18-20).

3. All of this was symbolic of the Covenant between God and His people.

Such is not required in Christendom, because Jesus has come, Who fulfilled all of this symbolism, and which now, we have a *"circumcision of the heart,"* which all comes by Faith (Rom. 2:29; Gal. 5:6).

(6) "AND WHEN THE DAYS OF HER PURIFYING ARE FULFILLED, FOR A SON, OR FOR A DAUGHTER, SHE SHALL BRING A LAMB OF THE FIRST YEAR FOR A BURNT-OFFERING, AND A YOUNG PIGEON, OR A TURTLEDOVE, FOR A SIN-OFFERING, UNTO THE DOOR OF THE TABERNACLE OF THE CONGREGATION, UNTO THE PRIEST:

(7) "WHO SHALL OFFER IT BEFORE THE LORD, AND MAKE AN ATONEMENT FOR HER; AND SHE SHALL BE CLEANSED FROM THE ISSUE OF HER BLOOD. THIS IS THE LAW FOR HER WHO HAS BORN A MALE OR A FEMALE.

(8) "AND IF SHE BE NOT ABLE TO BRING A LAMB, THEN SHE SHALL BRING TWO TURTLEDOVES, OR TWO YOUNG PIGEONS; THE ONE FOR THE BURNT-OFFERING, AND THE OTHER FOR THE SIN-OFFERING: AND THE PRIEST SHALL MAKE AN ATONEMENT FOR HER, AND SHE SHALL BE CLEAN."

The composition is:

1. Verse 6 typifies the solution for man's dilemma, the Cross of Christ, and as previously stated, the Cross alone!

2. The Offerings were designed that all may participate, even the poorest. If a lamb could not be afforded, then two turtledoves or young pigeons could be offered instead. These could be obtained for very little, or nothing.

3. The extreme poverty of the Lord's earthly parents was evidenced by their bringing two pigeons, the one for a Sin-Offering, the other for a Burnt-Offering (Lk. 2:24).

4. The Virgin Mary knew she was a sinner and needed the cleansing of atoning blood, for she brought the two pigeons, as commanded here (Williams).

THE CROSS OF CHRIST

Verses 6 through 8 read: *"And when the days of her purifying are fulfilled, for a son, or for a daughter, she shall bring a lamb of the first year for a Burnt-Offering, and a young pigeon, or a turtledove, for a Sin-Offering, unto the Door of the Tabernacle of the congregation, unto the Priest:*

"Who shall offer it before the LORD, and make an Atonement for her; and she shall be cleansed from the issue of her blood. This is the law for her who has born a male or a female.

"And if she be not able to bring a lamb, then she shall bring two turtledoves, or two young pigeons; the one for the Burnt-Offering, and the other for the Sin-Offering: and the Priest shall make an Atonement for her, and she shall be clean."

In the seven days after the birth of a little boy (14 if it was a girl), she made all that she touched unclean; in the second stage, which was 33 days, or 66 if it was a girl, she was only required to touch no hallowed thing, nor come into the Sanctuary, as she was progressing towards cleanness.

When in a state of impurity, the Hebrews were forbidden to enter the Sanctuary, to

NOTES

keep the Passover, and to partake of holy food, whether of sacrificial meat, of sacred offerings and gifts, or of Shewbread, because the clean only were fit to approach the Holy God and all that appertains to Him (Lev. 7:19-21; 22:3; Num. 9:6; 18:11; I Sam. 21:5).

As well, it is claimed by some that the reason why the duration of the mother's uncleanness is twice as long at a girl's birth as at a boy's, would appear to be that the uncleanness attached to the child as well as to the mother, but as the boy was placed in a state of ceremonial purity at once by the act of circumcision, which took place on the eighth day, he thereupon ceased to be unclean, and the mother's uncleanness alone remained; whereas in the case of a girl, both mother and child were unclean during the period that the former was *"in the blood of her purifying,"* and, therefore, that period had to be doubled (Pulpit).

When the length of the time required was fulfilled, whether it was for a son or a daughter, she was then to bring a lamb for a *"Burnt-Offering,"* and a young pigeon, or a turtledove, for a *"Sin-Offering."*

If she could not afford a lamb, she was to bring two turtledoves, or two young pigeons, the one for the *"Burnt-Offering,"* and the other for the *"Sin-Offering."*

In both of these Offerings, the *"Burnt-Offering,"* and the *"Sin-Offering,"* the two grand aspects of the Death of Christ are introduced here as the only thing which could possibly meet and perfectly remove the defilement connected with man's natural birth. The *"Burnt-Offering"* signified the Perfection of Christ offered up in Sacrifice, which God demanded, that is if the sin debt was to be forever settled. The *"Sin-Offering"* presents the Death of Christ as bearing upon the sinner's need. In other words, the Sin-Offering proclaimed the sinner's sin placed on Christ, while the Burnt-Offering portrayed the Perfection of Christ given to the sinner.

All of this tells us that nothing but blood-shedding could impart cleanness. The Cross is the only remedy for man's infirmity and man's defilement. Wherever that glorious work is apprehended by Faith, and we speak of the Sacrifice of Christ, there is perfect cleanness in joy (Mackintosh).

THE SACRIFICE OF THE CROSS

We find in this Twelfth Chapter the consideration of an ever-gracious God, Who is seen in the fact that He would accept the blood of a turtledove, if that was all the bearer could afford, just as He accepted the blood of the lamb or the bullock, as it regarded the rich. The full value of the atoning work was alike maintained and exhibited in each.

This means that the Sacrifice of the Cross is the same to every member of the Israel of God, whatever be his status in the assembly.

This means that Grace meets the needy one just where he is and as he is. The atoning Blood is brought within the reach of the very lowest, the very poorest, the very feeblest. All who need it can have it. One might say, *"To the poor the Gospel is preached."* None can say, *"The Blood of Jesus was beyond me."* (Mackintosh).

We also learn here that *"time"* did not heal the defilement of the woman. It was only meant to show the extent of her terrible problem, and in actuality, the terrible problem which besets the entirety of the race – both men and women. It was the Sacrifices Alone, which pointed to the Cross of Christ, which effected cleanness, and, thereby, the solution. There is no other, and which should by now be painfully obvious.

Were we speaking here of mundane matters, that would be something else altogether; however, inasmuch as we are speaking of the eternal consequence of the soul, and nothing could be more important, that is why I am adamant as it regards this subject. It is the Cross and the Cross alone which provides the solution. If I seem to stress this too much, I do so because the Church as a whole has drifted so far away from that perfect solution.

What does the Reader think that these Sacrifices represented? It is obvious as to what they represented. They represented Christ and the price that He would pay, as it regards the Redemption of lost humanity. They represent nothing else, as they can represent nothing else. That being the case, which is meant to provide for us a perfect symbolism, a perfect picture, of the One

Who was to come, and in fact did come. And in glaring portrayal, these Sacrifices picture the manner and the way in which man would be redeemed. It is the Cross alone that fulfills this symbolism, as ought to be overly obvious.

THE NEW COVENANT

The Old Covenant could only address itself to symbolism. The blood of bulls and goats could not take away sins (Heb. 10:4); and as we have stated several times, all of this was but *"a shadow of good things to come"* (Heb. 10:1).

Can the Reader see anything in these Sacrifices but the Cross? I think not!

It was to Paul that the meaning of the New Covenant was given. He gave it to us in his 14 Epistles. The meaning consisted of the Work of the Cross, in other words, what it meant to lost humanity.

In Romans, Chapters 4 and 5, the Holy Spirit, through Paul, proclaims to us the Work of the Cross as it regards Salvation. It is referred to as *"Justification by Faith."*

Chapters 6, 7, and 8 of Romans proclaim to us the part the Cross plays as it regards the Sanctification of the Saint. This was lacking under the Old Covenant, simply because animal blood was woefully insufficient. In fact, it was woefully insufficient as it regards Salvation. So, and as we've already stated, men were saved and sanctified in those days, one might say, on credit. It was done by symbolism, but yet by Faith in that which the symbolism represented, or to which it rather pointed, namely Christ. Men have never been saved any other way than by Faith in Christ, and the Cross has always been the means by which all of this comes to dying humanity.

The Cross opened up the way to the Holy of Holies, so to speak, which means that the Holy Spirit can now permanently abide in the heart and life of the individual Believer (Jn. 14:16-17).

THE VIRGIN MARY

As an aside from all of this, it was a poor woman's sacrifice which the Mother of our Lord offered, when, in accordance with these instructions, she offered a pair of turtledoves, or two young pigeons, on presenting herself for purification at the Temple with the child Jesus. This was done on the expiration of the prescribed term of uncleanness (Lk. 2:24), and the Priest, after sprinkling her with the blood of the humble sacrifice, declared her cleansed (Ellicott).

From this simple circumstance we learn that the reputed parents of our Blessed Lord Jesus were so poor as to be obliged to take advantage of the gracious provision made for those whose means could not afford *"a lamb for a Burnt-Offering."* What a thought! The Lord of Glory, the Most High God, the Possessor of Heaven and Earth, the One to Whom pertained *"the cattle upon a thousand hills"* – yes, the wealth of the universe, appeared in the world which His hands had made, in the narrow circumstances of humble eye. The Levitical economy had made provision for the poor, and the Mother of Jesus availed herself thereof. Truly there is a profound lesson in this for the human heart. The Lord Jesus did not make His appearance in this world in connection with the great or the noble. In fact, *"He became poor, that we through His poverty might be rich"* (II Cor. 8:9).

"Jesus, these eyes have never seen
"That radiant form of Thine,
"The veil of sense hangs dark between
"Thy blessed Face and mine."

"I see Thee not, I hear Thee not,
"Yet are you oft with me;
"And Earth has never so dear a spot
"As where I meet with Thee."

"Like some bright dream that comes
*   unsought,*
"When slumbers over me roll,
"Thine Image ever fills my thought,
"And charms my ravished soul."

"Yet though I have not seen,
"And still must rest in Faith alone;
"I love Thee, dearest Lord, and will,
"Unseen, but not unknown."

"When death these mortal eyes shall seal,
"And still this throbbing heart,
"The rending veil shall Thee reveal,
"All glorious as You art."

CHAPTER 13

(1) "AND THE LORD SPOKE UNTO MOSES AND AARON, SAYING,

(2) "WHEN A MAN SHALL HAVE IN THE SKIN OF HIS FLESH A RISING, A SCAB, OR BRIGHT SPOT, AND IT BE IN THE SKIN OF HIS FLESH LIKE THE PLAGUE OF LEPROSY; THEN HE SHALL BE BROUGHT UNTO AARON THE PRIEST, OR UNTO ONE OF HIS SONS THE PRIESTS:

(3) "AND THE PRIEST SHALL LOOK ON THE PLAGUE IN THE SKIN OF THE FLESH: AND WHEN THE HAIR IN THE PLAGUE IS TURNED WHITE, AND THE PLAGUE IN SIGHT BE DEEPER THAN THE SKIN OF HIS FLESH, IT IS A PLAGUE OF LEPROSY: AND THE PRIEST SHALL LOOK ON HIM, AND PRONOUNCE HIM UNCLEAN.

(4) "IF THE BRIGHT SPOT BE WHITE IN THE SKIN OF HIS FLESH, AND IN SIGHT BE NOT DEEPER THAN THE SKIN, AND THE HAIR THEREOF BE NOT TURNED WHITE; THEN THE PRIEST SHALL SHUT HIM UP WHO HAS THE PLAGUE SEVEN DAYS:

(5) "AND THE PRIEST SHALL LOOK ON HIM THE SEVENTH DAY: AND, BEHOLD, IF THE PLAGUE IN HIS SIGHT BE AT A STAY, AND THE PLAGUE SPREAD NOT IN THE SKIN; THEN THE PRIEST SHALL SHUT HIM UP SEVEN DAYS MORE:

(6) "AND THE PRIEST SHALL LOOK ON HIM AGAIN THE SEVENTH DAY: AND, BEHOLD, IF THE PLAGUE BE SOMEWHAT DARK, AND THE PLAGUE SPREAD NOT IN THE SKIN, THE PRIEST SHALL PRONOUNCE HIM CLEAN: IT IS BUT A SCAB: AND HE SHALL WASH HIS CLOTHES, AND BE CLEAN.

(7) "BUT IF THE SCAB SPREAD MUCH ABROAD IN THE SKIN, AFTER THAT HE HAS BEEN SEEN OF THE PRIEST FOR HIS CLEANSING, HE SHALL BE SEEN OF THE PRIEST AGAIN.

(8) "AND IF THE PRIEST SEE THAT, BEHOLD, THE SCAB SPREADS IN THE

SKIN, THEN THE PRIEST SHALL PRONOUNCE HIM UNCLEAN: IT IS A LEPROSY."

The construction is:

1. Acts of sins are the fruit of the sin nature.

2. The Sacrifices for the cleansing of the leper, as we shall see, foreshadowed the efficacy of the Sacrifice of Christ to deal with sin in the nature.

3. Considering all the minute attention given to this disease, we know that God intended for leprosy to be a type of sin.

THE LAW OF THE LEPER

Verses 1 and 2 read: *"And the LORD spoke unto Moses and Aaron, saying,*

"When a man shall have in the skin of his flesh a rising, a scab, or bright spot, and it be in the skin of his flesh like the plague of leprosy; then he shall be brought unto Aaron the Priest, or unto one of his sons the Priests."

Of all the things we will study concerning the Law of Moses, we will find that none demanded more attention, or more minute inspection, than the discernment and proper treatment of leprosy.

From this Chapter we will learn how absolutely horrible, putrefying, deadly, degradating, evil, destructive, and painful that sin actually is, which the Holy Spirit strongly desires that we learn. One of the great problems in the modern Church is that we do not know how vile, how awful, this dread malady actually is. We tend to think that small sins are insignificant. And as well, we are quick to label certain sins as small, therefore, insignificant.

We will find in the study of this Chapter that there are no insignificant sins with God. That the smallest sin will grow, exactly as leprosy spreads, until the individual is consumed.

And as well, not only will we learn how awful sin is, but we will also learn the remedy for sin, and that the remedy was not cheap, being the death of God's only Son, the Lord Jesus Christ. That death and that death alone could atone for the horror of sin.

It is said that there is no disease which produces so foul an appearance in the human form as leprosy. Consequently, it served as a suitable type for this dread malady.

First of all, we see that leprosy begins with

only a small spot. So does sin!

The ulcer of leprosy may continue unprogressive for months, or even for years, during which the person affected is able to do his ordinary business; but at the end of these periods, whether longer or shorter, it produces a more repulsive and foul disfigurement of the human face and frame than any known disease. The features of the face change their character, and part of the body occasionally mortifying, then dropping off. Death at last comes suddenly, when a vital part of the body has been affected.

All of this, as stated, is a perfect picture of sin. All lives that have been wrecked, dissipated, and destroyed by sin, started out rather with that which is labeled, *"a small sin."* No drunkard ever started out to be that way! No compulsive gambler ever began in that manner! No drug addict ever started as an addict! And the list goes on, but you get the point.

That's the reason that we must *"watch, as well as pray."* We must not allow ourselves to be placed in a position to where sin can take hold of our mind and spirit. To be sure, it is not nearly as easy to be made to go, as it is to come.

As an example, the Christian may think that he or she can frequent the movies, selecting only the best, but will soon realize that his selections grow more and more vile. In fact, it is the same with everything. One drink of alcoholic beverage is taken, and it must be remembered that millions have begun there, but ended up as blighted, wrecked, diseased drunkards. There comes a time when the person wants to quit, they want out, but they can't quit and they can't get out. Sin takes its awful toll.

As leprosy portrays the vileness of sin, perhaps it is easier to see just how vile it actually is, by observing the price that had to be paid in order for sin to be cleansed – the death of the Son of the Living God. If we minimize the Cross, we have minimized the only means by which sin can be eradicated. Notice that I said, *"The only means, there being no other"*; but sadly and regrettably, the modern Church seems to be very successful at denying the Cross, or ignoring the Cross, or registering a vote of no

confidence in the Cross, by accepting the wisdom of the world.

THE PRIEST

If it is to be noticed, if it was thought that the person possibly had contracted leprosy, he was to be brought to the Priest for inspection, and not to a physician. This further shows that God intended for this dread malady to be a portrayal, a type of sin. No, that doesn't mean that the leper was doomed spiritually. But it does mean that his disease was meant to portray the awful malady of sin.

The Priest was a type of Christ. He served as a mediator between God and man, and would do so, until Jesus came, the True Mediator. The Priesthood was made up of frail, flawed men, even the High Priest; however, they nevertheless stood for Christ, and were types of Christ, hence the leper being brought to the Priest.

This tells us that Christ is the only answer for sin, and in effect, Christ and Him Crucified, is the only answer.

If we accept the Virgin Birth of Christ, and ignore the Cross, we have forfeited Salvation. If we accept the Virgin Birth, and the Perfect Life of Christ, and ignore the Cross, we have forfeited Salvation. If we accept the Virgin Birth, the spotless Life, and the untold number of healings and miracles, but ignore the Cross, we have forfeited Salvation.

While all things pertaining to Christ were necessary and essential, and played their part, it was the Cross, and the Cross alone, which effected man's Redemption. We must not add anything to that, and neither must we take away anything from that.

A STROKE OF LEPROSY

Verse 3 reads: *"And the Priest shall look on the plague in the skin of the flesh: and when the hair in the plague is turned white, and the plague in sight be deeper than the skin of his flesh, it is a plague of leprosy: and the Priest shall look on him, and pronounce him unclean."*

The Priest alone could diagnose the plague of leprosy. (Actually, the word *"plague"* in the Hebrew could be translated *"stroke."*)

It really didn't matter what others said,

only what the Priest said. Likewise, it is what Christ, i.e., *"the Word,"* says, that provides the true course. It doesn't matter what man says about sin; it's what the Lord says about sin. Men have ever tried to change the definition of sin, or deny it altogether, but the Word teaches the following:

First of all, the Word teaches us that man is a sinner. He's born that way, due to the Fall. His entire being is depraved, meaning that he is spiritually dead. This means that he has no concept of God, at least that is correct and legitimate. That's the reason from time immemorial, men have worshipped stones, sticks, the moon, the stars, the sun, etc. In his unredeemed, spiritually dead state, man doesn't know Who God is, What God is, or How God is. This means that man is spiritually dead, which means that he's not merely spiritually sick.

This means he cannot save himself, cannot even have any idea as to how Salvation ought to be, and has no interest in God whatsoever. If he is to be saved, it has to be a work entirely of the Holy Spirit, which moves upon the Word of God, and convicts man through the Word, of his lost, undone condition. In fact, the Holy Spirit even has to give man saving Faith, for him to be able to believe, because he has none of his own, at least that which God will recognize.

Second, the Lord saves individuals from sin, not in sin. The idea that the only difference between the unsaved and the saved is Faith in Christ is spurious to say the least. The Lord doesn't save us in order that we might go on sinning. The business of the Holy Spirit is to get us out of sin. He works tirelessly toward that goal, which refers to Righteousness, Holiness, and Christlikeness. The idea that one can continue to live in sin, and continue to have Faith in Christ, is specious to say the least.

BELIEVERS AND SIN

Regarding the last statement made, I am not referring to Believers who do not understand the Cross, and are trying to live for the Lord with all of their heart, but because of improper knowledge of the Word, are living some way in spiritual failure. In fact, if the Believer doesn't understand the Message of the Cross as taught by Paul, no matter how hard he tries, no matter how sincere he might be, no matter how much he prays, etc., it is impossible for such a Believer to live victorious.

So what happens to such a Believer?

The sad fact is, almost the entirety of the modern Church falls into that category, and because almost the entirety of the modern Church understands the Cross not at all, as it regards Sanctification. In fact, most of the modern Church doesn't understand the Cross as it regards Salvation. The Word of Faith doctrine has so undermined the Message of the Cross, that millions of Believers any more little know what they actually do believe.

The truth is, sin is the problem! Whatever it may seem to be on the surface, if one digs enough, one will find sin as the problem. It can be denied, ignored, or falsely labeled, but the truth remains, it is sin.

Second, the only answer for sin is the Cross of Christ. Men may come up with their false sacrifices as Cain of old, but the answer is the Cross, and the answer alone is the Cross. There is no other remedy for sin, as there has never been another remedy for sin.

THE FALSE DOCTRINE OF
THE SINLESS SPIRIT

It is taught in many circles presently, and especially by the Word of Faith people, that when the person comes to Christ, their spirit is made perfect. In other words, they have a re-created spirit, which is perfect, and cannot sin, etc. They teach that the soul is being saved, whatever that means, and that they are to bring the physical body into line.

It is taught that their *"confession,"* brings the soul into line, and subdues the physical body. If their confession is right, they are taught, they have no problem with sin, and in fact, sin should not even be mentioned. To mention sin, they claim, brings about a sin-consciousness, which could lead to failure. So the Preacher, they teach, is to never preach about sin, never mention sin, and because sin is not a problem for the re-created man, who is the Righteousness of Christ.

They see no need for the Cross of Christ whatsoever, actually claiming that the Cross

169

plays no part whatsoever in the Believer's Sanctification. They actually teach that the Cross was the greatest defeat in human history. Consequently, they teach, the Blood does not atone. While they might, at times, say that it does atone, they will, at the same time, add something to the Blood, in effect stating that the Blood within itself, was merely a physical action, and has no bearing really on anything, unless it is connected with certain other things. To talk about the Cross, or to sing about the Cross in their thinking, constitutes weakness. Why not? Especially if we consider that the Cross was the greatest defeat in human history.

These are supermen and superwomen, who do not need anything about the Cross, and in actuality, do not even really need the Holy Spirit. While they certainly claim that the Holy Spirit abides within them, He in fact, has already done all He is going to do, and now it's left up to this superman and superwoman, who are to confess into existence whatever it is they want.

Is any of this stuff in the Bible?

No!

The Jews taught, and rightly so, that even though man was created spirit, soul, and body, he in fact, is a holistic being. In other words, whatever happens to the Believer happens totally, and they are right.

The Bible teaches that Salvation incorporates the entire being; hence the believing sinner is *"born again"* (Jn. 3:3). The Bible does not teach the foolishness of the soul being progressively saved, in other words, working towards some type of perfected state. Upon being born again, the soul is saved now, and is just as saved as it will ever be, along with the spirit of man. The human body is saved as well, but it is not yet glorified. In fact, the physical body is neutral, according to the teaching of the Apostle Paul. This means that if we understand the Cross, we can yield our physical body either to Righteousness or unrighteousness; however, if the Believer doesn't understand the Cross, he will find himself unable to yield his body to Righteousness (Rom. 6:13).

Paul also taught that the physical body is *"dead because of sin"* (Rom. 8:10).

This means that the physical body we now

have, due to the Fall, is not exactly like the physical body that Adam had. It has been ruined because of sin. This means that the Believer, irrespective as to how hard he might try, cannot make his physical body spiritually do what he wants it to do, and knows that it needs to do, unless the Holy Spirit helps him. Paul also said: *"But if the Spirit* (Holy Spirit) *of Him* (God the Father) *Who raised up Jesus from the dead dwell in you, He Who raised up Christ from the dead shall also quicken your mortal bodies by His Spirit Who dwells in you"* (Rom. 8:11).

As we've already explained some pages back, Paul is not speaking here of the coming Resurrection, for that will be the time when we will acquire a Glorified Body. He is speaking here of *"mortal bodies,"* therefore, the bringing of our physical bodies into proper spiritual line by the Power of the Holy Spirit.

He also stated: *"But if you through the Spirit do mortify the deeds of the body, you shall live"* (Rom. 8:13).

This tells us that the Believer can bring the physical body in line, in order that it yield to Righteousness and not yield to unrighteousness, only by the Power of the Holy Spirit.

However, the perfect spirit people claim that it's not the Holy Spirit here Who is being spoken of, but rather the re-created spirit of man. Their assumptions are made out of whole cloth. The proper translation of the Greek demands that Romans 8:9 be translated as the Holy Spirit, along with Verse 11 and Verse 13.

As well, the teachers of this false doctrine of the sinless spirit also claim that the word *"Spirit"* in Galatians 5:17 is not the Holy Spirit, but rather the human spirit. Again, nothing could be further from the Truth.

What they are doing is attempting to eliminate the need for the Cross, or the Holy Spirit, claiming that the re-created man can now do all that needs to be done. In other words, they claim that the Lord has already done all He is going to do, and now the rest is left up to us, which can be carried out by proper confession. In fact, this is the mainstay doctrine of the Word of Faith people, but is not limited to them.

WHAT DOES THE BIBLE SAY?

When it comes to Sanctification, which refers to our life and living on an everyday basis before the Lord, Paul wrote: *"And the very God of peace sanctify you wholly* (which refers to the whole man)*; and I pray God your whole spirit and soul and body be preserved blameless unto the coming of our Lord Jesus Christ"* (I Thess. 5:23).

Paul, as is obvious here, addresses the whole man, *"spirit and soul and body."* He does not separate them. In fact, whatever happens to one happens to the other. This means that when a Believer sins, or anyone for that matter, sin affects the spirit and the soul and the body.

The Apostle is saying here, unless certain things are done, that the spirit and soul and body will not be blameless; and we must remember, Paul is speaking here to Believers. So this debunks the idea that the spirit is perfect and cannot sin.

The Apostle also said: *"Having therefore these Promises, dearly beloved, let us cleanse ourselves from all filthiness of the flesh and spirit, perfecting Holiness in the fear of God"* (II Cor. 7:1).

Here, the Apostle says that the spirit of man, for that's what it's talking about here, can be either holy or unholy. So once again, this throws out the erroneous doctrine that the spirit cannot sin.

THE WHOLE MAN

As Righteousness affects the whole man, spirit and soul and body, likewise, sin affects the whole man, spirit and soul and body. Those who try to tell you that the human spirit of the Born-Again man cannot sin are denying the plain, clear, Word of God.

The Believer cannot properly live for God, unless he properly follows the prescribed order laid down by Paul. And what is that prescribed order?

I have devised a little diagram that will be given possibly several times in this one Volume. It will help us to understand what the Bible teaches as it regards our Sanctification.

FOCUS

The Cross of Christ. This means that the belief system of the Child of God should ever be focused on the Cross, should have the Cross as the foundation of all Doctrine (Rom. 6:3-14; I Cor. 1:17-18, 21, 23; 2:2; Eph. 2:13-18; Col. 2:14-15). In fact, you can include the whole Bible.

OBJECT OF FAITH

The Finished Work of Christ must ever be the object of our Faith. Satan will do his best to push our Faith from the Cross to other things. And as I've said over and over, he doesn't much care what the other things are, just as long as it's not the Cross. It was at the Cross and the Cross alone, where he was defeated (Col. 2:14-15; Heb. 1:3; 2:14-15; 7:25-26; 8:6; 9:14, 22, 24; 10:12).

POWER SOURCE

The Holy Spirit. Once the Cross is our focus, and remains our focus, and the object of Faith is the Finished Work of Christ, and remains the Finished Work of Christ, the Power Source will then be the Holy Spirit. He works exclusively within the parameters of the Finished Work of Christ, and through that Finished Work only. In fact, His manner of labor, so to speak, is so structured that it is referred to as a *"Law"* (Rom. 8:1-2, 11, 13; Gal. 5:5-6, 17-18).

RESULTS

The above is God's prescribed order of victory. If it is followed, perpetual victory will be ours. Paul said in respect to this: *"For sin shall not have dominion over you: for you are not under the Law, but under Grace"* (Rom. 6:14).

WRONG DIRECTION

I want to use the same guideline, but I want to show where erroneous doctrine takes us, and in fact, where much of the modern Church actually is. The Reader should check both diagrams, and take a long, strong look at yourself.

1. Focus: Works. These *"works"* can include about anything that one could begin to imagine. In other words, anything that is not Faith in the Cross must be constituted as works. Paul said if we do this, we will seek only in *"frustrating the Grace*

of God" (Gal. 2:21).

2. The Object of Faith: If works are our focus, then the object of our faith must be our performance. But again, Paul plainly says: *"If Righteousness come by the Law, then Christ is dead in vain"* (Gal. 2:21).

3. Power Source: Self. The only thing that will give us victory over the *"law of sin and death"* is the *"Law of the Spirit of Life, which is in Christ Jesus"* (Rom. 8:2). The Believer cannot live the Christian life without the help of the Holy Spirit. And to be sure, if we follow the diagram as laid out here, we are in fact, committing *"spiritual adultery,"* in which the Holy Spirit will have no part (Rom. 7:1-4). Self alone can <u>never</u> bring about spiritual victory.

4. Results: Failure in every capacity. Victory is found only in the Cross of Christ. Any other effort by man, even though it may look good on the surface, will never bring victory. And the reason is this:

God can give victory only to His Son, and our Saviour, the Lord Jesus Christ. He cannot give victory to fallen man; consequently, we have victory only as we are *"in Christ."* And that means that we must be *"in Christ,"* in the capacity of the Cross (Rom. 6:3-5). Any other capacity, any other direction, produces *"another Jesus"* (II Cor. 11:4).

THE WORD

Verses 4 through 8 read: *"If the bright spot be white in the skin of his flesh, and in sight be not deeper than the skin, and the hair thereof be not turned white; then the Priest shall shut him up who has the plague seven days:*

"And the Priest shall look on him the seventh day: and, behold, if the plague in his sight be at a stay, and the plague spread not in the skin; then the Priest shall shut him up seven days more:

"And the Priest shall look on him again the seventh day: and, behold, if the plague be somewhat dark, and the plague spread not in the skin, the Priest shall pronounce him clean: it is but a scab: and he shall wash his clothes, and be clean.

"But if the scab spread much abroad in the skin, after that he has been seen of the Priest for his cleansing, he shall be seen of

the Priest again.

"And if the Priest see that, behold, the scab spreads in the skin, then the Priest shall pronounce him unclean: it is a leprosy."

We learn from this that Holiness cannot permit anyone to remain in who ought to be out; and on the other hand, Grace will not have anyone out who ought to be in.

As the Priest minutely inspects the individual who seems to have leprosy, something which might seem to be insignificant, in reality can be serious, and then certain things which might look like leprosy, might prove to be nothing of the sort. This means that no case was to be hastily judged or rashly decided. No opinion was to be formed from mere hearsay.

The facts are, the Priest was not guided by his own thoughts, his own feelings, or his own wisdom. He was to be guided strictly by the Word of the Lord which had been given to him by Moses. Everything had already been spelled out in the *"Word,"* and he was to let that be his guideline totally and completely.

This means that his own prejudice, bias, or personal feelings, were never to enter into his judgment. The Word of God must be the judge, and the Word of God alone!

Unfortunately, Denominations tend to make up their own rules as it regards the problem of sin. They very little refer to the Word of God, but rather to their constitution and bylaws, etc., which they change almost yearly, if not sooner.

The Word and the Word only, must be the criteria in any and every case. It alone is the infallible guide.

If the Word is not the infallible guide, then terrible injustices will be done, people will be hurt, and souls could even be lost. It is incumbent upon Preachers, and in fact, all Believers for that matter, that the Word of God be the deciding factor in everything.

(9) "WHEN THE PLAGUE OF LEPROSY IS IN A MAN, THEN HE SHALL BE BROUGHT UNTO THE PRIEST;

(10) "AND THE PRIEST SHALL SEE HIM: AND, BEHOLD, IF THE RISING BE WHITE IN THE SKIN, AND IT HAVE TURNED THE HAIR WHITE, AND THERE BE QUICK RAW FLESH IN THE RISING;

(11) "IT IS AN OLD LEPROSY IN THE

SKIN OF HIS FLESH, AND THE PRIEST SHALL PRONOUNCE HIM UNCLEAN, AND SHALL NOT SHUT HIM UP: FOR HE IS UNCLEAN.

(12) "AND IF A LEPROSY BREAK OUT ABROAD IN THE SKIN, AND THE LEPROSY COVER ALL THE SKIN OF HIM WHO HAS THE PLAGUE FROM HIS HEAD EVEN TO HIS FOOT, WHERESOEVER THE PRIEST LOOKS;

(13) "THEN THE PRIEST SHALL CONSIDER: AND, BEHOLD, IF THE LEPROSY HAVE COVERED ALL HIS FLESH, HE SHALL PRONOUNCE HIM CLEAN WHO HAS THE PLAGUE: IT IS ALL TURNED WHITE: HE IS CLEAN.

(14) "BUT WHEN RAW FLESH APPEARS IN HIM, HE SHALL BE UNCLEAN.

(15) "AND THE PRIEST SHALL SEE THE RAW FLESH, AND PRONOUNCE HIM TO BE UNCLEAN: FOR THE RAW FLESH IS UNCLEAN: IT IS A LEPROSY.

(16) "OR IF THE RAW FLESH TURN AGAIN, AND BE CHANGED UNTO WHITE, HE SHALL COME UNTO THE PRIEST;

(17) "AND THE PRIEST SHALL SEE HIM: AND, BEHOLD, IF THE PLAGUE BE TURNED INTO WHITE; THEN THE PRIEST SHALL PRONOUNCE HIM CLEAN WHO HAS THE PLAGUE: HE IS CLEAN.

(18) "THE FLESH ALSO, IN WHICH, EVEN IN THE SKIN THEREOF, WAS A BOIL, AND IS HEALED,

(19) "AND IN THE PLACE OF THE BOIL THERE BE A WHITE RISING, OR A BRIGHT SPOT, WHITE, AND SOMEWHAT REDDISH, AND IT BE SHOWED TO THE PRIEST;

(20) "AND IF, WHEN THE PRIEST SEES IT, BEHOLD, IT BE IN SIGHT LOWER THAN THE SKIN, AND THE HAIR THEREOF BE TURNED WHITE; THE PRIEST SHALL PRONOUNCE HIM UNCLEAN: IT IS A PLAGUE OF LEPROSY BROKEN OUT OF THE BOIL.

(21) "BUT IF THE PRIEST LOOK ON IT, AND, BEHOLD, THERE BE NO WHITE HAIRS THEREIN, AND IF IT BE NOT LOWER THAN THE SKIN, BUT BE SOMEWHAT DARK; THEN THE PRIEST SHALL SHUT HIM UP SEVEN DAYS:

(22) "AND IF IT SPREAD MUCH

ABROAD IN THE SKIN, THEN THE PRIEST SHALL PRONOUNCE HIM UNCLEAN: IT IS A PLAGUE.

(23) "BUT IF THE BRIGHT SPOT STAY IN HIS PLACE, AND SPREAD NOT, IT IS A BURNING BOIL; AND THE PRIEST SHALL PRONOUNCE HIM CLEAN.

(24) "OR IF THERE BE ANY FLESH, IN THE SKIN WHEREOF THERE IS A HOT BURNING, AND THE QUICK FLESH THAT BURNS HAVE A WHITE BRIGHT SPOT, SOMEWHAT REDDISH, OR WHITE;

(25) "THEN THE PRIEST SHALL LOOK UPON IT: AND, BEHOLD, IF THE HAIR IN THE BRIGHT SPOT BE TURNED WHITE, AND IT BE IN SIGHT DEEPER THAN THE SKIN; IT IS A LEPROSY BROKEN OUT OF THE BURNING: WHEREFORE THE PRIEST SHALL PRONOUNCE HIM UNCLEAN: IT IS THE PLAGUE OF LEPROSY.

(26) "BUT IF THE PRIEST LOOK ON IT, AND, BEHOLD, THERE BE NO WHITE HAIR IN THE BRIGHT SPOT, AND IT BE NO LOWER THAN THE OTHER SKIN, BUT BE SOMEWHAT DARK; THEN THE PRIEST SHALL SHUT HIM UP SEVEN DAYS:

(27) "AND THE PRIEST SHALL LOOK UPON HIM THE SEVENTH DAY: AND IF IT BE SPREAD MUCH ABROAD IN THE SKIN, THEN THE PRIEST SHALL PRONOUNCE HIM UNCLEAN: IT IS A PLAGUE OF LEPROSY.

(28) "AND IF THE BRIGHT SPOT STAY IN HIS PLACE, AND SPREAD NOT IN THE SKIN, BUT IT BE SOMEWHAT DARK; IT IS A RISING OF THE BURNING, AND THE PRIEST SHALL PRONOUNCE HIM CLEAN: FOR IT IS AN INFLAMMATION OF THE BURNING."

The structure is:

1. A leper, white all over, was clean. He was a leper, but the disease was not active in him; it was, in a sense, dead. Thus, *"sin"* should be *"dead"* in the Christian (Rom., Chpt. 6).

2. Leprosy, as stated, vividly illustrates sin. It is loathsome, contagious, incurable, and fatal.

3. The minute directions given in this Chapter, and the care and patience enjoined upon the Priest, show how God distinguishes between sin and infirmity.

MINUTE INSPECTION

Verses 9 through 15 read: *"When the plague of leprosy is in a man, then he shall be brought unto the Priest;*

"And the Priest shall see him: and, behold, if the rising be white in the skin, and it have turned the hair white, and there be quick raw flesh in the rising;

"It is an old leprosy in the skin of his flesh, and the Priest shall pronounce him unclean, and shall not shut him up: for he is unclean.

"And if a leprosy break out abroad in the skin, and the leprosy cover all the skin of him who has the plague from his head even to his foot, wheresoever the Priest looks;

"Then the Priest shall consider: and, behold, if the leprosy have covered all his flesh, he shall pronounce him clean who has the plague: it is all turned white: he is clean.

"But when raw flesh appears in him, he shall be unclean.

"And the Priest shall see the raw flesh, and pronounce him to be unclean: for the raw flesh is unclean: it is a leprosy."

Leprosy was, for the most part, hereditary. After afflicting the parent, it was very apt to break out in the child. This is a perfect description of the terrible malady of sin.

Sin began in Adam, our first parent, and having worked its work in him for some 900 years, he then died, all as a result of sin. He was originally intended to live forever.

But the terrible problem that killed him has passed down to all who sprang from him, and in fact, all have sprung from him.

But leprosy was not contracted, necessarily by being hereditary. In other words, it could definitely break out on one whose parents had not the hint of such. But yet, sin, unlike leprosy in this respect, is always derived from our connection with a fallen, original parent.

But leprosy, whether hereditary, or contracted by contagion or otherwise, begins far within. Its seat is in the deepest interior of the physical body. In fact, it may bury itself in the system for a number of years before it shows itself. How exactly this describes sin!

How many of us know those who are now little more than brute beasts! But they were not always that way. They were once tender

NOTES

infants, the very personification of innocence. Who could look upon their innocent faces, and could tell that they would grow up to be a rapist, a murderer, etc.?

Who could have looked into the faces of those human beasts, who flew airplanes into the twin towers in New York City, and the Pentagon in Washington, and detected in their countenance that they would be masked murderers?

To show you the insidiousness of sin, let's shift our attention to one who is the very opposite of those we have mentioned. Think of Peter, who had been chosen by Christ, had walked with Him, shoulder to shoulder, for some three and one-half years, who, at the end of the Master's Ministry, even volunteered to die for our Lord. But yet, that's not what happened! There existed in his heart the root of the oaths and lies which broke from his lips on the porch of the palace of the High Priest. He would deny his Master!

Looking at ourselves, despite all of our good intentions, despite what the Lord has already done for us, little do we know of those depths of deceit which we carry in ourselves, or to what enormities of crime we are liable any day to be driven, that is, if our eyes are not forever fastened onto Christ! The Scripture says: *"Let him who thinks he stands take heed lest he fall"* (I Cor. 10:12). Those words were not given by the Holy Spirit to the Apostle Paul for nothing.

AN ERRONEOUS IDEA OF SIN

In previous paragraphs, I have directed your attention to the false doctrine proposed by some, claiming that when a person gets saved, their spirit is thereby perfect, which means their spirit cannot sin. In other words, they claim, sin is held within the soul and the physical body. Therefore, in their thinking, sin is not so bad.

Such thinking is grossly wrong, and for many reasons. The same error that proclaims this foolishness, as well, repudiates the Cross. Consequently, those who have bought into this false doctrine, and false it is, have not only bought into a false idea of sin, but as well, have repudiated the Cross, which is the only remedy for sin; consequently, Satan has boxed into a corner those who have embraced this error.

As we've said over and over again, and will continue to say over and over, the only answer for sin is the Cross. And for any Believer to claim that sin is no problem with them, exactly as I read this morning in a letter sent to me by a very deceived individual, they are being set up by Satan, who *"steals, kills, and destroys"* (Jn. 10:10). John said: *"If we say that we have fellowship with Him, and walk in darkness, we lie, and do not the Truth:*

"If we say that we have no sin, we deceive ourselves, and the Truth is not in us" (I Jn. 1:6, 8).

THE FIRST VISIBLE SIGNS OF LEPROSY

Those very first visible signs of this loathsome disease were often very small, very minute, in fact, not easily detected.

It is the same with sin! In fact, all the guilt that ever stained the Earth may be traced to *"a look"* – the admiring look of Eve upon the forbidden fruit. This tells us that no man can tell to what an issue the smallest sins may lead. Look at the results of Eve's *"look!"*

Many young people who claim Christ find it very difficult to understand how that a little of this, or a little of that, and we speak of the things of the world, can actually hurt them. It looks so innocent. As stated, it's very small indeed!

But let it be remembered, of the 20 million alcoholics in this country presently, who are living a life of unmitigated torture, and making a Hell on Earth for their loved ones, it all started with one drink. The same can be said for the gambler – it all started with one throw of the dice. In fact, I think one can say that sin always starts small, but it doesn't stay small for long.

WE SHOULD INSPECT THE FRUIT, BUT CAREFULLY!

Verse 13 deals with one who has had leprosy, and to such a degree, that it has covered all his flesh. But despite that fact, the scales have turned white, with no raw flesh showing. This tells the Priest that the leprosy is no more, and he now can pronounce him *"clean."*

Taking this into a spiritual meaning, it proclaims the fact that despite the ravages of

NOTES

sin which have taken their toll, the Blood of Jesus has cleansed the sinner, and done so to such a remarkable degree that Christ, through the Word, pronounces the individual, irrespective of the past, as *"clean."* And upon the heels of that statement, we hear the Voice of the Lord telling Simon Peter: *"What God has cleansed, that call not thou common"* (Acts 10:15).

CLEAN AND UNCLEAN

Verses 16 through 28 read: *"Or if the raw flesh turn again, and be changed unto white, he shall come unto the Priest;*

"And the Priest shall see him: and, behold, if the plague be turned into white; then the Priest shall pronounce him clean who has the plague: he is clean.

"The flesh also, in which, even in the skin thereof, was a boil, and is healed,

"And in the place of the boil there be a white rising, or a bright spot, white, and somewhat reddish, and it be showed to the Priest;

"And if, when the Priest sees it, behold, it be in sight lower than the skin, and the hair be turned white; the Priest shall pronounce him unclean: it is a plague of leprosy broken out of the boil.

"But if the Priest look on it, and, behold, there be no white hairs therein, and if it be not lower than the skin, but be somewhat dark; then the Priest shall shut him up seven days:

"And if it spread much abroad in the skin, then the Priest shall pronounce him unclean: it is a plague.

"But if the bright spot stay in his place, and spread not, it is a burning boil; and the Priest shall pronounce him clean.

"Or if there be any flesh, in the skin whereof there is a hot burning, and the quick flesh that burns have a white bright spot, somewhat reddish, or white;

"Then the Priest shall look upon it: and, behold, if the hair in the bright spot be turned white, and it be in sight deeper than the skin; it is a leprosy broken out of the burning: wherefore the Priest shall pronounce him unclean: it is the plague of leprosy.

"But if the Priest look on it, and, behold, there be no white hair in the bright spot, and it be no lower than the other skin, but

be somewhat dark; then the Priest shall shut him up seven days:

"And the Priest shall look upon him the seventh day: and if it be spread much abroad in the skin, then the Priest shall pronounce him unclean: it is the plague of leprosy.

"And if the bright spot stay in his place, and spread not in the skin, but it be somewhat dark; it is a rising of the burning, and the Priest shall pronounce him clean: for it is an inflammation of the burning."

As we observe in these Passages the minute inspection, as it regards this dread disease, we are again brought to the knowledge that only the Priest could diagnose this situation. The Priest being a type of Christ refers to the fact that our sin is diagnosed by Christ Alone, i.e., *"the Word,"* and it is cured by Christ Alone. As is painfully obvious here, the very smallest speck of leprosy was intolerable; likewise, the smallest amount of sin is intolerable with God. Most Christians do not understand that.

Why?

It's because far too many Christians function in the capacity of self-righteousness. Consequently, they compare themselves with others, and it's always easy to find someone who we think is worse than ourselves.

But God recognizes self-righteousness not at all! Beside that, Paul said: *"For we dare not make ourselves of the number, or compare ourselves with some who commend themselves: but they measuring themselves by themselves, and comparing themselves among themselves, are not wise"* (II Cor. 10:12).

The idea of all of this is, as there could not be one speck of leprosy on the person, there cannot be one speck of sin in the heart and life of the Believer. God cannot tolerate sin in any capacity, no matter how seemingly innocent it may be to us, or small in its observation. As someone has well said, the smallest sin is enough to damn the soul, and to do so forever.

(29) "IF A MAN OR WOMAN HAVE A PLAGUE UPON THE HEAD OR THE BEARD;

(30) "THEN THE PRIEST SHALL SEE THE PLAGUE: AND, BEHOLD, IF IT BE IN SIGHT DEEPER THAN THE SKIN; AND THERE BE IN IT A YELLOW THIN HAIR;

THEN THE PRIEST SHALL PRONOUNCE HIM UNCLEAN: IT IS A DRY SCALL, EVEN A LEPROSY UPON THE HEAD OR BEARD.

(31) "AND IF THE PRIEST LOOK UPON THE PLAGUE OF THE SCALL, AND, BEHOLD, IT BE NOT IN SIGHT DEEPER THAN THE SKIN, AND THAT THERE IS NO BLACK HAIR IN IT; THEN THE PRIEST SHALL SHUT UP HIM WHO HAS THE PLAGUE OF THE SCALL SEVEN DAYS:

(32) "AND IN THE SEVENTH DAY THE PRIEST SHALL LOOK ON THE PLAGUE: AND, BEHOLD, IF THE SCALL SPREAD NOT, AND THERE BE IN IT NO YELLOW HAIR, AND THE SCALL BE NOT IN SIGHT DEEPER THAN THE SKIN;

(33) "HE SHALL BE SHAVEN, BUT THE SCALL SHALL HE NOT SHAVE; AND THE PRIEST SHALL SHUT HIM UP WHO HAS THE SCALL SEVEN DAYS MORE:

(34) "AND IN THE SEVENTH DAY THE PRIEST SHALL LOOK ON THE SCALL: AND, BEHOLD, IF THE SCALL BE NOT SPREAD IN THE SKIN, NOR BE IN SIGHT DEEPER THAN THE SKIN; THEN THE PRIEST SHALL PRONOUNCE HIM CLEAN: AND HE SHALL WASH HIS CLOTHES, AND BE CLEAN.

(35) "BUT IF THE SCALL SPREAD MUCH IN THE SKIN AFTER HIS CLEANSING;

(36) "THEN THE PRIEST SHALL LOOK ON HIM: AND BEHOLD, IF THE SCALL BE SPREAD IN THE SKIN, THE PRIEST SHALL NOT SEEK FOR YELLOW HAIR; HE IS UNCLEAN.

(37) "BUT IF THE SCALL BE IN HIS SIGHT AT A STAY, AND THAT THERE IS BLACK HAIR GROWN UP THEREIN; THE SCALL IS HEALED, HE IS CLEAN: AND THE PRIEST SHALL PRONOUNCE HIM CLEAN.

(38) "IF A MAN ALSO OR A WOMAN HAVE IN THE SKIN OR THEIR FLESH BRIGHT SPOTS, EVEN WHITE BRIGHT SPOTS;

(39) "THEN THE PRIEST SHALL LOOK: AND, BEHOLD, IF THE BRIGHT SPOTS IN THE SKIN OF THEIR FLESH BE DARKISH WHITE: IT IS A FRECKLED SPOT THAT GROWS IN THE SKIN; HE IS CLEAN.

(40) "AND THE MAN WHOSE HAIR IS FALLEN OFF HIS HEAD, HE IS BALD; YET

IS HE CLEAN.

(41) "AND HE WHO HAS HIS HAIR FALLEN OFF FROM THE PART OF HIS HEAD TOWARD HIS FACE, HE IS FOREHEAD BALD: YET IS HE CLEAN.

(42) "AND IF THERE BE IN THE BALD HEAD, OR BALD FOREHEAD, A WHITE REDDISH SORE; IT IS A LEPROSY SPRUNG UP IN HIS BALD HEAD, OR HIS BALD FOREHEAD.

(43) "THEN THE PRIEST SHALL LOOK UPON IT: AND, BEHOLD, IF THE RISING OF THE SORE BE WHITE REDDISH IN HIS BALD HEAD, OR IN HIS BALD FOREHEAD, AS THE LEPROSY APPEARS IN THE SKIN OF THE FLESH;

(44) "HE IS A LEPROUS MAN, HE IS UNCLEAN: THE PRIEST SHALL PRONOUNCE HIM UTTERLY UNCLEAN; HIS PLAGUE IS IN HIS HEAD."

The construction is:

1. The minute directions given in this Chapter, and the care and patience enjoined by the Priests, show how God distinguishes between sin and infirmity.

2. A man might have a form of skin disease in appearance like leprosy, but the Priest was still to pronounce it other than leprosy. The Heavenly High Priest is a Priest for infirmity as well as for sin; and the instructed Christian will not confound these (Heb., Chpts. 4-5, 9).

3. The legislation of this Chapter reveals how tenderly, faithfully, and patiently Jesus the Lord acts toward the sinner.

SEVEN DAYS

Verses 29 through 34 read: *"If a man or woman have a plague upon the head or the beard;*

"Then the Priest shall see the plague: and, behold, if it be in sight deeper than the skin; and there be in it a yellow thin hair; then the Priest shall pronounce him unclean: it is a dry scall, even a leprosy upon the head or beard.

"And if the Priest look on the plague of the scall, and, behold, it be not in sight deeper than the skin, and that there is no black hair in it; then the Priest shall shut him up who has the plague of the scall seven days:

"And in the seventh day the Priest shall

look on the plague: and, behold, if the scall spread not, and there be in it no yellow hair, and the scall be not in sight deeper than the skin;

"He shall be shaven, but the scall shall he not shave; and the Priest shall shut him up who has the scall seven days more:

"And in the seventh day the Priest shall look on the scall: and, behold, if the scall be not spread in the skin, nor be in sight deeper than the skin; then the Priest shall pronounce him clean: and he shall wash his clothes, and be clean."

As is obvious, the number *"seven,"* or *"seventh day,"* are used quite a number of times. It referred to a quarantine period, in order that the Priest might inspect the infected region, to ascertain whether it was leprosy or not, or if it was leprosy, how bad it had progressed.

The number *"seven"* is God's number of totality, completion, and perfection. It speaks of totality in any and every respect.

The Bible teaches approximately 7,000 years of a sinful state. The last 1,000 years will be that referred to as the *"Millennial Reign."* Christ will Himself reign on this Earth at that time, but despite the fact that Satan, fallen angels, and all demon spirits will be locked away in the Bottomless Pit, there will still be sin on the Earth. It will not even remotely be to the degree it is presently, but it still will be present. In fact, it will not be thoroughly eradicated from this Earth until the prophecy of Simon Peter comes to pass: *"But the Day of the Lord will come as a thief in the night; in the which the heavens shall pass away with a great noise, and the elements shall melt with fervent heat, the Earth also and the works that are therein shall be burned up"* (II Pet. 3:10).

He then said: *"Looking for and hasting unto the coming of the Day of God, wherein the heavens being on fire shall be dissolved, and the elements shall melt with fervent heat?*

"Nevertheless we, according to His Promise, look for new Heavens and a new Earth, wherein dwelleth Righteousness" (II Pet. 3:12-13).

Picking up somewhat on what Peter said, John some years later wrote: *"And I saw a new Heaven and a new Earth: for the first*

Heaven and the first Earth were passed away; and there was no more sea" (Rev. 21:1).

These are the new Heavens and the new Earth of which Peter spoke, and *"wherein dwelleth Righteousness."*

It should sober one to realize that we are presently living at the very close of the sixth Millennium, and as well, the close of the Church Age. For some 2,000 years, the Lord has built His Church. But this time of Grace, at least as we now know it as it regards the Church Age, is about over. As well, the 6,000 years of terrible, sinful destruction, are about over as well. While, as stated, the seventh Millennium will continue to evidence some sin, it will be of small consequence, at least by comparison to that which we presently see and know.

THE LAST OF THE LAST DAYS

While every Believer ought to desire to know everything about the Word of God, and especially its prophetic overtones, inasmuch as we are at the very door of the fulfillment of the great predictions of the Book of Revelation, still, there is one thing even more important:

It is my belief that the modern Church is in worse condition spiritually than it has been since the Reformation.

The modern Church is the Laodicean Church, of which Jesus spoke in Revelation, Chapter 3. In other words, it is the Laodicean Age.

This Church says, *"I am rich, and increased with goods, and have need of nothing."* But what does the Lord say in respect to this?

The response of Christ is emphatic and to the point. He said, *"And knowest not that you are wretched, and miserable, and poor, and blind, and naked"* (Rev. 3:17).

If anyone has any degree of spirituality at all, then it becomes painfully obvious that this description fits perfectly the modern Church.

The Church of this present time is very similar also to the Israel at the time of Christ. While Israel was in bondage to Rome, they addressed this in several ways, from denying that there was any bondage (Jn. 8:33), to trying to rid themselves of this bondage by

physical force, which resulted in their total destruction. Paul said of them: *"For they being ignorant of God's Righteousness, and going about to establish their own righteousness, have not submitted themselves unto the Righteousness of God"* (Rom. 10:3).

The modern Church does the same thing. It is in bondage to Satan as never before. It addresses that bondage, exactly as Israel of old, by denying that it exists, which is the motif of the Word of Faith people, or else it tries to rid itself of such, by various man-instituted ways, i.e., *"humanistic psychology,"* etc. It goes about attempting to establish its own righteousness, and will not submit itself to the Righteousness of God.

WHAT IS THE RIGHTEOUSNESS OF GOD?

It is *"Jesus Christ and Him Crucified,"* or more particularly, the Righteousness of Christ which He gives to us according to our Faith in what He did for us at the Cross. In other words, it is the Cross which makes it possible for us to have the Righteousness of Christ, and the Cross alone. Without the Cross, it would be impossible for the Righteousness of Christ to come to any man or woman, and because all are sinners, without God, which means that we have no Righteousness within ourselves whatsoever, and furthermore, cannot obtain Righteousness in any capacity by our own strength or ability. Romans, Chapter 3 makes this painfully clear.

Therefore, the only Righteousness that a believing sinner can have is for the Righteousness of Christ to be freely imputed to him, which is done upon Faith, and we speak of Faith in Him, and what He has done for us at the Cross. It is always the Cross!

The Cross, and the Cross alone, is what makes it possible for God to bestow Grace upon any human being. Paul emphatically states this when he said: *"For if Righteousness come by the Law, then Christ is dead in vain"* (Gal. 2:21).

As should be obvious, this means that Christ had to go to the Cross, in order to pay the terrible sin debt. Upon simple Faith in Him, and what He did for us in the Sacrifice of Himself, a Perfect Righteousness, the Righteousness of Christ, is imputed to us.

THE CROSS OF CHRIST

In these last of the last days, as it regards the Church, the Holy Spirit is working mightily to bring the Church back to the Cross. The Message of the Cross is, in effect, the story of the New Covenant. In actuality, it is the New Covenant. The Lord gave this understanding to the Apostle Paul (Gal. 1:12).

He referred to any other message as *"another gospel,"* which is really a *"perversion of the Gospel of Christ"* (Gal. 1:6-7). The Apostle then said, and in no uncertain terms:

"But though we, or an Angel from Heaven, preach any other gospel unto you than that which we have preached unto you, let him be accursed."

For greater emphasis, the Holy Spirit through the Apostle repeats himself: *"As we said before, so say I now again, if any man preach any other Gospel unto you than that you have received, let him be accursed"* (Gal. 1:8-9).

Regrettably and sadly, the modern Church is in fact, preaching *"another gospel."* This means it has left its true foundation, which is the Cross of Christ.

When the Lord began to open up to me the Revelation of the Cross, which He did in 1996, I immediately sensed that what I had was that which was taught by the Apostle Paul. In other words, it matched up with the Word 100 percent, and which any true Revelation will always match up perfectly with the Word, and because it came from the *"Word."* So I keep saying that what I am preaching and teaching is not new, but rather that which was preached by Paul.

On that glorious day when the Lord began to open up to me that which changed my life, and in fact has changed the lives of untold millions, and in fact again is the only thing that's ever changed anyone, I knew that what I had was real, in other words, it was the Truth. Jesus said: *"You shall know the Truth, and the Truth shall make you free"* (Jn. 8:32).

But I sensed in my spirit that as wonderful and glorious as the initial confrontation was, I must not allow myself to stop, but must implore the Lord, which I did, that He ever keep this door open, that continued

NOTES

Truth would ever flow to me. I earnestly sought His Face in that respect.

Wondrously, He has answered that prayer, and continues to answer it, even unto this present hour. Very seldom does a week go by that the door doesn't open a little more, with more information being given.

Among other things, I have learned that the Cross, as previously stated, is not a mere doctrine, but rather the foundation on which all Doctrine is built. While it might be referred to as a doctrine, it very well must be understood, even in the fashion that I have mentioned. I am certain that Jesus looked at what He did for us on the Cross, and which was planned from before the foundation of the world (I Pet. 1:18-20), as more than just a mere doctrine.

I have learned more than ever that the Message of the Cross exposes false doctrine. And that's the greatest reason why the modern Church follows every fad in the world. Not understanding the Cross, it becomes a target for Satan and his insidious means. When the Believer begins to understand the Cross, false doctrine will stand out like the proverbial sore thumb. In other words, he will know the way of the Truth, and will walk therein.

SEPARATION

As well, the Cross of Christ will separate him from all things other than the Message of the Cross. Concerning this, Jesus said:

"If any man will come after Me, let him deny himself, and take up his cross daily, and follow Me.

"For whosoever will save his life shall lose it: but whosoever will lose his life for My sake, the same shall save it" (Lk. 9:23-24).

In connection with this, He also said: *"He who loves father or mother more than Me is not worthy of Me, and he who loves son or daughter more than Me is not worthy of Me.*

"And he who takes not his cross and follows after Me, is not worthy of Me" (Mat. 10:37-38).

So what am I saying?

I am saying that when one begins to hear the Message of the Cross, and begins to understand this Message, which in effect, is the New Covenant, he will soon find what it means to serve Christ. He may have to give up his Church, his Denomination, his loved ones, or whatever. Because the truth is this:

All type of people claim to serve Christ, but the Message of the Cross quickly divides those who are mere professors, from those who are true possessors. Many people are not willing to buck the tide.

I watch Preachers who are confronted by the Cross, and will back away, because to accept the Cross means they will have to give up their Church, or their Denomination, etc. They aren't willing to do that. So in their heart of hearts, they think they can serve both. They cannot!

If the Preacher begins to preach the Cross as he should, and the Believer begins to live the Cross as he should, the line of separation will quickly be drawn, and the neutrality will end.

When the modern outpouring of the Baptism with the Holy Spirit was given at the turn of the Twentieth Century, and is referred to as the *"Latter Rain,"* and is always accompanied by the speaking with other tongues, this separated men and women from cold, formal religion. The Cross likewise, is doing the same thing presently. This Message is separating the Church, and I speak of true Believers, from cold, formal religion. Sadly, even in the Denominations that came out of the great outpouring just mentioned, and refer to themselves as *"Pentecostal,"* the Holy Spirit is little evident in these particular Denominations. It is sad but true!

As stated previously in this Volume, at the turn of the Twentieth Century, the Denominational world has attempted to preach the Cross, at least to a certain degree, without the Holy Spirit. Presently, they are left preaching much of nothing. The Pentecostal Church world attempted to preach the Holy Spirit without the Cross, and they are left with nothing but *"spirits."*

THE HOLY SPIRIT AND THE CROSS

The Holy Spirit and the Cross of Christ, which latter provides the legal means for the Divine Spirit to do His Work, are so closely intertwined, that they, for all practical purposes, are one. Revelation 5:6 tells us this, along with Romans 8:2. So this means that the Holy Spirit cannot be properly preached

NOTES

and lived without the Cross, and the Cross cannot be properly preached and lived, without the Holy Spirit. This should be overly obvious from Paul's teaching in Romans, Chapter 8.

So if the Church drifts from the Cross, which it regrettably has, the Holy Spirit, at the same time, will cease His operations in the Church. In fact, that is the reason for our present dilemma!

If the Holy Spirit is not working within our lives, or else working very little, it will be virtually impossible to detect false doctrine; hence, the Church accepting that which is so obviously wrong.

THE GREAT WHORE

"And there came one of the seven Angels which had the seven vials, and talked with me, saying unto me, Come hither; I will show unto you the judgment of the great whore who sits upon many waters" (Rev. 17:1). This which John saw characterizes every false religion that has ever existed from the time of Cain, to the present, and which will continue even throughout the coming Great Tribulation.

To be more specific, it refers to any word, any message, any way claimed other than the Cross of Christ. So any Church, Denomination, Preacher, whoever or whatever, which proposes a way other than the Cross, all and without exception, come under the heading of the *"great whore."* To be blunt, that means that the Word of Faith doctrine is a part of the *"great whore."* Regrettably, one would probably have to say the same thing as it regards most religious Denominations. If they are not preaching the Cross, and precious few are, then they must be constituted as a part of the *"great whore,"* along with every other false religion and false way that have ever existed.

Paul said as much in Romans, Chapter 7. In the first four Verses of that illustrious Chapter, he spoke of a woman who was married to one man, and then turned and married another as well. He said, *"She shall be called an adulteress"* (Rom. 7:3).

He then tells the Believer that we are married to Christ. Then he said that we are *"dead to the Law by the Body of Christ,"* which refers to the Crucifixion of Christ, and Him giving His perfect body in Sacrifice. He was then raised from the dead (Rom. 7:4).

If we as Believers, in any way, attempt to live for God, outside of total Faith in Christ, and what Christ did at the Cross, we are labeled by the Holy Spirit, Who gave Paul these words to say, as committing *"spiritual adultery."* And to be sure, that is a serious offense, as ought to be obvious.

This means that in some way, we have sought the services of the *"great whore."* Once it is put in that terminology, and which terminology is definitely applicable, then it takes on a brand-new perspective.

The message always has been, is, and ever shall be, *"Jesus Christ and Him Crucified"* (I Cor. 1:23; 2:2; Gal. 6:14; Eph. 2:13-18). That being the case, this means that many Christians are actually supporting the *"great whore."* That should be a sobering thought indeed!

The definition of the *"great whore,"* is the religious system, whatever it might be, which is other than the Cross of Christ. Its *"pimps"* are those who support the system. The *"pimps"* get rich, and I speak of money, while the people get nothing, exactly as regular harlotry does. Look at the Word of Faith doctrine:

The Preachers, who are pimps for that particular system, get rich, while the people get nothing. Look at most religious Denominations as well:

The leaders perpetuate a system, which rewards them handsomely, while again, the people get nothing. It is the Message of the Cross alone that sets the people free, and in effect, enriches them spiritually. Everything else comes under the system of the *"great whore."*

UTTERLY UNCLEAN

Verses 35 through 44 read: *"But if the scall spread much in the skin after his cleansing;*

"Then the Priest shall look on him: and behold, if the scall be spread in the skin, the Priest shall not seek for yellow hair; he is unclean.

"But if the scall be in his sight at a stay, and that there is black hair grown up therein; the scall is healed, he is clean: and the Priest shall pronounce him clean.

"If a man also or a woman have in the skin of their flesh bright spots, even white bright spots;

"Then the Priest shall look: and, behold, if the bright spots in the skin of their flesh be darkish white: it is a freckled spot that grows in the skin; he is clean.

"And the man whose hair is fallen off his head, he is bald; yet is he clean.

"And he who has his hair fallen off from the part of his head toward his face, he is forehead bald: yet is he clean.

"And if there be in the bald head, or bald forehead, a white reddish sore; it is a leprosy sprung up in his bald head, or his bald forehead.

"Then the Priest shall look upon it: and, behold, if the rising of the sore be white reddish in his bald head, or in his bald forehead, as the leprosy appears in the skin of the flesh;

"He is a leprous man, he is unclean: the Priest shall pronounce him utterly unclean; his plague is in his head."

As should be obvious here, the very smallest speck of leprosy was intolerable to God. The truth is, the entirety of the human race, spiritually speaking, is covered with leprosy, i.e., *"sin,"* from head to toe. There are no exceptions (Rom. 3:10-18). So long as I think there is a single spot which is not covered with the direful disease, I have not come to the end of myself. It is when my true condition is fully disclosed to my view that I really understand the meaning of Salvation by Grace.

However, the more clearly I see myself as a sinner, as covered from head to toe with this dread disease called sin, the more clearly I understand my true condition, the more clearly is established my right to the Love of God and the Work of Christ. The Scripture says: *"For Christ also has once suffered for sins, the just for the unjust, that He might bring us to God"* (I Pet. 3:18). Mackintosh says, *"Now, if I am 'unjust,' I am one of those very people for whom Christ died, and I am entitled to all the benefits of His death."*

To which we have already alluded, the Scripture says, *"There is not a just man upon Earth"*; and inasmuch as I am *"upon Earth,"* it is plain that I am *"unjust,"* and it is equally plain that Christ died for me –

that He suffered for my sins.

If I accept Christ, which means that I accept what He did for me at the Cross, I am as safe as He is Himself. There is nothing against me: Christ met all. He not only suffered for my *"sins,"* but He *"made an end of sin."* He abolished the entire system, in which, as a child of the first Adam, I stood, and He, through the Cross, has introduced me into a new position, in association with Himself, and there I stand before God, free from all charge of sin and all fear of judgment. It is referred to as *"Justification by Faith."*

JUSTIFICATION BY FAITH

The term *"Justification by Faith,"* simply means that I am justified, by exhibiting Faith in Christ, and what Christ has done for me in the Sacrifice of Himself on the Cross.

The word *"justify"* means, *"to prove or show to be just, right, or reasonable."*

So how can a person who is covered by sin be shown to be just, right, and reasonable? It is all by and through what Jesus did at the Cross.

Listen to Paul: *"You are complete in Him* (Jesus), *which is the Head of all principality and power:*

"In Whom also you are circumcised with the circumcision made without hands, and putting off the body of the sins of the flesh by the circumcision of Christ:

"Buried with Him in baptism (Rom. 6:3-5, referring to being baptized into the death of Christ, and buried with Him by baptism into death; it does not refer to Water Baptism), *wherein also you are risen with Him through the Faith of the operation of God, Who has raised Him from the dead.*

"And you, being dead in your sins and the uncircumcision of your flesh, has He quickened (made alive) *together with Him, having forgiven you all trespasses;*

"Blotting out the handwriting of Ordinances that was against us, which was contrary to us, and took it out of the way, nailing it to His Cross;

"And having spoiled principalities and powers, He made a show of them openly, triumphing over them in it" (Col. 2:10-15).

Christ was the *"Last Adam"* (I Cor. 15:45-50), Who came to this world to do what the

first Adam didn't do, which was to render a perfect obedience to God, and to undo what the first Adam did do, which was to destroy man spiritually, physically, and in every way.

Jesus satisfied the Righteousness of the Law, by keeping it perfectly, and never failing even one time. But what must be understood, and understood completely, is that He did all of this for you and me. None of it was done for Himself, for Angels, or for Heaven in any capacity. The entirety of God becoming man, coming to this world, living a perfect life, and dying on the Cross of Calvary, was all done for you and me. In other words, He did it all as my Substitute. He did for me what I could not do for myself.

Even though He kept the Law perfectly, thereby making us perfect Law-keepers, and by Faith in Him, that within itself did not satisfy the broken Law. And the truth is, every human being, as we've already stated, had broken the Law repeatedly, and the Scripture plainly says, *"The wages of sin is death"* (Rom. 6:23).

THE CROSS

To satisfy the broken Law, God demanded that a perfect life be given, which is the reason that God became man. God cannot die, and if justice was to be satisfied, and satisfied completely, a perfect life had to be offered up. Since no human being could qualify, considering that all were unrighteous, the Lord would have to pay the price Himself.

Death was demanded, but not the death of just anyone. As stated, it had to be Christ. In order to satisfy this sin debt, which hung over the head of every individual, and because all, due to Adam's Fall, are born in original sin, God would have to do for us what we could not do for ourselves.

We must understand that the Cross was not an incident, and not an accident; it was a Sacrifice. While the Jews and the Romans, and because of their evil hearts, plotted the death of the Son of God, even refusing to believe that He was the Son of God, still, no man could have killed Him, unless He allowed it. He had stated: *"Therefore does My Father love Me, because I lay down My Life, that I might take it again.*

"No man takes it from Me, but I lay it

down of Myself. I have power to lay it down, and I have power to take it again. This Commandment have I received of My Father" (Jn. 10:17-18).

In fact, the Cross was planned from before the foundation of the world; therefore, the Cross was the destination, the total destination, the complete destination. Peter said: *"Forasmuch as you know that you were not redeemed with corruptible things, as silver and gold . . . but with the precious Blood of Christ, as of a lamb without blemish and without spot:*

"Who verily was foreordained before the foundation of the world, but was manifest in these last times for you" (I Pet. 1:18-20).

So if any man belittles the Cross, demeans the Cross, or ignores the Cross, and does so in any way, let him understand that he is demeaning the very Plan of God, and which without that Plan, which is the Cross, no one can be saved.

When Jesus died, shedding His Life's Blood, which means that His Life was poured out, His shed Blood atoned for all sin, past, present, and future, at least for all who will believe (Jn. 3:16; Rom. 10:9-10, 13).

The moment He died, at that moment the price was paid. The sin debt was cancelled. That means that anyone who registers Faith in Him is instantly saved, i.e., *"justified."* And you can only get it by Faith. Paul said: *"For by Grace* (the Goodness of God) *are you saved through Faith* (Faith in Christ and what Christ did at the Cross)*; and that not of yourselves: it is the Gift of God:*

"Not of works, lest any man should boast" (Eph. 2:8-9).

Paul then said: *"But now in Christ Jesus you who in times past were far off are made near by the Blood of Christ."*

And then the Apostle said: *"Having abolished in His flesh the enmity* (hatred), *even the Law of Commandments contained in Ordinances; for to make in Himself of twain* (Jews and Gentiles) *one new man* (the Church), *so making peace;*

"And that He might reconcile both (Jews and Gentiles) *unto God in one body* (the Church) *by the Cross, having slain the enmity thereby"* (Eph. 2:13-16).

One cannot read these Passages and come

away with any conclusion but one, and that is, *"It was the Cross which satisfied every claim, paid every debt, and made it possible for sinful man to become perfectly clean."*

Now this completely debunks the fallacious idea, as taught by the Word of Faith people, that the Cross was insignificant, and that Blood did not atone. It completely debunks the idea that Jesus died as a sinner on the Cross, and went to the burning side of Hell as a sinner, suffered there for three days and nights, and then was *"born again"* as a sinner is born again, and then resurrected from the dead. Not a shred of that is found in the Word of God, and yet this foolishness, this absurdity, in fact, this nonsense that borders on the edge of blasphemy, is taught and believed by many. And let the Reader understand that we are not speaking here of a mere matter of semantics, which means that the same thing is explained in two different ways. No! When one misunderstands the Cross, or demeans it as this evil doctrine does, one is tampering with the very heartbeat of Christianity. In fact, any sinner who tries to come to Christ, and believes that foolishness, cannot be saved. That just might explain the reason that precious few people are saved in those particular Churches, and because of that particular doctrine. While some few may be saved in these Churches, to be sure, they are saved because of something they heard somewhere else which was correct, and not because of the doctrine of which I have just spoken, oftentimes referred to as the *"Jesus died spiritually doctrine."*

I have just quoted to you the Passages given by Paul, *"Having abolished in His flesh the enmity"* (Eph. 2:15). This means that Jesus paid for our sins, satisfying the terrible sin debt, by His physical death on the Cross, and not by dying spiritually. There is nothing in the Word of God that states He died spiritually.

WHAT DOES IT MEAN TO DIE SPIRITUALLY?

It means to die without God. When Adam and Eve fell, they died spiritually, which means that were cut off from God.

He had told them that they may eat of any tree in the Garden, but of the tree of the knowledge of good and evil they must not eat, and if they did so, they would die (Gen. 2:16-17). And the moment they ate of that tree, in that moment they died, which means they were completely separated from God.

So for Jesus to die spiritually, He would have had to have sinned, because nothing will separate man from God but sin.

The Scripture says of Christ: *"For He* (God the Father) *has made Him* (Christ) *to be sin for us, who knew no sin; that we might be made the Righteousness of God in Him"* (II Cor. 5:21).

"Making Him to be sin," does not mean that Christ sinned, but rather that He was the *"Sin-Bearer"* for all of humanity. In other words, He did bear the penalty for sin, which in His case was death (Rom. 6:23). God would accept as payment for sin a Perfect Life, which only Christ could fulfill.

The spiritual death of both Adam and Eve brought about physical death. There would have been no physical death, had there not been first a spiritual death. So the idea of Redemption didn't have to engage the spiritual results of sin, but rather what it caused, which was death. When Christ died, giving Himself as a Perfect Sacrifice, and shedding His Life's Blood in the process, this and this alone atoned for all sin.

HELL

While it is certainly true that Jesus, after He died, went down into the Paradise side of Hell, and as well, the prison part of Hell, there is no Scriptural record whatsoever that He went to the burning side of Hell.

During the three days and nights after His death, the Scripture says that He *"descended first into the lower parts of the Earth."* And what did He do there?

"He led captivity captive and gave gifts unto men" (Eph. 4:8-9).

This means that He liberated every single person who was in Paradise (the Paradise part of Hell), which refers to every single Believer who lived before the Cross. It includes all the Old Testament greats, etc. They were held captive by Satan in Paradise. While he could not get them over into the burning side of Hell, and because their Faith was in Christ, they were still his captives, and because of sin,

i.e., *"the sin debt."* The blood of bulls and goats could not take away sins, so Satan still had a right to hold these people captive.

But when Jesus died on the Cross, the moment He died, the price was paid, the debt was settled, and He would now make all of these people His captives, thereby liberating them from Satan.

But he did something else during that three days and nights. Peter said: *"Also He went and preached unto the spirits in prison;*

"Which in times past were disobedient" (I Pet. 3:19-20).

These *"spirits"* were fallen angels. They were not human beings. Human beings are never referred to in the Bible as *"spirits."*

As well, the word *"preached"* is a different Greek word than normally used. As it is normally used, it means to *"proclaim glad tidings."* As it is used here, it means, *"to make an announcement."*

In fact, there was no good news for these *"spirits."* What Jesus said to them we have no way of knowing. And if the Holy Spirit had wanted us to know, He would have told us. But I can well imagine what He may have said.

These fallen angels were evidently the ones who had tried to corrupt the human race by intermarrying with the daughters of men. (This is referred to in Genesis 6:4.) In other words, their sin was even greater than that committed by other fallen angels.

He might have informed them that their plan did not work. The Sacrifice, which they had tried to stop, had been carried forth as planned, and now all sin was atoned, and Redemption was a completed work.

That which we have given you is all that the Bible tells us, as it regards what Jesus did in His three days and nights in the heart of the Earth. The idea of Him dying as a sinner on the Cross, going to the burning side of Hell, and burning there for three days and nights, tormented by demon spirits and even Satan himself, is totally fictitious. And to make it even worse, some of these Word of Faith teachers claim that when Jesus died, His spirit went to be with the Father, and His soul went to Hell. It becomes more preposterous the further one goes with such erroneous thinking.

They are referring to the Words of Christ, when He said, *"It is finished"* (Jn. 19:30), *Father, into Thy hands I commend My spirit"* (Lk. 23:46).

They realize that if Jesus died a lost sinner, and that He was cut off from God, He could not have referred to God as His Father at the time of His death, and could not have committed His Spirit unto Him. Lost sinners do not refer to God as *"Father,"* and neither do they commend their spirits unto Him.

Jesus did say, while He hung on the Cross, *"My God, My God, why have You forsaken Me?"* (Mat. 27:46).

Jesus was put on the Cross at 9 a.m., which had been the time of the morning sacrifice for some 1,600 years, the entirety of the time of the Law of Moses. At 12 noon, He cried these words I have just mentioned, and at that time, the Scripture says: *"There was darkness over all the land unto the ninth hour,"* which refers to 3:00 in the afternoon (Mat. 27:45). That's the time that Jesus died, the time of the evening Sacrifice, which as well had been carried on for approximately 1,600 years. In other words, He fulfilled the type in every respect.

During those three hours when darkness covered the land, Christ was bearing the sin penalty of the human race. Due to the fact that He was bearing the sin penalty, God could not look upon Him, and in fact, pulled the blinds, as someone has said, that no one else at that time could look upon Him as well.

When He died, suffering in the flesh (I Pet. 3:18; Eph. 2:15; Col. 1:22; Heb. 10:20), this and this alone atoned for all sin. In this we must place our Faith; in this, the Cross, we are saved.

(45) "AND THE LEPER IN WHOM THE PLAGUE IS, HIS CLOTHES SHALL BE RENT, AND HIS HEAD BARE, AND HE SHALL PUT A COVERING UPON HIS UPPER LIP, AND SHALL CRY, UNCLEAN, UNCLEAN.

(46) "ALL THE DAYS WHEREIN THE PLAGUE SHALL BE IN HIM HE SHALL BE DEFILED; HE IS UNCLEAN: HE SHALL DWELL ALONE; WITHOUT THE CAMP SHALL HIS HABITATION BE.

(47) "THE GARMENT ALSO THAT THE PLAGUE OF LEPROSY IS IN,

WHETHER IT BE A WOOLEN GARMENT, OR A LINEN GARMENT;

(48) "WHETHER IT BE IN THE WARP, OR WOOF; OF LINEN, OR OF WOOLEN; WHETHER IN A SKIN, OR IN ANYTHING MADE OF SKIN;

(49) "AND IF THE PLAGUE BE GREENISH OR REDDISH IN THE GARMENT, OR IN THE SKIN, EITHER IN THE WARP, OR IN THE WOOF, OR IN ANYTHING OF SKIN; IT IS A PLAGUE OF LEPROSY, AND SHALL BE SHOWED UNTO THE PRIEST:

(50) "AND THE PRIEST SHALL LOOK UPON THE PLAGUE, AND SHUT UP IT THAT HAS THE PLAGUE SEVEN DAYS:

(51) "AND HE SHALL LOOK ON THE PLAGUE ON THE SEVENTH DAY: IF THE PLAGUE BE SPREAD IN THE GARMENT, EITHER IN THE WARP, OR IN THE WOOF, OR IN A SKIN, OR IN ANY WORK THAT IS MADE OF SKIN; THE PLAGUE IS A FRETTING LEPROSY; IT IS UNCLEAN.

(52) "HE SHALL THEREFORE BURN THAT GARMENT, WHETHER WARP OR WOOF, IN WOOLEN OR IN LINEN, OR ANYTHING OF SKIN, WHEREIN THE PLAGUE IS: FOR IT IS A FRETTING LEPROSY; IT SHALL BE BURNT IN THE FIRE.

(53) "AND IF THE PRIEST SHALL LOOK, AND, BEHOLD, THE PLAGUE BE NOT SPREAD IN THE GARMENT, EITHER IN THE WARP, OR IN THE WOOF, OR IN ANY THING OF SKIN;

(54) "THEN THE PRIEST SHALL COMMAND THAT THEY WASH THE THING WHEREIN THE PLAGUE IS, HE SHALL SHUT IT UP SEVEN DAYS MORE:

(55) "AND THE PRIEST SHALL LOOK ON THE PLAGUE, AFTER THAT IT IS WASHED: AND, BEHOLD, IF THE PLAGUE HAVE NOT CHANGED HIS COLOR, AND THE PLAGUE BE NOT SPREAD, IT IS UNCLEAN; YOU SHALL BURN IT IN THE FIRE; IT IS FRET INWARD, WHETHER IT BE BARE WITHIN OR WITHOUT.

(56) "AND IF THE PRIEST LOOK, AND, BEHOLD, THE PLAGUE BE SOMEWHAT DARK AFTER THE WASHING OF IT; THEN HE SHALL REND IT OUT OF THE GARMENT, OR OUT OF THE SKIN, OR OUT OF THE WARP, OR OUT OF THE WOOF:

(57) "AND IF IT APPEARS STILL IN

THE GARMENT, EITHER IN THE WARP, OR IN THE WOOF, OR IN ANY THING OF SKIN; IT IS A SPREADING PLAGUE: YOU SHALL BURN THAT WHEREIN THE PLAGUE IS WITH FIRE.

(58) "AND THE GARMENT, EITHER WARP, OR WOOF, OR WHATSOEVER THING OF SKIN IT BE, WHICH YOU SHALL WASH, IF THE PLAGUE BE DEPARTED FROM THEM, THEN IT SHALL BE WASHED THE SECOND TIME, AND SHALL BE CLEAN.

(59) "THIS IS THE LAW OF THE PLAGUE OF LEPROSY IN A GARMENT OF WOOLEN OR LINEN, EITHER IN THE WARP, OR WOOF, OR ANY THING OF SKINS, TO PRONOUNCE IT CLEAN, OR TO PRONOUNCE IT UNCLEAN."

The overview is:

1. On four occasions Christ endorsed Leviticus as having been written by Moses. The Modernist says the Book was foraged by Ezra. The Christian believes the Master and not the Modernist.

Leviticus 12:3 – John 7:22, 23.
Leviticus 14:3-22 – Matthew 8:4.
Leviticus 20:9 – Mark 7:10.
Leviticus 24:5-9 – Matthew 12:4.

2. The Priest alone could judge whether a man were a leper or no. Directly a person is declared to be a leper, he was placed without the camp, and compelled, by voice and clothing, to confess himself a leper.

3. Leprosy in a garment is a type of sin in a man's circumstances, or habits. The Priest was commanded to show the same patience and care in judging a garment as in judging a man.

4. Sometimes a Christian must abandon part of his business because of evil attaching to it, and sometimes he must abandon it altogether. This is a principle which affects the whole Christian life.

5. One *"bright spot"* revealed the disease as surely as an extensive and revolting eruption. So one pleasing sin reveals the fact of corruption in human nature as certainly as 100 revolting vices. There is, as to the nature, no moral difference.

6. The carnal mind finds this Chapter tiresome, uninteresting, and unpleasant. To the spiritual mind it is humbling and comforting.

NOTES

Love untiring and infinite wisdom are the foundation of these Statutes. The Reader finds himself as a moral leper in the tender, patient, wise, and loving hands of the Heavenly Priest; and, accordingly, he studies every word with humiliation and adoration. (The headings were provided by George Williams.)

UNCLEAN, UNCLEAN

Verses 45 and 46 read: *"And the leper in whom the plague is, his clothes shall be rent, and his head bare, and he shall put a covering upon his upper lip, and shall cry, Unclean, unclean.*

"All the days wherein the plague shall be in him he shall be defiled; he is unclean: he shall dwell alone; without the camp shall his habitation be."

The descriptions given portray stipulations not only for the leper, but present a spiritual meaning as well.

We will attempt to look past the plight of the leper which existed so long, long ago, and bring the application to the modern Christian.

HIS CLOTHES SHALL BE RENT

This speaks of the outer garment which had to be ripped down the back from collar to hem. It has a spiritual meaning for us presently. It means that man's righteousness is insufficient for acceptance by God. The leper's torn garment said, *"I am undone, useless, and I am separated from God. Furthermore, all my good works can never bridge the gap."*

HIS HEAD BARE

This signifies that the sinner had and has no protection against the anger and wrath of God. In those days, all of the men among the Jews wore a covering on their head as a sign to the world that God was their covering and their protection. Today, male Christians when worshipping do not wear any type of covering on the head, signifying that Christ is our covering. He needs no symbolism because He is ever present in our hearts in the Power of the Holy Spirit.

The *"head bare"* meant that there was no Covenant between God and the individual. He was a sinner, and, thereby, a declared enmity against God.

IN THE SIGHT OF GOD

The moment any individual came within approximately 100 feet of a leper, the leper was to cry, *"Unclean, unclean."* If the leper did not shout out these words, he could be stoned to death.

In reality, this terrible problem has not changed. Today, when asked, *"Are you saved?"*, and the individual says, *"I am a member of _____ Church,"* they are in effect saying, *"Unclean, unclean."*

If there is any answer other than, *"I am saved by Faith in the Lord Jesus Christ, and I accept the price paid for me at Calvary,"* or words to that effect, then the individual is shouting to the whole world, *"Unclean, unclean."* In fact, most of the world presently, when speaking of their religious affiliation is, without knowing it, shouting, *"Unclean, unclean."*

HE SHALL DWELL ALONE

There is a terrible loneliness to sin. Even in the midst of a crowd, the loneliness seems to increase rather than to decrease. Man was created by God to serve the Lord. Unless man knows the Lord, there is a void in his heart that all the money, power, prestige, and education can never fill. In fact, the soul of man is so big that only God can fill it. Without God, man is *"alone,"* and, oh, so lonely.

Thank God, there is a cure for sin, and that cure is the Lord Jesus Christ. In the First Chapter of the Gospel according to Mark, he beautifully illustrates the cry of the leper, *"If You will, You can make me clean."* The answer of the Lord Jesus Christ will ever reverberate across the annals of history, *"I will, be thou clean."*

Our Lord further cries, *"Whosoever will let him come and take of the water of life freely."* The leper can be cleansed; the sinner can be saved; sin can turn to Salvation; death can turn to life; sickness can turn to health; Hell can turn to Heaven, but only by the Lord Jesus Christ, and what he has done for us at the Cross. Salvation cannot be obtained any other way. There is no other Saviour.

Man cannot reach God through Buddha, Mohammad, Confucius, or through any

other way or method. Jesus said, *"I am the Way, the Truth, and the Life. No man comes to the Father but by Me"* (Jn. 14:6). To be sure, there is no other way.

THE WARP, OR THE WOOF

Verses 47 through 59 read: *"The garment also that the plague of leprosy is in, whether it be a woolen garment, or a linen garment;*

"Whether it be in the warp, or woof; of linen, or of woolen; whether in a skin, or in any thing made of skin;

"And if the plague be greenish or reddish in the garment, or in the skin, either in the warp, or in the woof, or in any thing of skin; it is a plague of leprosy, and shall be showed unto the Priest:

"And the Priest shall look upon the plague, and shut up it that has the plague seven days:

"And he shall look on the plague on the seventh day: if the plague be spread in the garment, either in the warp, or in the woof, or in the skin, or in any work that is made of skin; the plague is a fretting leprosy; it is unclean.

"He shall therefore burn that garment, whether warp or woof, in woolen or in linen, or any thing of skin, wherein the plague is: for it is a fretting leprosy; it shall be burnt in the fire.

"And if the Priest shall look, and, behold, the plague be not spread in the garment, either in the warp, or in the woof, or in any thing of skin;

"Then the Priest shall command that they wash the thing wherein the plague is, and he shall shut it up seven days more:

"And the Priest shall look on the plague, after that it is washed: and, behold, if the plague have not changed his color, and the plague be not spread, it is unclean; you shall burn it in the fire; it is fret inward, whether it be bare within or without.

"And if the Priest look, and, behold, the plague be somewhat dark after the washing of it; then he shall rend it out of the garment, or out of the skin, or out of the warp, or out of the woof:

"And if it appears still in the garment, either in the warp, or in the woof, or in any thing of skin; it is a spreading plague: you shall burn

that wherein the plague is with fire.

"And the garment, either warp, or woof, or whatsoever thing of skin it be, which you shall wash, if the plague be departed from them, then it shall be washed the second time, and shall be clean.

"This is the Law of the plague of leprosy in a garment of woolen or linen, either in the warp, or woof, or any thing of skins, to pronounce it clean, or to pronounce it unclean."

As I think the Reader will find, Verses 47 through 59, at least for the most part, deal with leprosy that is in a particular garment, whether it's made of wool, linen, or a skin of some type. As is obvious, there were special instructions given for inspecting such a garment, and instructions given as to what to do with the garment, should it be found to contain the disease of leprosy. It was to be burned.

The phrase *"warp or woof,"* refers to any and every part of the garment.

The idea is, leprosy infects not only the person, but all that pertains to the person.

This means that sin affects everything. It affects all that we are, all that we touch, in fact, everything.

The burning of the garment expressed the act of judgment upon evil, whether in a man's habits or circumstances. There must be no trifling with evil.

In certain cases the garment was to be *"washed,"* which expresses the action of the Word of God upon a man's habits.

The idea is, the *"Word"* and the *"sin"* cannot be both entertained. One or the other must go. Concerning this, John said:

"He who commits sin is of the Devil; for the Devil has sinned from the beginning. For this purpose the Son of God was manifested, that He might destroy the works of the Devil.

Whosoever is born of God does not commit sin; for his seed remains in him: and he cannot sin, because he is born of God" (I Jn. 3:8-9).

The word *"commit"* would have probably been better translated, *"practice,"* thereby reading, *"Whosoever is born of God does not practice sin; for His seed* (the Word of God) *remains in him: and he cannot practice sin, because he is born of God."*

NOTES

The *"Law of the plague of leprosy"* was to be upheld in all circumstances. By this Law, and this Law alone, the Priest was to *"pronounce it clean, or to pronounce it unclean."*

It is by the Word alone that the true condition is found out. It is not what my Church says, or such and such a Preacher says, or any man for that matter. The criteria must ever be the *Word of the Lord."* It is by that *"Word"* that all of us will be judged, and this we must not forget.

But the sad fact is, millions are basing their Salvation on what their Church says, or on what man says. We must never forget that we are speaking of our eternal soul. We must not leave the answer to our Salvation up to others. We must faithfully study the Word, and know what it says, because more is at stake here than the mind of man could ever begin to comprehend. To take a chance on something as important as your soul is foolish indeed!

"Why say you not, a word of bringing back the King?
"Why speak you not of Jesus and His reign?
"Why tell ye of His Kingdom, and of its glories sing,
"But nothing of His coming back again?"

"Do you not want to look up upon His loving face?
"Do you not want to see Him glorified?
"Would you not hear His welcome, and in that very place,
"Where years ago we saw Him Crucified?"

"O hark! Creation's groans, how can they be assuaged?
"How can our bodies know Redemption joy?
"How can the war be ended in which we are engaged,
"Until He comes the lawless to destroy?"

"Come quickly, Blessed Lord, our hearts a welcome hold!
"We long to see creation's second birth;
"The promise of Your coming to some is growing cold,
"O hasten Your returning back to Earth."

CHAPTER 14

(1) "AND THE LORD SPOKE UNTO MOSES, SAYING,

(2) "THIS SHALL BE THE LAW OF THE LEPER IN THE DAY OF HIS CLEANSING: HE SHALL BE BROUGHT UNTO THE PRIEST:

(3) "AND THE PRIEST SHALL GO FORTH OUT OF THE CAMP; AND THE PRIEST SHALL LOOK, AND, BEHOLD, IF THE PLAGUE OF LEPROSY BE HEALED IN THE LEPER;

(4) "THEN SHALL THE PRIEST COMMAND TO TAKE FOR HIM THAT IS TO BE CLEANSED TWO BIRDS ALIVE AND CLEAN, AND CEDAR WOOD, AND SCARLET, AND HYSSOP:

(5) "AND THE PRIEST SHALL COMMAND THAT ONE OF THE BIRDS BE KILLED IN AN EARTHEN VESSEL OVER RUNNING WATER:

(6) "AS FOR THE LIVING BIRD, HE SHALL TAKE IT, AND THE CEDAR WOOD, AND THE SCARLET, AND THE HYSSOP, AND SHALL DIP THEM AND THE LIVING BIRD IN THE BLOOD OF THE BIRD THAT WAS KILLED OVER THE RUNNING WATER:

(7) "AND HE SHALL SPRINKLE UPON HIM WHO IS TO BE CLEANSED FROM THE LEPROSY SEVEN TIMES, AND SHALL PRONOUNCE HIM CLEAN, AND SHALL LET THE LIVING BIRD LOOSE INTO THE OPEN FIELD."

The diagram is:

1. The leper was cleansed by blood, by water, and by oil. These symbolized the Blood of Christ, the Word of God, and the Holy Spirit.

2. This triple cleansing restored him to the camp, to his family, and to the Tabernacle.

3. All was based upon the preciousness and efficacy of the shed blood. Apart from the Blood of Jesus moral reformation and spiritual power are impossible.

THE LAW OF THE CLEANSING OF THE LEPER

Verses 1 through 3 read: *"And the LORD spoke unto Moses, saying,*

"This shall be the Law of the leper in the day of his cleansing: he shall be brought unto the Priest:

"And the Priest shall go forth out of the camp; and the Priest shall look, and, behold, if the plague of leprosy be healed in the leper."

We will find here in the Law of the cleansing of the leper beautiful types and symbols. We must realize that all of these things given did not cure the leper, but were ordained for his ceremonial cleansing after the cure. It was all meant by the Holy Spirit to be symbolic of the cleansing from sin, which in effect points to the Cross.

We have already seen the lonely place occupied by the leper, which meant that he had no part in the Sanctuary or the Tabernacle of God. He couldn't worship in the Tabernacle, and neither could he associate with those who could. He was outside the camp, in the place of moral distance from God, from His Sanctuary, and His assembly.

He dwelt alone, in a place of uncleanness, all of this typifying sin. And as well, there was absolutely nothing he could do to cleanse himself. Neither could any other human being cleanse him, only God.

We may think that sin is not as obvious presently as was the leper. If it isn't, it's only because we do not understand the horror of sin. To be sure, sin in the heart and life of anyone is as horrible in the eyes of God as leprosy was to the citizens of Israel.

In fact, the Holy Spirit gave to us in this Book of Leviticus, *"the Law of the leper,"* and *"the law of the cleansing of the leper,"* that we may understand the terrible depravity of sin, and as well, its only cure, which is the Cross, and as we shall amply see.

THE AWFULNESS OF SIN

Our problem in the modern Church is that we little understand, at least as properly as we should, the awfulness of this dread monster called *"sin."* We little realize, and as previously stated, that even as the slightest touch of leprosy meant that the person was a leper, likewise, the slightest sin means that the person is a sinner. In fact, there are no little sins in the eyes of God. They are all hideous, destructive, depraved, unclean, impure, etc.

If we properly knew how awful that sin really is, we would not promote some of the ridiculous schemes for the cleansing of sin, which have become prominent. For instance, to the person who truly understands what sin is, the idea that humanistic psychology holds an answer for this dread malady, we would look at it as a joke. But yet the modern Church has fallen for this lie, which means that it has abandoned the Cross.

In fact, how that any person who calls themselves a Believer, much less a Preacher, could read the Word of God, and come away with any conclusion other than the Cross as the answer for dying humanity, is beyond me.

THE CROSS AND THE BIBLE

The Cross, by no stretch of the imagination, is a hidden symbol in the Word of God, but is rather the glaring centerpiece of its proclamation, all the way from Genesis 1:1 through Revelation 22:21. It takes an acute deception to miss this glaring fact.

For instance, the Sacrificial System was introduced at the very beginning (Gen., Chpt. 4). All of this typified Christ, and the price that He would pay, in order to redeem Adam's fallen race.

As well, and as we have already said any number of times, the Law of Moses all, and without exception, pointed to the Cross. This speaks of every ceremony, every ritual, every law, every sacrifice, the Tabernacle with all of its Sacred Vessels, and this which we are presently studying, and that which we will yet study – all and without exception pointed to the Cross.

THE PRIEST AND THE LEPER

In this illustration, the leper is the sinner; the Priest is Jesus. The Priest *"went forth"* out of the camp to where the leper was, and the leper was *"brought"* to him. So Christ came down from Heaven to where the sinner is, and the Holy Spirit, through the power of conviction brings the sinner to Him.

In the Priest going forth from the camp – forth from God's dwelling-place – we behold the blessed Lord Jesus coming down from the bosom of the Father. He did not

come half-way. He didn't even come nine-tenths of the way; He came all the way.

All of this should be wondrous to us. God could call worlds into existence by the simple word of His mouth; however, when it came to the Redemption of fallen mankind, something else was needed, something that was beyond our comprehension. For sinners to be saved, God would have to give His Son, the Lord Jesus Christ (Jn. 3:16).

Even though God would become man, it was far more involved than the Incarnation, as miraculous, glorious, and wonderful as that was. As we shall see as it regards the leper, blood-shedding was necessary before leprosy could be removed. *"Without the shedding of blood is no remission"* (Heb. 9:22). And we should observe that the shedding of blood, as we shall see, was the real basis of the leper's cleansing. Likewise, the shedding of Blood is the real basis of the Salvation of the sinner. It could not be effected any other way. And for Preachers, or anyone, to negate that fact, that Truth, or to claim that the Blood of Jesus needed something else added, even as the Word of Faith people claim, in fact, borders on blasphemy.

TWO BIRDS

Verses 4 through 7 read: *"Then shall the Priest command to take for him who is to be cleansed two birds alive and clean, and cedar wood, and scarlet, and hyssop:*

"And the Priest shall command that one of the birds be killed in an earthen vessel over running water:

"As for the living bird, he shall take it, and the cedar wood, and the scarlet, and the hyssop, and shall dip them and the living bird in the blood of the bird that was killed over the running water:

"And he shall sprinkle upon him who is to be cleansed from the leprosy seven times, and shall pronounce him clean, shall let the living bird loose into the open field."

As we've already stated, the symbolism, which we will now look at, was given by the Holy Spirit in order to portray a truth. In fact, within itself, it had nothing to do with the cleansing of the leper. It was rather meant to portray the price of that cleansing, which was the Cross of Christ.

Two birds were selected. They were no doubt turtledoves or pigeons. One was to be killed, typifying the Cross, and the other was to be let loose into the heavens, typifying the Resurrection.

These particular birds are the gentlest of the most gentle. They are perfect types of Christ, Who was *"meek and lowly in heart"* (Mat. 11:29). In fact, those two words *"meek"* and *"lowly"* are the only two words used by Christ in describing Himself.

The fate of the one bird shows us how Christ was mangled for human guilt, crushed to death for the sins of others, and brought down to the depths of the Earth. The other, coming up out of the earthen vessel, out of the blood of its fellow, shows us how Jesus rose again from the rocky sepulchre, and ascended up out of the hand of His captor on strong and joyous pinions far into the high abodes of Heaven, scattering as He went the gracious drops of cleansing and Salvation (Seiss).

JUSTIFICATION AND SANCTIFICATION

To the unspiritual mind, these two turtledoves or pigeons mean nothing. But to those who understand the typology behind this symbolism, we must recognize that these two little birds show through Christ our Sanctification, as well as our Justification. Both proceed from His Cross and Resurrection.

While we know that it's the Holy Spirit Who sanctifies, and the Holy Spirit Alone Who does this; still, had not Christ died and rose again, the Holy Spirit could not have even taken up abode on a permanent basis within the heart and life of any Believer. It is the Cross that made all of this possible. That's what Jesus was speaking of when He addressed His Disciples, saying that the Holy Spirit was then with them, but after the Cross, would be *"in them,"* and would be so on a permanent basis (Jn. 14:16-17).

The teaching of the Holy Spirit, although sublime and perfect, would be as dead as man's philosophies without what Christ did at the Cross, which made it all possible. Not only were acts of sin addressed at the Cross, but as well, the very root, the very cause, the very principle of sin was addressed as well. To atone for acts of sin, which Christ definitely did, but not atone for the very root

cause of sin, would not really have properly addressed the problem, as ought to be obvious. But the Cross did address the entirety of the sin problem.

Paul said: *"Blotting out the handwriting of Ordinances that was against us, which was contrary to us, and took it out of the way, nailing it to His Cross."* This addressed acts of sin.

But then the great Apostle wrote: *"And having spoiled principalities and powers, He made a show of them openly, triumphing over them in it"* (Col. 2:14-15).

This tells us that not only did Jesus address the acts of sin, and did so by the shedding of His Life's Blood, the shedding of that Blood also addressed the cause, the very root of sin. I speak of Satan and all of his cohorts.

SATAN

Somewhere in eternity past, Lucifer, then one of the great and beautiful Archangels of God, fell from his lofty position, even as he was created by Christ. Isaiah and Ezekiel give us a smattering of knowledge regarding this revolution against God (Isa. 14:12-20; Ezek. 28:12-19). Satan is the fomenter of evil, the instigator of the wicked seed. He is the cause of all sin.

Satan's legal hold upon humanity is sin. But when Jesus died on Calvary, shedding His Blood, He atoned for all sin, past, present, and future, which took away Satan's legal right. In that manner, He addressed the very root cause of sin. This means the sin debt is forever paid, and all who exhibit Faith in Christ and what Christ has done at the Cross can be saved, and can live a victorious life.

SANCTIFICATION

Most Christians have at least a smattering of knowledge as it regards the Cross and Salvation, i.e., *"Justification"*; however, they have almost no knowledge at all as it regards Sanctification. This means they don't know how the Holy Spirit works, which means they don't know the part the Cross plays in the Sanctification process.

I won't go into detail, simply because we've addressed this subject several times already; however, the Believer must understand that not only does Salvation come to him through the Cross, but as well, everything thereafter comes through the Cross. Consequently, our Faith must rest totally and completely in the Cross of Christ, which then gives the Holy Spirit latitude to work in our lives, because it is the Cross which makes it possible for Him to do what He does (Rom. 8:1-2, 11, 13).

The *"cedar wood,"* which was to be used in this ceremony, as given to us in Verse 4, is a type of the Cross, on which Jesus died.

The *"scarlet"* from the same Verse, speaks of a piece of cloth that was the color of scarlet, which typified His shed Blood.

The *"hyssop"* of the same Verse, typified His humanity, i.e., *"Incarnation,"* God becoming man.

DEATH, THE EARTHEN VESSEL, AND RUNNING WATER

One of the birds had to be killed, which typified Christ and the Cross. It was *"to be killed in an earthen vessel over running water."* The *"earthen vessel"* also spoke of the humanity of Christ, just as the hyssop. The *"running water"* spoke of the Word of God, in which Jesus was the Living Word.

The *"running water"* probably referred to water poured out of a bowl into the *"earthen vessel."* The first bird, typifying the Cross, was to be killed in this *"earthen vessel."*

They were to then take the *"living bird,"* which symbolized the Resurrection of Christ, attach to the living bird the cedar wood, the scarlet cloth, and the hyssop, which could all be held in the hands of the Priest. He would then dip the entire concoction, *"in the blood of the bird that was killed over the running water."* Inasmuch as a little bird would not have much blood, more than likely, these things were dipped into the water in the *"earthen vessel,"* which had blood mixed with it.

SEVEN TIMES

The Priest was to then take the concoction and sprinkle the cleansed leper seven times, with the number *"seven,"* denoting a perfect cleansing. He was to then pronounce him clean, and then he would let the *"living bird loose into the open field."* The living bird flying away was a type of the Resurrection of Christ.

Birds serving as a type of Christ, and His Death on the Cross, portrayed the fact that He died in weakness (II Cor. 13:4).

The weakness mentioned does not mean that Christ was Himself weak, but that he purposely did not use His power to prevent the Crucifixion. He purposely allowed Himself to be weak (II Cor. 13:4).

As well, it didn't mean that the Cross itself was a place of weakness. In fact, the *"preaching of the Cross is the Power of God"* (I Cor. 1:18). And how is it the power?

Of course, and as should be obvious, there was no power in that wooden beam, even as there is no power in death. The power comes in as it regards the Holy Spirit.

Jesus having paid the sin debt made it possible for the Holy Spirit to work mightily within our hearts and lives, and the Power is resident within Him. But the Cross made it all possible.

Mackintosh said: *"Let us remember this. Sin is a dreadful thing in the estimation of God. He cannot tolerate as much as a single sinful thought. Before one such thought could be forgiven, Christ had to die upon the Cross. The most trifling sin (if any sin can be called trifling,) demanded nothing less than God's eternal and co-equal Son. But, eternal praise be to God, what sin demanded, redeeming love freely gave; and now God is infinitely more glorified in the forgiveness of sins than He could have been had Adam maintained his original innocency."*

(8) "AND HE WHO IS TO BE CLEANSED SHALL WASH HIS CLOTHES, AND SHAVE OFF ALL HIS HAIR, AND WASH HIMSELF IN WATER, THAT HE MAY BE CLEAN: AND AFTER THAT HE SHALL COME INTO THE CAMP, AND SHALL TARRY ABROAD OUT OF HIS TENT SEVEN DAYS.

(9) "BUT IT SHALL BE ON THE SEVENTH DAY THAT HE SHALL SHAVE ALL HIS HAIR OFF HIS HEAD AND HIS BEARD AND HIS EYEBROWS, EVEN ALL HIS HAIR HE SHALL SHAVE OFF: HE SHALL WASH HIS CLOTHES, ALSO HE SHALL WASH HIS FLESH IN WATER, AND HE SHALL BE CLEAN.

(10) "AND ON THE EIGHT DAY HE SHALL TAKE TWO HE LAMBS WITHOUT BLEMISH, AND ONE EWE LAMB OF THE

FIRST YEAR WITHOUT BLEMISH, AND THREE TENTH DEALS OF FINE FLOUR FOR A MEAT-OFFERING, MINGLED WITH OIL, AND ONE LOG OF OIL.

(11) "AND THE PRIEST WHO MAKES HIM CLEAN SHALL PRESENT THE MAN WHO IS TO BE MADE CLEAN, AND THOSE THINGS, BEFORE THE LORD, AT THE DOOR OF THE TABERNACLE OF THE CONGREGATION:

(12) "AND THE PRIEST SHALL TAKE ONE HE LAMB, AND OFFER HIM FOR A TRESPASS-OFFERING, AND THE LOG OF OIL, AND WAVE THEM FOR A WAVE-OFFERING BEFORE THE LORD:

(13) "AND HE SHALL SLAY THE LAMB IN THE PLACE WHERE HE SHALL KILL THE SIN-OFFERING AND THE BURNT-OFFERING, IN THE HOLY PLACE: FOR AS THE SIN-OFFERING IS THE PRIEST'S, SO IS THE TRESPASS-OFFERING: IT IS MOST HOLY:

(14) "AND THE PRIEST SHALL TAKE SOME OF THE BLOOD OF THE TRESPASS-OFFERING, AND THE PRIEST SHALL PUT IT UPON THE TIP OF THE RIGHT EAR OF HIM WHO IS TO BE CLEANSED, AND UPON THE THUMB OF HIS RIGHT HAND, AND UPON THE GREAT TOE OF HIS RIGHT FOOT:

(15) "AND THE PRIEST SHALL TAKE SOME OF THE LOG OF OIL, POUR IT INTO THE PALM OF HIS OWN LEFT HAND:

(16) "AND THE PRIEST SHALL DIP HIS RIGHT FINGER IN THE OIL THAT IS IN HIS LEFT HAND, AND SHALL SPRINKLE OF THE OIL WITH HIS FINGER SEVEN TIMES BEFORE THE LORD:

(17) "AND OF THE REST OF THE OIL THAT IS IN HIS HAND SHALL THE PRIEST PUT UPON THE TIP OF THE RIGHT EAR OF HIM WHO IS TO BE CLEANSED, AND UPON THE THUMB OF HIS RIGHT HAND, AND UPON THE GREAT TOE OF HIS RIGHT FOOT, AND UPON THE BLOOD OF THE TRESPASS-OFFERING:

(18) "AND THE REMNANT OF THE OIL THAT IS IN THE PRIEST'S HAND HE SHALL POUR UPON THE HEAD OF HIM WHO IS TO BE CLEANSED: AND THE PRIEST SHALL MAKE AN ATONEMENT FOR HIM BEFORE THE LORD."

NOTES

The composition is:

1. Excepting the washing of himself in water, the leper did nothing for his cleansing; the Priest did everything.

2. Directly the repentant sinner is cleansed by the Precious Blood of Christ, he is called upon to *"cleanse himself"* from all defilement of the flesh and spirit. This cleansing is effected by the Word of God, of which the washing with water was a type.

3. He is to judge himself, and his habits, by the infallible standard of the Holy Scriptures, and he resolutely must turn away from everything that standard condemns. Thus, he cleanses himself.

4. A Trespass-Offering, a Sin-Offering, a Meal-Offering, and a Burnt-Offering were required to make Atonement for him.

THE WASHING

Verses 8 and 9 read: *"And he who is to be cleansed shall wash his clothes, and shave off all his hair, and wash himself in water, that he may be clean: and after that he shall come into the camp, and shall tarry abroad out of his tent seven days.*

"But it shall be on the seventh day that he shall shave all his hair off his head and his beard and his eyebrows, even all his hair he shall shave off: and he shall wash his clothes, also he shall wash his flesh in water, and he shall be clean."

The former leper was now to undergo a seven day cleansing ceremony. On the first of the seven days, he was to wash himself, his clothes, and shave himself. During the seven days, if he was married, he was not to come near his wife. While he is cleansed from leprosy, he still is not allowed into the Sanctuary, until the seven days of purification are concluded. At the end of the seven days, he is to do the same thing all over again, regarding the washing and shaving.

While all of this was ceremonial, it pointed to that which would be spiritual, and would take place after the Cross. Concerning the sinner coming to Christ, and I speak of the time since the Cross, Paul listed about every type of sin that one could imagine, and then said, *"And such were some of you: but you are washed, but you are sanctified, but you are justified in the Name of the Lord Jesus, and by the Spirit of our God"* (I Cor. 6:9-11).

The believing sinner upon coming to Christ, thereby trusting Christ and His Sacrificial, Atoning Work, at the moment of Faith, and we speak of Faith in Christ and His Atoning Work on the Cross, the sinner is thoroughly cleansed, of which the cleansing of the leper of old was a type.

The *"born again"* experience, which refers to being born of the Spirit, is the most life-changing experience that any human being could ever undergo (Jn. 3:3, 5-6).

Once again, we go back to what Paul said regarding the ancient Jewish Law. It was *"a shadow of good things to come, and not the very image of the things"* (Heb. 10:1).

The seven days of purification typified the perfect Salvation and Sanctification that we now have in Christ, and because of the Cross.

THE TRESPASS-OFFERING

Verses 10 through 13 read: *"And on the eighth day he shall take two he lambs without blemish, and one ewe lamb of the first year without blemish, and three tenth deals of fine flour for a Meat-Offering, mingled with oil, and one log of oil.*

"And the Priest who makes him clean shall present the man who is to be made clean, and those things, before the LORD, at the Door of the Tabernacle of the congregation:

"And the Priest shall take one he lamb, and offer him for a Trespass-Offering, and the log of oil, and wave them for a Wave-Offering before the LORD:

"And he shall slay the lamb in the place where he shall kill the Sin-Offering and the Burnt-Offering, in the Holy Place: for as the Sin-Offering is the Priest's, so is the Trespass-Offering: it is most holy."

After the seven days of purification were ended, *"on the eighth day,"* which typified Resurrection, inasmuch as Jesus rose from the dead on the first day, or eighth day, one might say, the leper was to offer up four Sacrifices. They were, first of all, the *"Trespass-Offering,"* which was to be followed by the *"Sin-Offering,"* then the *"Burnt-Offering,"* and last of all, the *"Meat-Offering."* No Peace-Offering is mentioned.

Why was the Trespass-Offering required first, and the Peace-Offering omitted?

As I understand the Law of the cleansing of the leper, it is a type of the sinner coming to Christ. While it certainly can pertain to the Believer who sins, I think the greater thrust is toward the unsaved being *"born again."* If in fact that is the case, we are dealing here with sin in all its forms; consequently, the Trespass, Sin, and Burnt-Offerings must be offered, along with the Meat-Offering, which in essence was for thanksgiving.

While it is true that Peace is now given to the believing sinner, the primary objective is rather the cleansing from sin. Thereafter, when the former leper is completely restored to the Sanctuary, he can then offer up a Burnt-Offering to be followed by a Peace-Offering.

The Peace-Offering was primarily for those who were in Covenant with the Lord, but had sinned in some way, which had hindered fellowship. Then the Burnt, Sin, or Trespass-Offering could be presented, whichever was needed, and then followed by a Peace-Offering.

Once again we go back to the idea of thankfulness for the New Covenant, which put away all of these symbols, ceremonies, and rituals, which were types of Christ. Christ fulfilled them all; hence we have presently a *"Better Covenant,"* based on *"Better Promises"* (Heb. 8:6).

The two *"he lambs"* were for the Trespass-Offering and the Sin-Offering. The one female lamb was for the Burnt-Offering. All were to be without blemish, and because they typified Christ.

It seems that quite possibly, each one of the three Offerings was to be followed by a *"Meat-Offering,"* which very well could have been the case.

Ordinarily a Meat-Offering did not accompany the Trespass-Offering, or the Sin-Offering, but rather the Burnt-Offering (Num. 15:4).

In Bible days, the word *"meat"* referred to all type of food, whereas presently, it refers to the flesh of certain animals. In fact, the Meat-Offering contained no flesh, and was, therefore, the only bloodless Offering presented. It consisted of *"fine flour,"* which typified the perfect Life and perfect Body of the Lord Jesus Christ, *"mingled with oil,"* which typified the Holy Spirit. Some of it was to be burned on the Altar, and some of it eaten by the offerer. It was a Thanksgiving-Offering more than anything else.

THE DOOR OF THE TABERNACLE

The phrase, *"At the Door of the Tabernacle,"* as used in Verse 11, could be translated, *"At the entrance of the tent of meeting."*

As far as the Temple was concerned, which of course had not yet been built, since expiation had not yet been made for the former leper, the individual could not enter into the Court of the Israelites, which was the Court nearest the Temple. In back of this Court was the Court of Women, for women could not go into the Court of the Israelites, and in back of the Court of Women was the Court of the Gentiles, which was the furthest from the Temple. As well, between the Court of the Gentiles, and the Court of Women, there was a barrier placed, which was approximately four feet high, which the Gentiles under the pain of death, could not cross. That's what Paul was speaking about when He said:

"But now in Christ Jesus you (Gentiles) *who in times past were far off are made near by the Blood of Christ.*

"For He is our peace, Who has made both one (Jews and Gentiles), *and has broken down the middle wall of partition between us"* (Eph. 2:13-14). Of course, Jesus did this by the Cross.

THE WAVE-OFFERING

As the Trespass-Offering was presented by the Priest, it was done different than normally done for other Trespass-Offerings. In the case before us, not only did oil accompany it, but both the Trespass-Offering and the oil were waved by the Priest, which did not take place on any other occasion in connection with the Trespass-Offering and Sin-Offering. Actually, in no other case was the entire victim waved before the Lord (Ellicott).

The *"Wave-Offering"* was different from the *"Heave-Offering,"* inasmuch as it was held above the head of the Priest, and waved back and forth, signifying that Salvation came from God Alone, in essence, above. It made a statement, in effect, saying that all of this ritual originated with the Lord, and

NOTES

was done so for the purpose of serving as a type of what Christ would do, as it regards the Redemption of Adam's fallen race. It originated with the Lord, was instituted by the Lord, and carried out by the Lord. Man, as is obvious, had nothing to do with the origination, and if he attempted to tamper with the process, he automatically rendered it ineffective.

It is the same presently with Salvation. The Message is *"Jesus Christ and Him Crucified."* The entire basis of Christianity rests upon those five words, which is the number of Grace. If man attempts to take away from that Sacrifice, or add to that Sacrifice, the Sacrifice is made ineffective for those who would believe such error, whatever it might be.

There are many presently who feel that any type of belief system is satisfactory, that is, if it includes Christ in some loose way. Nothing could be further from the Truth! Millions are in Hell presently because of such thinking, and millions are on their way to Hell because of such thinking.

Whatever we may think of Christ, whatever we may attribute to Him, if we are wrong on any point, it had better not be the Atonement. To liken it to the physical body, other things might have to do with a broken arm or a hangnail, etc., but the Atonement has to do with the heart, and the heart can kill you.

MOST HOLY

Ordinarily, the offerer actually performed the killing of the animal. But in this case, it was the Priest who killed the animal.

Normally the animal was killed before the Altar; however, this could not be done in this case, simply because the former leper could not yet come before the Altar. So the lamb was, therefore, brought to the door of the Court where the leper stood, and then he placed his hands on the head of the victim, as he was required to do, thereby transferring his guilt to the innocent animal, which typified Christ.

The flesh of the Trespass-Offering and the Sin-Offering was to be eaten by the Priests, and members of their families, and eaten within the Court of the Sanctuary. These two Sacrifices were *"most holy,"* as was the

Meat-Offering (Lev. 2:3). They typified deliverance from sin and thankfulness for that deliverance.

Why were they *"most holy"* and the Burnt-Offering and Peace-Offering not labeled as such?

Once again, we go back to the real purpose as to why Christ came to this world. He came to set men free from the bondages of sin. While other things were definitely important, and in fact, anything He did was definitely important, still, the overriding thrust of all that He did, was deliverance from sin, hence these particular Offerings being *"most holy."*

As we've already previously stated, the fact that these three particular Offerings were *"most holy,"* completely debunks the idea that Jesus became a sinner on the Cross, and died and went to the burning side of Hell as a sinner. How could something be *"most holy,"* which Christ was, and especially as He was bearing the sin penalty of mankind, and at the same time, be unholy? Of course, the idea is preposterous! Nevertheless, this erroneous doctrine is taught by the Word of Faith people. And regrettably, many people who adhere to this particular doctrine little know or understand what it is they actually have accepted.

When we began to address this subject over our morning Radio Program, *"A Study In The Word,"* and Donnie began to preach it in his Messages, which was aired over Television, at first we received many letters and e-mails claiming that we were lying about this particular doctrine; however, many people who had believed this doctrine, or else were somewhat toying with this particular way, began to investigate for themselves, and found to their dismay that what we were saying was true.

THE BLOOD AND THE OIL

Verses 14 through 18 read: *"And the Priest shall take some of the Blood of the Trespass-Offering, and the Priest shall put it upon the tip of the right ear of him who is to be cleansed, and upon the thumb of his right hand, and upon the great toe of his right foot:*

"And the Priest shall take some of the log

of oil, and pour it into the palm of his own left hand:

"And the Priest shall dip his right finger in the oil that is in his left hand, and shall sprinkle of the oil with his finger seven times before the LORD:

"And of the rest of the oil that is in his hand shall the Priest put upon the tip of the right ear of him that is to be cleansed, and upon the thumb of his right hand, and upon the great toe of his right foot, and upon the blood of the Trespass-Offering:

"And the remnant of the oil that is in the Priest's hand he shall pour upon the head of him who is to be cleansed: and the Priest shall make an Atonement for him before the LORD."

As we see in this Law of the cleansing of the leper, while water and oil were also employed, and played their part, thereby, types of the Word and the Holy Spirit, all in effect was based upon the preciousness and efficacy (effectiveness) of the shed blood. As we've already stated, apart from the Blood of Jesus, moral reformation and spiritual power are impossible.

When the Blood of the Trespass-Offering was poured out into a basin from the slain victim, the Priest then took the blood and put some on the *"tip of the right ear of him who was to be cleansed,"* typifying that all his hearing had now been cleansed by the blood, and henceforth, he would hear only that which is of the Lord. Blood was then placed on *"the thumb of his right hand,"* signifying that all that he *"did"* would now be according to Christ, and *"the great toe of his right foot,"* signifying that his *"walk"* was now straight. So we have the *"hearing,"* the *"doing,"* and the *"walking,"* actually signifying our living. If we *"hear right,"* then we will *"do right,"* and, thereby, *"walk right."* But the *"doing"* and the *"walking"* cannot be right, unless the *"hearing"* is correct. That's why Jesus said, *"He who has ears to hear, let him hear"* (Mat. 11:15), and, *"He who has an ear, let him hear what the Spirit says unto the Churches"* (Rev. 3:13).

If one has a problem with the *"doing"* and the *"walking,"* this means that one has a problem with the *"hearing."* In other words, they are hearing the wrong thing. And regrettably, that is the case with most Christians presently.

THE CROSS, OUR FAITH, AND THE HOLY SPIRIT

Most Christians simply don't know how to live a Godly, Christian life.

The real problem is that they have made the wrong thing the object of their faith. Every Christian in the world has faith (Rom. 12:3). And many Christians, due to much error being preached through the Word of Faith doctrine in the last few decades, are busy trying to increase their faith, when that's not their problem at all. In fact, the Disciples said to Christ at one particular place and time, *"Increase our faith"* (Lk. 17:5).

Jesus answered them by saying that it really wasn't an increase of Faith that they needed, but rather a proper placement of Faith.

He told them, *"If you had Faith as a grain of mustard seed . . ."* (Lk. 17:6).

Of course, the *"mustard seed"* is a very small seed. So Jesus was saying that it's not the quantity of our Faith that counts, but rather the quality.

Paul said: *"For Christ sent me not to baptize, but to preach the Gospel: not with wisdom of words, lest the Cross of Christ should be made of none effect"* (I Cor. 1:17).

He then said: *"But we preach Christ Crucified"* (I Cor. 1:23).

In effect, he is stating that the Gospel of Christ is the *"Cross of Christ,"* which refers to the benefits of the Cross, what Jesus did there, all on our behalf. The idea is, the Cross of Christ must be the object of our Faith. That being the case, the Holy Spirit will then help us, and do so grandly, which will help us to *"do right"* and *"walk right,"* simply because we are now *"hearing right."*

Far too many Christians have made Water Baptism, or the Lord's Supper, or their particular Church, or their good works, or even themselves, the object of their faith. This done, the Cross of Christ is made of none effect, which means that we are now in deep trouble (I Cor. 1:17).

If it is to be noticed, the blood was applied to the ear first, followed by the thumb, and then the great toe. That was done for

NOTES

purpose. For everything else to be right, we must first of all *"hear right."*

THE HOLY SPIRIT

The *"log of oil"* represented the Holy Spirit, but notice that it followed the blood.

He would pour some of the oil in his left hand, would then dip his right finger in the oil, and would sprinkle it toward the Holy of Holies seven times. This is what is meant by *"before the LORD."*

The blood having been applied, the Holy Spirit could now effect His Work in the heart and life of the former leper, i.e., *"sinner."*

One of the greatest lessons that the Believer can learn is how the Holy Spirit works. From this typology, and from Romans 8:1-2, we learn that the Spirit of God functions entirely within the framework of the Finished Work of Christ, i.e., *"the Blood."* The Blood of Christ being shed atoned for all sin, past, present, and future, which lifted the debt from the head of the sinner, and upon Faith, lets him go free. Perfectly cleansed, the former sinner now becomes a fit habitation for the Holy Spirit, but only after the Blood has been applied, which it is by Faith (Gal. 5:6).

The problem of the modern Church is that it is trying to get the Holy Spirit to work on the premise of *"works"* of some kind, which He will not do. In fact, the Christian who depends on anything other than the Cross, is in effect, looked at by God as a spiritual adulterer (Rom. 7:1-4). Consequently, I should think that all should know and realize that the Holy Spirit will definitely not help someone commit spiritual adultery. But that's exactly what the modern Church attempts to get the Holy Spirit to do.

As a result, the Church is left not with the Holy Spirit, but rather with *"spirits."*

In fact, the modern Pentecostal and Charismatic varieties have gone proverbially crazy over manifestations. They are mistaking these things for the Holy Spirit, when in fact, the Holy Spirit will have nothing to do with such proceedings. How do I know that?

While some manifestations definitely are of the Lord, thereby of the Holy Spirit, one can be certain that in such cases, the Preacher, in some way, is preaching the

Cross. But the modern variety, by no stretch of the imagination, is preaching the Cross. While there may be one here and there who does, the far greater majority doesn't! And if the Preacher doesn't preach the Cross, the Preacher is actually not preaching the Gospel (I Cor. 1:17-18, 21, 23; 2:2, 5; Gal., Chpt. 5; 6:14; Eph. 2:13-18).

The oil being sprinkled before the Lord seven times proclaimed a perfect cleansing. This means that the Holy Spirit has put His seal of approval upon the Finished Work of Christ. In fact, it was the Holy Spirit Who superintended the death of Christ. Paul writes:

"How much more shall the Blood of Christ, Who through the eternal Spirit offered Himself without spot to God, purge your conscience from dead works to serve the Living God?" (Heb. 9:14).

THE OIL APPLIED

The blood having now been applied to the tip of the right ear, the thumb of the right hand, and the great toe of the right foot, the oil was then placed accordingly, in fact, *"upon the blood of the Trespass-Offering."*

But again please notice that the *"oil,"* a type of the Holy Spirit, could not be applied, until the *"blood,"* a type of the Sacrifice of Christ, was first applied. How much clearer can the type be!

This tells us unequivocally that the Holy Spirit bases all that He does on the Finished Work of Christ. Paul, some 170 times in his 14 Epistles, used the term *"in Christ,"* or one of its derivatives. Every time it refers to Christ and what He did at the Cross. He tells us in Romans 8:2 that the *"Law of the Spirit of Life* (which is the Holy Spirit) *is in Christ Jesus,"* referring to the Cross, which refers to how the Holy Spirit works.

THE OIL ON THE HEAD

The oil that was left in the hand of the Priest was then to be *"poured upon the head of him who is to be cleansed,"* signifying the Anointing.

But again we state, and unequivocally, that it's all based on the Blood, i.e., *"the Sacrifice of Christ."* For anyone to say that the Blood alone does not atone, their statements

NOTES

border on blasphemy!

(19) "AND THE PRIEST SHALL OFFER THE SIN-OFFERING, AND MAKE AN ATONEMENT FOR HIM WHO IS TO BE CLEANSED FROM HIS UNCLEANNESS; AFTERWARD HE SHALL KILL THE BURNT-OFFERING:

(20) "AND THE PRIEST SHALL OFFER THE BURNT-OFFERING AND THE MEAT-OFFERING UPON THE ALTAR: AND THE PRIEST SHALL MAKE AN ATONEMENT FOR HIM, AND HE SHALL BE CLEAN.

(21) "AND IF HE BE POOR, AND CANNOT GET SO MUCH; THEN HE SHALL TAKE ONE LAMB FOR A TRESPASS-OFFERING TO BE WAVED, TO MAKE AN ATONEMENT FOR HIM, AND ONE TENTH DEAL OF FINE FLOUR MINGLED WITH OIL FOR A MEAT-OFFERING, AND A LOG OF OIL;

(22) "AND TWO TURTLEDOVES, OR TWO YOUNG PIGEONS, SUCH AS HE IS ABLE TO GET; AND THE ONE SHALL BE A SIN-OFFERING, AND THE OTHER A BURNT-OFFERING.

(23) "AND HE SHALL BRING THEM ON THE EIGHTH DAY FOR HIS CLEANSING UNTO THE PRIEST, UNTO THE DOOR OF THE TABERNACLE OF THE CONGREGATION, BEFORE THE LORD.

(24) "AND THE PRIEST SHALL TAKE THE LAMB OF THE TRESPASS-OFFERING, AND THE LOG OF OIL, AND THE PRIEST SHALL WAVE THEM FOR A WAVE-OFFERING BEFORE THE LORD:

(25) "AND HE SHALL KILL THE LAMB OF THE TRESPASS-OFFERING, AND THE PRIEST SHALL TAKE SOME OF THE BLOOD OF THE TRESPASS-OFFERING, PUT IT UPON THE TIP OF THE RIGHT EAR OF HIM WHO IS TO BE CLEANSED, AND UPON THE THUMB OF HIS RIGHT HAND, AND UPON THE GREAT TOE OF HIS RIGHT FOOT:

(26) "AND THE PRIEST SHALL POUR OF THE OIL INTO THE PALM OF HIS OWN LEFT HAND:

(27) "AND THE PRIEST SHALL SPRINKLE WITH HIS RIGHT FINGER SOME OF THE OIL THAT IS IN HIS LEFT HAND SEVEN TIMES BEFORE THE LORD:

(28) "AND THE PRIEST SHALL PUT

OF THE OIL THAT IS IN HIS HAND UPON THE TIP OF THE RIGHT EAR OF HIM WHO IS TO BE CLEANSED, AND UPON THE THUMB OF HIS RIGHT HAND, AND UPON THE GREAT TOE OF HIS RIGHT FOOT, UPON THE PLACE OF THE BLOOD OF THE TRESPASS-OFFERING:

(29) "AND THE REST OF THE OIL THAT IS IN THE PRIEST'S HAND HE SHALL PUT UPON THE HEAD OF HIM WHO IS TO BE CLEANSED, TO MAKE AN ATONEMENT TO BEFORE THE LORD.

(30) "AND HE SHALL OFFER THE ONE OF THE TURTLEDOVES, OR OF THE YOUNG PIGEONS, SUCH AS HE CAN GET;

(31) "EVEN SUCH AS HE IS ABLE TO GET, THE ONE FOR A SIN-OFFERING, AND THE OTHER FOR A BURNT-OFFER-ING, WITH THE MEAT-OFFERING: AND THE PRIEST SHALL MAKE AN ATONE-MENT FOR HIM WHO IS TO BE CLEANSED BEFORE THE LORD.

(32) "THIS IS THE LAW OF HIM IN WHOM IS THE PLAGUE OF LEPROSY, WHOSE HAND IS NOT ABLE TO GET THAT WHICH PERTAINS TO HIS CLEANSING."

The diagram is:

1. Two great facts shine here with exceptional luster; and both were of Grace. First, the uniting together of God's House with the leper's house; and, second, the placing side by side of the High priest and the leper; for these two were sprinkled with blood and anointed with oil. Only Aaron's sons were similarly consecrated; and thus, ceremonially, was the leper *put among the sons."*

2. The Priest represented our Great High Priest passed into the heavens. His double cleansing of the leper illustrated Justification and Sanctification.

3. The first cleansing, one might say, pictured Christ's Atoning Work for the sinner; the second cleansing, the Holy Spirit's Work in the Believer, giving him assurance of Salvation, deliverance from his sins, and power to live a holy life, and to enter into the Presence of God. The blood was his title, and the Spirit (oil) his capacity.

4. Verses 21-32 legislated, in Grace, for those who were too poor to provide the more costly Sacrifices; but in such cases it was

NOTES

absolute that the Sacrifice must be a sacrifice of blood (Heb., Chpts. 9-10).

THE SIN-OFFERING, THE BURNT-OFFERING, AND THE MEAT-OFFERING

The other ewe lamb mentioned in Verse 10 is now offered as a Sin-Offering. Symbolically, this pictures Christ taking the sinner's guilt.

After the Sin-Offering was presented, the Priest was now to kill the *"Burnt-Offering."* As the Sin-Offering took the sinner's guilt and placed it on Christ, the Burnt-Offering, would now take the Perfection of Christ and give it to the believing sinner.

The Priest, who presented the Offering on behalf of the leper, would eat, along with others, most of the Sin-Offering, with the fat being burned on the Altar, thus becoming one with the sinner, so to speak. The Burnt-Offering was the only Offering which was burnt wholly on the Altar, along with the fat. As stated, it proclaimed the Perfection of Christ, which Perfection God could accept in Sacrifice, meaning that no sin could be found within or without the heart, life, and physical body of the Son of God.

The *"Meat-Offering"* was then offered up, with a small part of it burnt on the Altar, and the balance eaten by the Priest. In this manner the *"Priest,"* who was a type of Christ, would *"make an Atonement for the leper, and he shall be clean."*

This is a perfect picture of the believing sinner coming to Christ, and the Work that Christ carries out in order for the sinner to be cleansed. All of these intricate details were carried out at the Cross.

THE POOR

Verse 21 and following proclaim the fact that if the leper could not afford to bring three lambs, he could instead bring one lamb, and then two turtledoves. But in all cases, as stated, it was absolutely necessary that the Sacrifice be a Sacrifice of blood.

However, even though the Sacrifices may be altered somewhat, as stated, the ritual was identical for the poor man's sacrifices, as it was for the rich. Concerning this, Ellicott says, *"The solemnity and imposing nature of the service is not diminished as both rich and poor are alike in the Presence of the Lord."* There is no difference!

As someone has well said, *"The ground is level at the foot of the Cross,"* meaning that the Cross puts all men on an equal footing, which refers to their desperate need of Salvation, and, thereby, a Saviour, irrespective as to whom they might be.

AN EXAMPLE

I had the privilege of coming under the Ministry of one of the great men of God of the Twentieth Century, A. N. Trotter. I also had the privilege of ministering with him in a number of Campmeetings, even though, to be sure, I was woefully inadequate for the task. As the Lord used this man, seldom, if ever, have I seen it repeated. But that which I saw helped mold and make my own personal Ministry.

He often told of his experience of being baptized with the Holy Spirit. If I remember correctly, the year of this wonderful happening was 1914. And then somewhat as an aside, he related the experience as well of the dear lady who helped him go through to his own personal Baptism.

She was the wife of one of the most famous surgeons in the world of that day. Actually, he was noted to be at least one of the most authoritative cancer specialists. People came to him from all over the world.

And then his wife, the dear lady of our illustration, contracted cancer herself. Her husband secured for her surgery other surgeons of like qualifications. The day was set; they would try their best to save her life.

HER HEALING

Somehow, whether by an advertisement in the newspaper, or however, she heard of a meeting in town where they were praying for the sick. Knowing that her chances for survival were very poor, she made plans to attend this meeting.

Very wealthy, she arrived at the meeting in her big Packard, and was surprised to find that it was merely a storefront, and only a few people had gathered. Beside that, it was in a poor part of town.

She started not to go in, asking herself the question, what possible good could develop

NOTES

from this?

At any rate, she overrode her negative thoughts, with curiosity helping her to go into the Service.

She was Presbyterian, a member of the elite society of that city, very wealthy, very educated; therefore, she was not very much impressed by her surroundings, which were very humble, to say the least.

The Preacher brought forth his message, and after the Service, noting that she stood out in the crowd, walked over to her and introduced himself. In the course of the conversation, he asked her if she was saved.

Not wanting to be impolite, she mumbled something, as he handed her a little tract explaining Salvation, which she took with her as she left.

When she got in her car to go home after the Service, she was incensed. The very idea, this man asking her if she was saved! Didn't he know that she was a member of the Presbyterian Church! Didn't he know that she was, as well, a member of the elite society of that city! Beside that, he hardly prayed for her that night, as it regarded her healing. She resolved in her mind that this was a wasted effort.

But the next day, there was a tug at her mind and heart to once again go back to the meeting. She found herself dressing, and then driving toward this particular place across town. She couldn't understand the reason why she was going, and in fact, none of it made any sense. But she went!

That night, she was a little more receptive to the Message, as the Word of God was preached. And then at a given time in the Service, the Preacher asked for those who were ill to come forward, exclaiming that the Lord was able to heal the sick.

She felt herself arising and walking toward the front. In a moment's time, he anointed her head with oil, which she had never experienced before, and began to pray.

And then, something happened, like she had never known before in all of her life. For the first time, she felt the Power of God. It went through her physical frame like hot oil, and in some way, in some manner, she knew she was healed of cancer. Beside that, at that moment, she gave her heart and life to Jesus Christ, and now knew what it was to be saved. In fact, a few nights later she would be baptized with the Holy Spirit, with the evidence of speaking with other tongues as the Spirit of God gave the utterance (Acts 2:4).

Upon arriving home, she immediately testified to her husband and her son, with the latter, as well, being a surgeon, that she was healed. Their immediate thoughts were that the cancer had affected her mind.

The morning of the surgery, for they insisted that she go ahead with the procedure, they gave her a pill to take, which would prepare her for the coming ordeal. She took the pill and rolled it across the floor like a marble, not taking it.

The father and the son stood in a room overlooking the operating room, as their wife and mother underwent surgery. At a given point, one of the doctors left the operating room, and came to where the husband and son were. With a puzzled look on his face, he questioned the world-famous surgeon.

"I don't understand," he said! *"There is no trace of cancer in your wife."* And then he asked, *"What made you think that she had cancer?"*

The husband offered no explanation, but in his heart he knew what she had told him some hours before. *"I am healed. The Lord Jesus Christ has healed me completely, and I have no more cancer."*

She was right; she had no more cancer.

God used her in a mighty way in that part of the world. She saw many people saved, many people healed, and many baptized with the Holy Spirit. As previously stated, the great man of God, A. N. Trotter, was baptized with the Holy Spirit under her Ministry.

Yes, the rich and the poor must come alike!

(33) "AND THE LORD SPOKE UNTO MOSES AND UNTO AARON, SAYING,

(34) "WHEN YOU BE COME INTO THE LAND OF CANAAN, WHICH I GIVE TO YOU FOR A POSSESSION, AND I PUT THE PLAGUE OF LEPROSY IN A HOUSE OF THE LAND OF YOUR POSSESSION;

(35) "AND HE WHO OWNS THE HOUSE SHALL COME AND TELL THE PRIEST, SAYING, IT SEEMS TO ME THERE IS AS

IT WERE A PLAGUE IN THE HOUSE:

(36) "THEN THE PRIEST SHALL COMMAND THAT THEY EMPTY THE HOUSE, BEFORE THE PRIEST GO INTO IT TO SEE THE PLAGUE, THAT ALL THAT IS IN THE HOUSE BE NOT MADE UNCLEAN: AND AFTERWARD THE PRIEST SHALL GO IN TO SEE THE HOUSE:

(37) "AND HE SHALL LOOK ON THE PLAGUE, AND, BEHOLD, IF THE PLAGUE BE IN THE WALLS OF THE HOUSE WITH HOLLOW STRAKES, GREENISH OR REDDISH, WHICH IN SIGHT ARE LOWER THAN THE WALL;

(38) "THEN THE PRIEST SHALL GO OUT OF THE HOUSE TO THE DOOR OF THE HOUSE, AND SHUT UP THE HOUSE SEVEN DAYS:

(39) "AND THE PRIEST SHALL COME AGAIN THE SEVENTH DAY, AND SHALL LOOK: AND, BEHOLD, IF THE PLAGUE BE SPREAD IN THE WALLS OF THE HOUSE;

(40) "THEN THE PRIEST SHALL COMMAND THAT THEY TAKE AWAY THE STONES IN WHICH THE PLAGUE IS, AND THEY SHALL CAST THEM INTO AN UNCLEAN PLACE WITHOUT THE CITY:

(41) "AND HE SHALL CAUSE THE HOUSE TO BE SCRAPED WITHIN ROUND ABOUT, AND THEY SHALL POUR OUT THE DUST THAT THEY SCRAPE OFF WITHOUT THE CITY INTO AN UNCLEAN PLACE:

(42) "AND THEY SHALL TAKE OTHER STONES, AND PUT THEM IN THE PLACE OF THOSE STONES; HE SHALL TAKE OTHER MORTAR, AND SHALL PLASTER THE HOUSE.

(43) "AND IF THE PLAGUE COME AGAIN, AND BREAK OUT IN THE HOUSE, AFTER THAT HE HAS TAKEN AWAY THE STONES, AND AFTER HE HAS SCRAPED THE HOUSE, AND AFTER IT IS PLASTERED;

(44) "THEN THE PRIEST SHALL COME AND LOOK, AND, BEHOLD, IF THE PLAGUE BE SPREAD IN THE HOUSE, IT IS A FRETTING LEPROSY IN THE HOUSE; IT IS UNCLEAN.

(45) "AND HE SHALL BREAK DOWN THE HOUSE, THE STONES OF IT, AND THE TIMBER THEREOF, AND ALL THE MORTAR OF THE HOUSE; HE SHALL

CARRY THEM FORTH OUT OF THE CITY INTO AN UNCLEAN PLACE."

The exegesis is:

1. All of this, even as we have seen, and shall see, there is but one cure for sin, whether in an individual, or a community, or in nature, and that one cure is the cleansing Blood of Christ.

2. If the plague of leprosy was found to be in a part of a house, the entire house was not to be condemned, but only the leprous stones removed. We find parallels to this in the Church.

3. Sin, wherever found, must be dealt with, or else it will quickly spread until it envelops the whole.

THE PLAGUE IN THE HOUSE

Verses 33 through 38 read: *"And the LORD spoke unto Moses and unto Aaron, saying,*

"When you be come into the land of Canaan, which I give to you for a possession, and I put the plague of leprosy in a house of the land of your possession;

"And he who owns the house shall come and tell the Priest, saying, It seems to me there is as it were a plague in the house:

"Then the Priest shall command that they empty the house, before the Priest go into it to see the plague, that all that is in the house be not made unclean: and afterward the Priest shall go in to see the house:

"And he shall look on the plague, and, behold, if the plague be in the walls of the house with hollow strakes, greenish or reddish, which in sight are lower than the wall;

"Then the Priest shall go out of the house to the door of the house, and shut up the house seven days."

Bringing this up to the time of the Cross, we will attempt to apply it to our modern circumstances. The Church at Corinth is an excellent example. It was a spiritual house, composed of spiritual stones.

In that particular house at Corinth, there was found the plague of leprosy, i.e., *"a man who had taken up with his father's wife,"* evidently while the father was still alive (I Cor., Chpt. 5).

Paul informed the Church that this man had to repent, which means dissolving the relationship, as should be obvious, or else he

had to be excommunicated. He used *"leaven"* as an example. If it's not removed, it will ultimately infect the whole.

In his second Letter to the Corinthians, he faces the potential of a different type of leprosy, so to speak, but leprosy all the same.

In the Second Chapter of that Epistle, he deals with the Church, as it respects their forgiving a particular individual. Whether the man mentioned is the same as the one in Chapter 5 of I Corinthians, we aren't told; however, it actually makes no difference. In the first Epistle, the man was on trial, and now in the second Epistle, the Church is on trial.

It seems the man had repented, whomever he might have been, and now Paul is admonishing the Church that they must forgive him, and restore him. If they fail to do so, their sin of unforgiveness would be just as bad, if not worse, than the sin committed by the individual in question.

The moral of all of this is, sin cannot remain in the house. If it is an open type of sin, and the individual is a member of the Church, he must be admonished to repent, thereby leaving that particular sin. If he refuses, he has to be excommunicated.

But even then, he is not to be treated as an enemy, but rather *"Admonished as a brother"* (II Thess. 3:14-15).

BREAK DOWN THE HOUSE

Verses 39 through 45 read: *"And the Priest shall come again the seventh day, and shall look: and, behold, if the plague be spread in the walls of the house;*

"Then the Priest shall command that they take away the stones in which the plague is, and they shall cast them into an unclean place without the city:

"And he shall cause the house to be scraped within round about, and they shall pour out the dust that they scrape off without the city into an unclean place:

"And they shall take other stones, and put them in the place of those stones; and he shall take other mortar, and shall plaster the house.

"And if the plague come again, and break out in the house, after that he has taken away the stones, and after he has scraped the house,

and after it is plastered;

"Then the Priest shall come and look, and, behold, if the plague be spread in the house, it is a fretting leprosy in the house; it is unclean.

"And he shall break down the house, the stones of it, and the timber thereof, and all the mortar of the house; he shall carry them forth out of the city into an unclean place."

As is obvious, if the leprosy had spread throughout the house, the house was to be dismantled in every respect, with the ruins taken to an unclean place outside of the city.

Bringing the type unto the present, actually into the entirety of the Church Age, we must conclude that if a Fellowship or Denomination has left the ways of the Lord, and is going in another direction, there must be a clean break from that particular *"house."* While the house may continue to exist, and even thrive according to the standards of the world, as far as God is concerned, it is *"no more."* The leprosy, i.e., *"sin,"* began small; however, it was not properly addressed, and ultimately and eventually, it overtook the entirety of the house, with it then, at least spiritually speaking, slated for destruction.

Many, if not most, of the modern Pentecostal Denominations, sadly and regrettably, fall into that category. Only about one-third of the people associated with these particular Churches even claim to be Spirit-filled anymore. Scores in these Churches, even their Preachers, frown on *"speaking with other tongues,"* which means they little believe in the doctrine anymore, if at all! As well, most of these Denominations have followed their Denominational brothers, and have opted for humanistic psychology, which means, despite what they might try to say otherwise, that they have registered a vote of no confidence as it regards the Cross. That being the case, the Holy Spirit, Who is the sparkplug of any Move of God, is very little present, if present at all!

The last several years I was with a major Pentecostal Denomination, despite the fact that we were touching much of the world by Television, seeing hundreds of thousands brought to a saving knowledge of Jesus Christ, and was actually the cause of most of their growth, the leadership little

frequented our meetings, if at all. In fact, if not downright hostile, they were at least very noncommittal.

I pleaded with them to come to the meetings, some of which drew some of the largest crowds in the world of that time, and saw tremendous things done for Christ, even entire nations moved. They little responded.

And then they began to grow more and more hostile, claiming that I was wanting to split the Denomination. The truth is, I cared about as much for Denominational politics, as I did a bad case of the flu. In fact, I had no interest whatsoever. My business was and is the preaching of the Gospel, attempting to get people saved and lives changed. I have no interest in the other!

During this time of increasing hostility, I would plead with them to come to the meetings, believing in my heart that if they could see the Moving and Operation of the Holy Spirit, they would change their attitudes.

What I did not then know, but was to later find out, it was the Moving and the Operation of the Holy Spirit they did not want or desire. Why?

The Holy Spirit cannot be controlled, and the name of their game is *"control."*

Millions think it was the events of 1988 that fueled their animosity toward me with increasing intensity. It wasn't! That was merely an excuse.

It is my prayer that this particular Denomination, and in fact, all Pentecostal Denominations, will experience Revival. I know the Lord is able, if men will just give Him half an opportunity. But for Revival to come, two things have to happen:

1. There has to be a hunger for the things of God. They who hunger and thirst after Righteousness shall be filled.

2. For true Revival to come, the Church has to come back to the Cross. This is not optional, even as the first point is not optional. Outside of the Cross, there is no Moving of the Spirit, at least that is true, no souls saved, no lives changed, no Believers baptized with the Holy Spirit, no people healed by the Power of God, in short, nothing! There may be a lot of religious machinery, and in fact, there is always a lot of religious machinery; however, outside of the

Cross, nothing is truly done for God.

I wonder if the same thing will be said of the Church, as it was of Israel, when the Master said: *"O Jerusalem, Jerusalem, you who killed the Prophets, and stoned them which are sent unto you, how often would I have gathered your children together, even as a hen gathers her chickens under wings, and you would not!*

"Behold, your house is left unto you desolate" (Mat. 23:37-38).

THE CROSS AND THE CHURCH

In fact, the Holy Spirit is proclaiming the Message of the Cross to the modern Church, perhaps as never before, or at least since the time of Paul in the Early Church. Will the majority of the Church accept this Message?

Some will; most won't! So the truth is this:

As the Second Coming of Christ will in effect save the world, and I speak of saving the world from destruction, likewise, the Rapture will save the Church. Were it not for the Rapture, the facts are, there would be no True Church left. In other words, the situation is not getting better, but rather worse.

While some will wax strong in the Lord, and even do great and mighty things, the far greater majority who presently call themselves Christians, in fact, do not know the Lord.

(46) "MOREOVER HE WHO GOES INTO THE HOUSE ALL THE WHILE THAT IT IS SHUT UP SHALL BE UNCLEAN UNTIL THE EVENING.

(47) "AND HE WHO LIES IN THE HOUSE SHALL WASH HIS CLOTHES; AND HE WHO EATS IN THE HOUSE SHALL WASH HIS CLOTHES.

(48) "AND IF THE PRIEST SHALL COME IN, AND LOOK UPON IT, AND, BEHOLD, THE PLAGUE HAS NOT SPREAD IN THE HOUSE, AFTER THE HOUSE WAS PLASTERED: THEN THE PRIEST SHALL PRONOUNCE THE HOUSE CLEAN, BECAUSE THE PLAGUE IS HEALED.

(49) "AND HE SHALL TAKE TO CLEANSE THE HOUSE TWO BIRDS, AND CEDAR WOOD, AND SCARLET, AND HYSSOP:

(50) "AND HE SHALL KILL THE ONE OF THE BIRDS IN AN EARTHEN VESSEL OVER RUNNING WATER:

NOTES

(51) "AND HE SHALL TAKE THE CEDAR WOOD, AND THE HYSSOP, AND THE SCARLET, AND THE LIVING BIRD, AND DIP THEM IN THE BLOOD OF THE SLAIN BIRD, AND IN THE RUNNING WATER, AND SPRINKLE THE HOUSE SEVEN TIMES:

(52) "AND HE SHALL CLEANSE THE HOUSE WITH THE BLOOD OF THE BIRD, AND WITH THE RUNNING WATER, AND WITH THE LIVING BIRD, AND WITH THE CEDAR WOOD, AND WITH THE HYSSOP, AND WITH THE SCARLET:

(53) "BUT HE SHALL LET GO THE LIVING BIRD OUT OF THE CITY INTO THE OPEN FIELDS, AND MAKE AN ATONEMENT FOR THE HOUSE: AND IT SHALL BE CLEAN.

(54) "THIS IS THE LAW FOR ALL MANNER OF PLAGUE OF LEPROSY, AND SCALL,

(55) "AND FOR THE LEPROSY OF A GARMENT, AND OF A HOUSE,

(56) "AND FOR A RISING, AND FOR A SCAB, AND FOR A BRIGHT SPOT:

(57) "TO TEACH WHEN IT IS UNCLEAN, AND WHEN IT IS CLEAN: THIS IS THE LAW OF LEPROSY."

The structure is:

1. The cleansing of the house, which as is obvious, was a material structure, as it regards the plague of leprosy, for all practical purposes, was the same as the cleansing of the leper himself. In all cases, even material objects, the blood had to be applied.

2. For this second heading, I will quote Mackintosh: *"I do not doubt in the least that this whole subject of leprosy has a great dispensational bearing, not only upon the house of Israel, but also upon the professing Church."*

3. As another example, the Divine Priest stands in a judicial attitude with respect to his house at Pergamos (Rev. 2:12-16). He could not be indifferent to symptoms so alarming, but He patiently and graciously gives time to repent. If reproof, warning, and discipline prove unavailing, judgment must take its course.

THE CROSS AND CLEANSING

Of course we know that material things, at least within themselves, have no spiritual quality. They are lifeless, and, therefore, void of such; however, the disease in the house could conceivably infect those who would live in the house, hence the need for cleansing, and if the situation is bad enough, for the structure to be demolished, and taken to a place for contaminated material.

But if the plague had not spread sufficiently for the house to be destroyed, and it could be salvaged, and the appropriate steps taken to remove the infected parts, still, basically, the same type of ceremony had to be undergone in order for the house to be pronounced as *"clean."*

This shows to us the absolute significance of the Cross of Christ. Everything that is infected with sin, irrespective as to what it is, if the situation is to be rectified, it can only be rectified by the Cross.

This means that when a person comes to Christ, everything about that person, all that they own, including property, personal possessions, or whatever, must come under the scrutiny of the Gospel. It's somewhat like the answer that Moses gave to Pharaoh when the Egyptian Monarch demanded that all the cattle and sheep be left behind, when the Children of Israel vacated Egypt; *"Not one hoof shall be left behind"* was the response of the great Lawgiver.

In a humorous sort of way, one might say that when a person comes to Christ, not only do they get saved, but their car gets saved, their pets get saved, their personal possessions get saved, their money gets saved, their work gets saved, their hobbies get saved, that is if they have such, which means that everything must come under the scrutiny of the Gospel. And if a person truly gives their heart to Christ, that's exactly what will happen.

Now this might mean that some activities will have to cease; some things being done will have to change or even stop. But I'm afraid in many cases, regarding many who claim Salvation little, if anything, changes at all. This is a sure sign that such people have not truly met Christ. To be sure, when one has an encounter with the King of kings and the Lord of lords, there will definitely be a change in one's life, and in everything about one's life. If the Gospel is anything, the Gospel is that!

While we preach Christ Crucified, and that Salvation comes by Faith alone, simply because the Word proclaims that (Eph. 2:8-9), still, true Salvation will always point to a surrender of self to the obedience of Christ. In other words, there must be a total change in the whole manner of life.

We must come to the conclusion that if what we profess is not powerful enough to work a complete revolution in our lives, leading us to obey and follow Christ, it will avail us nothing before God.

"Mistaken souls, who dream of Heaven,
"And make their empty boast
"Of inward joys and sins forgiven,
"While they are slaves to lust!"

"Vain are our fancies, airy flights,
"If faith be cold and dead;
"None but a living power unites
"To Christ, the Living Head."

"A Faith that changes all the heart;
"A Faith that works by love;
"That bids all sinful joys depart,
"And lifts the thoughts above."

"Faith must obey our Father's Will,
"As well as trust His Grace:
"A pardoning God is jealous still
"For His Own Holiness."

CHAPTER 15

(1) "AND THE LORD SPOKE UNTO MOSES AND TO AARON, SAYING,

(2) "SPEAK UNTO THE CHILDREN OF ISRAEL, AND SAY UNTO THEM, WHEN ANY MAN HAS A RUNNING ISSUE OUT OF HIS FLESH, BECAUSE OF HIS ISSUE HE IS UNCLEAN.

(3) "AND THIS SHALL BE HIS UNCLEANNESS IN HIS ISSUE: WHETHER HIS FLESH RUN WITH HIS ISSUE, OR HIS FLESH BE STOPPED FROM HIS ISSUE, IT IS HIS UNCLEANNESS.

(4) "EVERY BED, WHEREON HE LIES THAT HAS THE ISSUE, IS UNCLEAN: AND EVERY THING, WHEREON HE SITS, SHALL BE UNCLEAN.

(5) "AND WHOSOEVER TOUCHES HIS

BED SHALL WASH HIS CLOTHES, AND BATHE HIMSELF IN WATER, AND BE UNCLEAN UNTIL THE EVENING.

(6) "AND HE WHO SITS ON ANYTHING WHEREON HE SAT THAT HAS THE ISSUE SHALL WASH HIS CLOTHES, AND BATHE HIMSELF IN WATER, AND BE UNCLEAN UNTIL THE EVENING.

(7) "AND HE WHO TOUCHES THE FLESH OF HIM WHO HAS THE ISSUE SHALL WASH HIS CLOTHES, AND BATHE HIMSELF IN WATER, AND BE UNCLEAN UNTIL THE EVENING.

(8) "AND IF HE WHO HAS THE ISSUE SPIT UPON HIM WHO IS CLEAN; THEN HE SHALL WASH HIS CLOTHES, AND BATHE HIMSELF IN WATER, AND BE UNCLEAN UNTIL THE EVENING.

(9) "AND WHAT SADDLE SOEVER HE RIDES UPON WHO HAS THE ISSUE SHALL BE UNCLEAN.

(10) "AND WHOSOEVER TOUCHES ANYTHING THAT WAS UNDER HIM SHALL BE UNCLEAN UNTIL THE EVENING: HE WHO BEARS ANY OF THOSE THINGS SHALL WASH HIS CLOTHES, AND BATHE HIMSELF IN WATER, AND BE UNCLEAN UNTIL THE EVENING.

(11) "AND WHOMSOEVER HE TOUCHES WHO HAS THE ISSUE, AND HAS NOT RINSED HIS HANDS IN WATER, HE SHALL WASH HIS CLOTHES, AND BATHE HIMSELF IN WATER, AND BE UNCLEAN UNTIL THE EVENING."

The composition is:

1. The lessons of this Chapter are: first, the Holiness of God and of His Dwelling place.

2. Second, the loving and minute interest that He takes in the habits of His children. Nothing was too small or too private for Him. Their clothing and their health concerned Him deeply.

3. Third, the corruption of fallen nature; it defiled. Walking or sleeping, sitting, standing, or lying, its every touch conveyed pollution – a painful lesson for proud humanity (Williams).

THE RUNNING ISSUE

Verses 1 through 3 read: *"And the LORD spoke unto Moses and to Aaron, saying,*

"Speak unto the Children of Israel, and

say unto them, When any man has a running issue out of his flesh, because of his issue he is unclean.

"And this shall be his uncleanness in his issue: whether his flesh run with his issue, or his flesh be stopped from his issue, it is his uncleanness."

The Hebrew word for *"issue"* is *"zuwb,"* and means, *"to have a sexual flux."* It probably refers to *"gonorrhea,"* or *"blenorrhea."*

This Chapter, as we shall see, deals with diseases caused by personal sin, but as well, deals with diseases not caused by personal sin.

But the main thrust is that we understand, due to the Fall, that the whole of nature is defiled, and in every capacity. That's why Paul said: *"For the earnest expectation of creation waits for the manifestation of the sons of God.*

"For the creation was made subject to vanity, not willingly (due to the Fall, but which it had no part), *but by reason of Him Who* (God) *has subjected the same in hope* (God because of man's sin subjected the creation to death; but He did so in hope, for He looks forward to its recovery when man shall be redeemed. Creation shares this hope and waits for it.),

"Because the creation itself also shall be delivered from the bondage of corruption into the glorious liberty of the Children of God.

"For we know that the whole creation groans and travails in pain together until now" (Rom. 8:19-22).

The giving of these ceremonial rituals, for they within themselves cleansed nothing, were given in order that we may understand not only the terrible power of sin, but as well the totality of the Fall, and above all, the cure for these terrible things, which alone is the Cross of Christ. When we read these Passages, these are the truths that the Holy Spirit means for us to comprehend and understand.

Among many other things, the lesson is taught here that we may be great sinners without anybody else knowing anything about it. There may be no word spoken, no act done, no voluntary motion put forth, and we'd still be unclean by a silent and unintentional oozing out of a carnal heart. In fact, there may be a very correct exterior life, and yet a secret cherishing of pride, lust, and unbelief, and a secret painting of the walls with imagery, so to speak, as much unfitting us for the society of the pure and good, as any open and out-breaking wickedness. Even the quiet and involuntary emotions of natural feeling are often to be numbered with the uncleanest things (Seiss).

THIS EVIL WORLD

As any Believer knows and understands, at least if he knows anything at all about the Word of God, this world, and I speak of its systems, is evil beyond comprehension. For instance, we get only basic cable in our house; but yet, several of those channels are so ribald as to be offensive, at least to a Believer. However, the truth is, the entirety of the system of this world is evil. Paul said:

"Who gave Himself for our sins, that He might deliver us from this present evil world, according to the Will of God and our Father" (Gal. 1:4).

UNCLEAN

Verses 4 through 11 read: *"Every bed, whereon he lies who has the issue, is unclean: every thing, whereon he sits, shall be unclean.*

"And whosoever touches his bed shall wash his clothes, and bathe himself in water, and be unclean until the evening.

"And he who sits on anything whereon he sat who has the issue shall wash his clothes, and bathe himself in water, and be unclean until the evening.

"And he who touches the flesh of him who has the issue shall wash his clothes, and bathe himself in water, and be unclean until the evening.

"And if he who has the issue spit upon him who is clean; then he shall wash his clothes, and bathe himself in water, and be unclean until the evening.

"And what saddle soever he rides upon who has the issue shall be unclean.

"And whosoever touches anything that was under him shall be unclean until the evening: he who bears any of those things shall wash his clothes, and bathe himself in water, and be unclean until the evening.

"And whomsoever he touches who has the issue, and has not rinsed his hands in water,

NOTES

he shall wash his clothes, and bathe himself in water, and be unclean until the evening."

It is amazing how deep-seated the contaminations of sin are. Even the Godliest Believer, who loves the Lord supremely, and is attempting to live for God to the best of his ability, who trusts in Christ and what Christ has done for us at the Cross, still, due to the contamination, will find sin unintentionally escaping from him, contaminating himself and those who come in contact with him, or touch what he has touched, spiritually speaking. In fact, the whole nature of the Believer is yet so full of remaining corruption, that the least agitation causes it to trickle over. The Believer, occasionally, even finds it in his dreams. He puts forth his hand to welcome a friend, and the very touch sometimes awakes wrong echoes in the soul. Depravity cleaves to the best of us, like an old sore. It defiles the solitude with unclean thoughts. Paul said: *"I find a law, that when I would do good, evil is present with me"* (Rom. 7:21).

The Believer has two powerful factors that apply to our lives and living. They are:

1. Paul said: *"For all have sinned, and come short of the Glory of God"* (Rom. 3:23).

It would seem that this statement refers to past times; however, the actual meaning in the Greek is that not only did we come short of the Glory of God in times past, but we're doing so on a continual basis at present, and in fact, will do so until we die, or the trump sounds. That being the case, and it definitely is, how can we stand justified before the Lord?

John said: *"But if we walk in the Light* (the Word of God), *as He* (Christ) *is in the Light, we have fellowship one with another* (we have fellowship with Christ), *and the Blood of Jesus Christ His Son cleanses us from all sin"* (I Jn. 1:7).

One might say that as we are constantly coming short of the Glory of God, the Blood is constantly cleansing.

This is done because Christ, as our Great High Priest, is constantly making intercession for us (Heb. 7:25-26).

This was typified in the Tabernacle of old, by the Golden Altar which sat immediately in front of the Holy of Holies. On that Golden

Altar, twice a day, the time of the morning and evening Sacrifices, coals of fire were to be taken from the Brazen Altar, placed on the Golden Altar, with incense poured over the coals, which would fill the Holy Place with a beautiful and wonderful aroma. This signified our person, in fact, our very being, being made acceptable to God, pleasant one might say, due to what Christ did at the Cross, and our Faith in that eternal work. In short, the Golden Altar typified Christ interceding for us, in His High Priestly role, which He occupies at present.

2. No matter how hard the Believer tries, no matter how sincere he is, no matter how zealous he might be, he cannot live a victorious, overcoming, Christian life, unless he understands the Cross, thereby properly placing his faith, which then gives the Holy Spirit latitude to work (Rom. 6:3-14; Gal. 5:6; 6:14; I Cor. 1:17-18, 23; Rom. 8:1-2, 11).

Everything, and I mean everything, is found in the Cross. The Cross is the solution to every problem; the Cross is the answer to every question; the Cross is the means by which all things are given to us by God. And when we speak of the Cross, as I'm sure the Reader understands, we're not speaking of a wooden beam, but rather, the benefits that come from that which Christ did for us. It is all found in the Cross. We are saved because of what Jesus did at the Cross, and our Faith in that Finished Work. Likewise, we are sanctified by what Jesus did at the Cross, and our continued Faith in that Finished Work.

SCRIPTURAL IGNORANCE

Unfortunately, far too many Christians, virtually all, little understand the Sanctification process. They little know that the Holy Spirit Alone can effect this process, which means they try to sanctify themselves. And even if they know that it's the Holy Spirit Alone Who can sanctify, they little know how He works. In fact, virtually all Christians think that the Work of the Holy Spirit is automatic in the lives of Believers. Nothing could be further from the truth.

The Spirit of God works entirely within the framework of the Sacrifice of Christ (Jn. 14:16-17; Acts 1:8; Rom. 8:1-2, 11).

NOTES

FAITH

The whole Plan of Redemption is built on the premise of *"Faith."* Paul said: *"For in Jesus Christ neither circumcision availeth anything, nor uncircumcision; but Faith which works by love"* (Gal. 5:6).

He also said: *"Therefore it is of Faith, that it might be by Grace"* (Rom. 4:16).

He then said: *"Therefore being justified by Faith, we have peace with God through our Lord Jesus Christ:*

"By Whom also we have access by Faith into this Grace wherein we stand" (Rom. 5:1-2).

So what is Paul talking about, when he continually speaks of *"Faith"*?

Many Christians talk constantly of Faith, but then try to earn everything by and through works. Our Word of Faith friends think that quoting Scripture over and over is what increases Faith. It won't! In this manner we turn the Scripture into *"works."*

The truth is, unless we understand what the correct object of Faith ought to be, we're really not going to get very much done for the Lord. Merely having Faith is not enough. In fact, every human being in the world has faith, but it's not the kind that God recognizes.

The only kind of Faith that God will recognize is Faith that's placed in Christ and in what He has done for us at the Cross. That is having Faith in the Word. The Word is the story of the Cross, as is obvious from Genesis through the Book of Revelation. That's why Paul also said: *"But God forbid that I should glory, save in the Cross of our Lord Jesus Christ, by Whom the world is crucified unto me, and I unto the world"* (Gal. 6:14).

In all of Paul's writings, you will not find one single time where he admonishes Believers to confess the Scriptures over and over, in order to obtain results from the Lord. He didn't say anything about this, because the Holy Spirit didn't want him to, and because it's not Scriptural.

While it's wonderful to quote Scripture constantly, which every Believer ought to do; nevertheless, the mere quoting of Scripture over and over again, thereby confessing the Word of God, does not move God to action. God is moved to action only by and through

His Son, the Lord Jesus Christ, and what Christ did at the Cross on our behalf. Faith in Him and what He has done for us grants us His Blessings, which are all brought by the Holy Spirit.

Once again, please allow me to reiterate that it's the object of Faith which is so very, very important, which without exception, must always be the Cross of Christ.

When the Believer places his Faith properly, and keeps it there, and we continue to speak of the Cross, the Holy Spirit will then help him to live the holy and Godly life, which he ought to live, and in fact, wants to live. But it can only be done one way, and that is through *"Jesus Christ and Him Crucified"* (I Cor. 1:23).

Remember, when you study this Fifteenth Chapter of Leviticus, we must ever understand that it was written for our learning. We are to read it in the Spirit, and then it will have a spiritual application. To read it any other way is to wrest it to our own destruction, which I'm certain we don't want to do.

(12) "AND THE VESSEL OF EARTH, THAT HE TOUCHES WHO HAS THE ISSUE, SHALL BE BROKEN: AND EVERY VESSEL OF WOOD SHALL BE RINSED IN WATER.

(13) "AND WHEN WHO HAS AN ISSUE IS CLEANSED OF HIS ISSUE; THEN HE SHALL NUMBER TO HIMSELF SEVEN DAYS FOR HIS CLEANSING, AND WASH HIS CLOTHES, AND BATHE HIS FLESH IN RUNNING WATER, AND SHALL BE CLEAN.

(14) "AND ON THE EIGHTH DAY HE SHALL TAKE TO HIM TWO TURTLE-DOVES, OR TWO YOUNG PIGEONS, AND COME BEFORE THE LORD UNTO THE DOOR OF THE TABERNACLE OF THE CONGREGATION, AND GIVE THEM UNTO THE PRIEST:

(15) "AND THE PRIEST SHALL OFFER THEM, THE ONE FOR A SIN-OFFERING, AND THE OTHER FOR A BURNT-OFFERING; AND THE PRIEST SHALL MAKE AN ATONEMENT FOR HIM BEFORE THE LORD FOR HIS ISSUE.

(16) "AND IF ANY MAN'S SEED OF COPULATION GO OUT FROM HIM, THEN HE SHALL WASH ALL HIS FLESH

NOTES

IN WATER, AND BE UNCLEAN UNTIL THE EVENING.

(17) "AND EVERY GARMENT, AND EVERY SKIN, WHEREON IS THE SEED OF COPULATION, SHALL BE WASHED WITH WATER, AND BE UNCLEAN UNTIL THE EVENING.

(18) "THE WOMAN ALSO WITH WHOM MAN SHALL LIE WITH SEED OF COPULATION, THEY SHALL BOTH BATHE THEMSELVES IN WATER, AND BE UNCLEAN UNTIL THE EVENING."

The structure is:

1. We find in this section that the cleansing power of the shed Blood, and the sanctifying virtue of the Word of God, is the only way of cleansing and Holiness.

2. The nature of sin is exhibited in this Chapter. Even that which was unavoidably defiled.

3. The saliva from the sinner's lip defiled; that from the Saviour's lip healed (Mk. 8:23).

THE SACRIFICES

Verses 12 through 15 read: *"And the vessel of earth, that he touches which has the issue, shall be broken: and every vessel of wood shall be rinsed in water.*

"And when he who has an issue is cleansed of his issue; then he shall number to himself seven days for his cleansing, and wash his clothes, and bathe his flesh in running water, and shall be clean.

"And on the eighth day he shall take to him two turtledoves, or two young pigeons, and come before the LORD unto the Door of the Tabernacle, and give them unto the Priest:

"And the Priest shall offer them, the one for a Sin-Offering, and the other for a Burnt-Offering; and the Priest shall make an Atonement for him before the LORD for his issue."

Concerning these things, Mackintosh says, *"We learn that human nature is the ever flowing fountain of uncleanness. It is hopelessly defiled; and not only defiled, but defiling. Awake or asleep, sitting, standing, or lying, nature is defiled and defiling: its very touch conveys pollution. This is a deeply humbling lesson for proud humanity; but thus it is.*

"The Book of Leviticus holds up a faithful

mirror to nature: it leaves 'flesh' nothing to glory in. Men may boast of their refinement, their moral sense, their dignity: let them study the third Book of Moses, and there they will see what it is all really worth in God's estimation."

We learn as well from these Passages that no matter what the problem as it regards sin, there is only one cure, and that is the shed Blood of the Lord Jesus Christ.

The person so infected would have to offer up two turtledoves as a *"Sin-Offering,"* and two *"young pigeons,"* as a *"Burnt-Offering."* All of this, as is obvious, typified Calvary.

As well, the infected one would have to bathe his flesh with running water, which was a type of the Word of God.

Every single victory which the Lord has given me has all and without exception come about through the Word. The Lord has pointed out to me certain Passages of Scripture, and has revealed to me what they truly meant. This is the manner in which the Revelation of the Cross was given.

First of all, the Lord took me to Romans, Chapter 6, telling me that the Cross was the answer and the solution to every problem. From that Chapter, He also revealed to me that the Cross must ever be the object of our Faith. Then, He took me to Romans 8:2, explaining to me that the Holy Spirit works exclusively within the Finished Work of Christ, thereby, demanding our Faith in that Sacrifice.

So, if anyone claims any type of Revelation from the Lord, and it doesn't coincide perfectly with the Word of God, while it might be a Revelation, it's definitely not from the Lord.

It is exceedingly troubling whenever certain Preachers who draw large crowds claim some particular Revelation from the Lord, and then say, *"You won't find this in the Bible; it has to be revealed to your spirit."* Let it ever be known that the Holy Spirit will never reveal anything to anyone that is not first found in the Word.

The Canon of Scripture is complete, which means that the Lord is not going to add anything to that which He has already said. The Covenant we now have is an *"Everlasting Covenant,"* which means it will

never have to be amended, and it will never come to an end (Heb. 13:20).

TYPES

Verses 16 through 18 read: *"And if any man's seed of copulation go out from him, then he shall wash all his flesh in water, and be unclean until the evening.*

"And every garment, and every skin, whereon is the seed of copulation, shall be washed with water, and be unclean until the evening.

"The woman also with whom man shall lie with seed of copulation, they shall both bathe themselves in water, and be unclean until the evening."

Studying this should make us take stock of ourselves. While we certainly realize that the Book of Leviticus was the Law of Moses, and we are living today under Grace, still, the principle has not changed. Sin is just as hurtful, just as destructive, at this present time, as it was then.

To bring it down to where we all live, I think that there would not be one of us, but who would blush and be mortified almost to death to have all our thoughts and feelings suddenly laid open to the inspection of those around us. But still, that is not all bad.

We need something to keep us humble, to drive us continually to the Throne of Grace, and to keep us ever mindful of our dependence upon the Mercy of God. If we were not troubled with these secret flows of sin, so to speak, we would be in great danger of growing spiritually proud, negligent, and over-confident.

But this keeps us at the foot of the Cross, and ever prompts us to more earnest prayer, which keeps the soul from stagnation. We must not be negligent as it regards the understanding of the presence and power of the foe. At the same time, we must ever understand and realize that there is only one answer, one solution, as it regards this foe, and that is *"Jesus Christ and Him Crucified,"* and our Faith in that Finished Work.

(19) "AND IF A WOMAN HAVE AN ISSUE, AND HER ISSUE IN HER FLESH BE BLOOD, SHE SHALL BE PUT APART SEVEN DAYS: AND WHOSOEVER TOUCHES HER SHALL BE UNCLEAN UNTIL THE EVENING.

(20) "AND EVERY THING THAT SHE LIES UPON IN HER SEPARATION SHALL BE UNCLEAN: EVERY THING ALSO THAT SHE SITS UPON SHALL BE UNCLEAN.

(21) "AND WHOSOEVER TOUCHES HER BED SHALL WASH HIS CLOTHES, AND BATHE HIMSELF IN WATER, AND BE UNCLEAN UNTIL THE EVENING.

(22) "AND WHOSOEVER TOUCHES ANY THING THAT SHE SAT UPON SHALL WASH HIS CLOTHES, AND BATHE HIM-SELF IN WATER, AND BE UNCLEAN UN-TIL THE EVENING.

(23) "AND IF IT BE ON HER BED, OR ON ANY THING WHEREON SHE SITS, WHEN IIE TOUCHES IT, HE SHALL BE UNCLEAN UNTIL THE EVENING.

(24) "AND IF ANY MAN LIE WITH HER AT ALL, AND HER FLOWERS BE UPON HIM, HE SHALL BE UNCLEAN SEVEN DAYS; AND ALL THE BED WHEREON HE LIES SHALL BE UNCLEAN.

(25) "AND IF A WOMAN HAVE AN IS-SUE OF HER BLOOD MANY DAYS OUT OF THE TIME OF HER SEPARATION, OR IF IT RUN BEYOND THE TIME OF HER SEPARATION; ALL THE DAYS OF THE ISSUE OF HER UNCLEANNESS SHALL BE AS THE DAYS OF HER SEPARATION: SHE SHALL BE UNCLEAN.

(26) "EVERY BED WHEREON SHE LIES ALL THE DAYS OF HER ISSUE SHALL BE UNTO HER AS THE BED OF HER SEPA-RATION: AND WHATSOEVER SHE SITS UPON SHALL BE UNCLEAN, AS THE UN-CLEANNESS OF HER SEPARATION.

(27) "AND WHOSOEVER TOUCHES THOSE THINGS SHALL BE UNCLEAN, AND SHALL WASH HIS CLOTHES, AND BATHE HIMSELF IN WATER, AND BE UNCLEAN UNTIL THE EVENING.

(28) "BUT IF SHE BE CLEANSED OF HER ISSUE, THEN SHE SHALL NUMBER TO HERSELF SEVEN DAYS, AND AFTER THAT SHE SHALL BE CLEAN.

(29) "AND ON THE EIGHTH DAY SHE SHALL TAKE UNTO HER TWO TURTLE-DOVES, OR TWO YOUNG PIGEONS, AND BRING THEM UNTO THE PRIEST, TO THE DOOR OF THE TABERNACLE OF THE CONGREGATION.

(30) "AND THE PRIEST SHALL OFFER

NOTES

THE ONE FOR A SIN-OFFERING, AND THE OTHER FOR A BURNT-OFFERING; AND THE PRIEST SHALL MAKE AN ATONE-MENT FOR HER BEFORE THE LORD FOR THE ISSUE OF HER UNCLEANNESS.

(31) "THUS SHALL YOU SEPARATE THE CHILDREN OF ISRAEL FROM THEIR UNCLEANNESS; THAT THEY DIE NOT IN THEIR UNCLEANNESS, WHEN THEY DEFILE MY TABERNACLE THAT IS AMONG THEM.

(32) "THIS IS THE LAW OF HIM WHO HAS AN ISSUE, OF HIM WHOSE SEED GOES FROM HIM, AND IS DEFILED THEREWITH;

(33) "AND OF HER WHO IS SICK OF HER FLOWERS, AND OF HIM WHO HAS AN ISSUE, OF THE MAN, AND OF THE WOMAN, AND OF HIM WHO LIES WITH HER WHO IS UNCLEAN."

The construction is:

1. Defilement is cleansed by the *"Blood"* (I Jn. 1:7), by the *"Spirit"* (Titus 3:3-5), and by the *"Word"* (Eph. 5:26), all working to-gether in a sense as one.

2. Justification assures of Salvation from the guilt of sin (Rom., Chpts. 4-5); Sancti-fication effects separation from the filth of sin (Heb.).

3. A simple knowledge of Christ as the slain and living bird suffices to assure the conscience to Justification, but a fuller knowledge of Him as the Burnt, the Meal, the Trespass, and the Sin-Offering is needed to cleanse the conduct and effect Sanctifica-tion (Williams).

THE DEFILEMENT OF SIN

As we read these Passages, we are reminded of the *"woman which had an issue of blood for some twelve years,"* and who touched Jesus, and was made totally whole.

The Master was going to the home of Jairus, in order to raise his daughter from the dead. And then the Scripture says: *"And a certain woman, which had an issue of blood twelve years, and had suffered many things of many physicians, and had spent all that she had, and was nothing better, but rather grew worse, when she had heard of Jesus, came in the press behind, and touched His garment"* (Mk. 5:25-27).

For 12 years this dear lady, because of her uncleanness, which seemed to have been a menstrual issue, which was unchecked, had not been allowed within the precincts of the Temple, and had been unable, therefore, to take part in the public worship of God as appointed in the Books of Moses. And during the whole of the same long period, she had been in a state of separation from all about her: whoever touched her became unclean; the bed she lay upon was unclean; the seats that she sat upon were unclean; whosoever touched the bed that she lay upon or the seat that she sat upon was unclean. No wonder if for this reason alone *"she had spent all her living upon physicians"* (Lk. 8:43).

Upon seeing Jesus, she said, *"If I may touch but His clothes, I shall be whole"* (Mk. 5:28). This she did, and this she was!

As the leper, after he had been healed by our Lord, had to *"go and show himself to the Priest, and offer the gift that Moses commanded"* (Mat. 8:4), so no doubt the woman cured of the issue of blood had to fulfill the legal requirement for her cleansing, by offering her *"Sin-Offering"* and her *"Burnt-Offering"* on the eighth day after her healing.

Once again, let us make the statement and boldly do so, Jesus Christ Alone is the answer for these horrible problems of sin, of which all of these things were but a type. What He did at the Cross answered the question, provided the solution, which it alone could do.

In truth, we are encouraged to come into a knowledge that sin is a much larger matter than we are conscious of; that, in fact, it goes beyond all our conceptions, but at the same time is within the reach and grasp of our Lord's atoning power. If He thus sets our sins, and even our secret sins, in the light of His countenance, it is that He may have them entirely removed.

Superficial views of sin would lead men to imagine that a sin done in ignorance is not a guilty thing. God says differently, because He looks into the heart and discerns the deep-seated source.

Even as I dictate these words, I sense the Presence of God. How guilty we are! But in the Trespass-Offering, He takes our guilt.

How imperfect we are! But in the Whole Burnt-Offering, He gives us His perfection.

"We would see Jesus, for the shadows lengthen
"Across this little landscape of our lives;
"We would see Jesus, our weak faith to strengthen
"For the last weariness, the final strife."

"We would see Jesus, the great rock foundation,
"Where-on our feet were set by sovereign Grace;
"Not life, nor death, with all their agitation,
"Can thence remove us, if we see His Face."

"We would see Jesus; other lights are paling,
"Which for long years we have rejoiced to see;
"The blessings of our pilgrimage are failing;
"We would not mourn them, for we go to Thee.

"We would see Jesus; this is all we're needing;
"Strength, joy, and willingness come with the sight;
"We would see Jesus, dying, risen, pleading;
"Then welcome, day! And farewell, mortal night!"

CHAPTER 16

(1) "AND THE LORD SPOKE UNTO MOSES AFTER THE DEATH OF THE TWO SONS OF AARON, WHEN THEY OFFERED BEFORE THE LORD, AND DIED;"

The structure is:

1. The Sixteenth Chapter of Leviticus concerns the Great Day of Atonement.

2. The Lord will give instructions to Moses concerning this Great Day, which instructions were to be followed minutely.

3. Mention is made here again of the two sons of Aaron, which were stricken dead by

the Lord, because of their offering up of *"strange fire,"* in order that Aaron might understand the total and complete seriousness of these rituals.

THE LORD SPOKE

The phrase, *"And the LORD spoke unto Moses,"* concerns itself with the single most important information that will be given to the Lawgiver, as it regards Atonement. Everything else, as important as it was, was but a preliminary to this which will now be given. It will serve as a type of what Christ will do at the Cross in order to redeem fallen humanity.

If the Reader is to notice, as surely he does, there is a voluminous amount of repetition in all of these instructions given to Moses by the Lord. Why the constant repetition?

In the words of Seiss, he says, *"There is often much gain by frequent repetition. It is by going over his lessons again and again, that the schoolboy masters his tasks, and becomes so much wiser than he was before. It is by the oft hearing of a thought, that it becomes rooted in our hearts, and welds itself to our souls as a part of our mental and spiritual life. The success of the pulpit, and the benefit of our weekly attentions upon the Sanctuary, depend much more upon the continuous reiteration of the same great Truths of the Gospel, than upon any power of invention in the Preacher. It is not so much the presentation of new thoughts and brilliant originalities that converts men and builds them up in Holiness, as the clear and constant exhibition of the plain doctrines of Grace.*

"And so God, in His Law, reiterates and repeats in details and in summaries, line upon line, and precept upon precept, to ground his people well in all the great facts of His Will and Purposes."

THE REVELATION

In 1996, when the Lord began to open up to me the great Revelation of the Cross, which in effect was that which Paul had already taught, but of which the Lord gave me a much clearer understanding, regarding my personal knowledge, which to say the least is a gross understatement. As He began to

NOTES

enlarge it in my heart, adding to it almost on a daily basis, He then began to move upon me to teach this to our Church, Family Worship Center, which Messages were then aired over Television, and as well, over our daily Radio Program, *"A Study In The Word."* This we began to do, and in fact continued for a period of time.

I then went to other material, but found that the Lord would keep bringing me back to the Message of the Cross.

I constantly seek the Face of the Lord, that I might always know His Will, and be led by Him in all things. But sometimes, it is not exactly easy to find the Will of God. Not only does He train us by the fact of His Will, but as well, in the finding of His Will. It teaches us trust, obedience, and Faith.

Several times I tried to go to other subjects as it regards our daily Radio Program, *"A Study In The Word."* This is a 90-minute program each day, aired live Tuesday through Friday, at 7 a.m. C.S.T. The programs from Wednesday, Thursday, and Friday are re-aired on Saturday morning, Sunday morning, and Monday morning. Therefore, the program is aired seven days a week. Also, the morning program is aired again at 7 p.m., with the exception of scheduled Service nights at Family Worship Center, which are Wednesday Night Bible Study, and Sunday evening. Thursday night is for our youth group, Crossfire.

In fact, the Ministry is purchasing Radio Stations all over the nation, and will continue to do so until it is possible for every person in the nation to hear the programming, that is if they so desire. At least that's our goal. Also, we broadcast all over the world, through the World Wide Web.

While SonLife Radio was raised up for the Lord for many purposes, the main theme is, *"the preaching and teaching of the Cross."*

REPETITION

Although it has taken me some time, I have found out through the years that when the Lord tells us to do something, He means for us to keep doing it, until He tells us different. Situations may come, and circumstances may change, but that in no way gives us the right to change direction, unless the

Lord plainly tells us to do so.

At any rate, at times in the past several years, it would seem to me that I should leave the subject of the Cross, at least as it regarded our daily Radio Program, and go to other subjects. Every time, the Lord would bring me back.

I remember one morning walking out of the office, in fact going to the Studio for the morning program, when the Lord spoke to my heart. I remember exactly where I was when this happened. I had just closed the door behind me to the main Administration Building, and was walking toward my car. Even though it was not in an audible voice, it was as clear as if the voice was audible.

The Lord spoke to my heart, saying, *"I have told you to teach on the Cross, and to continue to do so until I say otherwise."* From that moment on, we have continued exactly as the Lord has told us to do.

It is by repetition alone that we learn. And repetition is needed far more as it regards the Message of the Cross than anything else. I'll tell you why!

Pure and simple, the Cross is God's Way, and, in fact, His only Way. Due to the Fall, the world is geared in an entirely different direction – the direction of self. Unfortunately, the clinging vines of self cling even to the dedicated Believer, which is a source of constant difficulties, hence Jesus telling us that if we were to follow Him, we would have to *"deny ourselves, and take up the Cross daily"* (Lk. 9:23).

There is something in all of us that seeks to try to earn our Salvation, earn our victory, earn our way, and to do so by religious means. And because it is religious means, and even spiritual for that matter, it oftentimes fools us. But when the cover is pulled back, it's still the same old *"Self."* Let me say it another way:

Anything that we do as it regards the Lord, other than our Faith exclusively in the Cross of Christ, is looked at by God as an operation of *"self."* And I might quickly add, it's an operation which He cannot condone. That's why Paul said:

"For Christ sent me not to baptize, but to preach the Gospel: not with wisdom of words, lest the Cross of Christ should be made

NOTES

of none effect" (I Cor. 1:17).

Pure and simple, this tells us that the Cross of Christ is to ever be the central theme of our *"done"* and *"doing."*

The truth is, the Church has been so moved away from its proper foundation, which is the Cross, that anymore it hardly knows where it's been, where it is, or where it's going. Sadly, when it hears the Message of the Cross, most of the time, it either ignores it, or brushes it aside, as elementary, with the words, *"I already know that."* The continued truth is, the modern Church knows next to nothing about the Message of the Cross, which in essence means that they know next to nothing about the True Gospel. That is sad, but true!

I have found out, before the Church can shake its self-righteousness, its works program, it has to hear the Message of the Cross, over and over.

I've also learned that once the Believer truly understands the Message of the Cross, which as I've already stated is what Paul taught, that Message will become so dear to them that in fact, no matter how much they hear it, or how often they hear it, they can't get enough of this *"good news."* They come to realize that the Cross is the answer to every question, the solution to every problem, the direction for which the soul of man seeks (Rom. 6:3-14; 8:1-2, 11; I Cor. 1:17-18, 21, 23; 2:2, 5; Gal., Chpt. 5; 6:14; Eph. 2:13-18; Col. 2:14-15; in fact, the entire Bible).

A FALSE OFFERING

The phrase, *"After the death of the two sons of Aaron, when they offered before the LORD, and died,"* refers back to the Tenth Chapter of this Book, as the Reader knows. This is a further warning that the Ways of the Lord must not be trifled with, must not be ignored, must not be hindered, and must not be added to or taken from. To do so means death. And yet, that is the great sin of the modern Church, and possibly one can say without fear of contradiction, the great sin of all of us.

The Word of God is to be the criteria in all cases. As well, as a Believer, it is our responsibility to know and understand the Word, which can be done, if we diligently study the Word, asking the Lord to give us understanding. Upon such a petition, this He will always do.

Every single difficulty and problem in the life of the Christian is always brought about because of an erroneous or false interpretation of the Word of God. Considering how important all of this is, in fact, the single most important thing in the world, even one thousand times over, it is sadder still when we realize that many, if not most, Christians little know the Word as it regards their own understanding, but rather rely on what someone tells them. While the Lord has definitely placed in the Church, *"Apostles, Prophets, Evangelists, Pastors, and Teachers,"* and all of this, *"For the perfecting of the Saints, for the Work of the Ministry, for the edifying of the Body of Christ,"* still, every Believer is to learn the Word for himself, although aided by these Callings (Eph. 4:11-12).

When Believers one day stand at the Judgment Seat of Christ, to be judged for the life lived on this Earth, and I speak of our life and not our sins, for the latter was handled at Calvary, the Believer at that time will not be able to shift responsibility or blame to a Preacher who misinformed him. Every believer has the Holy Spirit as well as every Preacher. And the Holy Spirit stands ready and willing to *"Guide you into all Truth"* (Jn. 16:13). In other words, He will tell you if what you are hearing the Preacher or the Teacher say, is Truth or not (I Jn. 2:27).

For instance, I urge you to inspect very carefully that which you are reading on these pages. Do not take what I say, merely because I say it. Make certain that it lines up with the Word of God, and does so fully and completely.

THE WAY TO INTERPRET THE WORD OF GOD

I'm sure that you have heard it said, *"Scripture interprets Scripture."* That is exactly the truth. But what does that mean?

It means that to properly understand a Bible subject, we are to look at all the Passages in the Word that relates to that particular subject, and then interpret them accordingly. The Scripture will never contradict itself. And if we read something in one

NOTES

Scripture that seems to say one thing, but it doesn't match up with other Scriptures relating to the same subject, then we know that we are not properly interpreting that particular Scripture.

Whatever I teach on Faith must fit all Scriptures that pertain to Faith, contradicting none. If my interpretation seems to favor one Scripture but contradicts another on the same subject, then my interpretation is wrong. That goes for any subject in the Word of God. That's what we mean by *"Scripture interpreting Scripture."*

Now what I've just stated as it regards comparing Scripture with Scripture is not an easy thing to do. The Bible is a big Book. So that necessitates you the Reader making it your life's work to study the Word of God, and to do so on a daily basis. You should also avail yourself of all the aids given to you, such as this Commentary, to help you understand it better. In fact, that's why the Lord put in the Church, *"Apostles, Prophets, Evangelists, Pastors, and Teachers,"* among other things.

STRANGE FIRE

To refresh your mind, Aaron had four sons, all selected by God to be Priests, while Aaron was called by God to be the Great High Priest. All were types of Christ, but Aaron's position as High Priest was the greatest type in this regard of all.

The Lord gave clear instructions to Moses as to how all of the rituals concerning the Tabernacle, Sacrifices, and Sacred Vessels would be attended. Those instructions were not to be changed in any form. Because those instructions were changed, two of the sons of Aaron were stricken dead by the Lord. Their names were Nadab and Abihu.

Twice a day, coals of fire from the Brazen Altar were to be put in the censers of the Priests, with that fire then taken to the Golden Altar which sat immediately in front of the Veil, in the Holy Place. Those coals were to be placed on the Golden Altar, either by the censer itself placed on the Altar, or else the coals taken from the censer, and placed directly on the Altar. Incense was to be poured over the coals, which would then fill the Holy Place with a beautiful and wonderful fragrance. This typified the Intercessory Work of Christ, serving as our Great High Priest, which He in effect, is doing at this very moment for all Believers, and has done since His Ascension and Exaltation (Heb. 7:25-26; 9:24).

Instead of bringing the coals of fire from the Brazen Altar, which was a type of Christ and His great Sacrifice of Himself on the Cross, they instead took coals from another fire close by, which was ordained for other things. This means they ignored the Cross, in effect, whether they realized it or not, stating that they did not need the Blood of Christ, which the Altar represented, etc.

When they took this *"strange fire"* into the Holy Place, and placed it on the Golden Altar, or the Altar of Incense as it was mostly called, fire came out from the Holy of Holies, where God dwelt between the Mercy Seat and the Cherubim, went through the Veil without burning it, and struck them mortally dead. They had offered *"strange fire"* before the Lord, and the penalty was death.

Let the Reader understand that the same God Who did this is the same God we serve today. And as well, let not the Reader think that because we live in the dispensation of Grace, God no longer does such. He can no more ignore such now, than He did then. In fact, He demands even more now than He did then, and for all the obvious reasons. The Church, due to the Cross and the advent of the Holy Spirit, now has much more light than Israel of old; consequently, the Lord expects far more of us now than then. Paul said:

"And the times of this ignorance (before the Cross) *God winked at; but now* (since the Cross) *commands all men everywhere to repent"* (Acts 17:30).

Spiritual death always accompanies those who demean the Cross, ignore the Cross, or deny the Cross. Paul bluntly said this in Hebrews:

"For it is impossible for those who were once enlightened, and have tasted of the Heavenly Gift, and were made partakers of the Holy Spirit,

"And have tasted the good Word of God, and the powers of the world to come,

"If they shall fall away, to renew them

again unto repentance; seeing they crucify to themselves the Son of God afresh, and put Him to an open shame" (Heb. 6:4-6).

This Passage, plus its neighboring Passage in Hebrews 10:26-29, does not mean that a backslider, after turning his back on the Lord, cannot come back to Christ. The truth is, anyone who truly wants the Lord, irrespective as to what they have done in the past, can in fact, come to the Lord, and be saved, with the past completely washed away (I Cor. 6:9-11). The idea is this:

If the Believer, and Paul is addressing Believers here and not unbelievers, ceases to believe in Christ and what He has done for us at the Cross, and continues to register unbelief, that person is then lost. They have *"trodden under foot the Son of God, and have counted the Blood of the Covenant, wherewith they were once sanctified, an unholy thing, and* (consequently) *have done despite unto the Spirit of Grace"* (Heb. 10:29).

So, at the present, there are millions who claim Salvation, but who place no Faith in the Cross. Some of these people have never placed any Faith in the Cross, and in fact, have never been saved, despite their claims. Others once placed Faith in the Cross, exactly as did the Jewish Believers to whom Paul addressed in the Book of Hebrews, but have since shifted their faith to other things, and if they remain in that state, they are lost.

Let the Reader understand that both Salvation and Sanctification are based solidly on the great Sacrifice of Christ. There is no other sacrifice, no other way, no other means! That's the reason the Message of the Cross is the Message! In fact, there is no other, at least that the Lord will recognize.

Paul referred to other Messages as *"another gospel,"* which in effect he said, *"is not another"* (Gal. 1:6-7).

He then said: *"But though we, or an Angel from Heaven, preach any other gospel unto you than that which we have preached unto you* (the Message of the Cross), *let him be accursed"* (Gal. 1:8; I Cor. 1:23).

THE LORD'S SUPPER

As well, and to which we have already alluded in this Volume, there are millions of Christians who truly love the Lord, but who aren't properly *"discerning the Lord's Body"* (I Cor. 11:29).

As a result, Paul said: *"For this cause many are weak and sickly among you, and many sleep"* (I Cor. 11:30). What did he mean by *"sleep"*?

He was referring to Christians dying prematurely. While they didn't lose their souls, their lives were cut short; consequently, if the truth be known, many Christians who die at an early age do so for this very reason. It certainly does not apply to all, but it does apply to *"many."*

WHAT DOES IT MEAN TO NOT PROPERLY DISCERN THE LORD'S BODY?

It means that when we take the Lord's Supper, which epitomizes His death on the Cross, in the giving of His perfect body in Sacrifice, and the shedding of His precious Blood, which atoned for all sin, that we must understand, and do so at all times, that everything we have from the Lord, our Salvation, our Sanctification, in fact everything, comes to us totally and completely by what Christ has done for us at the Cross. If we attribute it to anything else, we are not properly discerning the Lord's Body, which as I think should be obvious, is an extremely serious offense.

Most modern Believers aren't properly discerning the Lord's Body presently, and because the modern Church, for all practical purposes, is Cross illiterate. In other words, the Church has been so moved away from the Cross, that anymore, it understands the Gospel little, if at all.

The reasons for this are many! But the greatest reason of all is the most dangerous reason of all, and it is *"unbelief."*

As an example, most of the leaders of modern Denominations have fully and totally embraced humanistic psychology, as the answer to the ills and the aberrations of man. In fact, in the two largest Pentecostal Denominations, the Assemblies of God, and the Church of God, if one of their Preachers has committed some particular types of sin, before he can be reinstated, he must undergo several months of psychological therapy by a Denominationally appointed Psychologist.

The truth is, humanistic psychology is *"the wisdom of the world."* As such, it *"comes not from above, but is earthly, sensual, devilish"* (James 3:15). In other words, humanistic psychology, and that's the only kind there is, holds no answer for anything. The Holy Spirit through James said that it is *"devilish,"* meaning that its ultimate source is the Devil. Jesus said, concerning the Devil: *"The thief cometh not, but for to steal, to kill, and to destroy"* (Jn. 10:10).

Understanding this, we know it's not possible for Believers to embrace humanistic psychology and the Cross at the same time. It cannot be done. Jesus said: *"If therefore the light that is in you be darkness, how great is that darkness!*

"No man can serve two masters: for either he will hate the one, and love the other; or else he will hold to the one, and despise the other. You cannot serve God and mammon" (Mat. 6:23-24).

The *"light that is turned to darkness"* describes the present situation perfectly. Many of these Preachers of whom I speak, who consider themselves to be leaders, once had the light. But as Israel of old, they have forsaken that light, and it has been replaced with darkness. Let's say it so that everyone will understand:

If it's not the *"Cross,"* then it's not *"Light."* Many of these men of whom I speak came in the right way. In other words, they gave their hearts and the lives to Christ, embracing Him and what He did for them at the Cross. But now they have abandoned the Cross, and they are left with *"another Jesus, fostered by another spirit, thereby proclaiming another gospel"* (II Cor. 11:4).

Unbelief is an awful thing. Paul further said concerning this subject: *"Let us therefore fear, lest, a promise being left us of entering into His rest, any of you should seem to come short of it.*

"For unto us (the Church) *was the Gospel preached, as well as unto them* (Israel)*: but the Word preached did not profit them* (Israel), *not being mixed with Faith in them who heard it"* (Heb. 4:1-2).

This being the case, which was an abandonment of the Cross, the Lord further said: *"So I swore in My wrath, they shall not enter into My rest.*

"Take heed, Brethren (the Spirit here through Paul is speaking to Believers), *lest there be in any of you an evil heart of unbelief, in departing from the Living God"* (Heb. 3:11-12).

The gist of all of this is an abandonment of Christ and the Cross. And let the Reader understand that one cannot accept Christ and then ignore the Cross. Both are accepted, or neither is accepted, irrespective of the claims.

ALL TRUTH IS GOD'S TRUTH?

There are many who promote the statement given in the heading, claiming that God gave the truth of psychology to the likes of Freud, etc. Nothing could be further from the Truth.

In the first place, the Lord doesn't reveal spiritual truths to unredeemed people. Such is impossible, they being spiritually dead (I Cor. 2:14).

Furthermore, *"Truth"* is not a philosophy, philosophy being a search for truth, but is rather a Person. That Person is the Lord Jesus Christ. He said: *"I am the Way, the Truth, and the Life: no man comes unto the Father, but by Me"* (Jn. 14:6).

As well, our Lord said: *"Sanctify them* (Believers) *through Your Truth: Your Word is Truth"* (Jn. 17:17).

Then John wrote: *"This is He Who came by water and blood, even Jesus Christ; not by water only, but by water and blood. And it is the Spirit Who bears witness, because the Spirit is Truth"* (I Jn. 5:6).

So from the Scriptures we learn that Jesus is the Truth, the Word is Truth, and the Holy Spirit is Truth.

As it regards this *"Truth,"* due to what Christ did at the Cross (Jn. 14:16-17), the Holy Spirit now abides within all Believers, and will *"guide us into all Truth"* (Jn. 16:13).

Again I emphasize, the Holy Spirit does not give Truth to unbelievers. Such thinking is ridiculous.

So this means that humanistic psychology, and again we state, there is no other kind, didn't come from God. And if it didn't come from the Lord, then it must have come from Satan. And if it came from Satan, it holds no good for the human race.

NOTES

The truth is, the leaders of most modern religious Denominations have long since abandoned the Cross. They have done so because of unbelief. Please notice, I didn't say *"all,"* but rather *"most."* As a result, those particular Denominations, whatever they might be, cannot lead people to the Lord, but will rather lead them in the other direction.

"Strange fire" kills today, exactly as it did so long ago. God has not changed, as God cannot change! The two sons of Aaron died then, and untold millions are likewise dying presently.

(2) "AND THE LORD SAID UNTO MOSES, SPEAK UNTO AARON YOUR BROTHER, THAT HE COME NOT AT ALL TIMES INTO THE HOLY PLACE WITHIN THE VEIL BEFORE THE MERCY SEAT, WHICH IS UPON THE ARK; THAT HE DIE NOT: FOR I WILL APPEAR IN THE CLOUD UPON THE MERCY SEAT."

The composition is:

1. Over and over again, we see the words, *"And the LORD spoke unto Moses. . . ."* The constant repetition of this phrase proclaims the fact that the Lord originated everything that was done, which means that man had no part whatsoever in the origination. Salvation is all of God, and none of man.

2. This Chapter describes the Great Day of Atonement. It occurred only once a year. There was no other day like it. It dealt with the sins of the whole nation for 12 months.

3. It foreshadowed the Lamb of God taking away the sin of the world (Jn. 1:29).

INSTRUCTIONS GIVEN TO MOSES

This is one of the most important Chapters in the entirety of the Bible. As stated, it foreshadows Christ, by His Work on the Cross, taking away the sin of the world (Jn. 1:29). Consequently, as I think by now is obvious, we are treating this Chapter a little different than the others. It is worthwhile, I think, to go into complete detail, at least as far as we can, as it regards the Great Day of Atonement.

By referring to Verse 29, we find that this Great Day of Atonement was appointed for *"the seventh month."* Seven, as you remember, is a symbol of completeness, as it relates to the Lord.

There is wisdom and order in all of God's

arrangements. Not only is the thing done that needs to be done, and whatever it might be, but it is done at the correct time. For instance, it was only *"when the fullness of time was come, that God sent forth His Son . . . To redeem them who were under the Law"* (Gal. 4:4-5). Had Christ come earlier than He did, though the intrinsic virtue of His Mediatorial Work would have been the same, yet, the absence of due preparation to appreciate, receive, and spread it, would have rendered it much less influential upon mankind. His coming was accordingly delayed until the particular time of the Augustan reign, when His Cross would necessarily stand in the center of history and in sight of all the nations of the Earth. His appearance, therefore, to take away our sin was in *"the fullness of time."* So the Day of Atonement was placed *"in the seventh month."*

So, we must rank the Sixteenth Chapter of Leviticus among the most precious and important sections of inspiration, if indeed it be allowable to make comparisons where all is Divine (Mackintosh).

THE APPOINTED TIME

The phrase, *"Speak unto Aaron your brother, that he come not at all times into the Holy Place within the Veil before the Mercy Seat, which is upon the Ark; that he die not,"* refers here to the *"Holy of Holies."*

The Tabernacle itself was a small affair. Its entire length was approximately 45 feet, and its entire width approximately 15 feet, figuring 18 inches to the cubit.

It consisted of two rooms, the first being 30 x 15, called the Holy Place. In this compartment, as one came through the front door, stood on the right the Table of Shewbread, in front of the Veil, the Altar of Incense, and to the left, the Golden Lampstand.

The Veil separated the Holy of Holies, which was the second room, 15 feet square, from the Holy Place. (Actually, at times, the *"Holy of Holies"* was referred to also as the *"Holy Place."*)

In this second compartment were the Ark of the Covenant and the Mercy Seat. Actually, the Mercy Seat served as a lid for the Ark of the Covenant. Attached to the Mercy

Seat on either end were the Cherubim, who constantly looked down at the Mercy Seat. The Mercy Seat and the Cherubim were all made of one slab of pure gold. God dwelt between the Mercy Seat and the Cherubim, signified by the Cloud which hovered over the Holy of Holies on the outside by day, and was symbolized by a flame of fire at night. It must have been an awesome sight!

While all of the Priests, at least in their appointed duties, could come into the Holy Place, which was the first room of the Tabernacle, there to attend their duties, they were not allowed to go into the second room, which was the Holy of Holies, with the exception of the Great High priest, in this instance, Aaron. And he could only go in one day a year, on the great Day of Atonement, and not without blood. To be sure, if these instructions were not carried out minutely to the letter, the High Priest would die, especially considering that this was the most significant of all the ceremonies and rituals associated with the Law of Moses.

THE HOLY OF HOLIES AND THE CROSS

All of this was fulfilled by Christ at the Cross, as everything about the Law of Moses was fulfilled in Christ, and more particularly, His Cross.

Now, and due to the Cross, and what it accomplished, any Believer can come directly into the very Presence of God, and do so with boldness, not fearing death. It is all because of Christ, and His Finished Work. Paul said concerning this:

"Let us therefore come boldly unto the Throne of Grace, that we may obtain Mercy, and find Grace to help in time of need" (Heb. 4:16).

While we take this for granted presently, to be sure, it came at great price. Paul again said:

"Having therefore, Brethren, boldness to enter into the Holiest by the Blood of Jesus,

"By a new and living way, which He has consecrated for us, through the Veil, that is to say, His flesh."

And then, *"Let us draw near with a true heart in full assurance of Faith, having our hearts sprinkled from an evil conscience, and our bodies washed with pure water"* (Heb. 10:19-22).

As stated, the *"Veil"* hid the Holy of Holies from the outer compartment. No individual could go past that Veil, except the High Priest, and that only once a year. But when Jesus died on the Cross, at the moment He said, *"It is finished; Father, into Your hands, I commend My Spirit"* (Jn. 19:30; Lk. 23:46), the *"Veil"* in the Temple *"was rent in twain from the top to the bottom"* (Mat. 27:51). This signified that due to His Sacrificial, Atoning Death, the way had now been opened into the very Presence of God, so, no Veil was now needed.

Incidentally, Josephus, the great Jewish historian, stated that this Veil, which hid the Holy of Holies in the Temple, was 30 feet tall, and four inches thick. It weighed over 2,000 pounds, and it is stated that four yoke of oxen could not have pulled it apart. But at the moment that Jesus died, thereby atoning for all sin, past, present, and future, God Personally ripped the Veil from top to bottom, opening up the way.

In fact, it would have been all but humanly impossible to have physically torn the Veil at the bottom, due to its great thickness; however, considering that it was torn from the top to the bottom signifies that man did not open up the way, but rather that God opened it up. It was all based on what Christ did at the Cross, hence Paul using the term *"the Blood of Jesus,"* in conjunction with *"His flesh,"* which referred to His Perfect Body given in death (Heb. 10:19-20).

This present way is referred to by Paul as *"a new and living way."* The other was only ceremonial, but the ceremonial typified that which Christ would do.

WHY COULDN'T SINFUL MAN COME INTO THE PRESENCE OF GOD BEFORE THE CROSS?

The question answers itself. It was because man was sinful; therefore, to come into the Presence of a thrice-Holy God would have immediately meant the death of such an individual, hence Nadab and Abihu dying instantly, and because they offered up *"strange fire."*

Man's sin has estranged him from God. And to be sure, this crime of sin is against God. In fact, man doesn't feel the weight of

this terrible situation near as much as does God. It is God Who has been insulted, Who has been maligned, Who has been affronted. Man doesn't realize that near as much as he ought, even redeemed man.

Not only has man's sin insulted God, and has done so to a degree that's beyond our comprehension, as well, it has placed man in a position to where he can have no fellowship with his Creator. Due to man being spiritually dead, which means he is separated from God, this hurts God much more than it does man.

The only way this problem could be rectified was for the debt, the terrible debt owed by man to God, to be forever satisfied. But how could that be done?

SATAN AND THE ATONEMENT

When man fell in the Garden of Eden, due to the manner in which man was created, Satan felt that man was beyond Redemption. Due to the fact of Adam being the federal head of the human race, his Fall meant that all who would follow after him would, in effect, be born fallen. The fountain was corrupted, and everything it produced would be corrupted as well.

That being the case, *"How could man be redeemed?"* was no doubt Satan's thought!

Immediately after the Fall, the Lord through the serpent gave Satan a hint as to how this would be done. He said:

"And I will put enmity (a war) *between you* (Satan) *and the woman, and between your seed* (mankind) *and her Seed* (the Lord Jesus Christ)*; it* (Christ) *shall bruise your head* (through the Cross), *and you shall bruise His heel* (the suffering of the Cross)*"* (Gen. 3:15).

The term used by the Lord, *"her Seed,"* must have been puzzling to Satan, because the woman has no seed, that being the prerogative of man.

Through foreknowledge, even before the foundation of the world, God knew that He would create man, and that man would fall. And in the high counsels of Heaven, it was ordained that man would be redeemed by God becoming man, going to the Cross, giving His Life's Blood, which would atone for all sin (I Pet. 1:18-20).

I'm certain that Satan had no knowledge of this at the beginning, but in fact, did come to the knowledge of a coming Redeemer, God becoming man, not long after the Fall. We know this from the fact that some of the fallen Angels cohabited with women, in order to so corrupt the human race, through which Christ would have to come, that such a coming would be impossible (Gen. 6:4). So, Satan's plan to destroy man, God's most prized creation, which he thought he could do by the destruction of Adam, didn't hold up. The Cross, even as the Lord predicted in Genesis 3:15, would be Satan's undoing, and, therefore, stands at the very apex of history.

THE MERCY SEAT

The phrase, *"For I will appear in the cloud upon the Mercy Seat,"* in effect, referred to the fact that this is where God dwelt at all times. In fact, it was the Holy Spirit, the third Person of the Godhead, so to speak, Who actually dwelt between the Mercy Seat and the Cherubim. Concerning this, Paul said: *"Know ye not that you are the Temple of God, and that the Spirit of God dwells in you?"* (I Cor. 3:16).

Before the Cross, God dwelt between the Mercy Seat and the Cherubim, in the Holy of Holies, whether in the Tabernacle or later in the Temple. Since the Cross, which atoned for all sin, thereby paying the sin debt in full, the Holy Spirit can now abide permanently within the heart and life of the Believer, actually making the Believer His Temple (Jn. 14:16-17).

As Aaron was given these instructions, and solemn instructions they were, with even his life at stake, these instructions were meant to apply to all the High Priests who would follow him.

It is said that during the time of the second Temple, which was the Temple built by the returning Jews from Babylonian captivity, which Temple lasted for about 500 years, that the preparation of the High Priest for his functions regarding the Great Day of Atonement was the responsibility of the Sanhedrin.

Seven days before the Day of Atonement, he was separated from his wife, and lodged

NOTES

in a chamber in the Temple, lest he should contract defilement, which might unfit him for the performance of his duties. The Elders or the representatives of the Sanhedrin read and expounded to him the Ordinances contained in this Sixteenth Chapter of Leviticus; he had to practice these in their presence, so as to make sure that he could rightly perform all the ceremonies.

This continued during the whole night previous to the Day of Atonement, when he was kept awake, so as to prevent any pollution arising from a dream or accident by night. He read, in the silent hours of darkness, the Books of Job, Daniel, Ezra, and Chronicles; and if he was no scholar, and could not read, the Elders read them to him.

As it was deemed important that he should not fall asleep, the Priests who surrounded him alternately snapped their fingers, and made him walk on the cold pavement of the Court. When the Chief of the 13 Priests who were appointed to perform the ordinary duties in connection with the service in the Sanctuary had ascertained that the morning had dawned, that the ashes had been removed from the Brazen Altar, and that the time of the early Sacrifice had arrived, the High Priest was conducted to the Great Laver, where he immersed his whole body in water, thereby washing himself, and then he would put on the required garments to begin this Great Day.

(3) "THUS SHALL AARON COME INTO THE HOLY PLACE: WITH A YOUNG BULLOCK FOR A SIN-OFFERING, AND A RAM FOR A BURNT-OFFERING."

The composition is:

1. Abel's lamb redeemed one man; the Paschal lamb, one family; the Day of Atonement lamb, one nation; the Lamb of Calvary, the whole world (Jn. 1:29)!

2. The phrase *"into the Holy Place,"* would probably have been better translated, *"within the Veil."* The term *"Holy Place"* mostly refers to the first room of the Tabernacle, instead of the second room, the *"Most Holy."*

3. *"Within the Veil"* was where God promised to appear and commune with Israel. The cloud veiled His holy form. No Priest could enter into this place at all, with the exception of the Great High Priest, and then only

once a year with blood.

4. The *"Sin-Offering"* and the *"Burnt-Offering"* were not for Israel but were rather for Aaron himself. He was ever reminded that even though he was the Great High Priest chosen of God, and chosen to stand between God and Israel, still, he was but a sinner, and, thereby, had to offer up Sacrifice the same as the lowest and most ungodly in Israel.

THE HOLY OF HOLIES

The phrase, *"Thus shall Aaron come into the Holy Place,"* i.e., *"within the Veil,"* signified the dwelling-place of God.

No nation in the world had this honor or privilege, and I refer to God dwelling among them, except Israel. Irrespective of the monetary riches, or the military might of other nations, still, they could not begin to hope to compare with Israel, who had the leadership of Jehovah.

In fact, all the other nations of the world worshipped sticks, stones, planetary bodies, or whatever, which means that all such religion was inspired by Satan, and was actually controlled by demon spirits. Israel alone had the privilege of being led by the Creator; consequently, in every capacity of life and living, they were, proverbially speaking, light years ahead of every other nation.

As well, when they obeyed the Lord, no nation in the world could overcome them. When they disobeyed, the Lord at times allowed other nations to overcome them for a short period of time, in order that they may see themselves, and come back to the Lord. Regrettably, Israel finally drifted so far from Jehovah that He was forced to abandon them, which took place about 600 years before Christ. They were consequently taken captive by the Babylonians, whom they served, along with the Medes and the Persians, for about 70 years. They were then restored to their country, and built the second Temple, to which we have already referred. (Solomon's Temple, which was the first Temple, was destroyed by the Babylonians.)

ENTERING THE HOLY OF HOLIES

One can well imagine the fear and trembling which accompanied Aaron, and all High Priests who followed him, on this Great Day. The slightest misdirection could, and more than likely would, result in instant death. And yet, there is no indication that any High Priest ever died accordingly.

At least part of the reason for this was because the Lord vacated the premises shortly before the Babylonians sacked the Temple, actually razing it to the ground. In fact, in a Vision, Ezekiel the Prophet saw the Holy Spirit leave (Ezek. 11:22-23).

Thankfully, the great Prophet also saw the Holy Spirit return to the Temple, which will actually be the Millennial Temple (Ezek. 43:1-5).

Israel, as would be obvious, will then have accepted Christ, which she will do at the Second Coming (Zech., Chpts. 12-14), and will then under Christ become the greatest nation on the face of the Earth – that which the Lord intended all along.

It is a sobering thought to realize that presently (2004, the time of the publishing of this book), we are nearing the very end of the Church Age. In fact, one could say that we are living in the last of the last days, as it regards this particular Dispensation. The Rapture of the Church could take place at any moment, with the Great Tribulation following, which the Prophet Jeremiah stated would be, *"the time of Jacob's trouble."* But he then added, *"He shall be saved out of it"* (Jer. 30:7). It's the time that Jesus spoke of when He said: *"For then shall be great tribulation, such as was not since the beginning of the world to this time, no, nor ever shall be"* (Mat. 24:21). At the conclusion of that Great Tribulation, in fact, during the middle of the Battle of Armageddon, Jesus will come back, referred to as the Second Coming (Ezek., Chpts. 38-39; Rev., Chpt. 19), at which time Israel will be saved, both as it regards her existence as a nation, and spiritually speaking as well. That's when the *"fountain shall be opened to the House of David and to the inhabitants of Jerusalem for sin and for uncleanness"* (Zech. 13:1).

THE SIN-OFFERING AND THE BURNT-OFFERING

The phrase, *"With a young bullock for a Sin-Offering, and a ram for a Burnt-Offering,"* presents the first time that Aaron will go into the Holy of Holies. The Offerings he will present will be for himself instead of Israel. Even though he is the Great High Priest, he is still a sinful man, and must come the same way as all other men, even the worst among men.

He had to offer a young bullock and a ram. Actually, these were more costly Offerings than that given later in the day, which would be offered for the whole of Israel. This was necessary, simply because Aaron was a type of Christ, actually, as High Priest, the highest type of all. That being the case, more costly Sacrifices were required. As well, he had to pay for these Sacrifices out of his own pocket, simply because these animals were to expatiate his own sins, since he, like the meanest sinner, required Divine Mercy and Forgiveness.

The bullock was offered first of all as a *"Sin-Offering."* This means that his iniquity and his penalty were transferred to the innocent victim, namely Christ, symbolized by the two year old bullock (Ex. 29:1). Only the fat of the Sin-Offering was burned on the Altar, with the balance of the carcass eaten, and the remainder burnt without the camp, as was done all Sin-Offerings.

A ram was then presented as a *"Burnt-Offering,"* which means, after it was killed, and its blood caught in a basin, as was the blood of the Sin-Offering, the skin was pulled from its carcass, with the entirety of the carcass then being burned on the Brazen Altar. The Burnt-Offering presents Christ as a Perfect Sacrifice, satisfying the demands of a thrice-Holy God, with His perfection then given to the sinner. So, as stated, in the *"Sin-Offering"* the sin of the sinner is given to Christ, while in the *"Burnt-Offering,"* the Perfection of Christ is given to the sinner.

(4) "HE SHALL PUT ON THE HOLY LINEN COAT, AND HE SHALL HAVE THE LINEN BREECHES UPON HIS FLESH, AND SHALL BE GIRDED WITH A LINEN GIRDLE, AND WITH THE LINEN MITRE SHALL HE BE ATTIRED: THESE ARE HOLY GARMENTS; THEREFORE SHALL HE WASH HIS FLESH IN WATER, AND SO PUT THEM ON."

The construction is:

1. The Great High Priest had garments

NOTES

designed by God that were more beautiful than any of the other Priests. They were called *"garments of glory and beauty"* (Ex. 28:2).

2. However, when he entered the *"Holy of Holies,"* he could not wear these garments of *"glory and beauty,"* the reason being that the Lord Jesus Christ did not redeem us by His Deity, but rather as a man, the Man Christ Jesus, and did so by dying on the Cross.

3. Therefore, the *"linen"* would be the proper attire; it represented the Righteousness of Christ.

THE HOLY GARMENTS

The phrase, *"He shall put on the holy linen coat, and he shall have the linen breeches upon his flesh, and shall be girded with a linen girdle, and with the linen mitre shall he be attired: these are holy garments,"* proclaims the attire that he would wear, upon entering the Holy of Holies. The Righteousness of Christ is in view here.

Christ came to this world to do what the first Adam did not do, which was to render a perfect obedience to God, which He did. As well, He had to undo what the first Adam had done, which was to wreck humanity, and which Christ rectified, by His Death on the Cross.

Christ came to this world *"made of a woman, made under the Law"* (Gal. 4:4). In other words, as a man, He had to keep the Law perfectly, which no human being had ever done.

The Law carried Righteousness, but for its Righteousness to be gained, a perfect obedience had to be rendered (Rom. 8:3-4).

Due to man's fallen condition, there was no way that he could keep the Law. The Fall had taken such a deadly toll that man was helpless to render the obedience that was required, which was a perfect obedience. In fact, man was shot down even before he was born, due to the fact that he is born in sin (Ps. 51:5).

Christ gained a Perfect Righteousness, and did so as a man, the *"Last Adam"* (I Cor. 15:45-50), which He did on our behalf.

Then He went to the Cross to satisfy the claims of the broken Law, which was death (Rom. 6:23; Gal. 3:13).

Upon simple Faith in Christ, the Perfect Righteousness of Christ is imputed to the believing sinner, of which these linen garments represented.

THE WASHING

The phrase, *"Therefore shall he wash his flesh in water, and so put them on,"* proclaims the fact that cleanliness in every respect was demanded. He must be *"personally"* and *"characteristically"* pure and spotless.

To be sure, Christ did not need any of these things, such as the particular type of dress, etc. He was, intrinsically and practically, *"the Holy One of God."* What Aaron did, and what he wore – the washing and the robing – are but the faint shadows of what Christ is. The Law was only a *"shadow,"* and *"not the very image of good things to come."* Blessed be God, we have not merely the shadow, but the eternal and Divine reality – Christ Himself (Mackintosh).

(5) "AND HE SHALL TAKE OF THE CONGREGATION OF THE CHILDREN OF ISRAEL TWO KIDS OF THE GOATS FOR A SIN-OFFERING, AND ONE RAM FOR A BURNT-OFFERING."

The overview is:

1. The two kids of the goats, or rather the two he-goats, constituted together but one *"Sin-Offering."*

2. One ram had to be offered for a Burnt-Offering.

3. These animals had to be provided by the Children of Israel, which refer to the public purse, who were probably represented by the Elders.

THE CHILDREN OF ISRAEL

The phrase, *"And he shall take of the congregation of the Children of Israel,"* referred to the fact that the sinner had to provide the Offering or Offerings. Inasmuch as these Offerings were for the entire nation of Israel, they had to be paid for out of the public purse.

In fact, this was the most important day of the entire year. All the sins of Israel, as a nation, were to be atoned on this particular day. So what did it exactly mean, in respect to the fact that the people continually offered up Sacrifices during the year, and as well, two Sacrifices were offered daily, one at 9 a.m., and the other at 3 p.m., with that number doubled each Sabbath?

In effect, the Sacrifices offered on this Great Day of Atonement ratified all the other Sacrifices, as numerous as they may have been. To say it another way, without these Sacrifices offered on this Great Day of Atonement, all the other Sacrifices would have been invalid, meaning that they were rejected by God, meaning that there would be no Atonement. The results would be that the Covenant between God and Israel would be voided. Understanding all of this, we can see just how important the Great Day of Atonement actually was. This particular day, when the High Priest entered the Holy of Holies, proclaimed the fact that the Cross worked, represented by the many Sacrifices, which opened up the way.

THE GOATS AND THE RAM

The phrase, *"Two kids of the goats for a Sin-Offering, and one ram for a Burnt-Offering,"* specifies the Offerings for the nation of Israel.

It may seem somewhat a puzzle to us to have the blessed Saviour typified by a goat; however, the animal familiar to us by this name is not what is meant here. The Syrian goat, for that is the type of goat mentioned here, is a graceful, dignified, and clean animal. It was often used as the symbol of leadership and royalty. In fact, it was very highly appreciated by the Jews, and was one of the most valuable, and in fact, one of the most beautiful of domestic animals. It had none of the associations which we attach to goats of our present knowledge.

Contemplating Christ through the animal then mentioned, one would have conceived of Him as a great leader, strong, virtuous, and exalted.

The two goats used in the ritual of the Great Day of Atonement were kids of the first year, without blemish, which pictures our Propitiation, spotless, perfect, Who is Christ, elected to bleed on God's Altar in the freshness, prime, and vigor of His manhood. They were, as stated, to be furnished by the congregation of Israel, procured at the expense of the public treasury, and brought forward by the people.

As well, there was a price paid by the Jewish officials for the apprehension of Christ.

At 30 pieces of silver they procured Him. And the people brought Him forward to the Altar, saying, *"Crucify Him, Crucify Him!"*

The sacred lot was to decide which goat should die. So, after all, it was God Who made the selection.

The Jews acted out of their own malicious counsel when they brought Him to the slaughter. They had the choice of sending Christ to the Cross or Barabbas. They chose Christ! But yet, it was God Who actually chose Him for this momentous task, but at the same time, never overlooking for a moment the malicious intent of the Jews. For the Scripture says that He was *"delivered by the determinate counsel and foreknowledge of God"* (Acts 2:23).

In a sense, the two goats would constitute one *"Sin-Offering."* The ram would serve as the Whole Burnt-Offering. Once again, the sinfulness of the people would be placed on Christ as the Sin-Offering. Regarding the *"Burnt-Offering,"* the Perfection of Christ would then be given to the people.

(6) "AND AARON SHALL OFFER HIS BULLOCK OF THE SIN-OFFERING, WHICH IS FOR HIMSELF, AND MAKE AN ATONEMENT FOR HIMSELF, AND FOR HIS HOUSE."

The exegesis is:

1. As stated, Aaron, even though High Priest, plus his family, needed Atonement just as much as the worst sinners in Israel.

2. This shows us the terrible effect of sin on the human race.

3. This is difficult for the self-righteous man to understand, and because he judges his personal righteousness by comparing it with others – others whom he fancies to be in worse spiritual condition than himself.

THE PREPARATION

The phrase, *"And Aaron shall offer his bullock of the Sin-Offering, which is for himself,"* does not refer at this particular stage to the actual slaying of the animal, but rather the solemn presentation. In other times, the following form of confession was used by the High Priest when he laid his hand upon the bullock, which he had to do, and because he was the sinner.

He said, *"O Lord, I have committed iniquity;*

NOTES

I have transgressed; I have sinned, I and my house. O Lord, I entreat You, cover over the iniquities, the transgressions, and the sins which I have committed, transgressions, and sins before You, I and my house; even as it is written in the Law of Moses Your servant, 'For on that day will He cover over for you, to make you clean; from all your transgressions before the Lord you shall be cleansed'" (Edersheim).

And please remember, these words or similar were uttered by the High Priests of Israel – the same words that the lowliest sinner, whomever he or she may have been, would have to say.

The petition is little different now than then. John said, as the Holy Spirit moved him to write: *"If we confess our sins, He is faithful and just to forgive us our sins, and to cleanse us from all unrighteousness"* (I Jn. 1:9).

Does this mean, as some claim, that Christians sin constantly? No, it doesn't! But for the Christian to claim that there is never any failure in his life, which needs confessing to the Lord, such a Christian is foolish indeed! He either doesn't understand himself, or else he doesn't understand sin, or both.

ATONEMENT

The phrase, *"And make an Atonement for himself, and for his house,"* proclaims him acting for the entirety of his family.

There is a sense in which the husband is the High Priest of the family. Now that can only be taken so far, as should be understood; however, as the High Priest of Israel made Atonement for his family, even in a sense, as every man did, likewise, the husband should do the same presently. In this day and age, the Age of Grace, what exactly would that mean?

It means that the husband should take the lead in the family, as it regards the family's walk with God. The *"husband is to love his wife, even as Christ also loved the Church, and gave Himself for it"* (Eph. 5:25).

This does not mean that the Priestly work of the husband, so to speak, will guarantee that the entirety of the family will do, be, and live as they ought to; however, it will definitely go a long way toward bringing this to pass.

While Aaron made Atonement for himself and his family, Atonement has already been made for us, and I speak of what Jesus did at the Cross. So the truth is, presently, we trust in the Atonement that's already effected, and we do so by *"Faith"* (Gal. 5:6).

(7) "AND HE SHALL TAKE THE TWO GOATS, AND PRESENT THEM BEFORE THE LORD AT THE DOOR OF THE TABERNACLE OF THE CONGREGATION.

(8) "AND AARON SHALL CAST LOTS UPON THE TWO GOATS; ONE LOT FOR THE LORD, AND THE OTHER LOT FOR THE SCAPEGOAT.

(9) "AND AARON SHALL BRING THE GOAT UPON WHICH THE LORD'S LOT FELL, AND OFFER HIM FOR A SIN-OFFERING.

(10) "BUT THE GOAT, ON WHICH THE LOT FELL TO BE THE SCAPEGOAT, SHALL BE PRESENTED ALIVE BEFORE THE LORD, TO MAKE AN ATONEMENT WITH HIM, AND LET HIM GO FOR A SCAPEGOAT INTO THE WILDERNESS."

The diagram is:

1. According to tradition, the two goats were to be the same in size, color, and value, and as nearly alike as possible.

2. Both were presented to the Lord by the High Priest, and then lots were cast to determine which one should die and which should live.

3. The one that would live (sent into the wilderness) was called the *"goat of departure."*

4. The two goats represented and completed one Atonement for sin. The goat that died typified the death of Christ, which addressed the root cause of sin. The scapegoat represented all acts of sin removed and taken away.

5. When the goat was led into the wilderness, Atonement was complete; the sins transferred figuratively on the goat were already atoned for, and the blood was sprinkled before the Lord.

THE TWO GOATS

Verses 7 and 8 read: *"And he shall take the two goats, and present them before the LORD at the Door of the Tabernacle of the congregation.*

"And Aaron shall cast lots upon the two goats; one lot for the LORD, and the other

NOTES

lot for the scapegoat."

It must be carefully noted that, as the two goats made one Sin-Offering, so they are both presented before the Lord at the Door of the Tabernacle of the congregation. By this solemn presentation they became the Lord's, one as much as the other (Pulpit).

The two goats, of the same size and appearance as far as possible, stood together near the entrance of the Court. By them was an urn containing two lots. These the High Priest threw out at the same moment, placing one on the head of one goat, the other on the head of the other goat. According as the lot fell, one of the goats was taken and at once offered to the Lord, with a view to being shortly sacrificed; the other was appointed for a scapegoat, and reserved until the expiatory Sacrifices had been made, when it too was offered to the Lord, and then sent away into the wilderness.

After the lot had been chosen, the two goats were distinguished from each other by having a piece of scarlet cloth tied, the first around its neck, the second around its horn.

To properly understand the *"two goats,"* and what they represented, we must first of all understand, as previously stated, that both animals represented <u>one</u> Sin-Offering. Understanding that, the meaning of the scapegoat will become much more clear, which we will address momentarily.

Having presented his own Sin-Offering, the High Priest, accompanied by the two chief Priests, now came to the north side of the Altar. One of the Priests placed himself on the right of the High Priest, and the other on the left. The Priests then turned and faced the west, where the Holy of Holies was, and where the Divine Majesty was especially revealed, placed their hands on the heads of these animals, thereby transferring the entirety of the sins of all Israel to these innocent victims.

THE SCAPEGOAT

Verses 9 and 10 read: *"And Aaron shall bring the goat upon which the LORD's lot fell, and offer him for a Sin-Offering.*

"But the goat, on which the lot fell to be the scapegoat, shall be presented alive before the LORD, to make an Atonement with

him, and to let him go for a scapegoat into the wilderness."

The goat on which the lot fell to be sacrificed was *"for the Lord."*

The term *"the LORD's lot"* presents God as having a particular portion in the Death of Christ – a portion quite distinct – a portion which would hold eternally good even though no sinner were ever to be saved.

To understand all of this, it is needful to bear in mind how God has been dishonored in this world. His Truth has been despised; His authority has been condemned; His majesty has been slighted; His Law has been broken; His claims have been disregarded; His Name has been blasphemed; His character has been maligned.

Concerning this, Mackintosh said: *"Now, the death of Christ has made provision for all this. It has perfectly glorified God in the very place (this Earth) where all these things have been done; it has perfectly vindicated the majesty, the truth, the holiness, the character of God; it has Divinely met all the claims of His Throne; it has atoned for sin; it has furnished a Divine remedy for all the destruction which sin introduced into the universe; it affords a ground on which the blessed God can act in Grace, Mercy, and forbearance toward all; it furnishes a warrant for the eternal expulsion and perdition of the prince of this world; it forms the imperishable foundation of God's moral government."*

THE CROSS

Even though the world regards the Cross not at all; still, this world survives to the present only because of the Cross. The most vile, the most blasphemous, the most evil, the most wicked of men, *"live, move, and have their being,"* simply because of what Jesus did at the Cross, even though they understand that not at all. In fact, the very morsel which the blaspheming infidel puts into his mouth, he owes to the Atonement, which he knows not, and what little he does know, he wickedly ridicules.

In fact, the atheist who spends his life blaspheming God's Revelation, or denying His existence, owes everything, even though he doesn't know it, to the Atonement of Christ. The truth is, were it not for the Atonement,

instead of blaspheming on Earth, the entirety of the world without God would be weltering in Hell.

A LIMITED ATONEMENT?

There are some who talk of a *"limited Atonement."*

They are meaning by this statement that when Jesus died on the Cross, He only died for those who would be saved. Nothing could be further from the Truth. If Jesus died for one, He died for all. Jesus commanded that His Gospel be preached *"to every person,"* and if it was not meant for *"every person,"* then He would have said so (Mk. 16:15).

As well, Jesus also said: *"For God so loved the world, that He gave His only begotten Son, that whosoever believes in Him should not perish, but have everlasting life"* (Jn. 3:16).

It didn't say that He loved a part of the world, or some of the world, but rather *"all of the world."*

THE SIN-OFFERING

The first part of the Sin-Offering, the animal that was sacrificed, addressed itself to the fact of sin. This is what John the Baptist was speaking of when he said, *"Behold the Lamb of God, which takes away the sin of the world"* (Jn. 1:29). The scapegoat sent into the wilderness represented acts of sin, which we will deal with momentarily.

To deal only with acts of sin, and not deal with the root cause of sin, really doesn't address the problem. Jesus addressed the entirety of the problem in its totality. Listen to what Paul said:

"Knowing this, that our old man is crucified with Him (what we were before Redemption), *that the body of* (the) *sin might be destroyed* (the root cause of sin), *that henceforth we should not serve* (the) *sin"* (Rom. 6:6).

The Sin-Offering presented to the Lord on the Great Day of Atonement addressed sin in a more complete way than the Sin-Offerings of other times. This is the reason for the two animals, instead of one.

The Lord addressed on the Cross the root cause of sin, by satisfying the legal claims which had been brought about because of sin (Rom. 6:23). The crime of sin in its totality was and is against God. It was birthed and instituted by Satan, who in effect originated sin, by his revolution against God in eternity past (Isa., Chpt. 14; Ezek., Chpt. 28). Jesus atoned for all sin, which refers to the paying of a debt owed to God by all of mankind, by giving His life, which He did by the shedding of His Blood. When He did this, this removed Satan's legal right to hold humanity in captivity and bondage. In other words, this totally and completely defeated Satan (Col. 2:14-15).

When Paul said in Romans 6:6 that the *"body of sin was destroyed,"* he was meaning that the power of sin was broken, and the guilt of sin was removed. The first (power) was represented by the goat that was sacrificed, and the second (guilt) was represented by the scapegoat.

WHAT DID THE SCAPEGOAT MEAN?

First of all, the word translated *"scapegoat,"* in the Hebrew is *"Azalzel."* It means *"the goat of departure."* The Hebrew word *"azal"* means, *"removed,"* while *"azalzal"* means *"removed by a repetition of acts."*

In simple terms, it means *"to be sent away, bearing upon him all the iniquities of the Children of Israel into the wilderness."* It properly denotes one that removes or separates.

As we have stated, the two goats were the single Sin-Offering for the people; the one that was offered in Sacrifice symbolized Atonement or covering made by shedding of blood, and the other symbolized the utter removal of the sins of the people, which were conveyed away and lost in the depths of the wilderness, whence there was no return. The Psalmist said: *"As far as the east is from the west, so far has He removed our transgressions from us"* (Ps. 103:12).

Micah said: *"He will turn again, He will have compassion upon us; He will subdue our iniquities; and You will cast all their sins into the depths of the sea"* (Micah 7:19). The first animal that was sacrificed covered sin, hence Atonement, while the second animal symbolically removed sin. The latter speaks of our acts of sin.

So, not only was the root cause of sin addressed at the Cross, but as well, every act of sin was addressed, as it regards each and every individual.

The Emancipation Proclamation freed the slaves, but it took a war to effect that freedom.

God has the power to set humanity free merely by His Word. But it took a war, i.e., *"the Cross,"* to effect that freedom.

To understand that Atonement was made for the sin of the world, which it definitely was, is one thing. That represented the sacrificed animal. To understand that it was personally for me, and that every act of sin I have ever committed is washed and cleansed by the Blood of Christ, and removed from me as far as the east is from the west, completes the picture. The latter was symbolized by the scapegoat.

Some have tried to claim that the scapegoat represented an offering to Satan, or some such foolishness. Nothing could be further from the truth. The truth is, Satan had absolutely nothing to do with the Cross. Jesus didn't die to appease Satan, to satisfy Satan, or because something was owed to Satan. As stated, Satan had nothing to do with the Cross, but to be sure, the Cross definitely affected him in a most negative way (Col. 2:14-15).

The Cross was necessary, in order that the wrath of God would be propitiated. It is God Who has been offended! It is God Who has been wronged! It is God against Whom the crime was committed! So the Cross was demanded by the Lord in order that His Justice and Righteousness be forever satisfied. It was a terribly high price to pay, but considering that He paid it, man is left with no argument.

THE SCAPEGOAT AND THE JESUS DIED SPIRITUALLY DOCTRINE

By interpreting the *"scapegoat"* as a gift to Satan, or something of that nature, which incidentally is blatantly wrong, still, this particular interpretation blends with the *"Jesus died spiritually doctrine."*

As we've already stated several times in this Volume, this doctrine claims that Jesus not only died physically, but as well, died spiritually. To die spiritually means that one dies without God, thereby, dying as a sinner.

They teach that Jesus, while on the Cross,

in effect became a sinner, and then died and went to Hell, as any sinner would do so. He was then, they claim, tormented by Satan and demon spirits for three days and nights, with God then saying, *"It is enough."* In other words, He had suffered enough in Hell, and now He was born again, and then raised from the dead.

This corresponds with the scapegoat being a presentation to Satan, etc.

As previously stated, Jesus paid all the price on the Cross, and there is not a shred of evidence in the Bible to the contrary. In other words, all of this stuff about Jesus dying spiritually and going to the burning side of Hell is pure fiction. It's not in the Bible!

(11) "AND AARON SHALL BRING THE BULLOCK OF THE SIN-OFFERING, WHICH IS FOR HIMSELF, AND SHALL MAKE AN ATONEMENT FOR HIMSELF, AND FOR HIS HOUSE, AND SHALL KILL THE BULLOCK OF THE SIN-OFFERING WHICH IS FOR HIMSELF:"

The structure is:

1. The Sacrifice first of all had to be presented to the Lord, which is proclaimed in Verse 6.

2. If the Sacrifice was what the Lord had instructed to be brought, it would be accepted by the Lord, providing the ritual was carried out exactly as He had commanded.

3. The Sacrifice, in this case, a bullock, had to now be killed, typifying the death of Christ.

THE SACRIFICE

Verse 11 reads: *"And Aaron shall bring the bullock of the Sin-Offering, which is for himself, and shall make an Atonement for himself, and for his house, and shall kill the bullock of the Sin-Offering which is for himself."*

The person who brought the animal for Sacrifice, irrespective if it was the lowliest sinner in Israel, or the Great High Priest himself, in this case Aaron, all and without exception had to personally kill the animal. This proclaims several things.

A. It first of all stated that an innocent victim was suffering for the sins committed by another.

B. Knowing that sin required death, the death of an innocent victim, we should learn

from this just how bad sin really is.

C. The one bringing the Sacrifice actually having to kill the animal personally, brought home his sin in a more vivid way, in effect stating, *"My sin did this."*

D. When one looks at Calvary and all of its horror, one should say, as we've just stated, *"Sin did this."*

(12) "AND HE SHALL TAKE A CENSER FULL OF BURNING COALS OF FIRE FROM OFF THE ALTAR BEFORE THE LORD, AND HIS HANDS FULL OF SWEET INCENSE BEATEN SMALL, AND BRING IT WITHIN THE VEIL:

(13) "AND HE SHALL PUT THE INCENSE UPON THE FIRE BEFORE THE LORD, THAT THE CLOUD OF THE INCENSE MAY COVER THE MERCY SEAT THAT IS UPON THE TESTIMONY, THAT HE DIE NOT:"

The composition is:

1. The *"coals of fire from off the Altar before the LORD"* in Verse 12 was the only fire acceptable, which was from the Brazen Altar where Atonement had been made.

2. Only this fire could be used for burning incense on the Golden Altar and in censers. All other fire was *"strange fire"* and would bring death. This typifies the Cross. If our Faith is not in the Cross, spiritual death will be the result.

3. The *"sweet incense"* was a symbol of the Intercession of Christ, which is carried on unto this very hour.

4. It was poured on the fire which consisted of coals from the Brazen Altar.

THE CENSER, THE BURNING COALS OF FIRE, AND THE ALTAR

The phrase, *"And he shall take his censer full of burning coals of fire from off the Altar before the LORD,"* referred to the Brazen Altar, which fires, incidentally, were to never go out. They were to burn 24 hours a day, and because Atonement was always needed.

Of all the items of sacred furniture, all designed by the Lord, perhaps one could say without fear of contradiction that the Brazen Altar was the most important. Not at all is this meant to take away from the other vessels, which of course, were of supreme significance themselves. Each played a vital role in the symbolism of the Redemption of man.

One might say, if one looks at this carefully, that surely the Holy of Holies, which typified the Throne of God, actually where God dwelt between the Mercy Seat and the Cherubim, was the most sacred, the most holy, and the most important. In a sense, of course, that is true; however, the idea is this:

The Brazen Altar alone made it possible for entrance to be effected into the Holy of Holies. Only the Sacrifice of Christ, which the Brazen Altar represented, has opened up the way to the very Throne of God, that Believers presently may enter boldly into this sacred precinct (Heb. 4:14-16).

This is typified more vividly in the Vision given to the Apostle John on the Isle of Patmos.

In this Vision, he saw the Throne of God, which is described in Revelation, Chapters 4 and 5.

Right in the midst of the Throne, he saw a *"lamb as it had been slain."* Of course, this typified Christ Jesus, Who Alone was worthy to open the Book and to loose the seals thereof.

I remind the Reader that it was the slain Lamb Alone Who was worthy, as it regards the task at hand. As well, it is the *"slain Lamb,"* typifying, of course, the Sacrifice of Christ, that opened the way to the Throne of God. This must never be forgotten. Let us say it again:

Access to the Holy of Holies is made possible only by Jesus Christ and Him Crucified, and our Faith in that Finished Work (Eph. 2:13-18).

SWEET INCENSE

The phrase, *"And his hands full of sweet incense beaten small, and bring it within the Veil,"* refers to the Holy of Holies.

The *"sweet incense"* was made from the particular spices of *"Stacte," "Onycha," "Galbanum,"* with *"pure Frankincense"* (Ex. 30:34).

It was to be used only in the Holy Place and the Holy of Holies. It was not to be used as a perfume to be placed on the physical bodies of anyone, but only in the service of the Lord (Ex. 30:37-38).

The *"Incense"* was crushed, in order that it might give forth its pungent aroma, which it

was intended to do. As stated, it symbolized the Intercession of our Lord, all on our behalf.

The High Priest was to have in one hand *"a censer full of burning coals of fire from off the Altar before the LORD,"* and in his other hand, a container *"full of sweet Incense beaten small."*

THE CLOUD

Verse 13 reads: *"And he shall put the Incense upon the fire before the LORD, that the cloud of the Incense may cover the Mercy Seat that is upon the Testimony, that he die not."*

Holding the censer in one hand containing the coals of fire from the Brazen Altar, and the container with the Incense in the other hand, the High Priest went through the Veil that separated the Holy Place from the Holy of Holies, and advanced to the Ark of the Covenant, where he deposited the censer between its two staves.

The High Priest now poured the crushed spices upon the coals in the censer, and stayed there until the whole place was filled with a cloud of smoke, taking special care that the Mercy Seat and the Cherubim should be enveloped in the cloud.

If this wasn't done properly, which refers to the entire Holy of Holies being filled with the cloud supplied by the Incense upon the coals of fire, he could be stricken dead.

Here we are taught the lesson of the Vision of God, as it regards Him appearing in His Holiness. In one way or the other, He must be veiled.

The High Priest would then turn his back on the Ark of the Covenant, which contained the *"Testimony,"* i.e., *"the Ten Commandments,"* on two slabs of stone, he then walked back into the Holy Place past the Veil. He would then utter a prayer.

Once again, the *"Incense"* typified the Intercession of Christ, which He has offered on behalf of all Saints, from the time of the Cross. And when we speak of Intercession, we are not actually saying that Christ does something, for it has all been done at Calvary. We are meaning that by His very Presence at the Throne of God, such Presence guarantees Intercession on behalf of all Saints (Heb. 4:14-16; 7:25-26; 9:24).

(14) "AND HE SHALL TAKE OF THE BLOOD OF THE BULLOCK, AND SPRINKLE IT WITH HIS FINGER UPON THE MERCY SEAT EASTWARD; AND BEFORE THE MERCY SEAT SHALL HE SPRINKLE OF THE BLOOD WITH HIS FINGER SEVEN TIMES."

The construction is:

1. The solemn ritual of the Great Day of Atonement declared that entrance into the Presence of God was barred to the sinner, and that the blood of bulls and of goats could not rend the Veil that shut men out from God.

2. It further declared that atoning blood was the basis of God's Throne; hence the nearer the worshipper approached to that Throne, the greater was the value attached to the Blood shed at the Brazen Altar.

3. The entire way from the Brazen Altar by the Brazen Laver, the Golden Altar, and the Veil, and up to the Throne, was a blood-sprinkled way.

THE BLOOD

The phrase, *"And he shall take of the blood of the bullock, and sprinkle it with his finger upon the Mercy Seat eastward,"* means the High Priest has now entered once again into the Holy Place, where he is met by another Priest who stands with the bowl of the blood of the bullock, stirring it, to prevent it from coagulating. The High priest takes the bowl, and then goes back into the Holy of Holies, to the same place where he stood on his first entry.

Standing before the Ark of the Covenant, in the midst of the cloud furnished by the Incense upon the coals of fire, he would dip his finger in the blood of the slain bullock, and sprinkle it upon the Mercy Seat. This was to atone for himself and his family. The value of this can be seen, in part, from the following statement:

In the Ark of the Covenant was, as stated, the Ten Commandments, which had been written or carved on two slabs of stone. The Cherubim, representative of the strange creatures portrayed by John in his Vision of the Throne, recorded in Revelation, Chapter 4, looks down on the Mercy Seat, in effect, seeing the *"broken Law."* The Ten Commandments given by God, which were His Standard of Righteousness, had all been broken, in one way or the other, by every human being.

The *"blood"* would provide a shield between the gaze of the Cherubim and the broken Law, hence, the great statement given by the Lord so long before, *"When I see the Blood, I will pass over you, and the plague* (of sin) *shall not be upon you to destroy you"* (Ex. 12:13).

Let the Reader understand that it is the Blood and the Blood alone, and we speak of the shed Blood of Christ, which stands between us and the Wrath of God. We must not forget that. If our trust is in anything else, there awaits *"a certain fearful looking for of judgment and fiery indignation, which shall devour the adversaries"* (Heb. 10:27).

Paul had just written: *"For if we sin willfully after that we have received the knowledge of the Truth* (which refers to a rejection of the Sacrifice of Christ, which is a rejection of the Blood),*there remains no more sacrifice for sins"* (Heb. 10:26).

SEVEN TIMES

The phrase, *"And before the Mercy Seat shall he sprinkle of the Blood with his finger seven times,"* proclaims the following fact:

Outside of the Veil, the blood was precious; but it was within the Veil that its preciousness was fully revealed. The great factors within the Veil were the Blood and the Incense. The Incense expressed the fragrance of the Person of Christ, and as well, it had to do with His Intercession, which He carries on at this very time, the Blood, the efficacy (effectiveness) of His Work.

The blood sprinkled *"seven"* times on the Mercy Seat signified that the Redemption afforded by Christ would be a perfect Redemption.

The number *"seven"* which denotes perfection, completion, and totality, emphasizes the fact that all that Christ would do would be so perfect, so whole, so complete, so total, that it would never have to be done again. That's the reason that Paul referred to it as *"the Everlasting Covenant"* (Heb. 13:20).

As well, the *"Blood"* was not only for Israel, but also for the Gentile world, which of course, includes the Church.

All of this means that there is one foundation on which all of this rests, in fact, one solitary pedestal, upon which the stupendous fabric of Glory shall rest forever, and that is the Blood of the Cross – that precious Blood which has spoken peace – Divine and everlasting Peace – to your heart and to mine, and as well, to the conscience of every Blood-bought Believer, all in the Presence of His infinite Holiness, typified by the Mercy Seat.

One might say that the Blood which is sprinkled upon the Believer's conscience has been sprinkled *"seven times"* before the Throne of God. In fact, the nearer we get to God, the more importance and value we find attached to the Blood, the shed Blood, of the Lord Jesus Christ. If we look at the Brazen Altar, we find the Blood there; if we look at the Brazen Laver, we find the Blood there; if we look at the Golden Altar, we find the Blood there; if we look at the Veil of the Tabernacle, we find the Blood there; but in no place do we find so much about the Blood as within the Veil, before Jehovah's Throne, in fact, in the immediate Presence of the Divine Glory.

THE CHURCH AND THE BLOOD

Whenever we speak of the Blood, of course, as should be overly obvious, we are speaking of the Cross. It was on the Cross where Jesus gave His Life, i.e., *"shed His Blood."* So when Paul mentions the *"Cross,"* in essence, He is at the same time, speaking of the Blood.

The Reader should understand that the Word of Faith people, which doctrine has greatly permeated the modern Church, do not actually believe in the efficacy of the Blood. While they might say that we are redeemed by His Blood, they will also add that something has to be attached to the Blood, and by that, they are speaking, as we've already stated several times, of Jesus going down into Hell and being tormented there for some three days and nights. So in effect, they really do not believe in the Blood of Christ, which means that their doctrine is bogus from beginning to end. The *"Blood"* is the very Foundation of the Faith. That removed, there remains nothing!

(15) "THEN SHALL HE KILL THE GOAT OF THE SIN-OFFERING, THAT IS FOR THE PEOPLE, AND BRING HIS BLOOD

NOTES

WITHIN THE VEIL, AND DO WITH THAT BLOOD AS HE DID WITH THE BLOOD OF THE BULLOCK, AND SPRINKLE IT UPON THE MERCY SEAT, AND BEFORE THE MERCY SEAT:

(16) "HE SHALL MAKE AN ATONEMENT FOR THE HOLY PLACE, BECAUSE OF THE UNCLEANNESS OF THE CHILDREN OF ISRAEL, AND BECAUSE OF THEIR TRANSGRESSIONS AND ALL THEIR SINS: AND SO SHALL HE DO FOR THE TABERNACLE OF THE CONGREGATION, THAT REMAINS AMONG THEM IN THE MIDST OF THEIR UNCLEANNESS."

The overview is:

1. The goat is killed for the Sin-Offering, and Atonement is made for the people of Israel.

2. The blood, as well, is brought into the Holy of Holies, and applied to the Mercy Seat, exactly as had been the blood of the bullock. The difference is, the blood of the bullock was for Aaron and his family, and the blood of the goat is for Israel.

3. This had to be done, because of *"the uncleanliness (spiritual uncleanliness) of the Children of Israel, and because of their transgressions in all their sins."*

4. Atonement had to be made as well for the Tabernacle, because the transgressions of the Israelites during the year not only defiled them, but also drew defilement upon the very Sanctuary with its utensils, which was pitched in the midst of them.

THE SIN-OFFERING

Verse 15 reads: *"Then shall he kill the goat of the Sin-Offering, that is for the people, and bring his blood within the Veil, and do with that blood as he did with the blood of the bullock, and sprinkle it upon the Mercy Seat, and before the Mercy Seat."*

Aaron will now enter the Holy of Holies for the third time. The first time he offered Incense, and the second time he offered the blood of the bullock for him and his family. This time he will enter in regard to Israel as a whole.

The blood is sprinkled on the Mercy Seat seven times, and it seems as well that it was now sprinkled also on the ground *"before the Mercy Seat."*

We learn from this, and by the entrance of the High Priest into the Holy of Holies, that Atonement could only be effected before the Throne of Jehovah. As well, only the Blood of Christ, typified by these particular Sacrifices, could make that Atonement. So this means, as ought to be obvious, that any other proposed way of Salvation, any other proposed means of Salvation, in fact, anything instituted by man, will instantly be unacceptable to God. Only the Blood of Jesus Christ, God's Son, can *"cleanse from all sin"* (I Jn. 1:7).

THE ABSOLUTE NECESSITY OF THE CROSS

Some of you reading this Commentary may at times think that we go overboard as it regards our insistence upon the Cross of Christ. The truth is, if in fact something is wrong with our presentation, it's that we do not stress enough the Cross of Christ. I would surely hope that the Reader would see this in the Book of Leviticus.

We must understand that we are talking about the eternal soul of man; consequently, there could be nothing more significant than that. Jesus said: *"For what is a man profited, if he shall gain the whole world, and lose his own soul? Or what shall a man give in exchange for his soul?"* (Mat. 16:26).

As we know from the Word of God, there is only one way for the soul to be saved, and that is by Faith in Christ, accepting what He has done for us at the Cross (Jn. 3:16; Rom. 5:1; Eph. 2:8-9; Rom. 10:9-10, 13).

If that in fact is true, and considering the weight of the subject, I don't think it would be possible to overstress the significance of the Cross.

The way of Christ is a simple way. Paul said as much: *"But I fear, lest by any means, as the serpent beguiled Eve through his subtilty, so your minds should be corrupted from the simplicity that is in Christ"* (II Cor. 11:3).

But religious men would attempt to corrupt that simple Faith, for that is what is actually being discussed. They would add to this simple Faith, or else detract from it. To do so leaves such a Believer worshipping *"another Jesus,"* which is promoted by *"another spirit"* which results in *"another gospel"* (II Cor. 11:4).

To use as an example, if medical scientists perfect a particular type of medicine which will stop a particular disease, it should go without saying, if the ingredients in that medicine are tampered with in any way, its effectiveness will be totally destroyed. It is the same way with the Plan of God as it regards Redemption. Everything pertaining to God is based 100 percent on the foundation of *"Jesus Christ and Him Crucified"* (I Cor. 1:17-18, 21, 23; Gal. 6:14; Eph. 2:13-18; Jn. 3:16). Anything else is bogus!

Considering presently that the Cross is little preached, where does that leave the modern Church?

SAVED OR UNSAVED?

The terrible truth is, due to the problems that we have mentioned, most people in the modern Church aren't really born again. Of course, some few are! And again, there are some few Churches where the far greater majority in those Churches are born again. But those Churches, regrettably, are few and far between. In fact, there are tens of thousands of Churches, perhaps even more, where there is not one single person in those particular Churches who is truly saved. In fact, many who are very religious aren't actually saved.

The reason is, their faith and trust is not really in Christ, but rather something else. They may think it is Christ, but the truth is, they have divorced Christ from the Cross. And Christ without the Cross, as ought to be overly obvious, is pure and simple, as stated, *"another Jesus"* (II Cor. 11:4).

Sometime ago I received a letter from a lady from a particular state several hundreds of miles from Baton Rouge. She had seen our Telecast, and had given her heart to Christ. But the amazing thing about this is the following:

She told me that she was a member of a Baptist Church. She went on to relate that she was so versed in Baptist doctrine, actually having been raised in a Baptist Church, that she was the one who taught the new members class, instructing new members of the Church in Baptist doctrine.

But she said, *"Brother Swaggart, as I watched your Telecast last Sunday Morning, for the first time in my life, I felt the convicting power of the Holy Spirit. I then realized, for all of my religiosity, I wasn't saved."*

She then said, *"I prayed the sinner's prayer with you at the conclusion of the Message, and then knew beyond the shadow of a doubt that I was truly born again. The joy that immediately filled my soul, and continues to do so unto this very moment, is beyond description."*

And finally she said, *"To think that I've been so close all of this time, but yet so very far away. But thank the Lord, I now know Jesus Christ in my heart, and not merely in my head."*

I haven't quoted the dear lady verbatim, simply because I don't have her letter before me. But what I have said is basically the gist of what she proclaimed to me in her correspondence.

I doubt, considering the religiosity of this dear lady, that many people would have considered her to be unsaved. She was a member of a prestigious Church; and incidentally, while she was the member of a Baptist Church, what was said could be said about almost any Church. She was faithful in her attendance, faithful in her tithing, faithful in her learning of Baptist doctrine, so almost anyone would have thought of her as definitely being saved. But she wasn't! I'm afraid that's the case with untold millions.

As well, one must understand, to be wrong about other things is one thing, but to be wrong about our soul's Salvation is another matter altogether. There is absolutely nothing more important than that.

UNCLEANNESS AND TRANSGRESSIONS

Verse 16 reads: *"And he shall make an Atonement for the Holy Place, because of the uncleanness of the Children of Israel, and because of their transgressions and all their sins: and so shall he do for the Tabernacle of the congregation, that remains among them in the midst of their uncleanness."*

The Children of Israel were at a great advantage as it regarded the other nations of the world, in that they knew the Lord, while the other nations didn't. At the same time,

at least by comparison to the New Covenant, they were at a great disadvantage. The blood of bulls and goats could not take away sins (Heb. 10:4), and this was their disadvantage. While it did serve as a stopgap measure, so to speak, it only delayed judgment.

By that I refer to the fact that had Jesus not gone to the Cross, judgment would definitely have come upon all the Old Testament Saints, which means they would have been eternally lost. They died in the Faith looking forward to One Who was to come, Who in fact could take away sin, to which all of these sacrifices and rituals pointed.

Sin defiles, and defiles greatly. Despite efforts to the contrary, the individual who is not washed by the Blood of Jesus can only be described as *"unclean."* In fact, this is what the terrible disease of leprosy represented, which we studied in Chapters 14 and 15. That being a symbol of sin, and used by the Lord accordingly, we should understand just how unclean the unredeemed person actually is.

Sin defiles the heart, the life, the mind, and in fact, every part of the human being. It leaves nothing untouched, unscarred, unsullied!

Someone asked me the other day as to what effect does sin have on a Believer?

The moment the Believer confesses his sin (I Jn. 1:9), at that moment he is perfectly cleansed by the Precious Blood of Christ (I Jn. 1:7). For things that we really do not know about, but yet which causes us to come short of the Glory of God, the Blood of Christ is constantly cleansing.

As it regards known sins, even though confessed before the Lord immediately, and cleansed immediately, still, there is always an after effect of sin, which is very negative. In some way it hurts us! And of that, one can be certain.

No person, redeemed or otherwise, sins and gets by. Always and without exception, sin takes its deadly toll!

So, for the Believer to think that sin doesn't really matter, at least as it regards a Believer, and because Grace abounds much more than sin (Rom. 5:20), they should read carefully Paul's answer:

"What shall we say then? Shall we continue in sin, that Grace may abound?

"God forbid, how shall we, who are dead

to sin, live any longer therein?" (Rom. 6:1-2).

(17) "AND THERE SHALL BE NO MAN IN THE TABERNACLE OF THE CONGREGATION WHEN HE GOES IN TO MAKE AN ATONEMENT IN THE HOLY PLACE, UNTIL HE COME OUT, AND HAVE MADE AN ATONEMENT FOR HIMSELF, AND FOR HIS HOUSEHOLD, AND FOR ALL THE CONGREGATION OF ISRAEL.

(18) "AND HE SHALL GO OUT UNTO THE ALTAR THAT IS BEFORE THE LORD, AND MAKE AN ATONEMENT FOR IT; AND SHALL TAKE OF THE BLOOD OF THE BULLOCK, AND OF THE BLOOD OF THE GOAT, AND PUT IT UPON THE HORNS OF THE ALTAR ROUND ABOUT.

(19) "AND HE SHALL SPRINKLE OF THE BLOOD UPON IT WITH HIS FINGERS SEVEN TIMES, AND CLEANSE IT, AND HALLOW IT FROM THE UNCLEANNESS OF THE CHILDREN OF ISRAEL."

The exegesis is:

1. *"Atonement for the Holy Place,"* referred to the Golden Altar, and the blood that was to be applied there.

2. When the High Priest atoned for the Holy Place, no man was to be present other than himself. This nullifies all the arguments and practices of pretentious Priesthoods that made claims of direct representation as mediators between God and the people, while Christ is in the Heavenly Tabernacle, as now, carrying on His Priestly Work (Heb. 4:14-16; 5:1-14).

3. Christ is the only Mediator between God and men (I Tim. 2:4-6; Heb. 9:24).

4. No man can sacrifice Christ anew, for He has been sacrificed *"once for all"* (Heb. 7:27; 9:26-28; I Pet. 3:18), and this means that His flesh cannot be mystically made into bread or wafers which are the creation of man.

NO MAN

Verse 17 reads: *"And there shall be no man in the Tabernacle of the congregation when he goes in to make an Atonement in the Holy Place, until he come out, and have made an Atonement for himself, and for his household, and for all the congregation of Israel."*

While the High Priest was performing this process of cleansing, no one, whether Priest

or Israelite, was permitted to be present, thus precluding the possibility of anyone being within the precincts who had unwittingly contracted defilement. The High Priest alone must carry out this task, who incidentally, was a type of Christ. Christ Alone can cleanse from all sin, and He does so by the application of His Blood, and our Faith in that Finished Work.

COVERING

In the last few years, we've heard a lot about *"covering."* What exactly does it mean?

It means that certain Preachers claim that they serve as a *"covering"* for other Preachers, or that Denominations serve as a *"covering"* for those who are associated.

While such statements sound good to the flesh, they are totally unscriptural. In fact, such thinking is so unscriptural that it is an insult to Christ.

For any person to claim that another man (or woman), or even a religious Denomination is their covering is, at the same time, saying that Christ is not sufficient. Paul emphatically states: *"For there is one God, and one Mediator between God and men, the Man Christ Jesus"* (I Tim. 2:5).

For a Preacher to claim to be a covering for other Preachers, or even a Denomination to serve as such, is at the same time to insult Christ. Do we realize just how much of an insult that is? Do we realize that is a complete abrogation of the Finished Work of Christ?

The truth is, no human being can serve as a *"covering"* for anyone else, and to think so shows a complete ignorance of the Word of God.

Listen to the Prophet Isaiah, through whom the Lord spoke, saying: *"Woe to the rebellious children, saith the LORD, who take counsel, but not of Me; and that cover with a covering, but not of My Spirit, that they may add sin to sin"* (Isa. 30:1).

Any time we go astray, which means to leave the Word of God for directions of our own making, in some way, it is because of an improper interpretation of the Cross, or else the ignoring of the Cross. And this particular sin of man-made coverings is worse than most, because it strikes at the very heart of the Plan of Redemption, respecting Christ as the Mediator, and the only Mediator.

So, no man could enter into the Tabernacle of the Congregation when Aaron was making Atonement for the very Tabernacle itself.

THE BLOOD AND THE HORNS OF THE ALTAR

Verse 18 reads: *"And he shall go out unto the Altar that is before the LORD, and make an Atonement for it; and shall take of the blood of the bullock, and of the blood of the goat, and put it upon the horns of the Altar round about."*

The Altar addressed here is the Golden Altar, which sat in the Holy Place, directly in front of the Veil. It was referred to at times as the *"Altar of Incense."*

It typified Christ in His Mediatorial, Atoning, and Intercessory role as the High Priest of His people. In fact, it speaks of what Christ is doing right now before the Throne of God, and doing so by His very Presence, and in fact, has been doing ever since the Cross, and will continue to do so until He comes back in Person to rule and reign (Rev., Chpt. 19).

Blood was placed by the High Priest on the four horns of the Altar, signifying the following:

Horns in the Bible signify dominion or rulership. The idea is, due to what Christ has done for us at the Cross, we can have total and complete victory in every aspect of our spiritual life. The fact that the horns pointed in all four directions of the compass also signifies that we can have, and in fact, are meant to have total and complete dominion over all works of the flesh.

We are told how to do this in the Sixth Chapter of Romans.

ROMANS, CHAPTER 6

Without a doubt, this particular Chapter (Rom., Chpt. 6) is at least one of the most important Chapters in the entirety of the Word of God. While every single part of the Word is significant beyond compare, as should be obvious, some particular Chapters are used by the Holy Spirit to bring to a head all which have been taught elsewhere. Romans, Chapter 6 is one of those Chapters.

THE CROSS

Verses 3 through 5 of this Chapter point to the Cross, and the Believer's part in that Finished Work. It is a part that has to do with the initial Salvation experience, and as well, our continued life and living before the Lord. There is nothing more important!

Paul takes us first of all to the Cross, and in fact, takes us no further, simply because every benefit comes by and through the Cross of Christ.

He tells the Believer how that we as believing sinners, when we accepted Christ, we were *"baptized into His death."* Now this doesn't pertain to Water Baptism, as some believe. In fact, it has nothing to do with Water Baptism. It speaks entirely of the Crucifixion of Christ, and our part in His death. In other words, in the Mind of God, we literally died in Him when He died. To explain that, the word *"baptized"* is used, because its actual meaning refers to the fact that Baptism speaks of the person being into that in which it is being baptized, and that in which it is being baptized, being in the person. An excellent example would be a ship at the bottom of the ocean. The water is in the ship, and the ship is in the water.

Jesus was our Substitute, which is the limit of our understanding. But in the Mind of God, He was so much a Substitute as the *"Last Adam,"* that we were literally in Him when He died (I Cor. 15:45-50).

We not only were baptized into His death, but as well, we were *"buried with Him by baptism into death."* This means that all that we were, and I speak of the evil, the wickedness, the transgression, all and in its entirety were buried with Him.

When the Romans put the stone over the tomb, they thought they were holding the body of Christ in that tomb, but in reality, they were sealing up our sins, and all of our past, for it to be buried with Him forever and forever. In other words, because of Faith in Him, these sins can never be brought up before us again. We (they) are buried with Him.

As well, not only were we *"baptized into His death,"* and *"buried with Him by baptism into death,"* but also, we were raised with Him *"in newness of life"* (Rom. 6:3-4).

THE POWER OF THE SIN NATURE IS NOW DESTROYED

Paul said: *"Knowing this, that our old man is crucified with Him, that the body of sin might be destroyed, that henceforth we should not serve sin.*

"For he who is dead is freed from sin" (Rom. 6:6-7).

At the Cross, the power of sin was destroyed, and the guilt of sin was removed. Consequently, due to what Christ there did, the sin nature, although remaining with me, no longer has any sway within my heart and life. In fact, although present, it is to be dormant, and in fact, will remain dormant if our Faith remains in the Cross.

Whenever Christ died, we died. This means that the old man died, and now in Christ, I am a *"new creation"* (II Cor. 5:17).

I now have the capacity to live the *"Resurrection Life."* This means exactly as those four horns on the Golden Altar portrayed, that I can have total and complete victory over the flesh, and all to which it pertains. In other words, I can live this *"Resurrection Life."*

However, I cannot do this unless I understand at all times that I *"have been planted together in the likeness of His death"* (Rom. 6:5).

In other words, my *"Resurrection Living,"* which pertains to victory over all things, depends on my understanding of *"the likeness of His death,"* and my part in that death. This is absolutely crucial, and is imperative that the Believer understands and learns what is being said here.

THE SIN NATURE

Some 17 times in Romans, Chapter 6, Paul mentions *"the sin nature."*

Fifteen of these times, the word *"sin"* in the original Text, has before it what is referred to as the definite article, which would make it read *"the sin,"* thereby, referring to a particular principle of sin, and not acts of sin.

The other two times, the sin nature is implied, although the definite article time is not present (vss. 14, 15).

If the Believer no longer has a sin nature, as some Preachers claim, then the Holy Spirit

through Paul, wasted a lot of time and space explaining something that so longer exists. To be sure, the sin nature definitely does continue to exist in the heart and life of the Believer, but as stated, if we function according to God's prescribed order of victory, it will remain dormant in our lives, and definitely will not overpower us.

The unsaved person has two natures, *"human nature, and the sin nature."* The Believer has three natures, *"human nature, the sin nature, and the Divine Nature"* (II Pet. 1:4). (Jesus had a human nature as well as the Divine Nature, but no sin nature. The Virgin Birth guaranteed this.)

The sin nature rules the unconverted person, and I mean rules and reigns totally and completely.

While the sin nature is present in the life of the Believer, it is not to rule and reign (Rom. 6:12-13). However, it will definitely rule and reign in the Believer's life, no matter how dedicated that Believer might be, no matter how zealous he might be, if the Believer doesn't understand the Cross as it refers to Sanctification. This is sad but true, especially considering that virtually all of the modern Church is ruled by the sin nature. I say that not from a perspective of judging, but from the perspective of knowing and understanding that the modern Church understands almost nothing about the Cross, as it regards Sanctification.

FAITH

Paul said: *"Likewise reckon ye also yourselves to be dead indeed unto* (the) *sin, but alive unto God through Jesus Christ our Lord"* (Rom. 6:11).

This Scripture proclaims the necessity of the Believer continuing to exhibit Faith in Christ, and what Christ has done at the Cross. Doing that, and continuing to do that, and in fact, continuing to do that until the Lord calls us home, or the trump sounds, will guarantee that we stay dead unto the sin nature, but *"alive unto God through Jesus Christ our Lord."* This is where Faith comes in.

The Believer reckons himself to be dead unto the sin nature, strictly because of what Christ did at the Cross, and our part in His atoning death. This has to do with the *"Law of the Spirit of Life in Christ Jesus."*

THE LAW OF THE SPIRIT OF LIFE

Romans 8:2 says: *"For the Law of the Spirit of Life in Christ Jesus has made me free from the law of sin and death."*

Actually, the original Text says: *"For the Law of the Spirit of the Life in Christ Jesus did set me free from the Law of the sin and of the death."*

The definite article in the Greek is in front of the word *"Life,"* and it's also in front of the word *"sin,"* and *"death."* So what does this mean?

First of all, *"the Life,"* refers to the benefits of what Christ did at the Cross. It is the only *"Life"* there is, and as well, the only way we can have this *"Life"* is through *"the Law of the Spirit."*

As well, the word *"sin"* also has the definite article in front, signifying *"the sin,"* which refers to the sin nature. *"The death"* refers to eternal separation from God.

The only way I can have victory over *"the sin,"* i.e., *"the sin nature,"* which produces *"the death,"* is through the manner and the way in which the Holy Spirit works, which is according to *"the Law."* Now what is this Law?

It's not the Law of Moses, but it is rather *"The Law of the Spirit of Life."*

We find that this *"Law"* is ensconced *"in Christ Jesus."* In other words, this particular *"Law"* has its foundation and its function in what Christ did at the Cross on our behalf. The Work of Christ on the Cross was a legal work, hence, the Holy Spirit using here the word *"Law."*

On the Cross, Jesus satisfied the legal demands of a thrice-Holy God. Man had sinned grievously against Him, in fact, spoiling and polluting the entirety of the creation of God, and this was a debt that had to be paid. It was a legal debt, which gave Satan the legal right to hold man in captivity. When Jesus died on the Cross, He legally paid that debt, which then set man free, at least all who will believe (Jn. 3:16).

Understanding this *"Law of the Spirit of Life in Christ Jesus,"* and applying it to my heart and life, which I do by Faith in Christ, and what Christ has done for me

NOTES

in His Sacrificial, Atoning Death, I now have the following Promise:

THE DOMINION OF SIN IS BROKEN

Paul said: *"For sin* (the sin nature) *shall not have dominion over you: for you are not under the Law, but under Grace"* (Rom. 6:14).

Instead of the sin nature now having dominion over me, I have dominion over it, typified by the four horns on the Golden Altar. But due to the fact that blood was applied to those horns, this tells me that this dominion that I have, and which Romans, Chapter 6 beautifully explains, comes to me only by the Sacrificial, Atoning Death of Christ on the Cross. I can have this victory in no other way, no other manner!

GOD'S PRESCRIBED ORDER OF VICTORY

This which I have briefly given unto you, and which was first given to us by the Apostle Paul, is God's prescribed order of victory. Let the Reader understand that this is the only order of victory that God has, which is ensconced in the Cross. All of it is totally *"in"* the Cross, totally *"of"* the Cross, and totally *"by"* the Cross.

If we as Believers attempt to live for God any other way, than by Faith in Christ and His great Sacrifice, we will, in effect, be committing spiritual adultery, which means the Holy Spirit, in such a case, will not help us, which translates into failure (Rom. 7:1-4). When we try to live for the Lord by any other means or way than Faith in Christ and His Cross, whether we realize it or not, we are being unfaithful to Christ, thereby, committing spiritual adultery, which God, as should be obvious, can never honor. Knowing precious little about the Cross as it regards Sanctification, most Christians presently, God forbid, are committing, and in fact, living in spiritual adultery.

Reading the first four Verses of Romans, Chapter 7, we realize that the Holy Spirit chose these words and did so very carefully. Inasmuch as the word *"adultery"* is used, but used to explain a spiritual position, it was done this way in order that we might understand the seriousness of the situation. The Lord does not look lightly upon one who places his faith and trust in self, or other things, rather than Christ and Him Crucified. Considering the price that He has paid, I think it should be obvious as to His anger. In fact, the Scripture says: *"For the Wrath of God is revealed from Heaven against all ungodliness and unrighteousness of men, who hold the truth in unrighteousness"* (Rom. 1:18).

Jesus paid a great price for my victory, and I want the total victory for which this price was paid, and every Believer should desire such. Considering the price, it is an insult to Christ not to have all of that for which He has paid.

SEVEN TIMES

Verse 19 reads: *"And he shall sprinkle of the blood upon it with his finger seven times, cleanse it, and hallow it from the uncleanness of the Children of Israel."*

In fact, in these two Verses, we are given a double promise.

First of all, and to which we have addressed ourselves, the blood on the four horns signified a total dominion. As well, the blood sprinkled seven times on the Golden Altar, as well, signifies a total and complete dominion, hence the double promise.

So this means that if we live beneath our spiritual privileges, then we are doing so needlessly. But yet, all of us have functioned far below the level in which we should function, and mostly because of not knowing what Jesus has done for us.

(There is some disagreement as to what Altar is being addressed in Verse 18. Some claim that it's the Brazen Altar; however, the authorities during the Second Temple (the one after Solomon's Temple) took this to denote the Golden Altar, or the Altar of Incense which stood in the Holy Place over against the Holy of Holies, as this was the Altar for which expiation was made once a year on this day (Ex. 30:10); hence it was cleansed next. From the Passage in Exodus, I must conclude as well that it is the Golden Altar, and not the Brazen Altar, which is mentioned in this Eighteenth Verse.)

(20) "AND WHEN HE HAS MADE AN END OF RECONCILING THE HOLY PLACE, AND THE TABERNACLE OF THE CONGREGATION, AND THE ALTAR, HE SHALL

BRING THE LIVE GOAT:

(21) "AND AARON SHALL LAY BOTH HIS HANDS UPON THE HEAD OF THE LIVE GOAT, AND CONFESS OVER HIM ALL THE INIQUITIES OF THE CHILDREN OF ISRAEL, AND ALL THEIR TRANSGRESSIONS AND ALL THEIR SINS, PUTTING THEM UPON THE HEAD OF THE GOAT, AND SHALL SEND HIM AWAY BY THE HAND OF A FIT MAN INTO THE WILDERNESS:

(22) "AND THE GOAT SHALL BEAR UPON HIM ALL THEIR INIQUITIES UNTO A LAND NOT INHABITED: HE SHALL LET GO THE GOAT IN THE WILDERNESS."

The diagram is:

1. Verses 20 through 22 proclaim the scapegoat, which was sent away.

2. Aaron was to lay both his hands upon the head of the live goat and confess that Israel, in fact, had committed many iniquities and transgressions.

3. The goat (goat of departure) would now go into the wilderness, signifying that the sins were gone. Consequently, it could be translated, *"the departure of the sins."*

THE LIVE GOAT

Verse 20 reads: *"And when He has made an end of reconciling the Holy Place, and the Tabernacle of the congregation, and the Altar, he shall bring the live goat."*

Pulpit Commentary says: *"The second part of the ceremonies of the day now commences. It was not enough that the defilement of the Sanctuary should be covered, and the sins of the Priests and people atoned for by the blood of the Sacrifices. There remained a consciousness of sin. How was this to be taken away?"*

The phrase, *"He shall bring the live goat,"* should have been translated *"offer the live goat."* It is the same word used above for the offering of the goat that was slain, and it is the same Hebrew word always used for offering Sacrifices to the Lord.

WHAT DO WE MEAN BY A CONSCIOUSNESS OF SIN?

Perhaps it would be better asked, *"What do we mean by the consciousness of the removal of sin?"*

Inasmuch as the blood of bulls and goats

could not take away sins (Heb. 10:4), the conscience of the people of Israel was not eased. There was still a nagging knowledge, so to speak, that the sins remained. Paul said: *"Which was a figure for the time then present, and which were offered both gifts and Sacrifices, that could not make him who did the service perfect, as pertaining to the conscience"* (Heb. 9:9).

This being the case, something else was needed, something visible, which could portray their sins being removed, even though the nagging consciousness of sin remained. That which filled this void was the scapegoat.

THE SCAPEGOAT

Verse 21 reads: *"And Aaron shall lay both his hands upon the head of the live goat, and confess over him all the iniquities of the Children of Israel, and all their transgressions and all their sins, putting them upon the head of the goat, and shall send him away by the hand of a fit man into the wilderness."*

The goat that had been sacrificed as a Sin-Offering had atoned for the sins of the nation of Israel, with its blood having been applied to the Mercy Seat in the Holy of Holies. But now the Children of Israel needed a visible figure, a sign, that these sins had been removed.

To carry this out, Aaron laid both hands on the head of the live goat. He then confessed over him all the iniquities, transgressions, and sins of the people of Israel. The following is one form of this prayer:

"O Lord, they have committed iniquity; they have transgressed; they have sinned – Your people, the House of Israel. O Lord, cover over, I entreat You, their iniquities, their transgressions, and their sins, which they have wickedly committed, transgressed, and sinned before You – Your people, the House of Israel.

"As it is written in the Law of Moses Your servant, saying, 'For on that day shall it be covered over for you, to make you clean; from all your sins before the Lord you shall be cleansed.'"

During this confession of sins, the people remained prostrate in humiliation and prayer in the Court of the Tabernacle, and it was the custom of the High Priest to turn

NOTES

toward them as he pronounced the last words, *"You shall be cleansed."*

The Temple enclosure in Jerusalem had three Courts. The first one, which was the closest to the Brazen Altar, was the Court of Israel, or Court of Men, as it was sometimes called. Immediately in back of that was the Court of Women; actually, this was as close as women could come as it regarded the sacred precincts of the Temple.

Immediately in back of the Court of Women was the Court of the Gentiles, separated from the Court of Women by a barrier, which was approximately four feet high. If a Gentile crossed that barrier, he could be stoned to death.

In all three of these Courts, many thousands of people could stand, and witness the proceedings, or at least some of them. As well, on the Temple Mount proper, possibly one million people could occupy this vast space. Actually, I've personally been on this Mount several times, and it could easily hold this many people.

As it regards the Tabernacle, it had only one Court or enclosure, which wouldn't hold many people. But untold thousands, as would be obvious, could stand nearby the white fence which enclosed the Tabernacle, which they no doubt did. I say, *"stand,"* but in reality, they were prostrate in humiliation and prayer.

When the prayer had ended, the supplication for mercy and forgiveness, the goat was placed into the care of a *"fit man,"* to be led into the wilderness. This *"fit man"* was one who had been appointed for the occasion.

THE WILDERNESS

Verse 22 reads: *"And the goat shall bear upon him all their iniquities unto a land not inhabited: he shall let go the goat in the wilderness."*

As stated, this goat was actually labeled *"the goat of departure,"* which referred to the sins of the people departing from them, which in a sense gave them a visible sign that their sins were now atoned.

One can very well imagine the joy that must have filled the hearts of the many thousands who observed this scene, watching the goat as it was led away, and in effect taking away their sins, typifying Christ Who bore the iniquity of mankind, thereby, *"taking away the sin of the world"* (Jn. 1:29).

HOW DID CHRIST TAKE AWAY OUR SIN?

He took away our sin by taking away the debt. He paid the price, and the price being paid, there is no more debt, and no more sin.

As we've already stated, the blood of bulls and goats couldn't take away sins, so this means that the debt was not actually paid at this time. Bulls and goats could not pay that debt, as would be obvious. They served as a stopgap measure until Christ would come, which He did. When He did come, He went to the Cross, did bear the terrible sin penalty, which was death, and did so by the shedding of His Life's Blood, which paid the debt, and because it atoned for all sin. It was a Sacrifice which satisfied the Divine Justice of a thrice-Holy God. The Sacrifice being accepted means that the debt was forever paid. There are three Greek words which rightly define Redemption. They are:

1. Garazo: It means that by the Sacrificial Death of Christ on the Cross, we were purchased out of the slave market. In truth, every unbeliever is a slave of Satan, whether he realizes such or not.

2. Exgarazo: We were purchased out of the slave market, never to be put up for auction again. In other words, *"If the Son therefore shall make you free, you shall be free indeed"* (Jn. 8:36).

3. Lutroo: This Greek word means that such a price was paid on the Cross of Calvary that in eternity future, no demon, fallen angel, or Satan himself will ever be able to say that the price was insufficient.

The goat bearing the iniquities of the people unto a land not inhabited would be more correctly translated, *"a land cut off."* This referred to complete isolation from the surrounding country by some barrier of rock or torrent, which would make it impossible for the goat to come back again. Thus, the sins were utterly lost, as though they had never been, and they could not return to the sanctified people.

It is said that the arrival of the goat in the wilderness was immediately telegraphed by the waving of flags, from station to station,

until a few minutes after its occurrence it was known in the Temple, and whispered from ear to ear, that the goat had borne upon him all their iniquities into a land not inhabited. Both the goat that was a sacrifice, and the goat that served as remover of sins typified Christ.

The first presents Him to our Faith as the Victim on the Cross; the other as the Sin-Bearer on Whom *"the Lord laid on Him the iniquity of us all"* (Isa. 53:4; II Cor. 5:21; Gal. 3:13).

Concerning this, Keil says: *"The reason for making use of two animals is to be found purely in the physical impossibility of combining all features that had to be set forth in the Sin-Offering in one animal."*

(23) "AND AARON SHALL COME INTO THE TABERNACLE OF THE CONGREGATION, AND SHALL PUT OFF THE LINEN GARMENTS, WHICH HE PUT ON WHEN HE WENT INTO THE HOLY PLACE, AND SHALL LEAVE THEM THERE:

(24) "AND HE SHALL WASH HIS FLESH WITH WATER IN THE HOLY PLACE, AND PUT ON HIS GARMENTS, AND COME FORTH, AND OFFER HIS BURNT-OFFERING, AND THE BURNT-OFFERING OF THE PEOPLE, AND MAKE AN ATONEMENT FOR HIMSELF, AND FOR THE PEOPLE.

(25) "AND THE FAT OF THE SIN-OFFERING SHALL HE BURN UPON THE ALTAR."

The diagram is:

1. The work of Atonement now being finished, Aaron could once again put on his garments of glory and beauty.

2. He was to now offer his Burnt-Offering, and the Burnt-Offering of the people, which signified the Perfection of Christ.

3. The only part of the Sin-Offering burned on the Altar was the *"fat,"* which signified the prosperity of Christ that was given to the people.

4. No *"Meal"* or *"Peace-Offering"* appeared on this day, because Atonement, and not fellowship, was the business of that day.

THE GARMENTS OF GLORY AND BEAUTY

Verse 23 reads: *"And Aaron shall come into the Tabernacle of the congregation, and shall put off the linen garments, which he put on when he went into the Holy Place, and shall leave them there."*

Aaron having gone into the Holy of Holies some three times, and which he had to wear only the linen garments, typifying the Righteousness of Christ, that glorious task now being finished, he will once again put on his garments of glory and beauty, designed by the Holy Spirit, and designed solely for the High Priest, who was a type of Christ.

THE BURNT-OFFERINGS AND THE FAT OF THE SIN-OFFERING

Verses 24 and 25 read: *"And he shall wash his flesh with water in the Holy Place, and put on his garments, and come forth, and offer his Burnt-Offering, and the Burnt-Offering of the people, and make an Atonement for himself, and for the people.*

"And the fat of the Sin-Offering shall he burn upon the Altar."

It is now time to offer the *"Burnt-Offerings,"* which will be two rams, one for themselves, and one for the people.

Along with the Burnt-Offerings, he will also place on the Altar, *"the fat of the Sin-Offering,"* which was a bullock (vs. 6) and of a goat (vs. 15).

While the skin was taken from the Burnt-Offering, and the fat removed from the carcass, the entirety of the carcass other than those things mentioned was to be burned on the Altar. The *"Burnt-Offering"* typified the Perfection of Christ, and His Perfect Sacrifice, which satisfied the demands of God.

With the blood having been applied to the Mercy Seat in the Holy of Holies, and as well, sprinkled some seven times on the Altar of Incense, Atonement had now been made. The *"Burnt-Offerings"* could now be offered up, and they would be accepted by God.

As stated, the *"fat,"* which was always burned on the Altar, regardless of the type of Offering, typified the prosperity of Christ, given to those who would accept Him as Lord and Redeemer. A sickly animal had very little if any fat, while a healthy animal, as would be obvious, would have fat surrounding the various internal organs.

WHY?

Upon reading the accounts of all of these

rituals and ceremonies, and especially the copious amount of blood that had to be shed, one may well wonder as to why all of this was necessary. Could not Almighty God have atoned for sin in a different way? Was all of this necessary?

Jesus answered this question in the Garden of Gethsemane.

When facing the terrible Crucifixion, and we're not speaking here of the pain and suffering, but rather Him being the Sin-Bearer of all mankind, He said: *"O My Father, if it be possible, let this cup pass from Me: nevertheless not as I will, but as You will"* (Mat. 26:39).

If the Justice and Righteousness of God were to be satisfied, and if His nature was to be upheld, these things had to be satisfied, the manner in which Redemption was brought about had to be done, and had to be done in this manner only.

Sin is an awful thing, much, much worse than the most ardent Bible Scholar could ever know. As previously stated, we know that from the price that was paid to cleanse man from sin – the Death and Resurrection of God's Own Son.

Without the system set up under the Levitical Law, no man could be right with God, and no man could be saved. Consequently, none of the Gentile nations that existed during all of this period of time could be saved. In fact, these nations were by and large controlled by demon spirits. Once again we go back to the nature of the Fall. If affected everything and everyone, and did so in a disastrous way.

While Gentiles could be saved before the Cross, they had to do so by entering into the Covenant that God had with Israel. In other words, they had to become a proselyte Jew, or in some way exercise believing Faith, which some few did. But other than that, there was no means or way of Salvation.

Along with all the other tremendous benefits of the Cross, that which surely was not least was the fact that Jesus died for the whole world, thereby, making it possible for all to come in, and to do so by Faith (Jn. 3:16; Gal. 5:6).

Paul said: *"And that He* (Christ) *might reconcile both* (Jews and Gentiles) *unto God in one body* (one Church) *by the Cross, having slain the enmity thereby*" (Eph. 2:16).

Every Gentile who lives and breathes should thank God one thousand times over for the Cross. That and that alone made it possible for us to come in.

(26) "AND HE WHO LET GO THE GOAT FOR THE SCAPEGOAT SHALL WASH HIS CLOTHES, AND BATHE HIS FLESH IN WATER, AND AFTERWARD COME INTO THE CAMP.

(27) "AND THE BULLOCK FOR THE SIN-OFFERING, AND THE GOAT FOR THE SIN-OFFERING, WHOSE BLOOD WAS BROUGHT IN TO MAKE ATONEMENT IN THE HOLY PLACE, SHALL ONE CARRY FORTH WITHOUT THE CAMP; AND THEY SHALL BURN IN THE FIRE THEIR SKINS, AND THEIR FLESH, AND THEIR DUNG.

(28) "AND HE WHO BURNED THEM SHALL WASH HIS CLOTHES, AND BATHE HIS FLESH IN WATER, AND AFTERWARD HE SHALL COME INTO THE CAMP.

(29) "AND THIS SHALL BE A STATUTE FOREVER UNTO YOU: THAT IN THE SEVENTH MONTH, ON THE TENTH DAY OF THE MONTH, YOU SHALL AFFLICT YOUR SOULS, AND DO NO WORK AT ALL, WHETHER IT BE ONE OF YOUR OWN COUNTRY, OR A STRANGER WHO SOJOURNS AMONG YOU:"

The structure is:

1. The Burnt-Offerings completed the extra Offerings on the Great Day of Atonement mentioned in this Chapter. The regular daily Sacrifices were also offered, but are not listed here.

2. The washing of Aaron, and the washing of the man who burned the Sin-Offerings outside the camp, signifies that contacting sin, even in a symbolic way, caused the High Priest to be so unclean that washing and more Sacrifices were required.

3. Contact with sin makes one unclean and sinful. The washing of Aaron took place after the goat had been sent into the open countryside outside the camp.

4. This Sin-Offering being sent outside the camp and burned typified Christ as a Sin-Offering, dying outside the camp (Heb. 13:11-12).

NOTES

WASHING

Verse 26 reads: *"And he who let go the goat for the scapegoat shall wash his clothes, and bathe his flesh in water, and afterward come into the camp."*

The man who led the scapegoat into the wilderness, even though all of this was merely symbolic, still, had to wash himself, and his clothes, before coming back into the camp.

We derive from this the fact of the defilement of sin. The scapegoat, symbolically, was bearing the sins of Israel, in effect, taking them away. As such, any contact with this animal defiled the one making the contact.

This is the reason as Believers that we should be careful about sin in any respect. As Paul said, *"All things are lawful for me, but all things are not expedient: all things are lawful for me, but all things edify not"* (I Cor. 10:23).

So it's not a matter so much of what we can and can't do, but rather, is what we're doing bringing Glory to God? While the Christian certainly should not be taken over as it regards concern for sin, at the same time, we must never fail to realize its deadly effect. To be sure, sin is just as hurtful and destructive to the Christian as it is anyone else – even more so!

BURN IN THE FIRE

Verse 27 reads: *"And the bullock for the Sin-Offering, and the goat for the Sin-Offering, whose blood was brought in to make Atonement in the Holy Place, shall one carry forth without the camp; and they shall burn in the fire their skins, and their flesh, and their dung."*

As we stated in the headings, Jesus suffered without the Camp. In other words, He was crucified outside the walls of Jerusalem. This was necessary in order that He might be the Sin-Offering.

The fat of the Sin-Offering was burned on the Altar, and as well, its blood was used *"to make Atonement in the Holy of Holies"*; however, its carcass had to be taken outside of the camp and burned. In fact, the Burnt-Offering alone was totally consumed, minus its skin, on the Altar. All the other Offerings, while the fat was burned, were consumed in other ways. In fact, the majority of the Sin-Offering was eaten by the Priests (Lev. 10:17-18).

THE GREAT DAY OF ATONEMENT

Verses 28 and 29 read: *"And he who burned them shall wash his clothes, and bathe his flesh in water, and afterward he shall come into the camp.*

"And this shall be a Statute forever unto you: that in the seventh month, on the tenth day of the month, you shall afflict your souls, and do no work at all, whether it be one of your own country, or a stranger who sojourns among you."

The ceremonies of the Day of Atonement are not appointed for once only, but they were to be annual observances.

The Day of Atonement is the single fast of the Jewish Church, occurring once a year only. The fast began on the evening of the ninth day of the month, and ended on the evening of the tenth, when it was succeeded by general feasting. During the whole of the 24 hours no work at all was to be done.

As well, these regulations applied to strangers who sojourned among them, as to themselves.

The purpose of the abstinence from food and labor was to bring the soul of each individual into harmony with the solemn rites of purification publicly performed not by themselves, but by the High Priest (Pulpit).

Incidentally, the Great Day of Atonement took place in the Jewish month which corresponds to our September. On the first of the month is the Feast of Trumpets (Lev. 23:24), on the tenth the Great Day of Atonement, and on the fourteenth begins the Feast of Tabernacles, which lasts eight days.

(30) "FOR ON THAT DAY SHALL THE PRIEST MAKE AN ATONEMENT FOR YOU, TO CLEANSE YOU, THAT YOU MAY BE CLEAN FROM ALL YOUR SINS BEFORE THE LORD.

(31) "IT SHALL BE A SABBATH OF REST UNTO YOU, AND YOU SHALL AFFLICT YOUR SOULS, BY A STATUTE FOREVER.

(32) "AND THE PRIEST, WHOM HE SHALL ANOINT, AND WHOM HE SHALL CONSECRATE TO MINISTER IN THE PRIEST'S OFFICE IN HIS FATHER'S STEAD, SHALL MAKE THE ATONEMENT, AND SHALL PUT ON THE LINEN CLOTHES, EVEN THE HOLY GARMENTS.

(33) "AND HE SHALL MAKE AN ATONEMENT FOR THE HOLY SANCTUARY, AND HE SHALL MAKE AN ATONEMENT FOR THE TABERNACLE OF THE CONGREGATION, AND FOR THE ALTAR, AND HE SHALL MAKE AN ATONEMENT FOR THE PRIESTS AND FOR ALL THE PEOPLE OF THE CONGREGATION.

(34) "AND THIS SHALL BE AN EVERLASTING STATUTE UNTO YOU, TO MAKE AN ATONEMENT FOR THE CHILDREN OF ISRAEL FOR ALL THEIR SINS ONCE A YEAR. AND HE DID AS THE LORD COMMANDED MOSES."

The composition is:

1. The Great Day of Atonement was observed more or less until the Babylonian captivity, and afterward in the Restoration until the destruction of Jerusalem in A.D. 70.

2. When Israel failed God and had to be judged, God was no longer obligated to fulfill His Covenant with them, inasmuch as they had broken the Covenant themselves.

3. The Great Day of Atonement is the most beautiful example of the Sacrificial, Atoning Work of Calvary. To understand what it meant helps us to understand Christ even more, and more particularly, what He did for us in the giving of Himself in Sacrifice.

ATONEMENT

Verses 30 and 31 read: *"For on that day shall the Priest make an Atonement for you, to cleanse you, that you may be clean from all your sins before the LORD.*

"It shall be a Sabbath of rest unto you, and you shall afflict your souls, by a Statute forever."

The Jews looked at this particular Day in the following manner:

They believe that the Law declared that only the sins which a man committed against the Lord are atoned for on the Day of Atonement; but the sins which man commits against his fellow man are not forgiven on this day, unless he has first satisfied his injured neighbor, and has obtained pardon from him.

As well, all who would sin willfully, thinking that they could obtain pardon on the

Day of Atonement, for that individual, and for this type of sin, there was no forgiveness on this day. This should teach us something:

The Great Day of Atonement, in a sense, was a symbol of the Dispensation of Grace. Unfortunately, many feel that because this presently is the time of Grace, sin doesn't matter that very much. Some even claim that due to the fact that they have a position in Christ, it really doesn't matter too very much what they do otherwise. Nothing could be further from the truth.

The idea that we can sin, and do so willfully, and then ask God to forgive us, and all is well, simply won't work. While it is true that God will forgive sin any time a Believer confesses that sin; however, the entire act of proper confession demands that we also turn away from sin. Otherwise, it is a farce (I Jn. 1:9).

While Grace is available to all, it's available to all only on God's terms, and not ours. His terms are simple and easy: He simply demands Faith on our part, and that speaks of Faith in Christ and what Christ did for us at the Cross. In effect, Grace makes no allowance for willful sinning (Heb. 10:26-29).

For any Believer to conclude that the death of Christ on the Cross makes an allowance for sinning simply doesn't understand that for which Christ died. Christ died on the Cross in order that we may be cleansed from sin, and delivered from sin. There is no provision made for a sinning Salvation. While Believers very often may have to ask the Lord to forgive them for sins committed, these are to never be willful sins.

By that, I'm not speaking of Christians who get caught in a trap, simply because they do not understand the Message of the Cross, which actually makes them a target for Satan. No matter how hard that particular Christian tries not to sin, having their faith placed in the wrong object, which is self, or whatever, guarantees that they are going to fail the Lord in some way. We can have victory over sin as a Christian only by making the Cross the object of our Faith, which then guarantees the help of the Holy Spirit, Whom all of us desperately need, that is if we are to live a holy life (Rom. 8:1-2, 11, 13).

THE HIGH PRIEST

Verse 32 reads: *"And the Priest, whom he shall anoint, and whom he shall consecrate to minister in the Priest's Office in his father's stead, shall make the Atonement, and shall put on the linen clothes, even the holy garments."*

The idea of this Verse pertains to the succession of High Priests, who would follow down through the centuries. Aaron, being human, would pass away, even as he eventually did. One of his sons would then become the High Priest of Israel. In fact, the entirety of the Priesthood was to remain in the family of Aaron, at least the Priesthood which would be recognized by the Lord. By the time of Christ, there were thousands of Priests, supposedly in that great family.

There were many other duties corresponding with the Temple, the Sacrifices, and the Feast Days, which were attended by the Levites, who were as well of the Tribe of Levi, the same as Aaron, but they were not Priests. To be a Priest, as stated, one had to be of the family of Aaron.

ATONEMENT

Verse 33 reads: *"And he shall make an Atonement for the Holy Sanctuary, and he shall make an Atonement for the Tabernacle of the congregation, and for the Altar, and he shall make an Atonement for the Priests, and for all the people of the congregation."*

All the High Priests who would follow Aaron were to perform the service of expiation of sin, as detailed in this Chapter, a summary of which is given here.

The idea is, anything and everything that man touched was defiled. That may come as a blow to the pride of the self-righteous, but it happens to be true. Of course, we're speaking of the time before the Cross. As a result, Sacrifices had to be offered constantly, all attended by the Priests. As well, on the Great Day of Atonement, cleansing for national Israel was brought about, that is, if the High Priest did exactly what the Law of Moses demanded. Sin can only be handled in one way, not ten ways, not five ways, not two ways, only one way. That one way is the precious Blood of Christ, shed at Calvary's

Cross, all typified by the slaying of these animals. The only meeting place between God and man is Calvary. It is the Blood, and the Blood alone, that makes an Atonement for sinners. It was Christ's death that rent the Veil, it is His Blood that procures forgiveness of sins and boldness to enter into the Holiest (Williams).

How so much I can sense the Presence of God, even as I dictate these words! But yet how much my heart breaks as I look at the Church, the modern Church, which for all practical purposes has abandoned the Cross, denied the Blood, which means that access to God has been shut off, and despite all the religiosity.

The far greater majority of the modern Church has opted for humanistic psychology as it regards the sins and perversions of mankind. This is the wisdom of the world, and is, therefore, devilish (James 3:15). It is impossible to place trust in both humanistic psychology and the Cross. It simply cannot be done. Either one cancels out the other. So the idea that the Church can trust in the Cross and the meanderings and superstition of humanistic psychology is on its face ridiculous, and in fact, an oxymoron.

And then the Word of Faith doctrine, which is no Faith at all, has cut a great swath through the modern Church. It is opposed to the Cross in every capacity, even though it may pay lip service to the Sacrifice of Christ. When you consider that they will entertain no songs or worship as it regards the Cross, Calvary, or the Blood, then one begins to realize just how insidious this deceptive doctrine really is.

Paul said, and concerning these things: *"For many walk, of whom I have told you often, and now tell you even weeping, that they are the enemies of the Cross of Christ:*

"Whose end is destruction, whose god is their belly, and whose glory is in their shame, who mind earthly things" (Phil. 3:18-19).

It's sad, when you realize that the far greater majority of the adherents to the Word of Faith doctrine have little understanding, if any at all, as it regards what their doctrine actually is. And to be sure, those adherents number into the millions. The reason they do not know is because the

emphasis is not on their doctrine, but rather on *"money."* The truth is, these people are *"enemies of the Cross of Christ."* It cannot be looked at in any other capacity than that which I have just said. And regrettably, the far greater majority of the modern Church as a whole falls into the same category. As stated, the acceptance of humanistic psychology is a vote of no confidence as it regards the Cross, whether the latter is admitted or not!

A THEOLOGICAL QUESTION OR A MORAL QUESTION?

What do we mean by the statement, *"A theological question, or a moral question"*?

What I'm meaning is this: *"Enemies of the Cross"* do not reject the Cross because of theological reasons, but rather because of moral reasons. In other words, the Cross is not a theological question, and in fact never has been. By that statement, I'm referring to the fact that the Cross is difficult to understand, and is, therefore, in great dispute among Theologians. Nothing could be further from the truth. The Cross of Jesus Christ is a simple principle. It can be summed up in the phrase, *"Jesus Christ and Him Crucified"* (I Cor. 1:23).

So the idea that people do not accept it because they can't understand it holds no validity whatsoever. How much simpler can it be than the following statement:

"For God so loved the world, that He gave His only Begotten Son, that whosoever believes in Him, should not perish, but have everlasting life" (Jn. 3:16).

No! The problem is not theological; the problem is *"moral."* And what do we mean by that?

We mean that the reason men reject the Cross is because of self-will, pride, envy, self-righteousness, or 101 other things that could be said in that same capacity. The problem of sin is a moral problem. It always has been, and it is presently. So, men reject the Cross because of moral problems within their lives. And to turn it around, the only answer to their moral problem, whatever it might be, is the precious, shed Blood of the Lord Jesus Christ, which can be summed up in the *"Cross."*

AN EVERLASTING STATUTE

Verse 34 reads: *"And this shall be an everlasting Statute unto you, to make an Atonement for the Children of Israel for all their sins once a year. And he did as the LORD commanded Moses."*

The same phrase, more or less, as it regards the word *"Statute"* referring to a Commandment or Law of the Lord, occurs three times within four Verses (vss. 29, 31, 34). The thrice repeated phrase emphasizes the abiding nature of this Law, and indicates the solemnity of the day.

The last phrase of this last Verse of the Chapter, *"And he* (Aaron) *did as the Lord commanded Moses,"* proclaims the fact that Aaron carried out these ceremonies and rituals, in obedience to the command which God gave to Moses. He did not assume any type of dignity to exalt himself, but rather did as he was instructed to do, which is what he should have done. Every evidence is that he functioned in his task in humility before the Lord, not thinking of himself at all, but rather thinking of the great solemnity of the situation, and what it meant to the whole of Israel.

The *"everlasting Statute"* lasted as long as the earthly Jerusalem lasted, and until the Heavenly Jerusalem, so to speak, was instituted, when it had a spiritual fulfillment once for all. In other words, Jesus Christ, by His life and living, and above all, by the Sacrificial, Atoning Sacrifice of Himself fulfilled all of the Law of Moses. In fact, Christ was, one might say, *"the Great Day of Atonement,"* referring to an enlightened day that will never end, and a darkness which has been dispelled forever.

Of old, exactly as we have been studying, there was a High Priest who cleansed the people with the blood of bulls and goats, but now that the True High Priest is come, the former Priesthood is no more. The Altar fires can be banked; the Levitical robes of the Priests can be discarded forever, they are no more needed. The throats of the little lambs will no more be slit, with the hot blood pouring out, considering that the blood of the Son of the Living God has once and for all sufficed.

NOTES

In fact, it is a providential dispensation of God that the city and Temple of Jerusalem have been destroyed; for if they were still standing, some who are weak in faith might be dazzled by the outward splendor of the literal types, exactly as some Christian Jews were in the Early Church, necessitating the writing of the Book of Hebrews by Paul.

As we have already stated several times, Paul said: *"For the Law having a shadow of good things to come, and not the very image of the things, can never with those sacrifices which they offered year by year continually make the comers thereunto perfect"* (Heb. 10:1).

And then the great Apostle said: *"Then said He, Lo, I come to do Your will, O God. He takes away the first, that He may establish the second.*

"By the which will we are sanctified through the offering of the Body of Jesus Christ once for all" (Heb. 10:9-10).

"It may be at morn, when the day is awaking,
"When sunlight through darkness and shadow is breaking,
"That Jesus will come in the fullness of Glory
"To receive from the world His Own."

"It may be at midday, it may be at twilight,
"It may be, perchance, that the blackness of midnight
"Will burst into light in the blaze of His Glory,
"When Jesus receives His Own."

"While hosts cry Hosanna, from Heaven descending,
"With glorified Saints and the Angels attending,
"With Grace on His brow, like a halo of Glory,
"Will Jesus receive His Own."

"O joy! O delight! Should we go without dying,
"No sickness, no sadness, no dread, and no crying,
"Caught up through the clouds with our Lord into Glory,
"When Jesus receives His Own."

CHAPTER 17

(1) "AND THE LORD SPOKE UNTO MOSES, SAYING,

(2) "SPEAK UNTO AARON, AND UNTO HIS SONS, AND UNTO ALL THE CHILDREN OF ISRAEL, AND SAY UNTO THEM; THIS IS THE THING WHICH THE LORD HAS COMMANDED, SAYING,

(3) "WHAT MAN SOEVER THERE BE OF THE HOUSE OF ISRAEL, WHO KILLS AN OX, OR LAMB, OR GOAT, IN THE CAMP, OR WHO KILLS IT OUT OF THE CAMP,

(4) "AND BRINGS IT NOT UNTO THE DOOR OF THE TABERNACLE OF THE CONGREGATION, TO OFFER AN OFFERING UNTO THE LORD BEFORE THE TABERNACLE OF THE LORD: BLOOD SHALL BE IMPUTED UNTO THAT MAN; HE HAS SHED BLOOD; THAT MAN SHALL BE CUT OFF FROM AMONG HIS PEOPLE:"

The composition is:

1. As the previous Chapter, which outlined the Great Day of Atonement, is one of the most important Chapters in the Bible, likewise, this Seventeenth Chapter follows in the same train.

2. This Chapter proclaims the preciousness of the blood, in that all life belongs to Jehovah; and second, that the power of Atonement is in the blood.

3. The Lord attached a powerful significance to these things. He would have them impressed upon every member of the congregation.

4. No animal could be offered up in Sacrifice, unless it was offered up at the Tabernacle, and later the Temple, that is, when the Temple would later be built.

THE THING WHICH THE LORD HAS COMMANDED

Verses 1 and 2 read: *"And the LORD spoke unto Moses, saying,*

"Speak unto Aaron, and unto his sons, and unto all the Children of Israel, and say unto them; This is the thing which the LORD has commanded, saying."

This Chapter, we will find, is so clear as it regards the fact, *"It is the blood that makes*

NOTES

an Atonement for the soul." Concerning this, Mackintosh said: *"If I look from the Third Chapter of Genesis down to the close of Revelation, I find the Blood of Christ put forward alone as the ground of Righteousness. We get pardon, peace, life, Righteousness – all by the Blood, and nothing but the Blood. The entire Book of Leviticus, and particularly the Chapter which we are now studying, is a commentary upon the Doctrine of the Blood. It seems strange to have to insist upon a fact so obvious to every dispassionate, teachable student of Holy Scripture; yet so it is. Our minds are prone to slip away from the plain Testimony of the Word. We are ready to adopt opinions without ever calmly investigating them in the light of the Divine Testimonies. In this way we get into confusion, darkness, and error."*

He then said, *"May we learn to give the Blood of Christ its due place. It is so precious in God's sight that He will not suffer ought else to be added to or mingled with it."*

THE BIBLE, THE STORY OF THE CROSS

One could just as easily turn the heading around and say, *"The Cross, the story of the Bible."* When one properly learns the Word, one has learned the Cross; and it might even be turned around and said, when one learns the Cross, one has learned the Word. They are synonymous, one and the same!

If one properly understands the Word of God, then one will properly understand the Cross. And if it becomes obvious that one doesn't understand the Cross, to be sure, one will have a misunderstanding at the same time of the Word. Such is the road to spiritual disaster.

From the time of the Fall (Gen. 3:15), through Revelation 22:21, we find the Cross as the central theme of the Word of God. To try to understand the Word in any other capacity is to misunderstand the Word.

Concerning the Cross, and even as we shall see, we will find, *"This is the thing which the LORD has commanded."*

LAST DAY APOSTASY

The last day apostasy, as is obvious, is the repudiation of the Cross. Paul said: *"Now* the Spirit (Holy Spirit) *speaks expressly* (pointedly), *that in the latter times* (the times in which we now live) *some shall depart from the Faith, giving heed to seducing spirits, and doctrines of devils"* (I Tim. 4:1).

"The Faith" is *"Jesus Christ and Him Crucified"* (I Cor. 1:23; 2:2).

In the last several decades, and especially the last decade (the 1990's), the departure from *"the Faith"* has been accelerated. But at the same time, the Lord is lifting up a standard against this evil, by once again giving to the Church, and the world for that matter, the Message of the Cross, perhaps in a more powerful way than it has ever before been presented. And let the Reader understand that the understanding of the Cross is, in reality, the understanding of the entirety of the New Covenant. This is the Word that the Lord gave to the Apostle Paul, which he gave to us in his 14 Epistles. So, the understanding of the Cross is not merely the understanding of a particular doctrine, but is really the understanding of the foundation of all doctrine. All doctrine must be built on the premise of the Cross, or else in some way, it will be spurious.

In Paul's day, the greatest opposition to the Message of the Cross was the Judaizers. These were so-called Christian Jews, who endeavored to attach the Law to Grace. In other words, while they may have paid lip service to the Cross, if that, their greater theme was that Gentiles had to also keep the Law in order to be saved. While this matter was partially settled at the great Counsel in Jerusalem (Acts, Chpt. 15), it was just that, only partially settled. While it was decreed that the Gentiles would not have the Law imposed upon them, certain among the Jews continued to press this issue, which caused Paul untold difficulties. As someone has well said, while Judaism in effect gave birth to the Church, it came very close as well to being its grave.

In a sense of the word, that problem of Law versus Grace is still with us, but in perhaps a more devious way.

THE LAW

While Preachers no longer advocate the Law of Moses, many are in fact advocating *"law,"*

NOTES

though it be a law of their own making, or the making of someone else. At any rate, the problem is the same, and as well, the damage is the same. Whether it's the Law of Moses, or a law made up by Preachers or Churches, or wherever, for that matter, it is still law, and it cannot be mixed with Grace. Again, Paul said: *"I do not frustrate the Grace of God: for if Righteousness come by the Law, then Christ is dead in vain"* (Gal. 2:21).

The great Apostle is telling us here that the only thing law or laws can do is to frustrate the Grace of God, which means that the Grace of God cannot function in an atmosphere of law.

What do we mean by that?

What I'm attempting to discuss is, without a doubt, the single most important factor in the heart and life of the Believer. The Believer, not knowing how to appropriate Grace, whether he realizes it or not, functions in law, which only tends to make a bad matter worse. No matter how hard he tries, no matter how zealous he might be, no matter how dedicated he might be, he will not come out to victory, only defeat – and to be sure, the defeat will get worse and worse.

THE GRACE OF GOD

The only way that the Believer can understand the Grace of God, and to have Grace flowing uninterrupted in his heart and life is to understand the Cross, and thereby place his Faith. The Holy Spirit, Who superintends all Grace, will then guarantee victory in one's life (Eph. 2:18).

It is impossible to have and enjoy the Grace of God, unless one properly understands the Cross. As the Cross and the Word are synonymous, one could as well say that the Cross and Grace are synonymous.

The Grace of God is merely the Goodness of God, extended to undeserving Believers. As already stated, that Grace or Goodness is superintended by the Holy Spirit, Who works exclusively within the parameters of the Finished Work of Christ (Rom. 8:1-2, 11).

But most Christians don't understand the Cross, simply because it's not properly taught behind most pulpits, and thereby, they function in law, because there is no place else for them to function. It is either law or Grace, and if one doesn't understand the Cross, which is the password to Grace, then law is the only other alternative.

If Believers have problems, and most all do, and they go to their Pastor, virtually all of the time, the Pastor will say to them, among other things, *"You've got to try harder."* He says that, because he doesn't know the right way himself. In fact, he's having problems just as the seeker is having problems, perhaps even worse.

Living for God, and walking in victory, has nothing to do with *"trying harder."* I don't care how hard a person tries, as stated, how dedicated he might be, how zealous he might be, he's not going to arrive at a place of victory by this method. In fact, the hurtful situation in his life will only get worse.

Not understanding the Cross, what does the Church do?

WRONG DIRECTIONS

If it is to be noticed, the Church jumps from one fad to the other. When Frances and I first began in Evangelistic work in the 1950's, the problem, it was said, was demon spirits. In other words, it was claimed by many that Christians who had problems had these problems because they had a demon spirit moving them in certain directions. In other words, if it was an uncontrollable temper, they had a demon of temper, etc. It was stated that this particular demon had to be cast out of these Christians, and then their problem would be solved.

Consequently, people were lining up by the scores at certain Churches, which were proclaiming this foolishness, trying to find victory by having this particular demon cast out of them. In fact, this thing continued well on up into the 1960's, and is still promoted in some circles.

In those years, I did not understand the Cross as it refers to Sanctification, but I knew that was wrong. And I said so, and I said so plainly and loudly. Many Preachers grew very angry with me because of my stand, but I knew this wasn't Scriptural.

While all Christians are troubled at one time or the other by demon spirits, as should be obvious, Christians are not possessed by demon spirits. The Holy Spirit will not share

NOTES

His Temple with demons (I Cor. 3:16).

Sometime back, I had the occasion to speak with two of the most famous names in Charismatic circles. Both of these men advocated this of which I have just addressed. Demon spirits were causing the problems, and had to be cast out, etc.

Has anyone ever stopped to think that nothing like this is found in the Word of God? It's not found in the Word, because it's not Scriptural. While demon spirits definitely are real, and while demon spirits definitely inhabit scores of unsaved people, and while they greatly trouble many Christians, they do so, simply because the Christian doesn't understand the Cross, which is the secret of all victory. Jesus said: *"You shall know the Truth, and the Truth shall make you free"* (Jn. 8:32). He didn't say anything about Preachers laying hands on Christians and casting out demons, but rather that the Truth be given to Believers, which in effect, is the Message of the Cross, which He later gave to Paul (Rom. 6:3-14). Please note the following:

Jesus said when He ministered in Nazareth: *"The Spirit of the Lord is upon Me, because He has anointed Me to preach the Gospel to the poor; He has sent Me to heal the brokenhearted, to preach deliverance to the captives . . ."* (Lk. 4:18).

If it is to be noticed, He didn't say *"to deliver the captives,"* but rather *"to preach deliverance to the captives."* In other words, the only way in which captives can be delivered is for the Truth to be preached unto them. And what is the Truth?

TRUTH

The Truth is: *"Jesus Christ and Him Crucified"* (Rom. 5:1; 6:3-14; 8:1-2, 11; I Cor. 1:17-18, 21, 23; 2:2, 5; Gal. 5:1-6; 6:14; Eph. 2:13-18; Col. 2:14-15). We are to preach the Cross!

In the 1970's, on up into the 1980's, the *"self esteem theory"* was promoted. The answer, some Preachers claimed, was a proper self esteem. In other words, if the person was having problems, it was because they had a low self esteem, and the way to correct it was to get them to increase the esteem of themselves.

That on the surface is so foolish as to beggar description, but yet, it seems that many Preachers fell for this foolishness, and foolishness it is.

The truth is, the problem is *"self,"* whether it be *"low self"* or *"high self."* Either way it's a problem. The only answer for self is that it be placed into Christ, which it can be at the Cross (Lk. 9:23-24). But many in the Church fell for that stupidity!

In the 1980's the *"buddy system"* came into vogue. This was the idea that every Believer ought to have a friend in who he can confide, and that the two of them joining their faith together can overcome all the problems, etc.

Once again I'll quote Paul, *"If Righteousness can come by these things, then Christ died in vain."*

In the early 1990's, we had the *"laughing phenomenon,"* with that claimed to be the thruway to victory. And then at about the midpoint of the 1990's, the *"falling out"* phenomenon was revived. In other words, if one could experience this manifestation, one could then find victory, etc.

While the latter is definitely, at times, valid before the Lord, at least as it regards the manifestation, that's as far as it goes. Victory cannot be found for the Child of God in any manifestation, as Godly and Scriptural as that manifestation might be. Once again, we go back to the Words of Christ: *"You shall know the Truth, and the Truth shall make you free"* (Jn. 8:32).

And in the midst of all of this, many in the Church were advocating humanistic psychology, to which we have already addressed ourselves. It's as if they have tried all of these *"fads,"* and seeing they didn't work, not knowing where else to turn, they turned to the world. Unfortunately, humanistic psychology, or anything else the world has to offer, contains no solution whatsoever, only harm!

THE ANSWER IS THE CROSS

The answer to every problem the sinner might have, or the Believer might have, is the Cross and the Cross alone!

The Cross is not a confused, convoluted theory, but is rather the answer to man's dilemma, as given to us by the Lord. In other

words, what Jesus did at the Cross addressed every single problem that faces humanity, irrespective as to what that problem might be, excluding none! I don't know how plainer or clearer I can be. The solution to the problems of the unbeliever, and no matter what those problems might be, and no matter how severe they are, is found in the Cross of Christ, and as stated, in the Cross of Christ alone. If the unredeemed soul will come to Christ, placing his Faith entirely in Christ, which Faith the Holy Spirit will give to him upon him hearing the Word, his whole life can be changed, as has the lives of untold millions. That is the only hope, the only solution for the sinner (Jn. 3:3, 16).

Likewise, as it regards the Child of God, the answer to every problem, to every dilemma, irrespective as to what it might be is found solely in the Cross of Christ. But what does Satan do?

He does his best to get the Christian to look elsewhere. He fights the Message of the Cross as he fights nothing else. He really doesn't care too very much as to what things we believe, just as long as it's not the Cross. He was defeated totally at the Cross, and only at the Cross. And he was defeated by Christ removing his legal right to hold man in captivity, which Christ did by shedding His Life's Blood, which atoned for all sin, which we will graphically study in this Seventeenth Chapter of Leviticus (Col. 2:14-15).

If the Believer will understand that every single thing he receives from the Lord, irrespective as to what it might be, comes solely through the means of the Cross, and thereby make the Cross the object of his Faith, and refuse to allow it to be moved to other things, the Holy Spirit will then begin to work within his life, will allow the Grace of God to have full play, and that Christian will then find victory, and victory as he has never known before, and I speak of perpetual victory. John the Beloved said: *"This is the victory that overcometh the world, even our Faith"* (I Jn. 5:4).

THE PRECIOUSNESS OF THE BLOOD

Verses 3 and 4 read: *"What man soever there be of the house of Israel, who kills an ox, or lamb, or goat, in the camp, or who kills it out of the camp,*

"And brings it not unto the Door of the Tabernacle of the congregation, to offer an Offering unto the LORD before the Tabernacle of the LORD; blood shall be imputed unto that man; he has shed blood; and that man shall be cut off from among his people."

The word *"killeth"* actually should have been translated *"sacrificeth."* To translate it *"kill"* or *"killeth"* makes it seem as if this command applies to the slaughter of domestic animals for foodstuff, etc. This is not what the Holy Spirit is referring to.

Before the Law of Moses was given, and the Tabernacle erected as the central place of worship, it had been the right and duty of the head of each family to offer sacrifice for his household, and this he did wherever he thought proper, according to the ancient Patriarchal practice, and most naturally in the open fields. This duty and liberty are now abolished.

The Aaronic Priesthood has superseded the older Priestly system, henceforth every Sacrifice is to be offered in the Court of the Tabernacle, and by the hand of Aaron's sons.

Concerning this, Mackintosh said: *"A man might say, Can I not offer a Sacrifice in one place as well as another? The answer is, Life belongs to God, and His claim thereto must be recognized in the place where He has appointed – before the Tabernacle of the Lord. That was the only meeting-place between God and man. To offer elsewhere proved that the heart did not want God."*

Mackintosh went on to say, *"The moral of this is plain. There is one place where God has appointed to meet the sinner, and that is the Cross – the antitype of the Brazen Altar. There and there alone has God's claims upon the life been duly recognized. To reject this meeting-place is to bring down judgment upon one's self – it is to trample under foot the just claims of God, and to arrogate to one's self a right to life which all have forfeited."*

ONLY ONE PLACE, THE CROSS

As we have said over and over, and will continue to say, the Cross of Christ is the focal point of the entirety of the Bible. Everything either looks forward to the Cross

(the Old Testament), or everything looks backward to the Cross (the New Testament).

If this Command of the Lord was ignored, with men insisting upon offering up Sacrifices in the open field, or anywhere else other than the Tabernacle, the Scripture is clear: *"That man shall be cut off from among his people."* This meant that the man would lose his soul.

That which was the *"type"* and points to the Cross, proclaims the fact that this Truth is still the same now as it was then. If the Cross is ignored, abrogated, or denied, *"that soul will be cut off from the people of God."*

Within itself, that fact is chilling enough, but when one realizes that the modern Church has all but abandoned the Cross, then it becomes chilling indeed! In fact, the primary reason for these Commentaries, for SonLife Radio, for the Jimmy Swaggart Telecast, for our Crusades, for all the teaching aids, such as CD's, etc., in fact the very reason for our teaching and preaching, is the Cross of Christ. While I'm sure the Holy Spirit is using others around the world, and I pray that number will increase daily, this I do know: this is the very purpose of this Ministry, *"to preach the Cross."* Paul said:

"For the preaching of the Cross is to them who perish foolishness; but unto us which are saved it is the Power of God" (I Cor. 1:18).

Let me echo the words of Mackintosh again, *"There is one place where God has appointed to meet the sinner, and that is the Cross – the antitype of the Brazen Altar."* The Word of Faith people may claim that they are now the Righteousness of God, and as such, there is no more problem with sin. If that is the case, and as I've already stated, then the Holy Spirit through Paul wasted a lot of space, dealing with the Church about the problem of sin. In fact, he mentioned sin, actually the sin nature, some 17 times in the Sixth Chapter of Romans alone. Let it be remembered that he is speaking directly to Believers, and not unbelievers. As well, I hardly think the Holy Spirit would have devoted this much time to a problem that no longer exists. No! Such thinking is silly; in fact, it is stupid! And what we've related is from the Sixth Chapter of Romans exclusively, not to mention the entirety of his 14 Epistles.

While it is certainly true that we are the Righteousness of God (II Cor. 5:21), which we hold as a position in Christ, and which we gained exclusively by what He did at the Cross, the added truth is, our *"condition"* must be brought up to our *"position,"* which is the Work of the Holy Spirit, and which He Alone can do (Rom. 8:1-2, 11, 13).

(5) "TO THE END THAT THE CHILDREN OF ISRAEL MAY BRING THEIR SACRIFICES, WHICH THEY OFFER IN THE OPEN FIELD, EVEN THAT THEY MAY BRING THEM UNTO THE LORD, UNTO THE DOOR OF THE TABERNACLE OF THE CONGREGATION, AND TO THE PRIEST, AND OFFER THEM FOR PEACE-OFFERINGS UNTO THE LORD.

(6) "AND THE PRIEST SHALL SPRINKLE THE BLOOD UPON THE ALTAR OF THE LORD AT THE DOOR OF THE TABERNACLE OF THE CONGREGATION, AND BURN THE FAT FOR A SWEET SAVOR UNTO THE LORD.

(7) "AND THEY SHALL NO MORE OFFER THEIR SACRIFICES UNTO DEVILS, AFTER WHOM THEY HAVE GONE A WHORING. THIS SHALL BE A STATUTE FOREVER UNTO THEM THROUGHOUT THEIR GENERATIONS."

The diagram is:

1. The words, *"No more"* in Verse 7, make it clear that the people had previously sacrificed to demons in the land of Egypt. In Isaiah 13:21 and 34:14, the word is translated *"satyrs,"* i.e., *"half man, half goat."* It was the great goat-god, Pan; afterwards worshipped by the Greeks and Romans (Josh. 24:14; II Chron. 11:15; Ezek. 20:7; 23:3).

2. The *"blood"* is the all-important aspect of the Sacrifice, which was to be poured *"upon the Altar of the LORD at the Door of the Tabernacle."*

3. This *"Statute,"* which is to be *"forever,"* translates into the Cross, and continues unto this hour, with the Cross the centerpiece of the great Plan of God, even into eternity future.

THE SACRIFICES

Verse 5 reads: *"To the end that the Children of Israel may bring their Sacrifices,*

which they offer in the open field, even that they may bring them unto the LORD, unto the Door of the Tabernacle of the congregation, unto the Priest, and offer them for Peace-Offerings unto the LORD."

In essence, some three times the warning is given concerning the offering up of Sacrifices in places except the Tabernacle, or Temple, that is, when the Temple would be built (Vss. 4, 7, 10).

Once again I emphasize the fact that all of this translates into the Cross. Any time the Holy Spirit says something one time, it is of vast significance, as should be obvious. When He says it two times, we should understand the import, and when He says it three times, it is all done for emphasis, that the injunction may not in any way be misunderstood.

Considering that a person would lose their eternal soul if they disobeyed this command, we should readily realize just how serious all of this actually is.

I would have the Reader to forget about the Sacrifices of old as it regarded animal offerings, but remember what they represented, which is the Cross. And so the command is just as binding today as it was then.

If individuals attempt to reach God except through Christ and His shed Blood, all access will be barred by the Holy Spirit (Eph. 2:13-18). This means there is no Salvation outside of Christ and Him Crucified, and our Faith in that Finished Work. Any other proposed means of reaching God, being saved, etc., is condemned by God, in fact, is cursed by God (Gal. 1:6-9).

And then when we realize that the Cross is being all but ignored at the present time, with that terrible travesty pandemic among almost all Denominations, the matter becomes frightfully fearful.

THE BLOOD

Verse 6 reads: *"And the Priest shall sprinkle the Blood upon the Altar of the LORD at the Door of the Tabernacle of the congregation, and burn the fat for a sweet savor unto the LORD."*

In fact, most of the Offerings presented by the people of Israel were *"Peace-Offerings,"* even as Verse 5 proclaims. While the other Offerings (Burnt, Sin, and Trespass) were definitely offered, it was mostly Peace-Offer-ings. And even if they offered one of the other Offerings, it was as well to be followed by a Peace-Offering, intimating that Peace with God had now been restored.

Two Sacrifices were to be offered by the Priesthood each day, which were Burnt-Of-ferings, the first one at 9 a.m., and the sec-ond one at 3 p.m. This was done everyday, actually with the number of animals doubled on the Sabbath.

As we find in the Sacrifices, the *"blood"* and the *"fat"* always belonged to God.

It is carefully noted, even as we shall see, that Atonement is always in the blood, and <u>only</u> in the blood. *"It is the blood that makes Atonement for the soul."* It is not the blood and something else. The Word is most ex-plicit. It attributes Atonement exclusively to the Blood. *"Without shedding of blood is no remission"* (Heb. 9:22). It was the *"death"* of Christ that rent the Veil. It is *"by the Blood of Jesus"* we have *"boldness to enter into the Holiest."* *"We have Redemption through His Blood, the forgiveness of sins"* (Eph. 1:7; Col. 1:14).

"Having made peace by the Blood of His Cross." *"You who were afar off are made nigh by the Blood of His Cross."* *"The Blood of Jesus Christ His Son cleanses us from all sin"* (I Jn. 1:7). John wrote: *"They washed their robes and made them white in the Blood of the Lamb"* (Rev. 7:14). *"They overcame him by the Blood of the Lamb"* (Rev. 12:11).

Concerning this, Mackintosh said: *"The Blood of Christ is the foundation of every-thing. It is the ground of God's Righteous-ness in justifying an ungodly sinner who believes on the Name of the Son of God; and it is the ground of the sinner's confidence in drawing near to a Holy God, Who is of purer eyes than to behold evil. God would be just in the condemnation of the sinner; but through the Death of Christ, He can be just and the justifier of him who believes – a just God and a Saviour.*

"The Righteousness of God is His consis-tency with Himself – His acting in harmony with His revealed character. Hence, were it not for the Cross, His consistency with Him-self would, of necessity, demand the death and judgment of the sinner; but in the

NOTES

Cross, that death and judgment were borne by the sinner's surety, so that the same Di-vine consistency is perfectly maintained, while a Holy God justifies an ungodly sin-ner through Faith. It is all through the Blood of Jesus – nothing less, nothing more, and nothing different."

THE BLOOD PLUS SOMETHING ELSE?

Satan very seldom peddles his wares by opening the door wide all at one time. He does it little by little, and does so by mixing Truth with error.

For instance, most of the modern Church leaders, at least those who still claim to be-lieve in the Blood of Christ, try to wed hu-manistic psychology with the Blood. The outcome is, as it always is, the Blood, i.e., *"the Cross,"* is little by little pushed to the side, with humanistic psychology becoming the great thruway. The truth is, it's not pos-sible to believe in both. Either one cancels out the other.

The Word of Faith people do the same thing. They claim to believe in the atoning efficacy of the Blood, but really they are only paying lip service to the Finished Work of Christ, if that!

They claim in order for Redemption to be complete, Jesus had to die on the Cross as a sinner (some claim He died as a sinner, and some claim that He didn't), then go to the burning side of Hell, which all unredeemed do, and be tormented there by demon spirits and even Satan himself for some three days and nights, with God then saying, *"It is enough."* They then claim that Jesus was then born again, and resurrected.

The emphasis of their faith is not on the Cross or the Blood, but rather on some fabri-cated account, which is not found in the Bible, of Jesus going to the burning side of Hell, where He redeemed mankind. It was Joyce Meyer who said, *"You won't find this in the Bible; it has to be revealed to your spirit."*

Our dear lady is right about one thing: you won't find it in the Bible, because such a thing never happened. It is made up out of whole cloth, so to speak, and is pure fiction.

Ken Copeland states the fact that many others died on crosses that day all across the Roman Empire, and the shedding of their

Blood didn't atone for anything.

The only conclusion I can draw from such a statement is that they are claiming that Jesus Christ was the same as any other man, and all these others, whomever they may have been, who died on crosses that day, were the same as Christ. I beg to disagree!

Jesus was the Son of the Living God, in fact, God manifest in the flesh (Isa. 7:14). He was and is *"holy, harmless, undefiled, separate from sinners"* (Heb. 7:26). In fact, the reason that the Blood of Jesus atoned, of which all the Old Testament Types grandly portrayed, is because Christ was Perfect in every respect. His Life was Perfect, His Body was Perfect, His Blood was Perfect, being untainted or unpolluted. He was Perfect in every respect, therefore, a Sacrifice which God could accept, and in fact, did accept. To try to equate other human beings with Christ is foolishness beyond compare.

If the Word of Faith people claim to believe in the Blood, why is it that they won't sing any songs about the Blood in their Churches? The truth is, and as stated, one cannot mix something else, in this case, Jesus supposedly burning in Hell, with the Blood, as it regards Atonement. It is the Blood alone, and nothing but the Blood!

In such a situation, the *"leaven"* of false doctrine, no matter how small it may be at the beginning, will ultimately corrupt the whole. Paul said: *"A little leaven leaveneth the whole lump"* (Gal. 5:9).

One bad apple put in a barrel of good apples will not turn out with the bad apple ultimately becoming good, but rather the opposite. The bad apple will infect all the good ones, until ultimately, all the apples are bad.

False doctrine must be rooted out, and rooted out completely. Some of you may think that I am a little too stringent as it regards the Cross. No! The truth is, I'm not stringent enough.

FOREVER

Verse 7 reads: *"And they shall no more offer their Sacrifices unto devils, after whom they have gone a whoring. This shall be a Statute forever unto them throughout their generations."*

NOTES

By the use of the words *"no more"* we know that the Children of Israel, or at least some of them, did sacrifice unto devils while in Egypt.

The danger was, and in fact it did happen, that when sacrifices were offered in the *"high places,"* despite the fact that they claimed they were to God, the truth was, they were being offered up to various demon spirits.

Sacrifices had to be offered in a certain way, and using only certain animals. And as well, these sacrifices had to be offered at the Door of the Tabernacle, and no place else.

Carrying this over to the present time, even though Jesus has already fulfilled all of the Law, which means that animal sacrifices are no longer needed, and neither is the Tabernacle needed any more, still, the principle is the same; it holds true, and in fact, will ever hold true.

By that, I'm referring to the Cross of Christ, of which the Sacrifices were but a symbol. This *"Statute forever"* means exactly what it says. The Cross is the Way of Salvation, and it will never change. Paul referred to it as *"the Everlasting Covenant"* (Heb. 13:20).

To trust in anything else other than the Cross, or to add something to the Cross, or take something away, in a sense, is classified as faith placed in demon spirits. To be sure, demon spirits are always the cause of false doctrine (I Tim. 4:1). And to tamper with the Message of the Cross is the worst offense of all!

The Reader must remember that Satan or his ministers (II Cor. 11:15), never come in their true form, but always as an *"angel of light."* As such, they deceive, even as they are intended to deceive.

TRUTH

While there is much error promoted as a result of a wrong interpretation of the Word of God, the worst error of all is that which pertains to the Atonement. In fact, I think that one can say without fear of contradiction that all error, in some way, is connected with a wrong interpretation of the Cross. If the Cross is rightly understood, then in essence, the entirety of the Word of God is rightly understood, at least as far as its basic foundation is concerned. Let me give you an example of the wrong interpretation of the Cross, taken from the Word of God.

A SINNING SALVATION

Paul taught, and rightly so, that where sin abounded, Grace did much more abound (Rom. 5:20). Some Christians heard his teaching on that particular subject, and then concluded that sin didn't really matter. If Grace was greater than sin, and it definitely was, then our sinning, so they concluded, was of no consequence.

His answer to that was clear, concise, and to the point. He said: *"What shall we say then? Shall we continue in sin, that Grace may abound?*

"God forbid. How shall we, who are dead to sin, live any longer therein?" (Rom. 6:1-2).

The Grace of God flows to the Believer, as the result of what Christ did at the Cross, and by no other means. What Jesus did at the Cross was a Finished Work, and guarantees total and complete victory over sin, that is, if we follow God's Prescribed Order of Victory (Rom. 6:14).

No, this doesn't mean sinless perfection, for the Bible doesn't teach such, but it does teach that sin shall not have dominion over us.

The very fact of the Cross, the very reason for the Cross, was that sin be totally and completely defeated. So the idea of Christians blatantly continuing in sin proclaims the fact that they were misunderstanding what Jesus did at the Cross.

THE JUDAIZERS

Another group during Paul's day were the Judaizers. While they didn't really deny the Cross, they more or less ignored it. Their emphasis was on *"Law,"* i.e., *"the Law of Moses."*

They were teaching that the Law had to be added to Grace, or at least some parts of the Law. Paul addressed this in Galatians, Chapter 5.

His answer was again to the point. He said: *"Stand fast therefore in the liberty wherewith Christ has made us free, and be not entangled again with the yoke of bondage.*

"Behold, I Paul say unto you, that if you

be circumcised (subscribe to the Law), Christ shall profit you nothing.

"For I testify again to every man who is circumcised, that he is a debtor to do the whole Law.

"Christ is become of no effect unto you, whosoever of you are justified by the Law (seek to be justified by the Law)*; you are fallen from Grace"* (Gal. 5:1-4).

The Judaizers, in effect, were denying that all was done at the Cross, in other words, that the Law of Moses was answered in totality. Consequently, the Law and all of its rudiments, having been fulfilled totally and completely in Christ, were no more needed. In fact, they were instituted in the beginning only as a stopgap measure, intending to last only until the reality came. At best, they were but a shadow (Heb. 10:1).

By trying to include Law, in other words, demanding that Believers keep the Law as well as trust Christ, the Judaizers, in effect, were claiming that what Christ did at the Cross was not quite sufficient, and needed things added to it, i.e., *"the Law."* As should be obvious, this was a gross error as it regarded the Finished Work of Christ, which would destroy those who followed this teaching.

Regrettably, the problem continues with us presently. The Church continues to try to add law to Grace. While it's not the Law of Moses that is being promoted, as the Judaizers of old, nevertheless, it is law – that made up by men. And just as the Judaizers were demanding that Gentile Believers adhere to the Law in their day, religious men continue to do the same presently.

Once again, it is a gross misunderstanding, or misinterpretation of the Cross.

Make no mistake about it, if the Cross is misunderstood, to the degree that it is misunderstood, to that degree will the Believer accrue problems to himself. It can cause the loss of the soul. There is no way that a person can be saved except by trusting in Christ, and what Christ did at the Cross. There is no way that a Believer can live a sanctified life, unless he continues to place his Faith in the Cross of Christ, which gives the Holy Spirit latitude to work in one's life. Otherwise, there is the loss of the soul, or at the least, the loss of all victorious living. Let me say it again:

If the Believer attempts to trust Christ by any method other than what He did at the Cross, he will conclude by trusting *"another Christ"* (II Cor. 11:4). I would certainly trust that one would see exactly how serious this is. Millions are in Hell presently because they believed in something other than God's prescribed way. Regrettably, millions are on their way to Hell because their faith is placed in something other than that which God will recognize, which is *"Jesus Christ and Him Crucified"* (I Cor. 1:23).

(8) "AND YOU SHALL SAY UNTO THEM, WHATSOEVER MAN THERE BE OF THE HOUSE OF ISRAEL, OR OF THE STRANGERS WHICH SOJOURN AMONG YOU, WHO OFFERS A BURNT-OFFERING OR SACRIFICE,

(9) "AND BRINGS IT NOT UNTO THE DOOR OF THE TABERNACLE OF THE CONGREGATION, TO OFFER IT UNTO THE LORD; EVEN THAT MAN SHALL BE CUT OFF FROM AMONG HIS PEOPLE.

(10) "AND WHATSOEVER MAN THERE BE OF THE HOUSE OF ISRAEL, OR OF THE STRANGERS WHO SOJOURN AMONG YOU, WHO EATS ANY MANNER OF BLOOD; I WILL EVEN SET MY FACE AGAINST THAT SOUL WHO EATS BLOOD, AND WILL CUT HIM OFF FROM AMONG HIS PEOPLE.

(11) "FOR THE LIFE OF THE FLESH IS IN THE BLOOD: AND I HAVE GIVEN IT TO YOU UPON THE ALTAR TO MAKE AN ATONEMENT FOR YOUR SOULS: FOR IT IS THE BLOOD THAT MAKES AN ATONEMENT FOR THE SOUL."

The construction is:

1. There must not be any eating of blood among God's people, and because of what the blood represents.

2. The life of the flesh is in the blood.

3. It is the blood that makes an Atonement for the soul, and the blood alone!

A DESECRATION OF THE TYPE

Verses 8 through 10 read: *"And you shall say unto them, Whatsoever man there be of the House of Israel, or of the strangers who sojourn among you, who offers a Burnt-Offering or Sacrifice,*

NOTES

"And brings it not unto the Door of the Tabernacle of the congregation, to offer it unto the LORD; even that man shall be cut off from among his people.

"And whatsoever man there be of the House of Israel, or of the strangers who sojourn among you, who eats any manner of blood; I will even set My face against that soul who eats blood, and will cut him off from among his people."

These Passages proclaim to us that Salvation is the same, be it Jew or Gentile. God has but one Plan, and it is for the entirety of the world. That one Plan is *"Jesus Christ and Him Crucified"* (I Cor. 2:2).

While the Covenant was given to Abraham, and thereby, to the nation that would be raised up from his loins and the womb of his wife, Sarah, still, Salvation was one way, and one way only.

Please let the Reader know and understand that it has not changed. The Gospel is the same for all, irrespective as to whom they may be. The problem of sin is the same the world over, and the solution, Who is Christ, is the same the world over.

A PERSONAL EXPERIENCE

I have conducted Crusades in many cities of the world. That would include most of the major cities of Central and South America. It would include many cities in Africa, and the Philippines, along with Australia, New Zealand, and parts of Europe. I have seen hundreds of thousands the world over brought to a saving knowledge of Jesus Christ. Irrespective as to where I was, I always preached the same Message, and that Message was Jesus Christ and what He did for us at the Cross. It didn't matter whether the people were rich, poor, educated, or uneducated, as stated, the problem was the same, and the solution was the same.

I remember going into certain countries, and Missionaries would, in effect, tell me that my Ministry wouldn't go over there, because I didn't understand their culture, etc. Well, every single time, my Ministry did go over there, the results were many people being saved.

I remember one man telling me once, while my Ministry might go over in certain places, it wouldn't go over in France at all. He went on to relate as to how they were a very sophisticated people, and they required a certain type of sophistication before they would pay any heed.

I suppose he was telling me that my Ministry was crude, therefore, lacking in sophistication.

I asked him as to just what kind of Ministry would go over in France.

He went on to relate as to how his son was working there as a Missionary, and how he was seeing great results. I probed a little deeper, asking, *"Just how many people are getting saved under your son's Ministry?"*

"Oh," he replied, *"he hasn't had anyone saved yet, but they really enjoy what he does."*

I then asked, *"Well then what does he really do?"*

"He plays classical piano, and they really go for that," he replied!

Well the truth is, a short time later, we went on television in France, and saw a tremendous harvest of souls. In fact, as I dictate these notes on September 25, 2002, my son Donnie has just closed a Meeting in one of the largest Charismatic Churches in Paris, France. He had over 100 people baptized in the Holy Spirit, and many brought to a saving knowledge of the Lord Jesus Christ. In fact, I think I can say without fear of exaggeration, that it was the most powerful Meeting that this particular Church had ever had.

CULTURE

The Church makes one gigantic mistake when they try to deal with people in respect to their culture. To be frank, all culture has been spoiled, polluted, jaded, and wrecked by the powers of darkness. So, to try to deal with people on that level is foolishness to say the least.

While it is true, as Paul, *"to the weak became I as weak, that I might gain the weak: I am made all things to all men, that I might by all means save some"* (I Cor. 9:22). This means only, however, that Paul would take an interest in people, and deal with them on their level, in order that he might be able to speak to them about Christ. It isn't meaning that he accepted their culture, etc.

As we've already stated, the problem with

individuals the world over, and despite their culture, is *"sin."* Consequently, the solution to sin alone is *"Christ,"* and irrespective as to whom the people might be.

If it is to be noticed, when Paul went into various different countries of the Roman Empire, it should be understood that he interfaced with all types of cultures. But Paul never changed his Message. Wherever he was, the Message was the same irrespective of the people, *"Jesus Christ and Him Crucified"* (I Cor. 1:23; 2:2).

The truth is, when a person comes to Christ, and irrespective as to whom that person might be, they enter into the culture of the Word of God, which means that they leave their old culture behind. In fact, during the time of Paul, the Romans referred to the human race in only two categories. They looked at all men as either Romans or Barbarians. In other words, if the person was not a Roman citizen, in the eyes of Romans, they were Barbarian.

But when Christianity began to make its weight felt, the Romans referred to Christians as the *"third race."*

Presently we refer to people in the category of five races – yellow, white, black, brown, and red. But when people come to Christ, they leave all those distinctions behind. We are all one in Christ. And in fact, we ought to be so much one in Christ that the world would refer to us, irrespective of skin color or nationality, as *"the sixth race."*

THE HOLY SPIRIT

Going back to the Brother who was speaking to me about the country of France and the French people, the amazing thing about all of this was, this man was Spirit-filled. But the sadness is, he wasn't Spirit-led.

It doesn't matter who the people are; it is the Holy Spirit and the Holy Spirit Alone Who can reach souls for Christ. He does it strictly on the preached or taught Word of God. He convicts man of man's fallen and thereby, lost condition. He then gives man, and again, irrespective as to whom the man might be, Faith to believe the Word, that is, if he desires to do so. Regrettably, most, I think, reject that call; nevertheless, the call is given.

For Preachers, and especially Preachers who are supposed to be Spirit-filled, to think that souls can be reached by means other than the Power of the Holy Spirit is spiritual ignorance gone to seed. Again I mention Paul in a sense, becoming all things to all men, that he might win some to Christ. And again I state that he wasn't entering into their culture, but was rather showing interest in them, and whatever it was that they did, etc.

I look today at the modern Church, and especially at the youth scene. How foolish, how downright stupid it is, for Preachers, or anyone for that matter, to think they can reach the youth by playing the ridiculous contemporary music, which has become so popular in most Churches. Let me ask this question:

Can you win the drunk to the Lord by giving him whiskey? Can you win the gambler by gambling with him in the casinos? Can you win the drug addict by giving him more drugs?

We don't win people to Christ, be they young people or whomever, by diluting the Gospel to make it sound, look, and seem like the world. How stupid can we be!

I was reading the other day in a so-called Christian magazine, of a particular Church in California, a Church incidentally which claims to be Spirit-filled, which had built a youth hall, and made it look like a night club. They had the bar, the dance floor, etc. They served drinks (non-alcoholic), but made them to look like they were alcoholic, just like you would get in a bar. And oh yes, they had a rock band, and the young people danced, but of course, as they put it, they were dancing to Christian music, so this made it alright.

As I read this stupidity, and stupidity it is, the truth is, while they may get many young people to attend such gatherings, they won't win anybody to Christ. In fact, they will shove them deeper into the morass of sin and shame, which is wrecking so many young people today. Again let me state what the truth actually is:

People are won to Christ, the youth included, only by the Moving and Operation of the Holy Spirit. He Alone can bring that young person to a saving knowledge of Christ. He Alone can convict of sin, of Righteousness, and of judgment. And to be sure,

He will not function in that which looks like the world, seems like the world, sounds like the world, is meant to imitate the world, and in fact is of the world. But yet, many Christians are so foolish as to believe this lie that is promoted by the Devil, and even to support it with their money.

The Holy Spirit functions alone in the Finished Work of Christ. The Message must not change. It is *"Jesus Christ and Him Crucified,"* whether to the young or the old, the rich or the poor, the educated or the uneducated, the black or the white, or anything in between. And if we try to do it any other way, the Scripture plainly says here that the person who does such, *"will be cut off from among his people,"* i.e., *"will lose his soul."* But regrettably and sadly, that's where much of the modern Church is presently.

IT IS THE BLOOD THAT MAKES AN ATONEMENT FOR THE SOUL

Verse 11 reads: *"For the life of the flesh is in the blood: and I have given it to you upon the Altar to make an Atonement for your souls: for it is the blood that makes an Atonement for the soul."*

The phrase, *"For the life of the flesh is in the blood,"* should actually be translated, *"For the soul of the flesh is in the blood."* The Hebrew word rendered here *"life"* occurs twice more in this very Verse, and is properly translated *"soul."*

All of this assigns the reason why blood must not be eaten. It is the principal of vitality; it constitutes the soul of animal and human life. Hence *"blood"* and *"life"* are used interchangeably in the Scriptures. Thus, when the Psalmist exclaims, *"What profit is there in my blood?"*, he is actually using it for *"life,"* hence, *"What profit is there in my life?"*

So we learn from this that the *"blood"* speaks for life, i.e., *"the soul,"* and inasmuch as life was forfeited when Adam fell, a perfect life would have to be given, which would necessitate the shedding of the Blood of Christ in order for the sin debt to be paid, and man to be saved.

THE ALTAR, WHICH IS, THE CROSS

The phrase, *"And I have given it to you*

upon the Altar to make an Atonement for your souls," has in the Hebrew the words *"upon the Altar,"* placed first in the sentence. It is done for emphasis, meaning, *"For I have ordained it upon the Altar to make Atonement for your souls."* Ellicott says, *"Because the blood is the principle of life, therefore, God has ordained it to be offered upon the Altar as an expiation for the offerer's life."*

This tells us, for Atonement to be made for lost mankind, Christ would have to go to the Cross, and there shed His Blood, of which the Altar of old was but a type. Just any blood wouldn't do; only His Blood. As well, it being shed any other way than the Cross, as stated, typified by the Altar, would have rendered it insufficient. It had to be the Cross!

This means that had Jesus been stoned to death, or thrust through with a spear and thereby died, it would have been a sacrifice that was unacceptable. It had to be the Cross!

WHY THE CROSS?

Which we've already explained elsewhere in this Volume, the Law of Moses stated that if someone committed a heinous sin, a sin that was worthy of death, he would be put to death, and then hung on a tree, but taken down before nightfall. Likewise, Jesus did not stay on the Cross but a little over six hours. His body was taken down before nightfall, totally fulfilling the Law of Moses in this respect (Deut. 21:22-23).

The idea is, a heinous sin and crime had been committed by the human race, which demanded this strenuous example.

When Christ died on the Cross, He had to atone for all sin, past, present, and future, and that means the worst type of sins that one could ever begin to imagine, plus the very root of sin, in essence, the cause of sin. Inasmuch as it was demanded in the Law of Moses that the worst type of criminal be treated in such a fashion, Christ had to be treated in the same manner, hence the necessity for the Cross. In fact, both Paul and Peter referred to the Cross also as a *"tree"* (Acts 5:30; 10:39; 13:29; Gal. 3:13; I Pet. 2:24). Once again, the *"Altar"* typified the Cross, before which the blood had to be poured out.

So, to demean the Cross, to ignore the

NOTES

Cross, and to deny the Cross, or to add something to the Cross, or take something from the Cross, is tantamount to blasphemy. It is an affront against the very Plan of Redemption, which Plan incidentally was formulated before the foundation of the world (I Pet. 1:18-20).

HOW IMPORTANT ARE THE TYPES?

The types were important enough for Christ to fulfill them in totality. In fact, nothing could be more important than these types.

Among all other things, the types were given in order to portray what Christ would do when He came, which He did! They proclaimed how He did it, and even the exact manner in which it was done.

The Scripture says: *"The Holy Spirit this signifying, that the way into the Holiest of all* (the Throne of God) *was not yet made manifest, while as the first Tabernacle was yet standing:*

"Which was a figure for the time then present, in which were offered both gifts and sacrifices" (Heb. 9:8-9).

So the Holy Spirit tells us here through Paul that all of the types were *"figures"* of the reality, namely Christ, Who was to come. In fact, the *"types"* or *"figures"* were given to us, as stated, in order that we might understand more perfectly Who Christ was and is, and What Christ would do as it regards the Redemption of humanity.

For instance, when Nadab and Abihu were stricken dead by the Holy Spirit for offering *"strange fire"* (Lev. 10:1-2), this was not to be taken merely as a happening. The Holy Spirit meant for us to know and understand why these men died, in essence telling us that God does not change, and if the same sin is committed now, even though we are living in the Dispensation of Grace, spiritual death, and maybe even physical death, will definitely be the result.

ATONEMENT

The phrase, *"For it is the blood that makes an Atonement for the soul,"* plainly and purely tells us that the Death of Christ on the Cross, which was brought about by the shedding of His Precious Blood, is not only the means of Salvation, but in fact, is the only means of Salvation.

Mackintosh said, *"When man duly takes his place as one possessing no title whatsoever to life – when he fully recognizes God's claims upon him, then the Divine record is, 'I have given you the life to make an Atonement for your soul.' Yes; Atonement is God's gift to man; and be it carefully noted that this Atonement is in the Blood, and only in the Blood. It is not the Blood and something else. The Word is most explicit. It attributes Atonement exclusively to the Blood"* (Heb. 9:22; Eph. 1:7; Col. 1:14; I Jn. 1:7; Rev., Chpt. 12).

The Blood of Christ, which is the same thing as speaking of the Cross of Christ, is in essence, the vital doctrine of Atonement. It is the foundation of everything. It is the ground of God's Righteousness in justifying an ungodly sinner who believes on the Name of the Son of God; and it is the ground of the sinner's confidence in drawing near to a Holy God, Who is of purer eyes than to behold evil.

HOW IMPORTANT IS THE BLOOD?

Considering that the Scripture plainly and clearly says, *"It is the Blood that makes an Atonement for the soul,"* we should at first glance realize just how important this actually is. The Holy Spirit didn't mince words, and, as well, neither did He make it difficult to understand. He said it clean and clear, leaving absolutely no room for doubt.

Yes, the shed Blood of Christ, which atoned for the sin of man, and did so in totality, is the single most important thing in the history of man. Nothing else even remotely comes close.

It is on that ground, the ground of the shed Blood of Christ at Calvary's Cross, that effects every single Salvation that's ever been brought about, and as well, all the Sanctification of the Saints, in fact, every single thing that the sinner or the Saint receives from God. All and without exception comes through the Cross. The Holy Spirit works exclusively within the Finished Work of Christ, which most Christians, regrettably, do not understand.

In about 1998, if I remember the timeframe correctly, we felt led of the Lord at

this Ministry to take a stand against some of the false doctrines which have made such inroads into the Church. Considering that these doctrines are very popular, our stand did not endear us too very well to many Christians. Nevertheless, our position is not to please people, but rather to please the Lord.

I have found that a correct knowledge of the Cross, which is the knowledge of Truth (Jn. 8:32; I Cor. 1:17-18), at the same time, exposes error. In fact, nothing exposes error quite like a proper understanding of the Cross. The truth is, most Christians get into doctrinal trouble, which can cause them innumerable problems, simply because they do not understand the Cross.

The Cross is Christianity. If the Cross is taken out of Christianity, one is left with nothing but a philosophy – and a philosophy I might quickly add, which will set no captives free. The power is in the Cross, or better said, is made possible by the Cross. Actually, all the power is in the Holy Spirit. Listen to Paul:

"For the preaching of the Cross is to them who perish foolishness; but unto us which are saved it is the Power of God" (I Cor. 1:18).

THE PREACHING OF THE CROSS IS THE POWER OF GOD

What did Paul mean by that statement? Actually, his meaning is twofold:

1. As stated, all power is vested in the Holy Spirit (Acts 1:8). Actually, there is no power per se in a wooden beam, and neither is there any power in death. So what did Paul mean?

What Jesus did at the Cross gives the Holy Spirit the latitude to work within our lives, and considering that He is God, and is Almighty, meaning that He has all power, through the Cross, His power can be used on our behalf. Considering, as stated, that He works exclusively through the Finished Work of Christ, we are then given to understand that it is the Cross which has made it possible for Him to work with us as He does, as it regards His Power.

2. The preaching of the Cross is the Power of God, simply because at the Cross, Satan, along with every demon spirit, fallen angel, principality, and power, along with

the rulers of the darkness of this world, and spiritual wickedness in high places, all and without exception, were defeated by Christ at the Cross.

Exactly how did He defeat them? Listen again to Paul:

"Blotting out the handwriting of Ordinances that was against us, which was contrary to us, and took it out of the way, nailing it to His Cross;

"And having spoiled principalities and powers, He made a show of them openly, triumphing over them in it" (Col. 2:14-15).

The Lord defeated Satan and all his cohorts on the Cross, by simply removing the legal right that Satan had to hold man in captivity. That legal right is *"sin."* When Jesus atoned for all sin, which He did, this removed that legal right, with Satan now having no more right to make captives of anyone. So in effect, what Jesus did there in the Atonement defeated Satan completely, and made it possible for every human being on the face of the Earth, at least for those who will believe, to be free from every bondage of darkness, every vice of every description, irrespective as to what it might be.

FREE INDEED!

That being the case, why is it that most of the world still lives in spiritual darkness, and why is it that even many Christians, if not most Christians, are living in a state of spiritual bondage of some nature?

The answer is this: Satan is able to impose his will on those he governs, by the consent of the governed. What do we mean by that?

The unsaved will not believe Christ; consequently, they remain in captivity, in effect, giving Satan consent to hold them in spiritual darkness, and which he readily does, *"stealing, killing, and destroying"* (Jn. 10:10).

In effect, it is the same with the Believer, but in a little different way. The Believer has accepted Christ, has been born-again, and is a new creation in Christ Jesus (II Cor. 5:17). But the tragedy is, most Christians do not understand God's prescribed order of victory, and I'm speaking of victory for the Saints, and not understanding that prescribed order,

they set about to bring about victory in all the wrong ways. Whether they realize it or not, they are giving Satan consent to govern them, which he readily does.

Now many Christians might counter by saying that they are not giving Satan consent to do anything. But the truth is, they are! In a sense, they are doing so by default. While they don't want any domination by Satan, and will vigorously fight any domination, the truth is, they are placing their faith in the wrong thing, and by default, so to speak, Satan takes advantage of that, and causes them all types of problems.

THE CHRISTIAN AND SANCTIFICATION

The word *"Sanctification"* or *"Holiness,"* simply means, *"to be set apart exclusively for the Lord."* The born-again Believer surely wants such a thing; however, most don't know how to go about obtaining this which is the single most important thing in the life of the Christian.

The truth is, Sanctification is hardly mentioned in most Churches any more, despite the fact that it is one of the great Biblical Doctrines (Jn. 17:17; Eph. 5:26; I Thess. 5:23; Heb. 13:12; I Pet. 3:15; I Cor. 1:30; I Thess. 4:3-4; II Thess. 2:13; I Pet. 1:2).

The Bible teaches that the Believer is sanctified, and is being sanctified. In fact, the moment the believing sinner accepts Christ, he or she is instantly sanctified (I Cor. 6:11). That's the *"standing"* that each and every Believer has in Christ, which is a standing of perfection, and because it is in Christ.

Even though that is our *"standing,"* which never changes, our *"state"* is something else altogether. Consequently, it is the business of the Holy Spirit within our lives to bring our *"state"* up to our *"standing."* This is the Sanctification process. That's what Paul was talking about when he said:

"And the very God of Peace sanctify you wholly; and I pray God your whole spirit and soul and body be preserved blameless unto the coming of our Lord Jesus Christ" (I Thess. 5:23).

The Sanctification of the Saint is a process of the Holy Spirit. Again, Paul said: *"But we are bound to give thanks always to God for you, Brethren beloved of the LORD, because*

God has from the beginning chosen you to Salvation through Sanctification of the Spirit and belief of the Truth" (II Thess. 2:13).

This means that we cannot sanctify ourselves, beyond making preparation, which regards our being willing to be properly sanctified. From there it is entirely a Work of the Holy Spirit.

HOW DOES THE HOLY SPIRIT SANCTIFY THE SAINT?

Once more, we go back to the Cross. The Holy Spirit requires that we place our Faith entirely in Christ and the Cross, and because it is Christ Who paid the price for our Salvation and our Sanctification (Gal. 5:6; Rom. 6:11, 14).

With our Faith properly placed in the Cross, and remaining in the Cross, which states that we know and understand that Jesus did for us on the Cross, what we could not do for ourselves. That being the case, the Holy Spirit will then bring about Sanctification, which is an ordered process. In that way and that way alone can the Believer walk in perpetual victory. In that way and that way alone, *"sin will not have dominion over you"* (Rom. 6:14).

It is all by Faith, but it's Faith that is properly placed, which is the key.

FAITH!

Almost every Christian will agree that Faith is the ingredient on which Christianity functions. But beyond that, most Christians do not really know and understand how Faith operates.

Were most Christians to be asked as to what Faith means, they would probably respond by claiming that it means to have Faith in the Word, or Faith in Christ, or Faith in God, etc.

While those statements are correct, they really don't say very much. Going no further than that in their thinking, most Christians will then try to trigger Faith, or put it into motion, by quoting Scripture. In fact, that's one of the favorite means by which most Christians think that their Faith is increased, or else, such quotations put God into motion, etc.

While quoting Scriptures is very good, and

NOTES

should be done by every Believer, if it's done in the way that it's mostly done by most Christians, it amounts to little more than white magic. In other words, we try to manipulate the spirit world of Righteousness, by doing certain things.

Black magic is when someone tries to manipulate the spirit world of darkness by doing certain things. In fact, most Christians have never heard of white magic. And in reality, that is not important. But it is important for you to understand that God cannot be manipulated. The idea that I can get God to do something by quoting certain Scriptures, by doing some certain right things, in effect, makes a little god out of the individual, which in fact, the Lord really cannot tolerate.

The truth is, when we speak of Faith, if it's not Faith in Christ and the Cross, never separating those two, then it's not Faith that God will recognize. While it might be faith, it's not Biblical Faith.

For Faith to be proper, it must have a proper object, and that object is *"Jesus Christ and Him Crucified"* (I Cor. 1:23; 2:2). So what does all of this tell us?

Millions of Christians are trying to increase their faith, thinking that if they can just get their faith level up, they can get certain things; such thinking is bogus. Whenever the Disciples asked the Lord to *"increase their Faith,"* His answer to them was very revealing:

He said unto them: *"If you had Faith as a grain of mustard seed, you might say unto this sycamine tree, Be thou plucked up by the root, and be planted in the sea; and it should obey you"* (Lk. 17:5-6).

In other words, it was not increased Faith that the Disciples needed, but rather the correct object of Faith. While He did not explain it then, and because they would not have understood it, the correct object is the Cross. Listen again to our Lord:

At a point in time, Jesus began to proclaim to His Disciples, *"How that He must go unto Jerusalem, and suffer many things of the Elders, and Chief Priests and Scribes, and be killed, and be raised again the third day."*

The Scripture then said that: *"Peter took Him, and began to rebuke Him, saying,*

Be it far from You, Lord: this shall not be unto You."

The answer of Christ was very cryptic and to the point. He said: *"Get thee behind Me, Satan: you are an offense unto Me: for you savor not the things that be of God, but those that be of men"* (Mat. 16:21-23).

Jesus then said, *"If any man will come after Me, let him deny himself, and take up his Cross, and follow Me"* (Mat. 16:24).

In effect, He tells His Disciples here as to what His Mission to this Earth actually was. He then closed it out by telling them to do something that must have seemed about as far out as anything possible, and I speak of them taking up the Cross. But that's where He was directing their Faith – it was to the Cross. That was the reason He came, which means that it was the foundation of all that He was to do.

(12) "THEREFORE I SAID UNTO THE CHILDREN OF ISRAEL, NO SOUL OF YOU SHALL EAT BLOOD, AND NEITHER SHALL ANY STRANGER WHO SOJOURNS AMONG YOU EAT BLOOD.

(13) "AND WHATSOEVER MAN THERE BE OF THE CHILDREN OF ISRAEL, OR OF THE STRANGERS WHO SOJOURN AMONG YOU, WHICH HUNTS AND CATCHES ANY BEAST OR FOUL THAT MAY BE EATEN; HE SHALL EVEN POUR OUT THE BLOOD THEREOF, AND COVER IT WITH DUST.

(14) "FOR IT IS THE LIFE OF ALL FLESH; THE BLOOD OF IT IS FOR THE LIFE THEREOF: THEREFORE I SAID UNTO THE CHILDREN OF ISRAEL, YOU SHALL EAT THE BLOOD OF NO MANNER OF FLESH: FOR THE LIFE OF ALL FLESH IS THE BLOOD THEREOF: WHOSOEVER EATS IT SHALL BE CUT OFF.

(15) "AND EVERY SOUL THAT EATS THAT WHICH DIED OF ITSELF, OR THAT WHICH WAS TORN WITH BEAST, WHETHER IT BE ONE OF YOUR OWN COUNTRY, OR A STRANGER, HE SHALL BOTH WASH HIS CLOTHES, AND BATHE HIMSELF IN WATER, AND BE UNCLEAN UNTIL THE EVENING: THEN SHALL HE BE CLEAN.

(16) "BUT IF HE WASH THEM NOT, NOR BATHE HIS FLESH; THEN SHALL

NOTES

BEAR HIS INIQUITY."

The structure is:

1. In Verses 10 through 14, we have the Law against eating blood.

2. We as well have the explanation, showing how serious this sin is, and why it is sin, *"For the life of the flesh is in the blood."*

3. The death penalty was placed on anyone who would dare eat blood, *"Whosoever eats it shall be cut off."*

THE SACREDNESS OF THE BLOOD

The atoning power of the Blood, as being the seat of life, is the reason that the eating of it is forbidden.

What, then, can be said for a Church which professes literally to drink the Blood of Christ in the cup of the Mass? Is not that Church thereby guilty of outraging the law of all the Dispensations? It would evade this impeachment by impudently authorizing the eating of blood. But no impudence can evade the penalty: *"But flesh with the life thereof, which is the blood thereof, shall you not eat. And surely your blood of your lives will I require."* Does not this plainly say that God will require the blood of the life of the blood-eater? David abhorred the practice of the Syrians, who made libations of blood to their gods, and prophetically denounces and rejects our anti-Christian idolaters (Ps. 16:4). Drunk as she is with the blood of the Saints and the martyrs of Jesus, God will give her blood to drink, for she is worthy of such.

Considering all of this, our Lord's Words must have sounded so much the more strange in the ears of the Jews, when He said, *"Except you eat the flesh of the Son of Man, and drink His Blood, you have no life in you"* (Jn. 6:53).

However, He was speaking symbolically and not literally. He said: *"Does this offend you?*

"It is the spirit that quickens; the flesh profits nothing: the words that I speak unto you, they are spirit, and they are life" (Jn. 6:61, 63).

Jesus was speaking of Faith being placed in what He would do at the Cross. Paul related how this is done in Romans 6:3-5. Having Faith in Christ and what He did at the Cross, which refers to the giving of Himself in Sacrifice, which He did by the shedding of His

Blood, constitutes that of which He spoke in St. John, Chapter 6.

"Complete in Thee!
"No work of mine may take, dear Lord,
*   the place of Thine;*
"Thy Blood has pardon bought for me,
"And I am now complete in Thee."

"Complete in Thee!
"No more shall sin, Thy Grace has con-
*   quered, reign within;*
"Thy voice shall bid the tempter flee,
"And I shall stand complete in Thee."

"Complete in Thee!
"Each want supplied, and no good
*   thing to me denied;*
"Since You my portion, Lord, will be,
"I ask no more, complete in Thee."

"Dear Saviour!
"When before Your Bar all tribes and
*   tongues assembled are,*
"Among Thy chosen will I be,
"At Your right hand, complete in Thee."

CHAPTER 18

(1) "AND THE LORD SPOKE UNTO MOSES, SAYING,

(2) "SPEAK UNTO THE CHILDREN OF ISRAEL, AND SAY UNTO THEM, I AM THE LORD YOUR GOD.

(3) "AFTER THE DOINGS OF THE LAND OF EGYPT, WHEREIN YOU DWELT, SHALL YOU NOT DO: AND AFTER THE DOINGS OF THE LAND OF CANAAN, WHITHER I BRING YOU, SHALL YOU NOT DO: NEITHER SHALL YOU WALK IN THEIR ORDINANCES.

(4) "YOU SHALL DO MY JUDGMENTS, AND KEEP MY ORDINANCES, TO WALK THEREIN: I AM THE LORD YOUR GOD.

(5) "YOU SHALL THEREFORE KEEP MY STATUTES, AND MY JUDGMENTS: WHICH IF A MAN DO, HE SHALL LIVE IN THEM: I AM THE LORD."

The composition is:

1. In the first five Verses, God reminded Israel that He was a Holy God, and that having called them into fellowship with Himself

they must be a holy people (Williams).

2. God was to be their standard of Holiness, in essence His Word, and not the culture of the Egyptians or Canaanites, or anyone else, for that matter.

3. The fact that He was Jehovah their God provided a relationship that demanded a separation from all that defiled.

I AM THE LORD YOUR GOD

Verses 1 and 2 read: *"And the LORD spoke unto Moses, saying,*

"Speak unto the Children of Israel, and say unto them, I am the LORD your God."

In this Chapter, we will have revealed to us the Character of God, and the character of man. We will see that the character of man is desperately evil. In fact, even as the Prophet Isaiah said, *"The whole head is sick, and the whole heart faint.*

"From the sole of the foot even unto the head there is no soundness in it; but wounds, and bruises, and putrefying sores: they have not been closed, neither bound up, neither mollified with ointment" (Isa. 1:5-6).

And then the great Apostle said: *"For we have before proved to both Jews and Gentiles, that they are all under sin;*

"As it is written, There is none righteous, no, not one:

"There is none who understands, there is none who seeks after God.

"They are all gone out of the way, they are together become unprofitable; there is none who does good, no, not one.

"Their throat is an open sepulchre; with their tongues they have used deceit; the poison of asps is under their lips" (Rom. 3:9-13). The Prophet Isaiah also said, *"All we like sheep have gone astray; we have turned every one to his own way"* (Isa. 53:6).

That is the condition of man without God, and as is painfully obvious, none are excluded. While some may be a little better than others, all in fact, have spiritual leprosy, even though the degree may vary somewhat.

CHANGED

The only way that man can be changed from this vile, degrading, ungodly, wicked, transgressing condition is to be *"born again"* (Jn. 3:3, 16). All the philosophies in the world cannot change him. All the religions in the world, which are merely the inventions of men, cannot change him. In fact, religion can be defined as the efforts and strength of man to make himself acceptable to God, or to improve himself in some way, or so he thinks. In other words, it is a way devised by man, and not by God, which God can never accept.

Regrettably and sadly, it is not only the pagan religions which are guilty of this, but also, Christianity is rife with a departure from God's Way, to a way devised out of their own minds.

WHAT IS GOD'S WAY?

God's Way is *"Jesus Christ and Him Crucified"* (Gen. 3:15; 4:4-5; Lev. 17:11; Isa., Chpt. 53; Rom. 5:1, 15, 17; 6:3-14; I Cor. 1:17-18, 21, 23; 2:2; Jn. 3:16).

Man can only be changed by the Power of God, because it is the Power of God alone which is greater than the power of Satan, the originator of evil. That power is extended to sinful man, on the basis of justice forever satisfied, by the Sacrificial, Atoning Death of Christ on the Cross, and the Faith of the believing sinner in that Finished Work. Peter said, and rightly so: *"Be it known unto you all, and to all the people of Israel, that by the Name of Jesus Christ of Nazareth . . . which is become the head of the corner.*

"Neither is there Salvation in any other: for there is none other name under Heaven given among men, whereby we must be saved" (Acts 4:10-12).

While it was definitely *"Who"* He was that effected Salvation, which means that He was the Son of the Living God (Jn. 3:16); however, it was more so *"What"* He did, which refers to the Cross, that effected Salvation.

Jesus has always been God, is God presently, and will always be God. But His being God didn't really save anyone, as necessary as it was that He be such, and simply because no other could perform this task but Him. Nevertheless, the fact of Him being God, as necessary as it was, didn't save anyone.

If the Justice, Righteousness, and Nature of God were to be vindicated, Christ would have to die on a Cross, thereby paying the debt that man owed, which He did. To receive

Salvation, man is obligated to accept what Christ has done for us on the Cross, which will guarantee Salvation, and which alone will guarantee Salvation.

THE ACCEPTANCE OF THE CROSS

Why is it so difficult for man to accept Christ and the Cross? Millions accept Christ, but they reject the Cross. In doing so, they are left with *"another Jesus"* (II Cor. 11:4). In other words, if Christ and His Cross are not accepted fully, God will not accept the seeker. Jesus said: *"If any man* (which means that none are excluded) *will come after Me, let him deny himself, and take up his Cross, and follow Me"* (Mat. 16:24).

Unredeemed man is loathe to accept the Cross, because the Cross tells man how Righteous God is, and how unrighteous man is. Unredeemed man is loathe to admit that! He doesn't want to admit the fact that he is so sinful, so wicked, so vile, that it would take such a price, the price of the Cross, in order to redeem him. Unredeemed man likes to think that he is good, he is kind, and while there might be a problem, it is insignificant, and can be addressed in many and varied ways. Man is wrong! Dead wrong!

Man is what the Holy Spirit said he is, through the Apostle Paul, and the Prophet Isaiah, and in fact, every writer of the Word of God.

Redeemed man is loathe to accept the Cross, because the Cross says that man, even redeemed man, cannot live this life, cannot be what he ought to be, cannot be Christlike, cannot know Righteousness and Holiness, cannot in fact, have victory over sin, without expressing Faith in Christ and what He has done for us at the Cross on a perpetual basis. It is not only true that unredeemed man thinks he can save himself, but redeemed man, who ought to know better, thinks he can sanctify himself. That is, as stated, the biggest problem in the Church presently.

But let the Redeemed understand that we can no more sanctify ourselves, and I'm speaking of doing so by our religious observance, etc., than the unredeemed can save themselves.

THE DOINGS OF THE WORLD

Verse 3 reads: *"After the doings of the land*

of Egypt, wherein you dwelt, shall you not do: after the doings of the land of Canaan, whither I bring you, shall you not do: neither shall you walk in their ordinances."

Emphatically, and even dogmatically, the Lord of Israel tells the Israelites that Egypt and Canaan, in effect, all the nations of the world were wrong. They were wrong about life; they were wrong about living; they were wrong about death; they were wrong about eternity. As well, they were wrong about God, in fact, they were worshippers of demon spirits.

So who says that these nations were wrong, and Israel was right? Bringing it up to the present, who says that the world is wrong, and the true Child of God is right?

To be sure, Egypt and Canaan, and the other nations of the world, certainly would not have concluded themselves wrong, even as the people of the world presently do not at all consider themselves to be wrong.

However, these are questions that need to be asked, and to be sure, as Israel of old could stand that test, so can modern Christendom, that is, Christendom which is truly Biblical.

The Word of the Lord was the Standard by which all questions of right and wrong were to be definitely settled in the judgment of every member of the Israel of God.

Mackintosh says: *"It was not, by any means, the judgment of an Israelite in opposition to the judgment of an Egyptian or of a Canaanite; but it was the Judgment of God above all. Egypt might have her practices and her opinions, and so might Canaan; but Israel was to have the opinions and practices laid down in the Word of God, even as we shall see in the next two Verses."*

CHRISTIANITY ON TRIAL

Sometime back I debated a Muslim at Louisiana State University. I didn't have the luxury of knowing what the debate was all about, until it actually began.

After the debate, I had the occasion to have a private conversation with the man whom I was debating, who incidentally, was one of the shining lights of Islam. He was from South Africa.

At any rate, I asked him why I could not go on Television in countries controlled by

Islam. I went on to remonstrate that Muslims, or anyone else for that matter, could go on Television or Radio in the United States, and be perfectly free to preach their message, etc.

His answer was very evasive. Finally I spoke up and said, *"Muslim countries will not allow me to go on Television in their countries and preach the Gospel, simply because in their heart of hearts, they know that Islam cannot compete with Biblical Christianity."*

Of course, he strongly opposed that particular statement; nevertheless, it is true. In fact, there is no religion in the world, no philosophy in the world, that can compete with Biblical Christianity. To be sure, the type of Christianity that is not truly Biblical, of which there seems to be an abundance, is not that of which I speak. I speak of that which is truly of the Lord, thereby, Scriptural, and thereby empowered by the Holy Spirit. Not being able to compete, these particular religions simply close the doors to Biblical Christianity. In fact, the position they take is a testimony to the entirety of the world, if they would only look at it objectively, that they cannot compete.

THE WAYS OF THE LORD AND THE WAYS OF THE WORLD

As well, in this one Passage of Scripture (vs. 3), Israel was emphatically told not to adopt the ways of the heathen. We in modern Christendom should take that word to heart, as well!

But the truth is, the modern Church has adopted so many ways of the world, i.e., *"the Egyptians and the Canaanites,"* that anymore, much of that which refers to itself as Church can little be looked as being any different than the world.

This becomes very clear when one sees the Church attempting to use the methods of the world to reach people for Christ. What a travesty!

A perfect example is the youth of our Churches. So-called Contemporary Christian Music is claimed to be the method.

Anyone who would listen to this type of music for any length of time at all, who is actually Spirit-filled, would instantly know, while people may in fact be being reached, it is definitely not for the Lord.

I saw an ad some time back of a particular Church advertising its Services, as being only 28 minutes in length. I don't know why they came up with 28 minutes. Why not 30? Why have Church at all!

Another major Church advertises that the way to build a big Church is to canvass the community, and find out what the people want, and then give it to them. Incidentally, the Church which promotes this method is one of the largest in the nation, which is copied by hundreds, if not thousands, of other Churches.

Incidentally, as they canvassed the neighborhood or city, they found out that the people didn't want anything said about the Cross, because that was somewhat intimidating. They wanted something to make them feel good when they came to Church. And that's what this silly Pastor gave them.

The true man of God doesn't really care what the people want. He cares only for what the Lord has said, and then that he deliver what the Lord has said, exactly as it has been said, adding not to it, or deleting from it. That is my business as a Preacher of the Gospel. Otherwise, the Preacher is nothing but a hireling.

THE SPIRIT OF GOD

If Preachers do not have the Spirit of God, they will then resort to the things of the world. And the sad truth is, there's not one Preacher out of one thousand who is truly led by the Spirit.

To make *"self"* the ground of action or the standard of ethics is not only presumptuous folly, but it is sure to set one upon a descending scale of action. If self be my object, I must, of necessity, sink lower and lower everyday; but if, on the other hand, I set the Lord before me, I shall rise higher and higher as, by the Power of the Holy Spirit, I grow in conformity to that perfect model which is unfolded to the gaze of Faith into sacred pages of Inspiration.

Again, Mackintosh says, and concerning this, *"I shall undoubtedly have to prostrate myself in the dust, under a sense of how infinitely short I come of the mark set before me; but then I can never consent to the setting up of a lower standard, nor can I ever be satisfied until I am conformed in all things to Him Who was my Substitute on the Cross, and is my Model in the Glory."*

THE WORD OF GOD

Verses 4 and 5 read: *"You shall do My Judgments, and keep My Ordinances, to walk therein: I am the LORD your God.*

"You shall therefore keep My Statutes, and My Judgments: which if a man do, he shall live in them: I am the LORD."

We find from this, as with Israel of old, so with modern Christendom presently, the Word of God must settle every question, and govern every conscience: there must be no appeal from its solemn and weighty decision. When God speaks, every heart must bow. Men may form and hold their opinions; they may adopt and defend their practices, but the foundation principle of all right living is a profound reverence for, and implicit subjection to, *"every Word that proceeds out of the Mouth of God"* (Mat. 4:4).

It must always be understood, so far as it may be, that we as Believers are totally and completely governed, not by our own opinions, but by the Word of God.

It might come as a shock to many Christians; however, most Denominations, and I do not think that I exaggerate when I use the word *"most,"* are not in fact, governed by the Word of God, but rather by their own constitution and bylaws, which they feel free to change constantly.

I remember once relating to the Superintendent of a major Pentecostal Denomination, that what they were proposing was not Scriptural. I will not go into any detail, but I'll never forget his response:

He stuttered around for a few moments, not at all denying what I had said, and then finally blurted out, *"But this is our tradition."*

In other words, I suppose that it didn't matter what the Word of God said, only what their tradition said, whatever that was!

If the Word of God is not the Standard, then there is no standard at all. Men can feel free, which they definitely do, to make up their own rules as they go along, with the Word of God being ignored altogether.

Jesus said: *"Thus have you made the Commandment of God of none effect by your tradition."*

He then said: *"You hypocrites, well did Isaiah prophesy of you, saying,*

"This people draws nigh unto me with their mouth, and honors me with their lips; but their heart is far from Me.

"But in vain they do worship Me, teaching for doctrines the commandments of men" (Mat. 15:6-9).

How much clearer can it be!

The question ought to always be, *"What does the Bible say?"* Or *"Is it Scriptural?"*

A PERSONAL EXPERIENCE

I have had to face this as possibly few human beings in the world, at least in modern times.

In the early 1990's, with my whole world crumbling around me, failing, despite all I could do otherwise, I will never forget the day, with my family and friends gathered around me, when I laid my Bible on the table, and said, *"I don't know the answer to victorious living, but I do know that it's in the Bible. And by the Grace of God, I'm going to find it."* That was one of the greatest statements I've ever made.

At that very moment, the Church world was demanding that I do certain things, which I knew to be totally and grossly unscriptural, and which I could not do, that is, if I was to obey the Lord. In fact, they told me in essence, if I trusted the Lord, thereby doing my best to abide by His Word, that they would blackball me, and do everything within their power to destroy me. I can say this one thing about the powers that be, they meant every word they said, and did everything they could do to carry out their threat. And if it had not been for a firm grip on the Lord, they would have succeeded.

Let the Reader understand that there is no evil in the world like religious evil. Let the Reader also understand that it was not the drunks or the gamblers, as vile as those sins might be, who crucified Christ. It was the religious hierarchy who crucified Him. It hasn't changed. While there are certainly some Godly men in positions of leadership around the world in various Denominations,

and I am personally acquainted with some of them, for the most part, that is not the case at all. It is sad, but true! Any time men leave the Word of God spiritual catastrophe is the result.

So-called Church leaders used as an example a particular Preacher whose Television Ministry was very popular. He was doing exactly what they told him to do, and I should follow his example. As stated, the Lord in no uncertain terms told me that if I followed that example, I would destroy myself.

I don't really know what the man's problem was, but I do know what they were demanding wasn't Scriptural.

At any rate, the end result of that decision was our Brother and his wife are now divorced, and by contrast, the Lord has blessed my particular Ministry in a tremendous way.

THE CROSS

Incidentally, in 1996, the Lord answered my petition and my prayer. He gave me the solution to victorious, overcoming, Biblical living. That solution was and is the Cross of Christ. At that particular time He began to show me what the Cross was, and how it affected us, as it regards Sanctification, in other words, victorious living. In fact, that Revelation continues unto this hour, opening up the Word more and more, and which I trust it will ever continue. Why not! Paul referred to the Cross as *"the Everlasting Covenant"* (Heb. 13:20).

While it took some five years of ardently seeking the Face of the Lord, both day and night, and with tears, thank the Lord, my petition was graciously answered, the solution was readily given. In fact, what the Lord gave to me has been so overwhelmingly glorious in my life, even as it has the lives of untold millions, as to defy all description.

The Cross of Christ is the solution to every problem. There Jesus died, and to be sure, the price He paid included every need that man might have. The Lord showed me how the Cross effects our Sanctification, in fact, our daily living. In this, He showed me how the Holy Spirit works, which we have addressed over and over in this Volume. Had I listened to men, I would have been completely destroyed. The reason is obvious!

What they were demanding was grossly unscriptural, which means that God can have no part in such. And to be sure, man cannot solve his own problems, and for any individual to think he can shows a complete lack of understanding of the Word of God, or at the worst, a position of total unbelief. In fact, gross unbelief is the problem of many, if not most, so-called religious leaders.

(6) "NONE OF YOU SHALL APPROACH TO ANY WHO IS NEAR OF KIN TO HIM, TO UNCOVER THEIR NAKEDNESS: I AM THE LORD.

(7) "THE NAKEDNESS OF YOUR FATHER, OR THE NAKEDNESS OF YOUR MOTHER, SHALL YOU NOT UNCOVER: SHE IS YOUR MOTHER; YOU SHALL NOT UNCOVER HER NAKEDNESS.

(8) "THE NAKEDNESS OF YOUR FATHER'S WIFE SHALL YOU NOT UNCOVER: IT IS YOUR FATHER'S NAKEDNESS.

(9) "THE NAKEDNESS OF YOUR SISTER, THE DAUGHTER OF YOUR FATHER, OR DAUGHTER OF YOUR MOTHER, WHETHER SHE BE BORN AT HOME, OR BORN ABROAD, EVEN THEIR NAKEDNESS YOU SHALL NOT UNCOVER.

(10) "THE NAKEDNESS OF YOUR SON'S DAUGHTER, OR OF YOUR DAUGHTER'S DAUGHTER, EVEN THEIR NAKEDNESS YOU SHALL NOT UNCOVER: FOR THEIRS IS YOUR OWN NAKEDNESS.

(11) "THE NAKEDNESS OF YOUR FATHER'S WIFE'S DAUGHTER, BEGOTTEN OF YOUR FATHER, SHE IS YOUR SISTER, YOU SHALL NOT UNCOVER HER NAKEDNESS.

(12) "YOU SHALL NOT UNCOVER THE NAKEDNESS OF YOUR FATHER'S SISTER: SHE IS YOUR FATHER'S NEAR KINSWOMAN.

(13) "YOU SHALL NOT UNCOVER THE NAKEDNESS OF YOUR MOTHER'S SISTER: FOR SHE IS YOUR MOTHER'S NEAR KINSWOMAN.

(14) "YOU SHALL NOT UNCOVER THE NAKEDNESS OF YOUR FATHER'S BROTHER, AND YOU SHALL NOT APPROACH TO HIS WIFE; SHE IS YOUR AUNT.

(15) "YOU SHALL NOT UNCOVER THE NAKEDNESS OF YOUR DAUGHTER-IN-LAW: SHE IS YOUR SON'S WIFE; YOU SHALL NOT UNCOVER HER NAKEDNESS.

(16) "YOU SHALL NOT UNCOVER THE NAKEDNESS OF YOUR BROTHER'S WIFE: IT IS YOUR BROTHER'S NAKEDNESS.

(17) "YOU SHALL NOT UNCOVER THE NAKEDNESS OF A WOMAN AND HER DAUGHTER, NEITHER SHALL YOU TAKE HER SON'S DAUGHTER, OR HER DAUGHTER'S DAUGHTER, TO UNCOVER HER NAKEDNESS; FOR THEY ARE HER NEAR KINSWOMEN: IT IS WICKEDNESS.

(18) "NEITHER SHALL YOU TAKE A WIFE TO HER SISTER, TO VEX HER, TO UNCOVER HER NAKEDNESS, BESIDE THE OTHER IN HER LIFE TIME.

(19) "ALSO YOU SHALL NOT APPROACH UNTO A WOMAN TO UNCOVER HER NAKEDNESS, AS LONG AS SHE IS PUT APART FOR HER UNCLEANNESS."

The exegesis is:

1. There was given to Israel, and in exact detail, directions, and specifications as it regarded what they were not to do.

2. Every possible moral situation was addressed. When we look at the three Chapters of Leviticus 18, 19, and 20, we see the total degradation of man.

3. There are things that God says which are wrong. And let it ever be understood that what was wrong then is wrong now.

MORAL IMPURITY

As is plainly obvious here, and I speak of the entirety of this Chapter, but at the present, more specifically Verses 6 through 19, the terrible sins of incest and adultery are addressed.

These people were God's people, and as such, their ethics were to assume a character and time worthy of Him. Concerning this, Mackintosh said, *"It was no longer a question as to what they were, either in themselves or in comparison with others; but of what God was in comparison with all."*

First of all, we know and realize that the Lord laid down these restrictions for many and varied reasons; however, the evidence is plainly clear, and because of what was said in Verse 3, that the other nations surrounding Israel were grossly guilty of the terrible sins of incest.

Concerning these things, Pulpit says,

"Verses 6 through 19 contain the law of incest, or the prohibited degrees of marriage. The positive law of marriage, as implanted in the human heart, would be simply that any man of full age might marry any woman of full age, provided that both parties were willing. But this liberty is at once controlled by a number of restrictions, the main purpose of which is to prevent incest, which, however much one nation may come to be indifferent to one form of it, and another to another, is yet abhorrent to the feelings and principles of mankind. The Hebrew restrictive law is contained in one Verse, 'None of you shall approach to any who is near of kin to him, to uncover their nakedness: I am the Lord.'

"All that follows is simply an amplification and an explanation of the words, 'Near of kin to him.'"

Reuben's sin, by which he forfeited his birthright, is connected with this offense. He committed an incestuous act with Bilhah, his father's concubine (Gen. 35:22). And as well, Jacob was alive at the time of this transgression (Gen. 49:4). As well, incest is one of the sins which Ezekiel enumerates as those which brought the Judgment of God on Israel (Ezek. 22:10).

Paul addressed this as well, by saying of the man at Corinth, who had committed incest with his father's wife, and seemed to have done so while his father was yet alive, that this was *"fornication,"* which type was so bad that it was even objected to by the Gentiles (I Cor. 5:1-5).

Absalom's *"going in unto his father's concubines"* was regarded as the final act which made reconciliation with his father David impossible (II Sam. 16:22; 20:3).

WHAT IS *"NEAR OF KIN"* AS MENTIONED IN VERSE 6?

It covers mother, father, step-mother, step-father, sister, brother, step-sister, step-brother, father-in-law, mother-in-law, son-in-law, daughter-in-law, aunt, uncle, niece, nephew, and first and second cousins, with the latter being outlined in Verse 17.

NAKEDNESS

This word is used over and over in these

Verses as is obvious, and refers to *"sexual intercourse,"* whether in the bonds of incestuous marriage, which marriage would be sinful, or outside of the bonds of marriage, which would be fornication.

This is the Law of Moses which was given about 2,500 years after Adam. During this period of time, these laws did not actually apply, in which we find Abraham marrying his half-sister (Gen. 20:12).

Even though the Lord allowed such at that time, for the necessity of the human race, He ultimately instituted these various laws, as it regards the Law of Moses.

In some of these cases, death would change the order of events. For instance, if a man died, and he and his wife had not had children, his brother, that is if he had a brother, and the brother was not married, was instructed by the Lord to marry the sister of the deceased brother, and raise up children in the name of his deceased brother (Deut. 25:5-6).

All of this is deeply humbling, in that it declares the truth that man, spiritually speaking, is a total wreck. From the crown of his head to the sole of his foot, there is not so much as a single speck of moral soundness, as looked at in the light of the Divine Presence. Concerning that which is sinful and wicked, there is very little, if anything, that man will not do. That is his nature, a fallen nature, I might quickly add, which was brought about by the Fall of Adam and Eve in the Garden. Inasmuch as Adam was the federal head, so to speak, of the human race, him being poisoned guaranteed that all who would follow after him would be poisoned as well. Paul said: *"As in Adam all die"* (I Cor. 15:22). He also said: *"They who are in the flesh cannot please God"* (Rom. 8:8).

THE HOLY SPIRIT

But Paul also stated that the Believer is *"not in the flesh, but in the Spirit"* (Rom. 8:9). This means, as Believers, we do not have to be controlled by the sin nature, but we can be controlled by the Divine Nature (II Pet. 1:4).

We might very well ask the question as to how we were brought out from under the control of the sin-nature, into control by the

Divine Nature.

It has been referred to as the *"grandest story ever told."*

To be brief, God would become man, born of the Virgin Mary, which means that He was not tainted by Adam's Fall, but in a sense, came as Adam originally came, which means *"without sin."* Every child since Adam is born in what is referred to as *"original sin."* David said, *"Behold, I was shaped in iniquity, and in sin did my mother conceive me"* (Ps. 51:5).

He wasn't meaning that his mother had played the harlot, but was rather speaking of original sin, which is the lot of all, due to Adam's Fall.

As previously stated, Adam and Eve were originally intended to bring sons and daughters of God into the world (Lk. 3:38). Inasmuch as they both fell, that could no longer be done. Consequently, all offspring born into the world after Adam are not born sons and daughters of God, but rather, *"in the likeness of Adam"* (Gen. 5:3).

Jesus came as the *"Last Adam"* (I Cor. 15:45). He came to undo what the first Adam had done, which was to lift man out of the abyss of sin and shame to which he had plunged, and to do what the first Adam had not done, which was to render a perfect obedience to God, which He gloriously did (I Cor. 15:45-50).

As a result of Adam's Fall, man, being born in original sin, has a sin nature. What does this mean?

THE SIN NATURE

It means that the nature of the individual is bent totally and completely towards sin, which means it's not bent at all toward Righteousness. In other words, everything the unredeemed man and woman does is turned toward sin and shame. Even if he does something which seems to be good, it is for a selfish reason. Unredeemed man is totally controlled by the sin nature, and within himself, has no way to extricate himself from this morass.

In fact, religion, which refers to that devised by man and not at all by God, is man's effort to lift himself out of this quagmire. And because it lends itself to that which the

world labels as *"good,"* it deceives man. In fact, the origin of all religion, all self-righteousness, all of man's efforts to redeem himself, and to do so by good works, etc., is derived from the good side of the *"tree of the knowledge of good and evil"* (Gen. 2:15).

THE TREE OF THE KNOWLEDGE OF GOOD AND EVIL

Adam and Eve were allowed to partake of any tree in the Garden, at least as far as its fruit was concerned, with the exception of *"the tree of the knowledge of good and evil."* Concerning that tree, the Lord said: *"Thou shall not eat of it: for in the day that you eat thereof you shall surely die."* He wasn't speaking of physical death, but rather spiritual death, which was separation from God, but which would ultimately lead to physical death.

Regarding the *"evil"* side of this tree, it is obvious as to what it is. That list is long, and speaks of murder, hatred, man's inhumanity to man, etc. Even unredeemed man knows these things are wrong, and passes laws to keep them in check, even as he should. But when it comes to the *"good"* side of this tree, man is totally deceived. Because it is *"good,"* he thinks it is right. And what is that *"good"*?

In brief, it is man attempting to be saved, attempting to address his evil, outside of God's prescribed order, which is the Cross. It is described perfectly with the account of Cain and Abel, as given to us in Genesis, Chapter 4.

The Lord had given to the first family the means by which sinful man could have his sins forgiven, and have fellowship with a righteous God. God had promised that a Redeemer was coming, but until the Redeemer came, which incidentally would be His only Son, a lamb, or a clean animal of the same type, could be used as a substitute. An Altar was to be built, typifying Calvary, and the lamb was to be killed, typifying the Death of Christ. It's blood was to be poured out, and applied to the base of the Altar, typifying that Christ would give Himself in the shedding of His Blood, regarding His Crucifixion. While the sacrifice of such within itself did not bring about forgiveness of sin or a restoration of fellowship, Faith in the One to Whom it pointed definitely would accomplish these tasks. But as Cain then did, millions have followed in his train, they do not desire to go God's Way, which is *"Jesus Christ and Him Crucified,"* but rather attempt to bring about another way. So the entirety of the human race falls into the category of either accepting God's prescribed order, which is the Cross, or their own fabricated way. That's why the Holy Spirit through Solomon said: *"There is a way which seems right unto a man, but the end thereof are the ways of death"* (Prov. 14:12).

VICTORY OVER THE SIN NATURE

The only way that sin could be properly addressed was by and through the Cross. That's why Paul said that the emphasis must always be on the Cross, and never on anything else, as important as those other things sometimes are (I Cor. 1:17). It is by and through what Jesus did at the Cross that effects the Salvation of the sinner, and the Sanctification of the Saint.

But the sad thing is, the greater majority of the Church, knowing little or nothing about the Cross as it regards Sanctification, walk not after the Spirit, but rather after the flesh (Rom. 8:1). And let us say it a little more bluntly:

If the Believer doesn't understand the Cross as it regards Sanctification, he simply cannot walk after the Spirit, no matter how hard he may try, but will rather, walk after the flesh, and despite the fact that he is trying not to do so.

We *"walk after the Spirit,"* not by doing something, but rather by trusting in something that's already done. So that means that it's not by *"works"* but rather by *"Faith."* Concerning this, Paul said:

"For if Abraham were justified by works, he has whereof to glory; but not before God." In other words, men may glory in their works, but God will have nothing to do with it. The true way is this:

"Abraham believed God (expressed Faith in God), *and it was counted unto him for Righteousness."*

The Apostle then said: *"But to him who works not, but believes on Him Who justifies*

the ungodly, his Faith is counted for Righteousness" (Rom. 4:2-5).

Paul then said: *"Therefore being justified by Faith, we have peace with God through our Lord Jesus Christ"* (Rom. 5:1).

In fact, the whole of Paul's teaching was that we are *"justified by Faith, and not by works"* (Eph. 2:8-9).

THE OBJECT OF ONE'S FAITH

When it says that *"Abraham believed God,"* it wasn't meaning that Abraham simply believed there was a God. It rather means that he believed in what God would do as it regards the Redemption of the human race. In other words, the object of Abraham's Faith was the *"Cross,"* even though that term would not have been understandable to him at that time. Concerning Abraham, Jesus said: *"Abraham rejoiced to see My day: and he saw it, and was glad"* (Jn. 8:56).

In other words, our Lord was saying that Abraham saw what God was going to do, as it regarded the sending of His Son, Who would die on the Cross, typified by the Altars built by the Patriarch, which would redeem the human race, at least those who would believe (Jn. 3:16). So what am I saying?

I'm saying, as I've already stated in every conceivable way that I can think as it regards commentary in this Volume, the object of one's Faith must always be *"Jesus Christ and Him Crucified"* (I Cor. 1:17-18, 21, 23; 2:2, 5). And this is where the majority of the Church gets confused.

It talks about faith constantly, but the type of faith it talks about is not really the type of faith which Paul talked about.

The Church all too often talks about faith which gets *"things."* While that in a sense is correct, it is like using an 18-wheeler to deliver papers door to door. In other words, it is a tremendous under-use of Faith.

When Paul spoke of Faith, without exception, he was speaking of what Jesus did at the Cross, which in essence is described as *"the faith"* (Gal. 2:20). This means that the object of Faith must always be the Cross of Christ. That understood, and that carried out, guarantees that we know and understand what Jesus has done for us at the Cross, and that we continue to derive benefits from that

Finished Work. But the Church all too often makes other things the object of its faith, and even though the other things may be good in their own right, this is not what God will accept. The emphasis must always be on the Cross (I Cor. 1:17).

A VICTORIOUS LIFE

There is only one way that the Believer can live a victorious, overcoming, Christian life. Not five ways, not three ways, not two, but rather just one. That one way is:

First of all, the Believer, even as we've already stated any number of times in this one Volume, must understand that everything he receives from God comes exclusively through the Cross of Christ. As Salvation came through the Cross, likewise, Sanctification comes through the Cross.

As we've as well stated, the Cross being the vehicle through which all things come to the Believer, it must ever be the object of our Faith. We must not allow our Faith to be moved to other things. This is the critical juncture in the Christian experience – the object of our Faith.

The object of our Faith being correct, and we speak of the Cross, the Holy Spirit, Who works exclusively within the parameters of the legal Work of Christ, can then work within our lives, and do great and mighty things. The Holy Spirit is God; consequently, there is nothing that He cannot do. Things which are impossible with us are of no consequence to Him. The terrible power of sin is beyond our control, but it's not beyond His control. Listen again to Paul:

"For the Law of the Spirit of Life in Christ Jesus (which pertains to what Christ did at the Cross) has made me free from the law of sin and death" (Rom. 8:2).

The second most powerful law in the world is "the law of sin and death." But there is a law that is more powerful than that particular law, and it is "the Law of the Spirit (Holy Spirit) of Life in Christ Jesus."

To understand "the Law of the Spirit of Life," we must always realize that it is ensconced "in Christ Jesus," which refers to what He did at the Cross, and exclusively to what He did at the Cross.

If the Believer doesn't understand this,

he will find the sin nature once again controlling him exactly as it did before conversion. And sadly, that is the state of most of the modern Church presently, and because they do not understand the Cross, as it regards Sanctification.

Regarding the sin nature, the Church addresses it in a variety of ways. These ways are as follows, with only one being correct:

IGNORANCE

Most of the modern Church understands not at all the manner of the sin nature. In fact, I would suspect that most Christians have never even heard a message on the sin nature. That is tragic, considering that the Holy Spirit, through Paul, gave us such a voluminous amount of instruction. For instance, in the Sixth Chapter of Romans alone, Paul mentions the sin nature 17 times. As we've already explained, in the original Greek Text, there is in front of the word "sin," that which is referred to as the "definite article." That simply means that the word "the" is placed in front of "sin," meaning that it's not referring to an "act" of sin, but rather to a "state" of sin. In other words, it is referring to the sin nature.

Only two times in this Chapter is the definite article lacking, and that is in Verses 14 and 15. Even then, it is implied, so one can actually include these two Verses as well.

When it comes to victory over the sin nature, it seems from the Sacred Text that the Lord gave to Paul first of all the meaning of the sin nature, as it refers to the New Covenant, and how that victory can be obtained over that terrible monster. Romans, Chapter 7 proclaims Paul trying to address this thing in the wrong way, and failing constantly (Rom. 7:15). But out of that desperation came Revelation, as the Lord explained to the Apostle, the meaning of the New Covenant, which in reality, is the meaning of the Cross. Regarding Sanctification, it seems that first of all, as stated, He explained to Paul the meaning of the sin nature.

I sought the Lord earnestly for some five years, for an understanding as it regards victory over the world, the flesh, and the Devil. In late 1996, the Lord began to open up to me this great Truth. First of all, He took me to Romans, Chapter 6, and revealed to me the meaning of the sin nature. That was the very first thing that He showed me. He then showed me that my victory over the sin nature was found, and is found, exclusively in the Cross. He then showed me how the Holy Spirit works, by taking me to Romans 8:2.

Before the Lord explained to me the meaning of the sin nature, I cannot recollect ever having heard one single message on this all-important subject. And if the pulpit is silent, to be sure, considering that Faith comes by hearing, and hearing by the Word of God, this means that Believers will live in perpetual failure. As Paul also said: *"How shall they believe in Him of Whom they have not heard? And how shall they hear without a Preacher?"* (Rom. 10:14).

Why is it that Preachers ignore the sin nature, considering that it is so very important?

It's not so much that they ignore the sin nature. The truth is, they do not know anything about the sin nature; and it's impossible for someone to preach something in which they have little or no knowledge. That's at least one of the reasons that I plead with people who get these Commentaries and give a copy to your Pastor, or any Preacher friend, of that matter.

DENIAL

And then there is a great segment of the Church that denies that Believers have a sin nature. While they may conclude that the unredeemed have a sin nature, they teach that once the person comes to Christ, they then become a new creature, with old things having passed away, and all things having become new; consequently, there is no more sin nature (II Cor. 5:17).

Regarding the Believer becoming a new creation, all of that is certainly correct; however, the Bible nowhere teaches that the sin nature leaves the individual at conversion. If it does, and as stated, why does the Holy Spirit give through Paul, so much teaching on the subject? We must remember that in Romans, Chapter 6, where this is purposely addressed, that Paul is dealing with Believers. I hardly think that the Holy Spirit would have wasted this much time and space dealing with something that no

longer exists. No! The sin nature definitely exists in the heart and life of the Believer. But the key is this:

While the sin nature is not dead within our hearts and lives, we are indeed *"dead unto the sin nature"* (Rom. 6:11). And if we are dead to the sin nature, then it will cause us no problem whatsoever. In fact, in the heart and life of the Believer, the sin nature is supposed to be dormant. And in fact, if our Faith is exclusively in Christ and the Cross, ever making it the object of our Faith, allowing the Holy Spirit to work, the sin nature will not cause us any problem at all, and will for all practical purposes, as stated, be dormant. But if the Believer doesn't understand what is said regarding the Cross, to be sure, the sin nature will be revived, and fast, and will once again control our lives, just as it did before conversion.

What is the sin nature?

It is merely the nature of the individual to do wrong. In fact, when the believing sinner comes to Christ, the Divine Nature comes into our heart and life (II Pet. 1:4). The Divine Nature is to rule us, and will do so, if we function properly according to our Faith.

But let the Reader understand that denying the sin nature in no way makes it less effective. In fact, to deny that it exists is like trying to deny an elephant in our living room. We may claim it's not there, but I would greatly suspect that its presence would quickly abrogate our denial. As well, denying the sin nature in no way abrogates its power.

CONTROL

Many Christians, not knowing the Power of the Cross, think they have no choice but to sin constantly. They refer to themselves as *"sinners saved by Grace."* While there is some truth in that statement, it's not exactly correct, at least in the way that it is generally presented.

They are actually saying that due to the sin nature, they can't help but sin, but they don't worry too much about it because *"where sin abounded, Grace did much more abound"* (Rom. 5:20).

They do not understand victory over sin, and in a sense, don't even believe in victory over sin. They actually claim that Believers are no different from unbelievers, with one exception; the Believer places his trust in Christ, and the unbeliever doesn't. Both sin about the same, at least this is what they claim.

Nothing could be further from the truth. The Lord doesn't save us in sin, but rather, from sin. The greater part of the Work of the Holy Spirit within our hearts and lives is to rid us of sin. He desires to get out every vestige of wrongdoing, every transgression, all iniquity, until sin no longer dominates us (Rom. 6:14). While the Bible doesn't teach sinless perfection, it definitely does teach, as just stated, that sin shall not have dominion over us.

So, the idea that the sin nature must control us, and that we have no choice in the matter, is totally unscriptural. But regrettably, that's where millions of Christians, or at least, professing Christians, live their lives.

STRUGGLE

There are millions of Christians, and I think I exaggerate not, who believe that the struggle against sin is constant, never ending, and something that we just simply have to live with until we die, or the trump sounds. These Christians, who in fact love the Lord supremely, but not knowing the Way of the Cross, and its power, try various different means to overcome the world, the flesh, and the Devil. They jump from one fad to the other, all without success.

The tragedy is, the struggle just gets harder and harder, and because they are going in the wrong direction, believing the wrong thing, with the results in one way or the other, being perpetual defeat.

Some of these people will be some of the best workers in the Church, simply because they are trying to atone for their failure. And yet most of the time, these same Believers will loudly proclaim to all who will listen, as to how victorious they are, etc. The truth is, their victory is only a façade. Now let me make this statement, even though it is blunt:

It is absolutely impossible, no matter how zealous a person may be, no matter how sincere he may be, no matter how dedicated he may be, to live a victorious, overcoming, Christian life, unless one understands the Power of the Cross. Listen again to Paul:

"For the preaching of the Cross is to them who perish foolishness; but unto us which are saved it is the Power of God" (I Cor. 1:18).

How is the Cross the Power of God?

Within the Cross itself, and we speak of the wooden beam, there is no power. And as previously stated, there is no power in death, and I speak of the death of our Saviour. In fact, He died in weakness (II Cor. 13:4). The power is in the Holy Spirit (Acts 1:8). But as we've already explained, His power is exhibited on our behalf, strictly through what Jesus did at the Cross, and our Faith in that Finished Work (Rom. 8:2).

It is sad to see Christians who truly love the Lord, placing their Faith in things other than the Cross. I know beyond the shadow of a doubt that they will find no victory in this capacity, and because there is no victory in this capacity. It doesn't matter how good the other things might be, and I speak of being good in their own place, if Faith is not exclusively in the Cross, victory is impossible for the Child of God. In that capacity, the struggle will continue, and get worse, which makes the Christian experience one of misery. Listen to our Lord:

"Come unto Me, all ye who labor and are heavy laden, and I will give you rest.

"Take My yoke upon you, and learn of Me; for I am meek and lowly in heart: and you shall find rest unto your souls.

"For My yoke is easy, and My burden is light" (Mat. 11:28-30).

The Lord is speaking here to Believers, who were trying to function according to the Law, and did so in much labor, and were heavy laden with its demands. Most modern Christians function in the same manner. It is a constant struggle! Let me ask this question . . .

What is your Christian experience? Is it, in fact, a struggle, or is it *"rest"*? It cannot be both!

But if you will place your Faith exclusively in the Cross of Christ, understanding that it is through the Cross in which all blessings come, you will find the Holy Spirit then working for you, and you will know and enjoy the *"rest"* in which Jesus guarantees.

GRACE

This fifth and final way, Grace, is the only

means and manner in which the Believer can function in perpetual victory. It is solely and exclusively by the Grace of God. And what do we mean by that?

The Grace of God is simply the Goodness of God extended to undeserving Believers. In other words, we don't deserve this Grace, can do nothing to merit this Grace, but upon simple Faith in Christ, and what Christ has done for us at the Cross, a constant river of Grace will flow to us, even on a daily, even an hourly basis, which we must have, if we are to live a victorious life.

But let the Believer understand that the source of Grace, the means by which Grace is given to us, is exclusively the Cross. Regrettably, many Christians have it in their minds that because we are living in the Dispensation of Grace, which is the truth, that is fact, Grace just automatically comes to us. The latter part isn't true. The truth is, most Christians are frustrating the Grace of God. Once again, listen to Paul:

"I do not frustrate the Grace of God: for if Righteousness come by the Law, then Christ is dead in vain" (Gal. 2:21).

Regarding this one Verse, I think it would be literally impossible to exhaust its great truths. Several things are said here:

1. It is possible to frustrate the Grace of God, which means to hinder it coming to us, and even to stop it altogether.

2. There is no way that Righteousness can come by the Law, by rules, by regulations, or by merit, or by works, etc. It is impossible, even as the Scripture proclaims here.

3. If Righteousness can come by these various means, then *"Christ is dead in vain."* This simply means that Jesus didn't need to come down here and die on a Cross, if man could come by Righteousness, by the means of his own machinations.

The sadness is, most Christians presently are frustrating the Grace of God, and this is what causes the terrible struggle in our lives, a struggle that we never win.

Let's say it another way: If the Believer doesn't understand that all is in the Cross, then he will try to obtain Righteousness by other methods, which will tend to do nothing, no matter how sincere he might be, but frustrate the Grace of God.

NOTES

The Grace of God doesn't come to us by our *"doing,"* but rather, by trusting in what Christ has already *"done."* And what has He done?

We speak again of the Cross! Ever of the Cross! This and this alone is where the *"rest"* in Christ is found.

Let the Reader understand that the Grace of God is not some magic potion, or some spiritual magic that takes place in our lives. It is simply the fact that the Lord does all of these good things for us, even though we don't deserve them. But He will do it only on one premise, and that premise is the Cross of Christ, and our Faith in that Finished Work. Faith there placed will guarantee the help of the Holy Spirit, which in reality is the Grace of God.

(20) "MOREOVER YOU SHALL NOT LIE CARNALLY WITH YOUR NEIGHBOR'S WIFE, TO DEFILE YOURSELF WITH HER.

(21) "AND YOU SHALL NOT LET ANY OF YOUR SEED PASS THROUGH THE FIRE TO MOLECH, NEITHER SHALL YOU PROFANE THE NAME OF YOUR GOD: I AM THE LORD.

(22) "YOU SHALL NOT LIE WITH MANKIND, AS WITH WOMANKIND: IT IS ABOMINATION.

(23) "NEITHER SHALL YOU LIE WITH ANY BEAST TO DEFILE YOURSELF THEREWITH: NEITHER SHALL ANY WOMAN STAND BEFORE A BEAST TO LIE DOWN THERETO: IT IS CONFUSION.

(24) "DEFILE NOT YOU YOURSELVES IN ANY OF THESE THINGS: FOR IN ALL OF THESE THE NATIONS ARE DEFILED WHICH I CAST OUT BEFORE YOU:

(25) "AND THE LAND IS DEFILED: THEREFORE I DO VISIT THE INIQUITY THEREOF UPON IT, AND THE LAND ITSELF VOMITS OUR HER INHABITANTS.

(26) "YOU SHALL THEREFORE KEEP MY STATUTES AND MY JUDGMENTS, AND SHALL NOT COMMIT ANY OF THESE ABOMINATIONS; NEITHER ANY OF YOUR OWN NATION, NOR ANY STRANGER WHO SOJOURNS AMONG YOU:

(27) "(FOR ALL THESE ABOMINATIONS HAVE THE MEN OF THE LAND DONE, WHICH WERE BEFORE YOU, AND THE LAND IS DEFILED;)

(28) "THAT THE LAND SPEW NOT YOU OUT ALSO, WHEN YOU DEFILE IT, AS IT SPEWED OUT THE NATIONS THAT WERE BEFORE YOU.

(29) "FOR WHOSOEVER SHALL COMMIT ANY OF THESE ABOMINATIONS, EVEN THE SOULS WHO COMMIT THEM SHALL BE CUT OFF FROM AMONG THEIR PEOPLE.

(30) "THEREFORE SHALL YOU KEEP MY ORDINANCE, THAT YOU COMMIT NOT ANY ONE OF THESE ABOMINABLE CUSTOMS, WHICH WERE COMMITTED BEFORE YOU, AND THAT YOU DEFILE NOT YOURSELVES THEREIN: I AM THE LORD YOUR GOD."

The diagram is:

1. We find in Verse 20 the prohibition against adultery.

2. Verse 21 prohibits the offering up of little children to idols.

3. Verse 22 proclaims the terrible abomination of homosexuality.

4. Verse 23 prohibits bestiality.

5. The morality of Israel, due to the fact that they were God's people, was to be far above the surrounding nations.

6. If they defile themselves, by committing these terrible sins, the Lord would vomit them out of the land, just as surely as He vomited out those who had previously occupied it. In fact, that's exactly what happened!

ADULTERY

Verse 20 reads: *"Moreover you shall not lie carnally with your neighbor's wife, to defile yourself with her."*

This Passage, as is obvious, prohibits adultery. While it speaks of another man's wife, even though not said here, the Seventh Commandment prohibits sexual intercourse with anyone outside of the marriage bond (Ex. 20:14).

Some people erroneously think that adultery has to do with sexual intercourse between married people, but who is not their husband or wife, while fornication has to do with sex between unmarried people. While fornication includes adultery, adultery does not include all types of fornication. Fornication pertains not only to sex outside of the bonds of marriage, but it also includes

homosexuality, incest, bestiality, and in fact, any type of sexual aberration or perversion. In other words, fornication has a much wider meaning, as is obvious, than adultery.

IDOLS

Verse 21 reads: *"And you shall not let any of your seed pass through the fire to Molech, neither shall you profane the Name of your God: I am the LORD."*

"Seed" refers here to children. Parents were not to sacrifice their children to idols. And to be sure, the idol *"Molech"* was one of the worst types of heathenistic gods.

MOLECH

This so-called deity is associated with Ammon, which was a neighbor of Israel (I Ki. 11:7). Actually, it bordered Israel on the east, and would have been the same, at least in part, as the northern part of modern Jordan. This idol was called *"the abomination of the Ammonites,"* and was associated with the sacrifice of children in the fire (Lev. 20:2-5; II Ki. 17:31; 23:10; Jer. 32:35). (Molech is also sometimes called Milcom.)

The following graphic description has been handed down traditionally of this idol and its worship.

It was a brass and hollow image, bull-headed, with arms stretched out like a human being who opens his hands to receive something from his neighbor. Its temple had seven compartments, into which the offerers went according to their respective gifts. If one offered a fowl, he went into the first compartment; if a sheep, to the second; if a lamb, into the third; if a ram, into the fourth; if a bullock, into the fifth; if an ox, into the sixth; and if he offered his son, he was conducted into the seventh compartment. He first kissed the image, as it is written, *"Let the sacrifices of men kiss the calf"* (Hos. 13:2).

The child that was to be offered in sacrifice was tied to the outstretched arms of the idol, with the fire then kindled in its belly, until its arms became red hot. Drums were then beaten loudly by the heathenistic priests in order to drown out the screams of the child. It was to this idol that Solomon erected a temple on the southern side of Mount Olivet (II Ki. 23:13).

This idolatrous worship was punished with death by stoning, which is what this sin rightly deserved (Lev. 20:2).

PROFANING THE NAME OF GOD

Any act which is done in violation of the Commands of the Lord, or that misrepresents God in any way, or by which He is put on a par with other gods, is called *"profaning the Name of God."*

In a sense, and quite possibly to a greater degree than we could begin to think, when the Believer attempts to live for the Lord, outside of Faith in the Cross, such a direction is sin in more ways than one. It is rebellion against God's prescribed order, which in effect, says that the Cross was not that much needed, if at all! In effect, it is man making himself into God, and because he is attempting to devise his own manner of Salvation or Sanctification. To disobey the Word, or to circumvent the Word in any way, which rebellion against God's order does, can be labeled as none other than a profanation of the Name of our Lord. In fact, this is the major sin of the Church, and in truth, has been the sin of man from the very beginning. Cain would not heed what the Lord demanded that must be done in order for sins to be forgiven and fellowship to be restored. He produced his own sacrifice, which God could not accept, and then Cain blamed his brother for that, and killed him. There is evidence according to the writings of John that Cain cut his brother's throat. He in effect stated, *"If blood is what you want, blood is what you will get."* This direction has been followed by man in the beginning, and as stated, this is the great sin of the Church (I Jn. 3:12).

Men, even the Church, are loathe to accept the Cross, but let the Reader understand that to reject the Cross places one in the position of a *"reprobate"* (II Tim. 3:8; II Cor. 13:5).

HOMOSEXUALITY

Verse 22 reads: *"You shall not lie with mankind, as with womankind: it is abomination."*

This is the sin of Sodom (Gen. 19:5), i.e., *"sodomy,"* i.e., *"homosexuality."*

NOTES

Surrounding nations to Israel were addicted to this sin, and as well, which was so prevalent in the time of the Apostles (Rom. 1:27; I Cor. 6:9; Gal. 5:19; I Tim. 1:10). By the Law of Christ those who are guilty of this sin are excluded from the Kingdom of God (I Cor. 6:9-10).

While the Lord will save homosexuals, exactly as He will alcoholics, drug addicts, murderers, etc., when the homosexual is saved, which goes for all other individuals as well, the particular sin to which they are addicted must cease. The idea that a homosexual can come to Christ, and continue to live in homosexuality, is totally anathema to the Word of God. As well, it would go for any other sin, as stated!

While a person after coming to Christ may have a struggle for a period of time with a vice that had held him in bondage, ultimately the vice, whatever it might be, must go.

I have known individuals who were alcoholics before coming to Christ, and for a period of time, even several years, would continue to have difficulties, with them at time yielding to this sin that had formerly bound them; however, ultimately, the sin must go.

At the moment the believing sinner comes to Christ, that individual, and without exception, is totally delivered from the guilt of sin and the power of sin (Rom. 6:6). But most Believers, having just come to Christ, little understand the Cross as it refers to their living for the Lord, and try to live for God in all the wrong ways. Regrettably, they copy other Christians they see, who have no knowledge of the Cross as well, which guarantees they are going to have problems. Regrettably, millions continue to try to live for God other than by God's prescribed order, and while they are definitely saved, they never quite know the victory they ought to know.

WHAT IS THE CAUSE OF HOMOSEXUALITY?

Of course, the homosexual claims that he is born that way. That is incorrect! While Satan might make his play while the child is of tender age, no person is born a homosexual.

And yet at the same time, every child is born in original sin, with all of its attendant problems and difficulties. Understanding that, some children are definitely born with a proclivity towards certain directions, more so than others, and homosexuality can definitely be one of those proclivities. But that's a far cry from being born a homosexual, or an alcoholic, or a criminal, etc.

A person, even a child, becomes a homosexual, in most cases because they are molested by an older person. And to be sure, demon spirits are definitely involved. While all children do not turn out to be homosexuals who are molested in this fashion, many do.

As I dictate these notes, the last day of September, 2002, the nation and the world have experienced the problems of the Catholic Church, regarding homosexual Priests, etc. Scores of people have come forward claiming that particular Priests have molested them, with most of the officials of the Catholic Church, after finding out about the sin, doing little or nothing about it, even continuing to keep the accused priests in positions where they could continue their sodomy.

The Catholic Church has done absolutely nothing about this situation, and because they cannot do anything. First of all, the Catholic Church is a haven for homosexual priests. And if they kicked out all the priests guilty of molesting children, they would be placed in a serious situation indeed, considering that there is already a terrible shortage of priests.

But above all of that, Catholic priests aren't saved; consequently, they have no knowledge of Christ and the Cross, which means they have no solution.

PSYCHOLOGY AND HOMOSEXUALITY

It should be understood that the Catholic Church has some of the best Psychologists in the world. So the question should be asked, if psychology is the answer to the aberrations and perversions of mankind, why hasn't it helped their priests?

To be sure, many, if not most, of these offending priests have submitted to months if not years of psychological counseling, all to no avail. To my knowledge, there is not one single priest who has ever stopped the vice which has embroiled him by the root of psychology. I've never heard of even one!

So the question must be asked, if humanistic psychology is in fact the answer to these problems, why doesn't it work in the Catholic Church?

It doesn't work in the Catholic Church, and neither does it work in the Protestant world; in fact, it doesn't work anywhere. And to be blunt, Preachers, especially those who claim to be Spirit-filled, who would advocate this travesty, are engaging pure and simple in blasphemy. But regrettably, that's where most of the modern Church is.

I have not meant to single out the Catholic Church, for the problem doesn't stop there. Homosexuality is pandemic in the non-Catholic world as well. It is the sin of the age, and getting worse almost by the hour.

To be sure, the answer is not in legalizing homosexual marriages, as some of our foolish lawmakers are prone to do. Neither is the answer, as stated, humanistic psychology. There is only one answer for the homosexual, as well as the drunk, the drug addict, and every sinner who has ever lived for that matter, and it is *"Jesus Christ and Him Crucified"* (I Cor. 1:23). The Cross of Christ is the only answer for sin, as it has ever been the only answer for sin. God has one way, and that is it!

BESTIALITY

Verse 23 reads: *"Neither shall you lie with any beast to defile yourself therewith: neither shall any woman stand before a beast to lie down thereto: it is confusion."*

Concerning this sin, Ellicott says: *"The necessity for the prohibition of this shocking crime, for which the Mosaic Law enacts the penalty of death (Lev. 20:15-16; Ex. 22:18), will appear all the more important when it is borne in mind that this degrading practice actually formed a part of the religious worship of the Egyptians in connection with the goat deities. In other words, the Israelites were very familiar with this perversion, having lived in Egypt for so long."*

It is said that the disease of syphilis originated with men cohabiting with sheep.

We see here how the sins of incest, adultery, fornication, homosexuality, and bestiality, are prohibited.

As we shall see, when these sins become

pandemic in a nation, God will turn them over to demon spirits, hence the condition of many modern nations. It is said that nearly 50 percent of the men in Egypt presently have the disease of syphilis, which greatly debilitates the nation, as would be obvious. And to be sure, in one form or the other, the terrible problem of venereal diseases in the United States is not much behind, for that matter.

DEFILEMENT

Verses 24 and 25 read: *"Defile not you yourselves in any of these things: for in all these the nations are defiled which I cast out before you:*

"And the land is defiled: therefore I do visit the iniquity thereof upon it, and the land itself vomits out her inhabitants."

The Scripture says: *"Righteousness exalteth a nation: but sin is a reproach to any people"* (Prov. 14:34).

From the creation, the Earth shared in the punishment of man's guilt (Gen. 3:17), and at the restitution of all things, she is to participate in his restoration (Rom. 8:19-22). The physical condition of the land, therefore, depends upon the moral conduct of man.

When man disregards the Word of God, as regrettably most nations do, at God's Command, the land is parched up and does not yield her fruit (Deut. 11:17). *"The land is defiled"* when man defiles himself.

Conversely, when man walks in the way of the Divine Commands, the land is blessed (Lev. 25:19; 26:24). In a sense, the Prophet Isaiah says, *"The Earth mourns"* when her inhabitants sin (Isa. 24:4-5), and, *"The Earth is glad"* when God avenges the cause of His people (Ps. 96:11-13).

I think that one can look at the nations of the world, and I speak of their prosperity and freedom, or the lack thereof, and tell the reason why, as it regards the Word of God. God blesses or withholds blessing, and can do so in any number of ways, according to obedience, or disobedience, as it regards His Word.

THE WORD OF GOD

Verses 26 through 30 read: *"You shall therefore keep My Statutes and My Judgments, and shall not commit any of these abominations;*

NOTES

neither any of your own nation, nor any stranger who sojourns among you:

"(For all these abominations have the men of the land done, which were before you, and the land is defiled;)

"That the land spew not you out also, when you defile it, as it spewed out the nations that were before you.

"For whosoever shall commit any of these abominations, even the souls who commit them shall be cut off from among their people.

"Therefore shall you keep My Ordinance, that you commit not any one of these abominable customs, which were committed before you, and that you defile not yourselves therein: I am the LORD your God."

As we see here, the Word of God, as stated, is the criteria. God has told us how to live, and if we ignore that which He has said, we do so at our own peril.

We must know and understand that God can do anything. He can bless, or He can withhold blessing. Man is very limited, but God is not limited at all. There is nothing too hard for Him, and in fact, I think one can say without fear of contradiction, that nothing period is hard for Him.

In these Passages, the Lord tells Israel why He is vomiting out the inhabitants of the land they are to possess. God always does right by everyone and in everything. And it's not right simply because He does it, but He does it, because it is right.

This tells us that He was not being unfair to the Canaanites and others who inhabited the land, but disposed them because of their acute evil.

One archeologist working in the Middle East stated that the God of the Old Testament Who gave instructions for entire tribes to be exterminated, did future generations in the world an untold service. This man was speaking of the terrible crimes of incest, homosexuality, and bestiality, which these people practiced, which stood to impair the human race. The terrible power of sin takes its deadly toll in every regard and in every respect. For instance, in our country alone, the nation is being weakened by untold thousands of babies born, addicted to drugs, and because their mother was addicted to drugs, or born with AIDS, because their mother had AIDS, etc.

So the Lord tells Israel that despite the fact that they are His chosen people, and despite the fact that He has raised them up, that if they commit the sins that the Canaanites committed before them, that He will vomit them out, exactly as He vomited out those who preceded them. Verse 29 says, *"For whosoever shall commit,"* and that means whosoever!

The phrase *"I am the LORD your God,"* lends a weight to these Commandments that is beyond compare. In other words, God in effect, says that Israel had better understand that He is able to do what He says that He will do. We had better understand the same presently!

"The Spirit breathes upon the Word
"And brings the truth to sight;
"Precepts and Promises afford
"A sanctifying light."

"What glory gilds the Sacred Page,
"Majestic like the sun!
"It gives a light to every age;
"It gives, but borrows none."

"The hand that gave it still supplies
"His gracious light and heat,
"His truths upon the nations rise;
"They rise, but never set."

"Let everlasting thanks be Thine
"For such a bright display
"As makes the world of darkness shine
"With beams of heavenly day."

"My soul rejoices to pursue
"The paths of truth and love,
"Till glory breaks upon my view
"In brighter worlds above."

CHAPTER 19

(1) "AND THE LORD SPOKE UNTO MOSES, SAYING,

(2) "SPEAK UNTO ALL THE CONGREGATION OF THE CHILDREN OF ISRAEL, AND SAY UNTO THEM, YOU SHALL BE HOLY: FOR I THE LORD YOUR GOD AM HOLY.

(3) "YOU SHALL FEAR EVERY MAN HIS MOTHER, AND HIS FATHER, AND KEEP MY

SABBATHS: I AM THE LORD YOUR GOD.

(4) "TURN YOU NOT UNTO IDOLS, NOR MAKE TO YOURSELVES MOLTEN GODS: I AM THE LORD YOUR GOD.

(5) "AND IF YOU OFFER A SACRIFICE OF PEACE-OFFERINGS UNTO THE LORD, YOU SHALL OFFER IT AT YOUR OWN WILL.

(6) "IT SHALL BE EATEN ON THE SAME DAY YOU OFFER IT, AND ON THE MORROW: AND IF OUGHT REMAIN UNTIL THE THIRD DAY, IT SHALL BE BURNT IN THE FIRE.

(7) "AND IF IT BE EATEN AT ALL ON THE THIRD DAY, IT IS ABOMINABLE; IT SHALL NOT BE ACCEPTED.

(8) "THEREFORE EVERY ONE WHO EATS IT SHALL BEAR HIS INIQUITY, BECAUSE HE HAS PROFANED THE HALLOWED THING OF THE LORD: AND THAT SOUL SHALL BE CUT OFF FROM AMONG HIS PEOPLE.

(9) "AND WHEN YOU REAP THE HARVEST OF YOUR LAND, YOU SHALL NOT WHOLLY REAP THE CORNERS OF YOUR FIELD, NEITHER SHALL YOU GATHER THE GLEANINGS OF YOUR HARVEST.

(10) "AND YOU SHALL NOT GLEAN YOUR VINEYARD, NEITHER SHALL YOU GATHER EVERY GRAPE OF YOUR VINEYARD; YOU SHALL LEAVE THEM FOR THE POOR AND STRANGER: I AM THE LORD YOUR GOD.

(11) "YOU SHALL NOT STEAL, NEITHER DEAL FALSELY, NEITHER LIE ONE TO ANOTHER.

(12) "AND YOU SHALL NOT SWEAR BY MY NAME FALSELY, AND NEITHER SHALL YOU PROFANE THE NAME OF YOUR GOD: I AM THE LORD.

(13) "YOU SHALL NOT DEFRAUD YOUR NEIGHBOR, NEITHER ROB HIM: THE WAGES OF HIM WHO IS HIRED SHALL NOT ABIDE WITH YOU ALL NIGHT UNTIL THE MORNING."

The composition is:

1. In Chapter 19, seven groups of laws end with the words, *"I am Jehovah your God,"* and eight groups with the words, *"I am Jehovah."*

2. This section of the Book sets forth the appalling degradation of man apart from God,

and the pity of God for little children, widows, and the poor.

3. The day laborer was to receive his pay each evening. What exquisite thought for so humble a member of society! (Williams).

HOLY

Verses 1 through 4 read: *"And the LORD spoke unto Moses, saying,*

"Speak unto all the congregation of the Children of Israel, and say unto them, You shall be holy: for I the LORD your God am holy.

"You shall fear every man his mother, and his father, and keep My Sabbaths: I am the LORD your God.

"Turn you not unto idols, nor make to yourselves molten gods: I am the LORD your God."

The Commandments which now will be given effect the life of the Israelites in all its bearings, both towards God and man.

Moses is to understand as to how important all of this is, because the Lord commands the Lawgiver to make these precepts known *"to all the congregation of the Children of Israel."* In fact, this phrase occurs nowhere else in this Book, that is, as it regards this particular formula, and which is only to be found once more in the whole of the Pentateuch (Ex. 12:3). Then it was at the institution of the Passover, the great national festival which commemorated the Redemption of the Israelites from Egypt (Ellicott).

By the phrase, *"I the LORD your God,"* the demand is given that the conduct of the Israelites must not be in contradiction to God's Holy Nature, and that the life of each Israelite should bear the impress and reflect the Image of God. God is holy, and He demands that His people be holy.

It is the same presently, with in fact the demand now being even greater, simply because we now have the Holy Spirit, due to the Cross, abiding permanently within our hearts and lives (Jn. 14:16-17).

Many modern Believers have it backwards. They think that because we are now living in the Dispensation of Grace, God winks at sin. Nothing could be further from the Truth. Paul said: *"And the times of this*

ignorance God winked at (before the Cross); *but now* (since the Cross), *commands all men everywhere to repent"* (Acts 17:30).

HOW TO BE HOLY

The moment the believing sinner comes to Christ, at that moment, he or she is perfectly holy (I Cor. 6:11). He is perfectly holy because he is in Christ, and because of that alone. While that is the Believer's *"standing,"* it in fact is not his *"state."* Therefore, the Holy Spirit sets about to bring the *"state"* up to the *"standing."* It's not an easy process, and neither is it a quick process. There is only one way it can be accomplished. Listen to Paul:

"I am crucified with Christ: nevertheless I live; yet not I, but Christ lives in me: and the life which I now live in the flesh I live by the Faith of the Son of God, Who loved me, and gave Himself for me" (Gal. 2:20).

In this one Verse of Scripture, the Apostle tells us how to live for God, i.e., *"how to be holy."*

By the statement, *"I am crucified with Christ,"* Paul takes us back to Romans 6:3-5. Being *"baptized into the death of Christ,"* and *"buried with Him by baptism into death,"* proclaims that of which the Apostle is addressing himself. As is obvious, it concerns the Crucifixion of Christ, and our part in that Finished Work.

The moment the believing sinner evidences Faith in Christ, in the Mind of God, we literally become one with our Substitute, and what He did at the Cross, all on our behalf.

Due to our Faith in the Finished Work of Christ, which makes us a part of that Work, Christ now lives in us, and does so through the Person, Office, Power, and Ministry of the Holy Spirit (Jn. 3:3, 8).

So the way that Paul now lives this life is to *"live by the Faith of the Son of God, Who loved him, and gave Himself for Paul,"* and as well, for all others who will dare to believe.

He is speaking here strictly of what Christ did at the Cross, and our Faith in that great Work, which guarantees us all of its benefits. This is the only way to live for God, the only way to be holy, the only way to live a sanctified life.

To try to be holy by rules and regulations,

by laws and commandments, etc., will only succeed in plunging one into self-righteousness, which is the bane of the modern Church. The sad thing is, most of the modern Church will little accept that which Paul gave to us, but will rather devise its own ways. When it comes to religious Denominations, most of their leaders refer to those who serve the Denomination, as being holy, or words to that effect. In other words, one's blind loyalty to the Denomination is the criteria. As should be obvious, the Lord has no part in such direction, and because it is grossly unscriptural. The only type of Righteousness that God will accept is that which comes exclusively through Christ, and what Christ has done at the Cross, adding nothing to that, nor taking from it.

When it comes to independents, the far greater majority of those, at least in the Pentecostal and Charismatic realm, their allegiance is primarily to *"self."* They speak of having faith in their faith, of memorizing certain Scriptures, quoting them over and over, which is supposed to bring God to a place of action, etc.

At any rate, neither direction is according to the Word of God, but rather according to rules and regulations made up by men. As stated, God will have no part in such, and thereby judges those who practice such as *"unholy."*

Let us never forget that we aren't holy because of what we *"do,"* but we are holy because of what He has already *"done,"* and our Faith in that Finished Work, and that alone!

The respect for both mother and father has to do with the Fifth Commandment (Ex. 20:12). The keeping of the Sabbath referred to the Fourth Commandment.

The *"Sabbath"* was a type of Christ and moreover what He would do for us respecting the great Sacrifice of Himself. The Sabbath was not really a day of worship as it regards the old Jewish economy, but rather a day of *"rest."* That's what Christ gives us, when we fully and completely place our hopes, past, present, future, and in fact, everything, totally in Him, and His Finished Work. It is a *"rest"* from one's efforts to try to live a holy life by one's own methods, which of course will not work, and because the Holy Spirit

NOTES

will not sanction such (Heb. 4:9-10).

REST

Having been on both sides of the fence, and in fact, with the whole world aware of that of which I speak, probably more so than any other man, I would think that what I would say would carry at least a modicum of weight. In other words, I know what I am talking about. There is no education like experience, and especially that which comes at great price.

Please do not misunderstand, I definitely do not wear failure as any type of badge of honor, but rather the very opposite. But I definitely do wear the victory that I now have in Christ as a badge of deep and abiding appreciation for what the Lord has done for me. As well, I want all others to know what I now know, and not have to experience the pain and suffering that I have had to experience.

On the dark side of that fence, trying to earn my way with the Lord, and because I did not know and understand the Cross as it refers to Sanctification, I know what it is to *"labor"* and be *"heavy laden."* Now lest you the Reader take these statements lightly, and claim that you automatically know what I didn't know in those years, I would seriously doubt that you do. And how do I know that?

In fact, the Cross has been so ignored, pushed aside, and even repudiated, in the last few years that the modern Church, for all practical purposes, is Cross illiterate. It knows a little bit about the Cross as it refers to Salvation, but to be factual, precious little even of that. When it comes to the part the Cross plays as it regards the Believer's Sanctification, there is almost a complete dearth of knowledge as it regards this all-important subject, and because it's not preached and taught behind the modern Pulpit. Why?

Several decades ago, the Church opted in favor of humanistic psychology, as the answer to the aberrations and perversions of mankind. In other words, the Church, at least for the most part, now claims that psychology holds the solution to man's behavior problems, whatever they might be.

One, let it be known, cannot embrace humanistic psychology, and the Cross at the same time. As we've already stated several times in this Volume, either one cancels out the other. So, the Church embracing this false philosophy has had to repudiate the Cross. Consequently, for the last several decades, most of the sermons preached behind most pulpits, and most of the material in Christian bookstores, are in the realm of psychological mishmash. If you go to your nearest Christian bookstore, and look through the book titles, I think you will find that just about all of them, in some way, address the human problem from the realm of psychology, whether it outwardly claims to do such or not. At any rate, you will find very little material that promotes the Cross.

In 1996, the Lord, in answer to soul-searching prayer, Prayer Meetings, incidentally, which lasted for about ten years, both day and night, began to open up to me the Message of the Cross. It changed everything! To make a long story short, I now know what it is to *"rest"* in Christ. And let the Reader understand, one can know this *"rest"* only by understanding, and what Christ did at the Cross.

To be sure, there are all type of *"rests"* as it regards the flesh. And by that, I'm meaning that which pertains to man's personal ability, strength, and power. In other words, it's man trying to do what only the Holy Spirit can do. And if we try to do it ourselves, the Holy Spirit will have nothing to do with our efforts, and because in effect, we are actually committing spiritual adultery (Rom. 7:1-4). Paul said, *"There remains therefore a rest to the people of God.*

"For he who is entered into His rest, he also has ceased from his own works, as God did from His.

"Let us labor (strive) *therefore to enter into that rest, lest any man fall after the same example of unbelief* (the example of Israel and their unbelief)*"* (Heb. 4:9-11).

IDOLS

Let the Reader know and understand that *"idols"* didn't die with the heathenistic past. In fact, *"idols"* are just as prominent now, although probably more subtle, than ever before.

Anything that comes between a person and God becomes an idol. It might be their family, money, their place and position in

the community, religion, etc. Within themselves, many, if not most, of these things are harmless. But they become very harmful when we give them precedent over our love and allegiance to the Lord.

Why do you think John the Beloved closed out his First Epistle by saying, *"Little children, keep yourselves from idols"* (I Jn. 5:21)?

PEACE-OFFERINGS

Verses 5 through 8 read: *"And if you offer a Sacrifice of Peace-Offerings unto the LORD, you shall offer it at your own will.*

"It shall be eaten on the same day you offer it, and on the morrow: and if ought remain until the third day, it shall be burnt in the fire.

"And if it be eaten at all on the third day, it is abominable; it shall not be accepted.

"Therefore every one who eats it shall bear his iniquity, because he has profaned the hallowed thing of the LORD: and that soul shall be cut off from among his people."

A *"Peace-Offering"* could include a lamb, a goat, or a bullock (Lev., Chpt. 3). Regarding this Offering, while the fat was burned on the Altar, the breast and the right shoulder were to be given to the Priests for their consumption (Lev. 7:30-32). The balance was given to the one bringing the Offering, for him to have a feast with his family and friends.

It signified that peace had now been restored between this particular individual who had brought the Offering, and God. Surely it is understood that all of this is symbolic of Christ and the Cross. The Priests were types of Christ, and as well, the animals used in sacrifice were types of Christ. The Altar was a type of the Cross.

The phrase in Verse 5, *"You shall offer it at your own will,"* would have been better translated, *"You shall offer it for your acceptance."* In other words, it was to be offered before God, in the manner in which He stated that it should be offered, in order that it might be accepted and, therefore, the offerer accepted.

If the Offering was accepted, the offerer was accepted as well. If the Offering was rejected, the offerer was rejected also. For a perfect example of this, we need only go back to Genesis, Chapter 4, as it regards Cain and

Abel. The Offering of Cain was rejected; therefore, Cain was rejected. The Offering of Abel was accepted, because it was carried out in the manner that God said it must be carried out; therefore, Abel was accepted. Let the Reader understand that it has not changed unto this moment.

If we come to the Lord with Faith and trust in Christ, and what Christ has done for us at the Cross, without exception, irrespective of the past, we will be accepted, and because Christ as our Sacrifice, has been accepted. If we come to God, placing our Faith otherwise than Christ and the Cross, such is a sacrifice, whether we understand it or not, that God will not accept; therefore, that particular sacrifice being rejected, the person making the Offering to God is rejected also.

We are not accepted before God on the premise of our merit, for we have none, at least that which God will recognize. We can only come on the merit of Christ and by that, I speak of the Cross (Gal. 1:4). This is a great truth, and in fact, the foundational truth of the entirety of the Word of God.

THE PROHIBITION

The part that the offerer was to eat had to be eaten on the first or at the latest, on the second day, after it had been offered. If it was eaten at all on the third day, it was looked at as *"abominable,"* with the statement following, *"It shall not be accepted."*

Why this prohibition?

Of the five Levitical Offerings, four of them were animal Offerings, with the Meat-Offering alone not being in that category. (In fact, *"Meat-Offering"* should have been translated *"Cereal-Offering,"* and because it contained no meat. The word *"meat"* was used in those days for all types of food, both animal flesh and otherwise.) All of these Offerings typified Christ, and in fact, every single thing that was instructed to be done with them, signified Christ in some part of His Mediatorial, Atoning, or Intercessory Work. Therefore, these instructions were to be followed minutely. The example of the two sons of Aaron, Nadab and Abihu, who were Priests, as given to us in Chapter 10, should be a warning.

All of the Offering was to be consumed in

the allotted time, which typified Christ being accepted. Some of the Offering being left over for the third day, or even later, in essence said that Christ was not being accepted totally in that which He did for us, which in fact, pertains to the Cross. All of it had to be consumed in the allotted time, which testified to the fact that Christ was accepted totally and completely, as it regarded the Sacrifice of Himself on the Cross, and all of its benefits.

Far too many Believers presently have accepted Christ, but not the Cross. That being the case, and if it remains that way, they will be *"cut off"* exactly as Israel was warned so long, long ago.

To not accept the Cross is to accept *"another Jesus,"* which God can never honor (II Cor. 11:4).

THE LOVE OF GOD FOR THE STRANGER AND FOR THE POOR

Verses 9 and 10 read: *"And when you reap the harvest of your land, you shall not wholly reap the corners of your field, neither shall you gather the gleanings of your harvest.*

"And you shall not glean your vineyard, neither shall you gather every grape of your vineyard; you shall leave them for the poor and stranger: I am the LORD your God."

The object of this Law is to inculcate a general spirit of mercy, which is willing to give up its own exact rights in kindness to others suffering from want.

It is to be done in the Spirit of Christ, Who has given us everything in fact, the greatest gift of all, Salvation, purchased at great price, and I continue to speak of the Cross.

In fact, all of this looks forward to the Cross, even as we now look back to the Cross. The very spirit, attitude, and personality of the Believer must always be in the capacity of the spirit of the Cross. And without that particular spirit, which Christ epitomized, the Believer cannot conduct himself as he should.

We find the Lord showing here utmost care and concern for the stranger and even the poorest of the poor. As I've stated in previous commentary in this Book, when the Believer is alone with a person of very poor position, how you treat that individual when no one else is looking, is what you are.

TREATMENT OF OUR FELLOW MAN

Verses 11 through 13 read: *"You shall not steal, neither deal falsely, neither lie one to another.*

"And you shall not swear by My Name falsely, neither shall you profane the Name of Your God: I am the LORD.

"You shall not defraud your neighbor, neither rob him: the wages of him who is hired shall not abide with you all night until the morning."

"You shall not steal," forms the Eighth Commandment (Ex. 20:15).

"Neither lie one to another," deals with the Ninth Commandment.

"You shall not swear," corresponds with the Third Commandment. As well, fraud and oppression by violence are forbidden.

Verse 13 deals with the common laborer, and how that he is to be paid each night at the end of his day's work. As he is dependent upon his wages for the support of himself and his family, the Law protects him by enjoining that the earnings should be promptly paid each evening. In fact, this care for the laborer, and the denunciation against any attempt to defraud him, are again and again repeated in the Scriptures (Deut. 24:14-15; Jer. 32:13; Mal. 3:5; James 5:4).

In far too much of the world, even presently, and which has gone on since the beginning of time, too many are made rich at the expense of the poor, even the poorest of the poor.

While the problem definitely persists in the United States, still, this nation has probably come closer than most nations of the world, in protecting the rights of the weak and the less fortunate. God has blessed this country because of that particular direction. As someone has well said, *"Much Bible, much freedom; little Bible, little freedom; no Bible, no freedom."*

(14) "YOU SHALL NOT CURSE THE DEAF, NOR PUT A STUMBLING BLOCK BEFORE THE BLIND, BUT SHALL FEAR YOUR GOD: I AM THE LORD.

(15) "YOU SHALL DO NO UNRIGHTEOUSNESS IN JUDGMENT: YOU SHALL NOT RESPECT THE PERSON OF THE POOR, NOR HONOR THE PERSON OF THE MIGHTY: BUT IN RIGHTEOUSNESS SHALL YOU JUDGE YOUR NEIGHBOR.

(16) "YOU SHALL NOT GO UP AND DOWN AS A TALEBEARER AMONG YOUR PEOPLE: NEITHER SHALL YOU STAND AGAINST THE BLOOD OF YOUR NEIGHBOR; I AM THE LORD.

(17) "YOU SHALL NOT HATE YOUR BROTHER IN YOUR HEART: YOU SHALL IN ANY WISE REBUKE YOUR NEIGHBOR, AND NOT SUFFER SIN UPON HIM.

(18) "YOU SHALL NOT AVENGE, NOR BEAR ANY GRUDGE AGAINST THE CHILDREN OF YOUR PEOPLE, BUT YOU SHALL LOVE YOUR NEIGHBOR AS YOURSELF: I AM THE LORD.

(19) "YOU SHALL KEEP MY STATUTES. YOU SHALL NOT LET YOUR CATTLE GENDER WITH A DIVERSE KIND: YOU SHALL NOT SOW YOUR FIELD WITH MINGLED SEED: NEITHER SHALL A GARMENT MINGLED OF LINEN AND WOOL COME UPON YOU."

The construction is:

1. The deaf, blind, the afflicted were all to be treated with the deepest compassion.

2. The person, and even the nation, which comes closer to heeding these Commandments as given by the Lord, without fail, will be blessed by God.

3. There has never been any legislation in history, nor will there ever be in the future, that even remotely begins to compare with that given by God, referred to as the *"Law of Moses."*

THE AFFLICTED

Verse 14 reads: *"You shall not curse the deaf, nor put a stumbling block before the blind, but shall fear your God: I am the LORD."*

Tremendous principles are presented in this one Verse. Some of them are:

1. We must not say behind a person's back what we wouldn't say to their face.

2. The sin of cursing another is in itself complete, whether the curse be heard by the other or not, because it is the outcome of sin in the speaker's heart.

3. We are to have a special compassion for those who are afflicted, irrespective as to whom they might be. The Lord, to be sure, is watching us!

4. The eye is directed by God, Who can see and punish, however little the blind man is able to help himself.

5. All of this becomes even more acute, realizing that the Holy Spirit now lives within our hearts and lives, and accordingly, must bear with us, when we sin against others. How so often we must grieve Him!

THE POOR AND THE RICH

Verse 15 reads: *"You shall do no unrighteousness in judgment: you shall not respect the person of the poor, nor honor the person of the mighty: but in Righteousness shall you judge your neighbor."*

When it comes to the Law, James said, *"If you have respect of persons, you commit sin, and are convinced* (convicted) *of the Law as transgressors"* (James 2:9).

The poor must not be allowed to break the Law because they are poor, and the rich must not be allowed to break the Law because they are rich. As a Believer, we must judge fairly, righteously, honestly, and with integrity.

TALEBEARER

Verse 16 reads: *"You shall not go up and down as a talebearer among your people: neither shall you stand against the blood of your neighbor; I am the LORD."*

The phrase, *"You shall not go up and down as a talebearer,"* would have been better translated, *"You shall not go about slandering."*

During the time of Christ, it is said that the three greatest sins were *"idolatry, incest, and murder."* But it was said that one sin surpassed them all, and that was *"slander."* They reasoned that it killed three persons with one act – the person who slanders, the person who is slandered, and the person who listens to the slander.

Regrettably, this is one of the most oft committed sins; and more than likely, every one of us have been guilty of the sin of slandering someone else. It is a dreadful sin, because it ruins the lives of others, and as just stated, the one doing the slandering is put in the position of having sunk to the lowest possible immoral level.

"Standing against the blood of one's neighbor," refers to talebearing of the worst kind, which in effect, bears false witness against him. Thus, the effect of the false witness of the two men of Belial against Naboth was that *"they carried him forth out of the city, and stoned him with stones, that he died"* (I Ki. 21:13; 26:60; 27:4).

It is sad, but some of the worst talebearers in the world are in the Church. I suppose that's the reason that the Holy Spirit through James said: *"And the tongue is a fire, a world of iniquities: so is the tongue among our members, that it defiles the whole body, and sets on fire the course of nature; and is set on fire of Hell . . . But the tongue can no man tame; it is an unruly evil, full of deadly poison . . . out of the same mouth proceeds blessing and cursing. My Brethren, these things ought not so to be"* (James 3:6-10).

HATE

Verses 17 and 18 read: *"You shall not hate your brother in your heart: you shall in any wise rebuke your neighbor, and not suffer sin upon him.*

"You shall not avenge, nor bear any grudge against the children of your people, but you shall love your neighbor as yourself: I am the LORD."

As simple as this Eighteenth Verse is, it is without a doubt, one of the single most important in the entirety of the Word of God.

Gossip, idle talk, and meddling with our neighbor, and more directly still, insinuating and hinting evil of him, are sins forbidden here.

If a brother defame us, or slight us, or give us cause for grief and anger, we are to tell it to the person face to face. The Master gave us instructions regarding this in Matthew, Chapter 18.

Jesus went on to say that if he would not hear us then, we are to take one or two other individuals with us, and once again go to him and try to solve the problem.

If still the problem is not solved, we are to gather the Elders of the Church together, and let them hear the problem, and make a decision.

If it can't be settled then, Jesus said: *"Let him be unto you as an heathen man and a publican"* (Mat. 18:15-17).

Looking at someone as a heathen and a publican, in today's terminology, would simply refer to the fact that we are to discontinue fellowship with such a person. But even this doesn't mean that we are to speak evil of them, or try to hurt them in some way. In fact, we should pray for them, but as should be obvious, if a difference cannot be settled, and we have tried every way to settle the difference, fellowship has to be discontinued, and in fact, fellowship will be discontinued.

"Loving our neighbor as ourself," in effect, fulfills the second half of the Ten Commandments. Properly loving the Lord will fulfill the first half. If you love someone, you're not going to steal from then, lie on them, etc. And if we properly love the Lord, we will not put any other gods before Him (Mat. 22:36-40).

JOSEPH

A perfect example of showing the Love of God toward those who are enemies, or at least have once been enemies, is found in the life of Joseph.

As all Bible students know, his brothers sold him into slavery, and had even discussed killing him. He was about 17 years old when this happened, and one can well imagine the consternation which followed such.

While he was initially blessed in Egypt, ultimately he was placed in prison, where he remained for several years, which, as should be obvious, was a very trying time.

By the direction of the Lord, he was released from prison, and was made the viceroy of Egypt, in fact, the second most powerful man in the world.

Due to the famine that gripped that part of the world, his brothers ultimately came to Egypt to buy grain, etc. When they came before him, because he was in charge of all of this, he recognized them, even though in no way did they recognize him. Now here's the point I wish to make:

Not knowing at this stage if they had changed or not, he would put them to the test. In other words, did they have the same murderous spirit which had sold him into slavery, or had they allowed the Lord to change them?

As any Bible student knows, he put them to a test that was very rigorous. He must be

NOTES

satisfied in his heart that they were changed men, before he would reveal himself to them. In truth, they were changed men.

But the point I wish to make is, when he first saw them, he didn't run and jump into their arms, as some Christians presently think ought to be done. He knew that if they had not changed, fellowship would be impossible.

If an individual has sinned against you the Reader, and they have not repented of that sin, while you are to love them, and pray for them, there is no way that you can have fellowship with them under such circumstances.

When a person truly repents, they acknowledged their wrong, and they then set out on a course which is right and Biblical. But unless true repentance is enjoined, there can be no right direction. Even though, as stated, we are to love the individual, fellowship in such a case is out of the question (II Chron. 7:14).

THE WORD OF GOD

Verse 19 reads: *"You shall keep My Statutes. You shall not let your cattle gender with a diverse kind: you shall not sow your field with mingled seed: neither shall a garment mingled of linen and wool come upon you."*

The idea of this Verse is to present the fact of the mingling of two different kinds, and, thereby, the prohibition of such. Its spiritual application has to do with the mixing of false doctrine with the true. Paul wrote: *"You cannot drink the cup of the Lord, and the cup of devils"* (I Cor. 10:21).

Hooker said: *"He cannot love the Lord Jesus with his heart, who lends one ear to His Apostles and another to false teachers."*

While the things mentioned, trying to breed cattle with diverse kinds, or sowing the field with mingled seed, or making a garment mingled with both linen and wool, which are total contrasts, are obvious according to their appearance, such are meant to be a lesson to us regarding the light of the eye being single (Mat. 6:22).

A perfect example is the Message of the Cross.

THE MESSAGE OF THE CROSS

Two things take place when the seeking

Believer first hears the Message of the Cross. If that Believer is seeking for Truth, the Holy Spirit, without fail, will witness to that Believer's heart, that what he is hearing is Truth. But there is a second part:

Convinced that what he is hearing is the Truth, he is now faced with the prospect of living the Cross life, which is the greatest life there is, but which demands everything. In other words, to fully embrace the Message of the Cross, many Christians will have to leave their respective Churches, or Denominations. Automatically, the prospect of losing all their friends, possibly even their family, comes before them. Regrettably, many are not willing to pay that price.

They reason in their minds that they can make the Cross the object of their Faith, while at the same time, continuing in their previous direction. In other words, they are *"mingling seed."* They are taking in false doctrine, and at the same time, attempting to believe correct doctrine. The Holy Spirit through Paul said: *"Wherefore come out from among them, and be separate, saith the Lord, and touch not the unclean thing; and I will receive you"* (II Cor. 6:17).

Paul had just said, *"Be ye not unequally yoked together with unbelievers"* (II Cor. 6:14). For the true Christian to fully understand what is being said here, one can judge *"Believers"* and *"unbelievers,"* in the realm of the Cross. Irrespective of the claims, if the Faith of the individual, whomever that individual might be, is not squarely in the Cross of Christ, they have to be looked as an *"unbeliever."* A *"Believer"* is the opposite; his Faith is totally and completely in Christ and what Christ has done at the Cross. If the Cross is eliminated, the person is worshipping and serving *"another Jesus,"* which of course, the Lord cannot accept (II Cor. 11:4).

The Cross of Christ is the dividing line between belief, i.e., *"Believers,"* and unbelief, i.e., *"unbelievers."* On one side is the True Church; on the other side is the apostate church. Listen again to Paul:

"Now the Spirit (Holy Spirit) *speaks expressly* (pointedly), *that in the latter times* (the times in which we now live) *some shall depart from the Faith, giving heed to seducing spirits, and*

NOTES

doctrines of devils" (I Tim. 4:1).

Continuing to use the *"mingled seed"* as an example, in the mingling, there are some seed that are proper. In other words, they are the right seed, but it's the mixture that causes the problem. In fact, Satan's greatest effort is to fasten error onto the back of Truth. One could probably say that most, if not all, error rides into the Church on the back of Truth. Once again, it's the *"mingled seed."*

(20) "AND WHOSOEVER LIES CARNALLY WITH A WOMAN, WHO IS A BONDMAID, BETROTHED TO AN HUSBAND, AND NOT AT ALL REDEEMED, NOR FREEDOM GIVEN HER; SHE SHALL BE SCOURGED; THEY SHALL NOT BE PUT TO DEATH, BECAUSE SHE WAS NOT FREE.

(21) "AND HE SHALL BRING HIS TRESPASS-OFFERING UNTO THE LORD, UNTO THE DOOR OF THE TABERNACLE OF THE CONGREGATION, EVEN A RAM FOR A TRESPASS-OFFERING.

(22) "AND THE PRIEST SHALL MAKE AN ATONEMENT FOR HIM WITH THE RAM OF THE TRESPASS-OFFERING BEFORE THE LORD FOR HIS SIN WHICH HE HAS DONE: AND THE SIN WHICH HE HAS DONE SHALL BE FORGIVEN HIM.

(23) "AND WHEN YOU SHALL COME INTO THE LAND, AND SHALL HAVE PLANTED ALL MANNER OF TREES FOR FOOD, THEN YOU SHALL COUNT THE FRUIT THEREOF AS UNCIRCUMCISED: THREE YEARS SHALL IT BE AS UNCIRCUMCISED UNTO YOU: IT SHALL NOT BE EATEN OF.

(24) "BUT IN THE FOURTH YEAR ALL THE FRUIT THEREOF SHALL BE HOLY TO PRAISE THE LORD WITHAL.

(25) "AND IN THE FIFTH YEAR SHALL YOU EAT OF THE FRUIT THEREOF, THAT IT MAY YIELD UNTO YOU THE INCREASE THEREOF: I AM THE LORD YOUR GOD."

The exegesis is:

1. The Law as given by God, and given solely to Israel, covered every aspect of life and living.

2. Considering that the Law was given by God, which means that it was perfect, which speaks of total equality and fidelity in all cases, puts Israel far ahead of any other nation.

3. As we have seen, and will continue to see, the Sacrificial System was at the very heart of the Levitical Commandments.

THE TRESPASS-OFFERING

Verses 20 through 22 read: *"And whosoever lies carnally with a woman, who is a bondmaid, betrothed to an husband, and not at all redeemed, nor freedom given her; she shall be scourged; they shall not be put to death because she was not free.*

"And he shall bring his Trespass-Offering unto the LORD, unto the Door of the Tabernacle of the congregation, even a ram for a Trespass-Offering.

"And the Priest shall make an Atonement for him with the ram of the Trespass-Offering before the LORD for his sin which he has done: and the sin which he has done shall be forgiven him."

This Law seems intended to prevent anyone claiming circumstances on the one hand, or, on the other, taking advantage of his superior station in society, by taking advantage of a bondwoman.

A bondwoman was a slave, or else a woman who was working in a certain household for a period of time in order to pay off a debt.

The case in question is that of a bondwoman, who has been betrothed to some other slave. In ordinary cases, both she and the man who seduced her would be put to death, according to the Law (Deut. 22:23-25). But there is to be a difference made here.

The woman might be intimidated by the man's authority, or tempted by his apparent right and claim that she must obey him, etc.; therefore, she is not reckoned so guilty as in ordinary cases.

Then, on his part, the man might be ignorant of the bondwoman being engaged to another man.

Yet there is still a penalty involved. *"She shall be scourged"* for not resisting and making the whole case known. And he shall publicly offer a Trespass-Offering, confessing his sin.

We find from this that the Lord is considerate and impartial, yet Holy and Righteous (Bonar).

THE FRUIT OF THE TREE

Verses 23 through 25 read: *"And when you shall come into the land, and shall have planted all manner of trees for food, then you shall count the fruit thereof as uncircumcised: three years shall it be as uncircumcised unto you: it shall not be eaten of.*

"But in the fourth year all the fruit thereof shall be holy to praise the LORD withal.

"And in the fifth year shall you eat of the fruit thereof, that it may yield unto you the increase thereof: I am the LORD your God."

It is said that fruit trees yield better fruit afterwards, if the blossoms be nipped off (*"circumcised"*) during the earliest years. It is even said the fruit of the first years is unwholesome.

In the fourth year, the fruit was to be dedicated to the Lord. It was offered up to Him with songs of praise; perhaps with festival songs, as in that scene in the vineyards of Shiloh (Jud. 21:19, 21).

This entire precept was in some way a memorial of the *"forbidden tree of paradise."* Every fruit tree was to stand unused for three years, as a test of obedience. Every stranger saw, in Israel's orchards and vineyards, proofs of their obedience to their supreme Lord – a witness for Him. And what a solemn shadow they cast over the fallen sons of Adam there, reminding them of the first father's sin (Bonar).

(26) "YOU SHALL NOT EAT ANYTHING WITH THE BLOOD: NEITHER SHALL YOU USE ENCHANTMENT, NOR OBSERVE TIMES.

(27) "YOU SHALL NOT ROUND THE CORNERS OF YOUR HEADS, NEITHER SHALL YOU MAR THE CORNERS OF YOUR BEARD.

(28) "YOU SHALL NOT MAKE ANY CUTTINGS IN YOUR FLESH FOR THE DEAD, NOR PRINT ANY MARKS UPON YOU: I AM THE LORD.

(29) "DO NOT PROSTITUTE YOUR DAUGHTER, TO CAUSE HER TO BE A WHORE; LEST THE LAND FALL TO WHOREDOM, AND THE LAND BECOME FULL OF WICKEDNESS.

(30) "YOU SHALL KEEP MY SABBATHS, AND REVERENCE MY SANCTUARY: I AM

THE LORD.

(31) "REGARD NOT THEM WHO HAVE FAMILIAR SPIRITS, NEITHER SEEK AFTER WIZARDS, TO BE DEFILED BY THEM: I AM THE LORD YOUR GOD.

(32) "YOU SHALL RISE UP BEFORE THE HOARY HEAD, AND HONOR THE FACE OF THE OLD MAN, AND FEAR YOUR GOD: I AM THE LORD.

(33) "AND IF A STRANGER SOJOURN WITH YOU IN YOUR LAND, YOU SHALL NOT VEX HIM.

(34) "BUT THE STRANGER WHO DWELLS WITH YOU SHALL BE UNTO YOU AS ONE BORN AMONG YOU, AND YOU SHALL LOVE HIM AS YOURSELF; FOR YOU WERE STRANGERS IN THE LAND OF EGYPT: I AM THE LORD YOUR GOD.

(35) "YOU SHALL DO NO UNRIGHTEOUSNESS IN JUDGMENT, IN METEYARD, IN WEIGHT, OR IN MEASURE.

(36) "JUST BALANCES, JUST WEIGHTS, A JUST EPHAH, AND A JUST HIN, SHALL YOU HAVE: I AM THE LORD YOUR GOD, WHICH BROUGHT YOU OUT OF THE LAND OF EGYPT.

(37) "THEREFORE SHALL YOU OBSERVE ALL MY STATUTES, AND ALL MY JUDGMENTS, AND DO THEM: I AM THE LORD."

The diagram is:

1. Blood was not to be eaten, and in fact, was in a sense, to be held sacred.

2. Any type of superstition was to be avoided.

3. Rounding the corners of the hair, and marring the corners of the beard, all had to do with superstition, and must not be engaged by God's people.

4. Prostitution, as would be obvious, is forbidden.

5. They were to keep the Sabbaths, which proclaimed a portrayal of the *"rest"* which one would find in Christ.

6. Under no circumstances were God's people to seek the advice and counsel of witches or wizards.

7. The aged were to be respected.

8. The stranger (Gentile) was to be respected, and treated kindly.

9. God's people were to be honest in all things.

NOTES

10. These Statutes were not given for the sole purpose of merely making Laws, but were meant to be obeyed.

11. The closing phrase, used over and over, *"I am the LORD,"* proclaimed the fact that these Commandments didn't come from men, but rather from the Lord.

SUPERSTITION

Verses 26 through 28 read: *"You shall not eat anything with the blood: neither shall you use enchantment, nor observe times.*

"You shall not round the corners of your heads, neither shall you mar the corners of your beard.

"You shall not make any cuttings in your flesh for the dead, nor print any marks upon you: I am the LORD."

The pagans were accustomed to making small incisions in their physical bodies, or to put marks upon their flesh, as a sign of mourning for their loved ones who had recently died. But the Lord forbade anything of this nature among His people.

The incision represented a separation, in fact, an eternal separation, in the minds of the pagans. In essence, by the Lord commanding His people to not engage in such activities, He in effect, was telling them that death, that is if they would faithfully serve Him, did not end it all. In other words, if their loved ones had been in the Covenant, and had Faith in the Covenant, and the ones living continued to have Faith in the Covenant, they would see them again.

By the use of the phrase, *"I am the LORD,"* He in effect was telling them, *"Trust Me, I am able to do all things which I say that I will do, and even far greater than you could ever imagine or think. In fact, there is nothing too hard for Me."*

PROSTITUTION

Verse 29 reads: *"Do not prostitute your daughter, to cause her to be a whore; lest the land fall to whoredom, and the land become full of wickedness."*

This Command had a twofold meaning:

1. It referred to the worship of heathen gods, which demanded temple prostitutes, and which was common among the heathen. And at times, during periods of spiritual

declension, it also broke out among the Jews. It was referred to as temple prostitution, and because these young women had to remain in these temples dedicated to pagan gods.

2. All adultery and fornication were a violation of the Second and the Seventh Commandments (Ex. 20:4, 14). In fact, there must be no form of sexual immorality among God's people. The people of the Lord were to be clean physically and morally.

SABBATHS

Verse 30 reads: *"You shall keep My Sabbaths, and reverence My Sanctuary: I am the LORD."*

Under the Mosaic Law, Sabbaths were very, very special. In fact, the Lord had more to say about this particular Commandment, than any of the other Commandments (Ex. 20:8-11).

The Sabbath was not actually a day of worship, but rather a day of *"rest."* It was so important, simply because it pictured in type the *"rest"* which would be afforded by Christ when He would come. This is what Jesus was referring to when He said: *"Come unto Me, all who labor and are heavy laden, and I will give you rest.*

"Take My yoke upon you, and learn of Me; for I am meek and lowly in heart: and you shall find rest unto your souls.

"For My yoke is easy, and My burden is light" (Mat. 11:28-30).

So, when a Christian presently serves the Lord, making Christ one's Lord and Saviour, in fact, entering into His *"rest,"* at the same time, by doing this, he is keeping the Sabbath.

We find from the New Testament (since the Cross), that Sabbath-keeping as a day was not the custom among the Gentiles, and rightly so. In fact, Sunday, the day of the Lord's Resurrection, became a day of worship, instead of the old Jewish Sabbath (Acts 20:7; I Cor. 16:2; Heb. 2:9).

The reverence that must be shown the habitation of the Lord referred then to the Tabernacle, and would refer later to the Temple, which would be built approximately 500 years later.

In the Tabernacle and the Temple, God dwelt between the Mercy Seat and the

NOTES

Cherubim, which were in the Holy of Holies. Considering the two Priests, Nadab and Abihu, who were stricken dead for offering up *"strange fire"* (Lev., Chpt. 10), and further considering Israel's spiritual declension in later years, one wonders as to why more Priests were not stricken dead.

The greatest reason of all, one might say, is that for a period of about 500 years before Christ, the Lord was no longer in the Temple. In fact, the Prophet Ezekiel, in a Vision, saw Him leave the Temple, and in fact, He never came back, with the Temple being destroyed shortly thereafter (Ezek. 11:22-24). This means that when Jesus came, the Lord was actually not in the Temple, except for the times that Christ was in its precincts. But Ezekiel also in a Vision saw the Holy Spirit return (Ezek. 43:1-5). This will be during the Millennial Reign, when the Millennial Temple will be built, and Christ, from Jerusalem, will rule and reign over the entirety of the world.

The Ark of the Covenant was taken out of the Temple shortly before the Babylonian Monarch, Nebuchadnezzar, invaded Jerusalem, burned the city, and destroyed the Temple. Tradition says that the Prophet Jeremiah took the Ark of the Covenant out of the Holy of Holies, and hid it; however, from then until now, it has never been found.

When the Children of Israel returned from Babylonian captivity, the Temple was rebuilt under Zerubbabel (Ezra 5:2). This is referred to as the second Temple, with Solomon's being the first. While there was a Holy of Holies in the second Temple, there was no Ark of the Covenant. Neither was there an Ark of the Covenant in the Temple built by Herod. When the Romans broke into the sacred precinct, it was empty.

THE TEMPLE OF THE HOLY SPIRIT

Paul said: *"Know ye not that you are the Temple of God, and that the Spirit of God dwells in you?"* (I Cor. 3:16).

Due to what Christ did at the Cross, the Holy Spirit can now reside within the heart and life of the Believer, and do so permanently, which He does (Jn. 14:16-17).

All of these Commands given referring to the physical body, the keeping of the Sabbath, and the respecting of the Sanctuary, now refers to the Believer, in whom the Spirit of God now dwells. This literally means that our physical and spiritual person, at least in a sense, becomes the Temple of God. As such, we should be ever mindful of this fact, thereby being careful as to our conduct in all matters. We must remember that these literal Commandments given in the Old Testament, in a sense, were types of what the Holy Spirit would carry out within our lives. This life can now be lived by the Grace of God, that is, if we properly understand God's prescribed order of victory.

Jesus said: *"If any man will come after Me, let him deny himself* (deny his own strength and ability) *and take up his cross daily, and follow Me"* (Lk. 9:23).

Denying oneself does not refer to asceticism, which is the denial of all things which are pleasurable or comfortable, etc., but rather one denying his own personal strength, ability, power, and personal efforts. And what does that mean?

It means that we cannot live for God, cannot be what we ought to be, in fact, cannot be what we must be, by our own strength and ability. No matter how hard we try, no matter how much effort we put forth, or how sincere we may be, that path is guaranteed of failure. The answer is in what Jesus told us to do, as it regards taking up the Cross, and doing so on a daily basis.

He is speaking here of the benefits of the Cross, which He paid for at Calvary. This means that our Faith and trust must ever have the Cross as its object. We must ever understand that all things come to us from God, strictly and purely by what Christ did for us at the Cross. This is the only way that we can live for God, at least in a victorious way. Every other way, as stated, is guaranteed of failure.

The Master then said: *"For whosoever will save his life shall lose it: but whosoever will lose his life for My sake, the same shall save it"* (Lk. 9:24).

This corresponds with Paul's statement when he said: *"I am crucified with Christ: nevertheless I live; yet not I, but Christ lives in me: and the life which I now live in the flesh I live by the Faith of the Son of God, Who loved me, and gave Himself for me.*

"I do not frustrate the Grace of God: for if Righteousness come by the Law, then Christ is dead in vain" (Gal. 2:20-21).

The *"saving of our life and then losing it,"* refers to a Believer attempting to live this life by his own machinations and ability. Thinking to save it, he will lose it. The reason is simple; one cannot live for God in this manner. Sin is too strong for our own personal strength and abilities. It yields only to the Cross of Christ and the power of the Holy Spirit.

If we lose our life for Christ's sake, which means that we place everything in Christ, letting Him live through us by the power of the Holy Spirit, which He definitely will do if we will put our Faith totally and completely in what He did at the Cross, then we will save our life.

In fact, this is the only way that a person can live for God. Any other way, as repeatedly stated, is guaranteed of failure.

In this manner alone, we can keep this Temple of God, and make it a fit place for the habitation of the Holy Spirit. Paul said:

"In Whom (Christ and His Cross) *you also are built together* (Christ and the Believer) *for an habitation of God through the Spirit"* (Eph. 2:22).

FAMILIAR SPIRITS AND WIZARDS

Verse 31 reads: *"Regard not them who have familiar spirits, neither seek after wizards, to be defiled by them: I am the LORD your God."*

A *"familiar spirit"* is a demon spirit that is invisible, which possesses the individual, and helps that person relate certain things to those who seek such counsel and advice.

"Wizards" functioned in much the same manner, pretending to tell people the answers to questions, etc.

According to ancient tradition, these wizards put in their mouth a bone of a certain bird. They burned incense, which was in effect a drug, thus producing fumes which sent them off into an ecstasy, in which then they foretold future events. In effect, the *"wizard"* was the one who had the *"familiar spirit."*

God's people were to have no association with such works of darkness, and works of darkness they were! The Believer is not to be led by horoscopes, signs of the zodiac, or omens of any nature. The Christian is not to associate himself with these things in any capacity.

The Believer is to be led and guided strictly by the Holy Spirit. Our Lord said: *"Howbeit when He, the Spirit of Truth, is come, He will guide you into all Truth: for He shall not speak of Himself; but whatsoever He shall hear, that shall He speak: and He will show you things to come.*

"He shall glorify Me: for He shall receive of Mine, and shall show it unto you.

"All things that the Father has are Mine: therefore said I, that He shall take of Mine, and shall show it unto you" (Jn. 16:13-15).

Jesus further said: *"Ask, and it shall be given you; seek, and you shall find; knock, and it shall be opened unto to you.*

"For every one who asks receives; and he who seeks finds; and to him who knocks it shall be opened.

"If a son shall ask bread of any of you who is a father, will he give him a stone? Or if he ask a fish, will he for a fish give him a serpent?

"Or if he shall ask an egg, will he offer him a scorpion (an egg containing a scorpion)*?*

"If you then, being evil, know how to give good gifts unto your children: how much more shall your Heavenly Father give the Holy Spirit to them who ask Him?" (Lk. 11:9-13).

A PERSONAL EXPERIENCE

In this particular Message as given by Christ, which I refer to as the *"Parable of the three loaves"* (Lk. 11:5-13), the Lord gave me a great Promise. Consequently, it is very dear to me personally.

If I remember the exact time of the year correctly, it was the early spring of 1992. We were then having two Prayer Meetings a day, morning, and night, which we kept up for over ten years. (I still personally maintain a morning Prayer Meeting, which I will continue, by the help of the Lord, until He calls me home, or the trump sounds.)

In prayer that particular night, the Spirit of the Lord came upon me heavily. It was a time of great consternation and difficulty for the Ministry. In fact, if one looked outwardly,

NOTES

there was no way we could survive. The Media, along with organized religion, were doing everything within their power to shut the doors to our efforts. All I knew to do was pray, and in fact, that's exactly what the Lord had told me to do. He told me in late October of 1991 to begin two Prayer Meetings a day, which we instantly did. During this time, He also related to me that I was not to seek Him so much for what He could do, but rather for Who He was.

In October of 1991, with a small group of friends and family, I laid my Bible on the table in front of me, and in effect said these words: *"I don't know the answer to a victorious, overcoming, Christian life. But I know the answer is in the Word of God, and by the Grace of God, I'm going to find that answer."* And by the Grace of God I did.

In late 1996, the Lord in answer to that petition, began to open up to me the Message of the Cross, in effect telling me, *"The solution for which you seek is found only in the Cross."*

But going back to the early Spring of 1992, in Prayer Meeting one particular night, the Lord opened up to me this Parable found in Luke, Chapter 11, concerning the man who sought bread from a friend, and because he had none.

The Lord so moved upon me that night, giving me this Parable for my own particular situation, as a Rhema Word to my heart. In other words, it was a special Word from the Lord, which would sustain me, and would do so greatly.

In my particular situation, the Holy Spirit made it real to me, that I was the man who needed bread, and had none.

In the Parable, Jesus related as to how a man on a journey had come to a certain friend, and had needed sustenance, but the man to whose home he had come, had no sustenance to give him.

Consequently, he had gone to a friend of his, seeking bread, that he might help his destitute friend. He said: *"For a friend of mine in his journey has come to me, and I have nothing to set before him."*

However, in asking for help, considering that it was midnight, and the man from whom he sought help was in bed, the answer came back upon his request for three loaves, *"Trouble me not: the door is now shut, and my children are with me in bed; I cannot rise and give to you."*

But Jesus then said that irrespective of the answer, the man in need would not leave, but continued to knock on the door, until it was finally opened, and he was given as much as he needed.

WHAT THE LORD WAS TELLING ME

That night in the early Spring of 1992, the Lord was telling me that even though it may seem as if though the answer would not come, and that circumstances would seem to be very adverse, I was to keep knocking at that door, and if I kept knocking, it would eventually open. He gave me that Promise.

That's when He said, *"Ask, and it shall be given you; seek, and you shall find; knock, and it shall be opened unto you."*

He then promised that what we were asking for is that which we would receive, and that He would guarantee it by the power of the Holy Spirit.

That night for a period of time, as the Spirit of God washed over me, and the Lord brought this particular Message from Christ to my heart, as stated, making it a Rhema Word to my soul, I knew what the Lord was telling me.

In the coming five years, at times I grew very discouraged, but every time, the Spirit of the Lord would bring me back to this particular Message given by Christ. In essence, He was telling me, *"Keep asking, keep seeking, keep knocking, and it shall be opened unto you."* And that I did!

And then, as stated, in late 1996, the Lord began to do exactly what He had promised that He would do. I had asked, and now I was to receive. I had sought His Face earnestly, and now I was finding that for which I had sought. I had knocked, and this door was now beginning to open.

In fact, the beautiful thing about this is, when He begins to give, He just continues to give. When we begin to find that for which we are seeking, we just keep finding more and more. And when He begins to open to us the door, it just opens wider and wider, seemingly never stopping.

As I dictate these notes on October 6, 2002, the Lord is doing great and mighty things, and I know in my heart that it's just beginning. What He is doing now is truly wonderful; however, what He is going to do in the near future, I personally believe will eclipse anything that He has done in the past, at least for this particular Evangelist, and this particular Ministry. As He told me a few days ago: *"It is time to go in and to possess the land, which the LORD your God has given you"* (Josh. 1:11).

THE HONORING OF AGE

Verse 32 reads: *"You shall rise up before the hoary head, and honor the face of the old man, and fear your God: I am the LORD."*

It is said to this day, when, among orthodox Jews, an aged person enters into a house where young people are, they all rise up, and will not sit down until he asks them to do so.

If a man lives for God, and the Lord allows him to grow old, as should be obvious, he has much wisdom, and because of much experience. That wisdom should be sought.

However, it is speaking only of those who truly know the Lord. Otherwise, I'm afraid the adage holds true, *"There is no fool like an old fool."*

Near the conclusion of this Verse, the Holy Spirit through Moses used the phrase, *"And fear your God,"* linking that with the command as it regards respect for the elderly. The idea is, if it's not done, this which the Lord has commanded, the Lord will not take kindly to such actions, and the results at some point in time, will definitely be negative. And then he concluded by saying, *"I am the LORD,"* meaning that He had the power to do what He was saying.

THE STRANGER

Verses 33 and 34 read: *"And if a stranger sojourn with you in your land, you shall not vex him.*

"But the stranger who dwells with you shall be unto you as one born among you, and you shall love him as yourself; for you were strangers in the land of Egypt: I am the LORD your God."

The *"stranger"* referred to here was actually a Gentile, but one who had joined the

Jewish faith. He had, therefore, to undergo the rite of circumcision; he had to fast on the Great Day of Atonement (Lev. 16:29); he had to submit to the regulations about Sacrifices (Lev. 17:8-9; 22:18); he had to abstain from eating blood in the flesh of animals torn by wild beasts; he had to practice the laws of chastity (Lev. 18:26); like the Israelite by birth, he had to refrain from blasphemy, and obey the moral precepts (Lev. 24:16-22). These were some of the conditions of his sojourning in the land (Ellicott).

Having been admitted into the community, the Israelites were forbidden to upbraid him regarding his nationality, or throw at him the fact that he was originally an idolater. They are thus prohibited from calling him a foreigner or neophyte, but rather were to treat him with dignity and respect. In other words, he was to be treated as one of them, i.e., *"You shall love him as yourself"* (vs. 34).

It was this human law which attracted many Gentiles to Israel. Hence we find that in the days of Solomon there were 153,000 Gentiles in Israel.

The Lord reminded them that they had once been slaves in Egypt, and the very thought of this was meant to soften their hearts, and enable them to see their duty as it regarded the Gentiles among themselves. This appeal is to be found three times more in the Pentateuch (Ex. 22:20; 23:9; Deut. 10:19).

HONESTY

Verses 35 and 36 read: *"You shall do no unrighteousness in judgment, in meteyard, in weight, or in measure.*

"Just balances, just weights, a just ephah, and a just hin, shall you have: I am the LORD your God, which brought you out of the land of Egypt."

In these Passages, the Lord brands all dishonesty as wicked, and as well, an abomination to the Lord.

According to the authorities during the time of the second Temple (built after returning from Babylon), he who gave false weight or measure, like the corrupt judge, is guilty of the following five things:

1. He defiles the land.
2. He profanes the Name of God.

NOTES

3. He causes the Glory of God to depart from him.
4. The departing of the Glory means that God will lift his hand from Israel, and they will be defeated in battle.
5. As a result, they will go into captivity. Hence the Jewish Scripture authorities stated that *"the sin of illegal weights and measures was greater than that of incest, and was equivalent to the sin of denying God Who had redeemed Israel out of Egypt."*

As a result, they appointed public overseers to inspect the weights and measures all over the country; they prohibited weights to be made of iron, lead, or other metal liable to become lighter by wear or rust, and ordered them to be made of polished rock, of glass, etc., and furthermore, enacted the severest punishment for fraud.

In matters of honesty, how can modern Believers look to these commands as anything less than incumbent upon them! We are to be honest in all things.

This means that we must pay our taxes, and not defraud anyone.

Some Christians have the ridiculous idea that it's not wrong to steal from the Federal Government, or a major corporation such as an insurance company, etc. But let the Reader understand that stealing is stealing, fraud is fraud, dishonesty is dishonesty, wherever it is practiced, and upon whomever it is practiced. As Believers we must ever understand that God says what He means, and means what He says.

The implication in Verse 36 is, if Israel in fact ignored these commands, they would once again, in fact, find themselves in captivity, just as they had in Egypt. The Lord Who brought them out of Egypt could put them back into Egypt, which He in essence actually did, i.e., *"Babylon."*

THE WORD OF GOD

Verse 37 reads: *"Therefore shall you observe all My Statutes, and all My Judgments, and do them: I am the LORD."*

The Lord didn't say that Israel was to observe some of His Statutes and Commandments, but rather all of them. Was it in fact, possible for Israel to do this?

In truth, it wasn't! However, they definitely

were to try to keep the Law, and to do so in every respect. Offering up Sacrifices for their sins, God would honor their effort.

Before the Cross, the Holy Spirit could not come into hearts and lives and abide there permanently; therefore, believing man at that time was, for all practical purposes, helpless. In other words, due to the clinging vines of the Fall, he really could not live as he ought to live. But again, he had to try, and God would honor that, and because it was done by Faith.

As long as Israel did that, God blessed them abundantly so. But when they began to ignore the Law, ignore His Statutes, treat His Commandments with disdain, there came a time that God did exactly what He said He would do – He took them out of the land, and put them into captivity. Again we state, *"God says what He means, and means what He says."*

THE CROSS HAS MADE
THE DIFFERENCE

Before the Cross, the terrible sin debt owed to God by all men hung heavily over the heads of all, even the most ardent Believers. The simple reason was, the blood of bulls and goats could not take away sins (Heb. 10:4). While animal sacrifices served as a stopgap measure, they were that only, and would be that only, until Christ came.

As a result of the sin debt remaining, the Holy Spirit could not come into hearts and lives to abide permanently.

But when Jesus came, fulfilling the Law in every respect, and thereby died on the Cross, being made a curse for us (Gal. 3:13), the sin debt was then forever paid, and for all time, at least for all who will believe (Jn. 1:29; 3:16). Now the Holy Spirit can come in to abide permanently (Jn. 14:16-17).

Let the Reader understand that it is the Holy Spirit Alone Who makes the benefits of the Cross real to the heart and life of the Believer. That's what Paul was talking about when he said: *"For the Law* (a Law made by the Godhead in eternity past) *of the Spirit* (Holy Spirit) *of Life* (that which He gives is life, and is made possible by the Cross) *in Christ Jesus* (referring to what Christ did at the Cross), *has made me free*

from the law of sin and death" (Rom. 8:2).

It is through the Power of the Holy Spirit Alone that the Believer can have victory over the world, the flesh, and the Devil.

BUT HOW DOES THE
HOLY SPIRIT WORK?

That is the great question!

Once again, we find that the manner and way in which He works are found exclusively within the parameters of the Finished Work of Christ. We are given this as well, and to which we briefly alluded, in Romans 8:2. It is all found in the words *"in Christ Jesus,"* which always, and without exception, refers to what Christ did at the Cross.

So what do we mean by the Holy Spirit working strictly within the confines of the Finished Work of Christ?

If it is to be noticed, the first part of the Second Verse of the Eighth Chapter of Romans speaks of the *"Law."* Paul is not speaking here of the Law of Moses, but rather, *"The Law of the Spirit of Life in Christ Jesus."* As we've already explained, *"in Christ Jesus,"* refers strictly to the Cross.

Sometime in eternity past, the Godhead knew They would make man, and that man would fall. They determined to redeem man by the Cross, even as Peter informed us (I Pet. 1:18-20). This Redemption Plan was set in concrete, so to speak, with it being referred to as a *"Law,"* meaning that God will not deter from what He has planned.

As I've already stated any number of times in this Volume, the Holy Spirit demands of us very little; however, He most definitely does demand one thing, and that is our Faith in the Cross of Christ. It means that the Cross must ever be the object of our Faith, and whatever we do, we must never allow the object of our Faith to change from the Cross to something else (I Cor. 1:17-18, 21, 23; 2:2; Rom. 6:3-14; 8:1-2, 11).

Unfortunately, most modern Christians don't have the foggiest idea as to the veracity of the Cross as it refers to Sanctification, or the manner and the way in which the Holy Spirit works. As a result, they place their faith in other things, mostly out of ignorance, but which denies them the help of the Holy Spirit, which means they are destined to live a spiritual life of constant failure. The entirety of the Seventh Chapter of Romans bears this out.

FRUSTRATING THE GRACE OF GOD

Paul said: *"I do not frustrate the Grace of God: for if Righteousness come by the Law, then Christ is dead in vain"* (Gal. 2:21).

Now the Reader must understand that the *"Law,"* to which Paul now refers is not the Law of which he spoke in Romans 8:2. In Galatians 2:21, he is speaking of the Law of Moses, or any Law made by man. And in effect, he is saying that Righteousness cannot become a force within our lives, if we try to bring it about by laws and rituals, etc. And let the Reader understand that if man could not bring about Righteousness by trying to keep the Law of Moses, which is the only legitimate law that's ever been given, at least as far as Statutes and Commands are concerned, then it surely should dawn upon us that we can't effect Righteousness by laws of our own making. But that's exactly, sad to say, what the modern Church is trying to do.

If a Believer attempts to live for God by the method of rules and regulations, which means that he is placing his faith in these things, as good as they may be in their own right, he will fail. And why will he fail?

He will fail simply because the Holy Spirit will not help him in such endeavors. In fact, such endeavors are an insult to Christ. In effect, it states that what Christ did is not sufficient, or else not needed. In the very Face of God, the Believer is in effect saying that Jesus really did not have to come down here and die on a Cross, because we can live for the Lord, and be what we ought to be, without that.

Of course, it should become instantly obvious that such thinking is ridiculous, and actually borders on blasphemy. But yet, that's where most are.

As repeatedly stated, the Holy Spirit works exclusively within the premise of the Finished Work of Christ. And what is that Finished Work?

It includes many things. First of all, Jesus in His Perfect Life, kept the Law of Moses perfectly, and in every respect, thereby

NOTES

gaining its Righteousness (Gal. 4:4-5).

This means that He did what no other human being could do, and in fact, what no other human being could ever do.

He then went to the Cross, and was made a curse for us, in order that the broken Law might be addressed as well. He did that perfectly, offering up Himself in Sacrifice, by the shedding of His Precious Blood, pouring out His Own Life, which the Lord accepted as payment for all sin (Gal. 1:4).

If one properly understands the Word of God, one then understands that the Cross is the central object. Everything, in one way or the other, points to the Cross. In fact, that's the story of the Bible. As a result, we are to place our Faith exclusively in Christ and what Christ has done for us. As stated, the Cross must ever be the object of our Faith, in fact, never allowing it to be moved elsewhere. This being the case, the Holy Spirit will definitely help us, and will help us so grandly that sin will no longer have dominion over us in any regard (Rom. 6:14).

Please allow me once again to give the following formula. I realize that we've already given it; however, this is so important, in fact, the most important thing in the life of any Believer, that I think we cannot address it too much.

1. Focus: The Cross of Christ (I Cor. 1:17; Gal. 5:1-6).

2. Object of Faith: The Finished Work of Christ, which He accomplished on the Cross (Rom. 6:3-14).

3. Power Source: The Holy Spirit (Rom. 8:1-2, 11).

4. Results: Victory (I Jn. 5:4).

THE WAY OF RELIGION

Let's use the same formula, but turn it around, which most Christians are presently doing.

1. Focus: Works.
2. Object of Faith: One's performance.
3. Power Source: Self.
4. Results: Failure (Gal. 5:1-9).

"Break Thou the Bread of Life, dear Lord, to me,
"As You did break the loaves beside the sea:

"Beyond the sacred page I seek You,
Lord;
"My spirit pants for You, O Living
Word."

"Bless Thou the Truth, dear Lord, to
me – to me,
"As You did bless the bread by Galilee:
"Then shall all bondage cease, all fet-
ters fall,
"And I shall find my peace, my all in
all."

"Thou are the Bread of Life, O Lord, to
me;
"Thy Holy Word the Truth that saveth
me:
"Give me to eat and live with Thee
above;
"Teach me to love Your Truth, for You
are Love."

"Thank You Lord for Your Spirit, given
unto me,
"He will touch my eyes and make me
see:
"Show me the Truth concealed within
Your Word,
"And in Your Book revealed I see the
Lord."

CHAPTER 20

(1) "AND THE LORD SPOKE UNTO MOSES, SAYING,

(2) "AGAIN, YOU SHALL SAY TO THE CHILDREN OF ISRAEL, WHOSOEVER HE BE OF THE CHILDREN OF ISRAEL, OR OF THE STRANGERS WHO SOJOURN IN ISRAEL, WHO GIVES ANY OF HIS SEED UNTO MOLECH; HE SHALL SURELY BE PUT TO DEATH: THE PEOPLE OF THE LAND SHALL STONE HIM WITH STONES.

(3) "AND I WILL SET MY FACE AGAINST THAT MAN, AND WILL CUT HIM OFF FROM AMONG HIS PEOPLE; BECAUSE HE HAS GIVEN OF HIS SEED UNTO MOLECH, TO DEFILE MY SANCTU-ARY, AND TO PROFANE MY HOLY NAME.

(4) "AND IF THE PEOPLE OF THE LAND DO ANY WAYS HIDE THEIR EYES FROM

NOTES

THE MAN, WHEN HE GIVES OF HIS SEED UNTO MOLECH, AND KILL HIM NOT:

(5) "THEN I WILL SET MY FACE AGAINST THAT MAN, AND AGAINST HIS FAMILY, AND WILL CUT HIM OFF, AND ALL WHO GO A WHORING AFTER HIM, TO COMMIT WHOREDOM WITH MOLECH, FROM AMONG THEIR PEOPLE.

(6) "AND THE SOUL WHO TURNS AF-TER SUCH AS HAVE FAMILIAR SPIR-ITS, AND AFTER WIZARDS, TO GO A WHORING AFTER THEM, I WILL EVEN SET MY FACT AGAINST THAT SOUL, AND WILL CUT HIM OFF FROM AMONG HIS PEOPLE.

(7) "SANCTIFY YOURSELVES THERE-FORE, AND BE YE HOLY: FOR I AM THE LORD YOUR GOD.

(8) "AND YOU SHALL KEEP MY STAT-UTES, AND DO THEM: I AM THE LORD WHICH SANCTIFY YOU."

The structure is:

1. In all of this, we find that each Statute teaches a double lesson, namely, a lesson with respect to nature's evil tendencies, and also a lesson as to Jehovah's tender care.

2. Considering the offering up of human sacrifices, this but reveals a most humiliat-ing amount of wickedness in human nature. It is this nature, the evil nature, which causes all war, all of man's inhumanity to man, and in fact, all crime, sin, and evil.

3. The only answer for this sinful nature is *"Jesus Christ and Him Crucified."* There is no other answer, and if man thinks there is, he is only fooling himself.

HUMAN SACRIFICE

Verses 1 through 5 read: *"And the LORD spoke unto Moses, saying,*

"Again, you shall say to the Children of Israel, Whosoever he be of the Children of Israel, or of the strangers who sojourn in Israel, who gives any of his seed unto Molech; he shall surely be put to death: the people of the land shall stone him with stones.

"And I will set My Face against that man, and will cut him off from among his people; because he has given of his seed unto Molech, to defile My Sanctuary, and to profane My Holy Name.

"And if the people of the land do any ways

hide their eyes from the man, when he gives of his seed unto Molech, and kill him not:

"Then I will set My Face against that man, and against his family, and will cut him off, and all who go a whoring after him, to commit whoredom with Molech, from among their people."

The death sentence is demanded for 18 particular capital crimes. They are:

1. A man who has sexual intercourse with his own mother (Lev. 20:11).

2. With his step-mother (Lev. 20:11).

3. With his daughter-in-law (Lev. 20:12).

4. A man who has sexual intercourse with a woman who is engaged to be married to someone else (Deut. 22:23-24).

5. A man who commits the sin of homosexuality (Lev. 20:13).

6. A man who has sexual intercourse with an animal (Lev. 20:15).

7. A woman who has sexual intercourse with an animal (Lev. 20:16).

8. A blasphemer (Lev. 24:10-16).

9. The worshipper of idols (Deut. 17:2-5).

10. The one who sacrifices his child to Molech (Lev. 20:2).

11. One who tries to contact the dead through one who has a familiar spirit, etc. (Lev. 20:27).

12. One who is a wizard (Lev. 20:27).

13. The false prophet (Deut. 13:6).

14. The enticer to idolatry (Deut. 13:11).

15. The witch (Lev. 20:17).

16. The profaner of the Sabbath (Num. 15:32-36).

17. He who curses his parent (Lev. 20:9).

18. The rebellious son (Deut. 21:18-21).

THE MANNER IN WHICH EXECUTIONS WERE CARRIED OUT

The execution, if demanded, was to take place outside the city limits (Lev. 24:14; Num. 15:36). As well, the witnesses upon whose evidence the criminal has been sentenced to death are to throw the first stone (Deut. 17:7).

The administrators of the Law during the second Temple decreed the following mode of carrying out the sentence:

On his way from the court of justice to the place of execution a herald preceded the criminal, exclaiming, *"So-and-so is being led*

NOTES

out to be stoned for this-and-this crime, and so-and-so are the witnesses; if anyone has to say anything that might save him, let him come forward and say it."

Within ten yards of the place of execution he was publicly admonished to confess his sins, within four yards he was stripped naked except a slight covering about his loins. After his hands had been bound, he was led upon a scaffolding about twice the height of a man. Here wine mingled with myrrh was mercifully given him to dull the pain of execution, and from here one of the witnesses pushed him down with great violence so that he fell upon his back. If the fall did not kill him, the other witnesses dashed a great stone on his breast, and if this did not kill him, all the people that stood by continued to throw stones until he was dead.

The corpse was then nailed to a tree, and afterwards burnt. Hereupon the relatives visited both the judges and the witnesses to show that they bore no hatred towards them, and that the sentence was just.

Not infrequently, however, the excited multitude resorted to taking the law into their own hands, when they wished to inflict summary justice. This description will explain why the Jews said to Christ that the woman had to be stoned, and why He replied to her accusers that he who is without sin should cast the first stone (Jn. 8:5-7); why the Jews wanted to stone Christ when they thought He was blaspheming (Jn. 10:31), and why they offered Him wine mingled with myrrh before His Crucifixion (Mat. 27:34, 38; Mk. 15:23) (Ellicott).

MOLECH

More specifically, the Text of our study is addressing children (seed) being offered to the heathenistic god, *"Molech."* The Old Testament often speaks of the fact that Israelites at times of apostasy made their children *"go through the fire to Molech"* (II Ki. 23:10; Jer. 7:31; 19:5). In some Passages the reference is clearly to a deity to whom human sacrifice was made, particularly in the Valley of Hinnom on the southwest of the Jerusalem hill (II Ki. 23:10; Jer. 32:35) at a site known as *"Topeth."* The deity is associated with Ammon in I Kings 11:7, where reference is made to *"the abomination of the Ammonites."* The worship of Molech seems to have been associated, as I think is obvious, with the sacrifice of children in the fire (Lev. 18:21; 20:2-5; II Ki. 17:31; 23:10; Jer. 32:35).

As we can see from the Text, the Law of Moses demanded the death of anyone who offered his child to Molech as a sacrifice. It is almost impossible to comprehend parents doing such a thing, but the further away that a person gets from God, the fact becomes painfully obvious that Satan takes over that person completely, with them becoming so deceived and warped that they will do almost anything, such as the sacrifice of their own children, and consider it to be a positive event.

Once more, we come face to face with the absolute depravity of the human nature, all brought about as a result of the Fall. And let the Reader understand that there is no way out of this dilemma, no way out of this horror, except through Christ and His Cross. Satan bows to no other power, but most definitely will bow to that power. That's why Paul said:

"For the preaching of the Cross is to them who perish foolishness; but unto us which are saved it is the Power of God" (I Cor. 1:18).

HOW IS THE PREACHING OF THE CROSS THE POWER OF GOD?

As we've already stated in this Volume, the Cross itself, as far as a wooden beam is concerned, has no power. As well, the death of Christ on the Cross contained no power, at least within itself. In fact, He died in weakness (II Cor. 13:4), but the Reader must understand that it was a contrived weakness. In other words, He could have used His power at any time to have stopped the Crucifixion. He said: *"Do you not know that I can now pray to My Father, and He shall presently give Me more than twelve legions of Angels?"* (Mat. 26:53). But He purposely didn't stop the Crucifixion, and because the Crucifixion was His purpose in coming to this world (Mat. 16:21; I Pet. 1:18-20).

The *"power"* of which Paul spoke, and which the Holy Spirit told him to say, had to do strictly with the Holy Spirit. Jesus paid the price at Calvary's Cross, thereby atoning for all sin, past, present, and future,

at least for all who will believe (Jn. 3:16). This completely destroyed Satan's right to hold man in bondage, inasmuch as sin has given him that legal right. But with all sin atoned, he has no more legal right, and is now helpless (Col. 2:14-15).

Upon Faith, evidenced by the Believer, and we speak of Faith squarely in the Cross of Christ (Rom. 5:1-2; Gal. 5:1-6; Eph. 2:8-9, 13-18), the Holy Spirit will then use His almighty power on our behalf (Rom. 8:1-2, 11). In fact, Paul told us exactly the type of power that He would use:

"But if the Spirit (Holy Spirit) *of Him* (God the Father) *Who raised up Jesus from the dead dwell in you, He Who raised up Christ from the dead shall also quicken your mortal bodies by His Spirit Who dwells in you"* (Rom. 8:11).

Now please understand, this is not speaking of the Resurrection which is yet to come, but rather, of power in this present life. Paul is speaking here of *"mortal bodies,"* which we now have, and not *"glorified bodies,"* which we will have in the coming Resurrection.

RESURRECTION LIFE

In the last few years we've heard much about *"Resurrection Living."* And regrettably, most of what we've heard has not been Scriptural. The reason I say that is because most of the people, virtually all of them, speaking of Resurrection Life, are doing so outside of the Cross. In other words, many of them are denigrating the Cross, or at least, giving the Cross no place. They think of themselves as having gone beyond the Cross, and thereby being people of the Resurrection.

In the first place, it's not possible to go beyond the Cross. If we do so, we lose our way, and do so totally!

The facts are, we can only *"be also in the likeness of His Resurrection,"* if we first understand that *"we have been planted together* (Christ and the Believer) *in the likeness of His death"* (Rom. 6:5). In other words, *"Resurrection Life,"* or *"Resurrection Living,"* which is the same thing, and which we all should have, is predicated totally and completely on our understanding that we have this solely because of what Christ did at the Cross. And if we do not understand that, to be sure, there will be no *"Resurrection Living."* The Holy Spirit Alone brings about all of these things in our lives, but He does so strictly on the premise of our understanding that everything comes to us solely through the Cross (Rom. 6:3-14). When the Believer understands this, and I continue to speak of understanding that everything comes to us through and by what Jesus did in the Sacrificial Offering of Himself on the Cross, and that our Faith must ever be in that Finished Work, the Holy Spirit, Who functions entirely within the parameters of that Finished Work will then exert Himself mightily on our behalf. The Believer now has *"Resurrection Living"* (Rom. 6:4).

TROUBLED CHRISTIANS

As I dictate these notes, there are millions of Christians who truly love the Lord, which means they are truly born-again, but are living less than victorious lives. This includes Preachers as well. The truth is, the Believer simply cannot live a victorious, overcoming, Christian life, unless the Believer fully understands that his victory comes solely through the Cross, and no other way (I Jn. 5:4). For a moment, let us address Preachers.

PREACHERS

Sometime back, I had the opportunity to address several hundreds of Preachers, most of them Pastors. I asked them the following question:

"When your people come to you, needing help as it regards sinful problems within their lives, what do you tell them?"

The place grew extremely quiet. Of course, I knew the answer to that question.

Some would tell these people that they need to read the Bible more, or pray more. Others would tell them that they need to get more involved in the Church. Others would say that the individuals in question simply need to *"try harder."* Others would even recommend a Psychologist.

While some of the things recommended would definitely be helpful, and I speak of prayer and Bible study, the truth is, none of these things will bring victory. While the Bible definitely will tell us where the victory

will be found, the mere fact of us reading it, thinking that such will guarantee victory, simply will not work. Someone has to tell the Believer what the Bible says as it regards perpetual victory, which means that he is now living as an overcomer.

The problem gets larger when we realize that the Preachers, at least for the most part, are having problems in their lives, the same as the persons they are trying to help. In fact, at this very moment, there are untold thousands of Preachers who truly love the Lord, and are doing their very best in the Ministry, but are bound by alcohol, by drugs of some nature, by gambling, by immorality, which can come in many stripes. In fact, if the Preacher doesn't understand the Cross as it regards Sanctification, and precious few do, in some way, the works of the flesh are manifesting themselves in their lives. While it may not be the vices I have mentioned, it will definitely be something. The list is long, even as Paul told us in Galatians 5:19-21.

Untold thousands of Preachers, whether they realize it or not, are preaching heresy. In fact, if they are not preaching the Cross, in some way, they are preaching heresy, which is a work of the flesh. But yet, very few Christians think of such as a work of the flesh, actually limiting the flesh to particular vices which we have named.

The truth is, unless one understands the Cross, Preachers included, as it regards our Sanctification, and the part the Cross plays in that tremendous work, which is the single most important work for the Christian, that particular individual simply cannot live, no matter how hard he tries, a victorious life. He may be sincere, earnest, honest, and very zealous. He may try harder and harder, but not only will there be no victory, Satan will be able to cause untold difficulties, with those difficulties, in fact, becoming worse and worse, and despite the individual trying harder and harder. Please let me be as blunt as I can:

Unless one understands what Paul taught as it regards the Cross and Sanctification, which is found in the Sixth Chapter of Romans, one simply cannot live a victorious life. Now the trouble is, most every Preacher will quickly tell you that they understand

Romans, Chapter 6. But the truth is, most don't!

What everyone seems to forget or fail to realize, the sin nature is of far greater power and strength than any one of us could begin to imagine. Incorporated with the sin nature is the *"law of sin and death."* And there is only one power on Earth that is more powerful than the law of sin and death, and that is *"The Law of the Spirit of Life in Christ Jesus"* (Rom. 8:2). If we think we can overcome the law of sin and death by any other method, to use a southern expression, we are whistling Dixie. And as the South lost that war, likewise, the Believer is going to lose his war.

WHY IS IT SO HARD FOR THE CHURCH TO FULLY ACCEPT THE CROSS?

In fact, most Churches would probably inform all and sundry that they believe in the Cross. And quite possibly they do, as far as it goes. But most people as it regards the Cross, limit it only to the Salvation experience, and have no knowledge at all as it regards the Cross concerning Sanctification. If you mention such a thing to them, you draw a blank. In other words, they don't know what you are talking about. In fact, and as we've already stated any number of times in this Volume, Satan has been so successful in moving the Church away from the Cross, that any more, it hardly knows where it is. The truth is, the modern Church is in worse condition spiritually than it has been at any time, I believe, since the Reformation. It's all because of an improper understanding of the Cross, or else an outright denial of the Cross, as do the Word of Faith people. When individuals refer to the Cross as the *"worst defeat in human history,"* which the Word of Faith people do, then we begin to get the idea as to how much opposed they are to the Cross of Christ. While in some certain circumstances they may pay lip service to the Cross, it will only be in passing. The truth is, they don't believe in the Blood, they don't believe in the Cross, they don't believe in the Sacrifice of Christ, rather making up some will-o-wisp story about Jesus dying as a sinner and going to the burning side of Hell, and there being

tormented for three days and nights, before finally being born-again. Never mind that there is nothing like that in the Word of God, it is still gulped down by a gullible Christian public. Why?

The main thrust of the Word of Faith people is not correct doctrine, but rather *"money."* Unfortunately, there seems to be enough greed in all of us to make the money gospel very successful. The further truth is, the only ones getting rich are the Preachers, with the people not only not getting rich, but losing what little they do have. In fact, the same spirit that pulls the gambler into the casinos pulls gullible Christians into this maw.

The addicted gambler doesn't seem to realize that these billion dollar casinos are not built by losing money, but rather by winning. And it's out of the pockets of the gullible gamblers that these great hotel-casinos are built.

Likewise, as it regards the *"money gospel,"* the money only goes one way, and that's, as stated, into the hands of the Preachers, who need it in order to buy a second or third Rolls Royce. God help us! But the poor people keep going and keep giving, even more and more, thinking their jackpot is just around the corner. That's the trouble; it's always just around the corner, and never in their personal pockets. And that's the way it's going to stay!

What is being preached in those circles, despite its popularity, is not the Gospel. In fact, these Preachers, pure and simple, are preaching *"another Jesus, promoted by another spirit, which plays out to another gospel"* (II Cor. 11:4).

While Israel was warned not to sacrifice their children to the heathenistic god, Molech, modern Christians are in fact, sacrificing their children to the heathen god of false doctrine (I Tim. 4:1). The only difference is, the deaths in most cases are slower with the modern counterparts.

The Scripture plainly says that God would set His Face against the followers of the heathenistic gods, and to be sure, He is definitely setting His Face against the followers of the gods of false doctrine. Demon spirits are, in fact, the instigators of both.

SANCTIFY YOURSELVES

Verses 6 through 8 read: *"And the soul that turns after such as have familiar spirits, and after wizards, to go a whoring after them, I will even set My Face against that soul, and will cut him off from among his people.*

"Sanctify yourselves therefore, and be ye holy: for I am the LORD your God.

"And you shall keep My Statutes, and do them: I am the LORD which sanctify you."

The Lord promises judgment upon all of His people, who would seek the help of the spirit world of darkness, and not help that comes from the Lord. In fact, any people, irrespective as to whom they might be, who seeks the help of evil spirits, for evil spirits are behind all such activity, such as fortune telling, etc., sooner or later, those people will suffer the Judgment of God. Unfortunately, there are many nations of the world, which have been totally taken over by demon spirits, which always result in poverty, lack of freedom, oppression, sickness, and disease. Jesus said of Satan that he, *"steal, kills, and destroys"* (Jn. 10:10).

The spirit world is just as real as the world in which we live, and in fact, even more so because it's much older. That world consists of the spirit world of light, headed up by the Godhead and Angels. The spirit world of darkness is headed up by Satan, who himself is a fallen angel, plus other fallen angels, referred to as *"principalities, powers, rulers of the darkness of this world, and spiritual wickedness in high places"* (Eph. 6:12). As well, there are myriads of demon spirits in the spirit world of darkness.

DEMON SPIRITS

Some have claimed that demon spirits are fallen angels; however, that is incorrect. There is no record in the Word of God of Angels inhabiting anyone, whether those Angels be righteous or unrighteous.

Sometime in eternity past, Lucifer led a revolution against God, of which we are given a small amount of information in Isaiah, Chapter 14, and Ezekiel, Chapter 28. Satan was then known as Lucifer (Isa. 14:12). According to Ezekiel, Chapter 28, he was at least

one of, if not the most powerful and beautiful Angel ever created by God. For an undetermined period of time, he served the Lord in Faithfulness and Righteousness. But there came a time that he rebelled against God, with one-third of the Angels falling with him (Rev. 12:4). From the moment of that revolution, a war has raged between the spirit world of light and the spirit world of darkness. Of course, God is Almighty, and could easily dispose of Satan in a moment's time, plus all of his fallen angels and demon spirits. But for reasons known only to Himself, the Lord has allowed the Evil One to continue for a period of time; however, the Word of God also proclaims his eternal doom, which is shortly to come to pass (Rev., Chpt. 20).

As to exactly how demon spirit originated, we aren't told. We know that God did not create them in this fashion, even as He did not create Satan and the fallen angels as they now are. So something happened that caused demon spirits to be what they presently are. So what was it?

Some Bible Scholars think, and I concur with this thought, that demon spirits came from the habitation of the Earth which was occupied before Adam. There is every evidence that there was a civilization on the Earth at that time, ruled over by Lucifer, when he was serving God in Righteousness and purity. Whenever he fell, trying to usurp authority over God, whatever type of created beings were on the Earth at that time, evidently threw in their lot with the Evil One, hence these bodiless beings, whom the Bible refers to as evil spirits.

THE GAP THEORY

As well, I subscribe to that which is oftentimes referred to as the *"gap theory."* I'm speaking of what transpired between Genesis 1:1 and Genesis 1:2. We know that God did not originally create the Earth *"without form and void."* It became that way after some type of cataclysmic convulsion. That convulsion had to be the revolution of Lucifer.

And more than likely, the pre-Adamite Earth accounts for the dinosaurs, and creatures of that particular nature (Jer. 4:23-27).

There is no record in the Word of God, at least since the time of Adam, which accounts for dinosaurs and such like creatures. But yet we know these things existed, and if they existed during Old Testament Times, it is positive that the Word of God would have had something to say about these creatures. It said nothing, because at that time, due to the upheaval that took place between Genesis 1:1 and Genesis 1:2, they were made extinct. We have no way of knowing from the Word of God, and because it is silent on the subject, just how long this revolution lasted, when Satan began to attempt to usurp authority over God. It could have been a few months, or a few years, or several decades, or even hundreds of years. But it is almost positive that this is what happened.

WHAT TYPE OF CREATURES WERE THEY WHO RULED WITH LUCIFER BEFORE HIS REBELLION?

If in fact our summation is correct, we know they were creatures of intelligence. But I think whatever they were, the record is clear that they were not created by God in the same class as man.

Originally, and I speak of the creation of Adam and Eve, their intelligence knew no bounds. For instance, Adam was able to give scientific names to all of the animals (Gen. 2:19-20), which name for each animal or fowl incorporated the characteristics of that particular creation. And those names have not changed from then until now. So it should go without saying that this man, the first Adam, and of course we are speaking of the time before the Fall, had an intelligence that literally defies all description. As well, all of this completely debunks the mindless prattle called evolution.

For us to see and know what man truly was intended to be, we have to look at Christ, Who was the True Man (I Tim. 2:5; I Cor. 15:45-49).

At the Fall, Adam fell from the high and lofty position of total God-consciousness, down to the far, far lower level of self-consciousness. Whereas the Divine Nature ruled him (II Pet. 1:4), now the sin nature rules him, and has ruled unredeemed man ever since. This is the cause of evil in the Earth, the cause of all wars, man's inhumanity to man, etc.

HOLINESS

Israel of old sanctified themselves, as Verse 7 demands, by obeying the Commandments of the Lord. But the truth was, before the Cross, individuals could only try, which they were obligated to do, but really could not effect Sanctification. Due to the Fall, man simply could not keep the Law, even believing man.

The Holy Spirit was then very limited as to what He could do for man, in that He could not dwell within him permanently, and because the blood of bulls and goats simply could not take away sins (Heb. 10:4; Jn. 14:16-17). So before the Cross, man was at a terrible disadvantage.

The Law was God's Standard of Righteousness. It was that which was right, and it was not merely right simply because God said it, but because in fact, it was and is right. But as stated, man in his helpless state, even in the best of environments, simply could not keep this which God demanded. So, not being able to keep the Law, even though some of them tried very hard, what was their recourse?

Their recourse was the Sacrificial System set up by the Lord, in order for sins to be atoned. And to be sure, the Sacrifices themselves could not sanctify anyone, but were meant to point the faith of the individual toward the One Whom the Sacrifices represented, namely our Lord. So in effect, Salvation then came by people looking forward to the Cross, as it now comes by people looking backward to the Cross; but however it is done, the Cross is the central point, the focal point, of history and of humanity. In fact, everything in the Bible, in one way or the other, drives toward the Cross. The Sacrificial, Atoning, Substitutionary, Efficacious Work of Christ in the giving of Himself in Sacrifice, and doing so by the shedding of His Precious Blood, alone is what salvaged humanity. That's why Paul told us that we must preach the Cross (I Cor. 1:17-18, 21, 23; 2:2).

True Sanctification, which refers to a person being set apart exclusively for God, can only be done by the Holy Spirit, Who performs His Work in our hearts and lives, according to what Christ has done at the Cross, and out Faith in that Finished Work. It is a terrible thing for a Believer to make something else the object of his faith. Paul addressed that in no uncertain terms.

CHRIST SHALL PROFIT YOU NOTHING

The entirety of the Epistle to the Galatians is to oppose the doctrine of Galatianism. And what is that doctrine?

It is that we are saved by the operation of Faith, and sanctified by the operation of self. In other words, we can sanctify ourselves, which means to do so by our own machinations, etc. This is what was happening:

The Galatians, who were Gentiles, had come to Christ under Paul, or else one of the Preachers who had been trained under the Ministry of the great Apostle. Consequently, they had been taught correctly as it regards the Cross.

But after Paul left the area, going elsewhere in order to establish Churches, false teachers from Judea came into these particular Churches in Galatia, however many there were, and began to demean and degrade the Gospel of Grace. While they paid lip service to Christ and the Cross, they told the people that in order to live the life they ought to live, they also had to keep the Law. They were speaking of the Law of Moses. That's why Paul said: *"If you be circumcised, Christ shall profit you nothing"* (Gal. 5:2). In other words, these Jewish teachers from Judea, and most likely from Jerusalem, were telling them that to be a good Christian, they had to add Law to Grace. Of course, it was impossible for these Gentiles to fully keep the Law, considering that they lived many hundreds of miles from Jerusalem. But even if they had lived in Jerusalem, this was an entirely wrong doctrine, inasmuch as Christ had already satisfied all the demands of the Law. These false teachers were telling the men that they had to be circumcised, and that the little boy babies had to be circumcised at eight days old, etc. They were not speaking of health advantages, but rather a religious ritual.

Circumcision had been the seal of the Covenant of God with the Jews. And now, these false teachers were attempting to continue to promote this practice, claiming that

NOTES

one had to do such if one was to be a good Christian, or whatever type of terminology they may have used.

Paul would counter all of this by bluntly saying: *"For in Jesus Christ neither circumcision availeth anything, nor uncircumcision; but faith which works by love"* (Gal. 5:6).

Unfortunately, the problem of Galatianism did not die with the Galatians. It is alive and well in our midst presently. In fact, due to a paucity of knowledge as it regards the Cross, most of the modern Church functions from a position of attempting to sanctify themselves in all the wrong ways.

Sanctification comes instantly to the believing sinner upon their accepting Christ. It is a work of Grace (I Cor. 6:11). That is the Believer's position and standing in Christ. It is a position that does not change, irrespective of our spiritual ups and downs.

But then the Holy Spirit attempts to bring our state up to our standing, which is a function that really never ends (I Thess. 5:23). And how does He do this?

THE MANNER IN WHICH THE HOLY SPIRIT SANCTIFIES THE BELIEVER

As Paul stated in Galatians 5:6, it is all done by Faith. And what do we mean by that?

The Believer is to constantly evidence Faith in Christ and the Cross, understanding, as we've already said repeatedly, that everything comes to him through and by what Jesus did at the Cross. Ever making that the object of his Faith, the Holy Spirit will then perform and work mightily within the Believer's life (Rom. 8:1-2, 11).

That's not hard at all; however, many Believers refuse to believe what I've just said. It's the age old problem of pride. It came with the Fall. Man thinks that he can do what only God can do.

There is no human being alive, no matter how Godly he is thought to be, who can sanctify himself by his own machinations, ability, and strength. As well, it doesn't matter how much he claims to be trusting Christ, unless his Faith is in the Cross, the truth is, and as again we've already said repeatedly, he will find himself serving and trusting *"another Jesus"* (II Cor. 11:4).

The major problem is unbelief! To fully

believe in the Cross, one has to see himself as helpless, and God as Almighty. While most Christians definitely look at God as Almighty, they do not at all think of themselves as helpless. They think they can whip sin, can beat sin, can whip the Devil, can do all the things that we trumpet so loudly, and then on top of that, we have the audacity to refer to what we do as *"Faith."* It's not Faith; it's mostly self-will, i.e., *"ego."* It is one of the clinging vines of the Fall. That's the reason that most, especially Preachers, have to have their back to the proverbial wall, before they will finally admit that they can't live the life they know they ought to live, and will then begin to fully trust Christ, which means that one is placing his Faith exclusively in the Cross, not allowing it to stray elsewhere. But regrettably, most of us don't come to that place easily. Most have to be brought to a place to where they are stripped of everything, before they will finally heed the Word of God, and conduct themselves in true Faith, which is to believe Christ, and His Cross.

I realize that what I am saying, I've already said it any number of times in this one Volume, and I've done it with deliberation.

In the last several years, I've learned how hard it is for some people to understand the great Message of the Cross. And I'm not saying that as a put-down, but rather as a matter of fact. There have been so little teaching and preaching on the Cross in the last several decades that for all practical purposes, the modern Church is Cross illiterate. And as well, the Cross demands a totally different way of life. It is a life of total trust in Christ, understanding that what He does for us is done totally and completely through the Sacrificial Offering of Himself, and our Faith in that Finished Work (Rom. 6:3-14; 8:1-2, 11; Eph. 2:13-18; Col. 2:14-15).

Once the Believer begins to understand the Cross, almost everything within his life will change. He will then begin to see just how much religion was actually ruling and guiding his life, which did not fall out to a positive result. As I've already stated, he may have to leave his Church, his Denomination, and his friends. Many, regrettably, are not willing to do that. But if we are to have what Christ wants us to have, we must deny

NOTES

ourselves, and take up the Cross daily, and follow Him (Lk. 9:23-24).

In Verse 7, the Lord told Israel to *"sanctify yourselves,"* and then in Verse 8, He says again, *"I am the LORD which sanctify you."* There is no contradiction!

They were to sanctify themselves by submitting themselves to the Commands of the Lord. In this, the Lord accomplished the Work, as He Alone can accomplish the Work.

(9) "FOR EVERY ONE WHO CURSES HIS FATHER OR HIS MOTHER SHALL BE SURELY PUT TO DEATH: HE HAS CURSED HIS FATHER OR HIS MOTHER; HIS BLOOD SHALL BE UPON HIM.

(10) "AND THE MAN WHO COMMITS ADULTERY WITH ANOTHER MAN'S WIFE, EVEN HE WHO COMMITS ADULTERY WITH HIS NEIGHBOR'S WIFE, THE ADULTERER AND THE ADULTERESS SHALL SURELY BE PUT TO DEATH.

(11) "AND THE MAN WHO LIES WITH HIS FATHER'S WIFE HAS UNCOVERED HIS FATHER'S NAKEDNESS: BOTH OF THEM SHALL SURELY BE PUT TO DEATH; THEIR BLOOD SHALL BE UPON THEM.

(12) "AND IF A MAN LIE WITH HIS DAUGHTER-IN-LAW, BOTH OF THEM SHALL SURELY BE PUT TO DEATH: THEY HAVE WROUGHT CONFUSION; THEIR BLOOD SHALL BE UPON THEM.

(13) "IF A MAN ALSO LIE WITH MANKIND, AS HE LIES WITH A WOMAN, BOTH OF THEM HAVE COMMITTED AN ABOMINATION: THEY SHALL SURELY BE PUT TO DEATH; THEIR BLOOD SHALL BE UPON THEM.

(14) "AND IF A MAN TAKE A WIFE AND HER MOTHER, IT IS WICKEDNESS: THEY SHALL BE BURNT WITH FIRE, BOTH HE AND THEY; THAT THERE BE NO WICKEDNESS AMONG YOU.

(15) "AND IF A MAN LIE WITH A BEAST, HE SHALL SURELY BE PUT TO DEATH: AND YOU SHALL SLAY THE BEAST.

(16) "AND IF A WOMAN APPROACH UNTO ANY BEAST, AND LIE DOWN THERETO, YOU SHALL KILL THE WOMAN, AND THE BEAST: THEY SHALL SURELY BE PUT TO DEATH; THEIR BLOOD SHALL BE UPON THEM.

(17) "AND IF A MAN SHALL TAKE HIS

NOTES

SISTER, HIS FATHER'S DAUGHTER, OR HIS MOTHER'S DAUGHTER, AND SEE HER NAKEDNESS, AND SHE SEE HIS NAKEDNESS; IT IS A WICKED THING; THEY SHALL BE CUT OFF IN THE SIGHT OF THEIR PEOPLE: HE HAS UNCOVERED HIS SISTER'S NAKEDNESS; HE SHALL BEAR HIS INIQUITY.

(18) "AND IF A MAN SHALL LIE WITH A WOMAN HAVING HER SICKNESS, AND SHALL UNCOVER HER NAKEDNESS; HE HAS DISCOVERED HER FOUNTAIN, AND SHE HAS UNCOVERED THE FOUNTAIN OF HER BLOOD: AND BOTH OF THEM SHALL BE CUT OFF FROM AMONG THEIR PEOPLE.

(19) "AND YOU SHALL NOT UNCOVER THE NAKEDNESS OF YOUR MOTHER'S SISTER, NOR OF YOUR FATHER'S SISTER: FOR HE UNCOVERS HIS NEAR KIN: THEY SHALL BEAR THEIR INIQUITY.

(20) "AND IF A MAN SHALL LIE WITH HIS UNCLE'S WIFE, HE HAS UNCOVERED HIS UNCLE'S NAKEDNESS: THEY SHALL BEAR THEIR SIN; THEY SHALL DIE CHILDLESS.

(21) "AND IF A MAN SHALL TAKE HIS BROTHER'S WIFE, IT IS AN UNCLEAN THING: HE HAS UNCOVERED HIS BROTHER'S NAKEDNESS; THEY SHALL BE CHILDLESS."

The exegesis is:

1. All of these are moral laws, and as such, they have not changed, even as they cannot change. It was sin then, and it is sin now.

2. These are God's Standard of Righteousness and Holiness. To be sure, they aren't of man. Man has repeatedly tried to change them, but the fact remains, if these laws are disregarded or ignored, the results will not be pleasant. A nation can destroy itself doing such!

3. If we are to notice, the penalty for committing these particular sins, i.e., "crimes," was harsh indeed! It is not known as to exactly how many people were actually executed. As we shall see, further rulings made it very difficult in many cases for execution to be carried out.

THE CURSING OF PARENTS

Verse 9 reads: "For every one who curses his father or his mother shall be surely put to death: he has cursed his father or his mother; his blood shall be upon him."

As we can see here, the Lord places the cursing of a mother or father by a child into a very heinous category. In fact, no civilization of the world, of which I am aware, places such emphasis accordingly. Why? Better yet, why did the Lord place such emphasis on this particular sin?

Actually, in the Hebrew, it actually says, "He has cursed his father!" "He has cursed his mother!" It is written thusly in order to mark the crime as eminently heinous. As asked, why?

I'm sure that most sane people would regard this thing as very wrong; however, precious few would think of the penalty as being death. And as well, under the New Covenant, even though the crime remains heinous, the death penalty is not called for now.

In one sense of the word, the people of Israel were different than the modern Church. While both belonged to God, and both were and are very important, the purpose of each was a little different.

Israel was being prepared to give the world the Word of God, of which the first five Books of Moses were the beginning, and as well, to serve as the womb of the Messiah. In other words, they were to bring the Messiah into the world, the Saviour of men, which they ultimately did. As a result, they were to be a "holy people."

The Church is called upon to live the Word of God, which was given to the Jews, but supplemented by the New Covenant, brought about by Christ on the Cross. While the Jews served as the womb of the Messiah, the Church is supposed to have the Messiah, i.e., "our Lord," living in our hearts, and doing so on a continuing basis (Gal. 2:20). The mission of the Church is not exactly the same as the mission was as it regards the Jews of old. While both are to be holy, it was the Jews alone who were to bring in the Messiah. If they had engaged in these crimes to any degree, they would have destroyed themselves as a people, which would have greatly hindered the Coming of Christ. So the penalties for breaking these particular laws were harsh, even as they had to be harsh. Much was at stake!

ADULTERY

Verse 10 reads: *"And the man who commits adultery with another man's wife, even he who commits adultery with his neighbor's wife, the adulterer and the adulteress shall surely be put to death."*

To break these laws would mean that the land had become a land of sin. Its cities and its plains would cry up to Heaven! Children cursed their parents! Neighbors and relatives live in adultery with each other! The son dishonors the bed of his step-mother; the father-in-law that of his daughter-in-law! Men burn in unnatural lust (Rom. 1:27); and the same man takes mother and daughter as his wives!

Under the New Covenant, should the penalty of death be imposed for such sins?

If they should have been, then the Lord would have done so. He didn't include these penalties in the New Covenant, and because they are no longer necessary. But let the Reader understand that adultery in the life of a Believer is just as hateful in the sight of God as it was with Israel of old. God does not change as it regards moral situations. And even though the death penalty is not demanded presently, spiritual death will definitely follow those who commit such sins, unless they are Scripturally delivered by the Power of God.

THEIR BLOOD SHALL BE UPON THEM

Verses 11 and 12 read: *"And the man who lies with his father's wife has uncovered his father's nakedness: both of them shall surely be put to death; their blood shall be upon them.*

"And if a man lie with his daughter-in-law, both of them shall surely be put to death: they have wrought confusion; their blood shall be upon them."

The idea of the statement, *"Their blood shall be upon them,"* which is used a number of times, pertains to the fact that the penalty for the crime is their fault. Men love to blame God, while at the same time, absolving themselves of all blame. The truth is, God is never to blame, and man is always to blame. Even when we sin through ignorance, such action

portrays the state of the heart. In some way that is true, which writes a dismal picture of the depravity of mankind.

Men are fond of saying that God has made them like they are. No He didn't! While it is true that all men are born in original sin, the Lord has made provision for man to get out of that sin. But man addresses that privilege in several ways:

First of all, he claims to be right with God, when all the time he isn't. man is fond of doing that, with this problem being very widespread. He is obviously going in the wrong direction, but claiming all the while to be going in the right direction. He claims to be right with God, while at the same time, opposing the Holy Spirit. But he does not seem to see the problem, simply because he is deceived. In fact, deception is one of Satan's greatest weapons. That's the reason the Lord warned all and sundry that if in fact they found themselves facing the death penalty, *"Their blood shall be upon them,"* i.e., *"It is their fault and not the fault of God."*

HOMOSEXUALITY

Verse 13 reads: *"If a man also lie with mankind, as he lies with a woman, both of them have committed an abomination: they shall surely be put to death; their blood shall be upon them."*

The Holy Spirit through Moses refers to the sin of homosexuality as *"an abomination."*

"Abomination" in the Hebrew is *"towebah,"* and means *"something disgusting, an abhorrence."*

Is it a worse sin than adultery or incest?

All of these sins demand the death penalty, but yet, as stated, the Holy Spirit did refer to homosexuality as *"an abomination."* This portrays men and women engaged in unnatural lust (Rom. 1:27).

ONLY ONE CURE

There is only one cure for homosexuality, and one can as well throw in all vices. That cure is the Cross! Make no mistake about it, man has no cure for these problems, and religion doesn't either. To be sure, the world of humanistic psychology holds no answer either. The best these particular efforts can do is to try to get the individual to live with the problem.

The Cross is the answer, and the only answer. In fact, every single person bound by the terrible darkness of homosexuality, plus gambling, plus alcohol, plus drugs in any capacity, plus envy, greed, unforgiveness, jealousy, etc., can have total, complete, and absolute victory within their hearts and lives.

HOW DOES VICTORY COME BY THE CROSS?

An acceptance of the Cross, of course, is an acceptance in totality of the Lord Jesus Christ. It is a way of life, a total consecration, a total dedication. It draws the line regarding worldliness, regarding false doctrine, regarding apostasy of any shape.

The Cross is not something that one can add to their present belief system. A proper understanding of the Cross of Christ is a complete and total belief system of its own. In fact, it will not in any way tolerate any additions or deletions.

A proper understanding of the Cross gives one a proper understanding of the Word of God. In fact, one cannot really understand the Word as one should, unless one understands the Cross. The story of the Cross is the story of the Bible. They are one and the same. And to the degree that one misunderstands the Cross, or ignores the Cross, or repudiates the Cross, to that degree will they misinterpret the Word of God. In fact, this is the major cause, an improper understanding of the Cross, of all false doctrine.

As well, the Cross cuts all religious ties. Dependence on Churches, Ordinances, so-called Sacraments, rules and regulations, Denominations, is out.

A proper understanding of the Cross is a proper understanding of Christ. In fact, one cannot really trust and serve Christ as one ought to, without properly understanding and embracing the Cross. To do so puts one in the place and position of serving *"another Jesus"* (II Cor. 11:4).

In fact, concerning all of this, Jesus said: *"If any man will come after Me, let him deny himself, and take up his cross daily, and follow Me.*

"For whosoever will save his life shall lose it: but whosoever will lose his life for My

NOTES

sake, the same shall save it" (Lk. 9:23-24).

But the sad truth is, most definitely want the victory the Cross brings, but they do not want to embrace the Cross. But if we are to have that which the Sacrifice of Christ brings, we must embrace Christ in this respect wholeheartedly.

BESTIALITY

Verses 14 through 16 read: *"And if a man take a wife and her mother, it is wickedness: they shall be burnt with fire, both he and they; that there be no wickedness among you.*

"And if a man lie with a beast, he shall surely be put to death: and you shall slay the beast.

"And if a woman approach unto any beast, and lie down thereto, you shall kill the woman, and the beast: they shall surely be put to death; their blood shall be upon them."

The necessity of the Lord having to give these commands and warnings portrays to us the glaring fact of man's total depravity. Man is not a little bit wrong; he is totally wrong! He is not a little bit out of the way; he is totally out of the way! He is not somewhat controlled by sin, but totally controlled by sin! And there is a glaring truth in all of this that must not be overlooked.

Sin is degenerative. In other words, sin steadily takes the individual ever downward. There is no such thing as coming to a particular place and stopping. That is not the nature of sin.

It should be understood that of the 20 million alcoholics in the United States, not a single one of these individuals started this terrible lifestyle by thinking they would be an alcoholic. Not a single compulsive gambler ever began as such. The drug addict is the same thing. In fact, every facet of evil or immorality always takes the person much, much further than he wants to go.

While at the beginning, sin may seem to be a lark, after awhile, it's like a merry-go-round, which keeps getting faster and faster, with the person wanting to get off, but unable to do so.

THE PLEASURES OF SIN

The Bible uses the term *"the pleasures of sin"* (Heb. 11:25). But it also states that those pleasures are only *"for a season,"* meaning that it's for a short time. It starts out as a pleasure, but very soon, it becomes a bondage. It starts out as a lark, but very soon becomes a liability. It starts out exciting, but soon becomes destructive. In fact, the Bible also says, *"The wages of sin is death"* (Rom. 6:23).

A WICKED THING

Verses 17 through 21 read: *"And if a man shall take his sister, his father's daughter, or his mother's daughter, and see her nakedness, and she see his nakedness; it is a wicked thing; and they shall be cut off in the sight of their people: he has uncovered his sister's nakedness; he shall bear his iniquity.*

"And if a man shall lie with a woman having her sickness, and shall uncover her nakedness; he has discovered her fountain, and she has uncovered the fountain of her blood: and both of them shall be cut off from among their people.

"And you shall not uncover the nakedness of your mother's sister, nor of your father's sister: for he uncovers his near kin: they shall bear their iniquity.

"And if a man shall lie with his uncle's wife, he has uncovered his uncle's nakedness: they shall bear their sin; they shall die childless.

"And if a man shall take his brother's wife, it is an unclean thing: he has uncovered his brother's nakedness; they shall be childless."

These things, as we shall see, were dominant in the surrounding nations. In fact, they were dominant in the occupants of the land of Canaan, before it was occupied by Israel.

Some would claim that we do not need this type of preaching. They refer to it as *"negative."*

I would suggest that they should read the Bible. They should tell the Holy Spirit that He doesn't know what He's talking about by *"preaching against sin."*

Others would claim that we are not to mention sin in any form, and by not mentioning it, we will experience victory over sin. How foolish can we be! Why do you think the Holy Spirit put all of these commands and warnings in the Word of God? If merely refusing to mention them, which means that

NOTES

we don't preach against them any more, guarantees that these sins will not afflict us, somebody needed to have told the Holy Spirit this great truth.

Well, the facts are, those things aren't true, therefore, aren't a Truth, but rather a lie!

Men have to be told what is right and what is wrong, and they have to be told what is right and what is wrong on the authority of the Word of God. That means the Preacher is to preach at times a positive Message, and at times he is to preach a negative Message. He who is for something is, at the same time, against something. He who loves something, at the same time, hates something. It cannot be any other way.

Some of these so-called Saints scream loud whenever we point out false doctrine, and even point out who is preaching it, and what they have said. The truth is, they squeal because they have been squeezed. In other words, their sin is being exposed to the full light of the Word of God, and darkness hates light. Let's say that again, and because it's very, very important!

DARKNESS HATES LIGHT

That means that those who walk in darkness seek to avoid the light at all costs, because, as stated, light always exposes what is in the darkness.

In the last few months (as I dictate these notes in early October of 2002), we have felt led of the Lord to expose particular false doctrines. I speak specifically of the so-called Word of Faith doctrine, which is so popular among some Pentecostals and virtually all Charismatics. It has even made inroads into the Baptist and Holiness directions. And because it is so popular, even though many Preachers know that it is wrong, deadly wrong, which means it's grossly unscriptural; still, they will not say anything publicly against this error. But the Lord has told us to say something, and that we are attempting to do.

To make it very clear as to what is being said, we have called the names of the principal Preachers who are upholding this doctrine, and giving quotes verbatim from their messages as it regards what they teach and believe. In other words, we are not hiding behind shaded phraseology that says everything, but at the same time, says nothing. We are doing our very best, and by the help of the Lord, to make our statements as clear as possible, so there will be absolutely no misunderstanding as to what is being said.

I'm speaking of our teaching and preaching over SonLife Radio, over our Telecast, and in Family Worship Center, and as well, in Donnie's Meetings all around the world.

To be sure, the howls of protest were loud and long, when we began to take this stand. As stated, darkness does not desire the light. When light is shown upon the darkness, it exposes what is there; and if there is anything that the Truth does, it exposes the lie. And let the Reader understand for *"Truth"* to be what it ought to be, in other words, for it to be the Truth and nothing but the Truth, one must not only know and see the positive side, but as well, the negative side. What is right must be proclaimed, and at the same time, what is wrong must be proclaimed. This is the method of the Word of God, which means it's the method of the Holy Spirit.

Look at Paul's writings; in His 14 Epistles, there is as much correction, which speaks of the negative side, as there is proclamation, which speaks of the positive side.

Some Preachers claim that all we have to do is preach the positive side of truth, and the other will take care of itself. Not so! They say that, because they don't want to take the heat that the negative side will bring.

Paul could have soft-peddled the negative side, and possibly he would have stayed out of prison. Jeremiah could have done the same thing, and possibly he would have stayed out of the dungeon. In fact, the list is long. Isaiah could have taken only the positive side, and more than likely he would not have died a martyr's death, being placed in a log, and sawed asunder, tradition tells us.

Our Lord could have easily taken only the positive side, but if one looks at the Twenty-third Chapter of Matthew, plus much of his other teaching, one will see that he struck the negative side far harder than any other Preacher or Prophet who has ever lived.

In every century, Satan comes up with a new wrinkle on an old lie. In fact, there are no new lies, just different ways of proposing

NOTES

and presenting them. In whatever form the lies take, the end result is to pull the Believer away from the Cross. Satan doesn't care too very much what we preach, just as long as we don't preach the Cross.

THE WHOLE BURNT-OFFERING AND THE MEAT-OFFERING

These two Offerings we have already studied; however, please allow me for a moment to refresh your mind.

As the Whole Burnt-Offering symbolized the Perfection of Christ in the Perfect Sacrifice of Himself, which satisfied the demands of a thrice-Holy God, and which perfection, incidentally, was given to the sinner, the Meat-Offering signified the Perfect Life of Christ. But as we note Chapters 1 and 2 of this Book of Moses, we note that the Whole Burnt-Offering came first, followed by the Meat-Offering. The order of these Offerings, as with all the Offerings, was designed by the Holy Spirit. The Perfect Life of Christ, symbolized by the Meat-Offering, as wonderful, glorious, and necessary as it was, had to be subordinate to the Whole Burnt-Offering, which typified the Cross. While a part of the Meat-Offering was burnt on the Altar, as well signifying the Cross, which in effect stated that this Perfect Life of Christ was to be offered up, still, the greater part of the Meat-Offering signified, as stated, the Perfect Life of Christ. But here is the truth we must not forget:

As wonderful as was the Life of Christ, as wonderful as was His Perfection, His healings, His miracles, and all that pertains to that Life, we must not forget that the major thrust and theme of His Life was to go to the Cross (Mat. 16:21-25).

As a Preacher of the Gospel, I must preach all that pertained to that Perfect Life of Christ, which pertains to healing, prosperity, miracles, etc. But my Messages in this capacity must never sustain the emphasis, that always being the Cross of Christ. Satan has achieved his purpose, if the major theme of our Ministry, of our understanding of the Word, and of our putting the Word into practice in our hearts and lives, is anything but the Cross of Christ. The emphasis must always be on the Cross, with everything else, as important as it might be in its own right, being subordinate to that great Finished Work of Christ. Again I quote Paul:

"For Christ sent me not to baptize, but to preach the Gospel: not with wisdom of words, lest the Cross of Christ should be made of none effect" (I Cor. 1:17).

The Church makes a grave mistake presently when it makes prosperity its theme, or Divine Healing, or anything else for that matter. These things mentioned, and many things we haven't mentioned, are very important in their own right. They should be preached and practiced. They should be believed and acted upon, and because the Meat-Offering, in essence, proclaims these things, the Perfect Life of Christ, as a definite part of the Ministry of our Lord. And as well, that Ministry, in its totality, was strictly for us. But again I emphasize, the emphasis, the center of attention, the major thrust, the all-important aspect of our preaching, our lives, and our living, must always, and without exception, be the Cross of Christ. Outside of the Cross, there is no victory; there is no life; there is no power; there is no deliverance; all and without exception are found in the Cross.

HOW IS VICTORY FOUND IN THE CROSS?

Do you realize that in the Word of God, and more specifically I speak of the New Covenant, we are not told outright to fight sin. Now think about that statement for just a moment! Many in the modern Church, and I speak of those who are truly born-again, would emphatically state that we are to unequivocally fight sin. No we aren't!

In the first place, within our own strength and ability, no matter how zealous we might be, we are unable to overcome this monster of the law of sin and death.

Second, we don't have to fight this monster, and for the simple reason that Christ has already overcome sin, and has done so in every capacity. He overcame sin by His Perfect Life, and He atoned for all sin by His Perfect Death. Paul said:

"Who gave Himself for our sins, that He might deliver us from this present evil world, according to the Will of God and our Father" (Gal. 1:4).

NOTES

So, when the Christian starts to fight sin, and I'm referring to trying to overcome things in his life, and to do so by any means other than Faith in the Cross, every single time, he will lose that fight. There is only one fight in which we are supposed to engage – it is the good fight of faith.

THE GOOD FIGHT OF FAITH

Paul said: *"Fight the good fight of Faith, lay hold on eternal life, whereunto you are also called, and have professed a good profession before many witnesses"* (I Tim. 6:12).

Our Faith is to ever be in the Cross of Christ; Satan will do everything within his power to move our Faith to something else, or to keep us from hearing the Truth, so we'll keep our faith in something that's wrong. If that happens, and which it is the case with most Christians, we're fighting the wrong fight, a fight we cannot win, and simply because it's a fight that Jesus has already fought and won. And us attempting to fight it all over again, in essence, is saying that what He did is not sufficient, and we need to finish the task ourselves. I'm certain that it is easy to see what an insult this is to the Christ of Glory, Who has given His all for us.

Concerning this, Paul said to Timothy: *"Keep that which is committed to your trust, avoiding profane and vain babblings, and oppositions of knowledge falsely so-called:*

"Which some professing have erred concerning the Faith" (I Tim. 6:20-21).

If we err, it is always *"concerning the Faith."* And when Paul uses the term *"the Faith,"* or even the term *"Faith,"* always and without exception, he is speaking of Christ, and what Christ has done for us at the Cross, and our Faith in that Finished Work.

ERRED FAITH!

Every human being in the world has faith. Even the atheist has faith. He has faith in the fact that he doesn't have any faith, which I trust one can easily see how foolish is such a direction.

Nevertheless, all the faith the world has, and regrettably, most of the faith held by the Church, is not recognized at all by God. He recognizes only one kind of faith, and that is Faith in Christ and what Christ did at the Cross (Rom. 5:1; 6:3-14; I Cor. 1:17-18, 21, 23; 2:2; Gal. 6:14).

For the sake of properly comprehending that which is being said, let's use the following scenario:

Let's say that John Christian has been attacked by Satan, and Satan has succeeded in causing John Christian to fail. Let's say that we're discussing an uncontrollable temper. It could be anything, i.e., *"alcohol, nicotine, immorality, drugs, gambling, jealousy, envy, etc."* But we're using *"temper."*

Knowing that this uncontrollable temper is very unchristlike, and that it's hurting his testimony, and if he's married, it's hurting his marriage. It's not very Christlike for an individual to blow up and kick a hole in the wall, or whatever it is that's being done. Inasmuch as he is a born-again Believer, he will be sorry for what he has done, and will seek forgiveness, both from the one who has been harmed by it, other than himself, and the Lord. The Word of God promises us that any time we confess our sin before the Lord, He will be Faithful and just to forgive us our sin, and to cleanse us from all unrighteousness (I Jn. 1:9). But he finds himself confessing the same thing over and over again, and in fact, it's getting worse.

So he sets about to control his temper. He has heard some *"Christian Psychologist"* say that if we are plagued with such, we should take a pillow or some such like item into a room, and then beat the pillow, and thereby vent our frustrations, etc. In fact, he has tried that, but it doesn't work.

He has gone to his Pastor, and had hands laid on him, and although blessed, the problem continued. He has fasted a day or two, and that blessed him as well, but the temper remained.

He has thought, *"I will pray 30 minutes a day."* This he did, and was blessed immeasurably, but the temper remained. At the advice of others, he has selected two or three Scriptures which seem to apply to his problem, memorized them, and has quoted them over and over, even many times during the day, but the problem of the temper continues.

Such a Christian is very frustrated by now. And regrettably, this description I've just given

NOTES

is not merely an isolated situation, happening only to one here and there, but rather, is the lot of almost all Christians, in one form of the other.

John Christian, although loving the Lord very, very much, and at the same time, very ashamed of his problem, and trying to hide it, doesn't really understand what is wrong. Is this what Christianity actually is? Does one have to live this way?

The answer to those questions is, *"No!"* Such a life and living is not Biblical Christianity. So what is wrong?

PROPER FAITH

Some of these things that John was doing, such as praying so much each day, and memorizing and quoting Scripture, fasting, etc., are all good things, and will greatly bless the Believer, and in fact, are things that every true Believer will do. But if we place our Faith in those things, thinking that the doing of such will give us victory in this life, that's misplaced faith, thereby, faith that God will not recognize. And that's what frustrates John Christian. He's doing everything he knows to do, but without any success, and in fact, with the problem even getting worse.

In all of this, he has begun to believe that something is wrong with him. Maybe he is a special case. In other words, maybe Satan is attacking him harder than he is anyone else. Or maybe it's something that he inherited from his parents, and there's simply nothing he can do about it. Maybe it's something he's got to live with the rest of his life! He even maybe thinks that he might be demon possessed! No, none of these things are correct.

John Christian is not demon possessed even though demon spirits are definitely involved, as they are always involved in all sin. Neither is this the way that Christianity is supposed to be.

John's problem is, his faith is misplaced. He's putting his faith in these other things, and God won't honor that, simply because it dishonors Christ.

When John understands the Message of the Cross, and places his Faith there, and does not allow his Faith to be moved elsewhere, he will then find the Holy Spirit beginning to help him, because his Faith is now right (Gal. 5:1-6). It may continue to be a struggle for awhile, but if he will keep his Faith placed in the Finished Work of Christ, and not allow it to be moved, ultimately, he's going to have total victory within his life over this temper, and everything else for that matter. The Scripture plainly and beautifully says: *"For sin shall not have dominion over you: for you are not under the Law, but under Grace"* (Rom. 6:14).

WHAT DID PAUL MEAN THAT WE ARE NO LONGER UNDER LAW, BUT RATHER UNDER GRACE?

The Grace of God is simply the Goodness of God extended to undeserving Believers. Grace is superintended by the Holy Spirit, and is made available to us in unlimited quantities, due to what Christ did at the Cross. God has always been a God of Grace. He hasn't changed, even as He cannot change. But the Cross made it possible for Him to extend to us a copious quantity of Grace, that could not be extended before the Cross. To be sure, Grace was definitely prevalent before the Cross, because that's the only way a person can be saved, or receive anything from God, for that matter. But due to the fact that the blood of bulls and goats could not take away sins, God was limited as to what He could do as it regards sinful man (Heb. 10:4).

But since the Cross, which has opened the door, God can dispense Grace in an unlimited quantity. That's the reason He told Paul that irrespective of the problems, *"My Grace is sufficient for you: for My strength is made perfect in weakness"* (II Cor. 12:9).

HOW IS THE STRENGTH OF CHRIST MADE PREFECT IN OUR WEAKNESS?

In the first place, every singly human being who has ever lived is *"weak."* We may not like to think so, but it is the truth. And when we say *"weak,"* we're speaking of weakness by comparison to the powers of the Evil One. We are no match for the Devil. That is, if we try to face him on his grounds, or by our own initiative, ability, and strength. There is only one way that he can be faced, and which way will guarantee total and complete victory, and that is by our Faith and Trust in the Cross of Christ. That's why Paul said: *"For the preaching of*

the Cross is to them who perish foolishness; but unto us which are saved it is the Power of God" (I Cor. 1:18).

The idea here, as given by Christ, is not that we are weak, or that we aren't weak, but rather that we recognize our weakness, and thereby place total dependence on Christ. Whether we think so or not, we are weak. It's getting the Believer to understand that within himself he cannot do these things that need to be done. Christ, even as we've already stated, has already done these things for us, and we need to understand that, and thereby place our Faith in what He has done.

When we realize that we are weak, and cannot overcome the *"law of sin and death,"* at least within our own strength and ability, then we will begin to depend on Christ, and do so as it regards His Cross (Rom. 8:2).

ANOTHER JESUS

Paul said something very telling, something that we should look at very closely. He said:

"For if he who comes preaches another Jesus, whom we have not preached, or if you receive another spirit, which you did not receive (from us), *or another gospel which you have not accepted* (which you didn't get from us), *you might well bear with him* (if you think that he is something special, you might accept what he is saying, even though it's another Jesus, etc.)" (II Cor. 11:4).

Unless our Faith is planted squarely in Christ and His Cross, never divorcing the Cross from Christ, we will find ourselves ultimately and eventually, serving *"another Jesus."* This *"other Jesus,"* might look good, might sound good, and might seem good to the carnal mind, but again allow us to state the truth that if it's not *"Jesus Christ and Him Crucified,"* then it's not the Jesus of the Bible (I Cor. 1:23; 2:2).

The entirety of the Old Testament proclaims Christ and the Cross. That is the emphasis of the entirety of the Bible. So whenever we ignore the Cross, or demean the Cross, or even repudiate the Cross, even as the Word of Faith people have, the Jesus that we will then be serving will not be the Jesus of the Bible, but a Jesus of our own making. And to be sure, it's a Jesus that

God will never recognize.

There is only one answer for the world, and that's the Cross. Listen to what Christ said: *"And I, if I be lifted up from the Earth, will draw all men unto Me.*

"This He said, signifying what death He should die" (Jn. 12:32-33).

As is obvious here, Christ is speaking here of the manner in which He would die, which was to be lifted up on a Cross. By us preaching this, in this manner and this manner alone will we draw men to Christ. While we might preach something else, and draw people to our message, it will not be to Christ. That's the reason that much, if not most, of what is preached behind modern pulpits is pure and simple, *"another gospel."* But to be sure, this gospel, this erroneous gospel, no matter how intellectual it might seem, no matter how pleasing it might seem to the carnal heart, will not set the captive free, will not liberate mankind, will not cleanse from sin. Only what Christ did at the Cross will affect sin, the Cross and the Cross alone!

CHRIST DOES NOT DEAL WITH US ACCORDING TO GOOD OR EVIL ON OUR PART

And what do we mean by that?

In the first place, we do not have any good that He will recognize. Second, if He rejected us because of evil, He would accept no one. In other words, *"All have sinned and come short of the Glory of God"* (Rom. 6:23). And let the Reader understand that even though this Text sounds like it's from the past, in the Greek, it actually means that even the Godliest of us, whomever that might be, are constantly coming short of the Glory of God. We may not think so, and may loudly crow that it's not so, but the Word of God says that it is so.

So if the Lord dealt with us strictly on the basis of good or evil, none of us would have a chance.

God deals with us strictly on the basis of Faith (Rom. 5:1-2; Eph. 2:8-9, 13-18; Gal. 5:6).

My statement is not meant to imply that the Christian can exercise Faith, and continue in evil. Such a thought is preposterous! The

NOTES

Lord doesn't save us in sin, but rather *"from sin"* (Rom. 6:13-14). The way of Faith, and we are speaking of Faith in Christ and His Sacrificial Offering of Himself, is the way to victory, the way over evil, the way to rid oneself of evil. In fact, it is the only way! John beautifully and wondrously said: *"This is the victory that overcometh the world, even our Faith"* (I Jn. 5:4).

(22) "YOU SHALL THEREFORE KEEP ALL MY STATUTES, AND ALL MY JUDGMENTS, AND DO THEM: THAT THE LAND, WHITHER I BRING YOU TO DWELL THEREIN, SPEW YOU NOT OUT.

(23) "AND YOU SHALL NOT WALK IN THE MANNERS OF THE NATION, WHICH I CAST OUT BEFORE YOU: FOR THEY COMMITTED ALL THESE THINGS, AND THEREFORE I ABHORRED THEM.

(24) "BUT I HAVE SAID UNTO YOU, YOU SHALL INHERIT THEIR LAND, AND I WILL GIVE IT UNTO YOU TO POSSESS IT, A LAND THAT FLOWS WITH MILK AND HONEY: I AM THE LORD YOUR GOD, WHICH HAVE SEPARATED YOU FROM OTHER PEOPLE.

(25) "YOU SHALL THEREFORE PUT DIFFERENCE BETWEEN CLEAN BEASTS AND UNCLEAN, AND BETWEEN UNCLEAN FOWLS AND CLEAN: YOU SHALL NOT MAKE YOUR SOULS ABOMINABLE BY BEAST, OR BY FOWL, OR BY ANY MANNER OF LIVING THING THAT CREEPS ON THE GROUND, WHICH I HAVE SEPARATED FROM YOU AS UNCLEAN.

(26) "AND YOU SHALL BE HOLY UNTO ME: FOR I THE LORD AM HOLY, AND HAVE SEVERED YOU FROM OTHER PEOPLE, THAT YOU SHOULD BE MINE.

(27) "A MAN ALSO OR WOMAN WHO HAS A FAMILIAR SPIRIT, OR WHO IS A WIZARD, SHALL SURELY BE PUT TO DEATH: THEY SHALL STONE THEM WITH STONES: THEIR BLOOD SHALL BE UPON THEM."

The composition is:

1. Israel is admonished to keep the Commandments of the Lord.

2. If they did not keep these Commandments, as the Lord spewed out the inhabitants before them, He would, likewise, spew them out, which He ultimately did!

3. Israel is to be separate from the evil of the world, and even the evil among them, such as unclean animals, etc. That admonition, at least in Spirit, holds true even unto this hour, for all Believers.

4. The Lord is Holy, and He demands that we as His people be holy as well. There is only one way this can be done, and that is by the Cross.

5. Israel was to be led by the Lord, not at all by familiar spirits or wizards, etc. They were people of God, and not of Satan.

STATUTES AND JUDGMENTS

Verse 22 reads: *"You shall therefore keep all My Statues, and all My Judgments, and do them: that the land, whither I bring you to dwell therein, spew you not out."*

The Lord did not inform Israel here that they were to keep some of His Commandments, but rather all of them.

The truth was, Israel was literally incapable of doing such, even the best among them. But they were definitely to try.

There is a great difference in one taking a cavalier attitude toward the Commandments, or trying to keep them, but yet failing. To the latter, the Lord will most definitely show the way to victory, at least the victory that one could have before the Cross.

He tells them plainly here that if they ignore His Commands, He will ultimately vomit them out of the land, exactly as He was going to do those who now inhabited it. We speak of the Canaanites, etc. Regrettably and sadly, that's exactly what ultimately happened!

THAT WHICH GOD HATES

Verse 23 reads: *"And you shall not walk in the manners of the nation, which I cast out before you: for they committed all these things, and therefore I abhorred them."*

All of the things that the Lord has commanded in these Chapters, stating that Israel must not do them, and if they did do them, the results would not be pleasant to behold, pictures that which God hates, as ought to be overly obvious.

All of these Passages tell us that a nation can go so deep into sin that God will ultimately take them to task. While it may

be a short time, or it may be a long time in coming, nevertheless, God sees all, knows all, and will ultimately take steps.

Nazi Germany is an excellent example. Their evil knew no bounds, as Hitler began to gain power. In fact, at that particular time, and I speak of the mid and late 1930's, the heroes of the young people in the nation were women who were performing on the stage the most lewd and immoral of acts. It seems inconceivable that such would happen among people who were as educated as the Germans, but it did! In this climate, Hitler was accepted, but which resulted in the total and complete ruin of Nazi Germany. Their cities were bombed into rubble, and rightly so! Millions of their people were slaughtered, and rightly so! It was the Judgment of God, and rightly so!

Japan basically fell into the same category.

The horrifying thing about all of this is, the United States is presently following along the same path. The heroes of the nation are the rock stars, and the viler they become, the more they are worshipped and adored.

As I dictate these notes in October of 2002, the nation is undergoing the major corporation scandals, where the Chief Executive Officers of many of these multinational corporations, are cooking the books, making it seem as though the company is doing great, when in reality, it's losing money. Consequently, billions of dollars invested by the *"little people,"* are lost, throwing untold thousands into poverty, all because of gross fraud and dishonesty.

The only thing that can stem the tide of evil is the Gospel preached in all of its power and authority, which refers to the preaching of the Cross, but sadly and regrettably, that is not being done any more in America. Most of the Television Preachers have degenerated to the point of abject hucksterism. In other words, send me your $50, and I'll send you my bottle of snake oil, which will perform all type of miracles for you. Gargantuan claims are made of mighty miracles and millions being saved, when in reality, there are no miracles and precious few are being saved. In other words, it's a scam from the word go.

The so-called Christian Television Network, T.B.N., serves as the vehicle which has gone a long way toward totally corrupting the modern Church. The Preachers on this Network all too often, serve as spiritual pimps for the *"great whore."* And please understand, the terminology is not mine, but rather belongs to the Holy Spirit. John said:

"And there came one of the seven Angels which had the seven vials, and talked with me, saying unto me, Come hither; I will show unto you the judgment of the great whore who sits upon many waters:

"With whom the kings of the Earth have committed fornication, and the inhabitants of the Earth have been made drunk with the wine of her fornication" (Rev. 17:1-2).

Notice the terminology used by the Holy Spirit.

The *"great whore"* is the name given by the Holy Spirit to all false systems and false ways, claiming to be of God, or in many respects, actually claiming to be God, but have greatly deceived the people. The phrase *"sitteth upon many waters,"* speaks of many people.

In Verse 2, the Holy Spirit uses the term, *"With whom the kings of the Earth have committed fornication."* More than anything else, this is speaking of *"spiritual fornication."*

WHAT IS SPIRITUAL FORNICATION?

It is the same in a sense as *"spiritual adultery,"* which Paul addressed in Romans 7:1-4. In those particular Passages, he is speaking of Believers who are attempting to live for Christ by trusting in things other than the Cross. He calls them *"spiritual adulterers."* In other words, they are being unfaithful to Christ.

The terminology used by the Holy Spirit in Revelation, Chapter 17, covers a much wider spectrum. While all fornication includes adultery, the meaning of adultery does not include all the meanings of fornication.

The word *"fornication"* as used here, in the Greek is *"porneuo,"* and means, *"to practice idolatry."* At least that is one of its meanings, and which meaning applies more to the manner in which it is used in this Text than anything else.

The modern Church has not only left the Cross, which is spiritual adultery, but as well, it is also practicing idolatry. In fact, religion

and all of its many forms have become the idol of the modern Church. And to be sure, the Catholic Church is not the only branch of that which refers to itself as *"Christendom,"* but is followed closely by many Protestant Denominations also.

The phrase, *"That sitteth upon many waters,"* refers to people. John also stated: *"The waters which you saw, where the whore sits, are of peoples, and multitudes, and nations, and tongues"* (Rev. 17:15). This speaks of controlling the people, which religion grossly does.

CONTROL

Control comes in many and various ways. But the two greatest ways concern *"money"* and *"fear."* We'll deal with the last one first.

Many Denominations make people believe that if they don't belong to that particular Denomination, they cannot be right with God, and might even suffer the Judgment of God. Many Churches practice the same type of control. If the people belong to that particular Church, they are told that great blessings will come, and if they leave, they will be cursed, etc.

There is more superstition in religion than in anything else. Many people will use good common sense when it refers to many things, and then go completely off the deep end when it comes to religion. Again, it is superstition that controls them, which means it's not of God. Any Denomination or Preacher that would try to hold its people through superstition, and that's exactly what it is, is not of God, and should be shunned, irrespective of their threats. The Believer must remember this:

If one is truly a Believer, they must understand that God Alone can bring about blessings or curses. And to be sure, if you are truly a Believer, there will be no curse. There may be chastisement, but definitely no curse. That was handled at the Cross of Calvary (Gal. 3:13).

Money is the next strong arm that controls people. The *"money"* or *"greed"* gospel has become very, very big in these last several decades. Thousands, if not tens of thousands, of Churches make *"money"* their chief emphasis. This is part and parcel of the Word of Faith doctrine, which in reality is of Satan. That's blunt, but it is true!

The people are told if they give large sums of money, they are going to get fabulously rich. Even though it's all dressed up in all type of religious garb, the truth is, they hold their people in the Churches, again through fear. And how is this done?

Of course, the people are not going to get back any money, and in fact, they are going to lose what little they do have. They are not giving for the right purpose; they are certainly not giving to the right cause, and in fact, they're not giving to the Lord at all, irrespective as to what they may be told. They are merely giving to a Preacher, to make him ever more rich.

In this scheme, and a scheme it is, people mortgage their houses, some even sell their houses, cause their children to do without, ever giving more and more money, because they continue to be told that the end of the rainbow is right around the corner, and there are pots of gold waiting. They fear to leave, and that's where the fear comes in, because they are made to think that they are so very, very close to that pot of gold. The truth is, they are not only not close to any gold, but further away than ever before, and because they've given away everything they presently have, as stated, even depriving their family. It is religion pure and simple, which means it's not of God, and which means that control is exercised in one way or the other, and when the bottom line is reached, it's generally through *"fear."*

DECEPTION

Playing on this fear is deception. Paul said: *"Now the Spirit speaks expressly, that in the latter times* (the times in which we now live) *some shall depart from the Faith, giving heed to seducing spirits, and doctrines of devils"* (I Tim. 4:1). In everything that pertains to false doctrine, seducing spirits are definitely involved. That's at least one of the reasons, and in fact, the primary reason, that it's so hard for people to break away from this erroneous course. They keep, proverbially speaking, beating their head against the wall, even when it's so obvious that they are going in the wrong direction. Others can

see it, but they can't!

The only ones who really get out of this terrible deception are the ones who are actually seeking for truth. No matter where the person is, if the person is honestly seeking for Truth, God will bring that person to Truth. But not many actually want Truth, but rather, their own particular way, whatever that way might be. Once again, that's the reason that the greed gospel is so successful. There is enough greed in all of us to keep the thing alive and prosperous.

And once again let the Reader understand that all who promote any type of Gospel, whether it's far out, or whether it seems like the True Gospel, but yet isn't, in fact, every religion on the face of the Earth falls under the category of the *"great whore."* God says, *"I abhor them."*

A LAND THAT FLOWS WITH MILK AND HONEY

Verse 24 reads: *"But I have said unto you, You shall inherit their land, and I will give it unto you to possess it, a land that flows with milk and honey: I am the LORD your God, which have separated you from other people."*

If the Lord said that this land of Canaan was a land *"flowing with milk and honey,"* one can be doubly sure that it was exactly that and more. In effect, he was telling Israel that He was going to give them something that was good, very good. So in effect, He was saying: *"Don't blow it."*

They were to ever remember that He was *"the LORD their God."* This means that they were to look to Him for all things, and they were to obey Him in all things. It seems easy enough, doesn't it?

The truth is, it's not as easy as it seems, and it was even harder for the Israelites, because they lived before the Cross.

But that was no excuse, considering that the Sacrifices pointed to the One Who was to come, and Faith in Him would grant them the victory they needed, but only Faith in Him.

Israel was to be a separated people. This meant they were not to act like the people of other lands, be like the people of other lands, and in fact, were to limit association with the people of other lands. They were a *"separate people."*

In fact, we as Believers, although different from the nation of Israel of old, still are to live a separated life (II Cor. 6:14-18).

While the Lord demands separation, that is not the same as isolation. In fact, as Believers, we are not to live isolated lives. We are a city, so to speak, which is set upon a hill, and our light is to shine, that others may see it (Mat. 5:13-16).

That's the reason that communities which have been set up in times past, where Christianity was going to be brought about by law, has never worked. It hasn't worked, because it's unscriptural. We are to be *"in"* the world, while at the same time, never being *"of"* the world.

THE CLEAN AND THE UNCLEAN

Verse 25 reads: *"You shall therefore put difference between clean beasts and unclean, and between unclean fowls and clean: you shall not make your souls abominable by beasts, or by fowl, or by any manner of living thing that creeps on the ground, which I have separated from you as unclean."*

Because the Lord has separated or distinguished the Israelites from all nations, and is about to give them the Promised Land, therefore the Israelites are to be separate, and are to distinguish between the clean and unclean animals, as ordained in Chapter 11.

The *"clean animals"* and *"unclean animals"* had to do with the Sacrifices they offered, and as well, their dietary laws. As we have explained in previous commentary, this had to do with the fact that they were the people of God, through whom the Messiah would come.

HOLY

Verse 26 reads: *"And you shall be holy unto Me: for I the LORD am holy, and have severed you from other people, that you should be Mine."*

Israel was to belong to the Lord, and to belong to the Lord exclusively. It is the same with Believers presently.

This is what Sanctification is all about. We are supposed to be separate from the world, and separate unto God. In other words, we are separated from something, unto something. The first is the world, and the

NOTES

latter is, as stated, God.

Presently, God's people can live a holy life only by looking exclusively to Christ, and what He has done for us at the Cross. With that ever being the object of our Faith, the Holy Spirit will then grandly help us, and help us to be what we ought to be. That is God's Way, and in fact, He only has one Way.

LOOK TO THE LORD ALONE

Verse 27 reads: *"A man also or woman who has a familiar spirit, or who is a wizard, shall surely be put to death: they shall stone them with stones: their blood shall be upon them."*

Although this Passage, as is overly obvious, contains a warning, and a warning in no uncertain terms, the greater gist of what is being said here is that Israel was to look exclusively to the Lord for leading and guidance, and surely not at all to these evil spirits. For all people who claimed to be able to tell fortunes, or to read the future, etc., or who claimed to be able to make contact with the dead, all and without exception are possessed by familiar spirits. They are referred to as *"familiar spirits,"* and because these spirits know some things in the spirit world which pertain to the particular individual in question. When these things are brought out, it makes the gullible person actually think that they are communicating with their dead loved one, etc. In reality, they are communicating with demon spirits. There is no communication with the dead. Let that ever be understood.

"Wizards" are those who claim to be able to tell fortunes by reading signs, etc. All of this particular world, including horoscopes, etc., have to do with evil spirits. This was so serious in the Mind of God that those who would practice such in Israel were to be *"put to death."* The Lord must be their leader and not evil spirits.

Back up in Verse 26, the idea was not that the Gentile world was being rejected, and Israel alone being accepted, but that Israel was in fact, to be a leader for other nations, in order that they might be brought to God. Regrettably, they were not too very good at this, but it was the intention all along as it regards the Lord that the entirety of the world would know Him, with Israel supposedly setting the example. The Scripture plainly says: *"For God so loved the world that He gave His only Begotten Son, that whosoever believeth in Him should not perish, but have everlasting life"* (Jn. 3:16).

"I have found a heaven below,
"I am living in the Glory;
"Oh, the joy and strength I know,
"Living in the Glory of the Lord."

"Storms of sorrow round me fall,
"But I'm living in the Glory;
"I can sing above them all,
"Living in the Glory of the Lord."

"Satan cannot touch my heart
"While I'm living in the Glory;
"This disarms each fiery dart,
"Living in the Glory of the Lord."

"I can triumph over pain
"While I'm living in the Glory;
"I can count each loss a gain,
"Living in the Glory of the Lord."

"I am poor and little known,
"But I'm living in the Glory;
"And I'm waiting for a throne,
"Living in the Glory of the Lord."

"Soon the King will come for me
"To be with Him in the Glory;
"Then my song shall sweeter be,
"Reigning in the Glory of the Lord."

CHAPTER 21

(1) "AND THE LORD SAID UNTO MOSES, SPEAK UNTO THE PRIESTS THE SONS OF AARON, AND SAY UNTO THEM, THERE SHALL NONE BE DEFILED FOR THE DEAD AMONG HIS PEOPLE:

(2) "BUT FOR HIS KIN, WHO IS NEAR UNTO HIM, THAT IS, FOR HIS MOTHER, AND FOR HIS FATHER, AND FOR HIS SON, AND FOR HIS DAUGHTER, AND FOR HIS BROTHER,

(3) "AND FOR HIS SISTER A VIRGIN, WHO IS NIGH UNTO HIM, WHICH HAS HAD NO HUSBAND; FOR HER MAY HE BE DEFILED.

(4) "BUT HE SHALL NOT DEFILE HIMSELF, BEING A CHIEF MAN AMONG HIS PEOPLE, TO PROFANE HIMSELF.

(5) "THEY SHALL NOT MAKE BALDNESS UPON THEIR HEAD, NEITHER SHALL THEY SHAVE OFF THE CORNER OF THEIR BEARD, NOR MAKE ANY CUTTINGS IN THEIR FLESH.

(6) "THEY SHALL BE HOLY UNTO THEIR GOD, AND NOT PROFANE THE NAME OF THEIR GOD: FOR THE OFFERINGS OF THE LORD MADE BY FIRE, AND THE BREAD OF THEIR GOD, THEY DO OFFER: THEREFORE THEY SHALL BE HOLY.

(7) "THEY SHALL NOT TAKE A WIFE WHO IS A WHORE, OR PROFANE; NEITHER SHALL THEY TAKE A WOMAN PUT AWAY FROM HER HUSBAND: FOR HE IS HOLY UNTO HIS GOD.

(8) "YOU SHALL SANCTIFY HIM THEREFORE; FOR HE OFFERS THE BREAD OF YOUR GOD: HE SHALL BE HOLY UNTO YOU: FOR I THE LORD, WHICH SANCTIFY YOU, AM HOLY.

(9) "AND THE DAUGHTER OF ANY PRIEST, IF SHE PROFANE HERSELF BY PLAYING THE WHORE, SHE PROFANES HER FATHER: SHE SHALL BE BURNT WITH FIRE."

The composition is:

1. Chapters 21 and 22, with great detail, portray the Divine requirements in reference to those who were Priests unto God.

2. All Priests had to be sons of Aaron.

3. All Priests under the Mosaic economy were as well, types of Christ. As a result, they were to be holy, even as the Lord is holy.

PRIESTLY STANDARDS

Verses 1 through 4 read: *"And the LORD said unto Moses, speak unto the Priests the sons of Aaron, and say unto them, There shall none be defiled for the dead among his people:*

"But for his kin, who is near unto him, that is, for his mother, and for his father, and for his son, and for his daughter, and for his brother,

"And for his sister a virgin, who is nigh unto him, which has had no husband; for her may he be defiled.

"But he shall not defile himself, being a chief man among his people, to profane himself."

In the Passage, *"the Priests the sons of Aaron,"* we find it said a little different than the other six Passages in the writings of Moses where it is used. The other times it uses the phrase, *"the sons of Aaron the Priests"* (Lev. 1:5, 8, 11; 2:2; 3:2; Num. 10:8).

This no doubt was spoken in this manner in order that the Priests may know and understand that they are in fact, Priests by virtue of being sons of Aaron, and not because of any merit on their part.

They were to understand this, therefore, to impress it upon their children, who would be Priests as well.

As well, they had to meet a certain Standard, even as it is given in these particular Passages, and because they were types of Christ. They stood, in a sense, as mediators between God and men.

JESUS, OUR GREAT HIGH PRIEST

The Mosaic Priesthood was ordained by God. It was meant to fill a role and serve a purpose, until Christ would come, Who, through the virtue of His Cross, and thereby His Mediatorial, Atoning, Intercessory Work, would bring the Mosaic Priesthood to an end. In other words, this particular order was meant only to serve as a stopgap measure, until Christ would come. Upon His arrival, and His Atoning Work, the Aaronic Priesthood would no longer be needed. Jesus is now our Great High Priest (Heb. 4:14-16). Furthermore, Paul said: *"For there is one God, and one Mediator between God and men, the Man Christ Jesus"* (I Tim. 2:5).

This means that the Catholic priesthood of the present time, or any other Priesthood for that matter, is grossly out of order, and thereby, unscriptural. Such a priesthood actually says that the Atoning Work of Christ is insufficient, and needs the help of men. In fact, such a direction can only be labeled as *"blasphemy."*

Catholic priests attempt to serve as mediators between God and men, in some sense, as the Mosaic Priesthood of old, which is an insult to the Finished Work of Christ. If one surveys the New Testament, outside of the Jewish economy which refused to recognize

Christ, one will look in vain for any Priesthood. It no longer exists, and because it is no longer needed.

The greatest sin of the Church is usurping Christ, and which can be done, and in fact is done, in many and varied ways.

THE CROSS

For instance, whenever a Believer, any Believer, attempts to live for God by means other than God's prescribed order, which is based entirely upon the Finished Work of Christ, such a person is usurping Christ. In other words, they are denying His Work in some manner, even though most would do this in ignorance. But we must never forget, to sin in ignorance portrays a condition of the heart that's not quite right with God. In other words, the *"flesh"* is attempting to take the place of Christ.

God's prescribed order is very simple. As I've already said any number of times in this Volume, the Believer must understand that everything he receives from God has been made possible by the Cross. His Faith is to then make the Finished Work of Christ its object. Then the Holy Spirit will give him the necessary power to live the life he ought to live, which is the only way it can be lived (Rom. 6:3-14; 8:1-2, 11).

That is God's Way, even as Paul outlined it in Romans, Chapters 6, 7, and 8. To attempt to live for the Lord by any other means, as should be obvious, insults Christ, because it insults what He has done for us, which we could not do for ourselves. And for us to think we can, in essence, calls God a liar. Listen again to Paul:

"I do not frustrate the Grace of God: for if Righteousness come by the Law, then Christ is dead in vain" (Gal. 2:21).

In the statement, *"If Righteousness come by the Law, then Christ is dead in vain,"* every effort of man to live for God, outside of the realm of Grace, is shot down before it begins. The great Apostle is saying that if man can be righteous by any other way than trust in Christ and what He did at the Cross, then Jesus died unnecessarily. In other words, we are saying that God doesn't know how to redeem humanity, and in fact, what he did do, as it regards the Cross, was unnecessary.

Of course, we as Believers don't think in those terms, but that's the way that it comes up in the Face of God. It comes up to Him as self-righteousness, which God cannot tolerate.

Everything about the Christian experience must center up on Christ and the Cross. Christ must never be separated from the Cross, inasmuch as that was the very reason that He came. Without the Cross, man could not have been redeemed. Without the Cross, man could not have been set free. Without the Cross, there would be no Salvation, no Baptism with the Holy Spirit, no Grace, no peace, no hope, no power. Without the Cross there is nothing! With the Cross, we can have everything, because the Cross has made it possible.

KNOWING CHRIST AFTER THE FLESH

Paul said: *"Wherefore henceforth know we no man after the flesh: yes, though we have known Christ after the flesh, yet now henceforth know we Him no more"* (II Cor. 5:16).

What did Paul mean by this statement?

To know Christ *"after the flesh,"* is to judge things by the wisdom of the carnal mind. That wisdom knows Christ *"after the flesh,"* i.e., *"as the greatest religious Teacher, Moral Philosopher, and World Benefactor Who ever lived, and, perhaps, also as the Promised Messiah and Regenerator of Society."*

In this particular category, man is also judged in the light of the same wisdom and declared to be an emanation of God, and, as such, having a glorious history, is perpetually advancing to an ever higher level of moral and mental splendor. But these are the *"old things"* that pass away when the New Birth becomes a reality (II Cor. 5:17).

This type of worldly wisdom, *"after the flesh,"* doesn't recognize the Cross at all, doesn't believe in the Cross, and, thereby, counts it as nothing at all. In the thinking of worldly wisdom, the Death of Christ on the Cross was just an unfortunate end to the life of this great Moral Philosopher. Those who judge Christ in this manner do not think of Redemption at all, and because they really do not see man as being in need of Redemption. As stated, in the thinking of the world, and in the evolutionary process, man

NOTES

is getting better and better, etc.

But of course, any right thinking individual knows that is not true. Man is not getting better and better, but is actually on the very verge of destroying the whole of civilization. And in fact, were it not for the Second Coming, which will take place in the not too distant future, man would in fact, totally and completely destroy himself.

But if the Christian is not careful, as well, he will look at Christ *"After the flesh,"* which thinks of Him in a way that is not proper to think.

HOW SHOULD WE THINK OF CHRIST?

At the outset it should be understood that every single thing that Christ did, and all that He was and is (Christ is God), are significant beyond compare. Christ was God manifested in the flesh (Isa. 7:14). So to minimize anything He did presents itself as spiritual and Scriptural ignorance of the highest order.

But while everything that He did was of vast significance, and played a part in the great Redemptive process, the major theme of the Life and Ministry of Christ, the reason He came, was the Cross. In fact, the Lord, speaking to Satan through the serpent, and doing so immediately after the Fall, told the Evil One: *"And I will put enmity* (hatred and war) *between you* (Satan) *and the woman* (in other words, Satan hates the female gender, and for the reason that will now be given), *and between your seed* (fallen mankind) *and her Seed* (the Lord Jesus Christ); *it* (the Seed, the Lord Jesus Christ) *shall bruise your head* (meaning that Christ at the Cross, defeated Satan, and took away his dominion (Col. 2:14-15)), *and you* (Satan) *shall bruise His* (Christ's) *heel* (the suffering of the Crucifixion)*"* (Gen. 3:15).

So the prediction came forth immediately after the Fall, that Satan would be defeated by God becoming man and going to the Cross. In fact, Peter stated, as the Holy Spirit moved upon him: *"Forasmuch as you know that you were not redeemed with corruptible things, as silver and gold . . . But with the Precious Blood of Christ, as of a lamb without blemish and without spot:*

"Who verily was foreordained before the

foundation of the world, but was manifest in these last times for you" (I Pet. 1:18-20), proclaiming to us that the Cross was planned even before the foundation of the world. God through foreknowledge knew that He would make man, and that man would fall, and it was decided by the Godhead that man would be redeemed by the method of the Cross.

In the Fourth Chapter of Genesis, which in effect continues through the entirety of the Old Testament, we have the Sacrificial System instituted, which portrayed the One Who was to come, in effect serving as a Substitute. All of this pointed squarely to the Cross.

It was to Paul that the meaning of the New Covenant was given, which in effect was the meaning of the Cross. Paul explains it in beautiful, symbolic detail, as he gave us the complete explanation of that which we refer to as *"the Lord's Supper."* Totally and completely, it proclaims the Crucifixion of Christ, and the danger involved in not addressing that correctly (I Cor. 11:24-31). Paul also said, *"We preach Christ Crucified"* (I Cor. 1:23). He as well said: *"For I determined not to know anything among you, save Jesus Christ, and Him Crucified"* (I Cor. 2:2). Need we mention all the other times that Paul highlights and proclaims the Cross! (Rom. 5:1-2; 6:3-14; 8:1-2, 11; I Cor. 1:17-18, 23; Gal., Chpt. 5; 6:14; Eph. 2:13-18; Col. 2:14-15; etc.)

We should preach healing; we should preach prosperity; we should preach prophecy; in fact, we should preach everything about the Bible; however, our emphasis must always be on the Cross and nothing but the Cross.

HOW TO WALK IN VICTORY

On Thursday, October 10, 2002, incidentally, the Fiftieth Wedding Anniversary of Frances and myself, someone sent me an article entitled, *"Stopping the Sin Cycle."* I'm not acquainted with the author, but the individual who sent the article requested that I comment on the advice given.

As would be obvious from the title, the individual was telling people how to overcome sin.

Almost everything that was said in its own way was right and Scriptural, but regardless

of it being right and Scriptural in its own capacity, the advice given will not help anyone overcome sin in any degree at all.

All that the dear lady said pertained to things that we must do, such as, *"Put on the full armor,"* *"Choose to follow God,"* *"Renew the mind,"* *"Get a daily dose of God,"* *"Walk in the Spirit,"* *"Give burdens to God,"* etc. As stated, all of these things are good, that is, if they are done correctly. But what our dear sister was advising was erroneous direction, and the end result sought, which is victory over sin, cannot even remotely be obtained in this manner. She was turning these good and Scriptural things into *"works."*

THE CROSS

Not one single time did the dear lady mention the Cross. This tells me that she has no idea as to how to live a victorious, overcoming, Christian life. And in reality, she's not living a victorious life herself, or she wouldn't have given this type of advice.

But the sad thing is, virtually all of the modern Church would read what she wrote, and would think that it's exactly right. The truth is, it's exactly wrong!

There is only one answer for sin, and that's the Cross. God doesn't have 50 ways, 20 ways, or two ways, just one – the Cross of Christ. Paul wrote and said: *"But this Man, after He had offered one Sacrifice for sins forever, sat down on the Right Hand of God"* (Heb. 10:12).

This speaks of Christ, and His Sacrificial, Atoning Death on the Cross, and which will never have to be repeated, because the Sacrifice will suffice forever. Showing that the work is a Finished Work, He is *"sat down on the Right Hand of God."*

The modern Church is, for all practical purposes, Cross illiterate. This means that it doesn't know the Way of the Lord, but has rather devised its own way, which God can never accept. These ways we have chosen fool us, simply because they are religious. We paper them with Scriptures; we say some right things, so people read it and think it's right, and because they don't know any better. But the tragedy is, most Preachers don't know any better either.

DEATH

Priests were not to have any association with a dead body, or officiate at any funeral, with the exception of their nearest of kin.

Death is the result of sin, and actually the crowning achievement of Satan, as it regards the Fall of man. Had Adam and Eve not sinned, they would not have died. But tragically they did sin, and they died. First of all, they died spiritually, which refers to separation from God. This was immediate! It was then followed later, much later on their part, by physical death.

When one watches the physical body gradually age and wear out, ultimately followed by death, one is looking at the terrible result of the Fall. Medical Scientists tell us that they really do not know why the organs of the physical body age and ultimately cease operation. They state that the human body, in a sense, rejuvenates itself every seven years. It is somewhat like a snake shedding its old skin, and taking on a brand-new skin. In fact, they tell us that the organs of the physical body should last forever.

They have tried repeatedly to stop the aging process, but without any success. The reason being, the problem is not physical, although the physical is definitely affected, but rather spiritual. As stated, it is the result of the Fall.

By this very fact, we at least get some idea as to how bad sin actually is. It is powerful enough that from the beginning of recorded time, it has killed every one of the human race, with the exception of those who are presently alive, and we are dying.

But what Jesus did at the Cross, forever took away the fear of death. And when the Trump of God sounds, the Scripture tells us: *"So when this corruptible shall have put on incorruption, and this mortal shall have put on immortality, then shall be brought to pass the saying that is written, Death is swallowed up in victory.*

"O death, where is your sting? O grave, where is your victory?" (I Cor. 15:54-55).

THEY SHALL BE HOLY

Verses 5 through 9 read: *"They shall not make baldness upon their head, neither shall*

they shave off the corner of their beard, nor make any cuttings in their flesh.

"They shall be holy unto their God, and not profane the Name of their God: for the Offerings of the LORD made by fire, and the bread of their God, they do offer: therefore they shall be holy.

"They shall not take a wife who is a whore, or profane; neither shall they take a woman put away from her husband: for he is holy unto his God.

"You shall sanctify him therefore; for he offers the bread of your God: he shall be holy unto you: for I the LORD, which sanctify you, am Holy.

"And the daughter of any Priest, if she profane herself by playing the whore, she profanes her father: she shall be burnt with fire."

If a loved one died, or anyone, for that matter, Priests were not to alter their appearance in any manner as it regards mourning, as did the heathen of other nations. So the question could well be asked as to why the Lord prohibited such.

As we've already stated, death is an enemy. It is a result of the Fall, and in fact, the most horrendous result of all. By the Lord telling the Priests that they were not to disfigure themselves, or alter their appearance at all regarding death, even the death of a loved one, in effect made the statement, which the Lord desired to make, that death would ultimately be defeated. And if death is ultimately defeated, and it definitely shall be, with the process having already begun at Calvary, then to be sure, ever other aspect of Satan's revolution against God will be handled as well! The appearance of the Priests was to make that statement, and in fact did make that statement.

The *"bread"* of Verse 6 refers to the Sacrifices, whether the Whole Burnt-Offering, Meat-Offering, Sin-Offering, Trespass-Offering, or Peace-Offering. These were Offerings *"made by fire."* They all typified Christ, and were, therefore, the very heart of the Tabernacle program. Considering that the Priests officiated at these Sacrifices, and considering what the Sacrifices meant, they were never to *"profane the name of their God,"* by attending to these duties in any manner except that ordered by the Lord. While all things concerning the Tabernacle were of extreme significance, the Sacrifices, one could say, were the very heart of the Program of God. While the Priests were types of Christ, the Sacrifices were types of what Christ would do on the Cross.

Concerning the wife of the Priest, he was to select a lady who is in keeping with the Call of God on his life, who would conduct herself accordingly.

The implication was that he was to marry a virgin, but with one exception. The Scripture seems to imply that he could marry a woman who had been married, but that her husband had died.

If the daughter of any Priest profaned herself by *"playing the whore,"* she brings reproach upon her father, and upon his calling, and her punishment was to be that she would be *"burnt with fire."* Though the doom of the guilty man in the crime is not mentioned here, his sentence was death by strangulation.

Is it thought to be that the punishment is too severe?

First of all, we must understand that these laws were given by God. While they may be called the Law of Moses, in actuality, they all came from the Lord, and in totality. In other words, Moses contributed nothing, except to receive them.

It must be remembered, as stated, that these men were types of Christ; consequently, the entirety of their families in a sense, fell into the same category. To dishonor the Priesthood was to dishonor Christ, but more particularly, to dishonor the type. Therefore, the regulations and commandments were strong indeed, as it regarded the Priesthood, even as they should have been.

However, before any death sentence could be carried out, there had to be two witnesses to the crime or more (Deut. 17:6).

In fact, if there was one eyewitness to the crime or sin, and we speak of the particular type of sin that commanded the death penalty, even with an eyewitness, the person could not be put to death. As stated, there had to be two or more witnesses.

As would be obvious, it would not be often that two or more individuals would be witnesses to such a sin or crime. In fact, there is

very little evidence that many of these executions were actually carried out. While the sentence was very harsh, as is obvious, and of necessity, still, the Lord provided checks and balances, far more than we presently have, to protect the innocent, and in a sense, even to protect the guilty. Presently, there are very few courts in the land that would not convict upon the testimony of one eyewitness, that is, if the person seemed to be credible, but not the courts of the Old Testament.

(10) "AND HE WHO IS THE HIGH PRIEST AMONG HIS BRETHREN, UPON WHOSE HEAD THE ANOINTING OIL WAS POURED, AND WHO IS CONSECRATED TO PUT ON THE GARMENTS, SHALL NOT UNCOVER HIS HEAD, NOR REND HIS CLOTHES;

(11) "NEITHER SHALL HE GO IN TO ANY DEAD BODY, NOR DEFILE HIMSELF FOR HIS FATHER, OR FOR HIS MOTHER;

(12) "NEITHER SHALL HE GO OUT OF THE SANCTUARY, NOR PROFANE THE SANCTUARY OF HIS GOD; FOR THE CROWN OF THE ANOINTING OIL OF HIS GOD IS UPON HIM: I AM THE LORD.

(13) "AND HE SHALL TAKE A WIFE IN HER VIRGINITY.

(14) "A WIDOW, OR A DIVORCED WOMAN, OR PROFANE, OR AN HARLOT, THESE SHALL HE NOT TAKE: BUT HE SHALL TAKE A VIRGIN OF HIS OWN PEOPLE TO WIFE.

(15) "NEITHER SHALL HE PROFANE HIS SEED AMONG HIS PEOPLE: FOR I THE LORD DO SANCTIFY HIM."

The exegesis is:

1. The instructions now shift from what we might refer to as ordinary Priests to the *"High Priest."*

2. Although all Priests were designated as types of Christ, and because they were mediators, the High Priest was the greatest type of all.

3. That Holiness becomes God's House forever is true in all periods of time. God demanded an unblemished Priest and an unblemished Sacrifice. Such was Christ as Priest and Sacrifice.

THE HIGH PRIEST

Verses 10 and 11 read: *"And he who is the*

High Priest among his brethren, upon whose head the anointing oil was poured, and who is consecrated to put on the garments, shall not uncover his head, nor rend his clothes;

"Neither shall he go in to any dead body, nor defile himself for his father, or for his mother."

Whereas the ordinary Priest could attend his near kin who had died, the High Priest was forbidden to even go into the house where anyone had died, even his nearest relatives. As well, he was not to alter his appearance at all, not even when his father or his mother died.

This is the one on *"whose head the anointing oil was poured, and is consecrated to put on the garments."* As stated, there was no higher type of Christ!

THE SANCTUARY

Verse 12 reads: *"Neither shall he go out of the Sanctuary, nor profane the Sanctuary of his God; for the crown of the anointing oil of his God is upon him: I am the LORD."*

The idea is this:

If the High Priest was in the Sanctuary, and attending to a particular service, and the word came to him that one of his close loved ones had died, he was not to stop his service, not to leave the Sanctuary, in fact, not to do anything, but to continue the service exactly as it had begun. He was not to be a mourner, meaning that he was not to acknowledge death as far as sadness or sorrow were concerned, to any degree. Naturally as a man, and if a close loved one died, he felt it keenly, as would be obvious. He loved his wife, mother, or dad, etc., just like anyone else. But inasmuch as he was the High Priest, his duties at the Sanctuary must not be hindered or marred in any way. The implication is that he could not even attend the funeral service.

SANCTIFICATION

Verses 13 through 15 read: *"And he shall take a wife in her virginity.*

"A widow, or a divorced woman, or profane, or an harlot, these shall he not take: but he shall take a virgin of his own people to wife.

"Neither shall he profane his seed among his people: for I the LORD do sanctify him."

Whereas it seems an ordinary Priest could marry a widow, the High Priest could only marry a virgin.

As well, as Verse 15 proclaims, his children were to conduct themselves accordingly, because the oldest son among them was to be the next High Priest, at least when his father passed on. If something happened to him, then the next son in line was to be the High Priest. So they were to prepare from the time they were children. They were to live a sanctified life.

(16) "AND THE LORD SPOKE UNTO MOSES, SAYING,

(17) "SPEAK UNTO AARON, SAYING, WHOSOEVER HE BE OF YOUR SEED IN THEIR GENERATIONS WHO HAS ANY BLEMISH, LET HIM NOT APPROACH TO OFFER THE BREAD OF HIS GOD.

(18) "FOR WHATSOEVER MAN HE BE WHO HAS A BLEMISH, HE SHALL NOT APPROACH: A BLIND MAN, OR A LAME, OR HE WHO HAS A FLAT NOSE, OR ANYTHING SUPERFLUOUS,

(19) "OR A MAN WHO IS BROKEN-FOOTED, OR BROKENHANDED,

(20) "OR CROOKBACKED, OR A DWARF, OR WHO HAS A BLEMISH IN HIS EYE, OR BE SCURVY, OR SCABBED, OR HAS HIS STONES BROKEN;

(21) "NO MAN WHO HAS A BLEMISH OF THE SEED OF AARON THE PRIEST SHALL COME NEAR TO OFFER THE OFFERINGS OF THE LORD MADE BY FIRE: HE HAS A BLEMISH; HE SHALL NOT COME NIGH TO OFFER THE BREAD OF HIS GOD.

(22) "HE SHALL EAT THE BREAD OF HIS GOD, BOTH OF THE MOST HOLY, AND OF THE HOLY.

(23) "ONLY HE SHALL NOT GO IN UNTO THE VEIL, NOR COME NIGH UNTO THE ALTAR, BECAUSE HE HAS A BLEMISH; THAT HE PROFANE NOT MY SANCTUARIES: FOR I THE LORD DO SANCTIFY THEM.

(24) "AND MOSES TOLD IT UNTO AARON, AND TO HIS SONS, AND UNTO ALL THE CHILDREN OF ISRAEL."

The diagram is:

1. We find in these Passages that relationship is one thing; capacity is quite another.

2. Though a son of Aaron was a dwarf, or had a blemish in some other capacity, though curtailed in this manner, he was still a son of Aaron. While he would be shorn of many precious privileges and lofty dignities pertaining to the Priesthood, still, he was a son of Aaron all the while, and was permitted to *"eat the bread of his God."*

3. The relationship was genuine, though the development was defective.

THE SACRIFICES

Verses 16 and 17 read: *"And the LORD spoke unto Moses, saying,*

"Speak unto Aaron, saying, Whosoever he be of your seed in their generations who has any blemish, let him not approach to offer the bread of his God."

In order for the Priests to officiate in the offering up of Sacrifices, which are labeled here as *"the bread of his God,"* he must be without physical blemish. The reason for this was that his office served as a type of Christ. He could, in fact, function as it regarded other duties about the Tabernacle, but he could not officiate in the offering of Sacrifices, which pertained to the morning and the evening Sacrifices, and as well, for all of the people which constantly brought sacrifices to be offered up, and in which the Priests were to officiate and participate.

The Priests under the old Mosaic Law served as mediators between the people and God. The High Priest filled this role in a greater way than all. Of all their duties, the Sacrifices were the most holy, and simply because they typified the Crucifixion of Christ on the Cross, which would be necessary in order to redeem the fallen sons of Adam's race.

DO THESE COMMANDS HAVE ANY BEARING ON THE MODERN MINISTRY?

Only in a spiritual way, but most graphically in a spiritual way.

Preachers presently do not in any manner serve as mediators between God and men, that role being filled exclusively by Christ, in that His Work is now a Finished Work (I Tim. 2:5; Heb. 1:3). However, it is most definitely the obligation of every single Preacher of the Gospel to *"preach the Cross,"* which is

the same thing, in a sense, as the Priests of old, offering up Sacrifices, which were types of the Sacrificial Offering of Christ (I Cor. 1:21, 23; 2:2). If a Preacher preaches anything other than the Cross, which refers to making other things the emphasis of his message, he is then placed in the same class as the dysfunctional Priests under the Mosaic economy. While what he is doing might have some significance, even as those particular blemished Priests of old, it by no means is the central focus of the Gospel. That's why Paul graphically stated: *"For Christ sent me not to baptize, but to preach the Gospel: not with wisdom of words, lest the Cross of Christ should be made of none effect"* (I Cor. 1:17). The emphasis always must be the Cross of Christ, and nothing else. While other things definitely are important, they must never be the chief thrust or emphasis.

HOW MANY PREACHERS PRESENTLY ARE PREACHING THE CROSS?

Precious few!

That's the main reason why less people are presently being born-again than possibly any time in the history of the Church, since the Reformation. As well, fewer Believers are being Baptized with the Holy Spirit presently than any time since the Latter Rain outpouring at the turn of the Twentieth Century. Despite all the wild, boastful claims, fewer people are being truly healed today than any time since the Reformation. There is less spiritual victory as well, than ever.

This means that Churches are filled with people who aren't truly born-again. It means that most Believers have no idea as to the Function and Work of the Holy Spirit. It means as well that more Christians are bound by terrible vices of darkness than ever before. All of this is because of a lack of preaching of the Cross.

There is no Salvation outside of the Cross, no Baptism with the Holy Spirit outside of the Cross, no victorious living outside of the Cross. The answer to the ills of man is conclusively the Cross of Christ. There is no other answer, simply because no other answer is needed. It is *"Jesus Christ and Him Crucified"* (I Cor. 1:23; 2:2).

All of this means that almost all of the present Ministry is dysfunctional. It would be the same thing as almost all the Priests of the Mosaic Law being in some way blemished, which means they could not officiate as it regarded the Sacrifices. Had that been the case, and in fact, it ultimately did become the case, and Israel went to her doom.

THE VEIL AND THE ALTAR

Verses 18 through 24 read: *"For whatsoever man he be who has a blemish, he shall not approach: a blind man, or a lame, or he who has a flat nose, or anything superfluous,*

"Or a man who is brokenfooted, or brokenhanded,

"Or crookbacked, or a dwarf, or who has a blemish in his eye, or be scurvy, or scabbed, or has his stones broken;

"No man who has a blemish of the seed of Aaron the Priest shall come nigh to offer the Offerings of the LORD made by fire: he has a blemish; he shall not come near to offer the bread of his God.

"He shall eat the bread of his God, both of the most holy, and of the holy.

"Only he shall not go in unto the Veil, nor come near unto the Altar, because he has a blemish; that he profane not My Sanctuaries: for I the LORD do sanctify them.

"And Moses told it unto Aaron, and to his sons, and unto all the Children of Israel."

Although the blemished Priest could not officiate at the Sacrificial Altar, which pertained to the offering up of Sacrifices, and neither could he go into the Holy Place to apply incense on the Golden Altar; still, he could eat of the Peace-Offering, and even of the Offerings which were most holy, such as the Meat-Offerings, the Sin-Offerings, and the Trespass-Offerings.

Once again we emphasize the fact that this particular Office – the Office of the Priesthood – was intended to be fully a type of Christ. Christ was without blemish, and in every respect; therefore, those who served as *"types"* must function in the same manner, and we speak of the physical sense.

In fact, by the time of the second Temple, which was built by Zerubbabel, which was done after the Babylonian dispersion, the Sanhedrin laid down the rules that governed

NOTES

the Priests according to these commands given to Moses.

They examined all the Priests prior to their being received into the staff of those who officiated in the Sanctuary. At the conclusion of this examination, all the Priests were divided into two classes. Those who were pronounced physically disqualified *"put on black garments, wrapped themselves up in black cloaks, and went away in silence"*; while those who were declared qualified put on white garments and white cloaks, and forthwith joined their brethren to assist in the Sacred Office. They celebrated the day by giving a feast for all their friends, which they opened with the following benediction:

"Blessed be the Lord! Blessed be He because no blemish has been found in the seed of Aaron, the Priest; and blessed be He because He has chosen Aaron and his sons to stand and to serve before the Lord in His most holy Sanctuary."

The Priests who were declared physically unfit were employed in the chamber for wood at the northeast of the Court of the Women, which duty was to select the proper wood for the Altar, since any piece which was worm-eaten could not be burnt on it.

But let the Reader understand that physical blemishes, which put certain Priests into certain categories, had nothing to do with the spiritual. These men, even though they were limited in service, could in fact serve God with total Faithfulness, and could be used greatly of the Lord. In fact, none of this had anything to do with their true spiritual condition, as should be obvious.

But deriving the spiritual lesson taught us here by the Holy Spirit, as it regards the modern Ministry, the true meaning has the reverse effect. Then it was physical; now it is spiritual!

WHAT DO WE MEAN BY *"SPIRITUAL"*?

As we've already stated, the blemishes of the modern Ministry pertain only to the spiritual, and not at all to the physical. So, as stated, it is the very opposite of the Mosaic Law, and rightly so.

The spiritual part of the modern Ministry pertains solely to the emphasis of Faith. In other words, is the Faith of the modern Preacher exclusively in the Cross, or is it elsewhere?

In the last few years, Preachers all across the nation, and I speak of the United States, have formed certain groups, which pertain to recognition. In fact, entire Denominations function in the same capacity. In other words, if you belong to their Denomination, you are approved; but if you don't belong to their Denomination, you are not approved, or else you are less than you ought to be. In fact, coming up in a particular Pentecostal Denomination, I often heard the statement made or inferred that if Preachers were right with God, they would belong to our particular Denomination. If they didn't belong to our Denomination, while they might be Christians, they were definitely less than they ought to be. In other words, anyone who didn't belong to this particular Denomination was not a very good Christian.

Of course, the foolishness of such thinking beggars description! But unfortunately, that is the case with many religious Denominations.

The word *"covering"* has been used very extensively, as well, in the last few decades. The idea being, if you had certain famous Preachers as your covering, or a Denomination, this means that you were accepted, you were right with God, and you had great credibility, etc.

Of course, all of this, and without exception, is specious to say the least. In other words, it's all of the flesh, and not at all of God. All of this is man's righteousness, which is self-righteousness, which God can never honor or condone.

THE CROSS OF CHRIST IS
THE ONLY CRITERIA

The only spiritual disqualification regarding Preachers is the failure of the Preacher to *"preach the Cross"* (Rom. 5:1-2; 6:3-14; 8:1-2, 11; Gal., Chpt. 5; 6:14; Eph. 2:13-18; Phil. 3:18-19; Col. 2:14-15). If a Preacher places the emphasis of his Message elsewhere other than the Cross, he is spiritually disqualified. In fact, this is the only disqualification given in the Word of God. It doesn't matter how many Denominations with which the Preacher is associated, or how many famous Preachers

NOTES

he has for his *"covering,"* or with what groups he is associated, or how he is applauded by the Church or the world, if he doesn't preach the Cross, as far as the Holy Spirit is concerned, he is disqualified. Listen to Paul:

"I marvel that you are so soon removed from Him (the Holy Spirit) *Who called you into the Grace of Christ unto another gospel:*

"Which is not another (it won't do you any good)*; but there be some who trouble you, and would pervert the Gospel of Christ* (false apostles).

"But though we, or an Angel from Heaven, preach any other gospel unto you than that which we have preached unto you, let him be accursed.

"As we said before, so say I now again, if any man preach any other gospel unto you than that you have received, let him be accursed" (Gal. 1:6-9).

That's about as blunt as anything could ever be. *"Another gospel"* has to do with that, whatever it might be, which is other than the Cross. Not only is such a Preacher disqualified, but bluntly, clearly, and plainly, the Holy Spirit through Paul said that such Preachers and preaching are *"cursed by God."*

Therefore, under Grace, the rules, one might say, are far more stringent than they ever were under the Law, and as they should be.

There is no Law of Moses presently applicable to the modern Christian. Christ fulfilled it all at the Cross, and it, therefore, passed away. It served its purpose, but its purpose was completed upon the Sacrificial Offering of Christ.

Now it is all Faith. In fact, it has always been Faith. But Faith could not be properly realized, at least as it is now, before the Cross; consequently, the Law of Moses was given to show man the way. Now, we have Christ Who has shown us the way, and all that is required of us presently is that we have Faith in Him, and what he has done for us in the Sacrifice of Himself. It's a very simple thing, but even as Cain tried to change the Way of God, which was the Way of the Cross, into something else, likewise, modern Preachers seem to try to do the same.

ANGELS OF LIGHT

Paul also said: *"But I fear, lest by any*

means, as the serpent beguiled Eve through his subtilty, so your minds should be corrupted from the simplicity that is in Christ.

"For if he who comes preaches another Jesus, whom we have not preached, or if you receive another spirit, which you have not received, or another gospel, which you have not accepted, you might well bear with him . . .

"For such are false apostles, deceitful workers, transforming themselves into the apostles of Christ.

"And no marvel; for Satan himself is transformed into an angel of light.

"Therefore it is no great thing if his ministers also be transformed as the ministers of righteousness; whose end shall be according to their works" (II Cor. 11:3-4, 13-15).

As we have stated, Faith is simple, with Paul describing it as *"the simplicity that is in Christ."* But many attempt to change the simple Faith, which is the greatest story ever told, into something else; regrettably, many in the Church seem to respond very favorably to the bait.

The *"minds"* of modern Christians, at least for the most part, have been *"corrupted from the simplicity that is in Christ."* They have accepted *"another Jesus,"* which is brought by *"another spirit,"* which presents *"another gospel."* It is all done through *"angels of light."*

In other words, it looks like God, sounds like God, reads like God, and claims to be God. But the truth is, if the Preacher is not preaching the Cross, no matter how enticing his words might be, no matter how good he may look to the natural eye, the truth is, he is functioning as an *"angel of light,"* and is, therefore, accursed by God.

Once again allow me to emphasize, it's not the Denomination which is the criteria, or certain Churches, or even certain doctrines, although correct doctrine certainly is of vital significance, but rather, the criteria is totally and completely the Cross of Christ.

The Church, and I speak of Christians, is going to have to make a decision. Does it accept the Cross, or does it deny the Cross?

ACCEPTANCE OR DENIAL OF THE CROSS!

Almost every Christian would quickly and

readily exclaim their devotion to the Cross of Christ. However, most Christians little understand what they are actually saying. In fact, about all that most Christians know about the Cross is, *"Jesus died for me."* While that of course is certainly true, and while that of course is one of the greatest statements ever made, still, most Christians don't actually know what that really means.

In the lives of most Christians, the Cross is relegated solely to the initial born-again experience. And even that is falling into disrepute. The Word of Faith doctrine, which repudiates the Cross, has made such inroads into the modern Church, affecting basically every strata of religious society, that the Cross, in many circles, is looked at as an evil thing. With the Word of Faith people referring to the Cross as *"the greatest defeat in human history,"* one can readily understand as to the deterioration of the foundational doctrine of the Church. Incidentally, even though the title is *"Word of Faith,"* the truth is, it is not faith that God will recognize, and because it's not in the Cross of Christ.

As well, one cannot merely tack the Cross onto whatever it is that one is presently believing. The Cross of Christ must be the foundation of all doctrine, which means that it's not merely another doctrine. When one has a proper understanding of the Cross, as we've said repeatedly in this Volume, one will then have a proper understanding of the Word of God. To turn it around, one cannot have a proper understanding of the Word of God unless one has a proper understanding of the Cross. The first Promise of Redemption that came out of the Mouth of God after the Fall pertained to the Cross (Gen. 3:15). Thus, it became the foundation of the entirety of the Word of God. And in fact, the Word of God closes out in the Book of Revelation with the fulfillment of that Promise of Redemption, by saying, *"And there shall be no more curse: but the Throne of God and of the Lamb shall be in it; and His servants shall serve Him"* (Rev. 22:3).

So it begins with the Cross, and it ends with the Cross. The Cross alone, typified by the use of the title, *"Lamb,"* is what has lifted the curse. What a Promise! What a Blessing!

"Is your life a channel of Blessing?
"Is the Love of God flowing through
    you?
"Are you telling the lost of the Saviour?
"Are you ready His service to do?"

"Is your life a channel of Blessing?
"Are you burdened for those who are
    lost?
"Have you urged upon those who are
    straying
"The Saviour Who died on the Cross?"

"Is your life a channel of Blessing?
"Is it daily telling for Him?
"Have you spoken the Word of Salva-
    tion
"To those who are dying in sin?"

"We cannot be channels of Blessings,
"If our lives are not free from known
    sin;
"We will barriers be and a hindrance
"To those we are trying to win."

CHAPTER 22

(1) "AND THE LORD SPOKE UNTO MOSES, SAYING,

(2) "SPEAK UNTO AARON AND TO HIS SONS, THAT THEY SEPARATE THEMSELVES FROM THE HOLY THINGS OF THE CHILDREN OF ISRAEL, AND THAT THEY PROFANE NOT MY HOLY NAME IN THOSE THINGS WHICH THEY HALLOW UNTO ME: I AM THE LORD.

(3) "SAY UNTO THEM, WHOSOEVER HE BE OF ALL YOUR SEED AMONG YOUR GENERATIONS, WHO GOES UNTO THE HOLY THINGS, WHICH THE CHILDREN OF ISRAEL HALLOW UNTO THE LORD, HAVING HIS UNCLEANNESS UPON HIM, THAT SOUL SHALL BE CUT OFF FROM MY PRESENCE: I AM THE LORD.

(4) "WHAT MAN SOEVER OF THE SEED OF AARON IS A LEPER, OR HAS A RUNNING ISSUE; HE SHALL NOT EAT OF THE HOLY THINGS, UNTIL HE BE CLEAN. AND WHOSO TOUCHES ANYTHING THAT IS UNCLEAN BY THE DEAD, OR A MAN WHOSE SEED GOES FROM HIM;

(5) "OR WHOSOEVER TOUCHES ANY CREEPING THING, WHEREBY HE MAY BE MADE UNCLEAN, OR A MAN OF WHOM HE MAY TAKE UNCLEANNESS, WHATSOEVER UNCLEANNESS HE HAS;

(6) "THE SOUL WHICH HAS TOUCHED ANY SUCH SHALL BE UNCLEAN UNTIL EVENING, AND SHALL NOT EAT OF THE HOLY THINGS, UNLESS HE WASH HIS FLESH WITH WATER.

(7) "AND WHEN THE SUN IS DOWN, HE SHALL BE CLEAN, AND SHALL AFTERWARD EAT OF THE HOLY THINGS; BECAUSE IT IS HIS FOOD.

(8) "THAT WHICH DIES OF ITSELF, OR IS TORN WITH BEASTS, HE SHALL NOT EAT TO DEFILE HIMSELF THEREWITH; I AM THE LORD.

(9) "THEY SHALL THEREFORE KEEP MY ORDINANCE, LEST THEY BEAR SIN FOR IT, AND DIE THEREFORE, IF THEY PROFANE IT: I THE LORD DO SANCTIFY THEM.

(10) "THERE SHALL NO STRANGER EAT OF THE HOLY THING: A SOJOURNER OF THE PRIEST, OR AN HIRED SERVANT, SHALL NOT EAT OF THE HOLY THING.

(11) "BUT IF THE PRIEST BUY ANY SOUL WITH HIS MONEY, HE SHALL EAT OF IT, AND HE THAT IS BORN IN HIS HOUSE: THEY SHALL EAT OF HIS MEAT.

(12) "IF THE PRIEST'S DAUGHTER ALSO BE MARRIED UNTO A STRANGER, SHE MAY NOT EAT OF AN OFFERING OF THE HOLY THINGS.

(13) "BUT IF THE PRIEST'S DAUGHTER BE A WIDOW, OR DIVORCED, AND HAVE NO CHILD, AND IS RETURNED UNTO HER FATHER'S HOUSE, AS IN HER YOUTH, SHE SHALL EAT OF HER FATHER'S MEAT: BUT THERE SHALL BE NO STRANGER EAT THEREOF.

(14) "AND IF A MAN EAT OF THE HOLY THING UNWITTINGLY, THEN HE SHALL PUT THE FIFTH PART THEREOF UNTO IT, AND SHALL GIVE IT UNTO THE PRIEST WITH THE HOLY THING.

(15) "AND THEY SHALL NOT PROFANE THE HOLY THINGS OF THE CHILDREN OF ISRAEL, WHICH THEY OFFER UNTO THE LORD;

(16) "OR SUFFER THEM TO BEAR THE

INIQUITY OF TRESPASS, WHEN THEY EAT THEIR HOLY THINGS: FOR I THE LORD DO SANCTIFY THEM."

The structure is:

1. That Holiness becomes God's House forever is true in all periods of time. God demanded an unblemished Priest and an unblemished Sacrifice (Lev. 21:21; 22:20). Such was Christ as Priest and Sacrifice (Williams).

2. In the Christian life, God must have first place, then will the nearest and dearest relatives have their right place.

3. To beget souls for God, and nourish them in the Word of His Grace, the Believer must be equipped with full spiritual energy, and stand apart from everything that defiles.

SEPARATION

Verses 1 and 2 read: *"And the LORD spoke unto Moses, saying,*

"Speak unto Aaron and to his sons, that they separate themselves from the holy things of the Children of Israel, and that they profane not My Holy Name in those things which they hallow unto Me: I am the LORD."

In this Chapter, the Laws regulating the conduct of the Priests in their holy ministrations are continued. As the last Chapter concluded with the permission to disqualify Priests to eat of the Sacrifices, this Chapter opens with conditions under which even the legally qualified Priests must not partake of the Offerings (Ellicott).

As we shall see, there were many things that would disqualify a legally appointed Priest from carrying on his appointed duties, and because by the doing of those things, whatever they might have been, he would be declared by God as unclean; consequently, he would have to go through a particular ritual in order to once again become clean.

Now, we have both the perfect Priest and the perfect Sacrifice in the Person of our blessed Lord Jesus Christ. He having *"offered Himself without spot to God"* passed into the Heavens as our Great High Priest, where *"He ever lives to make intercession for us."* The Epistle to the Hebrews dwells elaborately upon these two points.

It throws into vivid contrast the Sacrifice and Priesthood of the Mosaic system and the Sacrifice and Priesthood of Christ. In Him

we have Divine perfection, whether as the Victim or as the Priest. We have all that God could require, and all that man could need. His Precious Blood has put away all our sins, and His all-prevailing intercession ever maintains us in all the perfection of the place into which His Blood has introduced us. As Paul said, *"We are complete in Him"* (Col. 2:10) (Mackintosh).

COMPLETE IN HIM?

While we definitely are *"complete in Him,"* and because all perfection is in Him, which we gain by Faith, still, even though that is our *"standing"* in Christ, it is hardly our *"state."*

We are, in effect, so feeble and faltering within ourselves, so full of failure and infirmity, so prone to err and stumble in our onward way, that we could not stand for a moment were it not that *"He ever liveth to make intercession for us"* (Heb. 7:25-26).

Now that which I have just stated is not admitted to by many in the modern Church. They have been so adversely affected by the Word of Faith doctrine, which I believe is Satan's last effort before the Rapture, that to make statements such as I have just made, although completely true, are judged as a *"bad confession."*

Let me quickly state that a true confession is not a bad confession. The truth is, we are perfect and complete in Christ. That is the positive side of Christianity, and a glorious side it is; however, the negative side is, and there is definitely a negative side, our *"state"* is not up to our *"standing."* And let the Reader full well understand that our *"state"* can never be brought up to our *"standing"* by merely confessing that our standing is perfect. It can only be brought to that place by Faith. And what do we mean by that?

When we speak of *"Faith,"* as we've already stated any number of times, we are speaking of *"Faith in the Cross of Christ,"* and that exclusively.

The Holy Spirit is given to us, Who works tirelessly, to bring us to the place that our *"state equals our standing."*

He doesn't do that merely by confession, as good as proper confession is, but rather by our Faith placed exclusively in Christ, and His Finished Work.

In this Twenty-second Chapter of Leviticus, we will study many things which would make a qualified Priest unable to carry out his duties. There is only one thing presently that can place the modern Preacher in such circumstances. That one thing is an incorrect object of Faith. The object must ever be the Cross of Christ, and if anything else is entertained, it disqualifies the man of God (I Cor. 1:17).

The Second Verse closes with the statement, *"I am the LORD,"* which refers to the fact that it's His Commandments that must be followed, and not those of men. Uncleanness in any form would *"separate"* these Priests from their sacred duties. Lack of Faith properly placed will presently do the same thing to modern Preachers.

UNCLEANNESS

Verse 3 reads: *"Say unto them, Whosoever he be of all your seed among your generations, who goes unto the holy things, which the Children of Israel hallow unto the LORD, having his uncleanness upon him, that soul shall be cut off from My Presence: I am the LORD."*

The Lord is speaking to Moses concerning Priests, and qualified Priests at that, proven by the phrase, *"Whosoever he be of all your seed* (the seed of Aaron) *among your generations."*

"Who goes unto the holy things," refers to the Priests approaching the Sacrifices in order to eat them, as proven in Verses 4, 6, and 12.

The greater part of the Meat-Offerings, the Sin-Offerings, and the Trespass-Offerings, was given to the Priests, as food for themselves and their families. The Peace-Offerings were included in these as well. The Burnt-Offering alone was consumed totally upon the Altar.

If a Priest was unclean in any manner, which uncleanness will be typified in coming Verses, he was not allowed to partake of these Sacrifices. If in fact he did so, ignoring the Commandments of the Lord, he would be *"cut off from the Presence of God."*

This means, if the Priest ventures to approach the Altar presumptuously to partake

in a defiled state of the Holy Sacrifices, God Himself will banish him from His Presence as He did Nadab and Abihu (Lev. 10:1-3).

CAUSES OF UNCLEANNESS

Verses 4 through 9 read: *"What man soever of the seed of Aaron is a leper, or has a running issue; he shall not eat of the holy things, until he be clean. And whoso touches anything that is unclean by the dead, or a man whose seed goes from him;*

"Or whosoever touches any creeping thing, whereby he may be made unclean, or a man of whom he may take uncleanness, whatsoever uncleanness he has;

"The soul which has touched any such shall be unclean until evening, and shall not eat of the holy things, unless he wash his flesh with water.

"And when the sun is down, he shall be clean, and shall afterward eat of the holy things; because it is his food.

"That which dies of itself, or is torn with beasts, he shall not eat to defile himself therewith; I am the LORD.

"They shall therefore keep My Ordinance, lest they bear sin for it, and die therefore, if they profane it: I the LORD do sanctify them."

The ceremonial matters against which the sons of Aaron were warned in the section before us, have their antitypes in the Christian economy. Mackintosh says: *"Had they to be warned against unholy contact? So have we. Had they to be warned against unholy alliance? So have we. Had they to be warned against all manner of ceremonial uncleanness? So have we to be warned against 'all filthiness of the flesh and spirit' (I Cor., Chpt. 7). Were they shorn of many of their loftiest Priestly privileges by bodily blemish and imperfect natural growth? So are we by moral blemish and imperfect spiritual growth."*

We should take a lesson from these things we are reading. Even though they pertain to a certain people, and a certain order, of long, long ago; still, they have, as already stated, great spiritual lessons for us.

The Holy Spirit is given to us in order that He may root out all sin within our lives. However, there are two distinct aspects to the Christian experience, on which the Holy

Spirit constantly works. Those two aspects are *"self"* and *"sin."*

SELF AND SIN

When Jesus died on the Cross, He died not only to save us from sin, but as well from self. The former is obvious, but the latter is not so obvious.

We cover *"self"* with Scriptures, make it very religious, and thereby, we are deceived. In fact, most in the modern Church little know what to do with *"self."* In other words, they address it in mostly wrong ways.

First of all, every human being is a *"self."* In the Church, we have heard about *"killing self,"* or *"dying out to self."* Perhaps the intention is correct, but both statements show a lack of understanding, as it regards *"self."*

As stated, we are a *"self,"* and will always be such. But there are some things we need to know, and because they are so very, very important.

CONQUERING SELF

No matter how hard we try, no matter what effort we may put forth, no matter how sincere we might be, if we try to conquer self by personal strength, which refers to bringing self into total and complete line with the Will of God, we will ingloriously fail. But yet, that's basically what we try to do.

"Self," which refers to our human nature, due to the Fall, cannot by our own strength and ability, function as we ought to. It just simply cannot be done. I realize Christians are fond of saying, *"I can do all things through Christ, which strengtheneth me"* (Phil. 4:13). But most completely misunderstand the Passage.

Paul was merely saying that if he had to, he could go hungry, or he could enjoy the plenty (Phil. 4:12). But many Christians love to stretch out the Passage, and make it mean anything. They are sadly mistaken! As well, just because we are saved and even Spirit-filled, doesn't mean that self is in its proper place.

In truth, most of the things attempted for the Lord are things which originated with *"self,"* which means the Holy Spirit did not give birth to these ideas, and which also means that it will do nothing for God, and

because the Holy Spirit will not help such an effort. He will only help that to which He has given complete birth (Rom. 12:1-3). But regrettably, many in the Charismatic world have the mistaken idea that now that they are saved, they are operating some type of spiritual franchise, and they can do whatever it is they want to do. In other words, whatever they say becomes the Will of God. Nothing could be further from the truth.

Paul said: *"For as many as are led by the Spirit of God, they are the sons of God"* (Rom. 8:14). There is only one way to be led by the Spirit, and we'll get to that in a moment.

THE DENIAL OF SELF

Jesus said: *"If any man will come after Me, let him deny himself, and take up his cross daily, and follow Me"* (Lk. 9:23).

What did Jesus mean by a denial of self?

First of all, He wasn't speaking of asceticism, which is a denial of all things that are comfortable and pleasurable. Unfortunately, that's what most Christians think He's talking about. So they have it in their minds that the more one suffers, or lives some type of cold, Spartan, abbreviated lifestyle, the holier they must be. Again, nothing could be further from the truth.

When Jesus spoke of one *"denying himself,"* He was referring to the Believer who must not trust self, must not depend on self, but entirely on Christ. Jesus also said: *"For without Me you can do nothing"* (Jn. 15:5). So if we are not to depend on self at all, then what are we to do?

He also stated, even as we've already quoted, that we must *"take up our cross daily, and follow Him."* What does that mean?

First of all, let's see what it doesn't mean.

To which we've already briefly alluded, it doesn't mean suffering. But yet, that's exactly what most Christians think it means, so they miss the point altogether.

When Jesus spoke of taking up our Cross, and doing so on a daily basis, He was speaking of us trusting in the benefits of the Cross, and doing so everyday. The Crucifixion is something that happened about 2,000 years ago. It was a completed task, which means it will never have to be repeated, or amended in any fashion. From what He did, great benefits flowed, and in fact, flow unto this very hour, and will never cease (Heb. 13:20). It's these benefits of which I speak. As Believers, we are to look to Christ and what He did for us at the Cross, and do so on a daily basis, which means that we ever make the Cross of Christ the object of our Faith, which is the only way that *"self"* can be properly approached.

Concerning this, Jesus said: *"For whosoever will save his life shall lose it: but whosoever will lose his life for My sake, the same shall save it"* (Lk. 9:24).

"Saving our life" refers to us trying to do this thing by our own strength, which means that we are going to lose. *"Losing our life for the sake of Christ,"* refers to placing our life and living, i.e., *"self,"* entirely into Christ. When we do that, we *"shall save it."*

The Master also said: *"At that day* (after the Cross and upon the Advent of the Holy Spirit) *you shall know that I am in My Father, and you in Me, and I in you"* (Jn. 14:20). We are in Christ, and Christ is in us. And how do we explain that?

BAPTIZED INTO HIS DEATH

Paul said: *"Know ye not, that so many of us as were baptized into Jesus Christ were baptized into His death?"* (Rom. 6:3).

Paul is not speaking here of Water Baptism, not at all! He is speaking of the Crucifixion of Christ, and how that our Faith in Him literally placed us in Christ when He died on the Cross. Of course we were not there, but the Holy Spirit through Paul is not speaking of something physical, but rather spiritual. Let me say it again:

The very moment that you as a believing sinner evidenced Faith in Christ, in the Mind of God, you were literally placed in Christ, as He hung on the Cross and died, literally baptized into His death. In fact, the word *"baptized"* is the strongest word that the Holy Spirit could use here. It means that we are completely in that into which we are baptized, and that into which we are baptized is completely in us. So is Christ!

Furthermore, *"We are buried with Him by baptism into death,"* and likewise, raised up with Him *"in newness of life"* (Rom. 6:4). This means that when Jesus died on the

Cross, we died with Him, and in effect, *"in Him."* We were buried with Him, and as well, raised with Him in newness of life, which refers to us being *"born again"* (Jn. 3:3, 8).

This is the reason we must look to the Cross; this is where it all was done. This is the only way that the Believer can properly address *"self."* Let us say it again:

When Jesus died on the Cross, He died not only to save us from *"sin,"* but as well, from *"self."* This means that every Believer has a twofold problem: *"sin and self."* They are both handled at the Cross, and they are both handled only at the Cross. There is no other way that victory can be achieved or obtained.

TO PROFANE THE HOLY THING

Verses 10 through 16 read: *"There shall no stranger eat of the holy thing: a sojourner of the Priest, or an hired servant, shall not eat of the holy thing.*

"But if the Priest buy any soul with his money, he shall eat of it, and he who is born in his house: they shall eat of his meat.

"If the Priests daughter also be married unto a stranger, she may not eat of an offering of the holy things.

"But if the Priest's daughter be a widow, or divorced, and have no child, and is returned unto her father's house, as in her youth, she shall eat of her father's meat: but there shall be no stranger eat thereof.

"And if a man eat of the holy thing unwittingly, then he shall put the fifth part thereof unto it, and shall give it unto the Priest with the holy thing.

"And they shall not profane the holy things of the Children of Israel, which they offer unto the LORD;

"Or suffer them to bear the iniquity of trespass, when they eat their holy things: for I the LORD do sanctify them."

We have here minute directions as to what the Priests could and could not do. They were to guard carefully the Word of God, as it related to their services at the Tabernacle. They must not add to that Word, and they must not take from that Word. They must do their very best to carry out that which the Lord had demanded, and because to do otherwise would bring upon themselves dire consequences.

Even though we are no longer under Law, in that Christ has satisfied and fulfilled all the demands of the Law, and did so by keeping it perfectly, and as well, addressed the broken Law by paying the price that it demanded. Still, we must understand that even though this is the Day of Grace, God's Word means exactly what it says, and says exactly what it means. We must obey the Word, or else we will suffer the consequences, just as the Priests of old.

And yet under Grace, which means we are no longer under Law (Rom. 6:14), even though the demands are few, those demands must be met. And exactly what are those demands?

FAITH

The demand is Faith (Rom. 5:1-2; Gal. 5:6; Eph. 2:8-9). The Holy Spirit simply demands that we exhibit Faith in Christ and what Christ has done for us at the Cross.

This morning (Oct. 14, 2002), I was on SonLife Radio, on the program hosted by Frances, taking questions from callers. One elderly lady called and asked this question: *"I do not fully understand what you are talking about as it regards the Cross and Sanctification. I just believe that the Lord died for me and paid the price for all that I need."* I related to the dear Sister that she was exactly right in what she was believing. That's really all that is required – that we trust Christ and what He did at the Cross for our Salvation, and continue to trust Him in this capacity for our Sanctification. Without going into a lot of detail, she had it right.

The object of her Faith was the Cross of Christ, and that's what is demanded of us, and that's all that is demanded of us.

However, if we attempt to live for God, and I speak now of the Sanctification process, by placing our Faith in something else other than the Cross, we will be violating the Word of the Lord, which means the Holy Spirit will not help us, without Whom we cannot survive, and failure will be the result.

A PERSONAL EXPERIENCE

I have preached the Cross all of my life, and have seen untold thousands brought to

NOTES

a saving knowledge of Jesus Christ. However, the preaching of the Cross, which I carried out, was limited to the Salvation of the sinner. As it regarded our everyday living for God, our Sanctification, I did not know or understand the part that the Cross played in this all-important process. Consequently, even as the far greater majority of the Church, I attempted to sanctify myself by my own doings, etc. The things I was doing were right in their own capacity. I speak of prayer, Bible study, witnessing to souls, etc. I was very diligent in this, and was blessed greatly by the Lord in these endeavors; however, despite my zeal, despite my sincerity, the Holy Spirit simply would not help me as it regarded my daily life and living, simply because my Faith was really not in Christ and what He had done for us at the Cross as it regards Sanctification, but rather in these particular works that I was carrying out. The things I was doing were correct, as far as those things were concerned. In fact, they were what any good Christian will do; however, once we begin to place our Faith and trust in those things, thinking that by the doing of them, it will bring us victory within our hearts and lives, we will be sadly disappointed.

Now I realize that many will read this and will automatically quip, *"Well, I knew that!"* But the truth is, they don't know that.

I've talked to too many, read too many Messages, taken too many e-mails, and watched and observed too many Christians, which make me to know that the far greater majority of the Church doesn't have the foggiest idea as to how to live a successful Christian life. Many may think they do! Others may claim they do! And while some precious few do know, the truth is, almost all don't know.

THE MODERN CHURCH

The Scripture plainly tells us, *"Faith comes by hearing, and hearing by the Word of God"* (Rom. 10:17). This means if we are to have Faith, we must hear the subject taught and proclaimed behind the pulpit. This is why the Lord has set in the Church, *"Apostles, Prophets, Evangelists, Pastors, and Teachers"* (Eph. 4:11-13). But the truth is, precious few Preachers understand the

Cross as they should. And if they don't understand it, they surely cannot teach it to those who would sit under them.

If you would turn on what passes for *"Christian Television,"* and listen long enough, thereby hearing Preachers tell us how to have victory, how to live a Godly life, etc., virtually all of them would tell us to do the very thing that I have mentioned earlier, concerning prayer and Bible study, etc. Or the Word of Faith people would tell you to find certain Scriptures that apply to your problem, memorize them, and then quote them over and over, which is supposed to stir God to action, etc.

While memorizing Scriptures are very good, and all the other things mentioned as well, the wrong comes in when we place our Faith in these things, instead of Christ and the Cross.

Satan is very subtle! He really doesn't care too very much about what we do, just as long as our Faith is not in *"Christ and Him Crucified."* Of course, he would rather us quit altogether; however, if he can't get the Christian to simply quit, which means to turn one's back on the Lord, he'll try to keep you from hearing the Truth, and thereby to anchor your Faith in something other than the Cross. He knows that when this is done, the Holy Spirit simply will not help the individual, which means that no matter how sincere the person might be, that person is going to fail.

SPIRITUAL ADULTERY

More than likely, most Christians have never heard the term *"spiritual adultery,"* in all of their lives. It is derived from Romans 7:1-4.

Paul gives the illustration of a woman who has a living husband, but marries another. In effect, she now has two husbands, at least in the Mind of God. Paul said that she would be called an *"adulteress."*

The Apostle is not teaching here on the subject of adultery, marriage and divorce, and remarriage, etc. There are Scriptural grounds for such. He is only referring to the woman that has no Scriptural grounds, and divorces her husband and marries someone else.

He is likening that to the Believer who is married to Christ, and should look to

Christ for everything, but rather looks to something else. Such action is *"spiritual adultery."* Even though Paul doesn't label it exactly as that, he heavily infers such. And the truth is, most Christians, simply because they do not know and understand the Cross as it regards their Sanctification, which refers to their everyday living for God, are in fact, committing *"spiritual adultery."* Such means that the Believer is not fully trusting the Lord, but in fact, is trusting something else as well. In other words, at least in the Mind of God, the Believer has two husbands, Christ and something else. This is what Paul is telling us in these first four Verses of Romans, Chapter 7.

We must understand that the Holy Spirit through Paul is the One Who explained it in this fashion, and He did so for purpose and reason. He wanted us to realize the seriousness of disobeying the Word of God.

The Sixth Chapter of Romans outlines to us the means and the way by which the Christian can live a victorious life. In other words, it tells us *"how"* the Holy Spirit works within our lives. He does so strictly by and through the Finished Work of Christ. One might say that the Sacrifice of Christ is His legal parameters.

Failing to adhere to Romans, Chapter 6, the Holy Spirit in Romans 7:1-4 then tells us what the outcome is – spiritual adultery.

AN INSULT TO CHRIST

All of this is meant to impress upon us how wrong it is to disobey the Word. And when we place our Faith in something else other than the Cross, we are definitely disobeying the Word (Gal. 6:14). To be sure, the results will definitely be negative.

Christ has paid such a price for us that what He did beggars description, and in fact, can never be exhausted as it regards its meaning (Heb. 13:20). And we must always remember that everything He did, He did it all for you and me. None of it was done for Himself, nothing for Heaven, nothing for the Godhead, all for sinners. So whatever it is He did, understanding that it was totally for us, we must realize how priceless His Sacrifice of Himself actually was and is. We should desire to understand what He did, why He did it, and what exactly was accomplished. And then realizing the tremendous price, we should certainly understand that He would want us to avail ourselves of all that He has done.

The insult of all insults is to demean what He did, to fail to properly understand what He did, or to ignore what He did, by registering unbelief. Such action, such direction, can only invite the wrath of God. Paul said:

"For the wrath of God is revealed from Heaven against all ungodliness and unrighteousness of men, who hold the truth in unrighteousness" (Rom. 1:18).

THE TRUTH

Our Lord said: *"You shall know the Truth, and the Truth shall make you free"* (Jn. 8:32).

What is the Truth?

In brief, the Truth is *"the Faith,"* or *"Jesus Christ and Him Crucified"* (Gal. 2:20; I Cor. 1:23).

If Believers know this *"Truth,"* which speaks of the Cross as it refers to Salvation, and as well, as it refers to Sanctification, they can live a life of perpetual victory. No, we are not teaching sinless perfection, because the Bible doesn't teach such. But as we've repeatedly stated, we are definitely teaching that, *"Sin shall not have dominion over you"* (Rom. 6:14).

This is the Truth, and anything else added to this Truth, or deleted from this Truth, makes this Truth ineffective.

So, as the Priests of old were commanded by the Lord to minutely follow His directions, we today are demanded to do the same thing. If we deviate from the Word of God, which is actually the true Word of Faith, we will accrue very negative results.

(17) "AND THE LORD SPOKE UNTO MOSES, SAYING,

(18) "SPEAK UNTO AARON, AND TO HIS SONS, AND UNTO ALL THE CHILDREN OF ISRAEL, AND SAY UNTO THEM, WHATSOEVER HE BE OF THE HOUSE OF ISRAEL, OR OF THE STRANGERS IN ISRAEL, WHO WILL OFFER HIS OBLATION FOR ALL HIS VOWS, AND FOR ALL HIS FREEWILL OFFERINGS, WHICH THEY WILL OFFER UNTO THE LORD FOR A BURNT-OFFERING;

(19) "YOU SHALL OFFER AT YOUR

NOTES

OWN WILL A MALE WITHOUT BLEMISH, OF THE BEEVES, OF THE SHEEP, OR OF THE GOATS.

(20) "BUT WHATSOEVER HAS A BLEMISH, THAT SHALL YOU NOT OFFER: FOR IT SHALL NOT BE ACCEPTABLE FOR YOU.

(21) "AND WHOSOEVER OFFERS A SACRIFICE OF PEACE-OFFERINGS UNTO THE LORD TO ACCOMPLISH HIS VOW, OR A FREEWILL OFFERING IN BEEVES OR SHEEP, IT SHALL BE PERFECT TO BE ACCEPTED; THERE SHALL BE NO BLEMISH THEREIN.

(22) "BLIND, OR BROKEN, OR MAIMED, OR HAVING A WEN, OR SCURVY, OR SCABBED, YOU SHALL NOT OFFER THESE UNTO THE LORD, NOR MAKE AN OFFERING BY FIRE OF THEM UPON THE ALTAR UNTO THE LORD.

(23) "EITHER A BULLOCK OR A LAMB THAT HAS ANYTHING SUPERFLUOUS OR LACKING IN HIS PARTS, THAT MAY YOU OFFER FOR A FREEWILL OFFERING; BUT FOR A VOW IT SHALL NOT BE ACCEPTED.

(24) "YOU SHALL NOT OFFER UNTO THE LORD THAT WHICH IS BRUISED, OR CRUSHED, OR BROKEN, OR CUT; NEITHER SHALL YOU MAKE ANY OFFERING THEREOF IN YOUR LAND.

(25) "NEITHER FROM A STRANGER'S HAND SHALL YOU OFFER THE BREAD OF YOUR GOD OF ANY OF THESE; BECAUSE THEIR CORRUPTION IS IN THEM, AND BLEMISHES BE IN THEM: THEY SHALL NOT BE ACCEPTED FOR YOU."

The composition is:

1. In these Verses, we are given instructions concerning the Sacrifice of certain animals. We are told that the animals with blemishes must not be given to the Lord. From this we learn that in the Christian life, God must have first place.

2. The Believer must stand apart from everything that defiles.

3. God has given His best unto us, and that refers to every capacity from His Son, to His Blessings; correspondingly, we must give our best to Him as well!

OF YOUR OWN WILL

Verses 17 through 20 read: *"And the LORD*

spoke unto Moses, saying,

"Speak unto Aaron, and to his sons, and unto all the Children of Israel, and say unto them, Whatsoever he be of the house of Israel, or of the strangers in Israel, who will offer his oblation for his vows, and for all his freewill Offerings, which they will offer unto the LORD for a Burnt-Offering;

"You shall offer at your own will a male without blemish, of the beeves, of the sheep, or of the goats.

"But whatsoever has a blemish, that shall you not offer: for it shall not be acceptable for you."

The laws about the physical features and ceremonial purity of the Priests, who are to be devoted to the services of the Altar, are now followed by kindred precepts about the animals which are to be offered upon the Altar (Ellicott).

The phrase, *"And unto all the Children of Israel,"* proclaims the fact that these instructions are meant not only for the Priests, but also for all the people as well.

First of all, all Sacrifices were to be offered of the *"freewill"* of the individual. Second, they were to offer animals, whichever clean animal was chosen, which was the best of the lot, and definitely not one that was blemished. If they did such, it would not be acceptable to God, would not be recognized by God, with in fact, the sacrifice being a waste of time.

AN OFFERING TO THE LORD

Verses 21 through 25 read: *"And whosoever offers a Sacrifice of Peace-Offerings unto the LORD to accomplish his vow, or a freewill Offering in beeves or sheep, it shall be perfect to be accepted: there shall be no blemish therein.*

"Blind, or broken, or maimed, or having a wen, or scurvy, or scabbed, you shall not offer these unto the LORD, nor make an Offering by fire of them upon the Altar unto the LORD.

"Either a bullock or a lamb that has anything superfluous or lacking in his parts, that may you offer for a freewill Offering; but for a vow it shall not be accepted.

"You shall not offer unto the LORD that which is bruised, or crushed, or broken, or

cut; neither shall you make an Offering thereof in your land.

"Neither from a stranger's hand shall you offer the bread of your God of any of these; because their corruption is in them, and blemishes be in them: they shall not be accepted for you."

The lesson that we are to presently learn from these instructions is that the Lord expects our best. And I suppose the great question must be asked, how many of us are actually giving the Lord our best?

I was speaking to a business man once who was very successful in his business enterprises, and for whom the Lord had done wondrous and glorious things. The Lord had saved his soul, healed him of cancer, and had blessed his business beyond his wildest dreams.

While this dear Brother had actually done much for the Lord, still, his greatest interest was on his business, and not the Lord's business. Now every business man ought to read that very carefully.

Somehow, many people have the idea that if God hasn't called them to preach, consecration is not too very much required of them. The truth is this:

THE CALL OF GOD

Every single person who has been saved has been called of God. In other words, the Lord has a particular work that He wants them to do. For some few it would be a pulpit Ministry, but for the greater majority, it would be other things. And to be sure, if such a Believer will earnestly ask the Lord as to what the Lord wants them to do, that is a prayer that most definitely will be answered.

I was greatly influenced in my Ministry by the great Full Gospel Preacher, A. N. Trotter. I've met few men in my life who knew the Word as he did, and who was anointed to preach the Gospel as he was anointed. I learned much from him. I had the privilege of preaching several Campmeetings with him, and saw firsthand the Moving and the Operation of the Holy Spirit, which in effect, changed my Ministry and my life. I heard him tell the following any number of times:

He related as to how his Father left his Mother and the several brothers and sisters he had, thereby doing nothing to support the family. He spoke of his Mother's determination, and how that she was ultimately Baptized with the Holy Spirit, and mightily healed by the Power of God. Upon being Baptized with the Spirit, she was drawn much closer to the Lord than she had previously known, and he related as to how she consecrated her life, asking the Lord as to what He wanted her to do.

Brother Trotter said that the Lord spoke to his Mother, and merely told her, *"Raise the children."*

She felt it strongly within her heart, but didn't put too much stock into what she was being told to do. As a Mother, she fully intended to raise them without the Lord having to relate such to her. But she soon found out that the Lord was speaking of far more than just providing for them, but rather meant that they be raised in the fear of the Lord, raised on the Scriptures, raised in an atmosphere of Godliness and Righteousness, which they were.

Now many may think that wasn't very much for a person to do. But anything that God tells us to do, no matter how small it may seem at the beginning, to be sure, is always great and grandiose.

She did exactly what the Lord told her to do, which means that she was faithful to the task.

As a result of such Godly upbringing, Brother Trotter became one of the great Preachers of the Twentieth Century, touching the hearts and lives of untold thousands. Putting several periods of time together, he spent nearly 12 years in Africa, and saw tremendous things done for God, so tremendous that they defied description.

His sister married H. B. Garlock, who actually opened up West Africa to the great Pentecostal Message. I had the privilege of meeting him not long before he died. His lovely wife Ruth, who has now gone on to be with the Lord, who lived incidentally to nearly 100 years of age, and as stated, was Brother Trotter's sister, saw miracles of unprecedented proportions in their field of labor in West Africa. They saw the dead raised, mighty healings of every description, but above all, they saw untold thousands brought to a saving knowledge of Jesus Christ, and thousands, as well, Baptized with the Holy Spirit.

So I think that one could look at that after it was played out to its conclusion, and could say that the Lord telling this dear lady so long ago to *"raise the children,"* which seemed so menial to begin with, proved to be of miraculous proportions. Little is much if God be in it.

This dear woman was not a Preacher, but she used her life for the Lord, and in doing so, she bettered this world.

While the business man may be involved in all type of businesses, or the layman may work even at menial tasks, still, God has a work for each and every Believer to do. If that Believer will only ask the Lord what it is, the Lord will definitely give direction. And when such direction is obeyed, that individual will be able to do a great Work of God. As stated, anything for the Lord is great!

But the problem is, far too many Believers, Preachers included, give God less than their best. To be sure, it is the same as Israel of old offering in Sacrifice that which was sick and disabled. After what the Lord has given for us, I don't think that such sets too well with Him, as should be obvious.

(26) "AND THE LORD SPOKE UNTO MOSES, SAYING,

(27) "WHEN A BULLOCK, OR A SHEEP, OR A GOAT, IS BROUGHT FORTH, THEN IT SHALL BE SEVEN DAYS UNDER THE CARE OF THE MOTHER; AND FROM THE EIGHTH DAY AND THENCEFORTH IT SHALL BE ACCEPTED FOR AN OFFERING MADE BY FIRE UNTO THE LORD.

(28) "AND WHETHER IT BE COW, OR EWE, YOU SHALL NOT KILL IT AND HER YOUNG BOTH IN ONE DAY.

(29) "AND WHEN YOU WILL OFFER A SACRIFICE OF THANKSGIVING UNTO THE LORD, OFFER IT AT YOUR OWN WILL.

(30) "ON THE SAME DAY IT SHALL BE EATEN UP; YOU SHALL LEAVE NONE OF IT UNTIL THE MORROW: I AM THE LORD.

(31) "THEREFORE SHALL YOU KEEP MY COMMANDMENTS, AND DO THEM: I AM THE LORD.

(32) "NEITHER SHALL YOU PROFANE MY HOLY NAME; BUT I WILL BE HALLOWED AMONG THE CHILDREN OF

ISRAEL: I AM THE LORD WHICH HAL-
LOW YOU,

(33) "WHO BROUGHT YOU OUT OF THE
LAND OF EGYPT, TO BE YOUR GOD: I AM
THE LORD."

The construction is:

1. In the life of separation unto God there
must be holiness, but not hardness (Williams).

2. Spiritual or physical wealth was not to
be separated from the precious blood that
bought it (vss. 29-30).

3. The Commandments of the Lord were
to be looked at in greatness, and must never
be profaned.

THE SACRIFICES

This Chapter closes with more instructions regarding the Sacrifices, what type of
animals were to be offered, and how they were
to be offered. All of it typified Christ and
what He would do at the Cross as it regards
the Redemption of lost humanity. That's
the reason the instructions were so minute,
so delicate, so detailed!

As we read these Passages, we should read
them with an eye on our present situation,
and how the instructions given point toward
us presently.

It is our business, presently speaking, to
*"offer up spiritual sacrifices, acceptable to
God by Jesus Christ"* (I Pet. 2:5).

While we certainly are no longer under
Law, but rather under Grace, and because of
what Christ did at the Cross, still, much is
demanded of us presently, and rightly so. In
fact, more is demanded of us now than ever
was under the Mosaic Legislation. We now
have the Holy Spirit abiding permanently
within our hearts and lives, which Old Testament Saints didn't have (Jn. 14:16-17). As
a result, there is no excuse for us not properly following the Word, and allowing the
Holy Spirit to bring us to the place of victory, which He Alone can do.

As those Sacrifices of old represented the
Cross in every respect, our lives today are to
be lived strictly by and through what Jesus
has done for us at the Cross. That is why
Paul said:

*"I am crucified with Christ: nevertheless
I live; yet not I, but Christ lives in me: and
the life which I now live in the flesh I live by*

NOTES

*the Faith of the Son of God, Who loved me,
and gave Himself for me.*

*"I do not frustrate the Grace of God: for
if Righteousness come by the Law, then
Christ is dead in vain"* (Gal. 2:20-21).

*"Master, the tempest is raging! The
billows are tossing high!*
*"The sky is over-shadowed with black-
ness, and no shelter or help is nigh;*
*"Carest Thou not that we perish? How
can You lie asleep,*
*"When each moment so madly is
threat'ning a grave in the angry
deep?"*

*"Master, with anguish of spirit I bow
in my grief today;*
*"The depths of my sad heart are
troubled; O waken and save, I pray!*
*"Torrents of sin and of anguish sweep
over my sinking soul!*
*"And I perish! I perish, dear Master; O
hasten, and take control!"*

*"Master, the terror is over, the elements
sweetly rest!*
*"Earth's sun in the calm lake is mir-
rored, and Heaven's within my
breast.*
*"Linger, O blessed Redeemer, leave me
alone no more;*
*"And with joy I shall make the blessed
harbor, and rest on that blissful
shore."*

CHAPTER 23

(1) "AND THE LORD SPOKE UNTO
MOSES, SAYING,

(2) "SPEAK UNTO THE CHILDREN OF
ISRAEL, AND SAY UNTO THEM, CON-
CERNING THE FEASTS OF THE LORD,
WHICH YOU SHALL PROCLAIM TO BE
HOLY CONVOCATIONS, EVEN THESE ARE
MY FEASTS.

(3) "SIX DAYS SHALL WORK BE DONE:
BUT THE SEVENTH DAY IS THE SAB-
BATH OF REST, AN HOLY CONVOCATION;
YOU SHALL DO NO WORK THEREIN: IT
IS THE SABBATH OF THE LORD IN ALL

YOUR DWELLINGS.

(4) "THESE ARE THE FEASTS OF THE LORD, EVEN HOLY CONVOCATIONS, WHICH YOU SHALL PROCLAIM IN THEIR SEASONS.

(5) "AND THE FOURTEENTH DAY OF THE FIRST MONTH AT EVENING IS THE LORD'S PASSOVER.

(6) "AND ON THE FIFTEENTH DAY OF THE SAME MONTH IS THE FEAST OF UNLEAVENED BREAD UNTO THE LORD: SEVEN DAYS YOU MUST EAT UNLEAVENED BREAD.

(7) "IN THE FIRST DAY YOU SHALL HAVE AN HOLY CONVOCATION: YOU SHALL DO NO SERVILE WORK THEREIN.

(8) "BUT YOU SHALL OFFER AN OFFERING MADE BY FIRE UNTO THE LORD SEVEN DAYS: IN THE SEVENTH DAY IS AN HOLY CONVOCATION: YOU SHALL DO NO SERVILE WORK THEREIN."

The exegesis is:

1. Israel's sacred year contained one weekly and seven annual Feasts.

2. The weekly Feast was the Sabbath.

3. The seven annual Feasts were Passover, Unleavened Bread, Firstfruits, Pentecost, Trumpets, Atonement, and Tabernacles.

THE FEASTS OF THE LORD

Verses 1 and 2 read: *"And the LORD spoke unto Moses, saying,*

"Speak unto the Children of Israel, and say unto them, Concerning the Feasts of the LORD, which you shall proclaim to be holy convocations, even these are My Feasts."

Without a doubt, this is one of the most important Chapters in the entirety of the Word of God. It contains the record of the seven great Feasts which marked Israel's year. But more particularly, it furnishes us with a view of Israel's history, from her beginning, to the time of her glory. Prophetically speaking, four of these great Feasts have come and gone, which we will deal with directly. Three are yet to be fulfilled, but just as surely as the first four have been fulfilled, so shall the last three be fulfilled.

These *"Feasts"* were *"Feasts of the LORD,"* and declared to be so. This was their true character, their original title; but in the Gospel of John, they are called *"Feasts of the*

Jews." They had long ceased to be Jehovah's Feasts. He was shut out. They did not want Him; and hence, in John, Chapter 7, when Jesus was asked to go up to *"the Jews' Feast of Tabernacles,"* He answered, *"My time is not yet come"*; when He did go up, it was *"privately,"* to take His place outside the whole thing, and to call upon every thirsty soul to come unto Him and drink (Mackintosh).

From this we catch the solemn truth as to how sacred things can be marred by men, until they no longer resemble what they were originally intended to be. In fact, almost everything given by the Lord falls into that category. Man adds to what the Lord has done, or He deletes from what the Lord has done, or changes it altogether.

CATHOLIC PRIESTS

I was discussing the Bible once with a group of Catholic Bishops.

They were making mention as to how the Catholic Church had changed some particular things. I very kindly (not at all sarcastically) asked them if what they had originally done was not that which they claimed to be Scriptural. I then added, *"If it was Scriptural the way you were first doing this particular thing, how could you change it?"* Their answer was very revealing.

One of the Bishops spoke up, and the others nodded their assent, that the Bible is whatever the Catholic Church says that it is.

That startled me for a moment, but I soon realized they were not joking, and were speaking that which was actually the case. Now think about that statement for just a moment.

"The Bible is whatever the Catholic Church says it is."

This means they can change the meaning as they so desire, and the Catholic people are supposed to accept it. I cannot really imagine a greater blueprint for spiritual disaster then that. But regrettably, I'm afraid that many Protestant Denominations are not far behind such awful departure from the Word of God. Whenever people begin to lose their way, whenever major Denominations begin to lose their way, it always begins with a departure from the Word. In other words, they replace the Word of God with their own ideas.

The leader of one Pentecostal Denomination was asked by a friend of mine that if the Word of the Lord said one thing, and their constitution and bylaws said something else, which would they follow? Without hesitation, the man quickly answered, *"We would follow our constitution and bylaws."*

It is not a question of that particular Denomination going into spiritual declension. They have already gone into spiritual declension. In fact, even as hurtful as it sounds, most religious Denominations have long since departed from the Word of God.

THE LORD SPOKE

Over and over again, we read in these texts of our study that it says, *"And the LORD spoke unto Moses, saying."* That which was spoken, as should be overly obvious, was and is the Word of the Lord. It was to be followed minutely in all things, or catastrophe would be the result, and catastrophe in every manner, be it spiritual, physical, domestical, and material. Let the Reader understand that it hasn't changed from then until now. The question must always be, *"Is it Scriptural?" "Is it according to the Word?"* The Word of God must be the criteria for all things. And if it's not the criteria, you as a Believer had better disassociate yourself from that particular direction, and do so as fast as possible.

One day, when we stand before the Lord, all of us will answer according to the Word. We will not be able to shift the blame to someone else, or to pass it off with the words, *"That's what they told me!"* It's what the Word of the Lord says, and not what *"they"* say, whomever *"they"* might be!

THE SEVEN GREAT FEASTS

In each Jewish year, there were seven great Feasts which were to be kept. They were:
1. The Passover.
2. The Feast of Unleavened Bread.
3. The Feast of Firstfruits.
4. The Feast of Pentecost.
5. The Feast of Trumpets.
6. The Great Day of Atonement.
7. The Feast of Tabernacles.

The first three were conducted in approximately our April. Pentecost was conducted in our May, with the last three conducted

in October.

The first three were connected with the *"barley harvest."* The Feast of Pentecost came during the time of the *"wheat harvest."* The last three in October came at the time of the *"fruit harvest."*

All of these Feasts pictured Christ in His Atoning, Mediatorial, Intercessory roles.

Passover figured Redemption.

Unleavened Bread figured His perfect, unspotted, unsullied life, which was offered up in Sacrifice.

Firstfruits figured His Resurrection.

Pentecost figured the outpouring of the Holy Spirit, made possible by what Christ did at the Cross.

The Feast of Trumpets portrays the Rapture of the Church, which will end the Church Age. Once again, all of this is made possible by the Cross. The trumpet call (I Thess. 4:13-18) will not only signal the end of the Church Age, but as well, will signal the beginning of God's dealings with Israel in a greater way than ever, to bring them back to the Lord, which will take place at the Second Coming (Zech. 12:10-12; 13:1).

The Great Day of Atonement prefigured the way to the very Throne of God being opened up by what Jesus would do at the Cross. Prophetically speaking as it regards Israel, it speaks of their cleansing. The Prophet Zechariah said: *"In that day there shall be a fountain opened to the House of David and to the inhabitants of Jerusalem for sin and for uncleanness"* (Zech. 13:1).

The Feast of Tabernacles, which was the last Feast of the Jewish year, and took place, as stated, in October, prefigured the coming Millennial Reign, when Christ will rule and reign on this Earth, along with the glorified Saints, and Israel as well, for 1,000 years (Rev., Chpt. 20).

The first four Feasts have been fulfilled in Bible Prophecy, and continue with their benefits unto this hour. The last three will be fulfilled according to what Christ has done at the Cross, which refers to the coming Rapture, the rebirth of Israel, so to speak, and the coming Millennial Reign.

THE SABBATH

Verses 3 and 4 read: *"Six days shall work*

be done: but the seventh day is the Sabbath of rest, an holy convocation; you shall do no work therein: it is the Sabbath of the LORD in all your dwellings.

"These are the Feasts of the LORD, even holy convocations, which you shall proclaim in their seasons."

The Sabbath is put forth here even before the Feasts are grandly proclaimed. That is done for purpose and for reason.

The Jewish Sabbath was a *"day of rest."* It was intended in this manner in order that it may portray the *"rest"* which can be found only in Christ. In other words, it typified all that Christ would do when He would come. In fact, and as previously stated, that's what Jesus was speaking about when He said: *"Come unto Me, all you who labor and are heavy laden, and I will give you rest.*

"Take My yoke upon you, and learn of Me; for I am meek and lowly in heart: and you shall find rest unto your souls.

"For My yoke is easy, and My burden is light" (Mat. 11:28-30).

In fact, this *"rest"* was portrayed even at the time of creation. The Scripture says: *"Thus the heavens and the Earth were finished, and all the host of them.*

"And on the seventh day God ended His work which He had made: and He rested on the seventh day from all His work which He had made.

"And God blessed the seventh day, and sanctified it: because that in it He had rested from all His work which God created and made" (Gen. 2:1-3).

If it is to be noticed, there is an evening to all the other days, but no evening to the Sabbath day. This means that it is eternal. It foretells Christ, the True Sabbath, in Whom God rests and in Whom Believers rest. This is *"God's Own rest"* of Hebrews, Chapter 4.

While the Lord sanctified that particular day in Old Testament times, and did so because it was a type of Christ Who was to come, we make a grand mistake now if we try to re-institute the type, as it was in Old Testament times, which is an insult to Christ. In effect, trying to keep the seventh day presently is an insult to Christ, which in effect, states that His Work was insufficient.

In the Book of Acts and the Epistles, while the Jewish Christians continued to keep the Sabbath, little by little, even as the Church as a whole came into being, that particular day was changed to Sunday, the first day of the week, the day that Jesus rose from the dead (Acts 20:7; I Cor. 16:2; Heb. 10:9).

CHRIST

To properly understand the Word of God, we must fully comprehend the fact that the entirety of the Word points strictly to Christ and His Work. That's the story of the Bible. All that was done in some way had a relationship to Him, and was meant to portray Him in His Sacrificial, Atoning, Mediatorial, Intercessory Work. So, if we get our eyes off Christ, and instead get them on the types and shadows, we miss the point altogether. In fact, one could probably say without fear of contradiction that the phrase, *"Jesus Christ and Him Crucified,"* is the theme of the entirety of the Word of God. Everything, and without exception, points to that.

So, the Sabbath is portrayed first in this Twenty-third Chapter of Leviticus, which speaks of the *"rest"* which Christ would provide, and now we will be told as to how He will provide it, and what it all means. For in these Feasts, we have the history not only of what Christ will do, but as well of Israel and the Church. That's the reason this is one of the most profound and comprehensive Chapters in the entirety of the Bible.

THE PASSOVER

Verse 5 reads: *"In the fourteenth day of the first month at evening is the LORD's Passover."*

The very first Passover celebrated by Israel, and because it was just then given by God, was in Egypt. It pertained to their deliverance from Egyptian bondage, and in fact, was the cause of their deliverance. The account is given to us in Exodus, Chapter 12.

A lamb was to be chosen for each house. It was to be a male animal, only in its first year. In other words, it couldn't be over one year old. They were to keep it for four days and inspect it minutely, making certain there were no blemishes, and because it was a type of Christ. It was to be killed on the evening of the fourteenth day of the month.

They were to catch the blood in a basin,

and put the blood on the two side posts and the upper doorposts of their houses.

They were to eat the flesh, roasted with fire, with unleavened bread, and with bitter herbs. All of this symbolized the Person of Christ, and the price He would pay for man's Redemption.

They were to eat all of the animal and let nothing of it remain until the morning. If in fact some did remain until the morning, it was to be burned with fire, signifying that one must accept all of Christ.

Future Passovers did not include applying blood to the doorposts, as would be obvious, simply because Israel had already experienced deliverance. But what happened on that particular night, and I speak of the death of the firstborn of all who did not have the blood applied, does in fact have a great spiritual meaning, even for the Child of God at present.

THE BLOOD APPLIED

The Israelites, as stated, were to apply the blood to the doorposts of their houses, and make certain that the entirety of the family remained in the houses, for in that manner only would they be safe. If they were outside of the houses, or if the blood had not been applied, which it was not applied to any of the houses of the Egyptians, at least that we know of, the firstborn in those particular homes would die, which even included the Palace of Pharaoh. This is what finally broke the will of the tyrant, and he allowed God's people to be released from their bondage. But let the Reader understand that the same power that effected the release of the Israelites, at that particular time so long ago, is the same power that effects the release of the believing sinner presently, and even the believing Christian. Let us explain:

The Israelites were to place their Faith in the blood, for the Lord had said: *"When I see the blood, I will pass over you"* (Ex. 12:13). The blood shielded the Israelites from the Judgment of God, while the houses that lacked the blood, experienced judgment in the death of the firstborn.

Whenever the believing sinner presently places Faith in the shed blood of the Lamb, and we speak of Christ and what He did at

the Cross, Salvation and protection are guaranteed to that person. As well, the Christian is to continue to express Faith in the Blood, and do so on a continuing basis, which means that his Faith is ever anchored in the Cross, which then guarantees such a Believer victory over sin, and in every capacity. In fact, there is no other answer for sin but the Blood of Christ. As we have commented on in Chapters back, I will quote it again: *"For it is the blood that makes an Atonement for the soul"* (Lev. 17:11).

While Christians do not keep the Passover, we do partake of the Lord's Supper, which is an outgrowth, so to speak, of the Passover. As the Passover commemorated the deliverance of the Children of Israel from Egyptian bondage, likewise, the Lord's Supper portrays in symbolic form the deliverance of every believing sinner from the clutches of Satan, typified by the broken bread, which symbolized Jesus' broken body, so to speak, given to us on the Cross in perfect Sacrifice, and the cup, which symbolized His shed Blood, which portrayed His poured out life. Faith in what Christ did guarantees victory over every power of darkness, and in effect, at least in the spirit world, carries out the same type of victory, as was carried out in Egypt so long, long ago! (Rom. 8:1; 6:3-14; 8:1-2, 11; Eph. 2:13-18).

THE LAST PASSOVER

In the last Passover celebrated during the time of Christ, which took place at the time of His Crucifixion; in effect, He was the Passover, the One toward Whom all previous Passovers had pointed.

During that Passion Week, Josephus, the Jewish Historian, tells us that some two million people crowded Jerusalem, with approximately 250,000 lambs offered up. The conduits running out from the Brazen Altar carried the blood, which flowed down into the Brook Kidron, with it running red for days, all typifying the One Who was to come, and in fact, had come. But sadly and regrettably, Israel did not know her Redeemer, did not understand the price that He paid, and in fact, wouldn't even admit that they needed what He had done. But let all the world know that every single person who died before the Cross, and died believing, and were taken down into Paradise, was dependent solely upon the Sacrificial Offering of Christ, which alone could loose them from the captivity of Satan. While they were comforted, and because of their Faith, which means that Satan only had a limited power over them, still, in a sense, they were his captives. That's the reason that Paul said: *"When He ascended up on high, He led captivity captive, and gave gifts unto men"* (Eph. 4:8).

The phrase, *"He led captivity captive,"* is a strange phrase. It means that all the Old Testament Believers were actually held captive by Satan down in Paradise, which was in the heart of the Earth. While because of their Faith in the coming Christ, He could not put them over into the burning side of Hell, actually with a great gulf that separated Paradise from that place (Lk. 16:26), but still they were his captives. But when Jesus died on the Cross, thereby being the great Passover, atoning for all sin, past, present, and future, at least for all who will believe (Jn. 3:16), He then went down into Paradise, with every single Believer there, made His captive, and there was nothing that Satan could do about it.

When Jesus died on the Cross, with all sin atoned, He removed the legal right that Satan had, which he could use to hold man in captivity, whether dead or alive. But with all sin atoned, he lost that legal right. Paul said of this occasion: *"Blotting out the handwriting of Ordinances that was against us"* (the Law of God which all had broken, and which condemned us), *which was contrary to us, and took it out of the way* (satisfied all of its just demands), *nailing it to His Cross* (it was at the Cross that this was done);

"And having spoiled principalities and powers, He made a show of them openly, triumphing over them in it" (Col. 2:14-15).

In effect, Jesus led all of those captives in Paradise to freedom, exactly as He had led the Children of Israel out of Egyptian bondage. Now when a Believer dies, and due to the price having been paid at the Cross, Satan has no hold on them whatsoever. They instantly go to be with Christ (Phil. 1:23). Let the Reader ever know that all of this was because of the Cross, and

solely because of the Cross.

THE PASSOVER, A PROCLAMATION OF THE CROSS

If one studies the Twelfth Chapter of Exodus, it becomes crystal clear that the Passover was symbolic totally and completely of Christ Who would ultimately come, in order to redeem humanity. Every phase of the Passover symbolized His Atoning and Mediatorial Work. In fact, all of the Feasts, even as we will study in this Chapter, pictured Christ, as did all the Sacrifices. In truth, the entirety of the Tabernacle, down to the smallest pin, all and in every respect symbolized the Atoning, Mediatorial, Intercessory Work of Christ, which He would accomplish, and in fact, did accomplish. One of the reasons that many in the modern Church do not understand the Cross, or relegate it to an insignificant position is because they do not understand the Old Testament types and shadows (Heb. 10:1).

THE FEAST OF UNLEAVENED BREAD

Verses 6 through 8 read: *"And on the fifteenth day of the same month is the Feast of Unleavened Bread unto the LORD: seven days you must eat unleavened bread.*

"In the first day you shall have an holy convocation: you shall do no servile work therein.

"But you shall offer an Offering made by fire unto the LORD seven days: in the seventh day is an holy convocation: you shall do no servile work therein."

Let the Reader understand that we can know nothing of *"rest,"* nothing of *"holiness,"* nothing of *"fellowship,"* save on the ground of the death of Christ. It is peculiarly striking, significant, and beautiful to observe that, directly God's rest is spoken of, and we speak of the Sabbath in Verse 3, the next thing introduced is the blood of the paschal lamb, symbolizing Christ.

While the Passover was on the fourteenth day of the month, on the fifteenth day commenced the *"Feast of Unleavened Bread."* For seven days, whatever bread was eaten was to be unleavened bread. As the Passover symbolized the death of Christ on the Cross, likewise, the unleavened bread, which was to be eaten for seven days, symbolized the perfection of Christ. As the Whole Burnt-Offering symbolized the Perfection of Christ on the Cross, likewise, the Meat-Offering, which followed the Burnt-Offering (Lev., Chpt. 2), symbolized the Perfection of Christ in His perfect life. Passover and Unleavened Bread symbolized the same.

"Leaven" was a type of fermentation, of rot, of pollution. It is that which makes grape juice into fermented alcohol, in other words, the kind that will make one drunk.

Jesus had no imperfection at all in Him, therefore, no leaven. He was perfect in every respect. His life knew no coarseness, unevenness, imperfection, or pollution in any manner. This was absolutely necessary in order that He might keep the Law, and keep it perfectly. And let the Reader understand that He did all of this totally and completely for you and me. He did it not at all for Himself, not at all for Heaven, not at all for Angels, but all for us. The Law of God must be kept, and kept perfectly, that is, if its Righteousness was to be obtained. To be sure, Jesus has always been Righteous. Jesus is God! As such, He didn't need any Righteousness, already being perfectly Righteous. But as the Last Adam (I Cor. 15:45), He must do what the first Adam did not do, which was to render a perfect obedience to God. This He did, and did so perfectly, thereby symbolized by the unleavened bread.

On the first day of the Feast of Unleavened Bread (vs. 7), there was to be an holy convocation, and man was to do no work whatsoever.

In addition to the daily ordinary Sacrifices, there were offered on this day, and on the following six days, two young bullocks, a ram, and seven lambs of the first year, with Meat-Offerings and a Burnt-Offering, and a goat for a Sin-Offering (Num. 28:19-23).

Beside these public Sacrifices, there were the voluntary Offerings, which were made by every private individual who appeared before the Lord in Jerusalem, that is, when the Temple was eventually built.

On the seventh day as well, there was to be no servile work. During the intervening days between the first and the seventh, the people indulged in public amusements, such as songs, enjoyment, worship, which filled up the time in harmony with the joyful and solemn character of the festival.

TWO CHARACTERISTICS OF THE FEAST OF UNLEAVENED BREAD

During this time, man's labor ceased, and the odor of the Sacrifice ascended, and this was a type of a Believer's life of practical holiness. What a triumphant answer is here to the legalist on the one side, and the antinomian on the other! The former is silenced by the words, *"no servile work"*; the latter is confounded by the words, *"You shall offer an Offering made by fire."* What does all of this mean?

On the two days, the first and the last, that no work was to be done, symbolized that *"Salvation is by Grace through Faith; and that not of yourselves: it is the Gift of God:*

"Not of works, lest any man should boast" (Eph. 2:8-9).

ANTINOMIANISM

We used the word *"antinomian"* in the text above. Many may wonder as to what it means.

It is a Greek word, with the English translation given here, that refers to one being against all law. The word *"anti"* means to be *"against"* or *"opposed to."* The word *"nomi"* means, *"law,"* which means *"against all law."*

There were some in Paul's day, after hearing the Message of Grace, who erroneously reasoned in their minds that since Grace was greater than sin (Rom. 5:20), which in effect it actually is, then we should not worry about sin at all. In other words, it is of no consequence. These individuals were against all law or restrictions of any kind, thinking that the Grace of God covered anything they did, whatever it was.

Paul answered this by saying: *"What shall we say then? Shall we continue in sin, that Grace may abound?*

"God forbid. How shall we, who are dead to sin, live any longer therein?" (Rom. 6:1-2).

The Sacrifices that were offered up during this time of Unleavened Bread signified the price that Christ would pay in order to deliver man from sin. We must always remember that we are saved from sin, and not in sin. The very fact of the Cross, the very purpose of the Cross, the very reason for the Cross was to destroy the power of sin, and to remove its guilt (Rom. 6:6). So for a Christian to treat sin lightly is to make a mockery of the Grace of God. The Grace of God never under any circumstance condoned sin, but rather grants us the power to overcome sin (Rom. 6:14; Gal. 2:21).

THE TYPE AND THE CROSS

In these simple statements, we find the Christian life. We find first of all that all of our personal efforts, ability, strength, and power, are woefully insufficient in order to live this Christian experience, hence the command that there be no *"servile work,"* on the first and seventh days. This corresponds with the Words of Christ, when He said: *"If any man will come after Me, let him deny himself"* (Lk. 9:23).

As we've already said in this Volume, He wasn't speaking of asceticism, which refers to the denial of all things which are pleasurable or comfortable. He was speaking rather of us denying our own ability and strength in order to obtain the richness of Salvation. Everything we receive from the Lord comes to us exclusively by Faith, and never by works. While true Faith always produces good works, good works will never produce Faith.

But when we speak of *"Faith,"* always and without exception, we must understand that it is Faith in Christ and what Christ has done for us at the Cross. As our Faith must be anchored in Christ, at least if it is to truly be Faith that God will recognize, at the same time, it must be Faith in what Christ has done at the Cross. As Faith must never be separated from Christ, Christ must never be separated from the Cross.

And then Jesus followed the statement about self denial by the phrase, *"And take up his cross daily, and follow Me."*

This shows our total dependence on what Christ has done for us at the Cross. No, we're not trying to put Jesus back on the Cross. In fact, Christ is presently seated with the Father in heavenly places (Heb. 1:3). And neither am I putting Believers on a wooden beam. In fact, Paul said: *"But God, Who is rich in mercy, for His great love wherewith He loved us,*

"Even when we were dead in sins, has quickened us together with Christ, (by Grace you are saved;)

"And has raised us up together and made us sit together in heavenly places in Christ Jesus:

"That in the ages to come He might show the exceeding riches of His Grace in His kindness toward us through Christ Jesus" (Eph. 2:4-7).

Rather, we're speaking of the benefits of the Cross. What Jesus did there broke the back of the powers of darkness, liberated mankind, at least for all who will believe. The purpose of Christ going to the Cross was to liberate man from sin. It is the Cross alone that addresses sin, and which in fact, has defeated it in every aspect. There our Lord not only dealt with all acts of sin, but as well, dealt with the very root or cause of sin, who is Satan (Col. 2:14-15).

HOW TO LIVE THE VICTORIOUS LIFE

I suppose I've had this same heading in one form or the other 10 or 15 times in this Volume. I have done so, addressing the issue, because this is the single most important issue as it regards the Child of God. Of course, *"Salvation"* is the most important issue as it regards the unredeemed; however, *"Sanctification"* is the most important issue as it regards the Redeemed. And to be sure, Sanctification, which pertains to our relationship with Christ, our belonging to Him, and the power that we derive from Him through the Holy Spirit, helps us to live a victorious, overcoming, Christian life. All of this is given to us strictly by our Faith in Christ and what He has done for us at the Cross. In that manner alone can the Believer live the victorious life.

As I dictate these words, and as you read these words, you're reading that which is written by someone who has been on both sides of the fence, so to speak. In fact, there are very few Christians in this world who are not aware of this of which I speak. And as every Christian knew of failure, they will at the same time know of victory. That victory is found only in the Cross of Christ.

I know what it is to try to live for the Lord without understanding the Cross as it refers to Sanctification. I know what it is to be as zealous as a human being can be, as dedicated as a person can be, as sincere as a person can be, in fact, trying with all of one's might, and as well, being used mightily of God to bring untold thousands to a saving knowledge of Jesus Christ, but despite all of that, failing just the same.

You see, the Church little understands what I've just stated. Most think that if God is truly using a person, then that person has all the answers. And if there is failure, they then say that God was not really using the person, and it was all a fake.

THE CALL OF GOD

Of course, such thinking, to which I have just alluded, portrays a terrible lack of knowledge as it regards the Bible. When God called Abraham out of Ur of the Chaldees, the call was just as real then as it would ever be; however, Abraham had to go through many years of testing, which were dotted with failures, before he finally knew the Way of the Lord, at least as he should know that Way. Let the Reader know and understand that such knowledge does not come quickly, and neither does it come easily.

David is another example. In fact, the Holy Spirit through Paul used these two men as examples of this of which I speak. Romans, Chapter 4 bears this out.

Abraham was used somewhat as a double illustration. His experience proclaimed the manner in which the believing sinner was to be saved. It is wrapped up in the words, *"Abraham believed God, and it was counted unto him for Righteousness"* (Rom. 4:3). And as well, this same Faith, despite the works that Abraham attempted to introduce, is what brought about the Promise of God, which was Isaac, which pertained to the coming Redeemer.

David is a type of the individual who comes to the Lord, is even greatly used of the Lord, is even said to be a man after God's Own heart, but still fails, and fails in a most shameful, ignominious way.

The Holy Spirit through Paul says of David, *"But to him who works not, but believes on Him Who justifies the ungodly, his Faith is counted for Righteousness."*

NOTES

It then says: *"Blessed are they whose iniquities are forgiven, and whose sins are covered"* (Rom. 4:5, 7).

Concerning these men, and all others who have ever lived and believed, Paul said: *"Therefore it is of Faith that it might be by Grace; to the end the promise might be sure to all the seed; not to that only which is of the Law* (the Jews), *but to that also which is of the Faith of Abraham; who is the father of us all"* (Rom. 4:16).

So what am I saying in all of this?

IT IS BY FAITH AND NOT BY WORKS

David, along with Abraham, were two of the most ardent Believers found in the entirety of the Word of God. Both of these men stand as foundations of all that we know in Christ Jesus. And yet, they had to learn the secret of victorious living, which secret is Faith, in order not to depend on their own works.

When the Lord began to show me the Cross, and emphatically related to me that the answer for which I had so long sought was solely in the Cross, I knew immediately that this was right. It was right because it is Scriptural (Gal. 6:14).

Back to our original subject, God used both Abraham and David mightily, as should be obviously understood, before they learned the true Way of the Lord, that is, as it referred to righteous living. I had to learn it the same way, and in fact, so does everyone else. If the Church is going to claim that God doesn't use people until they become perfect, or at least somewhere near perfection, to be sure, no one will ever be used. The simple fact is, there are no perfect Christians. While the Call of God on a person's life is one thing, living the life they ought to live is something else altogether. The two are distinct. Let me say it again:

Just because the Lord is using a person, and even doing so mightily, doesn't by any stretch of the imagination guarantee that such an individual knows the Word totally as he should know the Word. In fact, I think I can say without fear of exaggeration that at least at the beginning, none do. That person has to learn the Word, the same as everyone else. But the Church, as stated, seems to have a problem with that.

In this explanation of the Feast of Unleavened Bread, two very important things stand out to us. First of all, and as previously stated, the fact that the Children of Israel were to do no servile work on the first day and the seventh day of that holy convocation proclaims the fact of Salvation by Faith. Works are out! And then, the Sacrifices offered up proclaim the fact as well that sin can be addressed only by what was done at Calvary's Cross. We must not allow this lesson to be lost on us.

WORKS

Some paragraphs back, I made the statement that while works will never produce Faith, proper Faith will always produce good works. The problem is this:

If the Christian doesn't understand the Cross as it refers to one's Sanctification, in other words, how we are to live for God, then invariably, that Christian is going to resort to works. He may not understand it as such, but that's what it is. In fact, not understanding the Cross, invariably there is no other place to go but works.

Most of the time, the Christian doesn't understand that what he's doing is *"works,"* which God cannot accept, and because the works he is carrying out are good works. And what makes all of it so wrong is that he places his faith in this which he is doing, whatever it might be, thinking that it will bring about Righteousness, Holiness, and nearness to God. But no matter how good and righteous these works might be, they will not fall out to that which we've just mentioned. In fact, whatever problem the Believer is trying to overcome, if he continues with the method of works, not only will his problem not be solved, but it will steadily get worse, no matter how hard he tries otherwise.

If the Believer doesn't understand the Cross, in some way, works of the flesh will manifest themselves in his life. This is something that is inevitable! Listen again to Paul:

HOW THE SPIRIT WORKS

"For the flesh lusts against the Spirit, and the Spirit against the flesh: and these are contrary the one to the other: so that you cannot

do the things that you would" (Gal. 5:17).

First of all, let's establish the fact that the word *"Spirit"* as used here, pertains to the Holy Spirit, and not to a person's re-created spirit, as some teach. In fact, the word *"Spirit"* is mentioned in this Chapter eight times, and every time, it speaks of the Holy Spirit.

Most Christians, regrettably, do not understand how the *"Spirit"* works, neither do they understand what the *"flesh"* actually is.

The *"flesh"* speaks of our own personal strength, efforts, and ability. The Holy Spirit, as would be obvious, speaks of that which is totally of the Lord. Even as Galatians 5:17 proclaims, there is a struggle which constantly goes on between the Holy Spirit and the flesh.

As previously stated, many of the things we do are right and proper in their own way, and in fact, things such that a true Believer will always carry out. I speak of prayer, fasting, giving money to the Work of the Lord, being faithful to Church, witnessing to lost souls, etc. As is obvious, these things are of utmost significance; however, if we place our Faith in those things, thinking that by the doing of them it brings us Holiness and Righteousness, etc., this is wrong, and in fact, that which the Holy Spirit can never sanction. We have in effect turned these noble and righteous things into *"works,"* which will only produce self-righteousness.

The Holy Spirit demands that our Faith exclusively be in Christ and what Christ has done for us at the Cross, and not other things, irrespective as to how important those other things might be in their own right.

So, the Holy Spirit said to Moses of the two days in question, the first and the last of the holy convocation, no *"servile work"* was to be done. This typified our experience by Faith, with the Sacrifices, which were offered up during this time, signifying what Christ would do at the Cross, in order to deliver us from all sin.

(9) "AND THE LORD SPOKE UNTO MOSES, SAYING,

(10) "SPEAK UNTO THE CHILDREN OF ISRAEL, AND SAY UNTO THEM, WHEN YOU BE COME INTO THE LAND WHICH I GIVE UNTO YOU, AND SHALL REAP THE HARVEST THEREOF, THEN YOU SHALL

BRING A SHEAF OF THE FIRSTFRUITS OF YOUR HARVEST UNTO THE PRIEST:

(11) "AND HE SHALL WAVE THE SHEAF BEFORE THE LORD, TO BE ACCEPTED FOR YOU: ON THE MORROW AFTER THE SABBATH THE PRIEST SHALL WAVE IT.

(12) "AND YOU SHALL OFFER THAT DAY WHEN YOU WAVE THE SHEAF AN HE LAMB WITHOUT BLEMISH OF THE FIRST YEAR FOR A BURNT-OFFERING UNTO THE LORD.

(13) "AND THE MEAT-OFFERING THEREOF SHALL BE TWO TENTH DEALS OF FINE FLOUR MINGLED WITH OIL, AN OFFERING MADE BY FIRE UNTO THE LORD FOR A SWEET SAVOR: AND THE DRINK-OFFERING THEREOF SHALL BE OF WINE, THE FOURTH PART OF AN HIN.

(14) "AND YOU SHALL EAT NEITHER BREAD, NOR PARCHED CORN, NOR GREEN EARS, UNTIL THE SELFSAME DAY THAT YOU HAVE BROUGHT AN OFFERING UNTO YOUR GOD: IT SHALL BE A STATUTE FOREVER THROUGHOUT YOUR GENERATIONS IN ALL YOUR DWELLINGS."

The structure is:

1. The foundation of the seven Feasts was Grace. The Passover proclaimed Redemption through the blood, and the last Feast – Tabernacles – pictured the Millennium.

2. Between these two Feasts came the sheaf of the firstfruits, i.e., *"the Resurrection of Christ."*

3. The first three Feasts, *"Passover, Unleavened Bread, and Firstfruits,"* were all fulfilled by the Death and Resurrection of Christ.

THE WAVE-OFFERING

Verses 9 through 11 read: *"And the LORD spoke unto Moses, saying,*

"Speak unto the Children of Israel, and say unto them, When you be come into the land which I give unto you, and shall reap the harvest thereof, then you shall bring a sheaf of the firstfruits of your harvest unto the Priests:

"And he shall wave the sheaf before the LORD, to be accepted for you: on the morrow after the Sabbath the Priest shall wave it."

The Feast of Firstfruits could not really be

kept while the Children of Israel were in the wilderness, and for all the obvious reasons. So the Lord said, *"When you be come into the land which I will give unto you. . . ."* The Law concerning Firstfruits was given here, but could not be kept until Israel could in fact grow grain in their land which the Lord would give unto them.

They were to bring *"a sheaf of the firstfruits of their harvest,"* which spoke of barley. This time of the year, being April, the barley harvest was ready to be gathered.

The Priests were to wait until the sun had gone down, and then they were to cut a sheaf of grain, bring it to the Tabernacle or Temple, which could only be done after they were in the land of Israel. They would then stand facing the front of the Tabernacle, and wave the grain back and forth, which in a sense was a Wave-Offering of thanksgiving to the Lord for the barley harvest, and as well, consecrating it to the Lord.

THE SACRIFICE

Verse 12 reads: *"And you shall offer that day when you wave the sheaf an he lamb without blemish of the first year for a Burnt-Offering unto the LORD."*

On the day the Wave-Offering took place, the Priests were at the same time to offer a male lamb, which typified Christ, which was to be without blemish, which again typified Christ, with it being offered as a *"Burnt-Offering."*

The *"Burnt-Offering"* typified the Perfection of Christ, offered up to a thrice-Holy God, which then satisfied His justice.

THE MEAT-OFFERING

Verse 13 reads: *"And the Meat-Offering thereof shall be two tenth deals of fine flour mingled with oil, an Offering made by fire unto the LORD for a sweet savor: and the Drink-Offering thereof shall be of wine, the fourth part of an hin."*

The *"Meat-Offering,"* which consisted of fine flour, typified the Perfect Life of Christ. It was mingled with oil, which typified His being filled with the Spirit, and being filled as no other human being ever has, and then some of that was placed on the Brazen Altar, hence *"an Offering made by fire unto the*

LORD for a sweet savor."

While a small amount was burned on the Brazen Altar, the balance was eaten by the Priests.

This Passage (vs. 13), and Verses 18 and 37, are the only places in the Book of Leviticus where the Drink-Offering is mentioned. The Drink-Offering was normally poured out before the Lord.

The first time that the Jews ever waved the sheaf before the Lord must have been immediately on their entering the Promised Land. They entered and found the barley ripe for use. This was *"on the morrow after the Passover"* (Josh. 5:11). On that day they would eat the old corn and unleavened cakes; in that very day would cut down the sheaf of firstfruits, to be waved *"on the morrow after the Sabbath."* Thus, the first employment of Israel in Canaan was preparing the type of the Saviour's Resurrection, and their first spiritual act was *"holding up"* that type of a risen Saviour. Their land was to be renowned for this wonder more than any other – Resurrection! And that Resurrection implied Redemption and completed deliverance. The paschal lamb in Egypt showed deliverance begun; this showed it finished. But let it be understood that the Resurrection was never in doubt.

The wages of sin is death, but with all sin atoned, which Christ did at the Cross, Satan had no legal right to hold Jesus in the death world; consequently, His Resurrection was never in question (Rom. 6:23).

The Scripture says: *"But now is Christ risen from the dead, and become the 'firstfruits' of them who slept"* (I Cor. 15:20). The beautiful ordinance of the presentation of the sheaf of firstfruits typified the Resurrection of Christ, Who, *"at the end of the Sabbath, as it began to dawn toward the first day of the week,"* rose triumphant from the tomb, having accomplished the glorious Work of Redemption. His was a *"Resurrection from among the dead"*; and in it we have at once the earnest and the type of the Resurrection of His people. *"Christ the Firstfruits; afterwards they who are Christ's at His coming."* When Christ comes, His people will be raised *"from among the dead,"* that is, those of them who sleep in Jesus;

"But the rest of the dead lived not again until the thousand years were finished" (Rev. 20:5).

It must be evident to anyone who carefully ponders the subject in the light of Scripture that there is a very material difference between the Resurrection of the Believer and the Resurrection of the unbeliever. Both shall be raised; but Revelation 20:5 proves that there will be 1,000 years between the two, so that they differ both as to the principle and as to the time (Mackintosh).

THE COMMAND

Verse 14 reads: *"And you shall eat neither bread, nor parched corn, nor green ears, until the selfsame day that you have brought an Offering unto your God: it shall be a Statute forever throughout your generations in all your dwellings."*

Until the Wave-Offering was presented to the Lord, along with the *"Burnt-Offering,"* which typified the Perfect Offering of Christ on the Cross, and a *"Meat-Offering,"* which typified His Perfect Life, not so much as a single ear in the fields of Redemption could be gleaned. Then and then only could Israel partake of the harvest.

The sheaf waved before the Lord constituted the fact that recognition was given to Him for the entirety of Salvation. It is all of the Lord, and none of man.

Salvation has always come in the same manner. There has never been five, three, or even two ways of Salvation, only one. And that is by the *"Blood of the Paschal Lamb shed to screen us from the terrible Judgment of God, which must be poured out upon sin."* The Passover typified our Salvation; Unleavened Bread typified the One Who made it all possible, the Lord Jesus Christ, Who did such by His perfect life and perfect body, which was offered up in Sacrifice. As stated, the Feast of Firstfruits portray His Resurrection, which verified our Redemption.

(15) "AND YOU SHALL COUNT UNTO YOU FROM THE MORROW AFTER THE SABBATH, FROM THE DAY THAT YOU BROUGHT THE SHEAF OF THE WAVE-OFFERING; SEVEN SABBATHS SHALL BE COMPLETE:

(16) "EVEN UNTO THE MORROW AFTER THE SEVENTH SABBATH SHALL

YOU NUMBER FIFTY DAYS: AND YOU SHALL OFFER A NEW MEAT-OFFERING UNTO THE LORD.

(17) "YOU SHALL BRING OUT OF YOUR HABITATIONS TWO WAVE LOAVES OF TWO TENTH DEALS; THEY SHALL BE OF FINE FLOUR; THEY SHALL BE BAKED WITH LEAVEN; THEY ARE THE FIRSTFRUITS UNTO THE LORD.

(18) "AND YOU SHALL OFFER WITH THE BREAD SEVEN LAMBS WITHOUT BLEMISH OF THE FIRST YEAR, AND ONE YOUNG BULLOCK, AND TWO RAMS: THEY SHALL BE FOR A BURNT-OFFERING UNTO THE LORD, WITH THEIR MEAT-OFFER-ING, AND THEIR DRINK-OFFERINGS, EVEN AN OFFERING MADE BY FIRE, OF SWEET SAVOR UNTO THE LORD.

(19) "THEN YOU SHALL SACRIFICE ONE KID OF THE GOATS FOR A SIN-OF-FERING, AND TWO LAMBS OF THE FIRST YEAR FOR A SACRIFICE OF PEACE-OFFERINGS.

(20) "AND THE PRIEST SHALL WAVE THEM WITH THE BREAD OF THE FIRSTFRUITS FOR A WAVE-OFFERING BEFORE THE LORD, WITH THE TWO LAMBS: THEY SHALL BE HOLY TO THE LORD FOR THE PRIEST.

(21) "AND YOU SHALL PROCLAIM ON THE SELFSAME DAY, THAT IT MAY BE AN HOLY CONVOCATION UNTO YOU: YOU SHALL DO NO SERVILE WORK THEREIN: IT SHALL BE A STATUTE FOREVER IN ALL YOUR DWELLINGS THROUGHOUT YOUR GENERATIONS.

(22) "AND WHEN YOU REAP THE HAR-VEST OF YOUR LAND, YOU SHALL NOT MAKE CLEAN RIDDANCE OF THE COR-NERS OF YOUR FIELD WHEN YOU REAP, NEITHER SHALL YOU GATHER ANY GLEANING OF YOUR HARVEST: YOU SHALL LEAVE THEM UNTO THE POOR, AND TO THE STRANGER: I AM THE LORD YOUR GOD."

The construction is:

1. The command to do no servile work is repeated ten times in connection with these Feasts.

2. Man's activities were forbidden to in-trude themselves into a Salvation which was Divine and perfect. God desired happy redeemed

NOTES

children in His family, and not slaves.

3. The bread for the Feast of Pentecost was to be baked with leaven because that bread represented the redeemed.

4. But with the leavened bread seven lambs, one young bullock, two rams, a Meal-Offering, one kid for a Sin-Offering, and two lambs for a Peace-Offering were to be offered unto the Lord; thus proclaiming that an in-finite Saviour has been provided by God to engrace weak and erring men (Williams).

THE FEAST OF PENTECOST

Verse 16 reads: *"Even unto the morrow after the seventh Sabbath shall you number fifty days; and you shall offer a new Meat-Offering unto the LORD."*

The day after seven complete weeks was the fiftieth day, hence the name *"Pente-cost,"* which actually meant in the Hebrew, *"fifty,"* or *"fiftieth."* It would have fallen in our month of May. As the previous Feasts were in the time of the barley harvest, the Feast of Pentecost was in the time of the wheat harvest.

The phrase is used, *"A new Meat-Offer-ing unto the LORD,"* referring to the fact that this Offering was to be made of wheat, whereas the former was to be made of barley. This was a *"New Meat-Offering."* It was meant to commemorate the Feast of Pente-cost, or 50 days after the Passover.

THE WAVE-OFFERING

Verse 17 reads: *"You shall bring out of your habitations two wave loaves of two tenth deals; they shall be of fine flour; they shall be baked with leaven; they are the firstfruits unto the LORD."*

Incidentally, the Feast of Pentecost lasted only one day.

The two wave loaves were made out of wheat, which was ground into *"fine flour,"* typifying the Perfection of Christ.

They were to be baked with *"leaven,"* which was intended to foreshadow those who, though filled with the Holy Spirit, and adorned with His gifts and graces, had, nev-ertheless, *"evil"* dwelling in them. In other words, the sin nature is still in the Child of God (Rom., Chpt. 6). Although it dwells there, it is not to rule and reign (Rom. 6:12).

Concerning this, Mackintosh said: *"The assembly, on the Day of Pentecost, for this was the day that the Holy Spirit was outpoured, stood in the full value of the Blood of Christ, and was crowned with the Gifts of the Holy Spirit; but there was leaven there also. No power of the Spirit could do away with the fact that there was evil dwelling in the people of God. It might be suppressed and kept out of view, but it was there. This fact is foreshadowed in the 'type' by the leaven in the two loaves, and it is set forth in the actual history of the Church; for albeit God the Holy Spirit was present in the assembly, the flesh was there likewise. Flesh is flesh, nor can it ever made ought else than flesh."*

Mackintosh went on to say, *"The Holy Spirit did not come down on the Day of Pentecost to improve nature or to do away with the fact of its incurable evil, but to baptize Believers into one body, and connect them with their living Head in Heaven."*

Even as we've already stated, the fact of leaven being in the *"Meat-Offering,"* as presented on the Day of Pentecost, and which was a type of Christ, portrays the fact that despite what some Preachers say, the sin nature continues to dwell within the Child of God. Inasmuch as this particular Meat-Offering is presented on the Day of Pentecost portrays to us the fact that even the Presence of the Holy Spirit cannot do away with this fact. While every believer holds a position of perfection in Christ, that perfection is only in Christ, and not at all in ourselves per se. So the Holy Spirit proceeds to root out of our lives all sin and of every nature, from the moment that He comes in to abide, or at least, that's what he seems to do.

VICTORY OVER THE SIN NATURE

While the infilling of the Holy Spirit, and I refer to the Baptism with the Holy Spirit, which is always accompanied by the speaking with other tongues, is a definite help as would be obvious, as it regards victory, that within itself, however, will not guarantee victory.

The Holy Spirit works in conjunction with Christ and His great Sacrifice of Himself on the Cross of Calvary. In fact, the two, the Spirit and the Crucified Christ, are so closely

NOTES

intertwined, as to be indivisible one might say (Rev. 5:6).

As well, Paul plainly tells us: *"For the Law of the Spirit of Life in Christ Jesus has made me free from the law of sin and death"* (Rom. 8:2).

As we've already stated several times in this Volume, the phrase *"in Christ Jesus,"* always refers to the Sacrifice of Christ. So, we learn from this that what the Holy Spirit does is always done within the latitude of the Sacrifice of Christ. In other words, the work that He accomplishes within our lives is always within the framework of the legal work of Calvary. That's why it's referred to as a *"Law."*

Therefore, the only way that the Believer can have victory over the sin nature is to place his Faith 100 percent in Christ and what Christ has done at the Cross. Then, and only then, will the Holy Spirit work with His almighty power, thereby helping us to overcome the sin nature in every respect (Rom. 8:11).

Regrettably, most Christians do not know or understand this, thereby placing their faith in something else. In fact, most Christians don't even really understand Faith, but whether they understand it or not, if they do not understand the Cross as it regards Sanctification, inadvertently they will place their faith in something else. As a result, defeat will be the order of their lives, and because their faith is misplaced.

The *"firstfruits"* of the Seventeenth Verse mentioned here have to do with the firstfruits of the wheat harvest, and not the barley harvest of the Feast of Firstfruits.

THE SACRIFICES

Verses 18 and 19 read: *"And you shall offer with the bread seven lambs without blemish of the first year, and one young bullock, and two rams: they shall be for a Burnt-Offering unto the LORD, with their Meat-Offering, and their Drink-Offerings, even an Offering made by fire, of sweet savor unto the LORD.*

"Then you shall sacrifice one kid of the goats for a Sin-Offering, and two lambs of the first year for a sacrifice of Peace-Offerings."

Concerning all the Sacrifices being offered,

we have here an immediate connection with the leavened loaves, the presentation of an unblemished Sacrifice, typifying the great and all-important truth that it is Christ's perfection, and not our sinfulness, or sinlessness, that is ever before the view of God. In fact, the *"Sin-Offering"* was the answer to the *"leaven"* in the loaves.

Thus, on the Day of Pentecost, the Church was presented in all the value and excellency of Christ, and so have we been presented ever since, through the Power of the Holy Spirit. Though having in itself the leaven of the old nature, that leaven was not reckoned, because the Divine Sin-Offering had perfectly answered for it. The Power of the Holy Spirit did not remove the leaven, even as it could not remove the leaven, but the Blood of the Lamb had atoned for it. This is a most interesting and important distinction, and that which we must not overlook.

The work of the Spirit in the heart and life of the Believer, as important as it is, does not remove indwelling evil. It enables him to detect, judge, and subdue the evil; but no amount of spiritual power can do away with the fact that the evil is there – though, blessed be God, the conscience is at perfect ease, inasmuch as the Blood of our Sin-Offering has eternally settled the whole question; and therefore, instead of our evil being under the eye of God, it has been put out of sight forever, and we are accepted in all the acceptableness of Christ, Who offered Himself to God as a sweet-smelling Sacrifice, that He might perfectly glorify Him in all things, and be the food of His people forever.

THE TRUTH

This which I've just given to you is a truth that I did not always know and understand. In order to overcome sin, had you asked me the answer to this dilemma in the 1980's, I would have told you that it was the infilling of the Holy Spirit. While we dare not minimize the significance of the Holy Spirit Baptism, and in fact, it would be difficult to over-emphasize this great gift; still, I was frustrated at every turn trying to overcome the powers of darkness, and seemingly not able to do so. The Holy Spirit anointed me greatly to preach the Word, by which we saw hundreds

of thousands brought to a saving knowledge of Jesus Christ, and I exaggerate not. As well, He led me and guided me in many things, but when it came to overcoming the world, the flesh, and the Devil, such victory so desperately needed was not brought forth.

Until I understood exactly how the Holy Spirit worked, which has to do with the Sacrifice of Christ, and our Faith in that Finished Work, I did not, and in fact could not, know that victory. But once I understood this great Truth, this which Jesus said would make us free (Jn. 8:32), then I knew victory, and in every capacity. And here it is, all foreshadowed in the Feast of Pentecost, as it regards the *"leaven"* and the *"Sacrifices."*

Whenever the *"Sin-Offering"* is presented, which takes our sinfulness and places it upon Christ, then and only then can the *"Peace-Offerings,"* be effected, which refers to the fact that peace now comes to the troubled soul. It is all through what Christ did at the Cross.

A WAVE-OFFERING

Verse 20 reads: *"And the Priests shall wave them with the bread of the firstfruits for a Wave-Offering before the LORD, with the two lambs: they shall be holy to the LORD for the Priest."*

Two wave loaves were to be prepared in the following manner:

These sheaves of grain were beaten and trodden and ground into flour. They were made into two separate loaves. Each loaf was seven handbreadths long, four handbreadths broad, and five fingers high. These were offered to the Lord as firstlings (Ex. 34:17).

Then two lambs were brought into the Temple, and waved together or separately by the Priest while yet alive. They were then slain, and the Priest took the breast and shoulder of each one, laid them down by the side of the two loaves, put both his hands under them, and waved them altogether or separately toward the east side forwards and backwards, up and down.

He then burned the fat of the two lambs, after which the remainder of the flesh, which became the perquisite of the officiating Priests, was eaten by him and his fellow-Priests.

Of the two loaves which had been waved before the Lord, the High Priest took one, and the other was divided between the officiating Priests, who had to eat them up within the same day and half the following night, just as the flesh of the most holy things.

While the Priests were waving the *"bread of the firstfruits for a Wave-Offering before the LORD,"* along with the lambs, at that very moment, more than likely, and I speak of the Day of Pentecost, when the Holy Spirit came, Believers were in the Temple worshipping and praising God. And when the Day of Pentecost was fully come, which was probably immediately after sunrise, they were all filled with the Holy Spirit, and began to speak with other tongues.

The two loaves, and the two lambs, more than likely represented both Jews and Gentiles.

It should be noted that on the Day of Pentecost, about 3,000 people were saved (Acts 2:41). On the first Day of Pentecost, which took place at least 1,500 years before, on which day the Law was given, some 3,000 men were doomed (Ex. 32:28). Thus, the difference between Law and Grace. Understanding that, who would want to live under Law! That's the reason that Paul said: *"For sin shall not have dominion over you: for you are not under the Law, but under Grace"* (Rom. 6:14).

But regrettably, it seems like many Christians still enjoy attempting to live under Law. What a travesty!

WORKS ARE OUT

Verse 21 reads: *"And you shall proclaim on the selfsame day, that it may be an holy convocation unto you: you shall do no servile work therein: it shall be a Statute forever in all your dwellings throughout your generations."*

On this particular day, the Day of Pentecost, no *"servile work"* was to be done. The word *"servile"* means no work of any kind.

This signified that it was all of Grace and none of works.

The problem of *"works"* is a far greater problem than most Believers dare to realize. In fact, virtually all Christians, due to not understanding the Cross, are engaged in *"works,"* while all the time, thinking it's

Faith. When it comes to living for God, there are only two places where the Believer can be, and that is *"Faith"* or *"works."* There are no other alternatives. So if the Believer doesn't understand the Cross, which he must understand, that is if he is to have proper Faith, then inadvertently, he's going to rest his case in the realm of *"works."*

It's a terrible thing to think that we are engaging in Faith, or exercising Faith, when in reality, it's works. Let me explain!

The problem with most Christians is the turning of legitimate things into works. Now what do we mean by that?

It means that we place our Faith and confidence in the doing of things, which within themselves are not only not wrong, but are rather right. I speak of things such as prayer, the study of the Word, giving money to the Work of the Lord, witnessing to souls, etc. All of these things involve that which any good Christian will do. But when we place our Faith and confidence in the doing of them, then we turn them into works, which God can never honor.

PAUL AND FAITH

Paul explained Faith as no other man in the entirety of the Bible. Actually he used the word some 170 times in his 14 Epistles.

Every time he used the word, he was referring to Christ, and what Christ did at the Cross. In other words, for Faith to be that which God will recognize, it must be Faith that's anchored totally and completely in Christ and His Finished Work. Otherwise, it's Faith which God can never condone.

And to be sure, irrespective as to how good the works might be, if our Faith is anchored in those things, thinking that by the doing of such we merit something, we will find to our dismay that such will never be the case. God honors Faith and Faith alone. As we've already stated, while proper Faith will always produce good works, good works will never produce proper Faith. And for any Believer to have his Faith properly placed, he must understand the Cross, and I especially speak of the Cross as it refers to our Sanctification.

THE GLEANING OF THE HARVEST

Verse 22 reads: *"And when you reap the*

harvest of your land, you shall not make clean riddance of the corners of your field when you reap, neither shall you gather any gleaning of your harvest: you shall leave them unto the poor, and to the stranger: I am the LORD your God."

Williams says concerning this Verse, *"God would have the Gentile also at His festival board, and hence the command of Verse 22."*

In effect, Verse 22 proclaims God's welfare program. For those who did not own land, and found themselves on hard times, they, according to the Law, could reap the corners of the fields, and thereby obtain grain that they could use for food.

Some have claimed that the gleanings of the corners of the fields pertain to the Church, which allotment, of course, would be very small. However, let the Reader understand that what belongs to the Church is not merely the gleanings of Canaan, but the glories of Heaven – the glories of Christ. The Church is not merely blessed *"by"* Christ, but *"with"* and *"in"* Christ. The Bride of Christ, so to speak, will not be sent forth to gather up, as a stranger, the sheaves and clusters in the corners of Israel's fields and from the branches of Israel's vines. The truth is, the true Church tastes of higher blessings, richer joys, nobler dignities, than Israel ever knew. All of this is because of the Cross.

To be sure, Israel could have had all of this, had they accepted Christ. But they rejected Christ, and in doing so, the Church was brought in, actually grafted into the branch of Israel. Paul said: *"Because of unbelief they* (Israel) *were broken off, and you* (the Church) *stand by Faith. Be not high minded, but fear:*

"For if God spared not the natural branches, take heed lest He also spare you not" (Rom. 11:19-21).

The idea is, we must understand that the blessings we presently have in the Church are all because of the Cross, and if unbelief sets in, which regrettably it is beginning to do, we will lose our way exactly as Israel of old.

The truth is this: the Church presently is in worse condition than it has been at any time since the Reformation. As someone has well said, and rightly so, the Rapture is the only thing that will save the Church. In

other words, the longer the Rapture is delayed, the fewer there are who will be ready to go.

I realize that many in the modern Church are claiming that the Church is in better shape than ever; however, even though the Church says: *"I am rich, and increased with goods, and have need of nothing"*; the truth is, *"The Church doesn't even know that it is wretched, miserable, poor, blind, and naked"* (Rev. 3:17).

(23) "AND THE LORD SPOKE UNTO MOSES, SAYING,

(24) "SPEAK UNTO THE CHILDREN OF ISRAEL, SAYING, IN THE SEVENTH MONTH, IN THE FIRST DAY OF THE MONTH, SHALL YOU HAVE A SABBATH, A MEMORIAL OF BLOWING OF TRUMPETS, AN HOLY CONVOCATION.

(25) "YOU SHALL DO NO SERVILE WORK THEREIN: BUT YOU SHALL OFFER AN OFFERING MADE BY FIRE UNTO THE LORD."

The exegesis is:

1. We have in these three Verses an account of the Feast of Trumpets.

2. As well, no *"Servile work"* was to be done on this particular day.

3. The Feast of Trumpets pertains both to the Church and to Israel. It speaks first of all to the Church, which will signal the Rapture, and thereby, the close of the Church Age. But the same trumpets which signaled the end of the Church will, at the same time, signal the beginning of the restoration of Israel.

THE FEAST OF TRUMPETS

Verse 23 says: *"And the LORD spoke unto Moses, saying."* This represents the innumerable times this phrase is used. The idea is, all of this, all instructions, all commands, all directions, come strictly from the Lord, which means they are not at all of man. None of this should be lost on the Reader. Salvation is totally and completely of the Lord, and the moment that man attempts to add to, or take away, from that which the Lord has given us in His Word, is when the problems begin. And regrettably, the guilt of man in this capacity is horrendous. In fact, this is the great sin of both Israel and the Church.

HOW TO INTERPRET THE WORD OF GOD

The truth is, Scripture interprets Scripture. And what do we mean by that?

The way to interpret the Word of God is to compare every Scripture on any given subject. All Scriptures must harmonize, and in fact, will harmonize, if interpreted correctly. In other words, if I want to know what Redemption is, I look at all the Passages in the Word of God that relate to that subject, and the meaning will become clear.

The greatest problem that many Christians have is when they pull a Scripture out of context. In other words, at times, some Scriptures will seem to mean one thing, when they really mean something else. So to get the proper interpretation, all Scriptures, as stated, on any given subject, must be correlated. We must never forget, Scripture never contradicts itself. If it seems to mean one thing, when in reality it means another, it means that we are not properly interpreting it as we should. It's a tragedy that many false doctrines have been fostered off on the people, simply because of a misinterpretation of Scripture.

As well, many Christians little know what they actually do believe. They take the word of their Denominational hierarchy, or their Pastor, or whomever. In other words, they don't really seek out the Word for themselves, but take somebody else's word for the single most important thing in the world – their eternal soul. Nothing could be more foolish!

If the Preacher is relating the subject carefully and correctly, well and good! But if not, the individual who is believing the error can cause himself many problems, and can even lose his soul.

The Word of God is inviolate, which means that it cannot be changed. What it meant 3,000 years ago, it means the same thing now. Now there are some words, especially in the King James Text, which have changed their meaning over the years; however, those things can be easily ascertained.

THE MEMORIAL

Verses 24 through 25 read: *"Speak unto*

the Children of Israel, saying, In the seventh month, in the first day of the month, shall you have a Sabbath, a memorial of blowing of trumpets, an holy convocation.

"You shall do no servile work therein: but you shall offer an Offering made by fire unto the LORD."

The Feast of Trumpets was to be observed as a Sabbath, even though it did not fall on that particular day. It was to be a festival observed by rest, and a memorial of blowing of trumpets. In fact, the latter word should be rather rendered *"a memorial of a joyful noise."*

While every new moon trumpets were to be blown, that which was done on the first day of the seventh month was special. In fact, a different type of trumpet was to be used on this occasion. They were used to express a joyful emotion. That which they represent, the Rapture, will be a joyful time, at least for those who are ready.

Besides the blowing of trumpets, special Sacrifices were appointed for this particular time.

It was on this day, the first day of the seventh month, the Feast of Trumpets, that Ezra read the Book of the Law publicly to the people, and when *"the people wept when they heard the words of the Law,"* Nehemiah and Ezra and the Levites said, *"This day is holy unto the LORD your God; mourn not, nor weep . . . Go your way, eat the fat, and drink the sweet, and send portions unto them for whom nothing is prepared: for this day is holy unto our LORD: neither be ye sorry; for the joy of the LORD is your strength"* (Neh. 8:9-10).

The Feast of Trumpets, as all the other Feasts, portrayed a definite work of Christ, on behalf of His people. It has yet to be fulfilled. It portrays the Rapture of the Church, which will conclude the Church Age, and as well, the beginning of the Restoration of Israel. While Israel after the Rapture will see some dark days, in fact, the darkest they have ever known, all of this will be allowed for a purpose. The greater purpose of the coming Great Tribulation will be to humble Israel, and to ultimately bring her back to God. It will succeed (Mat. 24:21).

It is obvious that the Church is presently

coming to the end of the line. As well, it is overly obvious that Israel is being prepared for coming world events. While they are not aware of such presently, they soon will be.

The problems facing Israel presently are beyond the pale of mere mortals. I speak of Israel and the Palestinians. The best brains in America cannot seem to come to a successful conclusion regarding this situation, which actually began some 4,000 years ago.

But immediately after the Rapture of the Church, the Antichrist is going to step in and, miracle of miracles, solve that problem. Israel will then be able to rebuild her Temple, and will once again begin to offer sacrifices. She will herald the Antichrist as the Messiah, claiming he is the one for whom they have long looked. Many other nations will follow suit.

At this time, Israel will say, *"Peace and safety"*; the Scripture then says, *"Then sudden destruction cometh upon them, as travail upon a woman with child; and they shall not escape"* (I Thess. 5:3).

This will be at the midpoint of the Great Tribulation, called Daniel's Seventieth Week. It will be a week of years, or seven years.

The Antichrist will sign a non-aggression pact with Israel and other nations, which will institute the prosperity of the first half of the Great Tribulation. This is when they will cry *"peace and safety,"* thinking this man is truly the Messiah.

But then he will break his pact with Israel, actually attacking her, which refers to the *"sudden destruction,"* and for the first time since again becoming a nation in 1948, Israel will be defeated in battle. The latter half of the Great Tribulation will then begin, which will be the time of *"Jacob's trouble"* (Jer. 30:7). It's the time that Jesus predicted when He said: *"For then shall be great tribulation, such as was not since the beginning of the world to this time, no, nor ever shall be"* (Mat. 24:21).

But it will take this to bring Israel back to God. In fact, she will accept Christ as her Lord, her Messiah, and her Saviour, at the Second Coming (Zech. 13:1).

So the *"blowing of trumpets,"* and especially on this particular annual Feast Day, had great prophetic meaning, which is yet

to come to pass.

(26) "AND THE LORD SPOKE UNTO MOSES, SAYING,

(27) "ALSO ON THE TENTH DAY OF THIS SEVENTH MONTH THERE SHALL BE A DAY OF ATONEMENT: IT SHALL BE AN HOLY CONVOCATION UNTO YOU; AND YOU SHALL AFFLICT YOUR SOULS, AND OFFER AND OFFERING MADE BY FIRE UNTO THE LORD.

(28) "AND YOU SHALL DO NO WORK IN THAT SAME DAY: FOR IT IS A DAY OF ATONEMENT, TO MAKE AN ATONEMENT FOR YOU BEFORE THE LORD YOUR GOD.

(29) "FOR WHATSOEVER SOUL IT BE THAT SHALL NOT BE AFFLICTED IN THAT SAME DAY, HE SHALL BE CUT OFF FROM AMONG HIS PEOPLE.

(30) "AND WHATSOEVER SOUL IT BE THAT DOES ANY WORK IN THAT SAME DAY, THE SAME SOUL WILL I DESTROY FROM AMONG HIS PEOPLE.

(31) "YOU SHALL DO NO MANNER OF WORK: IT SHALL BE A STATUTE FOREVER THROUGHOUT YOUR GENERATIONS IN ALL YOUR DWELLINGS.

(32) "IT SHALL BE UNTO YOU A SABBATH OF REST, AND YOU SHALL AFFLICT YOUR SOULS: IN THE NINTH DAY OF THE MONTH AT EVENING, FROM EVENING UNTO EVENING, SHALL YOU CELEBRATE YOUR SABBATH."

The diagram is:

1. Verses 26 through 32 portray the Great Day of Atonement.

2. This was the sixth Feast of the Jewish year, but which the actual day contained no Feast at all. In fact, it was the only day in the Jewish year where Israel was ordered to fast. However, it was followed by a great Feast.

3. This Feast, along with the Feast of Trumpets, and the Feast of Tabernacles, took place in October, the time of the fruit harvest. All three of these Feasts covered a time span of approximately 23 days. On the first day of the seventh month was the Feast of Trumpets. On the tenth day of the seventh month was the Great Day of Atonement. The Feast of Tabernacles began on the fifteenth day of this seventh month, and extended for some eight days, totaling 23 days for all three Feasts.

THE GREAT DAY OF ATONEMENT

Verses 26 and 27 read: *"And the LORD spoke unto Moses, saying,*

"Also on the tenth day of this seventh month there shall be a Day of Atonement: it shall be an holy convocation unto you; and you shall afflict your souls, and offer an Offering made by fire unto the LORD."

The afflicting of the soul referred to the day being spent in fasting, and we speak of this Great Day of Atonement, which in a sense was at least one of, if not the most important day in the year as it regarded Israel. It was the day that the High Priest would go into the Holy of Holies, and offer up blood on the Mercy Seat, which would atone for the sins of Israel. In fact, this was the only day that he could go into this sacred place, this place where God dwelt between the Mercy Seat and the Cherubim. It was above this Holy of Holies that the cloud rested by day, and the fire by night. What a sight that must have been, as the many thousands of Israel looked toward the Tabernacle, always toward the Tabernacle. This was their strength, their power, their leading, their prosperity, their victory. It was their everything. This was where God dwelt. No nation on the face of the Earth could boast of this which Israel was privileged to have.

Likewise today, no people on Earth, no matter as to whom they might be, can boast as the true Believer can boast, as it regards the Lord literally living within our hearts and within our lives. Paul said: *"Do you not know that you are the Temple of God, and that the Spirit of God dwells in you?"* (I Cor. 3:16).

Actually, it was the High Priest, a type of Christ, Who Alone could go into the Holy of Holies, and then as stated, only one day during the year, which was denied all other Priests. That was the Old Covenant, but today, we have *"a better Covenant, which is established upon better Promises"* (Heb. 8:6). Now, even the weakest Believer, and at any time, can *"come boldly unto the Throne of Grace, that we may obtain mercy, and find Grace to help in time of need"* (Heb. 4:16). Then the Holy Spirit was with Israel; today, He lives within our hearts and lives, and does so on a permanent basis (Jn. 14:16-17).

On this day, this Great Day of Atonement, a Burnt-Offering, along with a Meat-Offering, were to be offered up, along with a Drink-Offering. As well, a kid of the goats was to be presented as a Sin-Offering, all pertaining to Christ (Num. 29:8-11).

The evidence is, the High Priest went into the Holy of Holies twice on this day, once for himself, and because he was a sinful man, even though the High Priest, and once for Israel. Some think he even went in three times; but be that as it may, he had to carry out his duties exactly as commanded by the Lord, or he could be stricken dead.

ATONEMENT

Verses 28 through 32 read: *"And you shall do no work in that same day: for it is a Day of Atonement, to make an Atonement for you before the LORD your God.*

"For whatsoever soul it be that shall not be afflicted in that same day, he shall be cut off from among his people.

"And whatsoever soul it be that does any work in that same day, the same soul will I destroy from among his people.

"You shall do no manner of work: it shall be a Statute forever throughout your generations in all your dwellings.

"It shall be unto you a Sabbath of rest, and you shall afflict your souls: in the ninth day of the month at evening, from evening unto evening, shall you celebrate your Sabbath."

On this Great Day of Atonement, several things were to be done as it regards the people:

1. They were to fast on this day. In fact, this was the only fast day in Israel's year.

2. They were to do no work whatsoever on this particular day.

3. It was to be a Sabbath of rest.

4. As stated, all of this represented Christ in His Atoning, Mediatorial, and Intercessory Work.

Atonement was made by the blood being applied to the Mercy Seat, and Atonement is still by the Blood, and only by the Blood. And of course, we speak of the shed Blood of Christ, which was shed once for all at Calvary's Cross, and need never again be repeated.

The fasting on this particular day represented the fact that *"man does not live by bread alone, but by every Word that proceeds out of the Mouth of God"* (Mat. 4:4).

The absence of all work on this particular day, to which we've already addressed ourselves, pertained to the fact that Salvation is all by Grace, and not at all by work or works.

Israel was to *"rest"* on this day, typifying the rest that Christ would bring, and which would come to the seeking soul. Whereas it was only one day of rest, typified every week by the Sabbath, now it is a perpetual rest, and because all is in Christ (Mat. 11:28-30).

(33) "AND THE LORD SPOKE UNTO MOSES, SAYING,

(34) "SPEAK UNTO THE CHILDREN OF ISRAEL, SAYING, THE FIFTEENTH DAY OF THIS SEVENTH MONTH SHALL BE THE FEAST OF TABERNACLES FOR SEVEN DAYS UNTO THE LORD.

(35) "ON THE FIRST DAY SHALL BE AN HOLY CONVOCATION: YOU SHALL DO NO SERVILE WORK THEREIN.

(36) "SEVEN DAYS YOU SHALL OFFER AN OFFERING MADE BY FIRE UNTO THE LORD: ON THE EIGHTH DAY SHALL BE AN HOLY CONVOCATION UNTO YOU; AND YOU SHALL OFFER UP AN OFFERING MADE BY FIRE UNTO THE LORD: IT IS A SOLEMN ASSEMBLY; AND YOU SHALL DO NO SERVILE WORK THEREIN.

(37) "THESE ARE THE FEASTS OF THE LORD, WHICH YOU SHALL PROCLAIM TO BE HOLY CONVOCATIONS, TO OFFER AN OFFERING MADE BY FIRE UNTO THE LORD, A BURNT-OFFERING, AND A MEAT-OFFERING, A SACRIFICE, AND DRINK-OFFERINGS, EVERYTHING UPON HIS DAY:

(38) "BESIDE THE SABBATHS OF THE LORD, AND BESIDE YOUR GIFTS, AND BESIDE ALL YOUR VOWS, AND BESIDE ALL YOUR FREEWILL OFFERINGS, WHICH YOU GIVE UNTO THE LORD.

(39) "ALSO IN THE FIFTEENTH DAY OF THE SEVENTH MONTH, WHEN YOU HAVE GATHERED IN THE FRUIT OF THE LAND, YOU SHALL KEEP A FEAST UNTO THE LORD SEVEN DAYS: ON THE FIRST DAY SHALL BE A SABBATH, AND ON THE EIGHTH DAY SHALL BE A SABBATH.

NOTES

(40) "AND YOU SHALL TAKE YOU ON THE FIRST DAY THE BOUGHS OF GOODLY TREES, BRANCHES OF PALM TREES, AND THE BOUGHS OF FIG TREES, AND WILLOWS OF THE BROOK; AND YOU SHALL REJOICE BEFORE THE LORD YOUR GOD SEVEN DAYS.

(41) "AND YOU SHALL KEEP IT A FEAST UNTO THE LORD SEVEN DAYS IN THE YEAR. IT SHALL BE A STATUTE FOREVER IN YOUR GENERATIONS: YOU SHALL CELEBRATE IT IN THE SEVENTH MONTH.

(42) "YOU SHALL DWELL IN BOOTHS SEVEN DAYS; ALL THAT ARE ISRAELITES BORN SHALL DWELL IN BOOTHS:

(43) "THAT YOUR GENERATIONS MAY KNOW THAT I MADE THE CHILDREN OF ISRAEL TO DWELL IN BOOTHS, WHEN I BROUGHT THEM OUT OF THE LAND OF EGYPT: I AM THE LORD YOUR GOD.

(44) "AND MOSES DECLARED UNTO THE CHILDREN OF ISRAEL THE FEASTS OF THE LORD."

The structure is:

1. Prophetically speaking, the Great Day of Atonement pictures Israel coming to Christ, and being cleansed by His Precious Blood, even as pictured by the Prophet Zechariah (Zech. 13:1). The Feast of Tabernacles, which we will now study, pictures Israel safe in Christ, and enjoying the coming Millennial Reign, when she will finally gain her place and position ordained by the Lord so long, long ago, as chief of the nations.

2. These Feasts, climaxing with the Feast of Tabernacles, runs the gamut of the entirety of the Plan of God for the human race. From the Feast of Tabernacles, we see the world at peace, with Israel in her rightful place, with Christ ruling from Jerusalem, with Satan, along with all his demon spirits and fallen angels, locked away in the bottomless pit.

3. But this great time that is coming, in which every Saint of God will take part, all the way from Abel to that coming time, all and in totality, are predicated on the Passover, i.e., *"the Shed Blood of the Lamb."* That and that alone is the foundation of the Gospel. In fact, *"Jesus Christ and Him Crucified,"* is the Gospel (I Cor. 1:23; 2:2).

THE FEAST OF TABERNACLES

Verses 33 through 35 read: *"And the LORD spoke unto Moses, saying,*

"Speak unto the Children of Israel, saying, The fifteenth day of this seventh month shall be the Feast of Tabernacles for seven days unto the LORD.

"On the first day shall be an holy convocation: you shall do no servile work therein."

The Feast of Tabernacles, as stated, took place in the month of October, the time of the fruit harvest. It began some five days after the Great Day of Atonement.

The last Chapter of Zechariah proclaims the institution of the Feast of Tabernacles, which will be faithfully kept in the coming Millennial Reign. The Scripture says: *"And it shall come to pass that every one who is left of all the nations which come against Jerusalem, shall even go up from year to year to worship the King, the LORD of hosts, and to keep the Feast of Tabernacles"* (Zech. 14:16).

This Passage means exactly what it says. Jerusalem will then be the principal city of the world, from which Jesus will rule and reign, and David will reign under Him. The nations of the world will come at the appointed time each year, and will do so in order to worship the Lord. It will be a time when peace will cover the Earth, and because the Prince of Peace will be reigning, the Lord Jesus Christ. Then all false religions will be gone. Their sponsor, Satan, will be locked away. Sickness will be no more, and neither will privation, want, or hunger, ever touch the brow of one single soul. There will be no more war, nor man's inhumanity to man. The world will see what it should be like, and in fact, what it will be like, when Christ rules and reigns, as He definitely shall.

In essence, there will be three classes of people on the Earth at that time. There will be the Glorified Saints, which will include every Saint of God who has ever lived, from the time of Abel, until the last person is raptured in the Great Tribulation. These will be those who are in the First Resurrection of life. All Saints with Glorified Bodies will be very much like Christ. In fact, John said: *"Beloved, now are we the sons of God, and it does not yet appear what we shall be: but we know that,*

when He shall appear, we shall be like Him; for we shall see Him as He is" (I Jn. 3:2).

There will as well be natural people on the Earth just as there are now, and always have been, who will be redeemed, but will not have Glorified Bodies. These are individuals who are born during the time of the Millennial Reign, or who accept Christ during that time. They will have families, just as at the present.

Also, there will be many at that time, regrettably so, although forced to serve God as far as keeping the laws are concerned, still will not give their hearts and lives to Him, and will be unsaved. There will be some during this time who will insist upon taking peace from the Earth, and will be summarily executed. But otherwise, the redeemed of the Earth will remain youthful, and in fact will not die, by virtue of the fruit that will grow on the trees that will line the river, which flows from the Sanctuary. The Scripture says, *"And the fruit thereof shall be for meat, and the leaf thereof for medicine"* (Ezek. 47:12; Rev. 22:1-2).

TABERNACLE CONSTRUCTION

Of course, this particular Feast could not be kept until the Children of Israel were safely in the land of Promise, which would be years later.

The Tabernacles, when they at long last would finally be erected, with the Feasts being kept, were to be temporary affairs, as would be obvious. It was done in this fashion, and we speak of the temporary structures, and the requirement that the people live in these structures for some seven days and nights, in order that Israel may not forget their deliverance from Egypt, and thereby thank the Lord for their present Blessings.

Our present-day Campmeetings would be similar events. However, of course, there is no requirement under the New Covenant for such habitations. But the principle should be similar. A Campmeeting, or a gathering of any nature of this type, should be the occasion when we thank the Lord for what He has done for us, in delivering us from the terrible bondages of sin and shame.

THE OFFERINGS

Verses 36 through 38 read: *"Seven days*

you shall offer an Offering made by fire unto the LORD: on the eighth day shall be an holy convocation unto you; and you shall offer up an Offering made by fire unto the LORD: it is a solemn assembly; and you shall do no servile work therein.

"These are the Feasts of the LORD, which you shall proclaim to be holy convocations, to offer an Offering made by fire unto the LORD, a Burnt-Offering, and a Meat-Offering, a Sacrifice, and Drink-Offerings, every thing upon his day:

"Beside the Sabbaths of the LORD, and beside your gifts, and beside all your vows, and beside all your freewill Offerings, which you give unto the LORD."

We find from these statements given in these Verses that this which is to come, and we continue to speak of the Millennial Reign, the greatest time of peace and prosperity the world has ever known, and one hundred times over at that, all and without exception are predicated, even as we've already stated, on the Sacrifice of Christ. As Believers, we tend to forget the cause and the reason for our great Salvation. We attribute it to one thing or the other, always being careful to give God the glory, or so we think! The truth is, unless we understand that every single thing we receive from the Lord, beginning with Salvation, continuing with the Baptism with the Holy Spirit, plus all freedom and prosperity, everything, and without exception, are given to us because of what Jesus has done at the Cross. Do we understand that? Or maybe I should ask, do we understand that as fully as we should?

THE GREAT DAY OF THE FEAST

It was at the Feast of Tabernacles, in fact, *"the last day, that great day of the Feast* (when) *Jesus stood and cried, saying, If any man thirst, let him come unto Me, and drink.*

"He who believes on Me, as the Scripture has said, out of his innermost being shall flow rivers of Living Water" (Jn. 7:37-38).

It is believed that the following occasioned the great statement made by the Master.

For this closing day of the Feast, Jerusalem, and especially the Temple Mount, would have been glutted with people. Jesus was standing somewhere in this crowd, with no

one there actually realizing that all of this ceremony that was taking place was, in reality, a figure or a symbol of the very One Who was in their midst, the Lord Jesus Christ. But regrettably, they didn't know that! They didn't know it simply because their leaders functioned in unbelief, refusing to recognizing Christ, even though the evidence as to Who He was, was incontrovertible.

Regrettably, millions are led astray because they have the wrong kind of leadership.

It is said by some that on this day, this last day, this great day of the Feast, when Jesus uttered forth that great statement, it was precipitated by a Priest holding a golden pitcher, who went to the pool of Siloam. He filled it there with water, returned with it to the Temple, and was then joined by another Priest who had a golden pitcher of wine, with both of them ascending the steps to the Great Altar. They then both poured their respective vessels on the Great Altar, and it was at this moment, when the water mixed with the wine touched the fires of the Brazen Altar, that Jesus cried aloud, *"If any man thirst. . . ."*

The great crowd, possibly numbering tens of thousands, if not more, would have stood in silence as the two Priests ascended to the Great Altar, watching the water and the wine being poured on the burning flame. So the cry of the Master must have charged through the people with a power that they had never sensed before.

This was the cry of the Son of the Living God, actually, the One Who said, *"Let there be light, and there was light!"* So what He said would have been accompanied by the greatest moving of the Holy Spirit that these people had ever known, witnessed, felt, or observed. As stated, He in reality was the *"Feast of Tabernacles."* And in just a few days, He would make it all possible, by what He would do at the Cross of Calvary.

BUT THIS SPAKE HE OF THE SPIRIT

Even as I dictate these notes, I sense the Presence of God. What Jesus made possible at the Cross defies all description. He made Redemption possible, which allowed the Holy Spirit to come into the hearts and lives of all Believers, and there to permanently abide. That's why Paul referred to the Divine Spirit as the *"Spirit of Life in Christ Jesus"* (Rom. 8:2).

Considering the price that was paid by Christ, and then for any Believer to deny the mighty Baptism with the Holy Spirit, which is always accompanied by the speaking with other tongues, is a travesty of the greatest proportions (Acts 2:4). As Salvation separates the sinner from the world, likewise, the Baptism with the Spirit separates Believers from cold, dead, formal religion. In fact, every single thing done on this Earth by the Godhead, but with one exception, has always been done by and through the Power and the Person of the Holy Spirit.

In fact, the Scripture opens with the words, *"And the Spirit of God moved upon the face of the waters"* (Gen. 1:2). It closes with the words: *"And the Spirit and the bride say, Come. And let him who hears say, Come. And let him who is athirst come. And whosoever will, let him take the water of life freely"* (Rev. 22:17).

It is ironical yet beautiful! The Scripture opens with the moving of the Spirit, and closes with the Spirit giving the great invitation.

The only thing on Earth that the Holy Spirit has not done is that which was done by Christ in the Redemption of lost humanity. But even then, the Holy Spirit was the instigator of the conception of Christ (Lk. 1:35). The Holy Spirit came into Christ at the beginning of His Ministry, and in a capacity never experienced before by any human being (Mat. 3:16; Jn. 3:34). As well, the Holy Spirit anointed Him mightily for Ministry (Lk. 4:18-19). In fact, the Holy Spirit worked so closely with Him that the evidence is that Christ did not give up His Life on the Cross until the Eternal Spirit said it was time (Heb. 9:14). As well, it was the Spirit of God Who raised Christ from the dead (Rom. 8:11). And in fact, just before the Ascension, our Lord told those who were assembled with Him to, *"Wait for the Promise of the Father, which, you have heard of Me.*

"For John truly baptized with water; but you shall be baptized with the Holy Spirit not many days hence" (Acts 1:4-5).

So, He was conceived by the Power of the Holy Spirit, anointed by the Power of the Holy Spirit, directed by the Power of the Holy Spirit, and the last thing He said

NOTES

before ascending was: *"But you shall receive power, after that the Holy Spirit is come upon you: and you shall be witnesses unto Me both in Jerusalem, and in all Judaea, and in Samaria, and unto the uttermost part of the Earth"* (Acts 1:8). From that, we certainly should learn just how important the Holy Spirit actually is, as it regards all that we are in Christ.

THE SIGNIFICANCE OF THE HOLY SPIRIT

Inasmuch as Jesus used the Feast of Tabernacles to proclaim the coming Advent of the Holy Spirit, and just how important all of this would be, we should not fail to recognize the significance of this Feast, as it regards this all-important aspect of the Divine Spirit. Even as the Feast of Tabernacles symbolizes and proclaims the coming Kingdom Age, it must be understood that during this thousand year Reign of Christ on Earth, the Holy Spirit will then work as He has never worked before. In fact, that coming Age might well be described as the Dispensation of the Holy Spirit. While He, this glorious Third Person of the Godhead, has worked mightily during the Dispensation of Grace, I personally feel that this is only a symbol of what He is actually going to do as it regards this coming time of unprecedented peace and prosperity.

THE FEASTS OF THE LORD

Verses 39 through 44 read: *"Also in the fifteenth day of the seventh month, when you have gathered in the fruit of the land, you shall keep a Feast unto the LORD seven days: on the first day shall be a Sabbath, and on the eighth day shall be a Sabbath.*

"And you shall take you on the first day the boughs of goodly trees, branches of palm trees, and the boughs of fig trees, and willows of the brook; you shall rejoice before the LORD your God seven days.

"And you shall keep it a Feast unto the LORD seven days in the year. It shall be a Statute forever in your generations: you shall celebrate it in the seventh month.

"You shall dwell in booths seven days; all who are Israelites born shall dwell in booths:

"That your generations may know that I

made the Children of Israel to dwell in booths, when I brought them out of the land of Egypt: I am the LORD your God.

"And Moses declared unto the Children of Israel the Feasts of the LORD."

At the close of this Chapter, we have the words which the Lord gave unto Moses, which declared these seven Feasts to be *"Feasts of the LORD."* Regrettably and sadly, by the time of Christ, they had merely become *"Feasts of the Jews."* This means they had long since ceased to be the Feasts of Jehovah. He was shut out. They no longer wanted or desired Him. However, that statement needs qualification:

One might could say that they did want the Lord, but they wanted Him on their terms, and that has ever been the problem of man. Religious man wants God, hence all the religions of the world. But he wants Him on terms devised and birthed out of his own brain and mind.

I would hope that it has become overly obvious, especially considering the great number of times that the word is used, *"And the LORD spoke unto Moses, saying,"* that all must come from the Lord, which means that none must come from man. Man must hear what God has to say, and do what the Lord has to say.

THE WAY OF MAN

Some years back, I was sent a questionnaire by the leadership of the National Religious Broadcasters, with certain questions they desired answered. They had sent them to all who were members of that particular organization.

Among the questions asked was the following: *"By the way of the Gospel, what do you think the people want?"*

My answer was somewhat cryptic, but definitely to the point. I answered, *"I really don't have any concern as to what the people want, only what God wants, and then His help to deliver that Word."*

The prostitution of the Gospel, and the exploitation of Believers, has ever been the bane of the Ministry. By *"prostituting the Gospel,"* we refer to putting it on the level of man; in other words, the Preacher becomes a hireling, inasmuch as he preaches what the people want to hear. Paul said concerning this: *"For the time will come when they will not endure sound doctrine, but after their own lusts shall they heap to themselves teachers, having itching ears;*

"And they shall turn away their ears from the Truth, and shall be turned unto fables" (II Tim. 4:3-4).

As is obvious, this speaks of the people who do not really want sound doctrine, and look for Preachers who will say what they want to hear said, and sadly, these type of Preachers are in plentiful supply.

THE PREACHING OF THE CROSS

In speaking to a Preacher over the phone the other day, I made mention of the fact that we were *"preaching the Cross."* There was a short silence on his end of the line, and then he finally responded by saying, *"The people won't accept that,"* or words to that effect. Regrettably, he is right!

But whether the people accept it or not is not my problem, or responsibility. As a Preacher of the Gospel, at least if I am to be true to my calling, my responsibility is to hear the Word of the Lord, as it is given to me by the Holy Spirit, and then to faithfully deliver that Word to the people. This is what the Lord told Ezekiel to do. Notice the Text:

"Son of man, I have made you a watchman into the House of Israel: therefore hear the Word at My Mouth, and give them warning from Me.

"When I say unto the wicked, You shall surely die; and you give him not warning, nor speak to warn the wicked from his wicked way, to save his life; the same wicked man shall die in his iniquity; but his blood will I require at your hand.

"Yet if you warn the wicked, and he turn not from his wickedness, nor from his wicked way, he shall die in his iniquity: but you have delivered your soul.

"Again, when a righteous man does turn from his Righteousness, and commit iniquity, and I lay a stumbling block before him, he shall die: because you have not given him warning, he shall die in his sin, and his Righteousness which he has done shall not be remembered; but his blood will I require at your hand.

"Nevertheless if you warn the righteous man, that the righteous sin not, and he does not sin, he shall surely live, because he is warned; also you have delivered your soul" (Ezek. 3:17-21).

The Word of the Lord given to the Prophet Ezekiel is abundantly clear. If he delivered the Word of the Lord to the wicked, and the wicked ignored it, the Prophet had done all he could. He had delivered his soul. But if he refused to deliver that Word, the wicked man would die in his sin, and without having an opportunity to repent, and the Lord bluntly and emphatically states: *"But his blood will I require at your hand."*

It is the same as it regards the Preacher delivering his soul to the righteous man. If the righteous man begins to turn from Righteousness, and go into iniquity, the Preacher is to warn him. If he rejects the warning, and dies in his sin, the Preacher has delivered his soul. But if he dies in his iniquity, without the Preacher having warned him, the Scripture once again is blunt: *"But his blood will I require at your hand."*

This is a frightful warning delivered to the Preacher of the Gospel. To both the unredeemed and the redeemed, he is ordered to deliver that which God tells him to deliver. It is his obligation to warn both the wicked and the righteous. Now let me ask this question:

DISOBEDIENT PREACHERS?

Beginning in the year 2000, that is if I remember the time correctly, the Lord began to move strongly upon this Ministry to address various false doctrines that have become prominent in the modern Church. Among those wayward directions are:

• A departure from the leading of the Holy Spirit.

• The acceptance of humanistic psychology as the answer to the aberrations of man.

• The rejection of the Cross.

• The Word of Faith doctrine, or as it is sometimes known, *"the Jesus died spiritually doctrine."*

• The denial of the Baptism with the Holy Spirit, with the evidence of speaking with other tongues.

• Justification by Faith and Sanctification by self.

• The denial of the Word of God as the criteria for all things.

• The unity gospel, with attempts even being made to wed Christianity and Islam.

• The greed gospel, which places money as the emphasis.

Even though these problems have been permanent from the very beginning, they are, I'm afraid, more prominent now than ever. The Holy Spirit through Paul said this would happen. Among the last words that he wrote, he said: *"And they shall turn away their ears from the Truth, and shall be turned unto fables"* (II Tim. 4:4).

Some weeks before he had also written: *"Now the Spirit speaks expressly* (speaks pointedly), *that in the latter times* (the times in which we now live) *some shall depart from the Faith* (the Cross of Christ), *giving heed to seducing spirits, and doctrines of devils"* (I Tim. 4:1).

When we begin to deal with these false doctrines, and especially the false doctrine of the Word of Faith, which in reality is no Faith at all, at least that God will recognize, we were met with a howl of protest. We called the names of the Preachers, and quoted them verbatim as to what they were teaching and preaching, and to be sure, when light shines upon darkness, it exposes the evil, and if there is anything the Devil doesn't like, it is to be exposed.

Especially considering some of the Messages preached by Donnie, which were most definitely given to him by the Lord, and delivered under an Anointing of the Holy Spirit, many Preachers heard what was said, for these Messages were aired over Television, and many admitted that what was being said was the Truth; however, they quickly added that they would not personally broach the subject themselves. Why?

POPULAR OR UNPOPULAR?

If it is to be noticed, most Preachers preach against false doctrines which are popular to be opposed. In other words, it's popular to expose nicotine, or drugs, etc. But if it's something that is popular, but still wrong, most won't touch that particular doctrine, because they don't want the abuse. Pure and simple, this makes them hirelings. It means they are not preaching what the Lord wants them to preach, which means that blood will ultimately be required at their hands.

TRUTH

Even though I have already addressed this subject, it is so important, I would pray that the Reader would bear with my dealing with it briefly again.

Some Preachers claim to preach only a positive gospel. While there definitely is a positive side to the Gospel, there is also a negative side. And if we preach only the positive side, or only the negative side, we're really not preaching the Truth, but only a part of the truth. Light must be given and darkness must be exposed. And a proper presentation of the light, at the same time, guarantees the exposure of the darkness.

False doctrine is so insidious, so wicked, so subtle, and so deceptive, refusal to point it out means that it will remain lodged in the hearts of those who have believed the error. In fact, this is one of the basic tenets of the Word of God. The Bible is about one-third history, one-third prophecy, and one-third instruction. At least half of it is devoted to pointing out error, with the other half devoted to proclaiming the light. The combination must not be omitted, if the True Gospel is to be given to the people.

Yes, to preach that which I have stated, and which the Word of God declares, will make some people angry. It will ruffle some feathers. In fact, Prophets of old were killed because of this of which I say. Do you think they were killed simply because they said nice things? I think not!

Someone said to a Preacher once, who was preaching the Gospel as he should have preached it, *"Why don't you say only nice things as Jesus did?"* His answer was cryptic and to the point, *"If He said only nice things, I wonder why they crucified Him?"* There are very few Preachers in the world who have ever preached as hard as Jesus did, and I offer the Twenty-third Chapter of Matthew as proof. And let it be understood that He said these things to the faces of these people whom He referred to as *"vipers and hypocrites,"* etc.

NOTES

Let the Reader understand that we are dealing here with matters of life and death. There is nothing more important! If a person is wrong about their insurance policy, they can change companies. If they are wrong about their Doctor, they can get another one. If their car turns out to be a lemon, they can change the make. But if one is wrong about one's soul, there is no way to rectify the situation. As the Lord said: *"He shall die in his iniquity"* (Ezek. 3:18).

In St. John, Chapter 7, when Jesus was asked to go up to *"the Jews' Feast of Tabernacles,"* He answered, *"My time is not yet come"*; and when He did go up, it was *"privately,"* to take His place outside of the whole thing, and to call upon every thirsty soul to come unto Him and drink.

Concerning this, Mackintosh said, *"There is a solemn lesson in this. Divine institutions are speedily marred in the hands of man; but how deeply blessed to know that the thirsty soul that feels the barrenness and drought connected with a scene of empty religious formality, has only to flee to Christ and drink freely of His exhaustless springs, and so become a channel of blessing to others."*

And so concludes our brief study of these seven great Feasts of the Lord. The first four, *"Passover, Unleavened Bread, Firstfruits, and Pentecost,"* have prophetically been fulfilled. The last three are at the very eve of fulfillment. And just as surely as the first four were fulfilled, just as surely will the last three be fulfilled. The Rapture is soon to take place (Trumpets, which proclaimed the conclusion of the Church, and the beginning of the Restoration of Israel). The full Restoration of Israel will signal the fulfillment of the Great Day of Atonement, which has included all who would come, from the time that Jesus died on the Cross, but which will then include Israel. This will take place at the Second Coming (Rev., Chpt. 19; Zech. 13). And then the Millennial Reign, which will fulfill the Feast of Tabernacles.

"I know not why God's wondrous
　　Grace to me
"He has made known,
"Nor why Christ, in His boundless love,
"Redeemed me for His Own."

"I know not how this saving Faith to
    me
"He did impart,
"Nor how believing in His Word,
"Wrought peace within my heart."

"I know not how the Spirit moves,
"Convincing men of sin,
"Revealing Jesus through the Word,
"Creating Faith in Him."

"I know not when my Lord may come,
"At night or noonday fair,
"No if I'll walk the vale with Him,
"Or meet Him in the air."

CHAPTER 24

(1) "AND THE LORD SPOKE UNTO MOSES, SAYING,

(2) "COMMAND THE CHILDREN OF IS-RAEL, THAT THEY BRING UNTO YOU PURE OIL OLIVE BEATEN FOR THE LIGHT, TO CAUSE THE LAMPS TO BURN CONTINUALLY.

(3) "WITHOUT THE VEIL OF THE TES-TIMONY, AND THE TABERNACLE OF THE CONGREGATION, SHALL AARON ORDER IT FROM THE EVENING UNTO THE MORNING BEFORE THE LORD CONTINU-ALLY: IT SHALL BE A STATUTE FOR-EVER IN YOUR GENERATIONS.

(4) "HE SHALL ORDER THE LAMPS UPON THE PURE LAMPSTAND BEFORE THE LORD CONTINUALLY."

The construction is:

1. The first nine Verses of this Chapter are repetitions from the Book of Exodus — the reason for that appears in the legislation now made concerning the man who dishon-ored the Name of Jehovah.

2. The *"pure oil"* represents the Grace of the Holy Spirit, founded upon the Work of Christ, as exhibited by the Lampstand of *"beaten gold."*

3. The *"olive"* was pressed to yield the *"oil,"* and the gold was *"beaten"* to form the Lampstand. In other words, the Grace and Light of the Spirit are founded upon the Death of Christ, and maintained in clearness and power by the Priesthood of Christ.

4. This lamp was to burn *"continually."*

THE GOLDEN LAMPSTAND

Verses 1 and 2 read: *"And the LORD spoke unto Moses, saying,*

"Command the Children of Israel, that they bring unto you pure oil olive beaten for the light, to cause the lamps to burn continually."

The words, *"Command the Children of Israel,"* is the second of two times this phrase is used (Ex. 27:20-21). In other words, this was not a suggestion!

Going forward to Acts 1:4, we read: *"And, being assembled together with them, com-manded them that they should not depart from Jerusalem, but wait for the Promise of the Father, which, said He, you have heard of Me.*

"For John truly baptized with water, but you shall be baptized with the Holy Spirit not many days hence."

In other words, due to the Cross, which has made it all possible, Believers could now receive what the Golden Lampstand prom-ised. Then it was a symbol, a ritual, a cer-emony, although extremely important. To-day, it is reality, at least for those who will believe and receive.

The olive oil of the Golden Lampstand was a symbol of the Holy Spirit. In fact, there were seven lamps on the Golden Lampstand, which number represents per-fection, totality, and completion. It is God's number! These seven lamps were a part of the Golden Lampstand. In other words, the entirety of the Lampstand was beaten or made out of one piece of gold. The three stems to the side were not merely attached to the main stem, but were part of the stem; likewise, the seven lamps were part of the entirety of the Lampstand. Nothing was welded or molded onto, but as stated, all was rather one piece.

All of this tells us many things:

First of all, we learn that Christ and the Holy Spirit are so inseparable as to be one. When John had his heavenly vision of the Throne of God, he said that he saw: *"In the midst of the Throne and of the four Living Creatures, and in the midst of the Elders, stood a Lamb as it had been slain, having seven horns and seven eyes, which are the seven Spirits of God, sent forth into all the Earth"* (Rev. 5:6). The seven lamps (Ex. 37:18) are the same as the seven Spirits of God. This doesn't mean that there are seven Holy Spirits, but rather refers to the seven attributes of the Holy Spirit. They are:

1. The Spirit of the Lord.
2. The Spirit of Wisdom.
3. The Spirit of Understanding.
4. The Spirit of Counsel.
5. The Spirit of Might.
6. The Spirit of Knowledge.
7. The Spirit of the Fear of the Lord (Isa. 11:2).

The Lampstand itself was of *"pure gold,"* signifying the Deity of Christ, and was *"of beaten work,"* typifying the Crucifixion of Christ (Ex. 37:17).

As stated, that in the Mosaic economy, which was symbolic, and could only be attended by the Priests, can now be had in all of its fullness by each and every Believer. We speak of the mighty Baptism with the Holy Spirit, which is always accompanied by the speaking with other tongues, as the Spirit of God gives the utterance (Acts 2:4; 10:46; 19:1-7; I Cor. 14:18).

THE LIGHT

The only light in the Holy Place, for there were no windows, was the light provided by the Golden Lampstand, i.e., *"the Holy Spirit."* Likewise presently, the only true light in this world is that which is provided by the Spirit. Otherwise, the age is dark!

Looking from the natural, virtually all of the technological advancement which has taken place in the world began at about the turn of the Twentieth Century. With some few exceptions, before that time, men lived pretty much as they had always lived. In other words, there was very little difference in the way people lived in the time of Abraham and in the 1800's. But beginning at about the time of the Twentieth Century, something happened, which has changed the complexion of the world. What was it?

Daniel prophesied: *"To the time of the end: many shall run to and fro, and knowledge shall be increased"* (Dan. 12:4). This refers to an increase in knowledge regarding

the Scriptures, and especially in the realm of prophesy, but as well that of technology.

This was brought about by the latter rain outpouring of the Holy Spirit, which began at about the turn of the Twentieth Century, which was predicted by the Prophet Joel. This concerned the outpouring of the Holy Spirit, which the Prophet spoke of as coming upon this Earth in a *"former rain,"* and a *"latter rain"* (Joel 2:23).

The *"former rain"* began on the Day of Pentecost, and included the time of the Early Church, with the account being given to us in the Book of Acts. To be sure, people continued to be baptized with the Holy Spirit, right on through the centuries, but in a limited way. But at about the time of the beginning of the Twentieth Century, hearts began to be hungry for what they read in the Book of Acts, and God rewarded that hunger, which He always does, with its fulfillment. The *"latter rain"* began, which has covered the Earth, resulting from then until now, in well over one-half billion people being baptized with the Holy Spirit, with the evidence of speaking with other tongues.

It is my contention that the outpouring of the Holy Spirit, although understood not at all by the world, and precious little by the Church, instigated the great technological advancement. This doesn't mean at all that those who are smart enough to develop scientific laws are redeemed people. In fact, the far greater majority isn't; however, it does mean that the *"light"* of the Holy Spirit has made all of this possible, even though understood not at all by the Scientists.

The two nations of the world that have contributed the most toward technological advancement have been the United States and England. While other nations have certainly contributed to a lesser extent, these two countries have been the achievers, and especially the United States. It just so happens that this great outpouring of the Holy Spirit basically began in these two countries.

LIGHT AS IT REGARDS THE CHURCH

While scientific light is one thing, of course, the greater thrust of the Holy Spirit, as always, is in the things of God, which pertains to the Church. Since the Advent of the latter rain outpouring, the far greater bulk of Missions work has been carried out in the world. In fact, this particular Ministry (Jimmy Swaggart Ministries) has had the privilege of having a part in this. The Gospel of Jesus Christ has literally girdled the globe, and even though every person hasn't had the opportunity to hear, every country has definitely had the opportunity to hear. Even as I dictate these words in late October of 2002, our Telecast is being aired in about 50 countries of the world. In fact, for approximately 25 years, we've been airing Television all over the world, in many cases, translating into the language of the particular country where the program was aired.

For instance, in 1989 we went on Television in one of the Soviet Republics. This was before the fall of Communism. Even though the KGB attempted to have the program taken off of the air, it remained in this particular city (Estonia). Immediately upon the fall of Communism, we began airing over T.V.1, which had been the principal propaganda Television Network of the old Soviet Empire. It went into all 15 Soviet Republics, in fact, going into virtually every town, city, and village, covering one-sixth of the world's land surface. It had over 2,000 Stations attached to this Network. We aired the Gospel of Jesus Christ over this Network for nearly two years. During that time, through the preaching of the Gospel, we saw a mighty Move of God all over the former Soviet Union, which resulted in untold numbers of people being brought to a saving knowledge of Jesus Christ.

One Pastor related to me as to how he and other Preachers had gone into Moscow, and had brought in Preachers from all over the former Soviet Union, actually paying their expenses, in order that they might be taught the Gospel, which all of them very much needed. He related to me that at the beginning of one of those sessions, they asked for Pastors to stand and relate as to how they had been saved.

He said to me, *"Brother Swaggart, over 75 percent of the Preachers who stood and gave their Testimony that day testified to the fact that they had been saved through your Telecast."* He went on to relate as to

NOTES

how some of these Pastors were now averaging several thousands in their Churches, etc.

All of this was made possible by the Holy Spirit. He provides the *"Truth,"* which of course is *"Light."* Jesus referred to Him as *"the Spirit of Truth"* (Jn. 14:17; 16:13).

And let me again emphasize, all of this was made possible by what Christ did at the Cross, symbolized by the Lampstand being of beaten gold.

THE LAMPS MUST BURN CONTINUALLY

Inasmuch as there is no other spiritual light in the world, it should be readily understood as to why the lamps must burn continually. Otherwise, there is nothing but darkness.

"Continually" covers not only the entirety of the time of the Law of Moses, but on up to the present as well, and in fact, forever. In truth, due to the Cross, which has made it possible for the Holy Spirit to function in a greater dimension, the lamps are burning brighter than ever. Or at least, they can if the Church so desires!

The tragedy is, while that light is definitely shining, it is not shining nearly as bright as it could. In fact, I'm afraid that it is shining less today than it has at any time since the great outpouring began at the turn of the Twentieth Century. I realize that's a shocking statement, but I believe it to be true.

But of course, the modern Church would claim the opposite. They are rather claiming that they are *"rich and increased with goods, and have need of nothing."* But what else did the Lord say of this modern Church?

He said: *"And knowest not that you are wretched, and miserable, and poor, and blind, and naked"* (Rev. 3:17).

One should notice that one of the condemnations is that of *"spiritual blindness."* For this He also said:

"I counsel you to buy of Me gold tried in the fire, that you might be rich (truly rich with spiritual things)*; and white raiment that you may be clothed, and that the shame of your nakedness do not appear* (the true Righteousness of Christ)*; and anoint your eyes with eye salve, that you may see"* (Rev. 3:18).

If the Cross is properly preached, the Holy Spirit can then properly work, and then spiritual sight will come back. But without the

Cross being properly preached, the Holy Spirit can little function as He so desires, and spiritual blindness will remain. It is the *"Law of the Spirit of Life which is in Christ Jesus, which alone can deliver us from the law of sin and death"* (Rom. 8:2).

THE PURE LAMPSTAND

Verses 3 and 4 read: *"Without the Veil of the Testimony, in the Tabernacle of the congregation, shall Aaron order it from the evening unto the morning before the LORD continually: it shall be a Statute forever in your generations.*

"He shall order the Lamps upon the pure Lampstand before the LORD continually."

As one would walk into the Tabernacle, to his left would be the Golden Lampstand. Immediately in front of it would have been *"the Veil of the Testimony,"* which hung between the Holy Place, where the Golden Lampstand was, plus other sacred vessels, and the Holy of Holies, which contained the Ark of the Covenant, i.e., *"the Testimony."*

The command given to Aaron as the High Priest in effect was given to all Priests, and in fact, all who would follow down the long line of succession. They were to attend to the Golden Lampstand every morning and every evening, actually at the time of the morning and evening Sacrifices, which were at 9 a.m., and 3 p.m. This was to be done *"before the LORD continually,"* and to never be neglected, although, eventually, it was neglected!

The phrase, *"Pure Lampstand,"* has to do with the arranging of the Lamps after having purified and being made clean, by trimming the wicks, and replenishing the oil. As stated, this was to be done twice every day.

While the Lampstand was of pure gold, the word *"pure"* as used here is not referring to that in particular, but rather, that which we have stated. The Lamps in their burning and their giving light were forever to be *"pure."*

THE HOLY SPIRIT

The Moving, Working, and Operation of the Holy Spirit within our hearts and lives are either enhanced or hindered by our consecration or the lack thereof. To be sure, there is nothing we can do that can earn His

help, but obedience is that which we can do, and which is definitely required.

Even though I have already dealt with the following in this Volume several times, due to the fact that many people study Commentaries only a Chapter at a time, etc., I feel compelled to again proclaim the following Truth, even though I am repetitive. If that which we will state is not understood and understood properly, the Holy Spirit will be greatly hindered in our hearts and lives, and the full potential of what He can do will only be partially realized.

Every Believer must understand that the Holy Spirit is God. As such, there is nothing He cannot do. In other words, He is Almighty. In fact, Paul told us that the following power is available to us. He said:

"But if the Spirit (Holy Spirit) *of Him* (God the Father) *Who raised up Jesus from the dead dwell in you, He Who raised up Christ from the dead shall also quicken your mortal bodies by His Spirit Who dwells in you"* (Rom. 8:11).

This plainly tells us that the same power that raised Jesus from the dead, which we certainly should know is almighty power, is available to us as Believers. No, Paul is not speaking here of the coming Resurrection, which most Believers think, but rather of our daily lives and living. He speaks here of *"mortal bodies,"* made alive, in other words, given the strength to live as we ought to. In the coming Resurrection, we will have Glorified Bodies, and will have no need of this which is addressed here.

So how can I have this almighty power to work perpetually within my heart and life?

THE CROSS

The Holy Spirit works exclusively within and through the Cross of Christ of Christ. This information is given to us in Romans 8:2, John 14:16-17, and John 16:13-15. This means that every single thing that He does for us, with us, of us, by us, and in us, is all done exclusively within the legal parameters of the Finished Work of Christ. In other words, the Cross is what made it possible for the Holy Spirit to abide within our hearts and lives, and to do so permanently (Jn. 14:16-17).

Now first of all, if the Believer fully understands the Cross, and we speak of its vast significance, and in every capacity, to be sure, the Believer will live a consecrated life. In other words, he will keep the wicks clean, and replenish the oil, so to speak.

FAITH

Understanding that everything comes to us through the Cross, our Faith must ever be in the Finished Work of Christ. In other words, the Cross of Christ must ever be the object of our Faith. This is of vital significance.

If Satan can move your Faith to other things, and he really doesn't care too very much what these other things are, in fact, how good they may be in their own right, just so it's not in the Cross, he will have defeated you. It was at the Cross and the Cross exclusively where he was totally and completely defeated. Listen again to Paul:

"Buried with Him in baptism (this speaks not of Water Baptism, but rather of His death – Rom. 6:3), *wherein also you are risen with Him* (Rom. 6:4-5) *through the Faith of the operation of God* (our part in Christ is realized by Faith in what He has done for us at the Cross), *Who* (God the Father) *has raised Him from the dead.*

"And you (Believers), *being dead in your sins and the uncircumcision of your flesh, has He quickened together with Him, having forgiven you all trespasses* (we were made alive in Him by what He did for us at the Cross. In fact, we were baptized into His death, which refers to the Crucifixion, buried with Him, and raised with Him in newness of life – Rom. 6:3-5)*;*

"Blotting out the handwriting of Ordinances that was against us . . . and took it out of the way (Jesus satisfied every demand of the Law, whether in the perfect keeping of its precepts, which He did, or paying the price the broken Law demanded, which was death), *nailing it to His Cross* (as stated, it was at the Cross that all of this was done, and Satan totally defeated)*;*

"And having spoiled principalities and powers, He made a show of them openly, triumphing over them in it" (Col. 2:12-15).

In what Christ did at the Cross, the legal right that Satan had to hold man in captivity was spoiled. In other words, by what Jesus did at the Cross, which was the atoning for all sin, past, present, and future, at least for those who will believe, this removed Satan's legal right to hold man in bondage. So anyone who is presently held in bondage by Satan is in this condition because they have given him consent.

WHAT DO WE MEAN BY CONSENT?

Every unsaved person in the world is a slave to his evil passions, therefore, to Satan. All of that, despite education, money, prestige, etc., ultimately leads to total destruction, i.e., *"the thief comes not but for to steal, kill, and destroy"* (Jn. 10:10). The unredeemed can be saved, as the Gospel is preached unto them, if they will only accept the Lord. The Scripture tells us, *"For God so loved the world. . . ."* That includes all (Jn. 3:16). It also says, *"Whosoever will"* (Rev. 22:17).

If the unredeemed remain in bondage, it is because they want to be that way, in other words, they give Satan consent to hold them in bondage, or else the Gospel has never been preached unto them, which is the case for so very many in the world today. Nevertheless, the price has been paid at the Cross of Calvary, for every single unredeemed person to be set free.

When it comes to Believers, it is basically the same thing. In fact, untold millions of Believers are presently in bondage to Satan, which means that in some way, sin has dominion over them. I speak of *"works of the flesh,"* which Paul dealt with in Galatians 5:19-21. This means that such Christians are not living up to nearly their potential in Christ. In fact, in such a state, Christianity is not a very pleasant experience. But regrettably, millions of Christians are held at this moment in Satanic bondage, whether they admit to it or not.

Once again, it is because they have given Satan consent to do so. Now I realize that many would take umbrage at that; however, it is true!

The major problem is, most Christians do not understand the Cross, which is where all victory is deposited; as a result, they try to live this life in all the wrong ways. Satan takes advantage of that, and please believe me, unless the Faith of the Believer is properly placed, which refers to the Cross ever being its object, the Believer cannot live a victorious, overcoming, Christian life. It is impossible! God has provided only one way of victory, and because only one way is required, and as well, that one way meets every need, and that way is the Cross. The solution for which mankind seeks, whether he realizes it or not, is *"Jesus Christ and Him Crucified"* (I Cor. 1:23).

THE POWER OF THE HOLY SPIRIT

When our understanding is correct as it regards the Cross, which refers to knowing that everything we receive from the Lord comes to us by and through what Jesus did at the Cross, and our Faith is properly placed there, and our Faith properly remains there, the Holy Spirit then has the legal right to do whatever needs to be done, and to be sure, He can do anything. This is the manner in which He works, and regrettably, this is the manner in which most Believers do not understand, simply because it is not taught from behind most pulpits. In fact, most Preachers don't have the foggiest idea as to how to properly tell a Believer how to walk in victory. In fact, they're not walking in victory themselves, so how can they tell others the truth?

Yes, some Preachers definitely do have the victory, but that number is few and far between. Just because a man or a woman has been called to preach the Gospel doesn't mean that these great Truths are automatically known by them. In fact, the Preacher of the Gospel has to learn the truth of the Word of God, like anyone else.

While all of the Word of God is of supreme significance, it is through Paul that we learn and thereby understand victorious, Christian living. It is this way simply because it was to Paul that the meaning of the New Covenant was given, which in effect is the meaning of the Cross (Gal., Chpt. 1).

What I have just given you in the above paragraphs, and which I have already related in this Volume, can change your life if you will only allow the Word to take its proper effect. That which I have taught you is not new. It is that which the Lord, as stated, gave to Paul. But Satan has been very successful

at moving the Church away from the Cross to other things. What a tragedy! What a liability! What defeat!

But if you the Believer will believe what the Word of God tells us, perpetual victory can be yours, which means that sin will no longer have dominion over you in any capacity (Rom. 6:3-14; 8:1-2, 11; I Cor. 1:17-18, 21, 23; 2:2, 5; Gal. 6:14; Eph. 2:13-18; Col. 2:14-15).

(5) "AND YOU SHALL TAKE FINE FLOUR, AND BAKE TWELVE CAKES THEREOF: TWO TENTH DEALS SHALL BE IN ONE CAKE.

(6) "AND YOU SHALL SET THEM IN TWO ROWS, SIX ON A ROW, UPON THE PURE TABLE BEFORE THE LORD.

(7) "AND YOU SHALL PUT PURE FRANKINCENSE UPON EACH ROW, THAT IT MAY BE ON THE BREAD FOR A MEMORIAL, EVEN AN OFFERING MADE BY FIRE UNTO THE LORD.

(8) "EVERY SABBATH HE SHALL SET IT IN ORDER BEFORE THE LORD CONTINUALLY, BEING TAKEN FROM THE CHILDREN OF ISRAEL BY AN EVERLASTING COVENANT.

(9) "AND IT SHALL BE AARON'S AND HIS SONS'; AND THEY SHALL EAT IT IN THE HOLY PLACE: FOR IT IS MOST HOLY UNTO HIM OF THE OFFERINGS OF THE LORD MADE BY FIRE BY A PERPETUAL STATUTE."

The composition is:

1. The Golden Lampstand with its sacred flame, and the pure table with its Presence Bread were figures, as already noted, of Christ as the Bread of Life and the Light of the world. They are inserted here by design by the Holy Spirit between the Feasts of Jehovah and the blasphemer of Jehovah.

2. The Bread, some 12 loaves in two rows of six, was to be eaten every Sabbath by the Priests. It was a type of our partaking of Christ as the Bread of Life.

3. Evidently the 12 cakes were stacked one upon the other, six in a stack, with a gold dish of frankincense at the top. Some say the cakes were square not round. The burning of the frankincense at the top of the stacks made the Shewbread an Offering made by fire unto Jehovah, as mentioned in

Verse 7 of this Chapter.

Actually, the loaves were not burned in the fire, for they were to be eaten by the Priests in the Holy Place as the most holy of the Offerings.

4. The stacks of Shewbread were to be upon the *"pure table"*; this was the Table covered with pure gold that stood before the Lord. Pure frankincense was to be burned upon the pure table. This signifies that all things connected with Jehovah and His worship were to be pure, thus typifying the purity of life and conduct of the worshippers who came before Him.

CHRIST, THE BREAD OF LIFE

Verses 5 and 6 read: *"And you shall take fine flour, and bake twelve cakes thereof: two tenth deals shall be in one cake.*

"And you shall set them in two rows, six on a row, upon the pure table before the LORD."

The *"fine flour"* of which the cakes were made, speaks of flour that has been sifted minutely in order that all impurities be removed. It is a type of the Perfect Life of Christ. There was no coarseness or unevenness about Him. His Life was perfect in every respect. In fact, it had to be this way, in order that He on our behalf, keep the Law perfectly, which He did.

We must ever understand that every single thing that He did was for us totally and completely, and not at all for Himself, or for Heaven in any capacity. He, one might say, was our Substitute. As the Last Adam, He did what the first Adam did not do, which was to render a perfect obedience to God. The Scripture says: *"Then said I, Lo, I come (in the volume of the Book it is written of Me,) to do Your Will, O God"* (Heb. 10:7).

As each one of us looks at our lives, and no matter how consecrated we may be to the Lord, if we are honest, we will find much unevenness and coarseness in our personalities. In other words, things which aren't Christlike! But Christ was perfect in His comportment, personality, demeanor, and in fact, in every action. In word, thought, and deed, He left nothing to be desired.

TWELVE CAKES

The *"twelve cakes"* represented the 12

Tribes of Israel, but in reality, they represented much more.

First of all, the bread, as is obvious, was totally and completely a type of Christ. But the number of loaves, being 12, represented His pure and perfect Government. In fact, the entirety of the Law of Moses was, in reality, the Government of God. It was that which the Lord required of the human race, inasmuch as it was His Standard of Righteousness. It was for the good of man everywhere, and totally for the good of man.

The biggest problem that Israel had was their circumventing the Government of God, thereby, instituting their own Government, which always, and without exception, brought ruin, as it always will bring ruin. In fact, that's the problem with the modern Church, and in fact, always has been. Men tend to take that which is given by God, which is His perfect Government, which is His Word, and then take from it, or add to it. As this was the tragedy of Israel, it is likewise the tragedy of the Church.

As we've already stated several times in this Volume, the criteria for all things must be, *"Is it according to the Word of God?"* If it's not according to the Word of God, and in every respect, then it's wrong, and must be shunned and put away. But men are fond of making rules, and especially religious men. They love to make rules, and they love to try to force others to obey those rules. In fact, the Earth has been soaked with blood over religious wars, more so than anything else. It is man attempting to have his religious way, instead of God's Way. Untold millions are in Hell at this moment because they chose man's way, thereby, forsaking God's Way. Listen to Solomon:

"There is a way which seems right unto a man, but the end thereof are the ways of death" (Prov. 14:12).

Modern religious Denominations are probably some of the worst offenders respecting this all-important subject. The constitution and bylaws of many Denominations are made without any thought as to whether they are Scriptural or not.

For instance, one major Pentecostal Denomination changed its rulings the other day as it regards a particular subject. If what they had done previously was Scriptural, how could they change it?

The truth is, what that had done previously was not Scriptural. I am persuaded that they have many more bylaws which aren't Scriptural as well. Somehow, these men seem to think that because it's a Denomination, which is incidentally man-instituted and man-directed, and that they vote on certain things, all of this makes it right. It doesn't! It doesn't matter what man votes or says; again we ask the question, *"Is it Scriptural?"*

I was a member of a particular Pentecostal Denomination for years, in fact, the very one I've just mentioned. While they have many Godly Preachers in that Denomination, and while there are many Godly people associated as well, the truth is, their Government is not Scriptural, and as such, it does great harm to the Work of God. Regrettably, most other Denominations fall into the same category.

God's Government cannot be changed, simply because it doesn't need to be changed. It was perfect when it was instituted, and it remains perfect.

FRANKINCENSE

Verse 7 reads: *"And you shall put pure frankincense upon each row, that it may be on the bread for a memorial, even an Offering made by fire unto the LORD."*

The Text seems to indicate that the frankincense was poured on the bread, but others who know the Hebrew claim that it really wasn't poured on the bread, but rather on the fire, hence, *"An Offering made by fire unto the LORD."* Incidentally, the frankincense would have been burned on the Golden Altar, which was immediately in front of the Veil. Until the time of the burning, the frankincense would have been kept in two bowls, with each bowl sitting near or on each stack of six loaves.

The phrase, *"For a memorial,"* had to do with the following:

As the frankincense would have been burned on the Golden Altar, it would have filled the Holy Place with a pungent aroma, signifying thankfulness to the Lord, and that all blessings came from Him. It would have signified also, due to the fact that it was

burned on the Golden Altar, the Intercessory Ministry of our Lord.

EVERY SABBATH

Verses 8 and 9 read: *"Every Sabbath he shall set it in order before the LORD continually, being taken from the Children of Israel by an Everlasting Covenant.*

"And it shall be Aaron's and his sons'; and they shall eat it in the Holy Place: for it is most holy unto him of the Offerings of the LORD made by fire by a perpetual Statute."

The *"Sabbath"* denoted *"rest,"* which of course pictured Christ. So each Sabbath, the Priests were to partake of this particular bread, thereby symbolizing the partaking of Christ, with it replaced by 12 fresh loaves. The following is an account as to how it was done:

"Four Priests entered the Holy Place, two of them carried on their hands the two stacks of the cakes, and two carried in their hands the two incense cups, four Priests having gone in before them, two to take off the two old stacks, and two to take off the two incense cups (frankincense). Those who brought in the new stood at the north side with their faces to the south, and those who took away the old stood at the south side with their faces to the north.

"As soon as the one party lifted up the old, the others put down the new, so that their hands were exactly over against each other, because it is written, 'Before My Presence continually' (Ex. 25:30).

"The authorities during the second Temple took the expression 'continually' to denote that the cakes were not to be absent for one moment. Hence the simultaneous action of the two sets of Priests, one lifting up the old, and the other at once putting down the new Shewbread."

The phrase, *"Being taken from the Children of Israel by an Everlasting Covenant,"* pertains to the fact that every person had to give a half shekel of silver each year, which contributed annually toward the maintenance of the service in the Sanctuary, the securing of ingredients, etc.

"Silver" represented Redemption, which is what Christ would bring about as a result of His death on the Cross.

As it regards the division of the 12 cakes,

it is said that the High Priest took six, and the other Priests had six, as well, among them. They were to eat the bread in the Holy Place. In fact, eight things were to be consumed within the precincts of the Sanctuary. They are as follows:

1. The remnant of the Meat-Offering (Lev. 2:3, 10).

2. The flesh of the Sin-Offering (Lev. 6:26).

3. The flesh of the Trespass-Offering (Lev. 7:6).

4. The leper's log of oil (Lev. 14:10).

5. The remainder of the omer (Lev. 23:10-11).

6. The Peace-Offering of the congregation.

7. The two loaves (Lev. 13:19-20).

8. The Shewbread (Lev. 24:9).

(10) "AND THE SON OF AN ISRAELITISH WOMAN, WHOSE FATHER WAS AN EGYPTIAN, WENT OUT AMONG THE CHILDREN OF ISRAEL: AND THIS SON OF THE ISRAELITISH WOMAN AND A MAN OF ISRAEL STROVE TOGETHER IN THE CAMP;

(11) "AND THE ISRAELITISH WOMAN'S SON BLASPHEMED THE NAME OF THE LORD AND CURSED. AND THEY BROUGHT HIM UNTO MOSES: (AND HIS MOTHER'S NAME WAS SHELO-MITH, THE DAUGHTER OF DIBRI, OF THE TRIBE OF DAN:)

(12) "AND THEY PUT HIM IN WARD, THAT THE MIND OF THE LORD MIGHT BE SHOWED THEM.

(13) "AND THE LORD SPOKE UNTO MOSES, SAYING,

(14) "BRING FORTH HIM WHO HAS CURSED WITHOUT THE CAMP; LET ALL WHO HEARD HIM LAY THEIR HANDS UPON HIS HEAD, AND LET ALL THE CONGREGATION STONE HIM.

(15) "AND YOU SHALL SPEAK UNTO THE CHILDREN OF ISRAEL, SAYING, WHOSOEVER CURSES HIS GOD SHALL BEAR HIS SIN.

(16) "AND HE WHO BLASPHEMES THE NAME OF THE LORD, HE SHALL SURELY BE PUT TO DEATH, AND ALL THE CONGREGATION SHALL CERTAINLY STONE HIM: AS WELL THE STRANGER, AS HE WHO IS BORN IN THE LAND, WHEN HE BLASPHEMES THE NAME OF THE LORD,

SHALL BE PUT TO DEATH.

(17) "AND HE WHO KILLS ANY MAN SHALL SURELY BE PUT TO DEATH.

(18) "AND HE WHO KILLS A BEAST SHALL MAKE IT GOOD; BEAST FOR BEAST.

(19) "AND IF A MAN CAUSE A BLEMISH IN HIS NEIGHBOR; AS HE HAS DONE, SO SHALL IT BE DONE TO HIM;

(20) "BREACH FOR BREACH, EYE FOR EYE, TOOTH FOR TOOTH: AS HE HAS CAUSED A BLEMISH IN A MAN, SO SHALL IT BE DONE TO HIM AGAIN.

(21) "AND HE WHO KILLS A BEAST, HE SHALL RESTORE IT: AND HE WHO KILLS A MAN, HE SHALL BE PUT TO DEATH.

(22) "YOU SHALL HAVE ONE MANNER OF LAW, AS WELL FOR THE STRANGER, AS FOR ONE OF YOUR OWN COUNTRY: FOR I AM THE LORD YOUR GOD.

(23) "AND MOSES SPOKE TO THE CHILDREN OF ISRAEL, THAT THEY SHOULD BRING FORTH HIM WHO HAD CURSED OUT OF THE CAMP, AND STONE HIM WITH STONES. AND THE CHILDREN OF ISRAEL DID AS THE LORD COMMANDED MOSES."

The diagram is:

1. This is a picture in type of the nation itself, represented by the son of the Israelitish woman, who would seek to kill the true man of Israel (vs. 10).

2. The subjection of mind that appears in Verse 12, and the anxiety to do what God wished, and not to act in the heat of their own judgment, is very gracious (Williams).

3. The Gentile (vs. 22) was to have an equal place with the Hebrews within the goodness and severity of the righteous law decreed in Verses 17-23.

THE SIN AGAINST GOD

Verses 10 through 12 read: *"And the son of an Israelitish woman, whose father was an Egyptian, went out among the Children of Israel: and this son of the Israelitish woman and a man of Israel strove together in the camp;*

"And the Israelitish woman's son blasphemed the Name of the Lord and cursed. And they brought him unto Moses: (and his mother's name was Shelo-mith, the daughter of Dibri, of the Tribe of Dan:)

"And they put him in ward, that the Mind of the LORD might be showed them."

The Reader might wander as to why the Holy Spirit would have Moses place the account of the apostasy of this young man at this juncture.

Tradition says that this woman, Shelo-mith, had married an Egyptian while she and her people were still in Egypt. Though the father's nationality is given expressly here, yet from the fact that he does not personally come before us in this incident, it is evident that he remained in Egypt, while the son was of the *"mixed multitude"* who followed the Israelites in their exodus (Ex. 12:38).

This incident, therefore, which is so difficult satisfactorily to connect with the preceding legislation, brings before us a picture of the camp-life of the Israelites in the wilderness.

According to tradition, the father of this blasphemer was the taskmaster under whom Shelo-mith's husband worked in Egypt, that he had injured Shelo-mith and then smote her husband, and that this was the Egyptian whom Moses slew (Ex. 2:11), for the injuries he had thus inflicted both upon the Hebrew and his wife, and that the culprit before us is the son of the outraged Shelo-mith by the slain Egyptian. This will explain the rendering here of the ancient Chaldee version, *"A wicked man, a rebel against the God of Heaven, had come out of Egypt, the son of the Egyptian who slew an Israelite in Egypt, and outraged his wife, who conceived, and brought forth this son among the Children of Israel."*

THE TRADITION CONTINUES

The cause and the manner of their quarrel or contention are not given here. But, according to tradition, the *"man of Israel"* was a Danite. The son of the Israelitish woman contended with this Danite that he had a right from the side of his mother to encamp among the children of Dan, while the Danite disputed this, maintaining that a son could only pitch his tent by the standard of his father's name (Num. 2:2).

This contention, moreover, took place before the rulers who tried the case (Ex. 19:21-22).

It seems that the Elders of Israel ruled against the son of the Israelitish woman. Hearing the sentence, he became very angry, and after leaving the court, *"Blasphemed the Name of the Lord, and cursed."*

Being vexed with the Divine enactments which excluded him from encamping in the Tribe of his mother, he both cursed God Who gave such Law, and reviled the judges who pronounced judgment against him.

Evidently a number of people overheard him, and they *"brought him to Moses."*

The contention about his right to pitch his tent among the Tribe to which his mother belonged was a minor point; however, blaspheming God was a very serious offense, and hence, the criminal was brought to Moses.

SON OF THE EGYPTIAN

Whether we accept the traditional explanation that Shelo-mith was no consenting party to her union with the Egyptian, or whether we regard her as having voluntarily married him, the fact that both her personal and tribal names are so distinctly specified here indicates that the record of this incident is designed to point out the ungodly issue of so unholy an alliance, and to guard the Hebrew women against intermarriage with heathen (Ellicott).

Though this was a transgression of the Third Commandment, and though it was ordained that he who cursed his earthly parents should be put to death (20:9), yet no law existed as to the exact punishment which was to be inflicted upon him who cursed his Heavenly Father (Ex. 22:28); nor was it known whether such an offender should be left to God Himself to execute the sentence. For this reason the criminal was detained until Moses had appealed to the Lord for instruction, in order that he might direct the people accordingly (Ellicott).

THE LAW

Verses 13 through 16 read: *"And the LORD spoke unto Moses, saying,*

"Bring forth him who has cursed without the camp; and let all who heard him lay their hands upon his head, and let all the congregation stone him.

"And you shall speak unto the Children

of Israel, saying, Whosoever curses his God shall bear his sin.

"And he who blasphemes the Name of the LORD, he shall surely be put to death, and all the congregation shall certainly stone him: as well the stranger, as he who is born in the land, when he blasphemes the Name of the Lord, shall be put to death."

We aren't told as to exactly how the Lord spoke to Moses. Possibly He used the Urim and Thummim, or maybe the Lord spoke to him from the Mercy Seat between the Cherubim (Ex. 25:22). Nevertheless, the Lord did speak directly to Moses, and gave him direction. He, in fact, laid down a general law for the punishment of blasphemers.

While under the New Covenant, such is no longer demanded; still, let not the Reader think that God has changed His rulings and commands. God doesn't change, and in fact, God cannot change, at least as it regards His Word. His Word is immutable, which means unchangeable, and to be sure, whatever is said is just as pertinent now as it was when it was uttered thousands of years ago.

Although physical death is not now demanded, and because Jesus fulfilled the Law in that respect, in effect, dying for all; but still, and to be sure, spiritual death definitely follows, for anyone who takes the Word of God lightly. Let that ever be understood!

INSTRUCTIONS REGARDING ONE'S FELLOWMAN

Verses 17 through 23 read: "And he who kills any man shall surely be put to death.

"And he who kills a beast shall make it good; beast for beast.

"And if a man cause a blemish in his neighbor; as he has done, so shall it be done to him;

"Breach for breach, eye for eye, tooth for tooth: as he has caused a blemish in a man, so shall it be done to him again.

"And he who kills a beast, he shall restore it: he who kills a man, he shall be put to death.

"You shall have one manner of Law, as well for the stranger, as for one of your own country: for I am the LORD your God.

"And Moses spoke to the Children of Israel, that they should bring forth him who had cursed out of the camp, and stoned him

NOTES

with stones. And the Children of Israel did as the LORD commanded Moses."

These Laws had already been given, and recorded in Exodus, Chapter 21. I'm sure they are given again here by the Holy Spirit for several reasons. One of those reasons would have to be that it should be known that the Law is applicable alike to the proselyte and to the Gentile, who does not even profess to believe in Jehovah.

The last Verse of this Chapter proclaims the fact, the Lord having told Moses what was to be done, Moses calls upon the people to execute the sentence which the Lord pronounced against the blasphemer.

MERCY AND GRACE

Some may read these words and think the sentence far too harsh. That would be easily thought when one considers that blasphemy against God now tumbles from the lips of the majority of mankind on an hourly basis. In other words, it is constant!

The truth is, it was the same in the world of Israel's day; however, Israel was different than any of the other nations of the world. They were to be a holy people, and because God was holy. If love, respect, and obedience for the commands of the Lord broke down, Israel would lose her way, which she eventually did. To whom much is given, much is required!

No, the Lord was not at all unmerciful. In fact, God cannot be unmerciful, considering that His Mercy endures forever. But He does say what He means, and means what He says!

"O Jesus, I have promised to serve You
    to the end;
"Be Thou forever near me, my Master
    and my Friend:
"I shall not fear the battle, if You are
    by my side,
"Nor wander from the pathway, if You
    will be my Guide."

"O let me feel You near me! The world
    is ever near;
"I see the sights that dazzle, the tempting sounds I hear;
"My foes are ever near me, around me
    and within;

*"But, Jesus, draw Thou nearer, and
shield my soul from sin."*

*"O let me hear You speaking, in ac-
cents clear and still,*
*"Above the storms of passion, the mur-
murs of self-will!*
*"O speak to reassure me, to hasten or
control!*
*"O speak, and, make me listen, Thou
Guardian of my soul!"*

*"O Jesus, You have promised, to all who
follow Thee*
*"That where You are in glory, there
shall Your servant be;*
*"And, Jesus, I have promised to serve
You to the end;*
*"O give me Grace to follow, my Master
and my Friend!"*

CHAPTER 25

(1) "AND THE LORD SPOKE UNTO MOSES IN MOUNT SINAI, SAYING,

(2) "SPEAK UNTO THE CHILDREN OF ISRAEL, AND SAY UNTO THEM, WHEN YOU COME INTO THE LAND WHICH I GIVE YOU, THEN SHALL THE LAND KEEP ITS SABBATH UNTO THE LORD.

(3) "SIX YEARS YOU SHALL SOW YOUR FIELD, AND SIX YEARS YOU SHALL PRUNE YOUR VINEYARD, AND GATHER IN THE FRUIT THEREOF;

(4) "BUT IN THE SEVENTH YEAR SHALL BE A SABBATH OF REST UNTO THE LAND, A SABBATH FOR THE LORD: YOU SHALL NEITHER SOW YOUR FIELD, NOR PRUNE YOUR VINEYARD.

(5) "THAT WHICH GROWS OF ITS OWN ACCORD OF YOUR HARVEST YOU SHALL NOT REAP, NEITHER GATHER THE GRAPES OF YOUR VINE UN-DRESSED: FOR IT IS A YEAR OF REST UNTO THE LAND.

(6) "AND THE SABBATH OF THE LAND SHALL BE MEAT FOR YOU; FOR YOU, AND FOR YOUR SERVANT, AND FOR YOUR MAID, AND FOR YOUR HIRED SERVANT, AND FOR THE STRANGER WHO SO-JOURNS WITH YOU.

NOTES

(7) "AND FOR YOUR CATTLE, AND FOR THE BEAST THAT ARE IN YOUR LAND, SHALL ALL THE INCREASE THEREOF BE MEAT."

The exegesis is:

1. The doctrine of this Chapter is that the people of Israel and the land of Israel belong to Jehovah, and that He, as the Divine Redeemer, has redeemed them both at the expense of His Own Precious Blood.

2. The legislation of this Chapter effects the Sabbatic year and the Jubilee year. These, together with the weekly Sabbath, pointed onwards to the Millennial rest that awaits Israel. But the greater meaning has to do with the rest that we find in Christ, and His Redeeming Work within our lives.

3. The principles that these Laws expressed are singular to the Bible, but yet, wonder of wonders, part of the great prosperity of the United States is based upon the teaching given in this Chapter. We will explain later.

GOVERNMENT

Verse 1 reads: *"And the LORD spoke unto Moses in Mount Sinai, saying."*

In the previous Chapter, we learned that Israel is being prepared for the Land of Israel, and in this Twenty-fifth Chapter, we learn that the land of Israel is being prepared for Israel.

Verse 1 of this Chapter reads a little different than the other similar statements. It says, *"The LORD spoke unto Moses in Mount Sinai."* The greater bulk of the teaching given in the Book of Leviticus emanated from the Tabernacle. This was understandable, and because it regarded the Sacrifices, the sacred vessels, and the duties of the Priests in carrying out the various ceremonies and rituals, which were so very important, as it regards the worship of God.

By now we should know that every single line, in fact, every single word in Scripture, are of vast significance. The great Law given in the Book of Exodus emanated from Mount Sinai, which one could say was the place of Government. While everything that pertains to the Lord in some way inculcates Government, still, there is a distinction as it regards the foundation of Government and the details of Government. The foundation is found in Exodus, and the remainder of the Chapters in Leviticus, beginning with this Twenty-fifth Chapter. Previous Chapters in Leviticus pertain to details of Government.

In the New Testament, we find the foundation of Government in the Book of Acts, and the details of Government found in the Epistles.

THE SEVENTH YEAR SABBATH

Verses 2 through 7 read: *"Speak unto the Children of Israel, and say unto them, When you come into the land which I give you, then shall the land keep a Sabbath unto the LORD.*

"Six years you shall sow your field, and six years you shall prune your vineyard, and gather in the fruit thereof;

"But in the seventh year shall be a Sabbath of rest unto the land, a Sabbath for the LORD: you shall neither sow your field, nor prune your vineyard.

"That which grows of its own accord of your harvest you shall not reap, neither gather the grapes of your vine undressed: for it is a year of rest unto the land.

"And the Sabbath of the land shall be meat for you; for you, and for your servant, and for your maid, and for your hired servant, and for the stranger who sojourns with you.

"And for your cattle, and for the beast that are in your land, shall all the increase thereof be meat."

The legislation in these Verses affects the Sabbatic year, which came every seventh year.

It is believed that after arriving in the land of Israel, about 20 years lapsed before this legislation began to be carried out, and then only partially.

The conquest of the Promised Land occupied them for some seven years (Josh. 14:10), and it seems that the division of the land between the different Tribes took another seven years (Josh. 18:1). So the real cultivation of the land began at the end of the 14 years. So six years of cultivation passed, with the seventh year then coming about, which would have been the twenty-first year after their entrance into Canaan.

In all of this, we find many things very interesting, not the least of them being the repetition of the Sabbaths. There was a

weekly Sabbath of one day, and then a yearly Sabbath of one year every seven years, which we are now studying, and then as we will study, a Jubilee Sabbath every fiftieth year.

Again as we will study, all of these Sabbaths spoke of *"rest,"* whether for the individual, or for the land, or for the nation as a whole.

While all of this pertained to the coming Millennial Earth, when Christ will rule and reign Personally from Jerusalem, even in a greater way it pertains to the great *"rest"* given by Christ, when the person makes the Lord his Saviour (Mat. 11:28-30). In fact, the latter is the greater symbol, and because it presupposes that which Christ will do at Calvary, in the shedding of His Precious Blood, which would liberate man from the captivity of darkness. While the Millennial Earth is definitely important, and for all the obvious reasons, to be sure, none of that could be enjoyed were it not for the Cross.

The Cross proclaims a Finished Work, which makes everything else possible. If a doctrine is not built on the foundation of the Cross, then in some way, it's not Scriptural, and must be avoided at all costs.

The seventh year being a Sabbath of rest for the land proclaimed two things: first of all, it portrayed the necessity of people trusting the Lord. They had to believe that the Lord would give them an abundance on the sixth year, that would tide them over for the seventh year.

Incidentally, in later years, Israel went about 490 years ignoring this Sabbath year, which would total 70 Sabbath years that they ignored the Command of the Lord. The land lay fallow that 70 years, while Israel languished in Babylon. That was not the only reason for their terrible situation at that coming time, but it was at least one of the reasons. Once again we state that God says what He means, and means what He says! (Lev. 26:43).

TITHES

The truth is, taking this subject a little further. Let's look at tithes as an example. The Believer either gives it to the Work of the Lord, as he should, or else the Lord extracts it in other ways. So as ought to be obvious, it is one thousand times better to simply obey the Lord.

Many Christians claim that they simply cannot afford to pay tithes. Well, the truth is, they cannot afford <u>not</u> to pay tithes. As stated, and to be sure, the Lord is going to get His portion. We should learn this from all of these Commands given in the Old Testament. We full well realize that we're living in the Dispensation of Grace, and not Law; however, the Word of the Lord doesn't change. In fact, under Grace, the Lord is far more demanding, than He ever was under Law. Listen to Paul:

"*And the times of this ignorance* (Old Testament times), *God winked at; but now* (the Dispensation of Grace) *commands all men everywhere to repent*" (Acts 17:30).

The second reason for the land to rest every seventh year was that it would replenish its nutriment value. The replenishment is now done in modern times by the use of certain chemicals applied to the soil, etc.

During the seventh year, whatever grew of its own accord, be it the fields or vineyards, could be gathered as food by all people alike, be they the owners of the land or slaves, etc. In other words, the produce of the land on the seventh year was to be used only as food, and was for the common good, anyone was welcome to gather what there was. To say it another way, every man had a right to everything in every place. And once again, it was not to be gathered in order to be sold, only to be consumed for one's own food, or food for the livestock.

(8) "AND YOU SHALL NUMBER SEVEN SABBATHS OF YEARS UNTO YOU, SEVEN TIMES SEVEN YEARS; AND THE SPACE OF THE SEVEN SABBATHS OF YEARS SHALL BE UNTO YOU FORTY AND NINE YEARS.

(9) "THEN SHALL YOU CAUSE THE TRUMPET OF THE JUBILEE TO SOUND ON THE TENTH DAY OF THE SEVENTH MONTH, IN THE DAY OF ATONEMENT SHALL YOU MAKE THE TRUMPET SOUND THROUGHOUT ALL YOUR LAND.

(10) "AND YOU SHALL HALLOW THE FIFTIETH YEAR, AND PROCLAIM LIBERTY THROUGHOUT ALL THE LAND UNTO ALL THE INHABITANTS THEREOF: IT SHALL BE A JUBILEE UNTO YOU; AND

YOU SHALL RETURN EVERY MAN UNTO HIS POSSESSION, AND YOU SHALL RETURN EVERY MAN UNTO HIS FAMILY.

(11) "A JUBILEE SHALL THAT FIFTIETH YEAR BE UNTO YOU: YOU SHALL NOT SOW, NEITHER REAP THAT WHICH GROWS OF ITSELF IN IT, NOR GATHER THE GRAPES IN IT OF YOUR VINE UNDRESSED.

(12) "FOR IT IS THE JUBILEE; IT SHALL BE HOLY UNTO YOU: YOU SHALL EAT THE INCREASE THEREOF OUT OF THE FIELD.

(13) "IN THE YEAR OF THIS JUBILEE YOU SHALL RETURN EVERY MAN UNTO HIS POSSESSION.

(14) "AND IF YOU SELL OUGHT UNTO YOUR NEIGHBOR, OR BUY OUGHT OF YOUR NEIGHBOR'S HAND, YOU SHALL NOT OPPRESS ONE ANOTHER:

(15) "ACCORDING TO THE NUMBER OF YEARS AFTER THE JUBILEE YOU SHALL BUY OF YOUR NEIGHBOR, AND ACCORDING UNTO THE NUMBER OF YEARS OF THE FRUITS HE SHALL SELL UNTO YOU:

(16) "ACCORDING TO THE MULTITUDE OF YEARS YOU SHALL INCREASE THE PRICE THEREOF, AND ACCORDING TO THE FEWNESS OF YEARS YOU SHALL DIMINISH THE PRICE OF IT: FOR ACCORDING TO THE NUMBER OF THE YEARS OF THE FRUITS DOES HE SELL UNTO YOU.

(17) "YOU SHALL NOT THEREFORE OPPRESS ONE ANOTHER; BUT YOU SHALL FEAR YOUR GOD: FOR I AM THE LORD YOUR GOD."

The composition is:

1. When the fiftieth year rolled around, the year of Jubilee began on the great Day of Atonement, by the blowing of trumpets throughout all the land.

2. This was a year, the fiftieth year, totally unlike any other year in any other nation of the world. At the beginning of this particular year, every prisoner went free; every debt was cancelled; all property went back to the original owner; in fact, the Jubilee voided all contracts and released all slaves.

3. As stated, the Trump of Jubilee, which proclaimed liberty to all was to be sounded on the Great Day of Atonement. The cancellation

of all debts and the liberation of all slaves were effected by the death of the atoning lamb. Thus was foreshadowed the world-wide Redemption purchased by the spotless Lamb of God.

4. The nearness or remoteness of the Jubilee increased or diminished the value of a sale or mortgage, simply because the land was to be returned on that fiftieth year to its original owners.

5. As the Christian realizes the nearness or remoteness of the Coming of the Lord, so does he place a low or a high value on earthly things.

THE YEAR OF JUBILEE

Verses 8 and 9 read: *"And you shall number seven Sabbaths of years unto you, seven times seven years; and the space of the seven Sabbaths of years shall be unto you forty and nine years.*

"Then shall you cause the Trumpet of the Jubilee to sound on the tenth day of the seventh month, in the Day of Atonement shall you make the trumpet sound throughout all your land."

At the end of the forty-ninth year, and the beginning of the fiftieth, and on the Great Day of Atonement, the year of Jubilee began. This would become obligatory only after the Israelites had taken possession of the Promised Land, and inasmuch as it took about 14 years to become established in the land, it would be the sixty-fourth year before the first Jubilee was celebrated.

When that particular day came, which as stated, began on the Great Day of Atonement, when the ceremonial obligations of that Great Day were concluded, and the Israelites knew that their Heavenly Father had annulled their sins, and that they were one with Him through His forgiving mercy, every Israelite was called upon to proclaim throughout the land, by nine blasts of the trumpet, that He, too had given the soil rest, that He had freed every encumbered family estate, and that He had given liberty to every slave, who was now to rejoin his kindred. Inasmuch as God has forgiven his debts, he also is to forgive his debtors (Ellicott). As stated, there has never been another law like this in the history of man

NOTES

in any nation of the world.

THE GREAT DAY OF ATONEMENT

As we have also stated, this great year of Jubilee was founded completely on the Great Day of Atonement, which signified that freedom rested solely in the shed blood of the lamb. Once again, it all spoke of the great Redemptive process which would take place when Christ would come. We are studying the material benefits of that, which now in Christ pertains to the spiritual, which latter is far more important! Once again the type proclaims the fact that every single thing as it regards Redemption's great and glorious Plan is built entirely on the Cross of Christ. There can be no jubilee, without the Cross! There can be no freedom without the Cross! There can be no Redemption without the Cross!

THE UNITED STATES

At the beginning of the study of this Chapter, I mentioned that the prosperity of the United States is based at least in part upon this command given to Israel so long, long ago, as it regards the Year of Jubilee, and what it all meant.

I cannot verify the following, but I read somewhere that those who originally enacted the federal income tax laws of the United States, did so, based at least in part on the Year of Jubilee. The idea was this, and rightly so:

The Year of Jubilee, as instituted by the Lord, kept the wealth of the nation of Israel from being gathered into the hands of a few, with the masses getting little or nothing. The federal income tax laws are based on the same principle. The Year of Jubilee redistributed the wealth, and the federal income tax laws are supposed to do the same, or at least drive toward that end.

LIBERTY

Verse 10 reads: *"And you shall hallow the fiftieth year, and proclaim liberty throughout all the land unto all the inhabitants thereof: it shall be a Jubilee unto you; and you shall return every man unto his possession, and you shall return every man unto his family."*

When the Children of Israel first went into

the Land of Promise, as stated, it took about seven years to subdue their enemies. It then took approximately seven years to distribute the land among the Tribes, and the various families. The account is given in the Book of Joshua.

The intention was that the land, as it was originally distributed, would remain in these particular families into perpetuity. This meant if they sold the land, they in effect only sold what remained of the fifty years, because at the end of that particular time, the land reverted to the original family. Even if they lost the land through bad investments, or whatever, at the next Year of Jubilee, the land was returned to the original family.

The phrase, *"And you shall return every man unto his family,"* refers in essence to slaves being released, which meant they were given their freedom. It functioned in somewhat the following manner:

From the time of the Feast of Trumpets to the Great Day of Atonement, a time frame of 10 days, the slaves were given this time to rejoice in their freedom. They ate, drank, rejoiced, and wore garlands, and when the Great Day of Atonement came, the judges blew the trumpet, and the slaves were free then to return to their homes, with no strings attached.

The phrase, *"And proclaimed liberty throughout all the land unto all the inhabitants thereof,"* is without a doubt one of the greatest phrases ever uttered.

From this one statement, and all of the particulars of the Year of Jubilee, I think it should be obvious that the Lord desires that His Children be free of every restraining force. I'm speaking of the physical, the domestical, the financial, and above all the spiritual. Provision at the Cross, in the great Finished Work of Christ, was made for all. There is no shortage of *"liberty,"* which means there is no shortage of *"Redemption."* If we don't have all for which Jesus died, then it's our fault in some way.

That doesn't mean that there will not be problems, and that Satan will not be allowed to attack us, etc.; however, it does mean exactly what it says, and that is *"liberty"* in every capacity, in every function, and every

state of our being.

THE PRICE THAT HE PAID

How so little we live up to that for which He paid such a price. And considering the price that He paid, it stands to reason that He wants us to have all that we can have. And how do we get it?

It all comes by Faith, but more particularly, it is Faith that must be anchored squarely in the Finished Work of Christ. As you the Reader can see in all of these types and shadows given to us in the Book of Leviticus, which is the great Book of Worship, in effect, which tells Israel how to worship, everything begins and ends with that which points directly toward the Cross. The types and the shadows are unmistakable! The meaning is unmistakable! In fact, if we do not understand what is being done, considering that it is done so repeatedly, it's because we simply don't want to understand (Heb. 10:1).

Man is loathe to admit that there is nothing he can personally do to save himself, or to sanctify himself. The sinner keeps claiming that he can save himself, and the Christian keeps thinking that he can sanctify himself. Both are doomed to failure.

Understanding the meanderings of the unredeemed, it's harder to understand the thinking of many, if not most, Christians. The Believer has the Divine Nature within his heart and life. The Holy Spirit, the Third Person of the Godhead, abides within. So there really is no reason that we should not fully understand the simplicity of the Gospel, and simple it is. Paul told the Corinthians: *"But I fear, lest by any means, as the serpent beguiled Eve through his subtilty, so your minds should be corrupted from the simplicity that is in Christ"* (II Cor. 11:3).

As the serpent beguiled Eve, Satan continues to beguile Believers. Seducing spirits become involved (I Tim. 4:1), and thereby, the wrong seems to be right, down seems to be up, black seems to be white, and unrighteousness seems to be Righteousness.

If any Preacher is to fully be what he ought to be, he has to as well be a student of people. Why do Believers do what they do? Why do they act as they act? Why do some take the position which they take, even though Scripturally, it is obviously wrong?

It's bad enough for Believers not to be able to hear, and thereby know and understand the Message of the Cross. But to have the opportunity and privilege of hearing it, and hearing it under the mighty Anointing of the Holy Spirit, and then to reject it, is tantamount to disaster. There is one sure thing: it will lead to disaster!

PRIDE

The basic problem with Believers, exactly as it is with the unredeemed, is *"pride."* We want to think that our doing produces Righteousness; or our association with other Believers produces Righteousness; or our good works produce Righteousness. In fact, the list is long. And then to be told that all of it is out, it is somewhat hard for most to swallow.

The only way that we can have all that Christ has done for us is for us to understand that everything we receive from the Lord, and I mean everything, comes exclusively by and through the Cross of Christ. Once we resign ourselves to that, and thereby place our Faith in the Finished Work of our Lord, wonderful things then begin to happen. The Holy Spirit can now work unhindered and unfettered. Oh yes, Satan will do all that he can do to throw in his doubts, to try to trip us up, to try to put unbelief in our minds, to try to get us to divide our Faith; in fact, he will do anything he can do to get us to veer away from the Cross of Christ. And the tragedy is, most of the time, he will use other Christians to bring about his devious ends. In fact, he works in a greater way through the Church than anything else. Most error rides into the Church on the back of Truth. Satan is a master at mixing Truth and error, with the Truth serving as bait.

The shed Blood of the Lamb is the foundational Truth of the Gospel of Jesus Christ. Everything is built upon that particular premise, and that premise alone (Rom. 6:3-14; 8:1-2, 11; I Cor. 1:17-18, 21, 23; 2:2; Eph. 2:13-18).

I have done my best, and am doing my

best in this Volume to address the Cross in every way that I know how. I have done so, and continue to do so, even to the extent, I'm afraid, of being overly repetitive. But I know how something must be constantly repeated, especially the Truth of the Gospel, if it is to be obtained and retained.

THE JUBILEE IS HOLY

Verses 11 through 17 read: *"A Jubilee shall that fiftieth year be unto you: you shall not sow, neither reap that which grows of itself in it, nor gather the grapes in it of your vine undressed.*

"For it is the Jubilee; it shall be holy unto you: you shall eat the increase thereof out of the field.

"In the year of this Jubilee you shall return every man unto his possession.

"And if you sell ought unto your neighbor, or buy ought of your neighbor's hand, you shall not oppress one another:

"According to the number of years after the Jubilee you shall buy of your neighbor, and according unto the number of years of the fruits he shall sell unto you:

"According to the multitude of years you shall increase the price thereof, and according to the fewness of years you shall diminish the price of it: for according to the number of the years of the fruits does he sell unto you.

"You shall not therefore oppress one another; but you shall fear your God: for I am the LORD your God."

Twice in the century the land was to lie fallow for two years in succession – from September to the second September following – special preparations having, of course, been made by, laying up a store of grain from the abundant harvest promised in the previous year, even as we shall see in Verse 21.

The Jubilee affected both land and men. Land could only be sold for fifty years, or for whatever number of years remained in the fifty before the Year of Jubilee would come about.

The other point chiefly affected by the Law of the Jubilee was slavery, or the working off of debts.

In case a brother Israelite became poor, it was the duty of his richer Brethren to help him, and to lend him money without interest, to get him back on his feet economically, so to speak. But if this did not succeed, the poor man might sell himself to another Israelite or even to a foreigner living in the land of Israel.

In the former case, it had been already enacted that his slavery was not to last beyond six years (Ex. 21:2). But to this enactment it was now added that he must be also set free whenever the Year of Jubilee occurred, that is, if it came before the six years had run their course.

If he sold himself to a non-Israelite, he must be set free, not as before on the seventh year of his slavery, so to speak, but still at the Jubilee.

He had also preserved for him the right of being redeemed by any kinsman, the price paid for him being the wages which would be paid up to the next Jubilee. In either case, he was to be treated well, and it was the duty of the Israelite magistrate to see that no undue harshness was used in any case.

THE PRINCIPLE OF THE
YEAR OF JUBILEE

The principle of all of this was, as the land was God's land, and not man's, so the Israelites, in whatever capacity, were slaves of God, and not of man, and that if the position in which God placed them was allowed to be interfered with for a time, it was to be recovered every seventh, or at furthest, every fiftieth year.

And when we use the term *"slaves,"* in no way did it mean that to which we think of presently. It was about the same as an individual working off a debt, and at the end of their servitude, some even elected to stay in the employ of their master, and that could be done as well.

The release of debts inculcated mercy. The command that the Law should be publicly read showed that the intention of the institution was not that the year should be spent in idleness, but that the time saved from ordinary labor was to be given to the worship of the Lord. But regrettably, it seems that Israel little acted upon the command of the Year of Jubilee. So the 70 years they spent in Babylon, to which we have already

alluded, was equal to the seventh year Sabbaths that were not kept, plus the Years of Jubilee. But after the time of their dispersion, it seems that they religiously kept these particular years, etc.

IN CHRIST

That we not lose sight of the primary objective, let us state again that the real meaning of this Year of Jubilee pertained to Christ, and what He would do to deliver humanity from the terrible bondages of sin and shame. How much Israel fully understood this is not clear; however, the insinuation was there, by the use of the word *"holy"* (vs. 12).

(18) "WHEREFORE YOU SHALL DO MY STATUTES, AND KEEP MY JUDGMENTS, AND DO THEM; AND YOU SHALL DWELL IN THE LAND IN SAFETY.

(19) "AND THE LAND SHALL YIELD HER FRUIT, AND YOU SHALL EAT YOUR FILL, AND DWELL THEREIN IN SAFETY.

(20) "AND IF YOU SHALL SAY, WHAT SHALL WE EAT THE SEVENTH YEAR? BEHOLD, WE SHALL NOT SOW, NOR GATHER IN OUR INCREASE:

(21) "THEN I WILL COMMAND MY BLESSING UPON YOU IN THE SIXTH YEAR, AND IT SHALL BRING FORTH FRUIT FOR THREE YEARS.

(22) "AND YOU SHALL SOW THE EIGHTH YEAR, AND EAT YET OF OLD FRUIT UNTIL THE NINTH YEAR; UNTIL HER FRUITS COME IN YOU SHALL EAT OF THE OLD STORE.

(23) "THE LAND SHALL NOT BE SOLD FOREVER: FOR THE LAND IS MINE; FOR YOU ARE STRANGERS AND SOJOURNERS WITH ME.

(24) "AND IN ALL THE LAND OF YOUR POSSESSION YOU SHALL GRANT A REDEMPTION FOR THE LAND.

(25) "IF YOUR BROTHER BE WAXED POOR, AND HAS SOLD AWAY SOME OF HIS POSSESSION, AND IF ANY OF HIS KIN COME TO REDEEM IT, THEN SHALL HE REDEEM THAT WHICH HIS BROTHER SOLD.

(26) "AND IF THE MAN HAVE NONE TO REDEEM IT, AND HIMSELF BE ABLE TO REDEEM IT;

(27) "THEN LET HIM COUNT THE

YEARS OF THE SALE THEREOF, AND RESTORE THE OVERPLUS UNTO THE MAN TO WHOM HE SOLD IT; THAT HE MAY RETURN UNTO HIS POSSESSION.

(28) "BUT IF HE BE NOT ABLE TO RESTORE IT TO HIM, THEN THAT WHICH IS SOLD SHALL REMAIN IN THE HAND OF HIM WHO HAS BOUGHT IT UNTIL THE YEAR OF JUBILEE: AND IN THE JUBILEE IT SHALL GO OUT, AND HE SHALL RETURN UNTO HIS POSSESSION.

(29) "AND IF A MAN SELL A DWELLING HOUSE IN A WALLED CITY, THEN HE MAY REDEEM IT WITHIN A WHOLE YEAR AFTER IT IS SOLD; WITHIN A FULL YEAR MAY HE REDEEM IT.

(30) "AND IF IT BE NOT REDEEMED WITHIN THE SPACE OF A FULL YEAR, THEN THE HOUSE THAT IS IN THE WALLED CITY SHALL BE ESTABLISHED FOREVER TO HIM WHO BOUGHT IT THROUGHOUT HIS GENERATIONS: IT SHALL NOT GO OUT IN THE JUBILEE.

(31) "BUT THE HOUSES OF THE VILLAGES WHICH HAVE NO WALL ROUND ABOUT THEM SHALL BE COUNTED AS THE FIELDS OF THE COUNTRY: THEY MAY BE REDEEMED, AND THEY SHALL GO OUT IN THE JUBILEE."

The composition is:

1. Plainly the Lord says, *"The land is Mine"* (vs. 23).

2. Land, or its fruits, might be mortgaged, but the mortgage became void at the Jubilee; and, at any time prior to the Jubilee, either might be redeemed at the option of the borrower.

3. A distinction was made between property created by man's industry (as for instance a house in a walled city), and property created by God, i.e., *"land."* The house could be sold in perpetuity; consequently bequeathed by will; land, never.

4. A house in a village was deemed to be an agricultural asset, and could not, therefore, become personal property. The Jubilee voided all contracts and released all slaves.

THE BLESSING

Verses 18 through 23 read: *"Wherefore you shall do My Statutes, and keep My Judgments, and do them; and you shall dwell in the land in safety.*

"And the land shall yield her fruit, and you shall eat your fill, and dwell therein in safety.

"And if you shall say, What shall we eat the seventh year? Behold, we shall not sow, nor gather in our increase:

"Then I will command My blessing upon you in the sixth year, and it shall bring forth fruit for three years.

"And you shall sow the eighth year, and eat yet of old fruit until the ninth year; until her fruits come in you shall eat of the old store.

"The land shall not be sold forever: for the land is Mine; for you are strangers and sojourners with Me."

Two great things are stated in these Passages: blessing, and the fact that the land belongs solely to the Lord.

At times, the land would have to remain fallow for some three years, which in fact did occur every Year of Jubilee. Every seventh year was to be a Sabbath year as well. And then when the Year of Jubilee rolled around, that would make two years in a row, that the land must remain fallow. And even though crops could be planted on the year following the Year of Jubilee, it would take nearly one year for the planted crops to come to harvest, and the vineyards to produce their fruit. To counteract this, the Lord said that He would *"command His Blessing upon Israel, in the sixth year, and it would bring forth fruit for three years"* (Vs. 21).

The Lord said, *"I will command My Blessing,"* and when the Lord commands something, it is commanded, which means it is done. But the Blessing was predicated solely on Israel obeying the Lord in every respect. In fact, blessing is always predicated on obedience.

THE BLESSING ON THIS MINISTRY

If I remember correctly the year was 1999. We were about to do a Television Special. Our director called over and asked me as to what music I desired to be used. I couldn't think of anything immediately, so I just told him to play the choir song that had aired the week before. In all honesty, I couldn't even remember what it was, only that it had been an excellent rendition.

The Special began with me addressing the people, and then we would go to the song, and after that I would come back and minister as had been previously planned.

The title of the song that was rendered by the choir was, *"Your Blessings Are Coming Through"*. The moment it began, I began to sense the Presence of the Lord. By the time the song ended, the Spirit of God was moving in a mighty way in the Studio, and what the Lord gave me that day was the beginning of that which is now happening, and which will continue to increase, until it touches, I believe, the entirety of the world.

In effect, the Lord spoke to my heart that, as it regards this Ministry, *"The blessings are beginning to come through."* It is the same as the Lord saying, *"I will command My Blessing upon you."* The Lord gave me other movings of the Spirit in the coming weeks and months, to verify what He gave me that day. And so it was, and so it is!

THE BLESSINGS FOR YOU

The Lord also related something else to me, which I think is very, very important. It is according to the following:

That which the Lord blesses extends to those who bless what He blesses. Let us explain further:

If God is blessing something, and His people stand behind and help carry forth that which is blessed, they too will experience the same blessing. This can be expected, and this will be realized!

Everyone wants blessings from the Lord. The conditions are as follows:

"Wherefore you shall do My Statutes, and keep My Judgments, and do them: and you shall dwell in the land in safety" (vs. 18). Even though the Year of Jubilee has long since been fulfilled in Christ and, thereby, set aside, still, the principle remains as it regards obedience, as should be obvious.

When we speak of obedience, we're speaking of obeying the Word of God. As we have said any number of times in this Volume, the criteria must always be the Word of God. What does the Word say?

Every Believer should strive to obey the Word. That means he should learn the Word,

should study the Word, and as well, ask the Lord to help him obey the Word.

This is at least one of the reasons that I believe these Commentaries are so very, very important. They, I think, will help you understand the Word of God just a little better. And anything that will do that is worth all of your time and effort.

THE LAND IS MINE

Emphatically and dogmatically, the Lord states that the land called *"Israel,"* even referred to as the *"Holy Land,"* belongs exclusively to Him.

And the Lord told the people that if they would obey His Statutes and Judgments, they would *"dwell in the land in safety."* They failed to obey Him, and ultimately were ejected from the land. But it still belongs to the Lord, and in every capacity.

There is more contention presently (2002) over the territory of the Land of Israel, than any other spot on the face of the Earth. The Palestinians and the Arab world are claiming the land, while at the same time Israel is claiming the land. According to the Word of God, and as is overly obvious, the Lord has reserved this land for the Israelites.

In A.D. 70, the Romans in their invasion of Judea, destroyed Israel, with it virtually ceasing to be a nation at that time. Another effort of nationhood was made by the Jews after that, but in the year A.D. 150, the Jews were defeated by the Romans once again, which destroyed any hopes they might have had for bringing the nation back.

Many Jews continued to live in the Land of Israel from then through the many centuries. I think one could say without fear of exaggeration that there have always been more Jews in the land than anyone else.

After World War II ended, the Jews once again were demanding their homeland. The world, feeling guilty because of the Holocaust, in which some six million Jews had died at the hands of the Nazi monster, Adolph Hitler, began to gradually work toward that conclusion. But unless the United States backed the desire of the Jews, for this ancient land, once called Israel, but now referred to as Palestine, to once again be their home, all would be in vain. And to be frank, all of this pretty much boiled down to the decision which would be made by Harry Truman, the President then of the United States.

At a point in time, the President put the full weight of his office behind the establishment of a nation for the Jews, and that this nation be in the same area as Israel of old, and in fact, that the State or nation would be called *"Israel."*

When Harry Truman made his decision thusly, the United Nations voted that the nation of Israel be established. However, the problems were only beginning:

ISRAEL

While many Jews occupied that ancient land, many Arabs did as well. Even though the United Nations had voted in favor of the Jews, they gave them no help in establishing this nation. On top of that, the Arabs banded together to keep the Jews from establishing what the United Nations said they could have.

In fact, nobody expected that Israel could win this conflict. What could they do, only a few thousand strong, against unlimited numbers of Arabs, who were well supplied?

In the natural they could do nothing, but with God they were able to do all things. Much to the surprise of the world, and especially the Arabs, the Jews established themselves in a tiny part of the land called Israel, and for the first time in nearly 2,000 years, the Star of David once again flew above that sacred soil.

From 1948 until the present, the Arabs have tried repeatedly to dislodge Israel, but failing each time. In fact, it is believed presently that Israel is the fourth most powerful nation in the world, militarily speaking. But yet the battle rages. Particular Jewish leaders have tried to appease the Palestinians, by offering them the West Bank, part of Jerusalem, and the Gaza Strip, plus other areas, all to no avail. The truth is, the Arabs want the entirety of the land of Israel. They will not be satisfied unless they have every foot of that land, and every Jew is dead. But several things must be said here:

First of all, the Arabs are fighting a losing battle. The land is not theirs; it belongs to the Lord. In fact, it's not even right for Israel

NOTES

to offer to the Arabs the West Bank, or any other portion. In effect, the land is really not theirs to give; it belongs to the Lord. He has emphatically stated, *"The land is Mine."* This means that God is going to do with the land exactly what He desires to do with the land. And it also means that it is no less His today, than it was when He uttered these words some 3,500 years ago.

ISRAEL, GOD'S PROPHETIC TIME CLOCK

Bible Prophecy can be interpreted to a great extend by the land of Israel, and the Jews who occupy that land. As stated, Israel is God's prophetic time clock. We can look at them and just about state as to what time it is, prophetically speaking. And to be sure, and as should be obvious, it's much later than most think.

World War II was fought, more than anything else, over the Jewish problem. Let me explain:

Satan, knowing that the time was drawing near that Israel was to be re-gathered, which is a miracle within itself, instigated that terrible conflict in order to extinguish the Jews. He would use Adolph Hitler and his evil henchmen to carry out his devious plan. In fact, he made long strides toward succeeding in this hellish endeavor. Of about 20 million Jews scattered all over the world, he slaughtered six million of them. Satan's idea was that if enough could be killed, they could not form a nation. When will man learn that to fight against God is a battle that one cannot win?

In fact, part of the fulfillment of the prophecy of Ezekiel was brought about by the formation of the nation of Israel in 1948.

The Lord showed Ezekiel *"the valley which was full of bones."* He then asked the Prophet: *"Son of man, can these bones live?"* The Prophet answered and said, *"O Lord GOD, You know"* (Ezek. 37:1-3).

Upon the terrible crematoriums being opened at the conclusion of World War II, one American General said, looking at the piles of corpses, that the words written in the Book of Ezekiel came to him, *"Can these bones live?"*

Well, those bones did live again. Out of the horror of the Holocaust, the Lord through miracle after miracle, reestablished the nation of Israel, even after nearly 2,000 years of them being wanderers all over the world.

Of course, the greater part of that prophecy regarding the Thirty-seventh Chapter of Ezekiel pertains to Israel once again becoming alive spiritually. But it does have part fulfillment in that of which I have spoken. Once again, that shows how late it really is.

Sometime back, while in the land of Israel, we came to a particular intersection, with a rusted tank sitting off to the side. I asked the Jewish guide as to what it was.

He mentioned one of the conflicts with the Arabs, and stated, *"They came this far, and no farther."*

While men argue over the land of Israel, and while the United Nations may think it has jurisdiction, and while America might even wish that the whole problem would just go away, the truth is, God is getting things ready for the complete restoration of Israel. We are told this in Romans, Chapters 9, 10, and 11, plus all the Prophets of the Old Testament.

In fact, the land originally promised to Abraham covered far more territory than the small nation of Israel presently. It included the entirety of the Sinai Peninsula, which in fact, Israel did take from the Egyptians in one of the past wars, but later gave it back. To the north it went all the way up to the River Euphrates. To the east, if it was to follow that River, it would also include the entirety of the Arabian Peninsula. Of course, all of this territory is several hundreds of times larger than present Israel. While the far greater part is desert, still, under that desert is the world's greatest deposit of oil. And as well, the Prophet Isaiah said: *"The wilderness and the solitary place shall be glad for them; and the desert shall rejoice, and blossom as the rose"* (Isa. 35:1). Actually, in the coming Millennial Reign, Israel will occupy all of this territory, and will be the ruling nation of the world, even as God originally intended.

But before that time comes, Israel is yet to face her hardest days. I speak of the coming Tribulation, which Jesus said would be worse than any, and so bad in fact, that there will

NOTES

never be anything like it again (Mat. 24:21).

THE ANTICHRIST

As we've already stated in this Volume, the Rapture of the Church is soon to take place. Not long after the Rapture, the Antichrist will make his debut (II Thess. 2:7-8). He will bring about peace between Israel and the Palestinians, thereby, solving one of the great problems of the world. Israel will think that he is the Messiah, and will herald such all over the world, with him in fact, being accepted by many as such. He will sign a seven year non-aggression pact with Israel and other nations, guaranteeing peace, with them even being able to rebuild their ancient temple. But at the midpoint of that seven-year pact, he will break his truce by attacking Israel, in which she will suffer her first defeat since becoming a nation in 1948. Then the trouble really begins. That's what Paul was speaking of when he wrote of this time and said: *"For when they shall say, Peace and safety; then sudden destruction comes upon them, as travail upon a woman with child; and they shall not escape"* (I Thess. 5:3).

It's what Jesus was speaking of when He said: *"When you therefore shall see the abomination of desolation, spoken of by Daniel the Prophet, stand in the Holy Place, (whoso readeth, let him understand:)*

"Then (the latter half of the Great Tribulation) *let them which be in Judaea flee into the mountains"* (Mat. 24:15-16).

THE GREAT TRIBULATION

The last three and one-half years of the Great Tribulation will be the worst time this world has ever known. The account is given to us in Revelation, Chapters 6 through 19. (Please see our Commentary on this Book.) In fact, this particular time will conclude with the Battle of Armageddon, which the Prophet Ezekiel describes in Chapters 38 and 39 of his Book. The Prophet Zechariah also described this time in Chapter 14 of his great Book. The Psalms allude to this over and over, as well as other Prophets. It is ironical; the first great organized rebellion against God began in the ancient city of Babylon. It will close out in the same manner (Gen. 10:8-10; 11:1-9; Isa. 14:4; Rev., Chpt. 18).

A REDEMPTION FOR THE LAND

Verses 24 through 31 read: *"And in all the land of your possession you shall grant a Redemption for the land.*

"If your brother be waxed poor, and has sold away some of his possession, and if any of his kin come to redeem it, then shall he redeem that which his brother sold.

"And if the man have none to redeem it, and himself be able to redeem it;

"Then let him count the years of the sale thereof, and restore the overplus unto the man to whom he sold it; that he may return unto his possession.

"But if he be not able to restore it to him, then that which is sold shall remain in the hand of him who has bought it until the Year of Jubilee: and in the Jubilee it shall go out, he shall return unto his possession.

"And if a man sell a dwelling house in a walled city, then he may redeem it within a whole year after it is sold: within a full year may he redeem it.

"And if it be not redeemed within the space of a full year, then the house that is in the walled city shall be established forever to him who bought it throughout his generations: it shall not go out in the Jubilee.

"But the houses of the villages which have no wall round about them shall be counted as the fields of the country: they may be redeemed, and they shall go out in the Jubilee."

The principle of all of these rulings pertains to individuals who have fallen on hard times, who had lost their possessions, with some even being reduced to slavery. The Year of Jubilee would rectify all of these situations, at least in a material, physical, and domestical sense. It would do so spiritually, if the person would fully trust the Lord.

All of this is a perfect picture of lost humanity. Man has lost his way, doesn't really know where he is, where he has been, or where he is going. He doesn't know where he has been when he leaves, and doesn't know where he is when he arrives. The future is a blank. His only hope is in the Lord, and if the Lord be accepted, he will enter into an eternity of Jubilee, for the Lord restores all.

RESTORATION

I think probably the theme of the Year of Jubilee would be *"restoration."* What a joy! The exiled can now return; the captive is now emancipated; the debtor is set free; each family opens its bosom to receive once more its long lost member; each inheritance receives back its exiled owner.

The sound of the trumpet was the welcome signal for the captive to escape, for the slave to cast aside the chains of his bondage, for the man-slayer to return to his home, for the ruined and poverty-stricken to rise to the possession of their forfeited inheritance (Mackintosh).

"Restoration" has to be one of the most beautiful words in any language. It means that which seems to have been forever lost has been regained. That is the story of the human race. It lost it all at the Fall. But God became man, and paid a price so staggering that it beggars all description, in order that man might be restored. Oh, how I sense His Presence, even as I dictate these words!

And even as I dictate these words, we must realize that the price He paid was enough to restore all of mankind, and forever. And yet, so few seem to take advantage of this *"eternity of Jubilee."* For when the lost sinner comes to Christ, he enters not merely a sabbatical year, but rather a sabbatical eternity. The chains are forever broken! The bondage is forever over! The darkness is forever past!

"Giving thanks unto the Father, which has made us meet to be partakers of the inheritance of the Saints in light:

"Who has delivered us from the power of darkness, and has translated us into the Kingdom of His dear Son:

"In Whom we have Redemption through His Blood, even the forgiveness of sins" (Col. 1:12-14).

(32) "NOTWITHSTANDING THE CITIES OF THE LEVITES, AND THE HOUSES OF THE CITIES OF THEIR POSSESSION, MAY THE LEVITES REDEEM AT ANY TIME.

(33) "AND IF A MAN PURCHASE OF THE LEVITES, THEN THE HOUSE THAT WAS SOLD, AND THE CITY OF HIS POSSESSION, SHALL GO OUT IN THE YEAR

OF JUBILEE: FOR THE HOUSES OF THE CITIES OF THE LEVITES ARE THEIR POSSESSION AMONG THE CHILDREN OF ISRAEL.

(34) "BUT THE FIELD OF THE SUBURBS OF THEIR CITIES MAY NOT BE SOLD; FOR IT IS THEIR PERPETUAL POSSESSION.

(35) "AND IF YOUR BROTHER BE WAXED POOR, AND FALLEN IN DECAY WITH YOU; THEN YOU SHALL RELIEVE HIM: YES, THOUGH HE BE A STRANGER, OR A SOJOURNER; THAT HE MAY LIVE WITH YOU.

(36) "TAKE THOU NO USURY OF HIM, OR INCREASE: BUT FEAR YOUR GOD; THAT YOUR BROTHER MAY LIVE WITH YOU.

(37) "YOU SHALL NOT GIVE HIM YOUR MONEY UPON USURY, NOR LEND HIM YOUR VICTUALS FOR INCREASE.

(38) "I AM THE LORD YOUR GOD, WHICH BROUGHT YOU FORTH OUT OF THE LAND OF EGYPT, TO GIVE YOU THE LAND OF CANAAN, AND TO BE YOUR GOD."

The structure is:

1. The Year of Jubilee reminded both buyer and seller that the land belonged to Jehovah and was not to be sold.

2. *"The fruits"* might be sold, but that was all: Jehovah could never give up the land to anyone.

3. It is important to get this point well fixed in the mind; it may open up a very extensive line of truth. If the land of Canaan is not to be sold – if Jehovah declares it to be His forever, then for whom does He want it? Who is to hold it under Him? Those to whom He gave it by an Everlasting Covenant, that they might have it in possession as long as the moon endures – even to all generations (Mackintosh).

I AM THE LORD YOUR GOD

Inasmuch as we will address ourselves to Verses 32 through 38, we will not bother to reprint the Text.

In Verse 38, the Lord made it clear to Israel that He had delivered them out of the land of Egypt, and that He did so that they might have a land of their own, the land of Canaan, the land which God would give to them. He was to be their God, and He must

NOTES

be their God Alone!

I think one can say without any fear of exaggeration that in the Mind of God, or we might say, in the Divine estimation, there is no spot on Earth like unto the land of Israel. It was there that the Lord set up His Throne in His Sanctuary. It was there that He raised up and nurtured His people, and made of them a great nation. It was there where He had His great Temple built, and His Priests ministered to Him on a continuing basis. It was there that the Prophets were given the Word of God, and thereby, gave it to the world. It was there that John the Baptist paved the way for the coming of Messiah, one of the very reasons for the existence of these ancient people. It was there, the land of Israel, by the Sea of Galilee, through its villages and towns, through its valleys and over its hills, that the Saviour trod, in the greatest mission that man has ever known, the Redemption of the whole of mankind. It is there that He died on a Cross, and rose from the dead, and ascended on high. But before He ascended, He promised to come back to this very land, even the exact spot was named, the Mount of Olivet. There His Throne will be reestablished and His worship restored. In a word, His eyes and His heart are there continually; its dust is precious in His sight; it is the center of all His thoughts and operations as touching this Earth; and it is His purpose to make it an eternal excellency, the joy of untold generations (Mackintosh).

(39) "AND IF YOUR BROTHER WHO DWELLS BY YOU BE WAXED POOR, AND BE SOLD UNTO YOU; YOU SHALL NOT COMPEL HIM TO SERVE AS A BONDSERVANT:

(40) "BUT AS AN HIRED SERVANT, AND AS A SOJOURNER, HE SHALL BE WITH YOU, AND SHALL SERVE YOU UNTO THE YEAR OF JUBILEE.

(41) "AND THEN SHALL HE DEPART FROM YOU, BOTH HE AND HIS CHILDREN WITH HIM, AND SHALL RETURN UNTO HIS OWN FAMILY, AND UNTO THE POSSESSION OF HIS FATHER SHALL HE RETURN.

(42) "FOR THEY ARE MY SERVANTS, WHICH I BROUGHT FORTH OUT OF THE LAND OF EGYPT: THEY SHALL NOT BE

SOLD AS BONDMEN.

(43) "YOU SHALL NOT RULE OVER HIM WITH RIGOUR; BUT SHALL FEAR YOUR GOD.

(44) "BOTH YOUR BONDMEN, AND YOUR BONDMAIDS, WHICH YOU SHALL HAVE, SHALL BE OF THE HEATHEN WHO ARE ROUND ABOUT YOU; OF THEM SHALL YOU BUY BONDMEN AND BONDMAIDS.

(45) "MOREOVER OF THE CHILDREN OF THE STRANGERS WHO DO SOJOURN AMONG YOU, OF THEM SHALL YOU BUY, AND OF THEIR FAMILIES WHO ARE WITH YOU, WHICH THEY BEGAT IN YOUR LAND: AND THEY SHALL BE YOUR POSSESSION.

(46) "AND YOU SHALL TAKE THEM AS AN INHERITANCE FOR YOUR CHILDREN AFTER YOU, TO INHERIT THEM FOR A POSSESSION; THEY SHALL BE YOUR BONDMEN FOREVER: BUT OVER YOUR BRETHREN THE CHILDREN OF ISRAEL, YOU SHALL NOT RULE ONE OVER ANOTHER WITH RIGOUR."

The construction is:

1. Only a relative could redeem a bondman and his inheritance. To redeem the slaves of sin it, therefore, was necessary that Christ should become man.

2. In Verses 38, 42, and 55 of this Chapter, and Verse 13 of the next Chapter, are found the words, *"brought forth."* Israel was brought forth out of Egypt to be free, to be rich, and to be Jehovah's servant.

3. We learn from all of this that Jehovah can never give up the land, nor those *"Twelve Tribes"* through whom He is to inherit it forever. God has not cast away His people, or the land which He swore to give unto them for an everlasting possession (Mackintosh).

THE PEOPLE OF GOD

We learn from this, as we certainly should, that the people of God were looked at in the eyes of God as totally different than anyone else. Of course, that should go without saying; however, inasmuch as strict instructions were given as it regarded their treatment, we should very well understand exactly what is being said.

If a fellow Jew fell on hard times, he was not to serve as a bondservant, i.e., *"slave."*

He was to be a hired servant.

Even when he was serving as *"an hired servant,"* he was not to be ruled over with austerity. In other words, every Israelite was to always remember that every other Israelite, no matter how lowly his state might be, was still in the Covenant, and was looked at by God as totally different than the heathen. He was to be treated accordingly!

It is presently shameful when we observe many Christians who show less kindness to fellow Christians, even than that shown by the world. The truth is, the world is very slow to forgive, and the Church forgives not at all! That is tragic, but true.

Whatever the lot and state of a Believer, that particular individual, whomever he or she might be, belongs to the Lord. He paid a tremendous price for their Salvation, and in dealing with them, we must never forget that.

In the ancient world, while a slave may be a slave, therefore, holding no status whatsoever, still, many were treated with great dignity and respect, simply because of who owned them. That should not be lost on the Believer.

Do we not remember that Jesus said: *"Verily I say unto you, inasmuch as you have done it unto one of the least of these My Brethren, you have done it unto Me"* (Mat. 25:40). That goes for either good or bad.

(47) "AND IF A SOJOURNER OR STRANGER WAX RICH BY YOU, AND YOUR BROTHER WHO DWELLS BY HIM WAX POOR, AND SELL HIMSELF UNTO THE STRANGER OR SOJOURNER BY YOU, OR TO THE STOCK OF THE STRANGER'S FAMILY:

(48) "AFTER THAT HE IS SOLD HE MAY BE REDEEMED AGAIN; ONE OF HIS BRETHREN MAY REDEEM HIM:

(49) "EITHER HIS UNCLE, OR HIS UNCLE'S SON, MAY REDEEM HIM, OR ANY WHO ARE NIGH OF KIN UNTO HIM OF HIS FAMILY MAY REDEEM HIM; OR IF HE BE ABLE, HE MAY REDEEM HIMSELF.

(50) "AND HE SHALL RECKON WITH HIM WHO BOUGHT HIM FROM THE YEAR THAT HE WAS SOLD TO HIM UNTO THE YEAR OF JUBILEE: AND THE PRICE OF HIS SALE SHALL BE ACCORDING UNTO THE NUMBER OF YEARS, ACCORDING TO

THE TIME OF AN HIRED SERVANT SHALL HE BE WITH HIM.

(51) "IF THERE BE YET MANY YEARS BEHIND, ACCORDING UNTO THEM HE SHALL GIVE AGAIN THE PRICE OF HIS REDEMPTION OUT OF THE MONEY THAT HE WAS BOUGHT FOR.

(52) "AND IF THERE REMAINED BUT A FEW YEARS UNTO THE YEAR OF JUBILEE, THEN HE SHALL COUNT WITH HIM, AND ACCORDING UNTO HIS YEARS SHALL HE GIVE HIM AGAIN THE PRICE OF HIS REDEMPTION.

(53) "AND AS A YEARLY HIRED SERVANT SHALL HE BE WITH HIM: AND THE OTHER SHALL NOT RULE WITH RIGOUR OVER HIM IN YOUR SIGHT.

(54) "AND IF HE BE NOT REDEEMED IN THESE YEARS, THEN HE SHALL GO OUT IN THE YEAR OF JUBILEE, BOTH HE, AND HIS CHILDREN WITH HIM.

(55) "FOR UNTO ME THE CHILDREN OF ISRAEL ARE SERVANTS; THEY ARE MY SERVANTS WHOM I BROUGHT FORTH OUT OF THE LAND OF EGYPT: I AM THE LORD YOUR GOD."

The exegesis is:

1. One of the lessons that we should learn from this Chapter is, if our hearts are cherishing the abiding hope of the Lord's return, we shall set light by all earthly things. It is morally impossible that we can be in the attitude of waiting for the Son from Heaven, and not be detached from this present world.

2. In Luke, Chapter 4, when Jesus said, *"The Spirit of the Lord is upon Me . . ."* and then when He closed the dialogue by saying, *"To preach the acceptable year of the Lord,"* this typified the Year of Jubilee when liberty was proclaimed to all people. When the Atonement of Christ is fully embraced, the sick, sinful, helpless, and needy are restored to health, holiness, power, and prosperity, as well as full dominion over Satan and membership and communion in God's family.

3. The new start in business at the end of Jubilee was based upon another year of release 50 years in the future, and, thereby, increased or diminished the value of a sale or mortgage. Likewise, as the Christian realizes the nearness or remoteness of the

Coming of the Lord, so he places a low or a high value on earthly things.

I AM THE LORD YOUR GOD

Some may ask the question as to whether the Ministry of our Lord was the Year of Jubilee being fulfilled. In a sense it was, but only in a sense. In effect, He announced the nearness of this great time by saying, *"The Kingdom of Heaven is at hand!"* That Kingdom which He preached brought in its train *"the opening of the prison door to the bound, deliverance to the captive,"* as well as *"glad tidings to the poor."* But then Jesus seems to have intended that this is what was coming, and that the actual time of the Jubilee had not yet come.

In part, and possibly one might even say in whole, it came when He died on the Cross of Calvary, which spiritually speaking was the fulfillment of the Great Day of Atonement. So we might say that Christ's First Coming gives the *"earnest"* of those blessings which His Second Coming shall give in full.

The Year of Jubilee will not be completely fulfilled until Israel accepts Christ as Lord, Saviour, and Messiah, and as well, the Kingdom is set up on this Earth, with Jesus Christ reigning supreme; however, we must ever remember that while this must be done, and in fact, will be done, it is all made possible by what He did at the Cross.

So we might say that the time of total fulfillment is thus indicated to be the time of Israel's final restoration, and the time of the Lord's Glorious Appearing.

The Jubilee which Christ's First Coming brings us is Redemption from the guilt of sin and its dominion. The Jubilee which His Second Coming brings is Redemption from all the bitter consequences of sin, and from sin's existence.

The Jubilee always began on the evening of the Day of Atonement. There was first given to the people a full display of the way of pardon, by all the ceremonies of that day. They were taught, and we by them are taught, that the full Atonement of our Lord – His Blood shed and sprinkled on the Mercy Seat, His entering in Himself, accepted and interceding, and His coming forth *"without sin unto Salvation,"* – is the foundation and groundwork of all other Blessings. No external blessing can be ours, whether now, or in that coming Millennial day, unless previously we have been accepted in the Beloved – forgiven, sanctified, made heirs with Christ (Bonar).

KINSMAN REDEEMER

If an Israelite fell on hard times, at the end of the 50 year time period, that which he had lost would be returned to him; however, at any time, if *"any of his kin"* so desired, and was willing and able to pay the price and restore him back his possession, this kinsman would have the liberty to do so.

In order to save fallen man, our Saviour had to become man, in effect, becoming our *"kinsman."* He did this in order to possess the right to offer the price of Redemption. Hence, He took our very nature, and was *"bone of our bone, and flesh of our flesh"* (Eph. 5:30). *"Forasmuch as the children are partakers of flesh and blood, He also Himself likewise took part of the same"* (Heb. 2:14). And by the coming thus related to us, He has the right, which He will enforce, and in fact, has enforced, of redeeming not only the persons of His Own, but the very Earth on which they dwell. On that coming day, and we speak of the coming Millennial Reign, Satan shall be driven from his long-usurped throne.

Concerning this, Bonar said, *"How joyful for us to traverse the plains, or stand on the hills, or trace the winding rivers of this Earth, and to remember that 'the Redeemer' of this decayed inheritance is living now, and soon to come again; and that He is One Who has all the affections, as well as ties, of relationship! How glorious our prospects – how sure our Redemption, spirit, soul, and body, as well as inheritance, when our Redeemer is such a one as would become our kinsman in very love to us!"*

"Out of my bondage, sorrow, and night, Jesus, I come, Jesus, I come;
"Into Thy freedom, gladness, and light, Jesus, I come to Thee;
"Out of my sickness into Thy health, out of my want and into Thy wealth,
"Out of my sin and into Thyself, Jesus,

I come to Thee."

"Out of my shameful failure and loss, Jesus, I come, Jesus, I come;
"Into the glorious gain of Thy Cross, Jesus, I come to Thee;
"Out of Earth's sorrows into Thy balm, out of life's storms and into Thy calm,
"Out of distress to jubilant Psalm, Jesus, I come to Thee."

"Out of unrest and arrogant pride, Jesus, I come, Jesus, I come;
"Into Thy blessed will to abide, Jesus, I come to Thee;
"Out of myself to dwell in Thy love, out of despair into raptures above,
"Upward for aye on wings like a dove, Jesus, I come to Thee."

"Out of the fear and dread of the tomb, Jesus, I come, Jesus, I come;
"Into the joy and light of my home, Jesus, I come to Thee;
"Out of the depths of ruin untold, into the peace of Thy sheltering fold,
"Ever Thy glorious face to behold, Jesus, I come to Thee."

CHAPTER 26

(1) "YOU SHALL MAKE YOU NO IDOLS NOR GRAVEN IMAGE, NEITHER REAR YOU UP A STANDING IMAGE, NEITHER SHALL YOU SET UP ANY IMAGE OF STONE IN YOUR LAND, TO BOW DOWN UNTO IT: FOR I AM THE LORD YOUR GOD.

(2) "YOU SHALL KEEP MY SABBATHS, AND REVERENCE MY SANCTUARY: I AM THE LORD.

(3) "IF YOU WALK IN MY STATUTES, AND KEEP MY COMMANDMENTS, AND DO THEM;

(4) "THEN I WILL GIVE YOU RAIN IN DUE SEASON, AND THE LAND SHALL YIELD HER INCREASE, AND THE TREES OF THE FIELD SHALL YIELD THEIR FRUIT.

(5) "AND YOUR THRESHING SHALL REACH UNTO THE VINTAGE, AND THE

VINTAGE SHALL REACH UNTO THE SOW-ING TIME: AND YOU SHALL EAT YOUR BREAD TO THE FULL, AND DWELL IN YOUR LAND SAFELY.

(6) "AND I WILL GIVE PEACE IN THE LAND, AND YOU SHALL LIE DOWN, AND NONE SHALL MAKE YOU AFRAID: AND I WILL RID EVIL BEASTS OUT OF THE LAND, NEITHER SHALL THE SWORD GO THROUGH YOUR LAND.

(7) "AND YOU SHALL CHASE YOUR ENEMIES, AND THEY SHALL FALL BE-FORE YOU BY THE SWORD.

(8) "AND FIVE OF YOU SHALL CHASE AN HUNDRED, AND AN HUNDRED OF YOU SHALL PUT TEN THOUSAND TO FLIGHT: AND YOUR ENEMIES SHALL FALL BE-FORE YOU BY THE SWORD.

(9) "FOR I WILL HAVE RESPECT UNTO YOU, AND MAKE YOU FRUITFUL, AND MULTIPLY YOU, AND ESTABLISH MY COVENANT WITH YOU.

(10) "AND YOU SHALL EAT OLD STORE, AND BRING FORTH THE OLD BECAUSE OF THE NEW.

(11) "AND I WILL SET MY TABER-NACLE AMONG YOU: AND MY SOUL SHALL NOT ABHOR YOU.

(12) "AND I WILL WALK AMONG YOU, AND WILL BE YOUR GOD, AND YOU SHALL BE MY PEOPLE.

(13) "I AM THE LORD YOUR GOD, WHICH BROUGHT YOU FORTH OUT OF THE LAND OF EGYPT, THAT YOU SHOULD NOT BE THEIR BONDMEN; I HAVE BRO-KEN THE BANDS OF YOUR YOKE, AND MADE YOU GO UPRIGHT."

The description is:

1. The first two Verses of this Chapter close the section of this Book dealing with weekly, annual, and Jubilee Sabbaths. A double injunction was given forbidding idolatry and enjoining true Sabbatic wor-ship (Williams).

2. In Chapter 26 are recorded God's sin-gular vows to His people, and in Chapter 27 His people's singular vows to Him. In these latter there might be failure, but never in the former (Williams).

3. Verses 3 through 13 promised blessing for obedience. Verses 40 through 45 assured restoration upon repentance.

NOTES

THE SABBATHS

Verses 1 and 2 read: *"You shall make you no idols nor graven image, neither rear you up a standing image, neither shall you set up any image of stone in your land, to bow down unto it: for I am the LORD your God.*

"You shall keep My Sabbaths, and rever-ence My Sanctuary: I am the LORD."

It is quite noticeable that the Lord com-bines idol worship with Sabbath breaking. While His statement covers many areas, I think the following is mostly intended:

If one is worshipping other gods, one is not worshipping Jehovah. To worship Jeho-vah refers to embracing the entirety of His Plan of Redemption, which would ultimately be the Cross. If that is ignored, and other gods embraced, then there could be no Sab-batical *"rest."* The *"rest"* we now have in Christ is based solely upon His Finished Work, and our anchored Faith in that Sacrifice.

MODERN IDOL WORSHIP

If the Preacher doesn't preach the Cross, thereby his hearers placing their faith in some-thing else, whether they realize it or not, they are serving *"another Jesus,"* which pure and simple is idol worship of some sort. And that is the great sin of the modern Church.

While it doesn't rear up its grotesque gods, fashioned with the engraver's tool, or out of molten metal, still, the principle of what is being done is the same. Anything that's not *"Christ and Him Crucified,"* which re-fers to the fact that all we have and know are based strictly on the Shed Blood of the Lamb, then we have fashioned an idol. As such, we cannot have the *"rest"* which Christ Alone can bring, and we might quickly add, Christ Crucified!

So in two Verses, the Holy Spirit has moved upon Moses to describe the sin of Is-rael, that which later came to destroy them, and as well, the sin of the modern Church, which in effect, is the sin of all of mankind.

OBEDIENCE

Verse 3 reads: *"If you walk in My Statutes, keep My Commandments, and do them."*

Following this condition, *"if,"* we find some of the most glorious Promises found anywhere in the Word of God. But as we've stated in Commentary on the previous Chapter, obedience is required. Now exactly what did obedience mean?

In truth, fallen man simply could not keep the Statutes and Commandments. Not even Israel, in the very best of circumstances, and the very best among them, could keep these Statutes and Commandments. So where did this leave Israel?

As we studied in the first Chapters of this Book, the Lord instituted the Sacrificial System, which in effect was at the very heart of the entire Levitical Legislation. In one way or the other, all of the Sacrifices address themselves to Christ, and in effect, to the Offering of Himself for sin, which He would do many centuries later, on the Cross.

The people of Israel were to make every attempt to keep the Laws. They were to guard themselves closely, asking the Lord to give them guidance, strength, and help in these matters, which He definitely would do, at least as much as the Holy Spirit could then do before the Cross. When they failed, they were commanded to offer up Sacrifices as it regarded that failure.

That's as close as Israel could come, even the best among Israel, before the Cross. Unfortunately, in later years, Israel made a religion out of trying to keep the Law. In doing this, they added some 600 oral laws, to the original Law of Moses, calling them *"fence laws"* and considered them to be even more important than the original Laws given to Moses. But man is that way! He thinks that which he does is more important than that which is done by the Lord.

God is merciful, kind, gracious, and patient. Were He not all of this, none of us would be here; however, He did expect two things from His chosen people, Israel:

1. He expected them to love Him with all of their heart, their mind, their soul, and their strength.

2. He expected them to love their neighbor as themselves.

When Jesus was asked to summarize the entirety of the Law, He did so by giving those two particular principles or Commandments (Mk. 12:29-31).

Now how could they do this, considering

that they didn't have the help of the Holy Spirit as we do at present?

PROPER FAITH

The Law of God was God's Standard of Righteousness. It's what He expected of man, and in fact, that which He had to expect from man. Anything less would have destroyed civilization. If man was to have even a semblance of sensible and right living, the Ten Commandments had to stand as the foundation of all principle.

But as stated, man was helpless to properly obey. But he definitely was to try to obey, and was to do so with all his strength. To be sure, if he truly loved the Lord, and his neighbor as himself, that he would try to do.

But when it was all said and done, his Faith had to be in what the Sacrifices represented. It's all wrapped up in the phrase, *"Abraham believed God, and God accounted it to him for Righteousness"* (Gen. 15:6).

Even though *"Faith"* is only mentioned two times in the Old Testament (Deut. 32:20; Hab. 2:4), the word *"believe"* or *"believing,"* which was commonly used, meant the same thing (Ex. 4:1, 5, 8; Num. 14:11; Deut. 1:32; II Ki. 17:14, etc.).

Had Israel functioned in the manner of love and of Faith, they would have never suffered loss, and neither will we presently.

BLESSINGS

Verses 4 through 13 read: *"Then I will give you rain in due season, and the land shall yield her increase, and the trees of the field shall yield their fruit.*

"And your threshing shall reach unto the vintage, and the vintage shall reach unto the sowing time: you shall eat your bread to the full, and dwell in your land safely.

"And I will give peace in the land, and you shall lie down, and none shall make you afraid: and I will rid evil beasts out of the land, neither shall the sword go through your land.

"And you shall chase your enemies, and they shall fall before you by the sword.

"And five of you shall chase an hundred, and an hundred of you shall put ten thousand to flight: and your enemies shall fall

before you by the sword.

"For I will have respect unto you, and make you fruitful, multiply you, and establish My Covenant with you.

"And you shall eat old store, and bring forth the old because of the new.

"And I will set My Tabernacle among you: and My soul shall not abhor you.

"And I will walk among you, and will be your God, and you shall be My people.

"I am the LORD your God, which brought you forth out of the land of Egypt, that you should not be their bondmen; and I have broken the bands of your yoke, and made you go upright."

The idea of all of this is, had Israel walked in obedience, they would have been blessed beyond measure, and would have been invincible regarding their enemies.

That being the case, the Presence of God would have ever been their shield and buckler. No weapon formed against them would have ever prospered. But then the Divine Presence was only to be enjoyed by an obedient people. Jehovah could not sanction by His Presence disobedience or wickedness.

The uncircumcised nations around might depend upon their prowess and their military resources: Israel had only the arm of Jehovah to depend upon, and that arm could never be stretched forth to shield unholiness or disobedience. Their strength was to walk with God in a spirit of dependence and obedience. So long as they walked thus, there was a wall of fire round about them, to protect them from every enemy and every evil (Mackintosh).

The following are some of the Blessings that the Lord promised them, if they would only render to Him proper obedience:

1. The Lord would give rain in due season, in other words, when it was needed.

2. The land would bring forth abundantly.

3. The vineyards would yield an abundance of fruit.

4. The crops would be so abundant that there would not be enough time to gather all the harvest before the fruit trees would begin to yield their fruit. And before all the fruit can be gathered, it would be time to plant for the next crop.

5. They would have so much to eat that

they could not consume it all.

6. They would not fear their enemies, but would dwell in their land safely. God would guarantee that safety and protection.

7. They would have peace and not war.

8. There would be no fear.

9. Beasts which were harmful would be taken out of the land.

10. No invading army would ever go through Israel.

11. If enemies did come against Israel, the Lord would make Israel so strong that five men would put 100 of the enemy to flight, and 100 Israelites would put 10,000 of the enemy to flight.

12. Because of their obedience, God would respect Israel, which means that He would bless them, and in every way.

13. They would have so much to eat that before it could be consumed, a new crop would come forth.

14. The Lord would set His Tabernacle among them, which means that His Presence would guarantee all of this.

15. He would walk among them, and they would feel His Presence, and because He was their God, and they were His people.

UNLIMITED BLESSINGS

As I think is obvious here, we're speaking of unlimited blessings. In fact, no nation in the world, or any group of nations, could even remotely boast of such that God promised Israel. In fact, as should be obvious, such was impossible as it regards other countries. It could only be with those who serve the Lord.

And then as we will study next, the Lord showed them what would happen to them, if they forsook His Ways; and the picture is not pretty. Yet the record shows that Israel did not obey, and came to the place that they did not even try to obey. They repudiated the Ways of the Lord, in effect, turning their backs upon Him, until there was no hope.

THE NEW COVENANT

In looking at these great Promises that God gave to Israel, what can we as Believers now expect? In other words, is that which was spoken to them applicable now to us, whether it was positive or negative?

I definitely believe that the New Covenant not only promises this which the Lord promised to Israel, but even more. Paul plainly stated: *"We now have a Better Covenant, which is established upon Better Promises"* (Heb. 8:6). And what does this New Covenant include?

First of all, and foremost, it includes spiritual blessings of untold proportions. Whereas Believers under the Old Covenant only had the Holy Spirit with them, we, since the Cross, have the Holy Spirit living within us, which opens the door for all type of blessings (Jn. 14:16-17).

With Faith anchored firmly in the Cross, which has made all of this possible, we can be victorious over sin in every capacity. No, we're not teaching sinless perfection, because the Bible doesn't teach such; however, we are definitely teaching that sin will not have dominion over us (Rom. 6:14). This is far and away of greater dimension than that which was under the Old Covenant.

Second, if the Lord promised healing under the Old Covenant, and He definitely did (Ex. 15:26), how can anyone think that we would be given less under the New Covenant! Yes and most definitely, Believers can ask the Lord for Divine Healing, and can expect Divine Healing, because it is definitely included in the New Covenant (James 5:14-16; Mat. 21:22; I Pet. 2:24; Jn. 14:14; 15:7, etc.).

Third, Believers can certainly expect financial prosperity, if they will believe the Lord, and be faithful to give to His Work. If the Lord would do such for Israel under the Old Covenant, and He definitely did, how much more will He do under the New Covenant? It is not that the Lord loves those under the New Covenant more than the Old, but rather, that the Cross has made all the difference.

That's why Jesus said of John the Baptist: *"Among them who are born of women there has not risen a greater than John the Baptist: notwithstanding he who is least in the Kingdom of Heaven is greater than he"* (Mat. 11:11).

He wasn't meaning that we were greater in character than John the Baptist, etc., but rather that under the New Covenant, the very least would have greater privileges even than

the great John the Baptist, or any other Prophet of the Old Testament. Let's say it this way:

Christians are not blessed financially because the Preacher behind the pulpit doesn't teach them to expect blessings from the Lord. Or they claim that such cannot be had today, etc. In fact, there are untold thousands of Churches that proclaim the idea that much of nothing can be had presently, everything having passed away with the Apostles, etc. Anyone who has the misfortune to be in such a Church is unfortunate indeed!

"Faith comes by hearing, and hearing by the Word of God" (Rom. 10:17). If we are to have Faith for something, the Word of God on that subject must be preached behind the pulpit. When it is preached, and people believe it, they can have what the Word says. And as well, we should as Believers only want and desire that which is God's Will for our lives. And a consecrated heart will definitely desire only that.

But please believe me, and above all believe the Word, God wants to bless His children, and He wants to do so in every way. We just must be ever conscious of the fact that emphasis must never be placed wrongly. The emphasis must always be on Righteousness and Holiness, i.e., *"Christ."* And Jesus plainly said that if we would *"seek first the Kingdom of God, and His Righteousness;* (then) *all these things shall be added unto you"* (Mat. 6:33). Now we can believe our Lord and Saviour, or not believe Him. I choose to believe Him.

Most definitely, everything that the Lord promised Israel, we can have it, and even much more. As the Lord delivered the Children of Israel from Egyptian bondage, most certainly He delivers no less presently. As He broke the bands of their yoke, He will break the bands of our yoke.

UPRIGHT

The phrase, *"And made you go upright,"* is a beautiful phrase, and carries a tremendous spiritual connotation.

Of course, the Lord was referring to the bondage of slavery to which the Children of Israel were submitted while in Egypt. They were bowed over, as a result of labor and slavery. As would be obvious, they were treated like animals, worked to death, robbed of all self-respect, and, thereby, given a slave mentality.

But when the Lord delivered them, He broke their chains of bondage, laid low their oppressors, and made of them a people of dignity, repose, strength, and power, or at least gave them the means to do so. It has not changed unto this hour:

Satan holds most of the world in bondage. As a result, they don't actually think upright, look upright, function upright, but rather in a distorted manner, and of course, we're speaking of spiritual values. But when Jesus comes into the life, He changes the person, and changes them so completely, until in reality, they are no longer the same person, but referred to by the Holy Spirit as a *"new creation"* (II Cor. 5:17). In other words, the Lord helps His Children to walk upright, look upright, and be upright.

(14) "BUT IF YOU WILL NOT HEARKEN UNTO ME, AND WILL NOT DO ALL THESE COMMANDMENTS;

(15) "AND IF YOU SHALL DESPISE MY STATUTES, OR IF YOUR SOUL ABHOR MY JUDGMENTS, SO THAT YOU WILL NOT DO ALL MY COMMANDMENTS, BUT THAT YOU BREAK MY COVENANT:

(16) "I ALSO WILL DO THIS UNTO YOU; I WILL EVEN APPOINT OVER YOU TERROR, CONSUMPTION, AND THE BURNING AGUE, THAT SHALL CONSUME THE EYES, AND CAUSE SORROW OF HEART: AND YOU SHALL SOW YOUR SEED IN VAIN, FOR YOUR ENEMIES SHALL EAT IT.

(17) "AND I WILL SET MY FACE AGAINST YOU, AND YOU SHALL BE SLAIN BEFORE YOUR ENEMIES: THEY WHO HATE YOU SHALL REIGN OVER YOU; AND YOU SHALL FLEE WHEN NONE PURSUES YOU.

(18) "AND IF YOU WILL NOT YET FOR ALL THIS HEARKEN UNTO ME, THEN I WILL PUNISH YOU SEVEN TIMES MORE FOR YOUR SINS.

(19) "AND I WILL BREAK THE PRIDE OF YOUR POWER; AND I WILL MAKE YOUR HEAVEN AS IRON, AND YOUR EARTH AS BRASS:

NOTES

(20) "AND YOUR STRENGTH SHALL BE SPENT IN VAIN: FOR YOUR LAND SHALL NOT YIELD HER INCREASE, NEITHER SHALL THE TREES OF THE LAND YIELD THEIR FRUITS."

The composition is:

1. Between these sections of the Chapter, i.e., from Verse 14 to Verse 39, are set out the five great judgments denounced upon disobedience. Compare with these the five visitations in wrath of Isaiah 5:25; 9:12, 17, 21; 10:4; and also the five lamentations of Amos 4:6-12 (Williams).

2. The glowing promises of Blessings for obedience are now followed by a catalogue of calamities of the most appalling nature, which will overtake the Israelites if they disobey the Divine Commandments (Ellicott).

3. The abhorrence by the people of God's Law is that which breaks the Divine Covenant with them. That done, they are then left at the mercy of Satan! And to be sure, he has no mercy.

THE BREAKING OF THE COVENANT

Verses 14 and 15 read: *"But if you will not hearken unto Me, and will not do all these Commandments;*

"And if you shall despise My Statutes, or if your soul abhor My Judgments, so that you will not do all My Commandments, but that you break My Covenant."

All of this means that the Covenant which God had with Israel was conditional. In fact, the far greater majority of all Covenants are in fact conditional.

The idea presented here is, if the Children of Israel would come to the place that they no longer regarded the Law of God, made no effort to abide by its precepts, and in fact, began to worship other gods, then these judgments would come upon them.

While God always demands perfection, we all know that such perfection is found only in Christ, Who was symbolized by the Sacrifices. Doing their very best to live for God as they should, and then offering up the Sacrifices for their sins, and believing in what the Sacrifices represented, namely Christ, would have guaranteed all the great blessings promised by the Lord. But failure to do that would break the Covenant, and bring upon them disastrous results, which it ultimately did.

WHAT IS THE DIFFERENCE IN THE NEW COVENANT AND THE OLD COVENANT?

In fact, the differences are great.

Any Covenant which God made with man, of whatever description, was always broken by man. Wherever man is placed, man fails.

While the New Covenant was made between God and man, just as all the other Covenants, still, there was a vast difference, which makes it a perfect Covenant, which means no other Covenant will ever have to be made, hence Paul referring to the New Covenant as *"The Everlasting Covenant"* (Heb. 13:20).

So if in fact the New Covenant was made between God and man, how could it be called perfect, considering that man has failed in every position in which he has been placed?

The answer is very complicated, but at the same time, exceedingly simple. God would become man, and thereby, satisfy both counts.

Jesus Christ is God, and Jesus Christ is man. That means that He is 100 percent God, so to speak, and 100 percent man. That's why at times He has been referred to by some Scholars as *"Very God,"* and *"Very Man."*

While the New Covenant was made between God and man, God becoming man, while never ceasing to be God, could fill both roles, which was done in Christ Jesus.

Paul said of Him, *"And He is before all things, and by Him all things consist"* (Col. 1:17).

And then Paul said: *"For it pleased the Father that in Him should all fullness dwell"* (Col. 1:19).

Man is brought into the New Covenant by Faith in what Christ did at the Cross, which was done entirely for Adam's fallen race. Paul again said: *"And, having made peace through the Blood of His Cross, by Him to reconcile all things unto Himself; by Him, I say, whether they be things in Earth, or things in Heaven"* (Col. 1:20).

Because this Covenant is totally and completely in Christ, it cannot fail. But believing man can fail, that is, if he ceases to believe. In fact, the entirety of the Book of Hebrews was written in regard to this very

thing. Christian Jews were getting discouraged, with some of them going back into Judaism, and, thereby, repudiating Christ. If they did that, and stayed in that condition, they would lose their souls, even though they had once been in the Covenant (Heb. 6:4-6; 10:26-31). It is Faith that gets us into the Covenant, and a lack of Faith can get one out of the Covenant. But the Covenant doesn't change, only the individual's disposition toward the Covenant. In other words, as the Covenant is all in Christ, this means that it cannot change, because God cannot change.

JUDGMENTS

Verses 16 through 20 read: *"I also will do this unto you; I will even appoint over you terror, consumption, and the burning ague, that shall consume the eyes, that shall cause sorrow of heart: and you shall sow your seed in vain, for your enemies shall eat it.*

"And I will set My face against you, and you shall be slain before your enemies: they who hate you shall reign over you; and you shall flee when none pursues you.

"And if you will not yet for all this hearken unto Me, then I will punish you seven times more for your sins.

"And I will break the pride of your power; and I will make your heaven as iron, and your earth as brass:

"And your strength shall be spent in vain: for your land shall not yield her increase, neither shall the trees of the land yield their fruits."

Failure to obey would result in the following judgments:

1. Fear will plague them, and continuously.

2. Sickness and disease will as well plague their physical bodies.

3. They will sow their seed for a harvest, but instead of reaping the harvest, the enemy will rather reap it. This is exactly what ultimately happened!

4. Instead of being victorious, their enemies would be victorious over them.

5. Instead of having Godly rulers, they would be taken over by ungodly nations, those who hated them.

6. Their fear would be so paramount that they would flee, even though none

were pursuing them.

7. If all of these things do not have the desired effect, which is to bring Israel back to God, then the Judgment will be multiplied seven times.

8. The Lord promised to break the pride of their power, which means that their trust would ultimately come to rest in their own army, instead of God. Their enemies would waste these armies that look mighty in their sight. With God, no nation or group of nations in the world could even think of overrunning Israel. Without God, the weakest nation could overcome them.

9. Instead of Heaven being opened to their prayers, it would be closed, *"as iron."* Instead of the Earth yielding its increase, it would be as *"brass."*

10. Even though they would work and labor, and do so with great vigor, their strength would be spent in vain.

(21) "AND IF YOU WALK CONTRARY UNTO ME, AND WILL NOT HEARKEN UNTO ME; I WILL BRING SEVEN TIMES MORE PLAGUES UPON YOU ACCORDING TO YOUR SINS.

(22) "I WILL ALSO SEND WILD BEASTS AMONG YOU, WHICH SHALL ROB YOU OF YOUR CHILDREN, AND DESTROY YOUR CATTLE, AND MAKE YOU FEW IN NUMBER; AND YOUR HIGH WAYS SHALL BE DESOLATE.

(23) "AND IF YOU WILL NOT BE RE-FORMED BY ME BY THESE THINGS, BUT WILL WALK CONTRARY UNTO ME;

(24) "THEN WILL I ALSO WALK CONTRARY UNTO YOU, AND WILL PUNISH YOU YET SEVEN TIMES FOR YOUR SINS.

(25) "AND I WILL BRING A SWORD UPON YOU, THAT SHALL AVENGE THE QUARREL OF MY COVENANT: AND WHEN YOU ARE GATHERED TOGETHER WITHIN YOUR CITIES, I WILL SEND THE PESTILENCE AMONG YOU; AND YOU SHALL BE DELIVERED INTO THE HAND OF THE ENEMY.

(26) "AND WHEN I HAVE BROKEN THE STAFF OF YOUR BREAD, TEN WOMEN SHALL BAKE YOUR BREAD IN ONE OVEN, AND THEY SHALL DELIVER YOU YOUR BREAD AGAIN BY WEIGHT: AND YOU SHALL EAT, AND NOT BE SATISFIED."

NOTES

The exegesis is:

1. In no uncertain terms, the Lord lays out the conditions for Blessing, and the cause of Judgment; consequently, there is no excuse.

2. In Deuteronomy, Chapter 28, once again blessings and curses are plainly and clearly stipulated.

3. Even though this is the Old Covenant, and which has been fulfilled by Christ, still, it would do us well to read very carefully these words stated so long, long ago. God hasn't changed!

SEVEN TIMES MORE PLAGUES

Judgment will at times bring people back to God. But if it doesn't, God has promised to increase the pressure, even seven times more than had previously been rendered. It is as follows:

11. Wild beasts would multiply in the land, even to the place of eating little children.

12. The wild beasts would also decimate their herds of cattle and sheep, etc.

13. Instead of the nation growing in population, it would rather be diminished.

14. The highways throughout the land would be desolate, because of the fear of bandits, etc.

15. If this did not turn Israel, the pressure would be multiplied again some seven times.

16. Their enemies would invade them, and put untold thousands to the sword.

17. Congregating in the cities, terrible diseases would break out among them. So there would be no safety in numbers.

18. Food would be in such short supply that ten families, represented by *"ten women,"* would have to exist or subsist on the amount that would normally be consumed by one family.

(27) "AND IF YOU WILL NOT FOR ALL THIS HEARKEN UNTO ME, BUT WALK CONTRARY UNTO ME;

(28) "THEN I WILL WALK CONTRARY UNTO YOU ALSO IN FURY; AND I, EVEN I, WILL CHASTISE YOU SEVEN TIMES FOR YOUR SINS.

(29) "AND YOU SHALL EAT THE FLESH OF YOUR SONS, AND THE FLESH OF YOUR DAUGHTERS SHALL YOU EAT.

(30) "AND I WILL DESTROY YOUR

HIGH PLACES, AND CUT DOWN YOUR IMAGES, AND CAST YOUR CARCASSES UPON THE CARCASSES OF YOUR IDOLS, AND MY SOUL SHALL ABHOR YOU.

(31) "AND I WILL MAKE YOUR CITIES WASTE, AND BRING YOUR SANCTUARIES UNTO DESOLATION, AND I WILL NOT SMELL THE SAVOR OF YOUR SWEET ODORS.

(32) "AND I WILL BRING THE LAND INTO DESOLATION: AND YOUR ENEMIES WHICH DWELL THEREIN SHALL BE ASTONISHED AT IT.

(33) "AND I WILL SCATTER YOU AMONG THE HEATHEN, AND WILL DRAW OUT A SWORD AFTER YOU: AND YOUR LAND SHALL BE DESOLATE, AND YOUR CITIES WASTE.

(34) "THEN SHALL THE LAND ENJOY HER SABBATHS, AS LONG AS IT LIES DESOLATE, AND YOU BE IN YOUR ENEMIES' LAND; EVEN THEN SHALL THE LAND REST, AND ENJOY HER SABBATHS.

(35) "AS LONG AS IT LIES DESOLATE IT SHALL REST; BECAUSE IT DID NOT REST IN YOUR SABBATHS, WHEN YOU DWELT UPON IT."

The diagram is:

1. There could be nothing worse than God walking contrary to a person, or a people.

2. Due to lack of repentance, the judgment now increases, even to the extent of driving Israel off her land, and scattering her all over the world, which is exactly what happened.

3. The *"Sabbaths"* were very important to the Lord, inasmuch as they portrayed the great *"rest"* which would be brought about as a result of what Christ would do on the Cross. So, to desecrate the Sabbath was to desecrate His Sacrifice. The idea is, the land would enjoy her Sabbaths, one way, or the other. Again we state, God said what He meant, and meant what He said!

THE SABBATHS

Failure to repent increases the judgments even more! Following point 18 of the previous commentary, they are:

19. If Israel walked contrary to God, He would walk contrary to them. This speaks, as should be obvious, of dire consequences.

20. The judgment increases seven times more. This makes the fourth time of a sevenfold increase in judgment, which means that God constantly would increase the pressure.

21. Food would be in such short supply that some would actually eat their own sons and daughters, which actually happened.

22. The judgment declared upon the idols in Verse 30 showed the helplessness of the gods worshipped. To prove His point, the enemies of Israel would slaughter tens of thousands of Israelites, even in the very presence of their idols, showing again their helplessness.

23. The cities would become waste, which is what happened.

24. The great Temple in Jerusalem, which had once been the House of God, was destroyed by the Babylonian Monarch, Nebuchadnezzar. This meant the sacrifices would now be stopped, which would signal the total doom of Israel, and because these Sacrifices represented the Cross. That repudiated and taken away, there was nothing left!

25. As a result, the land would be brought to desolation, which it was.

26. What had once been such a verdant garden will now become a cesspool, even to the extent that Israel's enemies would be astonished at it.

27. Israel would be scattered among the heathen, and again, that's exactly what happened.

The *"Sabbath"* of both days and years was so very important, and because of what it symbolized. In their totality, whether on the seventh day of the week, or the seventh year, or the fiftieth year, they all and without exception symbolized the *"rest"* which would come with Christ, and one's acceptance of Him. If we try to make less of the Sabbaths than this, we greatly misinterpret Scripture. If we try to make more, it is an impossible task, for there could be nothing greater than Christ, and what Christ would do at the Cross for Adam's fallen race.

The *"rest"* which comes with an acceptance of Christ, and especially when one knows and understands the price that has been paid for that *"rest,"* which was the death of Christ on the Cross, portrays the fact that the power of sin is broken, and the guilt of sin is removed (Rom. 6:6).

We make a grave mistake when we place emphasis presently on the *"day."* As the Brazen Altar was a type of the Crucifixion of Christ, and the Brazen Laver a type of Christ as the Living Word, and the Golden Lampstand as a type of Christ as the Light of the world, etc., likewise, the *"Sabbath"* was a type of the *"rest"* found only in Christ. In fact, every single thing about the Tabernacle, its sacred vessels, all the Feast Days, all the Sacrifices, and the Sabbaths, each and without exception perfectly portrayed Christ in His Atoning, Mediatorial, Intercessory Work. To add to that, or take from that, is to corrupt the *"types"* and the *"shadows"* (Heb. 10:1).

(36) "AND UPON THEM WHO ARE LEFT ALIVE OF YOU I WILL SEND A FAINTNESS INTO THEIR HEARTS IN THE LANDS OF THEIR ENEMIES; AND THE SOUND OF A SHAKEN LEAF SHALL CHASE THEM; AND THEY SHALL FLEE, AS FLEEING FROM A SWORD; THEY SHALL FALL WHEN NONE PURSUES.

(37) "AND THEY SHALL FALL ONE UPON ANOTHER, AS IT WERE BEFORE A SWORD, WHEN NONE PURSUES: AND YOU SHALL HAVE NO POWER TO STAND BEFORE YOUR ENEMIES.

(38) "AND YOU SHALL PERISH AMONG THE HEATHEN, AND THE LAND OF YOUR ENEMIES SHALL EAT YOU UP.

(39) "AND THEY WHO ARE LEFT OF YOU SHALL PINE AWAY IN THEIR INIQUITY IN YOUR ENEMIES' LANDS; AND ALSO IN THE INIQUITIES OF THEIR FATHERS SHALL THEY PINE AWAY WITH THEM."

The composition is:

1. Verses 36 through 39 predict the destruction of Israel by the Babylonians, and by the Romans.

2. They also predict these ancient people in great sorrow, scattered all over the world, and because of their forsaking the Lord their God.

3. This was occasioned by their treatment of Christ, when they said of Him: *"We have no king but Caesar"* (Jn. 19:15), and: *"His Blood be upon us, and upon our children"* (Mat. 27:25).

4. Verse 38 predicted not only the suffering of the centuries, but as well the horrible holocaust, where six million Jews died, at the hands of the Nazi monster, Adolph Hitler.

THE JUDGMENTS CONTINUE

28. For those who survive the slaughter, they would live in such fear that a *"shaken leaf would chase them."*

29. Death will stalk them in every conceivable fashion.

30. They will have no power whatsoever to stand before their enemies, which and who would be many.

31. As outcasts and vagabonds, they would perish among the heathen, and the land of their enemies would eat them up.

32. Irrespective as to where they went, sorrow and heartache would follow them.

33. And when one looks at the awful history, as we now see after the fact, the horror of it all beggars description. One can only conclude, *"Sin did this!"*

(40) "IF THEY SHALL CONFESS THEIR INIQUITY, AND THE INIQUITY OF THEIR FATHERS, WITH THEIR TRESPASS WHICH THEY TRESPASSED AGAINST ME, AND THAT ALSO THEY HAVE WALKED CONTRARY UNTO ME;

(41) "AND THAT I ALSO HAVE WALKED CONTRARY UNTO THEM, AND HAVE BROUGHT THEM INTO THE LAND OF THEIR ENEMIES; IF THEN THEIR UNCIRCUMCISED HEARTS BE HUMBLED, AND THEY THEN ACCEPT OF THE PUNISHMENT OF THEIR INIQUITY:

(42) "THEN WILL I REMEMBER MY COVENANT WITH JACOB, AND ALSO MY COVENANT WITH ISAAC, AND ALSO MY COVENANT WITH ABRAHAM WILL I REMEMBER; I WILL REMEMBER THE LAND.

(43) "THE LAND ALSO SHALL BE LEFT OF THEM, AND SHALL ENJOY HER SABBATHS, WHILE SHE LIES DESOLATE WITHOUT THEM: AND THEY SHALL ACCEPT OF THE PUNISHMENT OF THEIR INIQUITY: BECAUSE, EVEN BECAUSE THEY DESPISED MY JUDGMENTS, AND BECAUSE THEIR SOUL ABHORRED MY STATUTES.

(44) "AND YET FOR ALL THAT, WHEN THEY BE IN THE LAND OF THEIR

ENEMIES, I WILL NOT CAST THEM AWAY, NEITHER WILL I ABHOR THEM, TO DESTROY THEM UTTERLY, AND TO BREAK MY COVENANT WITH THEM: FOR I AM THE LORD THEIR GOD.

(45) "BUT I WILL FOR THEIR SAKES REMEMBER THE COVENANT OF THEIR ANCESTORS, WHOM I BROUGHT FORTH OUT OF THE LAND OF EGYPT IN THE SIGHT OF THE HEATHEN, THAT I MIGHT BE THEIR GOD: I AM THE LORD.

(46) "THESE ARE THE STATUTES AND JUDGMENTS AND LAWS, WHICH THE LORD MADE BETWEEN HIM AND THE CHILDREN OF ISRAEL IN MOUNT SINAI BY THE HAND OF MOSES."

The composition is:

1. *"If they shall confess their iniquity."* This is the one condition for personal and national restoration.

2. Verse 44 says: *"I will not cast them away,"* simply meaning that God has not utterly cast away His people whom He foreknew; He will yet bring them back to repentance and make a great nation out of them (Isa. 11:10-12; Zech. 12:10-13; Rom. 11:1-2).

3. It sobers one's mind to realize that all of these things have come to pass, exactly as the Lord said they would, and that as well, we are now living during the time of the beginning of the restoration of Israel, which will come to fruition at the Second Coming.

THE CONFESSION OF INIQUITY

Verses 40 and 41 read: *"If they shall confess their iniquity, and the iniquity of their fathers, with the trespass which they trespassed against Me, and that also they have walked contrary unto Me;*

"And that I also have walked contrary unto them, and have brought them into the land of their enemies; if then their uncircumcised hearts be humbled, and they then accept of the punishment of their iniquity."

This Passage is actually no different than that given in the New Covenant, when the Holy Spirit through the Apostle John said: *"If we confess our sins, He is faithful and just to forgive us our sins, and to cleanse us from all unrighteousness"* (I Jn. 1:9).

As should be obvious, under the Old Covenant, and even under the New, when

wrongdoing is committed by one of God's Children, if forgiveness is to be sought and received, we must first confess our iniquity, which means that we confess before God that we have done wrong, and that we deserve judgment, but that we plead for mercy.

The truth is, it is very difficult for unbelievers or Believers to admit that they have done wrong. All of us are so prone to blame others, or to blame circumstances. This is not new, having begun with Adam and Eve.

When the Lord asked fallen man, *"Have you eaten of the tree, whereof I commanded you that you should not eat?"*, Adam quickly shifted the blame by saying:

"The woman whom You gave to be with me, she gave me of the tree, and I did eat." So Adam blamed God and Eve.

When the Lord approached Eve, she as well attempted to shift the blame by saying, *"The serpent beguiled me, and I did eat"* (Gen. 3:11-13). Man has been trying to shift the blame ever since.

TRUE NEW COVENANT REPENTANCE

True repentance under the New Covenant demands not only that we confess iniquity, but as well that we confess our trust in good things, but not the Cross, which is possibly the worst sin of all. The evil side of the tree of the knowledge of good and evil is obvious. It's the good side of that tree that gives us the problems. So what am I saying?

The real cause of sin is our Faith and trust placed in that other than the Cross, and no matter how good these things might be in which we place our Faith and trust, God can never accept them, and they constitute a rebellion, in fact, the most serious rebellion of all, against God, and His prescribed Plan of Redemption. It is ironic that Believers will look at the unsaved as the latter attempt to do the same thing, which refers to trust in their good works, or the fact that they don't have a lot of bad works, or so they think, and will be quick to point out such error; however, all too often, Believers do the same thing, and do so oftentimes without realizing what they are doing.

There is only one Faith that God will recognize, and that's Faith in Christ and in His Sacrifice (I Cor. 1:23; 2:2). Therefore, when we place our Faith in other things, thinking that such brings about Righteousness and Holiness, etc., we sin, and we sin greatly! But it's hard for us to see that, simply because the things in which we have reposed our faith are in fact, good things, at least in their own right.

THE INIQUITY OF THE FATHERS

The phrase, *"And the iniquity of their fathers,"* proclaims the fact that the sin which has brought them to this evil state is not a new sin. It had begun a long time ago, even with their fathers and their fathers' fathers. In other words, Israel's condition was of long standing.

The phrase, *"And that I also had walked contrary to them, and had brought them unto the land of their enemies,"* refers to the fact that God was orchestrating the entirety of events, whether blessings or judgments.

Considering that all of this speaks of people who belong to God, whether Israel of old, or the Church at present, at least those who truly had known Him, where does this leave the nations of the world, which are primarily paganistic, irrespective of their religions?

As I'm certain we amply see in this presentation, the Blessings which follow from living a consecrated life to the Lord are above and beyond comprehension. As an example, the United States is by far the most powerful, the richest, and the nation with the greatest amount of freedoms, of any country in the world. This is the nation of destination for untold millions all over the world, who in fact, risk their lives, even on a daily basis, trying to gain entrance to the land of the brave and the home of the free. While many reasons may be given for these blessings, the truth is, it is the people in this nation who are truly born again, truly Spirit-filled, and Spirit-led, which are the secret of this nation's success. The Scripture plainly tells us: *"Righteousness exalts a nation: but sin is a reproach to any people"* (Prov. 14:34).

But the sadness is, the nation has long since been running on credit. Per capita, there are far less of the Righteous than there once was, and that number is growing smaller by the day. As someone has well said, if God doesn't judge the United States, He will have

to apologize to Sodom and Gomorrah. The terrible tragedy of September 11, 2001 should have been a wake-up call. But I'm concerned that it wasn't. So what will it take?

Regarding the nations of the world which do not know God, or else are paganistic regarding their so-called faith, while God oversees all, those nations are pretty much left to their own devices, except when those devices begin to impact the Kingdom of God. In fact, regarding these nations, demon spirits more or less control their activity, hence the lack of freedom and prosperity, etc.

But regrettably, the powers that be in the United States recognize not at all the actual secret of the prosperity of this nation. In fact, they would give no shift whatsoever to those who are truly of God.

That's at least one of the reasons that the leaders of our nation little understand the terrible evil of Islam. They keep trying to swallow the lie that the terrorists are merely misguided fanatics, and are not promoted at all by the religion of Islam. Actually, the President made the statement that the Koran was a book of love and peace. The truth is, it is anything but!

Trying to maintain the fallacy that the religion of Islam is a great religion, while the activities of the terrorists are merely that of a few misguided fanatics is, in fact, the very height of deception.

The truth is, the religion of Islam is totally and completely inspired by demon spirits (I Tim. 4:1), and it continues to be propelled by demon spirits. If that is not obvious, considering the terrorist activity all over the world, then I don't know what obvious actually is.

America is about to face what tiny Israel has been facing for years, and regrettably, we are facing this crisis with our policy based on a lie. Pure and simple, the problem is the religion of Islam. While all Muslims definitely aren't murderers, the religion of Islam most definitely inspires the spirit of murder, which once again is amply obvious all over the world.

In fact, Islam is a failed religion in every capacity. The nations of the world governed by the religion of Islam are among the poorest in the world. They have the least freedoms of most nations in the world, with education for the masses being almost nonexistent. All one has to do is to merely look at the results! But unfortunately, the unredeemed mind doesn't have the capacity to see that at which it looks.

THE COVENANT

Verse 42 reads: *"Then will I remember My Covenant with Jacob, and also My Covenant with Isaac, and also My Covenant with Abraham will I remember; and I will remember the land."*

The moment the people, through confession of their sins, attempt to come back into the Covenant, they will be readily accepted. This is what the Spirit of the Lord is saying through Moses.

God is merciful and gracious, but His Mercy and Grace cannot be shown to individuals who insist upon walking contrary to Him and His Ways. That should be forever understood.

Unfortunately, in this Dispensation of Grace, millions attempt to claim Christ, while at the same time living a life of constant, repetitive sinning. In fact, they have no relationship with the Lord, are not born again, and even though religious, are not saved. The Churches are filled with such, more today than at any time, I think, since the Reformation.

But it's hard, very hard, for people to admit they are wrong. Entire Denominations leave the Word of God, which once made them great, and stubbornly refuse to come back. They keep pushing on deeper and deeper into wrong direction, seemingly not realizing that judgment has already begun.

The truth is, the modern Church has forsaken the Cross of Christ. It little any more figures into the theology of most Churches. The pulpit is a Crossless pulpit. The pew is a Crossless pew. The preaching is Crossless preaching, and where does that leave the people?

If we understand all things, or at least think we do, and do not properly understand the Cross, then in actuality, we understand nothing! Let the Reader understand, as this Book of Leviticus so amply points out, always and ever, it is *"the Cross! The Cross!*

The Cross!" (Gen. 3:15; 15:6; Ex. 12:13; Isa., Chpt. 53; Rom. 6:3-14; 8:1-2, 11; I Cor. 1:17-18, 21, 23; 2:2; Gal. 6:14; Eph. 2:13-18; Col. 2:14-15).

THE PUNISHMENT OF THEIR INIQUITY

Verse 43 reads: *"The land also shall be left of them, and shall enjoy her Sabbaths, while she lies desolate without them: and they shall accept of the punishment of their iniquity: because, even because they despised My Judgments, and because their soul abhorred My Statutes."*

The phrase, *"The land also shall be left to them,"* would have been better translated, *"But the land shall be deserted by them,"* for this Passage pertains to the Children of Israel being driven from the land, which they were by Nebuchadnezzar, approximately 900 years later (II Chron. 36:17-21). In fact, the Scripture said: *"To fulfill the Word of the LORD by the mouth of Jeremiah, until the land had enjoyed her Sabbaths: for as long as she lay desolate she kept Sabbath, to fulfill threescore and ten years"* (II Chron. 36:21). Exactly what the Lord said would happen, happened as He said it would, which is guaranteed of the Word of God in any and every capacity. Israel ignored these commands concerning the seventh year Sabbaths, and as well the Year of Jubilee Sabbaths, so the Lord added all of those years together, which totaled 70 years, which time they spent in captivity in Babylon. Let us again emphasize this point:

The *"Sabbaths"* which were very important in the Law of God, all and without exception represented Christ, exactly as everything about the Law of God represented Christ.

THE REST PROVIDED BY CHRIST

A Seventh Day Adventist Brother wrote me sometime back, in essence, asking my definition of the Old Testament Sabbaths, etc.

My answer to him was very brief, in that I proclaimed to him that the Sabbaths totally and completely represented Christ, were symbols of Christ, and what Christ would provide by His Sacrificial, Atoning Death on the Cross of Calvary, which would give *"rest"* to the troubled soul, at least for all who would accept Him as their Lord and Saviour.

He wrote me back, in essence saying, *"Is that all?"*

In other words, he wasn't satisfied with my answer, which showed that he was missing the import and the intent of the Old Testament Sabbaths altogether. By his very answer he was relegating what Christ did on the Cross as relatively insignificant. I'm certain he didn't mean it that way, but that's actually what he was saying, whether he meant it or not.

There could be nothing greater than the Sacrifice of Christ. It is so absolutely great, so absolutely wonderful, so absolutely eternal, that it defies all description. What more could one say about the Sabbath, that would be greater than the fact that the Sabbath represents Christ and His Finished Work. In fact, the Sabbath was a day of *"rest."* It was meant to be that. The people were to do no work, all which represented Christ. Listen to Paul:

"Let us therefore fear, lest, a promise being left us of entering into His rest, any of you should seem to come short of it (the *'rest'* which Christ provides as a result of His Sacrificial Death on the Cross, and our acceptance of that Finished Work).

"For unto us was the Gospel preached, as well as unto them: but the Word preached did not profit them, not being mixed with Faith in them who heard it (Faith is the key, and by that, we speak of Faith in Christ and His Cross).

"For we which have believed do enter into rest, as He said, as I have sworn in My wrath, if they shall enter into My rest: although the works were finished from the foundation of the world.

"For He spoke in a certain place of the seventh day on this wise, and God did rest on the seventh day from all His works (the seventh day on which God rested, after bringing the Earth back to a habitable state, represented Christ and what Christ would do at the Cross).

"And in this place again, if they shall enter into My rest.

"Seeing therefore it remains that some must enter therein, and they to whom it was first preached entered not in because of unbelief (speaking of the Jews, who refused to accept Christ):

NOTES

"Again, He limited a certain day, saying in David (the Psalms), *Today, after so long a time; as it is said, Today if you will hear His voice, harden not your hearts.*

"For if Joshua had given them rest, then would he (David) *not afterward have spoken of another day.*

"There remains therefore a rest to the people of God (that *'rest'* is Christ).

"For he who is entered into His rest, he also has ceased from his own works, as God did from His" (Heb. 4:1-10).

Our Seventh Day Adventists friends, all too often, place Salvation in the *"day"*, i.e., *"the Sabbath,"* instead of what the Sabbath represented. Pure and simple, and as repeatedly stated, it represented Christ and His Finished Work, Who provides total and complete *"rest"* for the individual who makes Him Lord and Saviour of their life. As well, He brought all of this about by His Sacrificial, Atoning Death on the Cross.

IT IS ALL IN CHRIST

Let the Reader understand that the entirety of the Word of God, and we mean the entirety, is the story of Christ and Him Crucified. That is its theme, its foundation, its principal, its very purpose.

In Genesis 3:15, we read of the Lord telling Satan through the serpent that the dominion which had now been lost would be regained by the One Who was to come, and Who would bruise the head of Satan, which He would do by His effecting Work on the Cross (Col. 2:14-15), and that Satan would bruise His heel, referring to the suffering of the Crucifixion. So the very first Word given after the Fall as it concerns Redemption spoke of Christ and the Cross.

In the Fourth Chapter of Genesis, we find the Lord instituting the Sacrificial System, which was to serve as a stopgap measure, until Christ would come.

We then find Him through Abraham, Isaac, and Jacob, raising up a people unto His Name, all for the purpose of bringing the Redeemer into the world, Who would deliver the world, at least those who would believe, by His effecting Work on the Cross.

We then find the Lord giving Moses His great Law, which was His Standard of

Righteousness, with all of it in its entirety, representing Christ in His Atoning, Mediatorial, Intercessory Work. The whole of the Tabernacle, all of its Sacred Vessels, the entirety of the Sacrificial System, the Feast Days, the Sabbaths, all and without exception, pointed to Christ and His Atoning Work. If we do not see that, then we do not understand the Bible.

And then after this great Work was accomplished, which speaks of the New Covenant, the Lord then gave to the Apostle Paul exactly what the New Covenant meant, and how it is applicable to our hearts and lives. It can all be wrapped up in one phrase used by Paul: *"We preach Christ Crucified"* (I Cor. 1:23), and *"For I determined not to know anything among you, save Jesus Christ, and Him Crucified"* (I Cor. 2:2).

PROMISED RESTORATION

Verse 44 reads: *"And yet for all that, when they be in the land of their enemies, I will not cast them away, neither will I abhor them, to destroy them utterly, and to break My Covenant with them: for I am the LORD their God."*

Several things are said in this one Verse. Some of them are:

1. In essence, the Lord plainly predicted here that Israel would in fact ignore His Word.

2. He also predicted that they would be carried captive into a heathen land, which is exactly what happened.

3. But for all of that, He would not cast them away, at least as it regards His Promises to them. While those who disbelieved His Word definitely died lost, the overall Plan of God for Israel will ultimately be realized.

4. God's Covenants cannot be broken, at least as far as His part is concerned. While men may break the Covenant, which Israel definitely did, and which many do as it regards the New Covenant, the Covenant stands, but to be sure, those, whomever they might be, who register unbelief toward the Covenant, will definitely be lost. This was proven by Israel of old, and as well, proven by the Jews who were in the Early Church, with some of them turning their backs on Christ, in which if they continued in that state, occasioned the loss of their souls. The

entirety of the Book of Hebrews was written as it regards this very thing. And of course, that also means that every Gentile who has been born again, if they lose Faith in the Covenant, which pertains to Christ and Him Crucified, they are no longer in the Covenant, because it is Faith which gets one into the Covenant, and Faith which keeps one in the Covenant (Heb. 4:2). But yet the Covenant remains, and all may enter in who so desire (Rev. 22:17).

REMEMBER THE COVENANT

Verse 45 reads: *"But I will for their sakes remember the Covenant of their ancestors, whom I brought forth out of the land of Egypt in the sight of the heathen, that I might be their God: I am the LORD."*

In these Passages, plus many others given in the Word of God (Rom., Chpts. 9-11), we find the Lord promising that the Covenant He made with the Patriarchs will ultimately and in totality be fulfilled.

This completely abrogates the foolish notion held by some in the modern Church, claiming that Israel is no longer of any spiritual significance. I find that as difficult to believe as I do the denial of the Cross.

At this very moment, every time we turn on our television sets and look at the news, or read the periodicals, and hear and read reports of Israel's present struggle, we are hearing and reading the fulfillment of Bible Prophecy. These are all the beginning stages of the Lord bringing the Covenant that He made with Abraham, Isaac, and Jacob, to fulfillment. And what in essence was that Covenant?

THE COVENANT OF GRACE

First of all, the Covenant that God made with Abraham, Isaac, and Jacob, was most definitely a Covenant of Grace. It stated that from these men, all recorded in the Book of Genesis, that the Lord would raise up a people for His Glory. As well, He would give them a land, a specific land, the land which would ultimately be called *"Israel,"* which in fact it was. And that from that land they would be the Priestly nation of the world (Gen. 12:1-3; 13:14-17; 15:4-21; 22:1-18). As stated, all of this was strictly on the merit of the Grace of God (Gen. 15:6).

Israel is now being brought back into the possession of the land of Canaan, and done so on the ground of unqualified and unchangeable Grace – Grace exercised in Divine Righteousness, through the Blood of the Cross, even though she does not now understand that at all.

It is not by works of law, nor yet by the institutions of any other type of economy, but by the Grace which *"reigns through Righteousness, by Jesus Christ our Lord."*

Israel is now facing the coming Great Tribulation, predicted by the Prophets of old, and foretold by Christ (Mat. 24:21). This terrible time, which will be the worst time that Israel has yet known, when the Antichrist will seek to destroy them once and for all, will climax with the Second Coming, when Israel will then accept Christ as Lord, Saviour, and Messiah. Wherefore, never again, will Israel be driven forth from their possession. No enemy ever again shall molest them. They shall then enjoy undisturbed repose behind the shield of Jehovah's favor.

Their possession of the land, and their tenure of the land, will be according to the eternal stability of Divine Grace and the efficacy of the Blood of the Everlasting Covenant (Heb. 13:20). So considering that the Covenant will never fail, and we speak of the New Covenant, we know then that Israel shall be saved with an everlasting Salvation.

THE LAW OF GOD

Verse 46 reads: *"These are the Statutes and Judgments and Laws, which the LORD made between Him and the Children of Israel in Mount Sinai by the hand of Moses."*

Every one of these Laws was instituted by God, which means that man had no part in their formation at all. Inasmuch as these were the Laws of God, they were perfect in every respect. But unfortunately, man, due to his fallen state, could not keep these Laws, as simple as they might seem on the surface.

When one reads the Ten Commandments (Ex., Chpt. 20), which provides the heart of these Laws, and in fact, is the Moral Law of God, they seem so simple, and, thereby, so easily kept; however, even though they are simple, which means they are very easy to understand, still, due to the sin nature which

came into man at the Fall, man is unable to keep even these most simple laws.

Regrettably, far too many Christians presently think that because this is the New Covenant which we presently possess, and because we have the Holy Spirit in a dimension that those under the Old Covenant didn't have (Jn. 14:16-17), most surely we presently can obey the Lord in every respect.

The truth is, we definitely are to obey the Lord. In other words, total and complete obedience is required. But the great question is, how do we render that total and complete obedience? That's the question!

WALKING AFTER THE SPIRIT

Paul said: *"There is therefore now no condemnation to them which are in Christ Jesus, who walk not after the flesh, but after the Spirit"* (Rom. 8:1).

It is regrettable, but most Believers don't have the foggiest idea as to what *"walking after the flesh"* actually is, or *"walking after the Spirit."* And being bereft of this information, the Christian, without fail, will *"walk after the flesh,"* which always brings failure and condemnation (Gal. 5:19-21).

To *"walk after the flesh"* is to trust in our own strength and ability, which mostly is anchored in rules and regulations, in effect, more laws, etc. Religious men love to make laws, and they also love to try to force others to obey those laws.

"Walking after the Spirit," is the key to victorious, Christian living. It simply refers to the Believer understanding that every single thing that we receive from the Lord, all and without exception come to us through Christ and what He has done for us at the Cross.

Our Faith is to be planted firmly in that great Finished Work (Heb. 1:3). In fact, the Cross of Christ is to ever be the object of our Faith. This is the center, the key, the very foundation if you will, of all Biblical understanding. The Cross of Christ, although sometimes referred to as a doctrine, is in fact, much, much more. It is in reality, the foundation of all doctrine. I am absolutely certain that Jesus considered what He did on the Cross of far greater significance than a mere doctrine. So in the Cross of Christ, our Faith is to ever be anchored.

That being done, the Holy Spirit, Who works exclusively within the framework of the Sacrifice of Christ, will work mightily on our behalf (Rom. 8:1-2, 11).

Only in this manner can the Believer walk in Righteousness and Holiness; only in this manner can we have the liberty to live a holy life. Paul also said:

"Stand fast therefore in the liberty wherewith Christ has made us free, and be not entangled again with the yoke of bondage" (Gal. 5:1).

Paul was warning the Galatians against attempting to institute something else other than the Grace of God, which is in effect, the benefits of the Cross. In other words, the great Apostle was telling them not to bring the Law into their relationship with Christ. Christ has already satisfied the Law, and in every respect. In other words, He did for us what we could not do for ourselves. And to have all of this which He has done, all that is required of us is to evidence Faith in Him, which refers again to His Finished Work. As repeatedly stated, we are to never separate Christ from His Cross; and by that, we are speaking of the benefits of the Cross. Due to those benefits, we are now *"heirs of God, and joint-heirs with Christ"* (Rom. 8:17).

"In the Blood from the Cross, I have been washed from sin;
"But to be free from dross, still I would enter in.
"Deeper yet, deeper yet, into the crimson flood;
"Deeper yet, deeper yet, under the Precious Blood."

"Day by day, hour by hour, blessings are sent to me;
"But for more of His power, ever my prayer shall be.
"Deeper yet, deeper yet, into the crimson flood;
"Deeper yet, deeper yet, under the Precious Blood."

"Near to Christ I would live, following Him each day;
"What I ask He will give, so then with

Faith I pray.
"Deeper yet, deeper yet, into the crimson flood;
"Deeper yet, deeper yet, under the Precious Blood."

"Now I have peace, sweet peace, while in this world of sin;
"But to pray I'll not cease, till I am pure within.
"Deeper yet, deeper yet, into the crimson flood;
"Deeper yet, deeper yet, under the Precious Blood."

CHAPTER 27

(1) "AND THE LORD SPOKE UNTO MOSES, SAYING,

(2) "SPEAK UNTO THE CHILDREN OF ISRAEL, AND SAY UNTO THEM, WHEN A MAN SHALL MAKE A SINGULAR VOW, THE PERSONS SHALL BE FOR THE LORD BY YOUR ESTIMATION.

(3) "AND YOUR ESTIMATION SHALL BE OF THE MALE FROM TWENTY YEARS OLD EVEN UNTO SIXTY YEARS OLD, EVEN YOUR ESTIMATION SHALL BE FIFTY SHEKELS OF SILVER, AFTER THE SHEKEL OF THE SANCTUARY.

(4) "AND IF IT BE A FEMALE, THEN YOUR ESTIMATION SHALL BE THIRTY SHEKELS.

(5) "AND IF IT BE FROM FIVE YEARS OLD EVEN UNTO TWENTY YEARS OLD, THEN YOUR ESTIMATION SHALL BE OF THE MALE TWENTY SHEKELS, AND FOR THE FEMALE TEN SHEKELS.

(6) "AND IF IT BE FROM A MONTH OLD EVEN UNTO FIVE YEARS OLD, THEN YOUR ESTIMATION SHALL BE OF THE MALE FIVE SHEKELS OF SILVER, AND FOR THE FEMALE YOUR ESTIMATION SHALL BE THREE SHEKELS OF SILVER.

(7) "AND IF IT BE FROM SIXTY YEARS OLD AND ABOVE; IF IT BE A MALE, THEN YOUR ESTIMATION SHALL BE FIFTEEN SHEKELS, AND FOR THE FEMALE TEN SHEKELS.

(8) "BUT IF HE BE POORER THAN

YOUR ESTIMATION, THEN HE SHALL PRESENT HIMSELF BEFORE THE PRIEST, AND THE PRIEST SHALL VALUE HIM; ACCORDING TO HIS ABILITY WHO VOWED SHALL THE PRIEST VALUE HIM."

The structure is:

1. The singular vows affected persons, animals, houses, and fields; together with property designated as *"devoted things."*

2. The land was Emmanuel's land; and He by a singular vow offered Himself and the land to God. He, therefore, fulfilled all the conditions of this Chapter. He is the True Priest pointed to in Verse 21 (Williams).

3. Israel valued Him at 30 pieces of silver, but He valued Israel and the land at the price of His Own Blood.

VOWS

The casual reader, that is if there could be such a thing as a casual reader as it regards the Book of Leviticus, may wonder as to the significance of this Twenty-seventh Chapter?

The great significance lay in the fact of who these people were, better yet, to Whom they belonged, namely the Lord. As a people they were birthed by the Lord, and done so for a particular principle and purpose. As such, they had to be taught the significance of all of their doings, and especially vows made to God. They had to understand that these were not just idle words made in the heat of necessity, but that the Lord looked at these vows as serious things indeed.

CHRIST

Every single thing in the Bible, irrespective as to what it is, pertains to the story of Christ and what He would do on the Cross in order to redeem the lost sons of Adam's fallen race. As it regards Israel, and all that pertained to Israel, such as the Tabernacle, Sacred Vessels, Sacrifices, Feasts Days, and Sabbaths, everything and without exception pointed to Christ, and in some way, symbolized Him in His Atoning, Mediatorial, Intercessory Work.

David said: *"Praise waits for You, O God, in Sion: and unto You shall the vow be performed"* (Ps. 65:1).

Inasmuch as all the Psalms point to Christ, once again in His Atoning, Mediatorial, or

NOTES

Intercessory Work, this tells us that Christ had vowed to the Father that humanity would be redeemed.

Paul wrote: *"For when God made promise to Abraham, because He could swear by no greater, He swear by Himself,*

"Saying, Surely blessing I will bless you, and multiplying I will multiply you.

"For men verily swear by the greater: and an oath for confirmation is to them an end of all strife.

"Wherein God, willing more abundantly to show unto the heirs of promise the immutability of His counsel, confirmed it by an oath:

"That by two immutable things, in which it was impossible for God to lie, we might have a strong consolation, who have fled for refuge to lay hold upon the hope set before us" (Heb. 6:13-18).

As Israel, in a sense, is a type of Christ, with Christ being the True Israel, a vow made by an Israelite is the same as the Lord Himself making the vow. Hence we have here all the stipulations concerning vows, and how serious they are in the mind and eyes of God. And anything that is serious with Him had better be serious with us.

TYPE OF VOWS

It is said that no vow mentally made or conceived was deemed binding. It had to be distinctly pronounced in words before the Lord and before the Priest.

A positive vow was that which a man bound himself to consecrate for spiritual purposes his own person, members of his family over whom he had control, or any portion of his property. And for this kind of vow the formula was: *"Behold I consecrate this to the Lord."*

The words, *"And thy estimation,"* proclaim the fact that it was taken for granted that by consecrating a human being to God by a vow is meant to substitute the monetary value for him.

As the Scriptural Text indicates, different amounts of money were to be given according to the age of the individual.

As is obvious in this Chapter, the amount of money demanded, which incidentally was to be given to the Priests for the care of the

Sanctuary, was entirely a question of ability, capacity, and worth.

But if the individual was so poor that he could not pay the required amount, which as stated differed with age, then he could present himself before the Priest, and the Priest would evaluate his situation, and according to his ability, would the Priest levy a certain amount.

In other words, if it be a question of man's undertaking to meet the claims of Righteousness, then he must meet them; but if, on the other hand, a man feels himself wholly unable to meet those claims, he has only to fall back upon *"Grace,"* which will take him up just as he is. Moses, one might say, was the representative of the claims of Divine Righteousness: the Priest, as a type of Christ, is the exponent of the provisions of Divine Grace. The poor man who was unable to stand before Moses with the required amount, so to speak, fell back into the arms of the Priest.

THE VOW OF JEPHTHAH

Concerning the vow of Jephthah, the Scripture says: *"Then the Spirit of the LORD came upon Jephthah . . . and Jephthah vowed a vow unto the LORD, and said, If You shall without fail deliver the children of Ammon into my hands,*

"Then it shall be, that whatsoever comes forth of the doors of my house to meet me, when I return in peace from the children of Ammon, it shall surely be the LORD's, and I will offer it up for a Burnt-Offering" (Judg. 11:29-31).

The Lord helped Jephthah to defeat the Ammonites, and when he arrived home, the Scripture says: *"His daughter came out to meet him with timbrels and with dances: and she was his only child; beside her he had neither son nor daughter"* (Judg. 11:34).

The argument has raged for at least 3,000 years as to whether Jephthah actually offered his daughter as a human sacrifice, or paid the redemption value that he should pay. As well, the indication is that she would not marry and have children. The Text seems to point to the fact that Jephthah, for some reason, whether the fault of himself or his wife, could not have other children. If in fact that was the case, then his name would be blotted out

in Israel, which was a tragedy in their thinking, and because of many things.

Even though many Scholars have argued that Jephthah actually offered her up as a human sacrifice (a Burnt-Offering), I do not feel the Scripture warrants such. In the first place, *"the Spirit of the LORD"* was upon Jephthah during this battle, and I hardly think such would have been the case if he in fact was going to offer up his daughter as a human sacrifice. Such a sacrifice was abominable in the Eyes of God.

Second, the Scripture also says that she *"bewailed her virginity,"* lending credence to the fact that she was not married, had no children, and now would never have any (Judg. 11:37).

Third, Verse 39 says, *"And she knew no man,"* which lends even more credence to the fact that she remained unmarried.

The word *"house"* in Judges 11:31 refers to what we think of as a domicile, but in the Hebrew language, much more. It referred to every single thing owned by the individual, where the house, land, slaves, sheep, cattle, children, etc.

As well, the word *"doors"* as used in Verse 31 could refer to several things; doors to the actual domicile, a gate to the entrance of the property, etc.

From these statements, I gather that Jephthah paid his vow to the Lord by his daughter being dedicated to God all the days of her life, meaning that she did not marry and have children, which as stated, was looked upon in those days as extremely serious.

Some who claim that she was indeed offered up as a Burnt-Offering claim that her *"bewailing her virginity,"* simply meant that she was saddened because she was not married, and thereby had no children, and now would never be able to do so, which would rob her family of much. But that idea is offset by the phrase, *"And she knew no man"* (vs. 39), which indicates that she remained single for the rest of her life, which also indicates that she wasn't offered up as a Burnt-Sacrifice, but rather redeemed for ten pieces of silver, and then consecrated to the Lord the balance of her life (vs. 5).

(9) "AND IF IT BE A BEAST, WHEREOF MEN BRING AN OFFERING UNTO THE

LORD, ALL THAT ANY MAN GIVES OF SUCH UNTO THE LORD SHALL BE HOLY.

(10) "HE SHALL NOT ALTER IT, NOR CHANGE IT, A GOOD FOR A BAD, OR A BAD FOR A GOOD: IF HE SHALL LET ALL CHANGE BEAST FOR BEAST, THEN IT AND THE EXCHANGE THEREOF SHALL BE HOLY.

(11) "AND IF IT BE ANY UNCLEAN BEAST, OF WHICH THEY DO NOT OFFER A SACRIFICE UNTO THE LORD, THEN HE SHALL PRESENT THE BEAST BEFORE THE PRIEST:

(12) "AND THE PRIEST SHALL VALUE IT, WHETHER IT BE GOOD OR BAD: AS YOU VALUE IT, WHO ARE THE PRIEST, SO SHALL IT BE.

(13) "BUT IF HE WILL AT ALL REDEEM IT, THEN HE SHALL ADD A FIFTH PART THEREOF UNTO YOUR ESTIMATION."

The composition is:

1. The animals mentioned here, except for the unclean beasts, were those which could be used as a sacrifice, but not by the man who had dedicated it to the Lord. It must be given to the Priests.

2. That type of Sacrifice was always judged as *"holy,"* and because it was symbolic of Christ, and what He would do at the Cross.

3. The unclean animals referred to the proper animals, but which had blemishes and, therefore, could not be used as Sacrifices.

4. If the former owner who had dedicated the animal to the Lord, and we continue to speak of an unclean animal, and he wanted to purchase it back, while anyone else could purchase the animal at the valuation put upon it by the Priest, its former owner had to pay one-fifth more than the valuation price.

ANIMALS USED FOR SACRIFICE

Two types of animals are mentioned here, those labeled as *"clean,"* and those labeled as *"unclean."* As stated, according to the authorities, the expression *"unclean beasts"* denotes defective sacrificial animals, such as oxen, sheep, and goats with blemishes, which were unlawful for the Altar.

If an individual asked the Lord for something, and thereby, vowed to give an animal to the Lord, if such and such a thing was granted, he was obligated, as would be

NOTES

obvious, to keep the vow.

If it was a clean animal, one that was fit for sacrifice, it must be delivered to the Sanctuary, and it could not be redeemed for money. The Priests would then sell the animal to other Israelites who required them as Sacrifices for the Altar, and the money was used for the maintenance of the Sanctuary and its service.

As well, whatever animal was promised the Lord must not be changed for another animal, whether better or worse.

One may wonder at these instructions regarding animals, etc. As stated, they represent Christ and what He would do at the Cross on behalf of lost humanity. Without that, there would have been no instructions, and in fact, there would have been no sacrifices at all.

(14) "AND WHEN A MAN SHALL SANCTIFY HIS HOUSE TO BE HOLY UNTO THE LORD, THEN THE PRIEST SHALL ESTIMATE IT, WHETHER IT BE GOOD OR BAD: AS THE PRIEST SHALL ESTIMATE IT, SO SHALL IT STAND.

(15) "AND IF HE WHO SANCTIFIED IT WILL REDEEM HIS HOUSE, THEN HE SHALL ADD THE FIFTH PART OF THE MONEY OF YOUR ESTIMATION UNTO IT, AND IT SHALL BE HIS.

(16) "AND IF A MAN SHALL SANCTIFY UNTO THE LORD SOME PART OF THE FIELD OF HIS POSSESSION, THEN YOUR ESTIMATION SHALL BE ACCORDING TO THE SEED THEREOF: AN HOMER OF BARLEY SEED SHALL BE VALUED AT FIFTY SHEKELS OF SILVER.

(17) "IF HE SANCTIFY HIS FIELD FROM THE YEAR OF JUBILEE, ACCORDING TO YOUR ESTIMATION IT SHALL STAND.

(18) "BUT IF HE SANCTIFY HIS FIELD AFTER THE JUBILEE, THEN THE PRIEST SHALL RECKON UNTO HIM THE MONEY ACCORDING TO THE YEARS THAT REMAIN, EVEN UNTO THE YEAR OF THE JUBILEE, AND IT SHALL BE ABATED FROM YOUR ESTIMATION.

(19) "AND IF HE WHO SANCTIFIED THE FIELD WILL IN ANY WISE REDEEM IT, THEN HE SHALL ADD THE FIFTH PART OF THE MONEY OF YOUR ESTIMATION UNTO IT, AND IT SHALL BE ASSURED TO HIM.

(20) "AND IF HE WILL NOT REDEEM THE FIELD, OR IF HE HAVE SOLD THE FIELD TO ANOTHER MAN, IT SHALL NOT BE REDEEMED ANY MORE.

(21) "BUT THE FIELD, WHEN IT GOES OUT IN THE JUBILEE, SHALL BE HOLY UNTO THE LORD, AS A FIELD DEVOTED; THE POSSESSION THEREOF SHALL BE THE PRIEST'S.

(22) "AND IF A MAN SANCTIFY UNTO THE LORD A FIELD WHICH HE HAS BOUGHT, WHICH IS NOT OF THE FIELDS OF HIS POSSESSION;

(23) "THEN THE PRIEST SHALL RECKON UNTO HIM THE WORTH OF YOUR ESTIMATION, EVEN UNTO THE YEAR OF THE JUBILEE: AND HE SHALL GIVE YOUR ESTIMATION IN THAT DAY, AS A HOLY THING UNTO THE LORD.

(24) "IN THE YEAR OF THE JUBILEE THE FIELD SHALL RETURN UNTO HIM OF WHOM IT WAS BOUGHT, EVEN TO HIM TO WHOM THE POSSESSION OF THE LAND DID BELONG.

(25) "AND ALL YOUR ESTIMATION SHALL BE ACCORDING TO THE SHEKEL OF THE SANCTUARY: TWENTY GERAHS SHALL BE THE SHEKEL."

The construction is:

1. As I think should be obvious, vows made to the Lord, any type of vows, must be taken very seriously.

2. No man was forced to make a vow, but he was under obligation to be true to the vow after making it (Num. 30:2).

3. If an individual rashly makes a vow before God and then finds that it's impossible to keep, the individual should repent before God of making the vow and ask His forgiveness, then lay it aside. However, as stated, if it's possible to keep it, it should be kept.

4. A person should not use vows to attempt to obtain an answer to prayer or to bring about some desire. Faith in the Word of God is the ingredient that will produce answers to prayer and not unnecessary vows before God.

5. The "shekel" was not actually a coin, but a particular weight of silver. In this case, "twenty gerahs." It was probably about one ounce of silver.

6. It would probably be next to impossible to attempt to compare the economy of that day with the economy of the present day.

7. Silver in the Old Testament was a type of Redemption.

8. The "Sanctuary" set the standard for all things, and rightly so!

HOUSES AND FIELDS

If an individual vowed to give the Lord his house, he could redeem it with money, according to the valuation placed upon it by the Priest. He would then have to add a fifth part on top of the estimation.

A field devoted to the Lord was to be valued according to the years left unto Jubilee. At any time, the man could redeem the field, by paying the stipulated amount. If he did not redeem it by the Year of Jubilee, he had forfeited his right to redeem it at all. It would then be turned over to the Priests, in which it would be used for the upkeep of the Sanctuary. But if a man did such a thing, he would forfeit his rights to his property, actually doing so forever.

(26) "ONLY THE FIRSTLING OF THE BEASTS, WHICH SHOULD BE THE LORD'S FIRSTLING, NO MAN SHALL SANCTIFY IT; WHETHER IT BE OX, OR SHEEP: IT IS THE LORD'S.

(27) "AND IF IT BE OF AN UNCLEAN BEAST, THEN HE SHALL REDEEM IT ACCORDING TO YOUR ESTIMATION, AND SHALL ADD A FIFTH PART OF IT THERETO: OR IF IT BE NOT REDEEMED, THEN IT SHALL BE SOLD ACCORDING TO YOUR ESTIMATION.

(28) "NOTWITHSTANDING NO DEVOTED THING, THAT A MAN SHALL DEVOTE UNTO THE LORD OF ALL THAT HE HAS, BOTH OF MAN AND BEAST, AND OF THE FIELD OF HIS POSSESSION, SHALL BE SOLD OR REDEEMED: EVERY DEVOTED THING IS MOST HOLY UNTO THE LORD.

(29) "NONE DEVOTED, WHICH SHALL BE DEVOTED OF MEN, SHALL BE REDEEMED; BUT SHALL SURELY BE PUT TO DEATH."

The exegesis is:

1. Two classes of objects were forbidden to be vowed: (A) the firstborn of beasts and, (B) devoted things.

2. The firstborn belonged already to the Lord by an express Statute (Ex. 13:2).

3. To vow, therefore, to the Lord that which was His Own is a mockery.

THE FIRSTBORN

The firstborn of man and beast, as well as the ten percent of one's income (the tithe) pointed toward the Firstborn Who was to come, namely the Lord Jesus Christ. Jesus was the Firstborn of His mother (Mat. 1:25). As such, He was taken to the Temple by Mary and Joseph to be offered to God (Lk. 2:22-24).

Since Luke omits mention of a price being paid to redeem the child, he may have intended the incident to be regarded as the dedication of the Firstborn to the service of God. Jesus is also the Firstborn of His Heavenly Father.

Paul said of Christ: *"Who is the Image of the invisible God, the Firstborn of every creature:*

"For by Him were all things created, that are in Heaven, and that are in the Earth, visible and invisible, whether they be thrones, or dominions, or principalities, or powers: all things were created by Him, and for Him" (Col. 1:15-16).

When Paul used the term *"Firstborn"* regarding Christ, this doesn't mean that He was a created being. It rather means that He is the Creator of all things, and as one might say, the father of all creation.

The Greek word for *"Firstborn"* is *"protokos."* The Greek Scholars claim that there is no adequate English word to properly translate that particular Greek word, the word *"firstborn"* being the closest that can be derived.

For instance, Paul also said: *"For whom He* (God the Father) *did foreknow, He also did predestinate to be conformed to the image of His Son, that He* (Christ) *might be the Firstborn among many brethren"* (Rom. 8:29).

In no way does this mean that Jesus was born-again as a sinner, as some teach. The phrase, *"Firstborn among many brethren,"* refers to the fact that Christ is the Founder, one might say, of the born-again experience, which can be had by all men, who exhibit

Faith in Christ. He made this possible by His Sacrificial, Atoning Death on the Cross.

If the firstborn animal was unclean, thereby blemished, which means that it could not be used as a Sacrifice, such an animal could be used in a vow, and could be redeemed according to the valuation of the Priest, with an addition of one-fifth over and above the fixed value. If it was not redeemed, the treasurer of the Sanctuary sold it to anyone who desired to buy it at this valuation, and the proceeds were devoted to the maintenance and repairs of the Sanctuary.

That which had been devoted to the Lord could neither be sold by the officials of the Sanctuary nor be redeemed by the one who made the vow. All gifts devoted to the Lord in this manner became the property of the Priests (Num. 18:14).

Such was the case with Samuel when he was born. The Scripture says of his mother:

"And she vowed a vow, and said, O LORD of hosts, if you will indeed look on the affliction of your handmaid, and remember me, and not forget your handmaid, but will give unto your handmaid a manchild, then I will give him unto the LORD all the days of his life, and there shall no razor come upon his head" (I Sam. 1:11).

The Lord did exactly what Hannah asked, and Hannah did exactly what she told the Lord that she would do. Whenever she weaned Samuel, the Scripture says: *"She took him up with her, with three bullocks, and one ephah of flour, and a bottle of wine, and brought him unto the House of the LORD in Shiloh: and the child was young."*

She told the High Priest, Eli: *"For this child I prayed; and the LORD has given me my petition which I asked of Him:*

"Therefore also I have lent him to the LORD; as long as he lives he shall be lent to the LORD. And he worshipped the LORD there" (I Sam. 1:24-28).

CHRIST

Regarding Verse 29, Christ was totally devoted to the Lord by His parents when a child, and rightly so, and was not redeemed, and was put to death. But He was put to death, not for His Own sins, for He had no sins, but for the sins of others; consequently, He made it possible for all of mankind to be redeemed, at least those who will believe (Jn. 3:16).

(30) "AND ALL THE TITHE OF THE LAND, WHETHER OF THE SEED OF THE LAND, OR OF THE FRUIT OF THE TREE, IS THE LORD'S: IT IS HOLY UNTO THE LORD.

(31) "AND IF A MAN WILL AT ALL REDEEM OUGHT OF HIS TITHES, HE SHALL ADD THERETO THE FIFTH PART THEREOF.

(32) "AND CONCERNING THE TITHE OF THE HERD, OR OF THE FLOCK, EVEN OF WHATSOEVER PASSED UNDER THE ROD, THE TENTH SHALL BE HOLY UNTO THE LORD.

(33) "HE SHALL NOT SEARCH WHETHER IT BE GOOD OR BAD, NEITHER SHALL HE CHANGE IT: AND IF HE CHANGE IT AT ALL, THEN BOTH IT AND THE CHANGE THEREOF SHALL BE HOLY; IT SHALL NOT BE REDEEMED.

(34) "THESE ARE THE COMMANDMENTS, WHICH THE LORD COMMANDED MOSES FOR THE CHILDREN OF ISRAEL IN MOUNT SINAI."

The diagram is:

1. It is said in Verse 30 that all *"tithe"* belonged *"to the LORD."*

2. All tithes are *"holy unto the LORD."*

3. Tithe did not begin with Moses. The first mention of tithing refers to Abraham giving tithes to Melchizedek (Gen. 14:20; Heb. 7:4). As well, Jacob vowed the tenth to the Lord (Gen. 28:22). Although included in the Mosaic institution, the fact is, tithing preceded the Law, and continues unto this hour.

TITHES

Tithing as the tenth, and that's what the word means, fell into the same category as the *"firstborn."* In other words, as the firstborn of both man and beast belonged to the Lord, likewise, tithe belonged to the Lord presently. As we've already stated, tithing preceded the Law, and continues unto this hour.

The Scripture says, as also stated, that Abraham paid tithe to Melchizedek. This man, even as Paul reiterates in Hebrews, Chapter 7, was a type of Christ. Abraham is a type of all Believers. Inasmuch as Abraham

paid tithe to this man, we as Believers, the children of Abraham, continue to pay tithe to Christ, of Whom Melchizedek was a type (Heb. 7:1-5).

Paul said of Christ: *"Thou art a Priest forever after the order of Melchizedek"* (Heb. 7:17). That being the case, we are to continue to pay tithe to the Work of God.

But regarding our giving, tithing is something we owe, thereby, not a part of our giving. All giving must be extra and beyond tithing. In other words, after we have paid the tenth to the Lord, whatever else is added can then be considered as a gift.

I would hope the Reader can understand that tithing is far more than just a payment of money. It represents Christ as the *"Firstborn."* That being the case, we should understand how holy tithing actually is (Lev. 27:30).

Incidentally, if any Israelite failed to pay his tithe as he should, in effect borrowing them from the Lord, when he in fact did pay them, he had to add 20 percent to the total (Lev. 27:31).

Paying tithe to the Lord is a privilege. He has given so much for our Redemption, and tithing is supposed to help us to ever remember that. This means that every time we place our tithing check in the Offering plate, plus a thanksgiving gift on top of that, we are doing such as a memorial of what the Lord has done for us, and in fact, the whole of humanity. Notice what Paul said: *"But I have all, and abound: I am full, having received of Epaphroditus the things which were sent from you, an odor of a sweet smell, a sacrifice acceptable, well pleasing to God.*

"But my God shall supply all your need according to His riches in Glory by Christ Jesus" (Phil. 4:18-19).

Paul received the gift that the Philippians had sent him while he was in prison, which in effect was tithe, and he likened it to the *"odor of a sweet smell, a sacrifice acceptable, well pleasing to God."*

This is Old Testament terminology used of certain of the Sacrifices, which were types of Christ and His offering up of Himself.

So now I would trust that we have a little better understanding of tithing, realizing how important it is, and because of Who and

What it represents. It represents Christ, and the price that He paid on the Cross of Calvary for our Redemption. And nothing could be holier than that!

"I heard the Voice of Jesus say, 'Come
    unto Me and rest;
"'Lay down, you weary one, lay down
    your head upon My breast.'
"I came to Jesus as I was, weary, and
    worn, and sad;
"I found in Him a resting place, and
    He has made me glad."

"I heard the Voice of Jesus say, 'Be-
    hold, I freely give
"'The living water; thirsty one, stoop
    down, and drink, and live.'
"I came to Jesus and I drank of that
    life giving stream:
"My thirst was quenched, my soul re-
    vived, and now I live in Him."

"I heard the voice of Jesus say, 'I am
    this dark world's light:
"'Look unto Me: your morn shall rise,
    and all the day be bright.'
"I looked to Jesus and I found in Him
    my star, my sun;
"And in that light of life I'll walk till
    traveling days are done."

CONCLUSION

It is Monday afternoon, November 4, 2002, as I conclude my efforts regarding this wonderful Book of Leviticus. Even though it has taken only about three and one-half months to finish this Work, in reality, it has taken nearly 60 years.

The Bible, to be truly learned, has to be truly lived. It is not done quickly, for there are no shortcuts. Every tear, every hurt, every pain, every gladness, every joy, at least for those who live for God, are all a part of the learning experience. In essence, we are to be like Christ, at least as far as is possible, that we as He become the "Living Word."

NO OTHER BOOK QUITE LIKE LEVITICUS

After finishing this task, I feel I understand Christ just a little better. If that is the case, then your study of our efforts will help you to understand Christ a little better as

NOTES

well. If in fact that is so, your efforts in studying this Volume will have been well worth your while.

Of all things that we learn of Christ, and He did tell us, "Learn of Me," the greatest of all is that He "gave Himself for our sins, that He might deliver us from this present evil world, according to the Will of God and our Father" (Gal. 1:4).

Leviticus has been called the "Book of Worship," and so it is! But we learn from this Book of Worship that true worship is that alone which is based on the Sacrifice of Christ. Anything else is unacceptable to God. So of consequence, and because this Book of Moses bears it out so strongly, we have done our best to teach you in every way we know how, "Jesus Christ and Him Crucified."

I will close with a short poem that I learned years ago, which was a great blessing to me, and even this morning while in prayer, the Lord once again made it real to my heart. May it be the same to you as it was, and is, to me.

"I can see far down the mountain, where
    I've wandered many years.
"Often hindered on my journey, by the
    ghost of doubts and fears.
"Broken vows and disappointments,
    thickly strewn along the way,
"But the Spirit has led unerring to the
    land I hold today."

INDEX

The index is listed according to subjects. The treatment may include a complete dissertation or no more than a paragraph. But hopefully it will provide some help.

As well, even though extended treatment of a subject may not be carried in this Commentary, one of the other Commentaries may well include the desired material.

For information concerning the *Jimmy Swaggart Bible Commentary*, please request a Gift Catalog.

You may inquire by using Books of the Bible.

- Genesis (656 pages) (11-201)

- Exodus (656 pages) (11-202)

- Leviticus (448 pages) (11-203)

- Numbers
  Deuteronomy (512 pages) (11-204)

- Joshua
  Judges
  Ruth (336 pages) (11-205)

- I Samuel
  II Samuel (528 pages) (11-206)

- I Kings
  II Kings (560 pages) (11-207)

- I Chronicles
  II Chronicles (528 pages) (11-226)

- Ezra
  Nehemiah
  Esther (288 pages) (11-208)

- Job (320 pages) (11-225)

- Psalms (688 pages) (11-216)

- Proverbs (320 pages) (11-227)

- Ecclesiastes
  Song Of Solomon (288 pages) (11-228)

- Isaiah (688 pages) (11-220)

- Jeremiah
  Lamentations (688 pages) (11-070)

- Ezekiel (528 pages) (11-223)

- Daniel (416 pages) (11-224)

- Hosea
  Joel
  Amos (496 pages) (11-229)

- Obadiah
  Jonah
  Micah
  Nahum
  Habakkuk
  Zephaniah (544 pages) (11-230)

- Haggai
  Zechariah
  Malachi (448 pages) (11-231)

- Matthew (888 pages) (11-073)

- Mark (24 pages) (11-074)

- Luke (736 pages) (11-075)

- John (736 pages) (11-076)

- Acts (832 pages) (11-077)

- Romans (704 pages) (11-078)

- I Corinthians (656 pages) (11-079)

- II Corinthians (608 pages) (11-080)

- Galatians (496 pages) (11-081)

- Ephesians (576 pages) (11-082)

- Philippians (496 pages) (11-083)

- Colossians (384 pages) (11-084)

- I Thessalonians
  II Thessalonians (512 pages) (11-085)

- I Timothy
  II Timothy
  Titus
  Philemon (704 pages) (11-086)

- Hebrews (848 pages) (11-087)

- James
  I Peter
  II Peter (736 pages) (11-088)

- I John
  II John
  III John
  Jude (384 pages) (11-089)

- Revelation (592 pages) (11-090)

For telephone orders you may call 1-800-288-8350 with bankcard information. All Baton Rouge residents please use (225) 768-7000.

For mail orders send to:
Jimmy Swaggart Ministries
P.O. Box 262550
Baton Rouge, LA 70826-2550

Visit our website: www.jsm.org

NOTES

NOTES

NOTES

NOTES

NOTES

NOTES

NOTES

NOTES

NOTES

NOTES

NOTES

NOTES